THE POLICE DICTIONARY
AND ENCYCLOPEDIA

ABOUT THE AUTHOR

John Fay is a former police officer, investigator, instructor, and training administrator.

In 1980, he left law enforcement to seek a second career in the corporate world where he is presently a manager of security in the world's third largest oil company.

Mr. Fay earned the Bachelor of General Studies degree from the University of Nebraska at Omaha, and the Master of Business Administration degree from the University of Hawaii.

He is the author of several publications, one of which is a companion piece recently published by Charles C Thomas, Publisher, entitled *The Alcohol/Drug Abuse Dictionary and Encyclopedia*. His other works include *Approaches to Criminal Justice Training* (University of Georgia, Athens, GA), *Managing Drug Abuse in the Workplace* (Forward Edge, Houston, TX), and *Butterworths Security Dictionary* (Butterworths Publishers, Stoneham, MA).

THE POLICE DICTIONARY AND ENCYCLOPEDIA

By

JOHN J. FAY

C H A R L E S   C   T H O M A S   •   P U B L I S H E R
Springfield • Illinois • U.S.A.

Published and Distributed Throughout the World by

CHARLES C THOMAS • PUBLISHER
2600 South First Street
Springfield, Illinois 62794-9265

© *1988 by* CHARLES C THOMAS • PUBLISHER

ISBN 0-398-05494-0

Library of Congress Catalog Card Number: 88-10133

Printed in the United States of America
SC-R-3

Library of Congress Cataloging-in-Publication Data

Fay, John 1934–
        The police dictionary and encyclopedia / by John J. Fay.
                p.   cm.
        Bibliography: p.
        ISBN 0-398-05494-0
        1. Police — Dictionaries.   2. Law enforcement — Dictionaires.
I. Title.
HV7901.F39   1988
363.2'03'21 — dc19   88-10133
                                                                                                 CIP

As much as any profession, law enforcement has a language of its own. It is a composite language which reflects on the one hand fundamental concepts descended from law, criminology, and other disciplines, and, on the other hand, a great number of specialized and sometimes unique practices that have evolved from the demands of the work itself.

For the entry-level officer, learning the idioms of the job is essential. Learning will begin in recruit school where the officer is exposed to the basic terms of reference contained in constitutional law, deviant behavior, emergency care, and similar core subjects. Language development will continue to expand as the officer assumes his first assignment and encounters tasks that embody ideas and techniques not covered earlier in entry-level training. As he undertakes different assignments and moves into positions of supervision and management, the maturing officer is exposed to higher, frequently abstract concepts. Many of these are driven by new laws, new methods, and new technologies. The now experienced officer discovers that to keep pace with the growing complexity of law enforcement he must constantly update his working vocabulary. He comes to understand that law enforcement is becoming increasingly sophisticated and that it is no longer enough to merely know the language of patrol, investigations, or any single specialty within the field.

Whether generalist or technician, subordinate or supervisor, the professional seeking to excel has a need to communicate. Communications are enhanced when an officer has an ability to articulate, but the critical element is to have a grasp of the terms of reference. Mastery of the rules of speaking and writing have no value until applied to logically arranged knowledge.

This book is more than a compilation of meanings. The major effort has been to explain and amplify rather than to simply define. Examples have been provided where they seemed to be needed, and applications of important practices have been delineated. Much of the material is sufficiently detailed to permit direct transfer to lesson plans, student handouts, and standard operating procedures.

A publication of this type is not a one-time project. It has been undertaken with an expectation of later editions. The rapid changes occurring in law enforcement certainly indicate a need for periodic updating. A reader who may be disappointed at not finding a particular term or who may disagree with an entry is encouraged to send comments to me or the publisher. If worthy, the next edition will reflect these views. This is a constructive way to refresh and clarify the language of our profession.

I make no pretension or claim that this work is the final authority on any of its entries. The language of law enforcement is developmental, dynamic, and in constant flux. Definitions change with time, custom, and in many cases are open to interpretation. My aim has been to report the most common usage of a term at the time it was selected for inclusion.

John Fay
4820 Spruce Street
Bellaire, Texas 77401

CONTENTS

THE POLICE DICTIONARY
AND ENCYCLOPEDIA

ABA transit numbers. a number code developed by the American Bankers' Association (ABA) which facilitates the routing of a check back to the bank of origin. The code, which appears in the upper right corner of the check, indicates the city or state of the bank it was drawn against, the name of the bank, and the Federal Reserve Bank District. ABA transit numbers are useful in tracing cashed or deposited checks. The code key can be obtained from the ABA.

abandonment. deserting a pregnant or dependent wife or dependent children without providing proper support; discontinuation of an intended crime before its commission.

abandonment of a child. the desertion of a child (usually under 16 years of age) by a parent or other person having the care or custody for nurture or education. This crime, which is most often a felony, is shown when the child is left in destitute circumstances without proper food, clothing, or shelter, or is wholly abandoned. This latter provision requires a desertion of the child under circumstances which render it probable that its life or health may be imperiled, or it may be subject to suffering or bodily harm.

abandonment of wife. the act of a husband who abandons his wife without adequate support, or leaves her in danger of becoming a burden upon the public. Also, the desertion of a wife by her husband while she is pregnant and in destitute circumstances.

abatement. suspension of a legal proceeding.

abatement of nuisance. the removal of a nuisance by a court order. For example, if a person is maintaining a nuisance by storing explosives without a license, the court may direct its abatement by issuing an order to the sheriff to impound the explosives.

ABC sheet. a form used in an illegal horse race gambling operation. It contains columns representing win, place, and show, and serves as a record of bets made.

ABCD steps of CPR. an acronym indicating the basic steps of cardiopulmonary resuscitation. The letters stand for Airway, Breathing, Circulation, and Definitive therapy.

ABC surveillance. a surveillance technique in which a vehicle trails the subject, with a vehicle on each of the parallel streets. The surveillance is not interrupted if the subject turns right or left.

abduct. to restrain a person against his will with intent to prevent his liberation by hiding or holding him in a place where he is not likely to be found.

abet. to encourage, support, or countenance an offense or offender. The term implies that at least two persons are concerned in the commission of the offense: one who directly commits the act and a second who abets its commission. An abettor can be, but is not always, charged in a crime as a principal.

ab initio. a Latin term meaning "from the beginning." A trespasser ab initio is one who has committed trespass from the very beginning.

A-bomb. a marihuana cigarette laced with heroin or opium.

abjuration of allegiance. the renouncing under oath of all allegiance and fidelity to any foreign nation. An abjuration of allegiance is required in an application for American citizenship.

abortifacient. anything used to procure an abortion, including medicines, drugs, or instruments.

abortion. the unlawful destruction of the human fetus before the natural time of its birth; the procuring of a miscarriage of a woman, unless the same is necessary to preserve her life, or that of the child with which she is pregnant. Prescribing, supplying, or administering to a woman, or advising or causing her to take any medicine, drug, or substance, constitutes abortion, whether she is actually pregnant or not. An induced abortion is one caused artificially, either by the woman or by someone else. A therapeutic abortion is one artificially induced to save life and is therefore legal.

abrasion. a wound in which the outer layers of the skin have been scraped away; excoriation; a circumscribed removal of the epidermis of the skin or mucous membrane.

abrasion collar. a narrow ring in the skin around the entry of a bullet hole. Being elastic, the skin will stretch as the bullet passes through. The abrasive action of the bullet will form a circular discoloration which may also contain residues from the surface of the bullet.

abrasion tool mark. a mark made when a tool cuts into or slides against a softer surface. Such marks are typically caused by pliers, bolt cutters, knives and axes.

abrogate. to abolish or nullify; to set aside.

abscond. to go away secretly or hide in order to avoid legal proceedings; to flee with the property of another; to depart without authorization from a geographical area or jurisdiction in violation of the conditions of probation or parole.

absolute liability. liability that arises from extremely dangerous operations. For example, a police officer could be held liable for damages caused by the use of a sidearm. A claimant would not have to prove that the use of a sidearm is inherently dangerous.

absolute privilege. a prohibition against prosecution for criminal libel, regardless of malice. It is generally limited to official participation in governmental affairs. Absolute privilege is based on the belief that the public benefits by allowing officials to exercise their functions without fear of litigation.

absolve. to free from an accusation or from guilt.

absorption-elution test. a test that determines the blood group antigen present in a sample of blood.

absorptometer. an instrument used to compare and classify objects by measuring the light and colors reflected from them.

abstinence syndrome. the group of physical symptoms experienced by an addict when the addictive drug is withdrawn. The syndrome varies according to the drug abused. In narcotics abuse, the symptoms include watery eyes, runny nose, yawning, and perspiration from 8 to 12 hours after the previous dose. This is followed by restlessness, irritability, loss of appetite, insomnia, goose flesh, tremors, and finally yawning and severe sneezing. These symptoms peak at 48 to 72 hours, and are followed by nausea, vomiting, weakness, stomach cramps, and possibly diarrhea. Heart rate and blood pressure are elevated. Chills alternating with flushing and excessive sweating are characteristic. Pains in the bones and muscles of the back and extremities occur as do muscle spasms and kicking movements. Suicide is a possibility, and without treatment the symptoms may continue for 7 to 10 days. Also called the withdrawal syndrome.

Acapulco gold. a potent strain of marihuana, so named for its color and the region where it is grown.

accelerant. any highly flammable substance that operates to accelerate a fire. Commonly used accelerants are gasoline, kerosene, naptha, and jet fuel.

accelerant marks. in arson investigations, characteristic burn patterns caused by a liquid accelerant, such as gasoline. A surface struck by a Molotov cocktail will show "finger patterns" around and below the spot where the device shattered and ignited. In set fires, an accelerant will sometimes pool on a large, level floor and burn from the outside of the pool toward the center, leaving a distinctive mark on the floor. Flammable liquids will leave marks on furniture legs, rugs, and on the under portions of flooring. As an accelerant burns it will cause deep charring marks that neatly point to its flow. Tracing the flow marks back to the place of spillage helps the investigator locate the origin of the fire.

acceleration scuff. in traffic accident investigation, a scuffmark on a road surface made by a spinning wheel.

accessory. a person who was not present

when a crime was committed, but who was involved as a guilty party.

accessory after the fact. a person who, knowing that another has committed a felony, subsequently aids the felon to escape or prevents the felon's arrest and prosecution. An accessory after the fact must have an intention to assist and must actually do so.

accessory before the fact. a person who, before the time a crime is committed, knows of the contemplated crime, assents to or approves of it, and expresses a view of it in such a way as to encourage the principal to perform the act. An accessory before the fact is similar to a principal in the second degree. The difference turns on where the accessory was at the time of the act.

access time. in electronic data processing, the time interval between the instant at which an instruction control unit initiates a call for data and the instant at which delivery of the data is completed.

accidental whorl. a fingerprint pattern consisting of a combination of two different types of patterns, one of which is not the plain arch, and having two or more deltas.

accident analysis. a critical review of information developed in an accident investigation, usually for the purpose of identifying the cause and formulating measures to prevent recurrence.

accident proneness. a personal predisposition, as opposed to environmental influences, that leads some persons to have more accidents than others, within the same time period and under conditions where all confront the same risks.

accomplice. a person who aids another to commit a crime.

accountability. the state of being responsible and punishable for a crime. Accountability is reduced or abolished in certain instances because of age, mental defect, or other reason.

account executive. a provider of high-priced prostitutes.

accusation. a formal charge made to competent authority against someone who is alleged to have committed a crime.

acetone. a volatile ketone hydrocarbon commonly used as a solvent in such products as fingernail polish remover and plastic cements. It is a commonly abused inhalant.

acetone breath. breath characterized by a sweet, fruity odor, found especially in persons suffering from diabetic keto-acidosis.

acid. LSD.

acid head. a user of hallucinogenic drugs, such as LSD.

acid phosphatase. an enzyme found in large quantities in the seminal fluid of man and ape. There are also small quantities of acid-reacting phosphatase in vaginal fluid, feces, red blood cells, and in rare instances in saliva. Differentiation between the various types of phosphatase may be done by using a variety laboratory tests, quantification analysis, and separation by electrophoresis.

acid phosphatase reaction test. a crime laboratory test which determines the presence of semen in a suspect stain or substance. The test produces a chemical reaction for semen that is considered specific.

acid test for silver content. a field test in which a solution of silver nitrate, nitrate acid, and water is applied to a suspect silver coin to determine if it is counterfeit.

ack-ack. to dip the end of a cigarette in heroin powder, light it, and smoke it.

acoustic coupler. a telecommunication device that permits use of a telephone handset as a connection to a telephone network for data transmission by means of sound transducers.

acoustic fuse. a bomb sensitive to sonic or subsonic variations. The fuse operates from an influence exerted by the target on a sensor within the fuse.

acoustic pickup. a microphone, sometimes conventional and sometimes specially designed, that is easily concealed and employed for use in electronic eavesdropping operations.

acquisitive vandalism. damage to property accompanied by a theft, such as breaking into a car and stealing contents or the smashing and looting of a vending machine.

acquit. to set free, release, or remove an accusation of crime.

acquittal. a judgment of a court, based either on the verdict of a jury or a judicial officer, that the defendant is not guilty of the offense for which tried.

action. gambling play, as in betting or wagering. Also, that assembly of parts in a gun which cocks the hammer, moves the cylinder or slide, and fires the cartridge.

action ex delicto. an action at law to recover damages for the breach of a duty existing by reason of a general law. For example, an action to recover damages for an injury caused by negligence is an ex delicto action.

action message. in telecommunications, a message issued because of a condition that requires an operator response.

activation analysis. an analysis to determine chemical elements in a material by bombarding it with neutrons to produce radioactive atoms whose radiations are characteristic of the elements present. The technique has many forensic applications; for example, to determine the presence of a poison, such as arsenic, in the hair of a person believed to have died from poisoning. Also called neutron activation analysis.

active ingredient. the alkaloid or chemical in a plant that produces mind-altering and toxic effects. Cocaine, for example, is the active ingredient of coca leaf. Although active ingredients may be responsible for many of the effects of drug plants, they do not exactly reproduce those effects and in pure form have higher toxicity and potential for abuse. Also called active principle or active constituent.

active listening. an interviewing technique in which the questioner attentively listens to both the facts and the expressed feelings of the speaker.

active supervision. guidance, treatment or regulation by a probation agency of a person who is subject to adjudication or who has been convicted of an offense. Active supervision can be instituted by a formal court order or a probation agency decision.

Act of God. an accident-causing event generally interpreted as being beyond human control. Lightning, hurricane, flood, tornado and earthquake are regarded as Acts of God.

actus reus. criminal act. The "doing" part of the crime.

acute brain disorder. a disease syndrome resulting from temporary impairment of brain tissue function due to drugs, injury, or organic disease. Sometimes called acute brain syndrome.

acute situational maladjustment. an inability to cope with new experiences that are especially difficult or trying.

Adamism. exhibitionism by a male.

Adamsite. the popular name for diphenylaminechloroarsine (DM), a nauseating agent developed in 1918 by U.S. Army major Roger Adams. Originally produced for military applications, it has since been used in riot control operations. Adamsite produces severe discomfort and sickness, but because it takes several minutes to reach full effect it is sometimes combined with chloroacetephenone (CN) to produce a more rapid result.

ADAPT. an acronym representing a five-step approach for guiding the first patrol officer to arrive at the scene of a homicide. The five steps are: Arrest the perpetrator, if possible, Detail and identify witnesses and suspects, Assess the crime scene, Protect the crime scene, Take notes.

addict. one who has acquired the habit of using narcotics to such an extent that reasonable self-control has been lost; a nebulous term that generally refers to one who habitually uses drugs, especially morphine or heroin, to the extent that cessation causes severe physical or psychological trauma or both.

addict files. files kept by the Drug Enforcement Administration (DEA) which identify persons arrested by any law enforcement agency for illegal drug use.

addiction. a state of periodic or chronic intoxication produced by the repeated consumption of a drug. Addiction characteristics include an overpowering desire or need to continue taking the drug and to obtain it by any means, a tendency to increase the dose, a psychic and generally a physical dependence on the effects of the drug, and an effect detrimental to the individual and to society. Also, to give or bind a person to one thing or another. Generally used in the drug field to refer to chronic, compulsive, or uncontrollable drug use, to the extent that a person cannot or will not stop the use of some drug. Beyond this, the term is ambiguously used with a wide variety of often arbitrary meanings and connotations, and sometimes used interchangeably with, sometimes in contrast to, two other ill-defined terms, habituation and (drug) dependence. The former imprecisely refers to some lesser form of chronic drug use, the latter refers to a psychological or physical origin, often in varying combinations depending on the drug. It usually implies a strong (psychological) dependence and (physical) dependence resulting in a withdrawal syndrome when use of the drug is stopped. Many definitions place primary stress on psychological factors, such as loss of self-control and overpowering desires, i.e., addiction is any state in which one craves the use of a drug and uses it frequently. Others use the term as a synonym for physiological dependence. Still others see it as a combination.

addiction-prone theory. a theory of addiction holding that only certain kinds of individuals with specific psychological affinities that are satisfied by opiate narcotics will take favorably to these drugs and will continue to use them in the face of severe social opposition. More recently, the addiction-prone theory has been discounted by researchers who argue that addicts do not make up a homogeneous group but, rather, reflect divergent personality configurations.

addictive effect. the action obtained when the combined effect of two separate entities, such as drugs, taken together is the sum of the two separate effects.

add-on prescription. a prescription that has been used by a dishonest pharmacist to add-on drugs not authorized by the prescribing physician. Add-on prescriptions are used by unscrupulous pharmacists to account for drugs they have diverted to illegal channels.

adipocere condition. an after-death condition in which the buttocks, abdomen and other fleshy parts of the body turn into fatty acids and soaps. Adipocere fat is yellowish-white in color, has a greasy feel, and a strong, musty odor. It results from hydrolysis, a chemical process induced by enzymes and water in moist climates where bacteria can survive without air.

adjective law. a term relating to the practice of organizing all laws in two divisions: substantive and adjective. Substantive laws relate to rights and duties, and this includes practically all laws except those that are procedural. Adjective law is concerned with the procedures involved in carrying out substantive law, such as the laws of arrest, trial and bail. Also called procedural law.

adjudicate. to settle a matter through the course of judicial authority.

adjudication withheld. a court decision, made after a criminal complaint has been filed, to continue court jurisdiction short of pronouncing judgment. The usual purpose in stopping criminal proceedings prior to judgment is to avoid conviction when conviction is likely to bring unnecessary harm to the offender and/or unnecessary harm and expense to the public interest.

adjudicatory hearing. the fact finding process in which a juvenile court determines whether or not there is sufficient evidence to support the allegations in a petition. An adjudicatory hearing is analogous to a trial in criminal proceedings. Both proceedings determine matters of fact concerning alleged acts in violation of criminal law.

adjustment case. a juvenile offender who is in need of social, medical, psychiatric, or psychological treatment. A youth is considered an adjustment case when he is not released outright, but is entered into treatment according to a preliminary diagnosis and recommendation. Sometimes social, civic, or religious agencies may be called upon to lend their aid in restoring juveniles to normal and accepted attitudes.

ad litem. for the suit; for the litigation. For example, a guardian ad litem is a person appointed to prosecute or defend a suit for someone incapacitated by infancy or incompetency.

administrative judge. a judicial officer who supervises or performs administrative tasks for a court, sometimes in addition to performing regular judicial functions.

administrative law. the law governing powers and procedures of administrative agencies, including judicial review of administrative action; the rules and regulations framed by an administrative body created by a state legislature or by Congress to carry out a specific statute. For example, a state law requiring certification of peace officers might be administered by a peace officer standards and training council. The council would issue regulations and rules that have the weight of law as long as they keep within the scope of the authorizing state law. Such regulations often interpret in specific ways the legislature's general intent when it enacted the statute. In this way, an administrative body will take on powers that resemble legislative or judicial authority.

administrative reports. a general class of police reports which originate in staff or management units. They typically address issues relating to personnel, budgets, arrest rates, crime rates, and summaries of police activities.

admiralty. a court with exclusive jurisdiction over maritime cases, both civil and criminal; causes of action arising out of or in connection with the sea.

admiralty law. the code or system of law and procedure relating to maritime affairs; maritime law.

admissible. pertinent and proper to be considered in reaching a decision. As applied to matters in litigation, the term means that the evidence is of such character that the court must allow it to be introduced.

admission. a statement or an act by an accused before or after the commission of a crime which is inconsistent with a plea of innocence. An admission is not a confession, but when considered with other evidence may infer guilt. By contrast, a confession is an express acknowledgment of guilt. When a defendant has made prior statements, not amounting to a confession, but which admit facts in issue against him, such statements may be used in evidence against him as admissions. That the accused ran away or was in hiding after the commission of the crime is admissible as evidence of a guilty mind. Silence is an admission of guilt when the accused heard and understood the accusation made in the presence of others and did not rebut or deny it when he had an opportunity to do so. However, if the accused has already been placed in custody, his silence cannot be used against him for he is under no duty to explain his innocence. At trial, an admission is an acknowledgment by either prosecution or defense that a statement of fact made by the opposing side is true. Also, the entry of an offender into the legal jurisdiction of a corrections agency and/or physical custody of a correctional facility.

admission against interest. an admission of a fact which, though short of a confession, tends to suggest possible guilt; for example, that the subject had a motive or opportunity to commit the crime.

admonition. a reprimand from a judge to an accused, about to be discharged, warning him of the consequences of unacceptable conduct. Also, any authoritative oral communication or statement by way of advice or caution by the court.

ad quod damnum. to what damage; what injury. The phrase is often used in relation to a plaintiff's money loss or the damages he claims.

adrenal exhaustion. acute fatigue caused by extended or intense fear or other emotional stress. It can be a factor in administering a polygraph test.

adult. a person who is within the original jurisdiction of a criminal court because the age of the accused at the time of the alleged crime was above a statutorily specified limit.

adulteration. to make a drug inferior or impure by adding an improper substance; for example, the cutting of cocaine with sugars and cheap local anesthetics to make more of the substance available for sale. Drugs are often adulterated by more active (and less expensive) substances to make users think they are getting a more potent drug. In urine testing, the addition of a foreign substance to a urine specimen for the purpose of confounding the analysis.

adultery. an offense committed when one person engages in sexual intercourse with another person at a time when he or she has a living spouse, or the other person has a living spouse.

ad valorem. according to value.

advanced life support. basic life support plus definitive therapy. It includes the use of invasive procedures, drugs, and defibrillation by qualified medical practitioners.

advance fee scheme. a promotional scheme designed to procure fees in advance for services the promoter has no intention of providing. In many such schemes, the promoter will claim to have means of obtaining buyers or to have access to sources of loan financing. For example, a promoter will represent himself as an agent of a major lending institution that is willing to loan large sums at reasonable rates. In return for a fee paid in advance, the promoter will guarantee approval of a loan application.

adversary. the opposing party in a civil or criminal action.

adversary system. a system used in many countries for resolving both civil and criminal disputes. It features an adversarial relationship between an initiating party, called the plaintiff in civil proceedings and the prosecutor in criminal proceedings, and the responding party, called the defendant. It is presided over by a judge, who adjudicates and renders final judgment, sometimes with the aid of a jury for finding disputed facts on the basis of evidence presented in open court, and in light of the applicable law.

adverse action. an action considered unfavorable to a person; for example, a discharge or demotion of an employee.

adverse drug reaction. a negative somatic or psychological reaction to drug taking. A major problem in drug research has been the lack of agreement concerning what actually constitutes an adverse reaction. Many studies do not distinguish between types of adverse reactions, or they use subjective or poorly defined definitions.

adverse witness. a witness who is prejudiced against or hostile to the party who has called him to testify.

advice of rights form. any of the several varieties of forms used by police agencies when a suspect is advised of Miranda rights prior to questioning. The form typically contains the Miranda warnings, a place for the suspect to sign if he decides to waive his rights to remain silent and have counsel present, the name of the questioning officers, other persons present, the offense, time, date, and place of questioning.

aerosol irritant. any of the nonlethal chemicals used to subdue or temporarily disable resisting persons. Mace is an example.

affected class. that class of job applicants or employees with a common characteristic, such as race, color, religion, sex, national origin, or age, who have been denied equal opportunity in violation of Title VII of the Civil Rights Act of 1964, or an allied law.

affiant. the person who makes and signs an affidavit.

affidavit. a written statement which is signed and sworn to under oath before a judge or other official.

affirmant. a person who testifies on affirmation, or one who affirms instead of taking an oath.

affirmation. a solemn declaration made under penalty of perjury.

affirmative action. positive or active steps

taken to improve employment opportunities for minorities and women. Affirmative action is based on the rationale that past discrimination has put minorities and women far behind white males in competition for jobs and that such past discrimination will perpetuate the inequality of employment opportunities unless affirmative steps are taken.

affirmative action plan. a detailed plan of action for overcoming discriminatory policies in the hiring, employment and/or training of minority group members. Such a plan states an organization's goals for achieving equal employment opportunities and how those goals are to be accomplished. It is usually submitted for approval to the Equal Employment Opportunity Commission.

aforethought. in criminal law, deliberate; planned; premeditated.

a fortiori. by a stronger reason. The phrase is often used in court judgments to say that since specific proven facts lead to a certain conclusion, there can be other facts that logically follow which strengthen the conclusion.

African black. marihuana so called because of its color and origin.

after-accident situation map. a drawing of a traffic accident scene, usually to scale; a graphical summary of results of an accident, usually without indication of assumptions or inferences concerning fault or cause.

aftercare program. a supervisory and/or treatment program for juveniles who have been conditionally released from a treatment or confinement facility.

agar composition. a plastic-like substance used in moulage and casting. It is more elastic than plaster, and is particularly useful in picking up delicate impressions. When mixed with water, it will melt at the boiling point of water, and will solidify at about 100 degrees C. When agar composition sets, it is fluid enough to pick up undercut impressions and for this reason is highly favored for crime scene processing.

agent buy. a purchase of an illegal drug by an undercover police officer from a street peddler or dealer.

agent provocateur. an individual who is specifically hired by one organization to create trouble in a rival organization; a person who surreptitiously seeks to incite others to criminal behavior so that the police may intervene and the offenders may be prosecuted.

agent transmitter. a small radio transmitter concealed on a person working on behalf of law enforcement. The transmitter is used to secretly capture information from criminals or to give early warning to backup agents if a threat is made against the person wearing the transmitter. Also called a body bug or body wire.

age of consent. the chronological age of a female, usually 16 or 18, after which it is no longer felonious for another to have voluntary sexual relations with her.

agglutinogens. properties contained in the red blood cells which correspond to antibodies, or agglutinins, in the serum. Agglutinogens (also called antigens) are named A and B. Four combinations are possible. If a person has antigen A in his red cells, he is classified as having Group A blood; if he has antigen B, he is in Group B; if he has both antigens, he is Group AB; and if he possesses neither A nor B, he is classified Group O.

aggravated assault. unlawful intentional causing of serious bodily injury with or without a deadly weapon; unlawful intentional attempting or threatening of serious bodily injury or death with a deadly weapon.

aggravating circumstances. circumstances relating to the commission of a crime which increase its seriousness beyond that of the average instance.

aggregate maximum release date. the calendar date on which a prisoner is to be fully discharged; the date that marks the end point of the time that a given prisoner can be under correctional jurisdiction.

aggressive patrol. a patrol technique in which many officers are deployed in a high-crime area. They often use field inquiries and, where indicated, stop-and-frisk tactics. The objective is to apprehend wanted persons, confiscate contraband, and generally reduce criminal opportunities.

agonist. in drug abuse treatment, a substance that can bind at the molecular level with a receptor site to produce a pharmacological action. The interaction of the agonist at the receptor site can be displaced by its antagonist, which has the effect of completely or partially nullifying the pharmacological action of the agonist. Heroin, for example, is an agonist and naltrexone is a pure antagonist to heroin. Cyclazocine is a mixed antagonist to heroin having some slight agonist properties of its own.

agitation. excessive restlessness suggestive of severe internal tension. It is manifested by pacing, hand wringing, fidgeting, and other forms of constant motor activity, and is one of the major symptoms of nonfatal drug overdose.

Aguilar v. Texas. a case in which the U.S. Supreme Court ruled that it is not sufficient for a police officer seeking a search warrant to simply tell the issuing judge that an informant, whose information is included in the application for the warrant, has previously proved to be reliable or that the officer knows the informant is reliable. In reviewing an affidavit based on informant information, a court will look for evidence of the informant's credibility and reliability. An affidavit may be based on hearsay information and need not reflect direct personal observations of the officer swearing out the warrant, but the judge considering the request for a warrant must be informed of some underlying circumstances on which the informant's conclusions are based and some of the underlying circumstances from which the requesting officer concluded the informant was credible or the information reliable.

aid and abet. help, assist, or facilitate the commission of a crime, or encourage, counsel, or incite a crime to its commission.

aider (or abettor). an accomplice who solicits or knowingly assists another person to commit a crime. An aider is often actually or constructively present at the commission of the crime.

acquired immune deficiency syndrome (AIDS). a syndrome caused by a virus known as the human immunodeficiency virus (HIV) which infects and destroys certain white blood cells, thereby undermining the body's ability to combat infection. A victim can be infected with the HIV for years without ever developing symptoms of AIDS, and can transmit the virus even in the absence of symptoms. AIDS victims do not die from AIDS itself, but from "opportunistic infections" such as pneumonia, malignancies, and a type of skin cancer.

The AIDS virus is difficult to transmit and is quite fragile when outside the body. It can be destroyed by heat, many common household disinfectants and bleaches, and by washing with soap and hot water.

AIDS is transmitted through exposure to contaminated blood, semen, and vaginal secretions. This occurs primarily through sexual intercourse and needle-sharing by intravenous drug users. Transmission from infected mother to fetus or infant has also occurred.

Transmission of the AIDS virus has also been traced to blood transfusions and to blood products given to hemophiliacs. This source of infection, however, has almost nearly been eliminated through changes in screening and treating donated blood products.

The AIDS virus is not transmitted through casual contact. Studies have confirmed that the virus is not spread by sneezing, coughing, breathing, hugging, handshaking, sharing eating and drinking utensils, using the same toilet facilities, and other forms of nonsexual contact. There is no evidence of AIDS virus transmission in schools, offices, churches, or other social settings, and there are no known cases of police officers and other public safety employees becoming infected through performance of their duties. Except for a very small number of cases of infection in health care workers attributed to accidental needle sticks or other exposure to infected blood, there are no reports of infection as a result of occupational contact.

Law enforcement concerns related to AIDS include the following.

Human bite: Transmission through saliva is highly unlikely. Milk the wound to make it bleed, wash thoroughly, and seek medical attention.

Spitting: Transmission through saliva is highly unlikely.

Urine/feces: Virus is in very low concentrations in urine, and not at all in feces. Transmission is highly unlikely.

Cut/wound: Needle stick studies show low risk of infection. Use caution in handling sharp objects and searching in areas hidden from view.

CPR/first aid: Minimal risk associated with CPR. Use mask/airway, and avoid blood-to-blood contact by keeping open wounds covered and wearing gloves when in contact with bleeding wounds.

Body removal: Those who must come into contact with blood or other body fluids in connection with a dead victim should wear gloves.

Blood/body fluids: Wear gloves if contact with blood or body fluids is considered likely. Afterwards, wash thoroughly with soap and hot water. Clean up blood spills with one part water to nine parts household bleach.

Dried blood: Despite low risk of infection, caution dictates wearing gloves, a mask, and protective shoe coverings if exposure to dried blood is likely, for example, at a crime scene investigation.

Aikido. the Japanese art of self-defense which employs locks, holds and the principle of nonresistance to cause an opponent's own strength and momentum to work against him.

Air Force Law Enforcement Terminal System. a U.S. Air Force communications system that interfaces with NCIC and the various statewide computerized criminal information systems.

Air Force Radiation Assessment Team. a U.S. Air Force team made up of health physics technicians trained in the use of air transportable equipment. The team responds to radiation accidents/incidents for the purpose of providing on-site health consultation and instrumentation to detect, identify and quantify radiation hazards.

airhead. a drug user who has difficulty thinking or talking.

Air Opium. a nickname given to air operations that transport opium out of areas in Southeast Asia.

air pack. a portable oxygen unit. It is usually worn on the back, and consists of an oxygen canister, flow regulator and face mask.

air pressure sensor. a sensor that reacts to changes in air pressure. Such devices are used as the triggering mechanisms in anti-personnel bomb.

airway. the breathing passage in the head or throat; a device used to keep the breathing passage open.

AKA. an abbreviation for "also known as."

Al-Anon. a group that helps wives, husbands, and friends of alcoholic persons cope with related difficulties within and outside of the home.

alarm condition. a threatening condition, such as a fire or hold-up, reported by an alarm.

alarm response time. the time that elapses between activation of an alarm and arrival of a responding unit.

alarm station. a general term referring to any of several types of manually operated devices used to generate alarm signals. Alarm stations are used in public areas for reporting emergencies, such as a fire alarm pull station, or in concealed applications, such as a holdup button.

Alateen. a sub-group of Al-Anon which assists young people whose lives have been affected by the alcoholism of a family member or close friend.

Alco-Analyzer Gas Chromatograph. a breath testing device that measures alcohol concentrations in the blood of persons suspected of being under the influence of alcohol.

Alcohol, Drug Abuse, and Mental Health Administration (ADAMHA). an umbrella agency within the Public Health Service of the U.S. Department of Health and Human Services. In addition to its own administrative staff, ADAMHA consists of the National Institute on Alcoholism and Alcohol Abuse, the National Institute on Drug Abuse, and the National Institute of Mental Health.

alcoholic. a person unable to correct the physiological and other bodily disturbances which have accumulated as the result of his drinking.

alcoholic beverage. any beverage that contains ethyl alcohol (ethanol), the intoxicating sedative-hypnotic in fermented and distilled liquors. Made synthetically or produced naturally by fermentation of fruits, vegetables, or grains, alcohol is the oldest and the most widely used social drug in the world. A CNS depressant, depending on the concentration consumed, alcohol acts as an analgesic, tranquilizer, sedative-hypnotic, soporific, intoxicant, anesthetic, or narcotic. At low doses, it can act as a stimulant. At high doses, it can create stupor. Use with other depressants, or with antihistamines or solvents, can be extremely dangerous. Alcoholic beverages are usually classified into the fermented drinks beer and wine and distilled spirits. Fermented drinks contain about 2 percent to 17 percent alcohol. Distilled spirits contain over 90 percent alcohol (e.g., grain alcohol).

alcoholic personality. a generally discredited term used loosely to describe a composite of personality traits which predispose a person to alcohol addiction. Such traits include maladjustment, sexual and emotional immaturity, low self-esteem, and low tolerance to frustration or tension.

alcoholism. a ubiquitously used term with a wide variety of ambiguous meanings about which there is little consensus. Sometimes used narrowly as a synonym for addiction and at other times to refer to alcohol abuse generally. Alcoholism is sometimes viewed as a disease syndrome, other times not. It is sometimes regarded as having physical dependence characteristics and sometimes as having psychological dependence characteristics. Other definitions include: a chronic and usually progressive disease, or a symptom of an underlying psychological or physical disorder, characterized by dependence on alcohol (manifested by loss of control over drinking) for relief from psychological or physical distress or for gratification from alcohol intoxication itself, and by a consumption of alcoholic beverages sufficiently great and consistent to cause physical or mental or social or economic disability; a learned or conditioned dependence on alcohol that irresistibly activates resort to alcohol whenever a critical internal or environmental stimulus occurs; any use of alcoholic beverages that causes any damage to the individual or society or both; a chronic disease, manifested by implicative drinking, so as to cause injury to the drinker's health or his general functioning.

Alcohol Safety Action Program. a state-level program administered in cooperation with the National Highway Traffic Safety Administration. It is designed to reduce highway deaths, injuries, and property damage resulting from motor vehicle traffic accidents in which alcohol is a major contributing factor.

Alco-tector. a breath testing device that measures alcohol concentrations in the blood of persons suspected of being under the influence of alcohol.

ALGOL. an acronym for algorithmic language, a language used to express algorithms in computer programs.

alias. a false name that has been substituted in some official connection for a correct legal name. A nickname is not an alias unless it is used in some official way, such as on a driving license.

alias dictus. otherwise called.

alibi. a defense used by one charged with a crime that he could not have committed the crime because he was elsewhere at the time.

alibi witness. a person who testifies in

support of a defendant's alibi, usually claiming to have been with or to have seen the defendant someplace other than at the place of the crime.

Alice B. Toklas. a brownie with marihuana baked in it.

alidade. a rule equipped with simple or telescopic sights and used for determining direction. An alidade is sometimes used in preparing sketches of crime and accident scenes.

alienation. an individual's feeling of dissociation or estrangement from the surrounding society. Alienation may arise from feelings of powerlessness, normlessness, meaninglessness, depersonalization, isolation, or self-estrangement.

Alien Registration Act of 1940. a federal law, also called the Smith Act, that requires the annual registration of aliens. It also prohibits advocating the violent overthrow of the U.S. government.

alien reports file. a file maintained by the Immigration and Naturalization Service. It is used mainly for locator purposes.

alkaloids. a diverse group of some 5,000 bitter compounds of plant origin containing nitrogen as well as carbon, oxygen, and hydrogen, that are usually physiologically or pharmacologically active. Most medical plants owe their biological activity to alkaloids. Examples include caffeine, morphine, and nicotine. The term is also applied to synthetic alkaloids, which have structures similar to plant alkaloids.

alkalosis. an abnormal condition of acid-base balance that results when the body loses too much carbon dioxide by hyperventilation (respiratory alkalosis) or too much acid from vomiting, for example (metabolic alkalosis). It may also be caused by excessive intake of alkaline substances, such as antacids or sodium bicarbonate.

allegation. a statement by a party to a legal proceeding setting out what will be proved; a charge; an accusation.

Alliance for Cannabis Therapeutics (ACT). an alliance of patients, their families and physicians, researchers, administrators, and politicians organized for the purpose of ending the federal prohibition against using cannabis for medical applications. ACT works to repeal federal laws which prohibit the medical availability of cannabis; encourages and supports the enactment of state and federal laws which properly define cannabis as a drug with medical value; encourages aggressive and neutral scientific study of the cannabis plant for its therapeutic applications; provides the public with factual information on cannabis, its history, medical applications, and the laws governing its use; helps individuals, physicians, state agencies, and others regarding the proper legal procedures used to obtain access to cannabis and its derivatives under existing federal regulations.

alligator effect. in arson investigations, the checkering of charred wood, giving it the appearance of alligator skin. When the alligator effect appears as large rolling blisters the wood was exposed to rapid, intense heat. Small, flat alligator marks indicate long, low heat. When a fire is extinguished quickly, the charring is only slightly below the surface and the checkering pattern has large squares. As the fire continues, the charring goes deeper into the wood and the checkered squares become smaller. Alligator marks can also help the investigator find the origin of the fire, determine if an accelerant was used, and reveal if the arsonist set two or more separate fires.

allocution. in victim's rights, the right of a victim to attend and speak at restitution and/or felony sentencing proceedings concerning the person who committed the crime. In some cases, allocution includes victim participation in hearings on dismissals and pleas.

all-out. a fireman's signal that indicates a fire is out or under control and that all or most of the fire fighting units are ready to be withdrawn.

all points bulletin (APB). a message transmitted to all receivers within a given communications network. An APB transmitted on LETS, for example, is transmitted to law enforcement agencies nationwide.

alphamethyl fentanyl. a derivative of fentanyl that is about 200 times as potent as morphine. Because it has no approved medical use and carries a high potential for addiction, it is classified as a Schedule I controlled substance. When first synthesized, this drug was technically legal and was a popular "designer drug." It is much sought after by addicts for its heroin-like effects.

alphanumeric. a term relating to groups of characters that consist of numbers and letters.

alphanumeric key pad. a device similar to a push button telephone dial. When the buttons on the key pad are pressed in a particular coded sequence a signal is generated. The signal may cause, for example, a door lock to be released or an alarm system to be turned on or off.

also known as (AKA). a term used to denote an alias, false name, nickname or moniker.

alternate juror. a person added to a jury panel. The alternate juror is substituted for a juror who during the trial becomes unable to continue.

alternatives concept. a concept developed as a major prevention approach to drug abuse. The underlying assumption is that illicit drug use becomes a less attractive outlet for individuals who are involved with constructive activities of their own choosing. The key element in the alternatives concept is process rather than product. The specific activities and outlets are secondary. Of primary importance is the process that takes place within the individual of exploring and searching for ways to satisfy inner needs.

altimeter bomb. a bomb triggered by a change in atmospheric pressure relative to the altitude and the earth's surface. The altimeter bomb is a terrorist tool, frequently homemade.

AMAC 1. a commercially manufactured riot control vehicle featuring grenade launchers, water cannon, electrified body, CCTV, hermetically sealed air conditioning, firefighting systems, heavy armor, built-in drinking water supply, and toilet facilities.

amanita mushrooms. a family of large mushrooms that grow in many parts of the world. Some are poisonous and deadly, and a few are edible and delicious. Two varieties, the Amanita muscaria and the Amanita pantherina, are used as psychoactive drugs. The muscaria (also called the fly agaric) grows in the western United States. It is also the traditional intoxicant of a number of primitive tribes of Siberia. The red peel of the mushroom's cap is easily removed and can be dried and smoked. The whole mushroom can be eaten fresh, cooked, dried, or brewed into a tea. The strength and effect depend on where and when they grow. Generally, the strongest pharmacological power is found in mushrooms with red caps.

Moderate doses cause a dreamy intoxication, but there are often uncomfortable physical symptoms as well. High doses can produce delirious excitement and toxicity. The effect starts in about 30 minutes and lasts for 4–8 hours. The responsible chemicals are ibotenic acid and muscimol, substances that resemble gamma-aminobutyric acid (GABA), a natural brain chemical that facilitates nerve impulse transmissions.

The Amanita pantherina (also called the panther mushroom) contains higher doses of ibotenic acid and muscimol, but like the muscaria variety its effects are variable. It can cause sickness for up to 12 hours and has been linked to serious injuries caused while users were delirious.

amapola. a poppy grown in Mexico from which opium is extracted.

amateur burglar. a burglar who tends to act on impulse and opportunity, and whose targets are vulnerable buildings, such as schools, churches, and small businesses. The amateur burglar will generally steal readily usable items, such as cash and postage stamps.

ambient noise. acoustic noise existing in a defined space such as a protected room or area. In some intrusion detection applications, ambient noise is measured and evaluated electronically. When the ambient noise matches predefined characteristics, an alarm signal is annunciated.

ambush code. a special code used by an officer to report a duress situation. Also called a duress code.

ambush evidence. surprise evidence presented at trial; secret evidence presented at the last minute in a trial, usually for the purpose of swaying the jury.

amenable. answerable to the law; liable to punishment.

amercement. the act of punishing by an exactment, assessment, or deprivation; a pecuniary penalty in the nature of a fine. For example, if a fiduciary steals what he has been entrusted to protect, his punishment could include, in addition to the punishment for the crime, a fine equal to the value of the property plus interest.

American Council on Marijuana and Other Psychoactive Drugs. a nonprofit organization established to help reverse national trends in drug abuse. The council is concerned about all abused psychoactive drugs but has especially targeted marijuana.

amicus curiae. a Latin term meaning "friend of the court." An amicus curiae is a person or organization permitted to participate in a court action who does not otherwise have a right to do so.

amino acid. in forgery detection, the residue of perspiration left on paper when the hand, fingers or other parts of the body come into contact with it.

ammonal. a compound consisting of ammonium nitrate, ammonium powder, and TNT. It is used in the manufacture of explosive shells.

amnesty. a form of executive clemency, usually extended to a class or group of offenders, such as illegal aliens. An amnesty has the effect of saying that the offense did not occur. An amnesty is distinct from a pardon in that a pardon applies to only one person, and does not necessarily include the abolition of all legal recognition that the offense occurred.

amobarbital. the generic name for a barbiturate regulated under the Controlled Substances Act as a Schedule II drug. It is a common, intermediate-acting barbiturate manufactured as Amytal and, in a different form, as Amytal Sodium. The prescription drug Tuinal contains amobarbital. It is usually taken orally or injected. Also called barb, downer, blue, yellow jacket and sleeping pill.

amotivational syndrome. a condition sometimes seen in chronic drug users. It is characterized by a general lack of motivation and loss of personal will, rendering the victim highly susceptible to suggestions and manipulation by other persons. The condition is associated with regular marijuana use by youths in which the individual adopts an attitude and behavior that is asocial, nondirectional and "cops out" on established values. The amotivational syndrome is characterized by apathy; loss of effectiveness; and a diminished capacity to carry out complex, long-term plans, endure frustrations, concentrate for long periods, follow routines, or successfully master new material.

amped out. fatigued from the use of amphetamines.

amphetamine psychosis. a reaction seen in chronic users of amphetamines. It is characterized by vivid visual, auditory and olfactory hallucinations and delusions. A model psychosis that closely resembles paranoid schizophrenia has been seen to result from long-term amphetamine use. There is often difficulty in distinguishing amphetamine psychosis from schizophrenia, but it appears that visual hallucinations are more usual in amphetamine psychosis cases, while thought disorder is more usual in schizophrenia cases. There is conflicting evidence in the relative personality factors in precipitation, but many researchers believe that amphetamine psychosis is produced primarily in persons who already manifest a personality disorder or predilection for paranoid reaction.

amphetamine relatives. synthetic drugs, such as methylphenidate hydrochloride

(Ritalin) and phenmetrazine hydrochloride (Preludin), that have characteristics similar to the amphetamines, with which they are often used interchangeably for recreational purposes. Also called amphetamine analogues or amphetamine congeners.

amphetamines. a family of stimulants whose medical use is currently limited to narcolepsy, attention deficit disorders in children, and obesity. They constitute a class of synthetic sympathomimetic amines that are similar in some ways to the body's own adrenaline (epinephrine) and that act with a pronounced stimulant effect on the central nervous system. Chemically there are three similar types: racemic amphetamine or amphetamine sulfate (Dexedrine), and methamphetamine hydrochloride (Methedrine, Desoxyn), with amphetamine sulfate being the least potent and methamphetamine the most, and dextroamphetamine having the fewest side effects. Varying only in the degree of control over peripheral effects and potency, the amphetamines have been used medically as an aid in dieting by depressing appetite, as an energizer and euphoriant, as an antidepressant, to combat narcolepsy (involuntary sleep), hyperkinesis, and to promote alertness, retention, and wakefulness. Widespread use and abuse of amphetamines occurred following World War II when war-time stockpiles became available and were marketed on a nonprescription, over-the-counter basis, with use reaching epidemic proportions. The illicit use of amphetamines closely parallels that of cocaine, and despite broad recognition of risks, abuse continues. Vast quantities of amphetamines, such as methamphetamine and dextroamphetamine, are produced in clandestine laboratories. Other names include Biphetamine, Delcobese, and Mediatric. Amphetamines appear in the Controlled Substances Act as Schedule II and III stimulants.

amphetamine sulfate. the least potent of the amphetamines, manufactured as Benzedrine. Synthesized in 1927, it was first used in 1932 as an inhaler decongestant and in the treatment of narcolepsy. During World War II it was used on troops to counteract fatigue.

amphetamine variants. hallucinogens that are chemical variations of amphetamine synthesized in a laboratory. These drugs are numerous and differ from one another in their speed of onset, duration of action, potency, and capacity to modify mood with or without producing hallucinations. They are usually taken orally, sometimes snorted, and rarely injected. The common variants are DOM, STP, DOB, MDA, TMA, PMA and 2,5-DMA. Amphetamine variants appear in the Controlled Substances Act as Schedule I hallucinogens.

amylase azure test. a crime laboratory test that seeks to identify the presence of amylase in or on an object. Amylase is an enzyme peculiar to saliva and its detection can be significant to an investigation.

amyl nitrite. a quick-acting volatile inhalant that dilates certain small blood vessels (primarily in the brain and heart), lowers high blood pressure, and relaxes (involuntary) muscles. Effects take place within 30 seconds and last only 2 to 3 minutes. Unlike other inhalants, amyl nitrite is a stimulant rather than a depressant, and may be dangerous for people with low blood pressure, glaucoma, or anemia. Among illicit users, the drug is prized for its alleged sexual stimulation or prolongation of orgasm effects. It is usually sold in small glass vials. Slang names include pearls, snappers, amys, and poppers.

anabolic steroid. any of a group of compounds, derived from testosterone or prepared synthetically, which aid in constructive metabolism, including the building of cell components such as proteins and fats. They are used to treat certain anemias and malignancies, to promote body growth and weight gain, to strengthen bones in osteoporosis, to countereffect estrogen, or to promote masculinizing characteristics. Anabolic steroids are sometimes used illegally by athletes in an attempt to improve their strength and performance.

anachronism. in forgery detection, something appearing in a suspect document that could not have been present when the document was originally prepared.

analeptics. drugs that act as stimulants or restoratives to the central nervous system, such as caffeine or amphetamine.

analgesia. absence of sensibility to pain, while remaining conscious, due to nerve damage, hypnosis, acupuncture, the use of pain-relieving drugs (analgesics), or anything that activates the body's natural pain-relieving system.

analgesics. a major classification of drugs that produce relief from, or diminished sensitivity to pain without loss of consciousness. Analgesics may be divided into three basic categories: (1) the opiate narcotics, e.g., opium, codeine, morphine, meperidine hydrochloride (Demerol), hydromorphone hydrochloride (Dolophine); (2) nonnarcotic, prescription drugs; and (3) nonnarcotic, nonprescription, mild analgesics, e.g., aspirin (acetylsalicylic acid) and acetaminophen (Tylenol).

analog. a thing or part that is similar or comparable in certain respects with something else; in biology, similar in functions but not origin and structure. The opioids are often referred to as opiate analogs. Also spelled analogue.

analyte. in drug testing, the substance to be measured.

analytical confirmation. in drug investigations, the confirmation of a field test made of a suspect sample in which the finding was "positive." The field test is analytically confirmed by a second test which uses procedures as sensitive or more sensitive than the field test.

anaphylactic shock. a severe and sometimes fatal hypersensitivity reaction to the injection or ingestion of a substance (e.g., a drug) to which the organism has become sensitized by a previous exposure. Symptoms, including anxiety, weakness, shortness of breath, laryngeal edema, cardiac and respiratory abnormalities, hypo-tension, and shock, may occur within minutes of exposure. Treatment must be prompt and usually involves the use of epinephrine, the maintenance of an open airway, and the treatment of cardiac and other problems.

anaphylaxis. a lessened resistance to a substance (such as a drug) resulting from a previous inoculation of the same material; a sensitivity that can result in a profound state of shock.

anarchy. action to overthrow an organized government, usually by the use of force, violence or subversion.

anesthesia. loss of sensation to the point that pain is wholly abolished.

anesthetics. a class of inhalant drugs that abolish the sensation of pain. Local anesthetics produce loss of sensation only at the area of drug injection and are not used recreationally. General anesthetics affect the entire body and may produce loss of consciousness. While a number of drugs have anesthetic properties, the principal anesthetics are the vaporous chloroform and ether, and the gaseous nitrous oxide.

ANFO. a low explosive made of ammonium nitrate fertilizer and fuel oil.

angel dust. a form of phencyclidine (PCP) sprayed on marihuana or tobacco for smoking purposes.

angel grass. parsley dusted with PCP.

angina pectoris. acute pain in the chest caused by reduced blood supply to the heart muscle, usually caused by coronary artery disease.

angle of field. in police photography, the greatest angle between two light rays passing through the objective lens into the optical system. Also called the field of view or FOV.

angle of view. in police photography, the angle in degrees between the axis of the barrel of an optical system's scope and the centerline of the field of view. Also called the direction of view or DOV.

anilingus. the act of orally stimulating the anus of another.

animo. a Latin term relating to intent, disposition, design, or will.

animo furandi. intent to steal.

ankle belt. any of several types of leg-restraining devices applied to the ankles of violent subjects. The device typically consists of a braided line passed around each ankle and then secured.

anomie. a state of society characterized by a condition of relative normlessness, a general breakdown or absence of norms governing individual and group behavior, developed out of instability and change and is characterized by elements of anxiety, isolation, and purposelessness.

anorectic drug. a drug that causes loss of appetite. Phenmetrazine, benzphetamine, and phendimetrazine are examples of anorectics.

answer. a document which the defendant in a civil lawsuit serves on the plaintiff or his attorney in answer to the summons or complaint.

Antabuse. the trade name for disulfiram, a drug used in the treatment of alcoholism.

antagonist. a drug that blocks or counteracts the effect of another drug.

ante mortem. prior to death.

antemortem wound. a wound inflicted prior to death.

anthropometry. a system of human identification which uses body measurements, e.g., length of arms, fingers, and feet, size of skull, and overall body height. The system was created by Alphonse Bertillon and is often referred to as bertillonage.

anthropophagy. cannibalism; in deviant behavior, the eating of the victim's flesh.

antianxiety tranquilizers. those tranquilizers prescribed as sedatives to reduce anxiety and tension, sometimes called minor tranquilizers, as distinct from the major or antipsychotic tranquilizers. They are widely prescribed as sedatives that have relatively few other significant effects on emotional, cognitive, or perceptual processes, although there is much disagreement surrounding the extent to which they achieve this goal. Unlike the antipsychotic tranquilizers, which do not produce euphoria or other pleasant effects and are rarely used nonmedically, the antianxiety tranquilizers produce effects subjectively similar to alcohol and barbiturates and are often used nonmedically. In much of the scientific literature, the term is restricted to use of the benzodiazepine derivatives chlordiazepoxide hydrochloride (Librium) and diazepam (Valium), and of the propanediol derivative meprobamate (Equanil and Miltown). Sometimes the term is used in a broader sense to refer to other of the new nonbarbiturate sedatives such as glutethimide (Doriden) and methaqualone (Quaalude or Mequin). The antianxiety tranquilizers should not be confused with the antidepressants.

antibug. a device that defeats the operation of a clandestine listening device. An antibug usually operates on the principle of noise generation.

anticipatory offense. an offense that is a step toward the intended commission of another offense. Also called an inchoate offense.

anti-climax dampening effect. in polygraphy, an effect upon a subject being tested in which all questions other than the one feared by the subject will be anti-climactic. By comparison to the feared question, the responses to the anti-climactic (non-feared) questions will be dampened in the measurements recorded by the polygraph instrument.

anti-contamination clothing. specially constructed clothing that provides protection from alpha-beta (nuclear) radiation and which helps to prevent the spread of contamination. Also called anti-C's.

antidepressants. a major classification of drugs sold only by prescription, and used medically to improve mood in severely depressed patients. Generally divided into the tricyclic compounds amitriptyline hydrochloride (Tofranil), and the MAO inhibitors, the antidepressants are rarely used for nonmedical purposes since they have little immediate pleasurable effect on normal mood states. This varied group of drugs seems to have a stimulant effect in cases of pathologic depression but appears to have little effect in normal states. Chronic usage, however, has been shown to have clearly defined stimulatory action. While some of the stimulants have been medically used as antidepressants, their effects are inconsistent.

anti-disturbance device. a device built into a bomb that will trigger the explosive charge if the bomb is jarred, moved or disturbed. The principle of operation may be mechanical, as in the case of release of spring tension, or chemical, as in the case of a reaction caused by chemicals coming into contact with each other.

antidote. a substance used to counteract the effects of a drug or combat the effects of a poison.

anti-eavesdrop device. a device that scans radio frequency transmissions in search of covert listening devices.

anti-human test. a crime laboratory test which examines stains and other materials to detect the presence of blood or other body fluids of human origin.

anti-personnel bomb. a bomb intended to primarily injure or kill people. It is frequently home-made, as in a pipe bomb, and designed to fragment upon explosion.

anti-pick latch. a type of spring latch bolt designed to resist entry attempts with the use of thin-bladed tools.

antipsychotic tranquilizers. a major classification of drugs commonly used to treat psychiatric problems falling under the rubric of psychosis. The classification has four groups: (1) phenothiazines, such as chlorpromazine (Thorazine); (2) Rauwolfia compounds, such as reserpine (Serpasil); (3) butyrophenones, such as haloperidol (Haldol); and (4) thioxanthines, such as Navane. Because they lack euphoric properties and generally produce unpleasant side effects, they are rarely used nonmedically.

Anti-Racketeering Act of 1934. a federal law that prohibits the use of extortion or violence that in any way obstructs, delays, or affects interstate commerce. Also called the Hobbs Act.

anti-shim device. a mechanism in a lock which prevents the bolt from being shimmed or forced open.

antisocial personality. a personality disorder characterized by a basic lack of socialization and by behavior patterns that bring the individual repeatedly into conflict with society. Also, a diagnostic category recommended by the American Psychiatric Association for persons over age 15 who demonstrate a history of continuous and chronic antisocial behavior in which the rights of others are violated. This diagnosis is recommended in place of the older psychiatric categories "sociopathic personality disorder" and "psychopathic personality disorder."

Anti-Strikebreaker Act of 1936. a federal law that prohibits employers from transporting strikebreakers across state lines. As amended in 1938, the statute also prohibits the interstate transportation of persons for the purpose of interfering with peaceful picketing. Also called the Byrnes Act.

anti-surveillance equipment. equipment designed to detect or prevent the use of electronic surveillance devices.

antitrust laws. those federal laws designed to prevent restraint of trade, monopoly, and unfair practices in interstate commerce. The antitrust statutes include the Sherman Act (Antitrust Act of 1890), the Clayton Act, the Federal Trade Commission Act, the Robinson-Patman Act, the Miller-Tydings Act, and the Wheeler-Lea Act.

anxiety attack. an acute episode of intense anxiety and feelings of panic, accompanied by symptoms such as palpitations, breathlessness, sweating, gastrointestinal complaints and feelings of imminent disaster. The attacks usually occur suddenly, may last from a few seconds to an hour or more, and may occur infrequently or several times a day. Treatment includes reassurance, the use of anxiolytic and ataraxic drugs, sedation, and often psychotherapy.

anxiety disorder. a human condition in which severe and persistent anxiety interferes with normal, daily functioning.

anxiolytic. a drug that relieves anxiety; anxiety relieving.

aorta. the great artery arising from the left ventricle; the main trunk from which the systemic arterial system proceeds.

aortic regurgitation. in polygraphy, an expected and natural phenomenon observed as a notch in the pen tracing of the cardiosphygmograph component of the polygraph instrument. It results from measurement of blood pressure changes that occur naturally in the human body as blood is expelled through the semilunar valves in the left ventricle of the heart.

apnea. cessation of breathing; partial asphyxia. In death investigations, a condition associated with the sudden infant death syndrome (SID). In polygraphy, a phenomenon frequently observed in the reactions of deceptive persons or persons who attempt to distort measurements during testing by engaging in irregular breathing.

apoplexy. the sudden reduction or loss of consciousness, sensation, and voluntary motion caused by rupture or obstruction of an artery of the brain. Also called stroke.

appeal. an application of one found guilty of a crime by a lower court to have the case reviewed by a higher court.

appeal of right. an appeal which must be heard and decided on its merits. In criminal cases, defense appeals of final judgments are most frequently appeals of right, i.e., the defendant's right to appeal from a conviction is guaranteed by law.

appeal proceedings. a set of orderly steps by which an appellate court considers the issues and makes a determination in a case before it on appeal. The major steps are: (1) the appeal is initiated by the filing of a formal document, (2) a record of the original proceedings in the trial court is transferred to the appellate court, (3) briefs are filed by the opposing parties, (4) a hearing is scheduled and the arguments heard, and (5) the appellate court deliberates, reviewing the record of the earlier proceedings and considering the allegations and arguments of the parties, and announces its decision.

appearance. the act of coming into a court and submitting to the court's authority.

appellant. the person who protests the correctness of a court order, judgment, or other decision and who seeks review and relief in a court having appellate jurisdiction.

appellate court. any court that reviews a trial court's actions or the decisions of a lower-level appellate court.

appetite suppressant. a drug used to curb the desire to eat. The prescription varieties of appetite suppressants usually contain amphetamines. The nonprescription varieties usually contain phenylpropanolamine and/or caffeine.

applied stimulus. in polygraphy, a stimulus applied to an examinee for the purpose of adjusting polygraph instrument controls. An example of an applied stimulus would be to ask the examinee to add a simple series of numbers. As the examinee does so, the polygraphist observes the instrument's tracings and adjusts the controls.

apprehend. to take, seize, or arrest.

a priori. from what goes before; from the cause to the effect; a generalization resting on presuppositions and not upon proven facts.

aqueous suspension. a mixture or emulsion containing a drug suspended in a liquid. When standing, the mixture will separate (i.e., solids will settle to the bottom) and when shaked, it will evenly mix.

area sketch. a type of rough sketch which depicts the physical surroundings closest to the crime scene. Area sketches might be made of the house containing a room where a crime occurred, the area immediately around the house, the neighborhood, and routes of entry and departure.

arborescent mark. a mark on the body of a person hit by lightning. It is so-called because of its tree-like shape.

Architectural Barriers Act of 1968. a federal statute which specifies that buildings and facilities designed, constructed, altered or leased with federal funds are to be usable by and accessible to physically disabled persons.

arch pattern. one of the three basic groups of fingerprint patterns, the other two being the loop and whorl. The arch pattern has two subgroups: the plain arch and tented arch.

area control. the coordinated management of traffic over a large area.

area sketch. a type of rough sketch which depicts the physical surroundings of a crime scene. Area sketches might be made of the house containing a room where a crime occurred, the area immediately around the house, and the neighborhood.

arecoline. an alkaloid with CNS-stimulant properties found in the betel nut.

argument of counsel. the final statements given to a court or jury by a prosecutor and defense attorney.

Arkansas v. Sanders. a case in which the U.S. Supreme Court ruled in 1979 that the police have no right to search luggage taken from an automobile when there is no risk to themselves or danger of loss of evidence. In this case, after receiving a tip that Sanders was to arrive on a certain flight, the police set up a surveillance at the airport. The officers watched Sanders arrive, retrieve his luggage, and enter a taxi with a second individual. The taxi was stopped, the trunk was opened, and the luggage searched without a search warrant. The luggage contained approximately 10 pounds of marihuana.

armed propaganda. a term used by terrorists to describe their acts of violence.

armed robbery. the unlawful taking or attempted taking of property that is in the immediate possession of another, by the use or threatened use of a deadly or dangerous weapon.

arming signal. a signal, transmitted from a protected premises, such as a bank, to a central station or other monitoring location, which informs that the alarm system has been armed by an authorized person.

armor piercing bullet. a high-velocity bullet usually jacketed with steel. In larger calibers, armor piercing bullets are manufactured with chemicals that ignite and burn through a target upon impact.

armpit carrying. a shoplifting technique in which the thief places an item under the armpit inside a jacket or coat.

army disease. an expression often used as a synonym for morphine addiction after the Civil War; also called "soldier's illness." During the Civil War the hypodermic needle was first used to inject morphine, which was employed indiscriminately as an analgesic. Because only soldiers were so widely effected, the addiction became known as the army disease.

arraign. to bring an arrested person before the court, where the charge is explained and a plea is taken. If later indicted, the same process is repeated in a higher court.

arrest. the taking of a person into custody to answer for a crime. It may be effected by "an actual restraint of the person or by his submission to custody." Police officers, however, may detain persons for any of several purposes without the detention becoming custodial and thereby an arrest. Also, a stoppage of circulation or ventilation.

arrestee dispositions. a class of law enforcement or prosecutorial actions which terminate or provisionally suspend proceedings against an arrested person before a charge has been filed in court. Examples of arrestee dispositions include police release, complaint rejected, and prosecution withheld.

arrest rate. the number of arrests as a percentage of the crimes known to the police; the number of arrests as a percentage of the entire population or a cohort thereof, such as arrests of males within the total population or of male juveniles within the male population.

arrest record. a list of a person's arrests and or charges that have been made against him, usually including those that have been dropped and those of which he was found innocent. The arrest record also contains information on dispositions and sentences, where there was adjudication of guilt.

arrest register. a document containing a chronological record of all arrests made by members of a given law enforcement agency, containing the identity of the arrestee, the charges at time of arrest, and the date and time of arrest.

arrest report. the document prepared by the arresting officer describing an arrested person and the events and circumstances leading to the arrest. Information in an arrest report may be the basis for the complaint filed by the prosecutor.

arrest warrant. a document issued by a judicial officer which directs a law enforcement officer to arrest an identified person who has been accused of a specific offense. In order for the judicial officer to issue an arrest warrant, he must have had presented to him either a sworn complaint or evidence that probable cause exists. The person to be arrested must be identified by name and/or other unique characteristics, and the crime described. When a warrant does not identify a person by name, it is sometimes called a "John Doe warrant" or a "no name warrant."

arson. the intentional destruction, by fire or explosive, of the property of another, or of one's own property with the intent to defraud.

arson squad. a team of investigators, some of whom may be specially trained and experienced firemen, that investigates incendiary fires, fires of undetermined origin, and false alarms.

arrhythmia. variation from the normal rhythm or rate, especially of the heart beat.

arsonist profiling. an investigative technique designed to assist in the identification of an arsonist. A psychological profile is prepared from available clues, such as the ignition device and accelerants used, preparation, methodology, and entry/departure methods and routes.

artery. a vessel that carries blood away from the heart to various parts of the body.

artificial intelligence. the capability of a device to perform functions that are normally associated with human intelligence, such as reasoning, learning, and self-improvement.

artificial ventilation/respiration. any method of forcing air into and out of the lungs to start breathing in a person whose breathing has stopped; a life saving technique in which air is forced into and from the lungs by external means when natural breathing ceases. Also called rescue breathing.

artillery. paraphernalia for injecting drugs.

artnapper. a person who specializes in stealing art objects, by whatever method, and ransoms them back to owners or sells them to collectors, sometimes with the help of unscrupulous art dealers.

Ashuft v. Tennessee. a case in which the Supreme Court held that the police may not use prolonged and continuous interrogation to obtain a confession.

Asklepieion. a type of therapeutic community, frequently formed within penal institutions, so named after the temple of the Greek god of healing. This approach incorporates concepts from Synanon and transactional analysis into a self-help microcosm of inmates within the prison setting.

aspermis. the absence of spermatazoa.

asphyxia. a lack of oxygen or excess of carbon dioxide in the body that is usually caused by interruption of breathing and results in unconsciousness. Asphyxia can result from an injury, electric shock, and drowning.

asphyxiate. to suffocate; to deprive body tissue of oxygen.

aspirate. to inhale foreign material into the lungs; to remove by suction.

asportation. the unlawful removing or carrying away of the personal property of another.

assassinate. to kill for hire, or kill a prominent person.

assassin's special. a .22 caliber automatic fitted with a silencer.

assault. unlawful intentional inflicting, or attempted or threatened inflicting, of injury upon another.

assault with a deadly weapon. unlawful intentional inflicting, or attempted or threatened inflicting, of injury or death with the use of a deadly weapon.

assay. a procedure for analyzing and quantifying the chemical components of a substance.

assessment center method. a method of evaluating candidates for police jobs through the administration of various tests which often include simulation and performance techniques. The assessment center method is usually associated with the selection of seasoned police officers who are in competition for mid-level or higher positions within a department.

The term assessment center does not refer to a place, but to the process by which employees are evaluated so that they may be given appropriate assignments. The process typically involves placing the subject under intense observation in a variety of simulations and stress situations over a period of several days.

assignable cause. a causal factor designated as having a relationship to an accident.

assigned counsel. a defense attorney appointed or assigned by the trial judge for an indigent defendant who is not represented by counsel.

assigned risk. a risk which underwriters do not care to insure but which, because of a law or otherwise, must be insured. An example of an assigned risk is a motorist who has repeated convictions for moving violations.

Assimilative Crimes Act. an act which provides for the applicability of state criminal statutes to criminal acts committed within federal enclaves but not specifically covered under federal law. The purpose of this statute is to provide for the prosecution in the federal courts of offenses committed within federal enclaves to the degree and extent that such conduct would have been punished had the enclave remained subject to the jurisdiction of the state. Prosecutions under this act are not to enforce the laws of the state, territory, or district, but rather to enforce federal law, the details of which, instead of being delineated by statute, are adopted by reference.

Assizes of Clarendon. a session of the English superior courts held in 1166 at which the first traces of a grand jury system can be found. This Anglo-Saxon concept of a grand jury is believed rooted in the inquest feature of Norman law which was first introduced into England following the Norman conquest. The Assizes of Clarendon intended for the grand jury concept to serve as an instrument of monarchical power rather than to protect an accused from oppressive governmental conduct.

associative evidence. evidence that links a suspect to the crime scene or to the offense. Fingerprints, shoe and tire impressions, and matching hairs, fibers, fragments, and paint chips are examples.

assumed identity. a change of name, address and/or appearance for the purpose of avoiding detection.

assume the position. an order by a law enforcement officer to a suspect to assume a spread-eagle position preparatory to a search. The term is also used by correctional officers when conducting searches of prisoners.

asthenic reaction. a psychoneurotic reaction characterized by listlessness, lack of enthusiasm, and physical and mental fatigue.

Astro-Pak. a brand name for a two-part explosive used in blasting. A two-part explosive is composed of two chemicals each of which is not explosive until joined together.

"A" substance. the water soluble substance in body fluids that would be secreted by a person of blood group A or AB.

"A" switchboard. a manual telephone switchboard in a local central office, used primarily to receive subscribers' calls and to complete connections either directly or through some other switching equipment.

asylum state. the state or place in which a fugitive from justice seeks refuge.

ataraxic drug. a tranquilizer; a sedative drug that does not produce sleep.

atavism. a theory of criminal behavior which postulates that criminality diminishes in the evolutionary development of humanity, and that its appearance as a biological predilection in some persons is a hereditary throwback on the evolutionary scale.

ataxia. gross muscular incoordination, as in alcohol intoxication.

Ativan. the trade name for lorazepam, a depressant drug in the family of benzodiazepines. It is a commonly abused drug and is regulated under the Controlled Substances Act as a Schedule IV depressant.

Atmospheric Release Advisory Capability (ARAC). a capability of the Department of Energy in which a computer model projects the most probable path of radioactive contamination released at a nuclear accident site.

atomic absorption spectrometer. a device that determines a sample's elemental composition by identifying the wavelength of the light that the sample absorbs. It is used in criminal investigations, especially in respect to the evaluation of gunshot residue.

at-risk populations. subgroups within the population whose members have been identified as being particularly susceptible to becoming drug misusers. These subgroups are usually targeted by organized drug misuse prevention efforts and often include groups such as adolescents, the elderly, and middleaged housewives.

atrocity. the result of conduct that is outrageously or wantonly wicked, criminal, vile, cruel, extremely horrible or shocking.

atropine. a natural poison found in the nightshade plant and jimson weed. It causes respiratory paralysis and is sometimes seen in persons who consume nightshade and jimson for their psychoactive effects.

attachment. a proceeding by which a person or his property are restrained in accordance with a direction of a civil court to secure payment of a judgment or the presence of the person when the case is being tried.

attachment of property. a writ issued in the course of a lawsuit, directing the sheriff or a law enforcement officer to attach the property of the defendant to satisfy the demands of the plaintiff.

attempt. an act done with intent to commit a crime but falling short of its actual commission; a form of conduct, coupled with intent, which attempts to effect the commission of a crime. For example, one who aims at a person and pulls the trigger of a non-functioning pistol might be charged with attempted murder.

attestation. the act of signing a written instrument as witness to the signature of a party, at his request. For example, witnessing signatures to a contract or a will.

attorney general. the chief legal officer of the United States and head of the Department of Justice; the chief legal officer of a state.

Attorney General's list. a document which at one time listed suspected subversive organizations. The document was prepared by the Office of Attorney General of the United States.

attorney in fact. a person who has been appointed by another to transact business for him and in his name. The person does not have to be a lawyer.

attractive nuisance. a dangerous place, object or condition to which children may be attracted. The owner of an attractive nuisance has the legal duty of taking unusual care to prevent injury to those who may be attracted to it. Examples are construction projects, swimming pools and animals.

audible alarm. an alarm that is activated when predetermined events occur that require operator attention or intervention for system operation.

audio actuator. a sound actuated device used to turn on and off tape recorders or radio transmitters.

audio response unit. an output device that provides a spoken response to digital inquiries from a telephone or other device. The response is composed from a prerecorded vocabulary of words and can be transmitted over telecommunication lines to the location from which inquiry originated.

audit trail. a manual or computerized

means for tracing the transactions affecting the contents of a record.

aunt emma. morphine.

aura. a premonition of impending seizure that is commonly associated with epilepsy.

auscultate. to listen to the sounds made by the thoracic or abdominal viscera. This procedure may be performed with the unaided ear (direct or immediate auscultation) or with a stethoscope (mediate auscultation).

authentic act. that which has been executed before a notary public or other public officer, duly authorized, or which is attested by a public seal, or has been rendered public by the authority of a competent magistrate, or which is certified as being a copy of a public register.

authorization code. a code made up of a user identification and password, used to protect against unauthorized access to data and system facilities.

autoclave bomb. a bomb designed to explode when atmospheric conditions change. Also called an altimeter bomb.

autoerotic death. an accidental death, usually by strangling, in which the victim dies performing a bizarre sexual act. The victim, while trying to achieve sexual gratification, will typically use rope or cord to constrict the neck.

autointoxication. the poisoning of the body or parts of the body by toxic matter produced within the body.

Automated Regional Justice Information System. a computerized system that assists law enforcement by providing criminal history information.

Automated Reporting and Consolidated Order System (ARCOS). a comprehensive drug-tracking system that enables the Drug Enforcement Administration to monitor the flow of selected drugs from points of import or manufacture to points of sale, export, or distribution.

Automated Security Clearance Approval System. a computer system used by the US Air Force to transmit and record data pertaining to security clearances and investigations.

automatic calling unit. a dialing device which permits a machine to automatically dial calls over a communication network. The unit is frequently used to summon an emergency response agency (police, fire or medical) in conjunction with an alarm system.

automatic data processing (ADP). data processing performed by computer systems. It is achieved by means of one or more devices that: (1) use common storage for all or part of a program and also for all or part of the data necessary for execution of the program, (2) execute user-written or user-designated programs, (3) perform user-designated symbol manipulation, such as arithmetic operations, logic operations, or character-string manipulations, and (4) can execute programs that can modify themselves during their execution.

automatic dialing unit. a device capable of automatically generating dialing digits.

automatic firearm. a type of firearm that, after a shot is fired through the agency of a mechanism acted upon by the explosion, ejects the shell and pushes a fresh cartridge into the breech.

autonomic nervous system. the portion of the nervous system over which there is no voluntary control. This system regulates involuntary vital functions, such as the activity of the heart and smooth muscle. It is divided into two parts: the sympathetic nervous system, which, when stimulated, constricts blood vessels, raises blood pressure, and increases heart rate; and the parasympathetic nervous system, which, when stimulated, increases intestinal and gland activity, slows heart rate and relaxes sphincter muscles.

autopsy. an examination, using dissection and other methods, of a body after death to determine the cause of death, the extent of injuries, or other factors.

autoptic evidence. evidence that results from being seen.

autosadism. inflicting pain to one's self to obtain sexual pleasure.

auto theft squad. a team of police officers, not necessarily detectives, that focuses on the identification and suppression of organized professional automobile theft activities. An auto theft squad will typically conduct surveillances of areas where heavy losses occur, inspect used car lots and junk yards for evidence of stolen automobiles and parts, and maintain special files and equipment, such as known automobile thief and modus operandi indexes and tools for unlocking and starting vehicles.

auxiliary force. persons, not necessarily police personnel, who supplement the regular police force in emergency situations.

auxiliary support unit. an element in a police department whose primary function is to support law enforcement activities by performing various technical or housekeeping duties. Persons assigned to the auxiliary support unit are typically non-sworn employees.

available path. the entire area available in a trafficway in which a vehicle may maneuver without interfering with other vehicles. Road space is the area within which a vehicle is legally entitled to travel. Available path is road space plus whatever other space is present for a vehicle to maneuver without causing a hazard.

aversion therapy. a process in which undesirable behavior is treated by accompanying the behavior with a disagreeable experience, such as extreme nausea. The treatment has been used to help persons stop drinking alcohol or smoking tobacco.

avoidable accident. an accident which could have or can be prevented by proper behavior, or by environmental or equipment modifications or controls. All accidents are theoretically avoidable within the limits of our understanding of scientific and behavioral phenomena. However, not all accidents can be avoided by all individuals.

avoidance. a noninvolvement in order to defend against or free oneself from fear, anxiety, or other adverse feelings.

avulsion. a wound in which there is a tearing away of a structure or part.

ayahuasca. a strong psychedelic drink made from a woody vine of the Amazon forests. Indians pound lengths of the vine with stones, then cook them in water for several hours, sometimes adding other psychoactive plants to heighten the effect. Ayahuasca is consumed in night-long vision-seeking rituals with shamans or in large tribal ceremonies that celebrate the passage into manhood. The initial effect of the drink is intense vomiting and diarrhea, followed by a relaxed, dreamy state lasting from 6–10 hours. The plant owes much of its potency to harmaline, a natural drug. The leaves most commonly added to ayahuasca contain the hallucinogen dimethyltryptamine (DMT). Curiously, when DMT is eaten the stomach juices neutralize it, but recent research indicates that harmaline inactivates the stomach's neutralizing enzyme, thereby allowing the DMT to take effect. Also called yage and caapi.

Azene. the trade name for a depressant drug in the family of benzodiazepines. It is a commonly abused substance regulated under the Controlled Substances Act as a Schedule IV drug.

babble. the aggregate crosstalk from a large number of interfering communications channels.

baby pro. a child or teenage prostitute.

BAC. blood alcohol content.

back blows. an emergency measure for relieving an obstructed airway in which the first aider strikes the victim on the back between the shoulder blades.

backgate parole. the death of a prisoner.

background investigation. a personnel investigation consisting of records reviews and interviews with sources of information, usually for the purpose of determining a person's suitability for employment in a sensitive position.

backing-up alarm. a device that automatically sounds a continuous or intermittent signal whenever the vehicle is backing up. It is used on some trucks and buses and required on some off-road vehicles.

backlog. the number of cases awaiting disposition in a court which exceeds the court's capacity for disposing of them within the period of time considered appropriate. Backlog is not the same as pending caseload, which is the number of cases awaiting disposition in a given court. The pending caseload of a court could be very large but not represent backlog if the rate at which the court can dispose of cases is sufficiently high that the cases can be disposed of within a reasonable period of time.

backstop. to provide appropriate verification and support of cover arrangements for an undercover agent in anticipation of inquiries or other actions which might test the credibility of his or her cover.

backstrap. a telephone extension used in an illegal gambling operation.

backtrack. to pull back the plunger of a hypodermic syringe just before injecting a drug. It is done to facilitate proper insertion of the needle in the vein, and is believed to prolong the drug's effect.

backups. high-intensity backup lights installed in an armor-plated auto used for transporting a person who may be a kidnap or assassination target. Backups are designed to blind a pursuing driver.

bad bag. an oversize shopping bag used by shoplifters. Also called a booster bag.

badger game. any of several types of schemes in which the victim is drawn into a compromising situation and then threatened with exposure unless certain demands are met.

bad trip. an unpleasant reaction to a drug, usually an hallucinogen. It is characterized by overwhelming fear, intense anxiety, and possibly immobilization. This reaction accounts for many of the cases that come to the attention of psychiatric personnel. A bad trip may be triggered by any drug or may appear seemingly spontaneously without the drug having been taken again. Also called panic reaction, bum trip, and bummer.

bag. originally a small glassine envelope containing 50–100 milligrams of diluted heroin. Heroin is now generally sold in smaller amounts in aluminum foil or paper. The term currently applies to plastic and cellophane bags containing marihuana, cocaine, phencyclidine, and other drugs in powder form. Also, any quantity of leafy or powdered illicit drug that comes in a paper or glassine envelope or plastic bag. Local convention and prevailing illicit drug prices determine the quantities of drugs sold by the "bag." The terms "nickel" ($5) and dime ($10) bags have long been used as standard street retail units for the packaging of small quantities of drugs, but they have been made nearly extinct by inflation over the years.

bag cutter. a thief who specializes in stealing purses from lady shoppers in crowded stores by cutting the straps of purses carried from the shoulder.

bag job. a burglary or illegal break-in, sometimes made by law enforcement agencies in need of otherwise unobtainable evidence.

baglady. a woman who collects or pays off bets as part of a numbers racket.

bag thief. a thief who specializes in stealing momentarily unattended shopping bags or handbags from shoppers, usually in crowded stores or malls.

bagman. a person designated to collect bets, bribes or so-called loans or to pay off other racketeers or dishonest politicians; anyone holding or receiving money during the course of an illegal transaction; a peddler of dangerous drugs.

bag thief. a thief who specializes in stealing momentarily unwatched shopping bags or handbags from shoppers.

bail. security given to a court in exchange for the release of a person in custody to assure his presence in court at a later time.

bail bond. the bond taken with securities at the time a defendant is released, conditioned on due appearance of the defendant.

bail bondsman. one who posts bail for others for a fee, generally 10 percent of the value of the bond. The term is applied to those who post such bonds regularly for a livelihood.

bailiff. a court attendant who performs a variety of duties, for example, maintain order in the courtroom, guard prisoners, run errands for the judge, pass papers and exhibits to authorized persons, and guard the jury room.

bailiwick. the office, jurisdiction, or district of a bailiff; the limits of a bailiff's authority; the special district or territory of a peace officer. For example, the bailiwick of a state trooper may be the state highways.

bailment. the delivery of personal property to another for a special purpose. Such delivery is made under a contract, either expressed or implied, that upon completion of the special purpose, the property shall be redelivered to the bailor or placed at his disposal.

bail revocation. the court decision withdrawing the status of release on bail previously conferred upon a defendant. Bail status may be revoked if the defendant fails to appear in court when required, or is arrested for another crime, or violates a condition of the bail release, such as a requirement that he or she remain within a certain jurisdiction.

bait-and-switch. a technique of advertising a bargain sale and when a customer shows interest the seller offers a similar product alleged to be superior but which is more expensive. Frequently the seller will claim that the bargain item has been sold out or found to be faulty.

bait money. money in a bank teller's or cashier's drawer set to trigger a robbery alarm if it is removed; money that has been marked or recorded for identification after it has been taken.

balance of sentence suspended. a type of sentencing disposition consisting of a sentence to prison or jail, which credits the defendant for time already spent in confinement awaiting adjudication and sentencing, suspends the execution of the time remaining to be served, and results in the release from confinement of the defendant.

Balkan route. a route used by heroin and opium smugglers which begins in Afghanistan, Iran and Pakistan and transverses Turkey and the Balkans into Western Europe.

ball. to absorb a stimulant, such as cocaine, via the genitalia.

ballistics. the science of the motion of projectiles; the comparison of marks and striations from two different bullets or casings to determine whether they were fired from the same weapon; a branch of applied physics which deals with the motion of projectiles. In police science, there are two branches of ballistics. One is called internal ballistics and it deals with the motion of the projectile while it is still in the gun. The other is called external ballistics and it deals with the motion after the projectile has left the muzzle.

Since all firearms leave distinctive markings on bullets as well as on discharged shells, it is possible through microscopic examination by a firearms examiner to determine whether certain bullets or shells came from the same weapon. Bullets, shells, and firearms collected in the course of an investigation can be compared against one other as well as against corresponding items on file in the crime laboratory.

The term ballistics is also often used to describe the scientific examination of powder marks and powder burns as a means for identifying the firearms.

balloon. a quantity of powdered drugs, usually heroin, packaged in a balloon.

balloon effect. the phenomenon of drug users substituting the use of one type of drug for another when authorities clamp down on their original drug of choice. Like a balloon, when drug use is squeezed in one direction it often expands in another, often with adverse results. For example, heroin use increased in Southern California after Operation Intercept's blockade of Mexican marihuana.

balloon hazer. a homemade harassment device constructed of a balloon or condom filled with urine, bleach, ink or similar substance and thrown at or dropped upon law enforcement or security officers during disturbances.

balloon room. a place or room where marijuana is smoked; a meeting place for marijuana smokers and drug pushers.

bam. the street name for phenmetrazine hydrochloride. Also, a mixture of barbiturate and amphetamine.

Bangalore torpedo. a dynamite-filled length of pipe detonated by a blasting cap or a fuse.

Bangkok connection. the exportation of narcotics to the United States and Canada from Southeast Asia through the port of Bangkok, Thailand.

banji. a type of hashish plant grown in Arabia, Iran and other Middle Eastern countries.

bank. the degree to which the outside edge of a roadway is higher than the inside edge at a specified point on a curve; the change in elevation per unit distance across a roadway from the inside of its curve to the outside edge.

bank camera. a type of camera so named for its use in banks to obtain photographs during a robbery. It operates photomechanically as opposed to a television process, and is typically activated by a concealed switch or a money clip device.

bank craps. a dice game in which the house takes all bets.

banker. the person who finances a numbers game or who backs the house in dice, poker and other gambling games.

Bank Robbery Note File. a collection of holdup notes and other writings of known bank robbers maintained by the FBI Laboratory for use in identifying known writers and in determining if questioned notes originated from the same source.

bank routing transit number. a unique identification number that appears on checks issued by a bank. The number identifies the issuing bank.

Barberios test. a micro crystal test in which a solution of picric acid is added to a suspected seminal stain. If spermine is present in the stain, characteristic crystals will form which can then be viewed under a microscope. This is a preliminary chemical test that is regarded as not specific and not conclusive.

barbidex. a mixture of barbiturate and amphetamine.

barbital. a drug classified as a Schedule IV controlled substance. It is a long-acting barbiturate. Manufactured in 1883, barbital was one of the first barbiturates used in medicine. It is sold as Veronal.

barbiturates. the largest and most common group of the synthetic sedative/hypnotics. In small doses they are effective in sedation and in relieving tension and anxiety, and, like tranquilizers, they do not cause much drowsiness. In larger doses they are used as hypnotics (sleep inducers). Certain barbiturates are used for epilepsy and intravenous anesthesia. When large dosages are not followed by sleep, signs of mental confusion, euphoria, and even stimulation may occur, similar to that produced by alcohol, another sedative/hypnotic. Hence barbiturates are often used recreationally by people seeking similar effects to those produced by alcohol, often combining the two. Because alcohol potentiates the effects of barbiturates, this practice is extremely hazardous. Barbiturates are also used in combination with or as a substitute for other depressants, such as heroin, and are often taken alternately with amphetamines, as they tend to enhance the euphoric effects of amphetamines while calming the overwrought nervous states they produce. In large dosages they can cause severe poisoning, deep comas, respiratory and kidney failure, and death. Thus barbiturates play a leading role in fatal poisonings and suicides in the United States. Automatism has been identified as a potential cause of deaths due to excessive barbiturate use. Since first used in 1903, over 2,500 barbiturates have been produced, but only 50 commercial brands are now available and only 12 widely used. In 1970, barbiturates and their substitutes accounted for 28.6 percent of all prescriptions for psychoactive drugs in America. Although still considered indispensable in medicine, their medical applications have declined primarily due to the availability of other drugs with similar effects such as the antianxiety tranquilizers and other nonbarbiturate sedative-hypnotics.

The barbiturates are usually divided into three categories according to the rate of speed with which they are eliminated from the body: (1) long-acting (6–24 hours) phenobarbital (Luminal) and barbital (Veronal); (2) short-to-intermediate-acting (3–6 hours) pentobarbital sodium (Nembutal), secobarbital sodium (Seconal), a secobarbital sodium/amobarbital combination (Tuinal), and butabarbital sodium (Butisol Sodium or Buticaps); and (3) ultra-short-acting (under 3 hours) thiopental sodium (Pentothal). The most widely abused and dangerous are the short-to-intermediate-acting barbiturates. Primarily prescribed to treat sleep disturbances, they are the ones most likely to be used to produce intoxication, to be found on the illicit market, and to be used in suicide attempts. In Great Britain, the suffix "-al" is usually replaced by "-one," e.g., barbitone instead of barbital. Barbiturates are classified as sedative/hypnotics. They appear in the Controlled Substances Act as Schedule II, III and IV depressants. Slang names include: rainbows, blue devils, reds, yellows, yellow jackets, blues, blue heavens (based on the unique colors of their pharmaceutical capsules); barbs, downers, down, goofballs, sleeping pills.

barbiturism. a poisoning resulting from the use of barbiturates, marked by slurred speech, sleepiness, loss of memory, disorientation, and, in serious cases, depressed respiration, coma, and death.

barometric bomb. a bomb triggered by a change in air (barometric) pressure. Also called an altimeter bomb.

barratry. the act of encouraging lawsuits and inciting quarrels which ultimately end in litigation.

barrel striations. distinctive markings impressed on a projectile as it passes through the barrel in firing. Striations appear as minute lines and scratches, and have importance in firearms identification.

barrier line. a line, which when placed parallel to a center line or lane line, indicates that all traffic must not cross the line for purposes of overtaking or passing; a double line consisting of two normal solid yellow lines delineating the separation between travel paths in opposite directions where overtaking or passing is prohibited in both directions.

barrister. a lawyer in the United Kingdom and in certain British Commonwealth countries who is authorized to represent a party in court, in contrast to a solicitor, who is primarily an office lawyer.

base dealer. a card shark who deals from the bottom of the deck.

base man. that person situated at the leading position in an offensive riot control formation, such as the wedge, triangle (diamond), or echelon (diagonal). Also called the point man.

base house. a place where crack is sold and used.

base wad. the paper filler at the rear of the powder charge inside the head of a shotgun shell.

basic effect. the effect experienced during that period of time when a drug is maximally active in the plasma, causing the typical influence. Also called main effect.

basic life support. an emergency procedure consisting of the recognition of respiratory and/or cardiac arrest and the proper application of cardiopulmonary resuscitation (CPR) to maintain life until a victim recovers or advanced life support assistance is available.

baton. a short, heavy club or stick with an attached strap or handle typically used as a defensive weapon.

battered child syndrome. a general term describing the social phenomenon of child abuse; the misused and unconscionable beating of a helpless child.

battering ram. a tool used in to knock down walls or doors. It is usually pole-shaped with grasping handles that permit it to be swung in a pendulum fashion.

battery. an unlawful beating or wrongful physical violence or constraint inflicted on another without consent. Assault is the actual offer to use force or violence while the using of it is the battery.

bawdyhouse. a house of ill-frame; a house of prostitution; a brothel.

bazooka. a hand-held weapon which launches a missile capable of piercing armor. The bazooka is a favorite weapon of the terrorist.

bazooka paste. coca paste.

beam test. a chemical test for detecting marihuana. Cannabis is placed into a test tube and mixed with petroleum ether. After shaking the contents, the petroleum is left to stand and evaporate at room temperature. The residue remaining at the bottom of the test tube is removed and placed on filter paper. Alcoholic potassium hydroxide solution is added to the residue. The presence of cannabis is indicated if a violet color appears at the outer edge of the residue.

beard. a person whose job is laying off bets for bookmakers.

beat a mark. successfully pick the pocket of a victim.

beat it. to run, flee; to have successfully avoided arrest or conviction or to win an appeal following conviction.

beat the gong. smoke opium.

beat the machine. to lie during a polygraph examination and not be detected.

Beckwith v. United States. a 1976 case in which the U.S. Supreme Court decided whether a special agent of the Internal Revenue Service, investigating potential criminal income tax violations, must, in an interview with a taxpayer not in custody, give the Miranda warnings. In this case, Beckwith invited the IRS agents into his house, the conversation was friendly and relaxed, and the agents did not press Beckwith on any question he could not or chose not to answer. At trial, Beckwith argued that Miranda should be extended to cover interrogation in noncustodial circumstances after a police investigation has focused on a suspect. The Supreme Court held that an interview with government agents in such a situation does not present the elements which would be so inherently coercive as to fit within the custody aspect of Miranda and thus does not require Miranda warnings to be given. Quoting from another decision, the Court added that "it was the compulsive aspect of custodial interrogation, and not the strength or content of the government's suspicions at the time the questioning was conducted, which led the Court to impose the Miranda requirements with regard to custodial interrogation."

bee. a cherry bomb with tacks glued to the outside.

beef. a complaint, or to complain.

beeper warrant. a search warrant that allows the police to covertly place a beeper (transponder) on a suspect's airplane, vehicle, package or the like for the purpose of tracking its movements. Also called a transponder warrant.

behavioral pharmacology. the branch of

pharmacology that deals with the effects of drugs on behavior, particularly operant behavior processes.

behavioral tolerance. a negative change in the effect of a drug due to alteration of environmental constraints; a decrease in response to a drug dose resulting from behavioral mechanisms in the user's surroundings.

behavior disorder. a broad term that describes a behavior abnormally believed not to be associated with specific organic causes or symptoms. In general, the term is used for abnormalities that affect general and social adjustment, such as drug use, antisocial behavior, and crime.

behaviorism. a branch of psychology concerned with objective observations of behavior, as evidence of such processes as intent and drive, without influence from personally biased statements.

behavior modification. the changing of human behavior through conditioning or other learning techniques. It generally uses a system of rewards and punishments to elicit the desired or appropriate behavior. Behavior modification is one of the major concepts employed by therapeutic communities.

behavior therapy. the systematic application of learning principles and techniques to the treatment of behavior disorders that focuses on attacking the symptoms rather than tracing the history of the problem as in traditional forms of psychotherapy.

belly gun. a short-barreled handgun, such as a snub-nose revolver.

belt boosting. a shoplifting technique in which the thief places several items against the stomach and holds them in place with a belt. A loose fitting topcoat conceals the stolen items from view.

bench trial. a trial without a jury, in which the verdict is handed down by one or more judges.

bench warrant. a document issued by a judicial officer directing that a person who has failed to obey an order or notice to appear be brought before the court. A bench warrant is also sometimes issued when there has been no failure to obey,

such as when a person is first named in an indictment, or when issued to transfer an accused person from jail to court for trial. Also called an order for arrest, a capias, and an alias warrant.

benny. a Benzedrine (amphetamine) pill.

Bent Spear. a Department of Defense term used when identifying or reporting a significant incident involving a nuclear warhead, weapon and/or component.

Benzedrine. the trade name for amphetamine sulfate, a commonly prescribed and abused drug, which is regulated under the Controlled Substances Act as a Schedule II stimulant.

benzidine test. a screening test used for the detection of blood. It is based on the ability of a chemical (in blood or other substances) called peroxidase to change a colorless reagent to blue when hydrogen peroxide is added. It is extremely sensitive, making it a very valuable negative test. If used properly in a two stage test, under certain conditions, some experts consider it to be almost specific for blood.

benzodiazepines. a family of depressants that relieve anxiety, tension, and muscle spasms, produce sedation and prevent convulsions. They are marketed as anxiolytics (mild tranquilizers), sedatives, hypnotics or anticonvulsants. The forms of benzodiazepine currently sold in the U.S. are alprazolam (Xanax), chlordiazepoxide (Librium), clanazepam (Clonopin), clorazepate (Tranxene), diazepam (Valium), flurazepam (Dalmane), halazepam (Paxipam), lorazepam (Ativan), oxazepam (Serax), prazepam (Centrax), temasepam (Restoril), and triazolam (Halcion). Benzodiazepines appear in the Controlled Substances Act as Schedule IV depressants. They are widely abused and prolonged use can produce physical and psychological dependence and withdrawal symptoms.

benzphetamine. the generic name of a stimulant sold legally as Didrex. It is a sympathomimetic amine used as an anorectic and is regulated as a Schedule III drug.

bequeath. to give personal property by will to another.

bertillonage. the name given to a technique for identifying criminals or others based upon measurements of certain unchanging parts of the skeleton. Also called anthropometry.

Bertillon system. an identification system developed by Alphonse Bertillon using anthropometric measurements, standardized photographs, notation of markings, color, thumb line impressions and other data.

best evidence rule. a rule of law requiring that only the original of a document or an object is admissible evidence. A copy or facsimile is admissible only if the original is not available.

bestiality. a sexual connection between a human being and an animal.

beveled dice. dice which have been beveled on their edges to increase the chances of certain point combinations.

beveled wound. a wound in which the skin is penetrated at an angle. One margin of the wound is beveled and the other margin overhangs it.

beyond a reasonable doubt. a term referring to the evidence that must be shown by the state in a criminal case for the accused to be found guilty of the charge; the standard of proof required under America's adversary system of law. A prosecutor must establish facts sufficient to convince an ordinary person that a defendant has committed a crime as charged.

B girl. a female employed in a drinking establishment to entice male patrons to purchase expensive drinks. A B girl will frequently engage also in prostitution.

bhang. a powder made from ground hemp leaves which is often mixed with spices, honey, or water and ingested; the name used in India for marijuana. Also the name for a beverage drunk in India that is made with marijuana and often contains milk.

bifurcated trial. in criminal proceedings, a special two-part proceeding in which the issue of guilt is tried in the first step, and if a conviction results, the appropriate sentence or applicable sentencing statute is determined in the second step.

bifurcation. in fingerprint science, the forking or dividing of one line into two or more branches.

bigamy. the criminal offense of willfully and knowingly contracting a marriage while being married to a third party.

big con. a large scale confidence game.

Big Five. the five most commonly abused drugs, i.e., cocaine, methamphetamine, heroin, PCP, and marihuana. The Big Five will change as user preferences change.

Big John. a drug abuser's term for the police.

Big Seven. the Big Five drugs plus alcohol and nicotine.

bill of attainder. originally, the complete loss of rights and privileges on being condemned of treason or another felony. In recent times, it is a legislative conviction without a criminal trial. The effect is to pronounce upon the guilt of the person without regard to the rules of evidence or of any of the judicial trial, and it affixes the degree of punishment according to its own concept of the gravity of the offense. An example occurred in 1865 when Congress passed a law providing that no person should practice as an attorney unless he should take an oath that he had not in any way aided the Confederate cause. The Supreme Court held this to be a bill of attainder, and hence contrary to a specific prohibition in the U.S. Constitution.

bill of exception. a legal procedure by which a defendant protests a particular ruling of the court or question of law. An exception may be taken by the defendant to a decision of the court upon a matter of law, by which his substantial rights are prejudiced, such as disallowing a challenge to a juror, admitting or rejecting witnesses or testimony, or deciding a question that is not a matter of discretion. An exception taken during the progress of a trial is a protest against the ruling of the court upon a question of law. It is also designed to be a notice to the court so that it may reconsider its action, and to protect the opposing counsel so that he may consent to a reversal of the ruling.

bill of indictment. the written response of a grand jury which accuses a person of a crime. If a grand jury finds that an accusation is supported by probable evidence, a bill of indictment is returned to the court with the words "true bill," and thereupon the accused is said to stand indicted of the crime and is bound to make answer to it. If the grand jury does not find sufficient evidence to support the bill, it will be returned to the court with the words "no bill," or "not a true bill," whereupon the accused may be discharged. Also called a true bill.

bill of particulars. a statement by the prosecution filed by order of the court, at the court's own request or that of the defendant, of such particulars as may be necessary to give the defendant and the court reasonable knowledge of the nature and grounds of the crime charged, such as the time and place, means by which it was alleged to have been committed, or more specific information. Also, a defendant who intends to rely on an alibi defense may be required to furnish the prosecuting officer with a bill of particulars as to such alibi. This bill sets forth in detail the place or places the defendant claims to have been, together with the names and addresses of witnesses upon whom he intends to rely to establish his alibi. The purpose of this procedure is to prevent the sudden and unexpected appearance of alibi witnesses whose testimony in the latter stage of a trial could cast reasonable doubt on the state's case. By compelling advance notice, the prosecutor is afforded time to investigate the alibi and the credibility of the alibi witnesses, and be in a position to refute their testimony.

Bill of Rights. the first ten amendments to the U.S. Constitution. Several of them govern criminal trial procedures and rights of the accused, and were applied to state criminal courts in a series of Supreme Court decisions. Some state constitutions contain provisions similar to those in the Bill of Rights.

billy. a small bludgeon that may be carried in the pocket.

binary system. a numbering system that uses 2 as a base, as opposed to the decimal system which uses 10. The binary system uses only two symbols, 0 and 1, to represent any number.

bind over. to require by judicial authority that a person promise to appear for trial, appear in court as a witness, or keep the peace.

bindle. a small paper folded to transport heroin or other illegal drugs in powder form.

bingler. a seller of narcotics.

biological death. the period beyond 4 to 6 minutes after clinical death has occurred in which the cells and tissues of the body deteriorate as the oxygen supply ceases; the time at which irreversible damage to the cells of the brain begins to occur.

Biphetamine. the trade name for a stimulant that combines amphetamine and dextroamphetamine which are regulated under the Controlled Substances Act as Schedule II drugs. Street names include speed, upper, black beauty, crank, meth, bam, and pink.

bird dog. that member of a pickpocket team who looks for and distracts the police while the team in operating.

birdie powder. a mixture of heroin and morphine.

birefringence. in crime laboratory analyses, the difference between two refractive indices. Birefringence is determined by first placing a sample parallel to polarized light and then measuring the refractive index. The sample is then placed perpendicular to polarized light and the refractive index is measured. Birefringence is determined by computing the difference between the indices.

bite. money paid by a loan shark to a middleman who lines up a borrower.

black. a term used to indicate reliance on illegal concealment of an activity rather than on cover.

black bag job. warrantless surreptitious entry, especially an entry conducted for purposes other than microphone installation, such as physical search and seizure or photographing of documents.

black box. a device for bypassing a telephone company's switching system so that calls can be made without charge by, or knowledge of, the telephone company; any technical device used in gathering intelligence, which may range from a telephone wire tapping apparatus to an aerial satellite.

black gungi. marijuana grown in India.

black gunpowder. an explosive mixture consisting of 75% saltpeter, 10% sulphur, and 15% charcoal. The explosive quality of gun powder derives from its ability to burn rapidly in the absence of air and that in the process of burning liberates large volumes of gas. Black powder is called a low explosive, i.e., the rate at which the explosive travels is never more than 1200 feet per second.

black intelligence. information obtained through espionage.

black leg. a card cheat; a swindler; an employee who continues to work for an organization while it is being struck by co-workers.

black light. an ultraviolet light used to detect fluorescent dyes, dust or paints which transfer to the skin or clothing of persons suspected of handling decoy objects such as bait money.

black list. an official counterintelligence agency listing of actual or potential hostile collaborators, sympathizers, or other persons viewed as threatening to friendly military forces; in business, a list of persons to be denied employment or to be punished in some other manner, or a list of vendors or suppliers to be avoided; to put on a blacklist.

blackmail. to obtain something of value from a person by means of threatening to expose them to injury, disgrace, libel, or other harm.

black maria. a prison van or police patrol wagon.

black market. an imprecise term referring to the underground market in which illegal items, such as illicit drugs and stolen property, are trafficked, or in which goods and services are bought and sold without payment of taxes.

black money. funds not reported to tax collectors, usually because they were gained by gambling or illegal operations.

black powder. an explosive frequently used in the construction of homemade bombs. In its usual form it consists of a mixture of potassium nitrate, carbon, and sulfur in the ratio 75/15/10.

black propaganda. disinformation consisting of lies combined with some distortions, half-truths and even bits of the whole truth; propaganda which purports to emanate from a source other than the true one.

black Russian. a very dark and very potent variety of hashish.

black tar heroin. a form of heroin having at the street sale level a purity between 60–90 percent, as compared with white (Asian) heroin and brown (Mexican) heroin having purities between 2–6 percent. Black tar heroin is manufactured at clandestine laboratories in Mexico.

blank check. a check no longer acceptable to most banks due to the Federal Reserve Board regulations that prohibit standard processing without encoded characters. A blank check may be used, but it requires a special collection process on the part of the bank. Also called a universal check.

blanket lift. a technique for lifting an injured person onto a stretcher with the use of a blanket. A pleated blanket is placed beneath the victim's head, and through a series of lifting motions, the blanket is unfolded beneath the victim. On signal, the blanket is lifted as a stretcher is slid beneath the victim.

blast tube. a steel tube fitting over and extending beyond the barrel of a gun so as to provide added protection against blast.

blast wave. in bomb incident investigations, a movement of air away from the point of detonation that reaches velocities up to 1100 fps and pressure up to 1.5 million pounds psi. In an explosion, more damage is done by blast than by any other effect.

bleached note. a counterfeit bill created by bleaching a low denomination genuine note and then printing on it, with a counterfeit plate, a high denomination note.

bleeder. in a numbers operation, a bet on any combination of two of the three digits. Also called a bolita, bleeder, or double action.

blind panic. a type of reaction seen in situations of mass casualties in which individual human judgment is severely impaired by uncontrollable fear.

blind tiger. a place where liquor is sold illegally. Also called a blind pig.

blind wagon. a moving van without the name or address of the owner imprinted thereon.

blockbusting. the illegal practice of introducing a nonconforming user or undesirable into a neighborhood for the purpose of causing an abnormally high turnover of property ownership in the area.

blocking. the intentional full or partial concealment of an item intended to be shoplifted. A purse in a shopping cart is commonly used to block the targeted item; in polygraphy, a characteristic tracing on the pneumograph chart caused by cessation of breathing by the person being tested.

blockout cards. playing cards having altered back designs.

block watch. a neighborhood program in which residents actively look for and report criminal activity.

blood alcohol concentration (BAC). the relative proportion of ethyl alcohol within the blood, based upon the number of grams per alcohol per millimeter of blood, and often expressed as a percent.

blood alcohol tester. an instrument for capturing and analyzing for alcohol content a deep lung breath sample. A tester typically has components for collecting a breath sample, holding the sample in a chamber, sensing any hydrocarbons that may be present in the sample, emitting a readout display of the well-established relationship between the concentration of alcohol in blood and deep lung breath, calibrating controls, and energy source.

blood alcohol zones. standards which are commonly employed as measures of intoxication. In this measure, the parts of alcohol per thousand parts of blood are expressed as a percentage. Three zones are used: Zone 1 includes blood alcohol values from 0.00 to 0.5 percent and is considered fairly good evidence that the person is sober. Zone 2 ranges from 0.5 to 0.15 percent and is inconclusive as to whether or not the person is under the influence. Zone 3 relates to findings above 0.15 percent. At this level a person is considered to be intoxicated. Its equivalent is to drink 8 ounces of whiskey or eight 12-ounce bottles of beer.

blood groups. the four different types or groups of human blood. Blood grouping is based on the fact that in blood the red cells contain two antigens and the serum contains corresponding antibodies. The two antigens are named A and B and the two antibodies are called anti-A and anti-B. Persons are placed into blood groups according to four possible combinations: Group A persons have antigen A; Group B have antigen B; Group AB have both antigen A and B; and Group O persons possess neither A or B but instead have both antibodies in the serum. About 40 percent of adults have Group A blood; 7 percent have Group B; 43 percent have AB; and 10 percent have Group O. Antigens are also called agglutinogens and antibodies are also called agglutinins.

blood pressure cuff. in polygraphy, a fabric arm cuff containing an inflatable rubber bladder. It is typically attached to the arm of the examinee during a test for the purpose of detecting blood pressure changes. The cuff is part of the sphygmomanometer component of the polygraph instrument.

blood pressure tracing. in polygraphy, the inked tracing that represents changes in the blood pressure of a person being tested. The tracing appears on a polygram created by the movement of chart paper beneath a stylus. The polygraphist interprets the tracing.

blotter. the daily record of arrests and other enforcement activities made by a police department.

blotter acid. LSD impregnated in paper.

blow. to inhale or snort a drug, particularly cocaine or heroin; to smoke a marijuana cigarette. Also, that step in a confidence game when the victim is permitted to win or gain something in order to build the victim's confidence and set him up for a final "score."

blowback. an exposure of espionage activity due to an unsuccessful attempt to recruit a secret agent.

blown. destroyed, as when an undercover agent's identity has been discovered.

blown away. to be in a narcotically-induced euphoria.

blown cover. the discovery of an undercover agent's identity.

blow off. that point in time during a confidence game when the victim's money or property is taken.

blow snow. to snort cocaine.

bludgeon. a short clublike weapon with one end loaded or thicker than the other.

blue acid. pale-blue liquid LSD-25.

blue angels. amytal (barbiturate) tablets.

bluebirds. capsules of sodium amytal.

blue box. an electronic device used illegally to dial toll-free exchanges. Once the original call is completed, the device holds the line open so that additional calls can be placed at no cost to the caller.

blue devils. amobarbital capsules.

blue flu. a form of illegal strike by police officers. When police officers strike by calling in sick, they are said to be suffering from a disease so unique it affects only persons who wear blue uniforms.

blue laws. rigid laws or religious regulations that prohibit certain activities on Sunday, such as shopping or drinking alcoholic beverages in public places. This term derives from certain strict laws in the early Colonial government of Connecticut. The object of the laws was to stamp out heresy and preserve the sanctity of the Christian Sabbath. Today the term is applied to any severe religious law especially in regard to Sunday amusement. Many laws of this character remain on the statute books of the eastern United States. Some are enforced while others are neglected. Pennsylvania still retains and enforces many of its blue laws, while New York has a less restrictive enforcement policy.

blue ribbon jury. a special jury selected from the upper or upper middle socioeconomic strata, or from persons with some special expertise. Such selection was sometimes used to form grand and petit juries, but is no longer legal in the United States.

blue-sky laws. laws that have been enacted by most of the states to protect the public from fraud in the offering of securities. Such laws are an exercise of the police power of the states. They supplement interstate regulation of securities offerings, securities exchanges, and speculative practices, through the Securities and Exchange Commission. Protection is achieved through specific legislation of blue-sky laws, and through enforcement of the statute of frauds.

blue tip. an incendiary bullet identified by its blue-painted tip.

BNDD. Bureau of Narcotics and Dangerous Drugs. A law enforcement agency created in 1968 and replaced in 1973 by the Drug Enforcement Administration.

bodily harm. any touching of the person of another against his will with physical force, in an intentional, hostile, and aggressive manner, or a projecting of such force against his person.

body armor. a device, often called a bulletproof vest, consisting of a vest or jacket filled with a shock-and-impact-absorbing material designed to protect the wearer from the impact of bullets or other projectiles.

body-cavity search. an anal or vaginal search for contraband such as diamonds or narcotics.

body transmitter. a small radio transmitter concealed on a person's body. Generally used to provide instant communication to back-up persons nearby, or for consensual monitoring.

Boggs Amendment. a 1951 amendment to the Harrison Narcotics Act of 1914, the Narcotic Drugs Import and Export Act of 1922, and the Marijuana Tax Act of 1937. Reflecting the increased concern over drug addiction following World War II, the amendment increased penalties for all drug violations and, for the first time in federal criminal legislation, lumped together marijuana and narcotic drugs, establishing uniform penalties for violations of both the Narcotic Drugs Import and Export Act and the Marihuana Tax Act. Also for the first time, a mandatory minimum sentence of 2 years was established for first narcotic violators and up to 10 years imprisonment for repeat offenders. In 1956, the Narcotic Drug Control Act further escalated penalties.

boilerplate. written materials characterized by excessive verbiage.

bolita. in a numbers operation, a bet on any combination of two of the three digits. Also called parlay, bleeder, or double action.

bolt attack. a category of burglary attack in which force, with or without the aid of tools, is directed against the bolt in an attempt to disengage it from the strike or to break it.

bomber. a very large marijuana cigarette.

bomb disposal unit. a team of experts trained in defusing, rendering harmless, and disposing of unexploded bombs, explosives, and similar dangerous materials or devices. In some departments, the bomb disposal unit is responsible for escorting and coordinating protection for especially hazardous materials, such as radioactive products, while they are in the local jurisdiction.

bombing incident. the detonation or attempted detonation of an explosive or incendiary device for a criminal purpose, or with willful disregard of the risk to the person or property of another.

bomb sniffer. a dog trained to detect the presence of bombs or narcotics; any mechanical, chemical or electronic device used for the detection of bombs.

bona fide. in good faith; without fraud or deceit; genuine.

bona fide occupational qualification. in an equal employment opportunity program, a job qualification that is genuine and reasonably necessary to the normal operation of the organization. This mechanism allows the employer to select or reject applicants without regard to considerations of race, sex, national origin, or age.

bond. an agreement by one person to guarantee that another person will appear in court.

bondsman. one who gives security to procure the release from legal custody of a person arrested or imprisoned.

bong. a cylindrical water pipe used to smoke marijuana.

bong juice. the water that cools the smoke in a bong.

booby trap. a disguised explosive device intended to cause human injury.

boodle. the stack of money used by confidence men in a switch game. On either end of the stack is a high denomination bill, with the middle of the stack being one dollar bills or pieces of paper made to look like currency. The switch consists of the boodle being exchanged for a stack of money belonging to the victim.

bookie front. a place of business, frequently a tavern, news stand or barber shop, that serves as a front for a bookie operation.

booking. a police administrative action officially recording an arrest and identifying the person, place, time, the arresting authority, and the reason for the arrest; the process of entering in the official arrest record a suspect's name, the offense charged, and the time and place of the occurrence. Booking usually takes place at a police station, under the guidance of the arresting officer.

bookmaker. a professional betting man who accepts wagers on sporting events, most frequently horse racing.

boost. that member of a confidence game team who encourages or builds up the victim prior to the "score." Also called a shill.

booster. a shoplifter; a person who steals from cars, such as hub caps, radios, CB units and tape decks. Also called a car clout.

booster bloomers. pocket-fitted undergarments used by shoplifters to secrete stolen merchandise.

booster box. an innocuous looking box or package carried by a shoplifter and used to conceal stolen items. It is typically fitted with a hinged side or bottom.

booster explosive. an explosive material detonated by the primary explosive and which in turn detonates the main charge. It is the third element in the basic firing chain typical of most explosions. Examples of booster explosives are tetryl, PETN and RDX. A booster explosive is also called a secondary explosive.

booster pants. oversize pants with deep pockets used to hold shoplifted merchandise.

boosting an invoice. increasing the figures on a supplier's invoice, often done by an employee of the purchaser in collusion with the supplier.

booting. a procedure when injecting heroin of drawing blood into the syringe before injecting its contents to assure that the needle is in the vein.

bootleg turn. a pursuit driving tactic for rapidly reversing direction of travel. It is executed by a rapid stop with the nose of the vehicle pointed to the right, followed by a backup maneuver with the steering wheel turned full left so that the nose of the vehicle faces in the opposite direction. So called because of its use by bootleggers when attempting to escape pursuit by the police.

Borstal system. an English prison system in which young offenders are given industrial training and other instructions designed to help them succeed upon release. The system constitutes a halfway house between the adult prison and the juvenile reformatory. Offenders between 16 and 23 years of age are received for a period of two to four years. The Borstal Association follows up those

who have been released on parole and supervises them to see that they do not again fall into crime. This system is so named because it was first implemented at a juvenile reformatory located in the village of Borstal.

bottom-up method. a method of organizing and planning in which goals are set by managers for their own departments.

bouncer. a person employed to preserve the peace in night clubs and similar places of evening entertainment.

Bouquet reagent test. a chemical test for marijuana. The suspect materials is crushed to powder and placed in a test tube. After adding ethyl acetate, the contents are shaken. The ethyl acete solution is boiled and the residue dissolved in acetone. Concentrated sulfuric acid and ethyl alcohol (Bouquet reagent) are added to the test tube. The appearance of a brownish-red color is indicative of cannabis. When water is added to the solution a white opalescent color will appear.

box. a safe.

box man. a safe burglar.

bradycardia. slowness of heart beat, usually defined as a rate under 60 beats per minute.

brainstorming. a group effort structured to generate suggestions or ideas that can serve as leads to problem solving.

braking distance. the distance through which brakes are applied to slow a vehicle; the shortest distance in which a particular vehicle can be stopped from a specified speed on a particular surface; the distance from application of brakes to collision.

brass knuckles. a weapon worn on the hand over the knuckles and so made that in hitting with the fist considerable damage is inflicted. Originally made of brass, the term is now used without reference to the metal of which the weapon is made.

breach of peace. a violation of the public order, such as a riot, an unlawful assembly, or an illegal demonstration. To constitute a breach of the peace, the act must be public in character and such as to actually tend to disturb the public peace and quiet. A private annoyance, however exasperating or reprehensible, is not a breach of the peace.

breach of trust. to take for personal use anything of value which is being held in trust for someone else.

breach of warranty. a warranty made by a vendor which proves to be false. For the breach, the buyer has a choice of four remedies: (1) accept or keep the goods and set up the breach to reduce the purchase price; (2) keep the goods and recover damages for the breach of warranty; (3) refuse to accept the goods if title has not passed and bring an action for damages for breach of warranty; and (4) rescind the contract, or if the goods have been delivered, return them, and recover any part of the purchase price that had been paid. The buyer can claim only one of the remedies.

break-down revolver. a general class of revolver constructed to allow the breech end of the barrel, along with the cylinder, to be tilted forward and upward from the frame for loading and unloading.

breaking. as used in criminal law, forcibly separating, parting, disintegrating, or piercing any solid substance.

breaking and entering. illegal and forcible entry of a premises, as by breaking a lock or a window, removing a door, or cutting through a roof or wall. When the entry is for the purpose of committing a theft, it is usually charged as burglary.

breath alcohol test. a test for determining blood alcohol concentration by analysis of a breath sample. A sample of deep lung breath is collected from the subject's air output and held captive in a device which measures hydrocarbons. Hydrocarbons will be present in the deep lung breath of a person who has recently consumed an alcoholic beverage. An exaggerated reading, however, can occur if in the 15 minute period immediately preceding the test the subject consumed or regurgitated alcohol. Thus, a 15 minute waiting period prior to testing is recommended to guard against an exaggerated reading. A breath alcohol test is regarded as a screening test which, if positive, should be immediately followed by a confirmation test using a more sensitive analytical technique.

Breathalyzer. a breath testing device used to determine alcohol concentrations in the blood of persons suspected of being under the influence of alcohol.

breech birth. delivery of a fetus with the buttocks, knees, or feet appearing first. It may be associated with a traumatic delivery and with asphyxia. Breech births occur at a significantly higher rate among deliveries by narcotic addicted mothers.

breech block. the solid mass of metal behind the bore of a gun. Its principal function is to sustain the shock of the explosion. All small sporting and military arms are breech loaders. The breech block is often finished by hand and, as a consequence, some of the filing marks remain on the face of the block. When a bullet is discharged, the force of the explosion causes a backward reaction of the shell, pressing the base of the shell against the breech block. In the process, the shell picks up indentations formed by the filing marks. These indentations on the shell can be used to identify the weapon that fired the bullet.

breechblock marks. unique tooling marks permanently affixed to a weapon during the process of manufacture; the marks placed upon an expended cartridge by the unique breechblock characteristics of a weapon. Also called breechface marks.

Brewer v. Williams. a case in which the U.S. Supreme Court ruled that a person is entitled to the help of a lawyer at or after the time that judicial proceedings have been initiated against him, whether by way of formal charge, preliminary hearing, indictment, information, or arraignment. In this case, the right-to-counsel doctrine (under the Sixth Amendment) was found to be the basis for suppressing statements in what was thought to be a custodial-interrogation situation (under the Fifth Amendment/Miranda procedures).

Williams had been arrested for murder pursuant to a warrant and given full Miranda warnings during an appearance before a magistrate as well as by the police officers. He was represented by two attorneys, neither of whom accompanied him during a 160-mile automobile trip even though one attorney asked to ride along but permission was denied. Both lawyers insisted that no interrogation take place during the trip, and the police agreed to this. But during what was described by the police as a "conversation" during the trip, Williams revealed the location of the body of the victim and made certain incriminating statements. The statements and the finding of the victim's body were introduced at trial over defense objection. Williams was convicted and appealed. The Court ruled that Williams had been denied his Sixth and Fourteenth Amendment rights to counsel, and said "the right to counsel means at least that a person is entitled to the help of a lawyer at or after the time that judicial proceedings have been initiated against him . . . "

The Court went on to say that in this case (1) judicial proceedings had commenced against Williams, (2) Williams therefore had a right to counsel if the State wanted to interrogate him, (3) during the trip in the car, a police officer questioned Williams and he made statements to the police officer, and (4) the only way those statements could be admissible is if the State showed a valid waiver of the right to counsel on the part of the defendant.

This case established standards for showing a waiver of the right to counsel after judicial proceedings have been initiated: (1) it is incumbent on the State to prove an intentional relinquishment or abandonment of a known right or privilege, (2) the right to counsel does not depend upon a request by the defendant, and (3) courts must indulge in every reasonable presumption against waiver.

bribery. the giving or offering of anything of value with intent to unlawfully influence a person in the discharge of his duties, and the receiving or asking of anything of value with intent to be unlawfully influenced.

brick. a compressed brick-shaped block of hashish, marijuana, morphine or opium. A brick usually weighs one pound or one kilogram.

bridge tap. an unterminated length of line attached somewhere between the extremities of a telecommunication line.

brief. a concise statement in writing of the law and the authorities relied upon in trying a cause; a memorandum of all the material facts of a client's case prepared for instruction of the trial lawyer.

brief and casual detention. detention for an investigative purpose that is less than custodial in nature; detention that does not amount to sustained and coercive withholding of a person's freedom of movement. The term has practical meaning in the context of Miranda. When detention of a person for an investigative purpose is brief and casual, Miranda warnings need not be made, but when suspicion focuses sharply enough to provide probable cause for arrest, Miranda warnings must be given and a waiver obtained before continuing questioning. For example, an officer makes a brief and casual detention when he stops a person to inquire why the person is walking on the street late at night in a high crime area. A Miranda warning is not necessary for this purpose; however, if the person's answers or actions lead the officer to suspect that the person is involved in a crime, the detention passes from brief and casual to sustained and coercive. At this point, the person is considered to be in custody thereby triggering Miranda.

Brinegar v. United States. a case in which the U.S. Supreme Court established a workable definition of probable cause by ruling that a reasonable ground for belief may be based on evidence less than that required to justify conviction, but more than mere suspicion. The court stated: "Probable cause exists where the facts and circumstances within the officers' knowledge of which they had reasonable, trustworthy information, are sufficient in themselves to warrant a man of reasonable caution to believe that an offense has been or is being committed."

brisance. the shattering effect of an explosive. The higher the velocity of an explosive, the more brisant it is said to be.

British system. a term referring to the medically oriented treatment of opiate users in Great Britain, which has allowed users to obtain and use opiates legally. This medical, noncriminal approach has been credited with limiting heroin use, preventing the development of a black market, reducing drug-related crime, and enabling addicts to lead more useful lives, and has been recommended as a model for implementation in the United States. It has been widely praised by advocates of heroin maintenance. However, several problems surround the use of this concept. First, British policy has undergone significant changes in the course of the 20th century. Before 1968 the system was not a government-sponsored program but rather a policy that allowed private physicians to treat opiate users and prescribe maintenance doses. However, in the 1960s when heroin use among young males began to increase, this approach was altered and a new government-sponsored program was established that imposed stricter controls on the manufacture, sale, and possession of opiate drugs, and instituted a program of addict notification and treatment through clinics. Addicts could still get maintenance doses of low-cost heroin, but only from government-authorized treatment centers or from licensed physicians. Second, the very nature and effectiveness of British policy before the 1967 act and afterward, and its applicability or comparability to the American situation (particularly the concept of heroin maintenance) are still controversial. While some observers view the clinics as a maintenance system, others maintain they are presently abstinence oriented. Others observe that the clinics are in fact moving from using heroin to using methadone.

Broken Arrow. a Department of Defense term used when identifying or reporting a significant incident involving a nuclear weapon, warhead and/or component.

bromides. nonbarbiturate sedative drugs that were first introduced into medicine in 1857 for the treatment of epilepsy. Unlike most depressants, bromides do not effectively induce sleep in large, single doses. Overdosages of bromides can cause serious mental disturbances similar to alcoholism and a disturbance of sleep. Replaced since 1900 by the barbiturates and other more effective, less toxic drugs, bromides are still employed as headache remedies and nonprescription sleeping pills.

bromocriptine. a drug sold as Pavlodel and usually prescribed to treat Parkinson's disease. Early research suggests that bromocriptine reduces cocaine craving and acts more quickly than the antidepressants. This drug appears to mimic dopamine, a natural brain chemical, and is reported as being successful in restoring sexual potency among some cocaine users.

Brompton cocktail. an analgesic drug concoction used in British hospices to control chronic, intractable pain associated with cancer. It contains heroin, cocaine, phenothiazine, and other drugs such as prochlorperazine, promazine, and chlorpromazine. Hospital-prepared variations of the Brompton cocktail have undetermined shelf life stability depending upon pH, alcohol concentration, and other variables. An oral solution of morphine that contains 10mg of morphine sulfate per 5 ml in a nonflavored vehicle that contains 10 percent ethanol is approved for commercial distribution in the United States.

broom. a member of the bean family whose blossoms are dried and smoked for their mildly intoxicating effects. The active stimulant ingredient in broom is cytisine, a substance that is harmless when smoked but is toxic when taken orally.

brothel. a house kept for the purpose of prostitution.

brown sugar. the street name for a type of heroin that is frequently grown in Asia and often adulterated with caffeine and strychnine.

Brown v. Illinois. a case in which the U.S. Supreme Court ruled inadmissible a confession obtained following an illegal arrest even though the defendant received a Miranda warning. The court held that not only must the confession meet the Fifth Amendment voluntariness standard, but that the illegal arrest be broken sufficiently to purge the confession of its primary taint.

The Court identified two factors to be considered in determining whether a confession is to be purged of an illegal arrest: (1) the time that elapses between the arrest and the confession, and (2) the presence of intervening circumstances and, particularly, the purpose and flagrancy of the official misconduct.

Brown v. Mississippi. a 1936 case in which the Supreme Court ruled that the use of physical coercion to obtain a confession was in violation of the Fourteenth Amendment. This case involved a man arrested and charged after having confessed murder to the police. His attorneys, however, felt strongly that the manner in which the police had obtained the confession "shocked the conscience," and appealed Brown's conviction. After finding that Brown had been held by the police in a field, where he was beaten, threatened, hanged by the neck from a tree, and released for a few days before undergoing the same treatment, the Supreme Court reversed the conviction.

"B" substance. the substance in body fluids that would be secreted by a person of blood group B or AB.

bucket shop. an office or place (other than a regularly incorporated or licensed exchange) where persons engage in pretended buying and selling of commodities as part of some fraudulent operation; a place which accepts wagers on market price fluctuations; an establishment maintained for placing bets on the fluctuation of the market prices of stocks, grain, or other commodities. In this latter definition, the methods of operation are nominally those of brokerage, the difference being that the operation is unlicensed and therefore illegal.

budget cycle. the series of events that include the development, approval, execution, and evaluation of a budget.

bufotenine. an intoxicant snuff obtained from the pods and seeds of a shrub found in parts of South America and the West Indies. It produces intoxication and hallucinations, and is classified as a Schedule I controlled substance.

bug. a clandestine listening device, usually consisting of a hidden microphone and radio transmitter; a computer programming error; an alarm sensor, especially of the type attached to surfaces to detect vibrations.

bugging. the process of monitoring conversations by electronic means; the interception of orally transmitted communications without the consent of participants.

bullet. a projectile encased in a metallic cartridge and fired from a rifle or a pistol. The diameter of a bullet is measured in hundredths of an inch in the U.S. and in millimeters in foreign countries. The caliber of a firearm is the diameter of the bore between grooves (formed by the lands of the bore). The grooves in a firearm, usually spiral, cause the bullet to spin as it passes through the muzzle. A cannelured bullet is an elongated bullet with grooves at the base for the purpose of holding the lubricant or crimping the shell to the bullet base. An elongated bullet is a bullet that is longer than it is wide. A flat-point bullet is a bullet with a flat nose. A hollow-point bullet is one with a hollow point or a hole at the point to assure a mushrooming effect upon impact. A soft-pointed bullet is metal-cased with a lead tip so that it will mushroom upon impact, causing a more damaging wound.

bullet entrance wound. typically a neat, round hole made by a bullet entering the body or head of the victim.

bullet exit wound. typically a ragged or

torn hole made by a bullet leaving the body or the head of the victim. It is usually much larger than the size of the bullet.

bullet identification. a function performed in the crime laboratory by a firearms examiner who seeks to match bullets with the firearms that fired them. The process of bullet identification is based on the fact that a bullet is slightly larger in diameter than the bore through which the bullet passes. As the bullet moves through the bore, it picks up certain tell-tale markings called striations. These markings are unique in that they correspond only to the rifling characteristics of the particular weapon that fired the bullet. There are many such characteristics, such as the width, depth, and pitch of grooves inside the bore.

A bullet removed from the body of a victim can be compared against bullets fired from a firearm taken from a suspect. If the suspect weapon is small-caliber firearm (such as a revolver or pistol), the firearms examiner discharges it into a cotton mass. If it is a large-caliber firearm, the discharge is made into water. The bullets retrieved from the cotton or water are then microscopically compared against the bullet removed from the victim. Spent bullets may also be identified as to type and manufacture because the makers of ammunition keep records as to the weights of the various bullets they produce.

bulletin. a periodically issued official document which summarizes a police agency's activities during a particular time period (such as one day or one week) and which usually includes other essential information for use by the personnel of the agency.

bullet resistant glass. glass consisting of two or more plates bonded with plastic interlayers, generally resistive to penetration by bullets from medium to high power arms.

bull jive. adulterated low-grade marijuana.

Bumner v. North Carolina. a case in which the U.S. Supreme Court ruled invalid a consent search made when police officers lied to the defendant by claiming to have a search warrant. In this case, an uneducated widow allowed law enforcement officers to search when they falsely told her they had a search warrant. This decision relates to the voluntariness of a consent to search. Courts will scrutinize the age and education of an accused, circumstances, time of day, place, and reason for a search when determining whether consent was voluntarily given.

bump-and-run. a mugging technique in which one mugger knocks the victim down while another mugger snatches the victim's handbag or valuables.

bumper beeper. a radio beacon transmitter hidden in or on a vehicle for use with radio direction finding equipment.

bumping. a method of opening a pin tumbler lock by means of vibration produced by a wooden or rubber mallet.

bunco artist. a card sharper, confidence man or swindler.

bunco game. any trick, artifice, or cunning calculated to win confidence and to deceive, whether by conversation, conduct, or suggestion.

buprenorphine. a mixed antagonist/agonist with a long duration of action. It requires less frequent administration than methadone; appears to block the toxic, euphorigenic, and dependence-producing effects of opiates; and acts as a competitive antagonist (like Naltrexone) while producing cross tolerance (like methadone). Buprenorphine itself appears to produce little physical dependence; therefore, maintenance therapy could easily be terminated.

Burdeau v. McDowell. a case in which the U.S. Supreme Court ruled that the Fourth Amendment is a limitation on the government and that evidence seized by a private illegal search does not have to be excluded from a criminal trial.

This case involved a search by a private security officer. The Constitution, on its face, does not limit the powers of private security personnel, like those of public law enforcement, to conduct searches of persons or property. While the common law authority for a private search is sparse and inconclusive, there appear to be four instances when a search by private security would be permissible: (1) consent, (2) implied consent as a condition of employment or as part of a contract (such as a union contract), (3) incidental to a valid arrest, and (4) incidental to a valid detention.

burden of proof. the duty to prove the facts in a case. The burden of proof is on the government in a criminal case.

Bureau of Drug Abuse Control. an enforcement agency created by the Drug Abuse Control Amendments of 1965 within the U.S. Department of Health, Education, and Welfare charged with controlling the illegal traffic in certain stimulant, depressant, and hallucinogenic drugs. In 1968 these responsibilities were transferred to the Bureau of Narcotics and Dangerous Drugs.

Bureau of Narcotics and Dangerous Drugs. a law enforcement agency created in 1968 in the U.S. Department of Justice in which were merged the responsibilities of the Treasury Department's Bureau of Narcotics and HEW's Bureau of Drug Abuse Control. In 1973, the bureau was replaced as the lead agency in drug law enforcement by the Drug Enforcement Administration.

burglar-resistant glazing. any glazing which is more difficult to break through than the common window or plate glass, such as glass designed to resist "smash and grab" burglary attacks. This glazing typically consists of two layers of plate bonded with a plastic interlayer.

burglary. unlawful entry of a fixed structure, or a vehicle or vessel used for regular residence, or a vehicle or vessel in a fixed location regularly used for industry or business, with or without force, with intent to commit a felony or larceny. The behavior which is specifically described as burglary may differ greatly from one state to another. However, acts not called burglary will be codified as other offenses under different names falling within the general crime type of "unlawful entry with intent to commit a crime."

burn. an injury caused by extremes of temperature, electric current, or chemicals.

burned. exposed as a surveillant or undercover operative; cheated in a drug transaction.

burning bar. a bar packed with aluminum and magnesium wire or rods, and connected through a regulator to an oxygen container. It burns like a high-powered sparkler and is consumed while being used. A burning bar is capable of defeating most safes currently manufactured. Also called a thermal lance.

burning grenade. a type of pyrotechnic grenade which upon ignition releases an opaque cloud of vaporized chemical agent. The release time may last for several minutes while the grenade continues to burn.

burn job. a safecracking method in which a cutting torch is used to burn a hole into the side of the safe. The cutting tool is usually an oxyacetylene torch, a thermal burning bar or a thermite grenade. Also called a torch job.

burnout. a term used to describe a condition experienced by chronic users who use a drug or drugs (mostly nonnarcotic) to the extent that their thought processes become impaired, and they take on a spaced out or "vegged out" appearance and manner. Also, the saturation point reached by chronic drug users, particularly addicts, when the maladaptiveness of the lifestyle becomes so salient that the "hassle" becomes more important than the satisfaction and the dependent person stops taking drugs.

burn time estimate. the time a fire started, as estimated by a fire investigator. It is based on an examination of the material burned, depth of char, presence of accelerants, wind, oxygen availability, moisture content and other factors.

bursting grenade. a grenade which upon delivery and ignition releases a relatively small but highly concentrated cloud of chemical agent. The instantaneous release renders the grenade ineffective if it is thrown back. Also called an expulsion grenade.

business entries. records which show the truth of their content and which may be admitted into evidence as an exception to the hearsay rule.

businessman's high. the street name for dimethyltriptamine (DMT), a hallucinogenic drug the effects of which are of short duration.

business opportunity scheme. any one of a number of fraudulent schemes and deceptions executed within the framework of an apparently lucrative business venture. Schemes of this type can occur in any type of financial arrangement, but they seem most often to be associated with franchises, distributorships, and partnerships.

business record or entry. an entry made in the conduct of regular business.

bust-out. a fraud in which a company declares bankruptcy immediately after diverting or concealing cash obtained from the sale of inventory purchased on credit.

busy air. airwaves cluttered with police or other radio calls.

"but for" rule. a rule of law which holds that a defendant's conduct is not the cause of an event if the event would have occurred without it. Also called the sine qua non rule.

Butisol. the trade name for butabarbital, a commonly abused intermediate-acting barbiturate, usually taken orally or injected. Also called barb, downer, blue, yellow jacket and sleeping pill.

buttress lock. a lock which secures a door by wedging a bar between the door and the floor. Some incorporate a moveable steel rod which fits into metal receiving slots on the door and in the floor. Also called a police bolt or police brace.

butyl nitrite. an inhalant drug that first appeared in 1969 after amyl nitrite was made a prescription drug. Like amyl nitrite, inhalation produces a brief but intense lightheaded feeling by lowering blood pressure and relaxing the smooth (involuntary) muscles of the body.

buy and sell bust. a police tactic designed to identify, arrest, and prosecute criminal fences. In this tactic, an undercover officer or informant will purchase stolen goods and then offer to sell them to one or more professional fences. Typically, the officer or informant will assume a role as a broker of stolen property. After much buying and selling over a period of several months, in which substantial evidence will have been gathered to assure successful prosecution, a "bust" is made of the criminal participants.

buy-bust. a police tactic designed to arrest and prosecute a specifically targeted criminal fence. In this tactic, a criminal fence is identified through routine intelligence operations (e.g., informant reports and surveillance). An undercover officer or informant will approach the fence and offer to sell him a "bait" item that is described as stolen. The negotiations between the undercover officer/informant and fence are monitored and recorded through the use of a body transmitter. After completing the deal, backup officers who have monitored the negotiations enter the premises with a warrant to search for the "bait" item.

buzz. drug-induced euphoria.

buzzwords. the technical vocabularies of an occupational specialty.

by color of office. acts committed by a public official acting in an official capacity although the acts are not authorized by the official position.

by social harm involved. a custom of classifying crimes according to the particular type of social harm resulting from their commission. A classification scheme by social harm involved might list offenses according to the objects of commission such as persons, habitations, property, public morals, and public authority.

Offenses against the person include murder, manslaughter, rape, assault, kidnapping, and the like.

Offenses against the habitation include arson, breaking and entering and burglary.

Offenses against property include the various forms of larceny and robbery.

Offenses against morals and public health include sodomy, adultery, incest, lewdness, illicit cohabitation, abortion, prostitution, indecent exposure, obscenity, nonsupport, desertion, gambling and drug offenses.

Offenses against public authority and government include escape, rescue, perjury, bribery involving public officials, resisting arrest, bail jumping, obstructing justice, misprison, compounding a crime, misconduct in office, criminal contempt, and the like.

bystander. a person, other than the perpetrator, police, or victim, in the vicinity of a crime. The bystander may be a witness, someone who is incidentally injured, or who intervenes as a Good Samaritan.

C. when appearing on a numbers slip, a symbol that indicates a three digit number to be played in any possible transposition.

C-4. a military plastic explosive that usually appears as a white, semi-soft, moldable plastic putty. It is typically used in shape charges.

Cabana v. Bullock. a case in which the U.S. Supreme Court ruled that the State of Mississippi judicial system was deficient relating to the determination of culpability of accomplices to capital murder. Mississippi subsequently adopted a statute that required a trial jury to determine whether an accomplice actually killed, attempted to kill, or intended to kill or use lethal force.

cacodyl. a garlic-like odoriferous poison used as an explosive because it ignites spontaneously in dry air.

cadaveric spasm. stiffening of the arms or hands at the time of death. In violent, sudden deaths associated with extreme emotional tension, the muscles in active concentration just prior to death may undergo instantaneous rigidity. Most frequently, only a small group of muscles are affected, usually those of the hand. For example, a person who dies under tension while holding something might clutch it tenaciously. Such a condition is tantamount to proof that the object was held in the deceased's hands at the time of death.

cafe coronary. a choking incident, so named because its suddenness may lead observers to mistake it for a heart attack.

calendar. the list of cases established in a court to determine their orderly disposition and trial.

caliber. the diameter of the bore of a rifled firearm. The caliber is usually expressed in hundredths of an inch, or millimeters, e.g., .22 caliber and 9 mm. Firearms are frequently referred to by their caliber designations.

caliber designation. a descriptor denoting a specific cartridge case size and configuration. While some cartridges will interchange, most are specific for particular weapons. Examples of caliber designations are the .38 Special, .44 Magnum and 6 mm Remington.

calumny. defamation; slander; false accusation of a crime or offense.

camera. the judge's chamber or private room. A judge who decides an issue in camera decides the cause in his private chambers as opposed to open court.

Camorra. a group of Italian-dominated organized crime leaders and their followers that originated in Sicily. Also called the Mafia.

camouflet. an underground cavity created when an explosive ordnance penetrates the earth and explodes at a depth not sufficient to rupture the earth's surface.

cancellation ink. a special ink having forgery prevention qualities, typically used on official documents and legal tender.

cannabinoids. the highly potent, rapid-acting psychoactive ingredients of cannabis products such as marijuana and hashish.

cannabinoid screen. a field test or preliminary test used to detect the presence of cannabinoids in a sample.

cannabis. the generic name for marijuana; a major classification of drugs derived from the botanical plant class of the same name. Cannabis is the Latin word for hemp. Both cannabis and marijuana are often used interchangeably as general terms to refer to all of the various associated preparations that are consumed for their intoxicating properties. Cannabis has been cultivated for thousands of years for its intoxicating flowering tops and leaves, its fibrous stems and branches, and its nutritious seeds. A strain that is high in one of these qualities tends to be low in the other two. Cannabis Indica, for example, is very low in fiber content but generates the most potent marijuana. Cannabis Sativa high in fiber content contains very little THC (less than 0.5

percent). The seeds of Cannabis Sativa can also be harvested for use as animal feed and for producing oil that is used in cooking and in making paint. The psychoactive effects from ingesting cannabis vary considerably depending on such factors as potency, the set (mood and expectations) of the user, and the environment in which the drug is consumed. Effects similar to the depressants, stimulants, and hallucinogens have all been associated with Cannabis Sativa.

Cannabis sativa. the hemp plant from which cannabis products are obtained. It is a single species that grows wild throughout most of the tropic and temperate regions of the world. Also called the cannabis plant or marihuana plant.

cannelure. small channels or grooves on a cartridge case; indentation rings on a bullet.

cannon. a revolver or pistol. Also, the member of a pickpocketing team who does the actual stealing.

can opener. a large prying tool used in a safe ripping job. The tool is used to rip or peel the safe's outer covering.

canvass. a door-to-door inquiry or the stopping of persons on the street by police officers for the purpose of ascertaining whether or not anyone at or near a particular location witnessed something or can supply information concerning a specific crime.

cap. the street name for a capsule of narcotic drug.

capacity to commit. a concept of law which demands that a person should not be held criminally punishable for his conduct unless he is actually responsible for it. Young persons and mentally afflicted persons, for example, may be recognized as not having the capacity to commit crimes.

capax doli. capable of committing crime, or capable of criminal intent; the condition of one who has sufficient intelligence and comprehension to be held criminally responsible for his or her deeds.

capias. an order or writ directing the arrest of a person.

capital crime. any crime for which a convicted person can be sentenced to death.

capo. a Mafia boss, frequently the head of a Mafia family or Mafia core group. A capo's authority over the family or core group is absolute, possibly subject only to authority administered by the Mafia's national advisory group.

capo di tutti capi. a Mafia term meaning "boss of all bosses." This person is the head of the leading Mafia family.

caporegime. a Mafia functionary who operates below the level of a sotocapo (underboss) and above the soldato (soldier or rank and file member). He is equivalent to a manager or senior supervisor, and carries out orders as opposed to making decisions.

capper. an agent of gamblers who seeks new trade. Also, in some swindles based on gambling, the capper will aid in deceiving the victim by appearing to win large sums.

caption. the taking element of theft; an acquisition of dominion and control over property taken; a certificate stating the time, place, and the authority of an instrument (such as that of taking a deposition or of the finding of an indictment), and such other particulars as are necessary to render the certificate legal and valid. Also, the title or introductory part of a legal instrument which shows time, place, circumstances, authority, and notary's affidavit.

carbine. a light, short-barreled rifle originally devised for mounted troops. A carbine is typically magazine-fed, gas-operated, and weighs about five pounds. It is for the most part intended for and limited to the use of military personnel.

carbon tetrachloride. a highly toxic, chlorinated hydrocarbon liquid, at one time widely used as a solvent in cleaning fluids, which when inhaled produces intoxication. Toxic reactions include headache, confusion, depression, fatigue, nausea, vomiting, and death. Both the vapor and the liquid irritate skin and eyes.

carborundum pencil. a tool used to inscribe identification marks on evidence items made of metal, such as firearms and knives.

carboxyhemoglobin test. a test that measures the amount of carbon monoxide present in the blood of a deceased person. A medical examiner can ascertain from this test whether the victim was conscious, unconscious, or not breathing immediately prior to death.

car clout. a person who steals parts from cars, such as hub caps, radios, CB units and tape decks. Also called a booster.

cardiac arrest. sudden and often unexpected stoppage of effective heart action. If resuscitation is not undertaken within minutes of the occurrence, permanent damage to other organs will result from insufficient blood supply, and the death of the individual is probable.

cardiac massage. an emergency measure to empty the ventricles of the heart in an effort to circulate the blood, and also to stimulate the heart so that it will resume its pump action; rhythmic compression and relaxation of the heart performed on the outside of the body in which the heart is squeezed between the sternum and the vertebrae.

cardiac output. the amount of blood pumped by the heart; at rest this is normally 4 to 5 liters a minute.

cardioactivity monitor. in polygraphy, a volumetric plethysmograph that records the radial pulse. It consists of a sensor unit containing a transducer, amplifier, and pen motor. It is commonly called a CAM.

cardiogenic shock. shock that results from inefficiency of the heart as a pump. It is frequently caused by disease or infection of the heart muscle, and in this condition the heart is unable to contract forcefully enough to eject sufficient volume or output of blood.

cardiopulmonary resuscitation (CPR). the reestablishment of heart and lung action following cardiac arrest, sudden cardiovascular collapse, electric shock, drowning, respiratory arrest, or other causes; the basic life support provided until more advanced life support is available; a com-

bination of artificial respiration (rescue breathing) and artificial circulation (external cardiac compression).

cardiosphygmograph. a major component of the polygraph instrument which mechanically records in ink, on paper, a subject's blood pressure and pulse rate variations. Measurements are made through a blood pressure cuff placed on the examinee's arm and inflated to sufficient pressure to produce a graph tracing of about one-half inch amplitude. The traced patterns, called a chart, are interpreted by the polygraph examiner.

cardiosphygmomanometer. a subcomponent of the polygraph instrument. It is an in-line pressure dial in a closed air circuit capable of representing the circuit's pressure in units of millimeters of mercury.

card stimulation test. a test which uses ordinary playing cards to stimulate a polygraph examinee and to demonstrate to the examinee the accuracy of the polygraph instrument. Typically, the examinee chooses a card from among several and is told to deny the selection when asked during a polygraph test. This technique tends to reduce the emotional tension of the innocent, and increase the tension of the guilty subject. A card stimulation test is a type of controlled peak of tension test.

career addict. a person who literally works at maintaining a drug supply for personal use. In addition to engaging in activities that provide drugs, the career addict strives to avoid arrest and imprisonment. The concept of career implies that addicts are not persons seeking escape from responsibility and psychological problems, but are frequently very capable individuals engaged in activities that are challenging, adventurous, and rewarding.

career criminal. a person whose principal activity or occupation is criminal; a person who makes his living through profits generated by crime; a person having a past record of multiple arrests or convictions for serious crimes, or an unusually large number of arrests or convictions for crimes of varying degrees of seriousness. Also called professional criminal or habitual offender.

career criminal program. a prosecution program designed to identify repeat offenders and to flag such cases for expeditious processing by specialized units or with intensive procedures.

carnal. pertaining to the body, its passions and its appetites; sensual; sexual.

carnal abuse of a minor. intercourse, sodomy, or other sexual relationship with a child under the legally stated age, with or without the consent of the child-victim.

carnal knowledge. sexual intercourse.

car opener. a thin-bladed jimmie with a curved end used to open a locked car door. It is inserted between the door window and the weatherstripping, forced down inside the door, and then manipulated until the lock mechanism is released.

carotid. the principal artery of the neck supplying blood to the head. This structure contains chemoreceptors that monitor oxygen content in blood and help to regulate respiration. The carotid pulse is felt at the side of the neck, below the jaw.

carotid restraining technique (CRT). a type of choke hold sometimes used by police officers to subdue violent subjects. Pressure is applied to the carotid artery, frequently with a baton or wand-type flashlight. Because the hold is lethal, it is banned by policy or law in many jurisdictions. Also called the carotid choke hold.

car pocketing. stealing the contents of a car, usually the glove compartment.

carriage trade. a prostitute's clientele.

Carroll v. United States. a 1925 case in which the U.S. Supreme Court decided that the mobility of a motor vehicle presents circumstances in which a police officer would not have the necessary time to obtain a search warrant and, upon showing of probable cause, a stop of a vehicle and subsequent search thereof without a warrant was legal. Several later cases restricted this decision, however. In Coolidge v. New Hampshire, a 1971 case,

the Supreme Court found illegal the search of the defendant's vehicle parked in his driveway while the defendant was being arrested in his home. The principles established by this decision are sometimes referred to as the Carroll doctrine.

carry away job. a criminal method in which a safe or similar container is carried from the scene to a remote, concealed location where it is forced open.

carrying. in shoplifting, the practice of carrying, usually in the hand, a concealable item just prior to concealment.

cartel. an unlawful association of companies within the same industry which exists to control prices and minimize competition.

cartwheel. the street name for an amphetamine sulfate tablet.

case-hardened lock. a lock having a strengthened metal casing to protect it from physical tampering.

case law. a body of law based on judicial decisions in specific prior cases.

caseload. the total number of cases assigned to one court, judge, or other agency or person; for example, the number of active cases under investigation by a police detective.

case officer. an intelligence agency staff officer who is responsible for handling agents.

cast. in criminal investigations, a positive impression made from a mold.

casual criminal. a generally law-abiding citizen who commits a crime out of some pressing need not necessarily related to greed.

casual supplier. a person who furnishes an illegal drug to another for the convenience of the user rather than for gain.

casual thief. a person who steals on impulse, without premeditation, when an opportunity is present.

catatonia. a state of muscular rigidity sometimes observed in schizophrenics.

catatonic schizophrenia. a mental disorder characterized by an intense withdrawal from reality. The illness is demonstrated in two distinct forms: (1) catatonic stupor in which the victim moves slowly or hardly at all, and (2) catatonic excitement in which the victim engages in short, wild, and disorganized outbursts.

cat burglar. a burglar who specializes in occupied dwelling places; a burglar who enters during the night when the occupants are sleeping. The cat burglar typically attempts to enter and depart without detection, taking with him relatively small items that were particularly targeted.

cathode ray tube display. the viewing screen of a computer terminal or television receiver. It is typically used to display operating instructions, alarm information, live video surveillance, and graphic maps.

cattle prod. an electric device sometimes used to control violent people in mobs and riots.

causal relationship. a relationship in which one phenomenon affects and is incidental to the occurrence of another phenomenon, rather than frequently appearing with but coincidental to the occurrence of the other. For example, prolonged injection of heroin has a causal relationship to heroin addiction. Heroin addiction is highly associated with liver disease, but there is no causal relationship as in the case of alcohol and liver disease. The liver disease associated with heroin use has a causal relationship with unsanitary injection procedures and not either the heroin or the addiction per se.

causa mortis. a legal term meaning imminent death; the prospect of imminent death, as relates to a dying declaration.

causation. the relationship that must be established to hold a person responsible for a consequence of his action; that element of a crime that indicates a causal relationship between an offender's conduct and the harm or injury sustained.

cause and origin expert. a qualified expert witness in arson cases, usually a fire investigator, who testifies as to a fire's cause and point of origin.

cause in fact. the causal connection between an act or omission of the tortfeasor and plaintiff's injury. It is a basic element in a tort cause of action.

cause of action. the legal basis on which the plaintiff relies for recovery against the defendant.

caveat emptor. a legal term meaning "let the buyer beware."

cease and desist order. a ruling, frequently issued in unfair labor practice cases, which requires the charged party to stop conduct held to be illegal and take specific action to remedy the practice.

ceiling hook. in firefighting operations, a pole with a pointed end and a hook. It is used to pull down ceilings or partitions and to create holes for ventilating purposes.

celerity. speed or swiftness in the apprehension, trial, and punishment of an offender. Believers in the concept of deterrence regard it as a major factor in the effectiveness of punishment.

center of mass. in police combat shooting, a term referring to the upper torso where the heart, lungs and major arteries are located.

center of the field. the point at which an object being examined by a magnifying glass or microscope is centered so as to attain the best image.

centralized case management. a coordinated strategy for dealing with investigations in which all cases are checked daily.

centrally acting drugs. drugs that exert effects on the central nervous system.

central nervous system (CNS). one of the two main divisions of the human nervous system (the other being the peripheral nervous system), consisting of the brain and the spinal cord. The main coordinating and controlling center of the body, the central nervous system processes information to and from the peripheral nervous system. The system is made up of gray matter (mostly nerve cells and associated parts) and white matter (mostly nerve fibers) and contains protective cerebrospinal fluid. The CNS is the primary bodily system affected by psychoactive drugs.

central pocket loop. in fingerprint science, a pattern which has two deltas and at least one ridge making a complete circuit. An imaginary line drawn between the two deltas will touch or cross at least one of the recurving ridges. This pattern is only slightly differentiated from a plain whorl.

central tendency. a characteristic of frequency distributions indicated by statistics such as the mean, mode, and median.

cerebrovascular accident (CVA). a disorder of the blood vessels serving the cerebrum, resulting from an impaired blood supply to that part of the brain. The resultant symptom of neurological damage is called the stroke syndrome.

certified copy. a copy of a written instrument, document, or writing which contains the identical information, record or transcript as the original, with an attached attestation by a certifying official (usually a notary public).

certiorari. an order or writ from a higher court ordering that a lower court send up the record of a case for review. A certiorari is a supreme court's method of accepting a particular case for judicial review.

chain and Ts. a steel chain fitted with steel Ts at either end, used to restrain unruly prisoners. As the Ts are twisted, the chain applies increasing pressure on the prisoner's wrists.

chain door interviewer. an auxiliary locking device which allows a door to be open slightly, but restrains it from being fully opened. It consists of a chain with one end attached to a keyed metal piece which slides in a slotted metal plate attached to the door. Some chain door interviewers incorporate a keyed lock operated from inside.

chain of custody. a written record listing the persons who had custody of a particular item from the time of initial custody to final disposition. The custody record also reflects the dates and reasons of custody.

chain referral scheme. a scheme that typically involves sales of grossly overpriced products through false representation that the cost will be recovered by commis-

sions the promoter will pay on sales to the purchaser's friends, if only the purchaser will permit them to be contacted with the same proposition.

chair carry. a technique for carrying an ill or injured person when a stretcher is not available. The victim is seated in a kitchen-type chair which is then carried by one person holding the back rest and one person holding the front legs.

challenge. an objection, usually regarding a specific prospective juror, made to the judge by a party to a case, requesting that the person in question not be allowed to serve on the jury. A challenge may be for cause or peremptory. Also, in military jurisprudence, the defendant in a court-martial may challenge a member of the court for cause.

challenge for cause. the right of a party to a lawsuit to object to a juror for a particular or general reason.

changeable characteristics. in observation and description, the alterable characteristics of a person, e.g., hair color and style, clothing, and cosmetics.

change of venue. the removal of a case by the court in a criminal action to a court in another location at the request of the defendant if, in the opinion of the court, an impartial trial cannot be had in the court where the case is pending.

Chaos. a CIA nickname for domestic security files and operations.

character evidence. objects or testimony demonstrating a defendant's character. It can be used to evaluate the credibility of a defendant, but not to show that he is the type of person likely to commit a crime.

character witness. a person called to testify that the defendant does or does not possess an upright character.

charas. the Indian name for hashish.

charge. a formal allegation that a specific person has committed a specific crime.

charge to jury. statements or comments given by a judge to the jury on a particular point of law so they might appreciate the matter in its proper perspective.

charged line. a line of hose or pipes filled

with water and under pressure and ready for operation in case of fire.

charging document. a formal written accusation submitted to a court, alleging that a specified person committed a specific offense. The charging document may be a complaint or a filing. If a grand jury or magistrate find probable cause, the charging document might be called an information, indictment, or true bill.

chart identification. an administrative procedure incident to a polygraph examination. The examinee's name, signature, date and time of test, name and signature of examiner, and other identifying details are placed on the examinee's polygraph chart. The purpose of the procedure is to create a record that links the chart with the examinee, the examiner, and the reason for the test.

chart markings. markings placed on a polygraph chart by the examiner during the course of a test to (1) show mechanical adjustment of instrument components, (2) identify artifacts introduced into the polygrams by the examinee, and/or (3) show the mechanical or electrical settings of components.

chart minutes concept. a concept which holds that the various components of the polygraph are differentially effective depending on how much chart time has elapsed during a test. Overall, the polygraph technique is considered most effective between the 4th to 12th minute of chart time.

chase the dragon. to use a mixture of heroin and barbiturates.

chaste. never voluntarily having had unlawful sexual intercourse; an unmarried woman who has had no carnal knowledge of men.

C-head. a cocaine addict or user of LSD.

checkering. a pattern inlaid or cut on the fore-ends and grips of rifles, shotguns, and handguns for ornamentation or to facilitate gripping.

check fraud. the issuance or passing of a check, draft, or money order that is legal as a formal document, signed by the legal account holder but with the foreknowledge that the bank or depository will refuse to honor it because of insufficient funds or closed account.

checkpoint. an entry point to a controlled area where persons seeking entry are required to provide an entry pass or some form of identification; a pre-designated location on a convoy route used to coordinate travel time and ascertain status and progress.

cheese box. an electronic device connected between two telephone lines for the purpose of preventing call tracing.

chemical breath testing device. an instrument which uses photoelectric or other sophisticated techniques to quantitatively determine blood-alcohol concentrations. Examples of such devices are the Alco-analyzer Gas Chromatograph, Alco-tector, Breathalyzer, Gas Chromatograph Intoximeter, and the Photo Electric Intoximeter.

chemical explosion. an explosion that results from an extremely rapid conversion into gases of a solid or liquid explosive compound, characterized by an instantaneous change normally called a detonation or deflagration.

chemical fuse. a bomb fuse which depends upon a reaction between a chemical and some other substance to initiate the firing action such as induced flame or induced mental fatigue. A chemical fuse depends upon the calculated reaction of various chemicals to produce electrical, mechanical, or chemical energy to function.

chemical initiator. a strong corrosive acid used to eat away in a predetermined time an item or material that restrains detonation.

chemical sensor. a device that evaluates air in a protected area. If suspicious effluvia are detected, the sensor can read and record the change, and signal as programmed.

chemical stability. in bomb investigations, the potential of an explosive to react with its container.

chemistry section. a unit within a crime laboratory that performs qualitative and quantitative chemical tests of evidence.

The testing techniques include thin layer chromatography (TLC), gas chromatography (GC), gas liquid chromatography (GLC), high-pressure liquid chromatography (HPLC), mass spectrometry (MS), radioimmunoassay (RIA), and enzyme immunoassay. Other analyses include infrared and ultraviolet spectrometry, microscopy, and macrophotography.

cherry test. in arson investigations, an examination of the discoloration in copper wiring that has been exposed to fire. When copper wire is subjected to high temperatures, whether internally from electricity or externally from an outside heat source, it takes on a cherry color. If the color permeates the wire completely, the heat was internal. If the cherry color is on the surface only, the heat was external.

chest drape. a shoplifting technique in which the thief drapes a garment across the chest under a loose fitting coat and by folding his arms is able to hold the garment in place until safely out of the store.

Chicago school. a major school of sociological thought in the United States between the two world wars. It had a strong impact on criminological theory and research, stressing particularly the need to study criminals, delinquents, vagrants, prostitutes, and other social outcasts in their natural environments and to perceive the world from their vantage points.

child abuse. physical assault inflicted on a young child, often by parents, endangering the child's life, health, and welfare; the malicious beating, striking, or otherwise mistreating of a person under the age of 16 years to such a degree to require medical treatment. The term is also used to imply other broad areas of neglect and mistreatment, including psychological mistreatment.

child molestation. any sexual solicitation, contact, or intercourse of an adult with a child. The term usually refers to children below the age of puberty. Child abuse can be heterosexual or homosexual.

chillum. an Indian-style cylindrical pipe held vertically while smoking hashish.

Chimel v. California. a 1969 case in which the U.S. Supreme Court ruled that a search incident to arrest must be confined to the person of the arrestee and the area within his immediate control. The ruling also makes it acceptable for an arresting officer to search the arrested person in order to remove any weapons that the arrestee might seek to use in order to resist or effect an escape. In addition, the ruling allows an arresting office to search for and seize any evidence or weapons on the arrestee's person or in his immediate control in order to prevent its concealment or destruction.

chimney effect. in arson investigations, the natural tendency of heat to flow upward through openings, such as stairwells and elevator shafts.

China White. high quality heroin, so named for its whiteness and for its origin in the Far East. Also, the street name for alpha-methylfentanyl, a drug that has no recognized medical use and about which there is little available pharmacological information. It appears to be a potent morphine-like narcotic analgesic drug at least 100 times stronger than morphine. This extreme potency makes the strength of illegal street preparations difficult to control, and abuse of this drug can result in overdose. Alpha-methylfentanyl may produce euphoria, physical dependence, and severe respiratory depression, effects similar to other narcotic drugs. The respiratory depression may be reversed by a narcotic antagonist such as naloxone (Narcan).

Chinese connection. Chinese controlled and operated narcotic smuggling, extending from the Golden Triangle and Hong Kong to Amsterdam and to U.S., Canadian, Central American and Mexican airports and seaports.

chipping. using drugs occasionally.

chippy. a part-time drug user.

chi-square. a statistical procedure that estimates whether the observed values in a distribution differ from the expected distribution and thus may be attributable to the operation of factors other than chance.

chloral hydrate. the oldest of the hypnotic, or sleep-inducing drugs. Its popularity declined after introduction of the barbiturates. Chloral hydrate is a liquid, marketed in the form of syrups and soft gelatin capsules. It is not a street drug of choice, and its main misuse is by older adults. Chloral hydrate appears in the Controlled Substances Act as a Schedule IV depressant. Chloral hydrate is a hypnotic or sedative technically known as trichloroacetaldehyde, but more popularly called joy juice, knockout drops or Mickey Finn.

chlorazepate dipotassium. an antianxiety tranquilizer derived from benzodiazepine. It is also known generically as chlordiazepoxide and is regulated under the Controlled Substances Act as a Schedule IV depressant. It is legally sold as Librium.

chloroacetophenone (CN). a chemical agent used to effect the capture of criminals and to disperse rioters. Within seconds after exposure to it, CN irritates the upper respiratory system and eyes, causing tears. In heavy concentrations, this agent is irritating to the skin and can cause a burning, itching sensation on moist parts of the body.

chlorpromazine. an antianxiety tranquilizer derived from phenothiazine, which is used for treating severe psychosis, acting to reduce the patient's fear and hostility. It also reduces hallucinations and delusions and has often been used as an antagonist in the treatment of LSD-induced panic reactions. It is manufactured as Thorazine.

choke. constriction at or near the muzzle of a shotgun. The extent of choke determines the size of the spread of shot. Little or no constriction will allow the shot to spread out as it leaves the muzzle, whereas maximum constriction (full choke) will deliver the shot in a tight or restricted pattern.

choke hold. a self-defense technique used by the police to overcome or control violent persons.

choline. a chemical found in seminal fluid which is tested for by means of a crystal test called the Florence test. Because it is also found in other body fluids, this chemical alone is not specific for seminal fluid. However, if it is found in a stain which also contains acid phosphatase and spermine, the stain is or contains seminal fluid.

chop job. a safecracking method in which a chopping tool, such as an ax or chisel, is used to penetrate a safe, usually through the bottom.

chopper. a pickpocket who uses a razor to cut the pockets or purses of victims. Also called a slitter.

chop shop. a criminal operation in which stolen autos are dismantled and the parts sold.

Christmas ball hazer. a homemade device in the shape of a hand-size ball and made of styrofoam or similar material. The sharp points of needles and nails protrude from the ball. It is sometimes soaked with urine or other irritant and thrown at law enforcement and security officers during disturbances.

chromatic aberration. a condition that occurs when the characteristics of a lens are such that different wavelengths of light are focused at varying distances from the lens. The result is color-fringing or halos around objects in the image.

chromatography. a crime laboratory method of analysis in which the various components in a specimen are identified and measured by separating them according to their chromatographic properties. Several different types of techniques are used: thin layer chromatography (TLC), gas liquid chromatography (GLC), and high-pressure liquid chromatography (HPLC). The combination of GLC with mass spectrometry (GC/MS) provides a highly specific and accurate analysis.

chronic. lasting a long time or recurring often, as in the case of drug addiction.

chrysoidine. a tracing powder used to mark objects likely to be touched by a culprit. The powder is converted to an orange-colored dye by the skin's natural moisture.

churning. excessive trading in a client's account for the purpose of increasing the stockbroker's commissions.

ciphertext. data that are unintelligible until transformed by secret keys into intelligible data (plaintext).

circuit net message. a message transmitted only within the local area of a large communication network. For example, a circuit net message sent on LETS is directed only to those local stations or areas having a responsibility to act on the information.

circulating main. a water main designed to supply water for firefighting purposes in such a way that water can be supplied from more than one direction and with greater force and volume.

circumstantial evidence. evidence which tends to prove a fact, but does so indirectly.

circumstantial-situational drug use. drug use that is usually task specific and self-limited. Use is motivated by the perceived need or desire to achieve an effect deemed desirable to cope with a particular situation that is personal or vocational in nature. Examples would be athletes who use drugs to improve performance, and students who use drugs while preparing for examinations.

circus grifter. a person holding a concession with a circus or carnival to run a rigged game of chance. Games include the shell game, eight dice cloth, three-card monte, and spindle. Circus grifters often obtain the cooperation of dishonest circus managers and public officials.

citation. a written notice which orders a person to be in court at a stated time and place to answer for a crime.

citizen's arrest. the arrest, without a warrant, of an alleged offender by a person who is not a law enforcement officer, for a felony or a breach of the peace committed in the citizen's presence.

citizen's complaint. a complaint of a citizen against a government official, usually a law enforcement officer.

Citizens Crime Watch. a neighborhood non-profit effort in which citizens cooperate with local police by reporting crimes in progress and suspicious activities.

citizens' review board. a group, generally made up of persons not in law enforcement, that makes decisions about law enforcement problems that affect the community. The police may or may not have a representative on the board.

civil arrest. an arrest made pursuant to a written order signed by a judge of competent jurisdiction in a civil action or proceeding. Civil arrests may be ordered by a supreme court, family court, surrogate's court, and the district court of a county, and are carried out by the county sheriff. The civil arrest process is made includes four circumstances: (1) a provisional remedy called an order of arrest which may be granted at the discretion of the court without notice, (2) commitment for contempt, (3) attachment against person which may be bailable or non-bailable, and (4) warrant of arrest.

civil action. a proceeding for the redress of a private grievance or the enforcement of a private right.

civil commitment. the action of a judicial officer or administrative body ordering a person to be placed in an institution or program for custody, treatment or protection. In the treatment of drug addicts, commitment is for a specified period in a special treatment facility (sometimes only a modified prison) for detoxification and rehabilitation. Civil commitment is not a treatment mechanism per se but rather a vehicle for retaining individuals while they participate in a given course of treatment. It is this forced and prolonged supervision that distinguishes it from voluntary programs.

The concept of civil commitment developed out of the procedures established in the middle of the 19th century in which the state committed the mentally ill to public asylums where they often remained until "cured." By the turn of the century the procedure had been adopted for the cure of "inebriates," meaning chronic users of alcohol or any other drug. In the 1920s the responsibility for dealing with the users of prohibited substances was surrendered to the criminal process, but the noncriminal commitment process attracted revived interest following the 1962 landmark Supreme Court decision that held that narcotic addiction itself constituted an illness rather than a crime and could not be punished as a criminal offense.

Although various programs exist employing different therapeutic techniques for drug abusers, what uniquely characterizes such civil commitment programs is the involuntary manner in which addicts are recruited into the program through the criminal justice system. An addict who has been arrested for a crime can choose to stand trial or enter a rehabilitation program lasting about three years. If the addict does not choose to enter the program and is found guilty while standing trial, authorities can still send the addict to the rehabilitation center. Most programs incorporate provisions for the courts to dismiss criminal charges upon successful completion.

Civil commitment programs are not limited just to addicts charged or convicted of crimes. Programs generally also include noncriminals (committed on the basis of suspected future criminal activity) and volunteers. Commitment is sometimes referred to as "certification." Supporters argue that in order for treatment to be successful, compulsory confinement is essential and that it is the duty of the state to safeguard and treat those who are unable or unwilling to do so voluntarily. Critics argue that: (1) the program is not really nonpunitive or different from imprisonment; (2) it has caused court congestion; (3) it is an infringement on the right of noncriminals to be free, an inherent contradiction to the notion of individual liberty; (4) it has not been successful in treatment; (5) commitment for treatment has not been proven effective, is cruel and unusual punishment; and (6) the whole program is a subterfuge around the protection afforded to a person accused of a crime but not afforded to those suffering from an illness.

civil contempt. an offense against the party in whose behalf the mandate of the court was issued. A penalty of fine or confinement can be imposed. The purpose of the penalty is to enforce the court's original order, and the penalty can be avoided by compliance with that order.

civil death. the loss of numerous rights and privileges as a result of a sentence of death or life imprisonment. Such losses may include nullification of a marriage, distribution of an estate, or denial of the right to sue or be sued.

civil disabilities. rights or privileges denied a person as result of a conviction or a guilty plea, in addition to or other than the imposed legal penalty.

civil disobedience. deliberate, overt, and nonviolent lawbreaking in which the perpetrator justifies his action on the ground that a particular law is immoral; for example, activities conducted in violation of the segregation laws. Those engaged in civil disobedience seek to change an immoral law by focusing attention on it.

civil disturbance system file. a file maintained by the Department of Justice as an intelligence aid. A subject index lists persons involved in civil disturbances, and the incident index contains records of civil disorder events. The indexes are cross-referenced.

civilianization. the use of civilians to perform functions traditionally conducted by police officers.

civil law. the system of law that adjusts conflicts and differences between persons in private and civil matters; the body of law relating to the rights of citizens.

civil liberty. freedom from restraint of or interference with the affairs, opinions, or property of a person except in the interest of the public good.

civilly dead. a principle of law which holds that an individual who is not legally dead can forfeit his/her civil rights upon conviction of treason or imprisonment for life.

civil process. the serving of summonses, subpoenas, and other documents issued by or under the authority of a court in civil matters.

civil rights. the rights of every citizen which are guaranteed under the Constitution.

Civil Rights Acts of 1866, 1870 and 1971. laws intended to insure equality before the law in a variety of functional areas (ability to enter into contracts, sue, give evidence, and secure equal protection of persons and property) and establish that individuals or governments denying any rights or privileges shall be liable for legal action. These acts are often used in conjunction with, but are not replaced by, other civil rights acts as the basis for suits.

Civil Rights Act of 1957. a law generally considered to be the beginning of contemporary civil rights legislation. It established the U.S. Commission on Civil Rights and strengthened the judiciary's ability to protect civil rights.

Civil Rights Act of 1960. a law intended mainly to correct errors in the Civil Rights Act of 1957.

civil wrongs. wrongs that infringe on private rights and duties. Remedy against them is sought by private action. Tort and breach of contract are among the more common civil wrongs.

claims adjuster. a person employed or hired by an insurer to investigate the facts surrounding a loss and to also determine the extent of damage. A claims adjuster is usually authorized to either negotiate a settlement or equitably adjust the loss to its correct value.

clandestine operations. intelligence, counter-intelligence, and other information collection activities; covert political, economic, propaganda and paramilitary activities, conducted so as to assure secrecy.

class action. a search for judicial remedy that one or more individuals may undertake on behalf of themselves and all others in similar situations. For example, a person who has been discriminated against as the result of an unfair employment practice may seek through a class action to eliminate the unfair practice and to obtain compensation for himself and all other persons similarly affected.

class characteristics. properties of evidence that can only be associated with a group and never with a single source. The term also relates to marks made on an object as a result of the manufacturing process. Such manufacturing marks may have significance to the analysis of foot and tire prints, tool marks, and similar forms of physical evidence.

class conflict. the struggle between competing classes, specifically between the class that owns the means of production and the class or classes that do not.

classical conditioning. a process whereby a neutral stimulus that normally evokes a reflexive response comes to elicit that response when presented by itself.

classical school of criminology. a dominant trend in the history of political and philosophical thought on crime that flourished for about a century beginning in the 1760s. The classical school assumed the existence of free will, imputed responsibility and accountability to all perpetrators, and stressed the necessity of meting out punishment sufficiently severe to deter would-be criminals, but not so severe as to be cruel, unjust, or unnecessary.

classification. procedures during which a new inmate of a penal institution is assigned a security status, an educational, work or therapeutic program, and appropriate institutional housing; a method of categorizing fingerprints for easier storage, retrieval and comparison.

classification authority. the authority vested in an official of the originating or user agency to make a determination that certain information requires protection against unauthorized disclosure.

classified destruction. the process of destroying or rendering unintelligible materials that are classified or contain classified information.

clean. not carrying illicit drugs or not using illicit drugs, particularly narcotics. Also used to describe the process of removing the seed and stems from marijuana.

clearance. in Uniform Crime Reports terminology, the event where a known occurrence of a Part I offense is followed by an arrest or other decision which indicates a solved crime at the police level of reporting.

clearance by arrest. in Uniform Crime Reports terminology, an instance where a known offense is solved by the arrest and charging of at least one person, the summoning, citing or notifying of at least one person, or the citing of a juvenile to appear before juvenile authorities, in connection to the offense.

clearance by exceptional means. in Uniform Crime Reports terminology, a case where police know the identity and location of a suspect and have information to support arrest, charging, and prosecution, but are prevented from taking action by circumstances outside police control.

clearance rate. the number of offenses cleared divided by the number of offenses known to police, expressed as a percent. For example, if within a particular time period the police make 300 arrests in connection with 500 reported offenses, the clearance rate is .6 or 60 percent.

clear and present danger. a concept that gives to the government a right and a duty to curtail otherwise constitutionally protected speech when utterance of the words in a specific context threaten imminent and grave harm.

cleartext. data that are intelligible until transformed by secret keys into unintelligible data. Also called plaintext.

cleavage line wound. a gaping wound produced by cutting or stabbing perpendicularly to a cleavage line. The wound will appear to have been caused by a large blade or a deep cutting action. The gaping aspect, however, results from a distortion of the muscle fibers that provide a normal tension to the skin.

clemency. executive or legislative action where the severity of punishment of a single person or a group of persons is reduced or the punishment stopped, or a person is exempted from prosecution for certain actions. The chief forms of clemency are pardon, amnesty, commutation, reduced sentence, reprieve, and remission of fine or forfeiture. Grounds for clemency include mitigating circumstances, post-conviction evidence of innocence, dubious guilt, illness of prisoner, reformation, services to the state, turning state's evidence, reasons of state, and correction of an unduly severe sentence or injustice stemming from imperfection or misapplication of penal law.

clicker. a marijuana cigarette soaked in formaldehyde (embalming fluid). Also called a cricket.

clinical death. an event that occurs when a person's heart stops beating and breathing ceases.

clonidine. an effective non-opiate drug for controlling withdrawal from opiates and opioids. Subjects experience only mild discomfort when detoxifying with clonidine, and its use has been proposed as a transition drug to bridge the gap in moving addicts from methadone treatment to antagonist (e.g., naltrexone) treatment.

Clonopin. the trade name for clonazepam, a depressant in the family of benzodiazepines. It is a commonly abused drug and is regulated under the Controlled Substances Act as a Schedule IV depressant.

closed bomb. a bomb in which none of the component parts are visible to the naked eye.

closed case. an investigation that has been closed because it is completed or because there are no further investigative leads to follow.

closed fracture. a fracture in which the skin is not penetrated by fractured bone; a break in a bone in which the injury is entirely internal with no break in the adjacent tissue or skin. Also called a simple fracture.

close-range gunshot wound. a wound caused when the muzzle at time of discharge is 2–24 inches from the victim. As the distance between a gun and the skin is increased, the flame burns diminish and powder grains embedded in the skin (tattooing) are spread in a widening circle around the bullet entry hole. Eventually, the tattooing effect disappears. When a bullet fired at close range first passes through clothing or some other substance, the tattooing effect may not be visible at all, thereby giving the appearance of a distant shot.

closing arguments. arguments by the prosecutor and defense counsel in which each side attempts to persuade the jury to reach a favorable verdict.

cloudy hairline. a tell-tale sign of a counterfeit bill as evidenced by an indistinct hairline on the head of the person depicted on the bill.

CN agent. the descriptor for chloroacetophenone, a riot control chemical agent that causes severe weeping or tearing of the eyes. CN is a commonly used tear gas that produces a characteristic apple blossom odor and is released as a particulate cloud, or dissolved and released as a liquid aerosol.

COBOL. the acronym for Common Business-Oriented Language, an English-like programing language designed for business data processing applications.

cocaine. an alkaloid refined from the coca plant that is a short-acting but powerful stimulant pharmacologically similar to the amphetamines. Isolated in the 1850s, it was hailed by many as a wonder drug and was also widely valued and used as a local anesthetic and nerve-blocking agent. Now stronger anesthetics with fewer stimulant side effects have virtually eliminated its medical usefulness, including such synthetic cocaine-like compounds as procaine (Novocain). By the late 19th century cocaine had also achieved considerable popularity in the United States as a general tonic and addiction cure. Its exhilarating properties made it a favorite ingredient of medicine, soda pop (including Coca-Cola), and wine (Vin Mariani). In 1914 its use was controlled by the Harrison Narcotics Act, in which it was incorrectly classified as a narcotic. Effects include euphoria, restlessness, excitement, and a feeling of well-being. Users view it as a social drug in terms of convenience of use, bulk, effects, safety,

minimal side effects, and no after effects. As with the amphetamines, cocaine users often go on "runs" and chronic heavy use can lead to a "paranoid syndrome" in which the user is highly suspicious or nervous. Many of cocaine's therapeutic applications are obsolete as the result of the development of safer anesthetics. Illicit cocaine is distributed as a white crystalline powder, often diluted by a variety of other ingredients, the most common of which are sugars such as lactose, inositil, mannitol, and local anesthetics such as lidocaine. The drug is most commonly administered by being "snorted" through the nasal passages. Less commonly, for heightened effect, the drug is injected directly into the bloodstream. It is also smoked by a method called "freebasing" in which cocaine hydrochloride (the usual form in which it is sold) is converted to cocaine base. Inhalation of the fumes produces a rapid and intense effect. Cocaine has a potential for extraordinary psychic dependence. Although technically a stimulant, cocaine appears in the Controlled Substances Act as a Schedule II narcotic. The street names for cocaine include coke, flake, and snow.

cocaine base (or freebase). a form of cocaine converted from its normal form, usually for the purpose of smoking it, called "free basing." The process of converting street cocaine (cocaine hydrochloride) into its freebase, or more purified form involves heating ether, lighter fluid, or similar flammable solvents, which can be extremely hazardous. Since cocaine in its normal street form is not effective when smoked, an elaborate do-it-yourself chemical process is used to convert it to a purified form. This purified cocaine base is smoked in a water pipe or sprinkled on a tobacco or marijuana cigarette for a two minute, sudden and intense high. The substance is rapidly absorbed by the lungs and carried to the brain in a few seconds. However, the euphoria quickly subsides into a feeling of restless irritability. The freebase post-high is so uncomfortable that cocaine smokers—in order to maintain the high—often continue smoking until they are exhausted or run out of cocaine. The smoking of cocaine originated in Peru during the early 1970s. The custom quickly spread to several other South American countries, eventually traveling to the United States. The South American practice involves smoking coca paste, an extract produced during the manufacture of cocaine from coca leaves. Also called freebase, white tornado, baseball, snowflake.

cocaine blues. an intense depression that results from discontinuing the use of cocaine.

cocaine paste. a white, semi-solid or solid preparation containing cocaine sulphate and other coca alkaloids. It can be mixed with tobacco or marihuana and smoked. Also called coca paste, cocaine sulphate, and cocaine basic paste.

cocaine psychosis. a psychological reaction to prolonged cocaine use characterized by hallucinations. The diagnosis of psychosis often emerges from the presence of tactile sensations. However, psychosis involves more than hallucinations and usually implies dysfunction in an individual's mental processes, emotional responses, memory, communication skills, sense of reality, and behavior. The presence of such a wide range of phenomena in cocaine intoxication is less clear than the presence of hallucinations; therefore, the use of the term is questionable.

cocked striker. in bomb construction, a firing pin held under tension. Upon release of the tension, the pin initiates the bomb's firing train.

Code 1. an emergency call usually prompted by a report of an officer in danger, a shooting, an explosion or bombing, robbery or felony in progress, a major accident, or other situation in which human life is in danger.

Code 2. an urgent call usually prompted by a public disturbance, a citizen's request for help, an injury, a major fire, or other situation that is serious but not life threatening.

Code 3. a call for routine police services that does not require an emergency or urgent response.

codefendant. one of the accused in a trial in which two or more persons are charged with the same criminal act or acts and are tried at the same time. A defendant in such an instance may request a separate trial, or severance.

codeine. an alkaloid found in raw opium. Although it occurs naturally, most codeine is produced from morphine. As compared with morphine, codeine produces less analgesia, sedation, and respiratory depression. It is widely distributed in products of two general types. Codeine for the relief of moderate pain may consist of codeine tablets or be combined with other products such as aspirin or acetaminophen (Tylenol). Some examples of liquid codeine preparations for the relief of coughs (antitussives) are Robitussin AC, Cheracol, and elixir of terpin hydrate with codeine. It is also manufactured to a lesser extent in injectable form for the relief of pain, and is by far the most widely used naturally occurring narcotic in medical treatment. Codeine products appear in the Controlled Substances Act as Schedule II, III and V drugs.

code of ethics. a statement of professional standards of conduct to which the practitioners of a profession say they subscribe.

Code of Hammurabi. Babylonian laws of the twenty-second century BC, generally regarded by historians as a moderate and humanitarian code for its period. It is one of the oldest codes of law.

Code of Justinian. the codification of Roman law by Justinian I in the sixth century AD in the form of a body of law.

codicil. an addition to a will.

coding siren. a siren with the capability of emitting controlled bursts of sound.

Cody v. Brombrowski. a 1973 case in which the U.S. Supreme Court held that a search warrant is not required to conduct an inventory search of vehicle seized at the time of a legal arrest or impounded for police caretaking.

coefficient of friction. the friction constant

of two moving surfaces in contact. This principle is applied in the determination of motor vehicle speed from the measurement of skid marks. For level surfaces, the coefficient of friction equals friction force divided by weight. For example, if the force required to move a 4000-pound vehicle is 3200 pounds, then the coefficient of friction is 0.8 (3200 divided by 4000). The coefficient of friction for average paved roadways in dry weather is 0.6 to 0.8; for wet roads, 0.5; for packed snow or mud, 0.2; for ice, 0.1; for very wet, muddy, or icy roads, less than 0.1; for sand or cinders on concrete, 0.4 to 0.6. The coefficient of friction decreases when speed is increased on dry surfaces, and decreases on wet roads. However, on snow and gravel, the coefficient of friction increases slightly with increased speed.

coerced confession. an admission of guilt obtained by threat or the use of force.

coercion. compelling a person to do that which he does not have to do, or to omit what he may legally do, by some illegal means such as by threat or force.

cognitive interview. a type of interview used in obtaining information from witnesses and victims of crime. It features four general methods for jogging memory: (1) reconstructing the circumstances, (2) reporting everything, (3) recalling the events in different order, and (4) changing perspectives. In addition, this interview technique seeks to obtain specific information relating to physical appearance, names, numbers, speech characteristics, and things said.

cohabit. to live together.

cohort. in statistics, the group of individuals having one or more statistical factors in common in a demographic study.

Cointelpro. a now defunct FBI counterintelligence program that monitored the activities of suspected subversives.

coitus. sexual intercourse.

coke-head. cocaine addict.

coke out. to become incoherent from excessive use of cocaine.

coke spoon. a small spoon, sometimes expensive and elaborate, used for spooning out cocaine incidental to snorting.

cold hardware. an unregistered or untraceable firearm.

cold surveillance. secretive tailing or bugging of a target.

cold turkey. to quit using heroin or morphine and go through the resulting abstinence syndrome without the aid of pharmacological agents. The term supposedly comes from the onset of gooseflesh associated with abrupt withdrawal.

collapsed vein. venous thrombosis. A malady, not uncommon among veteran heroin users, caused by repeated injections in a vein often precipitated by contaminants in the injected material and unsanitary procedures. After a regularly used vein collapses, other veins are usually sought in new areas of the body, including the arms, hands, legs, feet, and neck.

collateral consequence. any harm that may result from a guilty plea or a conviction, addition to the preordered punishment. Examples include deportation, disenfranchisement, disbarment, or loss of license to practice certain professions.

collateral fact. a fact not directly related to an issue; extraneous information.

collected standards. handwriting specimens collected for comparison purposes. Typically, they are not in direct connection to the crime and are obtained from various public and private files.

collection. the acquisition of information by any means and its delivery to an intelligence processing unit for use in the production of intelligence.

collision diagram. a schematic drawing of a street intersection or other roadway location showing, by symbols, the traffic unit movements and conflicts that have occurred in a given time period. The symbols represent vehicle types, travel directions, pedestrians, bicycles, manner of collision, and indicate where the collisions were fatal or caused injury or property damage.

collusion. an agreement between two or

more persons to proceed fraudulently to the detriment and prejudice of an innocent and ignorant third party.

Collyer v. S.H. Kress and Company. a 1936 case in which the U.S. Supreme Court ruled that a detention of a suspected shoplifter by a store detective was permitted if the detention was reasonable in both time and manner.

Colombian. a potent strain of marijuana, so named for its place of origin.

color of authority. authority based on a prima facie right; that which is presumed because of apparent legal authority. For example, the actions of law enforcement officers take place under color of authority.

comatose. the state of partial or complete unconsciousness.

combination tool mark. a tool mark consisting of an abrasion and a negative impression. The abrasion is caused by the movement of the tool against a surface. The impression is formed when the tool is applied as a lever. Combination tool marks are frequently made by crowbars and jimmies.

combustible. capable of undergoing combustion; apt to catch fire; inflammable.

come-along. a type of body hold or a device used by a police officer when taking a resisting person into custody. A come-along body hold is usually applied to a finger, hand, wrist, or arm. A come-along device is the wrist chain, which when wrapped around the wrist and twisted, will produce intense pain. The police flashlight can also be used as a pressure-applying device in certain come-along holds.

come down. to begin to come off the influence of a drug.

come home. an undercover agent's withdrawal from active operations.

command. in computer usage, an instruction, generally an English word, typed by the user or included in a command procedure that requests the software to perform some well-defined activity such as copy, delete, transfer, or print.

commercial bribery. conferring or offering or agreeing to confer benefit upon an employee, without consent of the employer, with intent to influence the employee's conduct in relation to his employer's affairs. The crime is also committed when the employee solicits, agrees or accepts such benefit. It is a crime separate from traditional bribery and usually applicable to conduct involving non-public, business persons.

commercial burglary. the unlawful or forcible entry or attempted forcible entry of a commercial establishment, usually, but not necessarily, attended by a theft.

commercial robbery. the theft or attempted theft of money or property from a commercial establishment, by force or threat of force.

commercial sex offense. unlawfully performing, or causing or assisting another person to perform, a sex act for a fee, or causing or assisting another person to obtain performance of a sex act by paying a fee, or receiving money known to have been paid for performance of a sex act or attempting such acts.

comminuted fracture. a break in a bone in which the bone is fragmented.

commission. doing or perpetration; the performance of an act.

commit. to order into custody, either to a correctional facility or a mental institution.

commitment. the written order by which a court or magistrate directs an officer to take a person to prison; authority for holding in jail one accused of crime.

common carrier. a person or company who carries or holds itself out as carrying persons and/or goods for hire to all who apply.

common entry door. any door in a multiple dwelling which provides access between the semi-public, interior areas of the building and the out-of-doors areas surrounding the building.

common knowledge. matters which a court may declare applicable to action without necessity of proof. It is knowledge that every intelligent person has.

common law. a system of law, or body of

legal rules, derived from decisions of judges based upon accepted customs and traditions. It originated in England and is based on centuries of case decisions. It is known as the common law because it is believed that these rules were generally recognized and were in full force throughout England. Common law is now the basis of the laws in every state of the United States, except Louisiana, which bases its laws upon the early laws of France. Statutes have been enacted to supplement and supersede the common law in many fields. The common law, however, still governs where there is no statute dealing with a specific subject. Although the common law is written, it is called the unwritten law in contradistinction to statutory law enacted by the legislatures.

common-law marriage. a union not solemnized in the ordinary way, but created by an agreement to marry, followed by cohabitation.

common nuisance. a danger or damage threatening the public.

Commonwealth of Pennsylvania v. Harry Mimms. a 1977 case in which the U.S. Supreme Court found that once a motor vehicle has been lawfully detained, the officer may order the driver out of the vehicle for the officer's personal protection. This face-to-face contact may prevent a motorist from making any sudden moves for weapons and, at the same time, may negate the necessity of having the officer stand on the roadway side of the vehicle during the encounter.

communications security. the protective measures taken to deny unauthorized persons information derived from telecommunications and to ensure the authenticity of such communications.

communicator. a device that electronically dials one or more prerecorded telephone numbers using digital codes and reports alarm or supervisory information to a receiver.

community-based treatment. a treatment program that takes place in a community setting, such as a Halfway House. The term also applies to parole and probation programs, outpatient methadone maintenance programs, and other therapeutic approaches not involving incarceration.

community-centered policing. a concept of police operations in which a police agency and the community it serves maintains mutually supportive relationships. In some contexts the term indicates control of a police agency by politically active individuals in the community.

community corrections. any type of supervision over a person convicted of delinquent or criminal activity in which the supervision takes place outside an institution of confinement. Examples include probation and parole.

community profiling. a community-oriented method of policing that holds individual officers accountable for delivering services as required by the expressed needs of the community.

community restitution. public work done for the community, in lieu of or in addition to other criminal sanctions, as punishment for a crime. Vandalism is an offense for which community restitution is sometimes ordered.

community service officer. a person other than a commissioned police officer who performs certain non-enforcement duties in such programs as community relations and crime prevention. Community service officers range from paid to nonpaid, part-time or full-time employees, and in some cases recruits and applicants who have not yet met all of the requirements for commissioned employment.

commutation of sentence. an act of clemency in which a sentence of death is changed to a term in prison, or in which a prison sentence is lessened, sometimes to time already served, in order to permit the convict's release without delay.

companionate crime. crime committed by two or more persons against another, as in a holdup or a mugging.

comparative negligence. a principle of law which takes into account the negligence of both sides in an accident.

comparison microscope. a microscope having an optical bridge that permits an examiner to view and thereby compare two samples at the same time. It is often used to identify bullets. If when the ends of two bullets are brought together in a single fused image and their separate striations match, the ballistics examiner would conclude that both bullets were fired from the same weapon.

comparison spectrum. a spectrum which contains a number of sharply defined, well identified lines of standard wavelength, which is used as a standard of comparison in studying other spectra.

compelling impulse. an accused's claim (but not a legal defense) that the crime committed was done because of an irresistible urge.

compensation. a human condition characterized by actions that serve to conceal personal weaknesses by emphasizing desirable traits. A person who compensates is likely to make up for frustration in one area by over-gratification in another area.

compensatory damages. a sum of money awarded to a plaintiff by a court or jury as a fair and just recompense for injury sustained to a person, property, or reputation.

competency. as used in the law of evidence, the presence of those characteristics, or the absence of those disabilities, which render a witness legally fit and qualified to give testimony in a court of justice. The term is applied in the same sense to documents or other written evidence.

competency to stand trial. the concept that a defendant should be tried only if he has sufficient ability at the time of trial to understand the proceedings against him, to consult with his lawyer with a reasonable degree of understanding, and to assist in his own defense.

competent evidence. that which the very nature of the thing to be proved requires, as the producing of a writing where its contents are the subject of inquiry.

competent court. a court having lawful jurisdiction.

complainant. the person who, as a victim of a crime, brings the facts to the attention of the police.

complaining witness. in criminal proceedings, the person who originally causes the case to be prosecuted, or who initiates the complaint against the defendant. The complaining witness is usually the victim.

complaint. in general criminal justice usage, any accusation that a person has committed an offense, received by or originating from a law enforcement or prosecutorial agency, or received by a court. In judicial process usage, a formal written accusation made by any person, often a prosecutor, and filed in a court, alleging that a specified person has committed a specific offense. Also called a filing or a charging document.

complaint denied. the decision by a prosecution agency to not file a complaint or information in court, or to not seek an indictment. Also called complaint rejected, complaint declined, and declination.

complaint granted. the decision by a prosecution agency to grant a request for complaint by filing a complaint or information in court, or by seeking an indictment from a grand jury. Also called complaint accepted.

complaint modified. the decision by a prosecution agency to initiate prosecution in relation to an alleged criminal event, but to alter some or all of the charges or to omit some of the charges in the document requesting the complaint.

complaint requested. a request by a law enforcement or other government agency, or a private citizen, that a prosecution agency file a complaint or information or seek an indictment alleging that a specified person has committed a specified offense.

compliance agency. an agency that has been given the power to enforce the equal employment opportunity laws. Such agencies include the Office of Federal Contract Compliance Programs, the Equal Employment Opportunity Commission, the U.S. Department of Labor, and the various state level commissions on human rights.

complicity. conduct on the part of a person other than the chief actor in the commission of a crime, in which the person intentionally or knowingly serves to further the intent to commit the crime, aids in the commission of the crime, or assists the person who has committed the crime to avoid prosecution or to escape from justice. Complicity is the name of a pattern of behavior, and not the name of an offense.

component failure. a cause for failure or improper operation of an element in a system.

composite. a forged document made from piecing or recombining other documents.

composite drawing. a drawing of a suspect made by a police artist from information provided by witnesses.

Composition C. a powerful plastic explosive used for military and demolition purposes.

compounded larceny. a larceny accompanied by another offense such as battery.

compound fracture. a break in a bone in which the bone is severed and at least one end damages adjacent tissue and protrudes through the skin. Also called an open fracture.

compounding a crime. the taking, or agreeing to take, money, property, gratuity or reward upon an understanding to conceal a crime, or violation of statute, or to abstain from, discontinue or delay prosecution, or to withhold any evidence thereof, except in a case where a compromise is allowed by law; the offense of receiving or offering to give a monetary or other consideration in return for a promise not to prosecute or aid in the prosecution of a criminal offender. Also known as misprision of a felony.

compound microscope. a normal-light microscope used for making crime laboratory examinations. It has two lenses or sets of lenses, the first being the eyepiece or eyepiece assembly, and the other the objective or objective assembly.

Comprehensive Drug Abuse Prevention and Control Act. a 1970 law that superseded all other federal narcotics laws. Title II is concerned with control and enforcement, and is called the Controlled Substances Act.

compress. a clean or sterile pad or folded cloth used for applying pressure to a hemorrhaging wound.

compression mark. a mark made by the application of pressure by a tool on a softer material. For example, a pry bar used to force open a window is likely to leave a compression mark on the sill.

compromise. the disclosure of classified information to persons not authorized access thereto.

compulsion. forcible inducement to the commission of an act; an impulse or feeling of being irresistibly driven toward the performance of some act.

compulsion defense. a defense which argues that a person should not be charged with a crime when the act was committed in response to an imminent, impending and overwhelmingly coercive influence. For example, a person who is ordered to drive a getaway car under the threat of immediate death would not be punishable as a principal to the crime. Also called the necessity defense.

compulsive drug use. a classification of drug use that is characterized by both high frequency and high intensity levels of relatively long duration, producing physiological or psychological dependence such that the individual cannot discontinue such use at will without experiencing physiological discomfort or psychological disruption. It is viewed as primarily psychologically motivated and reinforced, stemming from the need to elicit a sense of security, comfort, or relief related to the person's initial reasons for regularly using the drug.

compulsive neurosis. a condition characterized by obsessive ideals and desires to perform complicated and senseless acts.

compulsory. involuntary; forced; coerced by legal process or by force of law.

compulsory treatment. treatment in which the patient is compelled to begin and/or continue treatment; any treatment program that does not require consent of the client.

compurgation. a process, used at the time of the origin of the jury system, in which a defendant attempted to prove his innocence by calling witnesses who testified as to their belief in his innocence.

computer. a functional unit that can perform substantial computerization, including numerous arithmetic operations or logic operations, without intervention by a human operator during a run. Computers are also identified by the functions they perform or other unique characteristics, for example, analog computer, arbitrary sequence computer, digital computer, general purpose computer, hybrid computer, parallel computer, self-adapting computer, self-organizing computer, sequential computer, serial computer, simultaneous computer, special purpose computer, stored program computer, and synchronous computer.

computer abuse. a category of undesirable or unethical, but not illegal, behavior involving computer equipment.

computer-aided dispatching. a system in which police dispatchers are assisted by computer technology in assigning cases to patrol officers. The term also refers to a dispatching system that is enhanced by the use of computer equipment at the communications center or in patrol units.

computer crime. a popular term for crimes committed by use of a computer or crimes involving misuse or destruction of computer equipment or computerized information, sometimes specifically theft committed by means of manipulation of a computerized financial transaction system, or the use of computer services with intent to avoid payment.

computerese. jargon used by computer specialists.

computer network. the interconnection of communications lines (including microwave or other means of electronic communication) with a computer through remote terminals; a complex consisting of two or more interconnected computers.

computer program. a set of data fed into a computer to be evaluated or to be used to process other data or solve a problem; a series of instructions or statements, in a form acceptable to a computer, that permits the functioning of a computer in a manner designed to provide appropriate products from the computer system.

computer-related crime. any illegal act for which knowledge of computer technology is essential for performance of the act.

computer science. the branch of science and technology that is concerned with methods and techniques relating to data processing performed by automatic means.

computer system. a functional unit, consisting of one or more computers and associated software, that (1) uses common storage for all or part of the data necessary for execution of the program, (2) executes user-designated data manipulation, including arithmetic operations and logic operations, and (3) that can execute programs that modify themselves during their execution.

concentrated explosion. an explosion characterized by an extremely rapid combustion, known as detonation reaction, which occurs through the action of explosives such as dynamite, TNT, nitroglycerin, pentaerythritoltetranitrate, and various plastic explosives.

concentration. the amount of a substance in a unit volume of fluid, expressed as weight/volume. Concentrations are usually expressed either as nanograms per milliliter (ng/ml), as micrograms per milliliter (ug/ml), or milligrams per liter (mg/l). There are 28,000,000 micrograms in one ounce, and 1000 nanograms in a microgram. Also, in equal employment opportunity programs, the presence of a greater number of individuals of a particular race or sex in a job group than would be reasonably expected in the external work force.

concentric circle search. a type of crime scene search in which the investigator begins at the apparent center of the scene and searches in ever-widening circles until satisfied that all available evidence has been detected.

concentric-zone theory. a theory of urban development which holds that cities grow around a central business district in concentric zones, with each zone devoted to a different land use.

concertina. a coil of barbed wire typically used as a temporary fence.

conclusion of fact. a determination by a jury based on facts produced in evidence.

conclusion of law. a determination arrived at by applying to the facts pleaded certain artificial rules of law.

conclusive. shutting up a matter; shutting out all further evidence; not admitting of explanation or contradiction; beyond question or beyond dispute.

conclusive evidence. that which is incontrovertible, either because the law does not permit it to be contradicted, or because it is so strong and convincing as to overbear all proof to the contrary and establish the proposition in question beyond any reasonable doubt.

conclusive presumption. a presumption which cannot be challenged no matter how strong the evidence to the contrary may be.

concubinage. the act or practice of cohabiting, without the authority of law or a legal marriage.

concurrent jurisdiction. a jurisdiction that applies when the federal government and a state have all the rights accorded them under the Constitution with the broad qualification such rights run concurrently. Exact equivalence of rights is not present, however. At all times the federal government has the superior right to carry out federal functions unimpeded by state interference. State criminal laws are, of course, applicable in the area of enforcement of the state. The same laws are enforceable by the federal government under the Assimilative Crimes Act, which is applicable to areas under concurrent and exclusive jurisdiction of the United States. Other federal criminal laws also apply. Most crimes fall under both federal and state sanction and either the federal or state government, or both, may take jurisdiction over a given offense.

concurrent sentences. two or more sentences to be served simultaneously. Concurrent sentencing effectively reduces the severity of a sentence, while also ensuring the state the right to continue confinement if a court of appeals should overturn the guilty verdict on one of the charges.

concurring opinion. an opinion which states the reasons and reasoning of one or more judges who agree with the majority decision of a court, but on different grounds.

concussion. an injury to a soft structure, such as the brain, resulting from a blow or violent shaking. It is characterized by immediate and transient impairment of neural function, such as altered consciousness, mental disequilibrium, and disturbed vision.

condescending counsel. a cross-examination tactic sometimes used by an attorney for the defense as a means to discredit the testimony of a prosecution witness. This technique subjects the witness to ridicule and attempts to create an impression that the witness is inept and unreliable. The defense attorney's general approach is to assume an air of benevolence and sympathy in which the prosecution witness is portrayed as bumbling and incompetent.

condemnation. the legal machinery by which an authorized governmental agency takes private property for public use.

conditionally suspended sentence. a court disposition of a convicted person specifying a penalty of a fine or commitment to confinement but holding execution of the penalty in abeyance upon good behavior. In some jurisdictions, a conditionally suspended sentence is equivalent or complementary to a grant of probation.

conditional pardon. an executive act releasing a person from punishment, contingent upon his or her performance or non-performance of specified acts.

conditional plea. a plea of guilty or nolo contendere which is entered on the understanding that the defendant will still be allowed to appeal a prior adverse ruling which otherwise would be forfeited by entry of the plea.

conditional privilege. a defense in criminal libel which contends that the defendant has made the allegedly libelous statement in order to fulfill a public or private duty to speak.

conditional release. the release by executive decision from a correctional facility of a prisoner who has not served his or her full sentence and whose freedom is contingent upon obeying specified rules of behavior.

condition diagram. a map drawn to scale of a street intersection or other roadway location that shows pavement widths, curbs or shoulders, sidewalks, view obstructions, grades, traffic controls, lighting, access driveways, and other important features that can affect traffic movements.

conditioning. political agitation caused by the successful use of disinformation.

condonation defense. a defense that is used in some rare cases where the law allows an accused to be not prosecuted if certain conditions are met. For example, a charge of seduction might be dropped if the parties involved subsequently marry.

conduct unbecoming an officer. in police and military disciplinary proceedings, a charge involving violation of the rules and regulations or professional and ethical standards of the department or service.

cone fracture pattern. a cone shaped pattern that appears in glass plate fractured by a penetrating force. In a cross sectional view, the tip of the cone is on the entering side of the glass with the large end of the cone on the exiting side. In addition to the crater being formed, flaking of the glass takes place, which upon close examination may reveal the angle of direction of the missile. For example, in the case of a bullet fired straight into the glass, the flaking will appear uniform. Flaking that is heavy on one side of the crater indicates that the missile came from the opposite direction. Also called saucer pattern.

confabulation. the filling in of memory gaps with false and often irrelevant details.

confess. to admit as true; to admit the truth of a charge or accusation.

Confessing Sam. a person who regularly confesses to sensational crimes he or she has not committed.

confession. a voluntary statement of guilt; a complete acknowledgement of guilt.

confession distance. the distance between the interrogator and the person being interrogated within which the interrogator establishes feelings of friendship, acceptance, intimacy and reassurance.

confidence game. a popular term for false representation to obtain money or any other thing of value, where deception is accomplished through the trust placed by the victim in the character of the offender.

confidential communication. an oral or written communication between two persons which because of their relationship may not be divulged unless waived. The law forbids the disclosure of such confidential communications, particularly in the cases of husband and wife, clergyman and penitent, doctor and patient, and lawyer and client.

confidential information. information protected by statute or by rules of an organization. Examples of confidential information might be military secrets, or a company's trade secrets.

confidential source. a person from whom valuable information is obtained and whose identity is known only to one or a few officers. Also called an informant.

confidential vehicle identification number. a number placed on certain major assemblies of a vehicle at the time of manufacture and which is known only to designated persons within the Federal Bureau of Investigation and the National Automobile Theft Bureau.

confinement. the restraint or restriction of a person's freedom of movement; in correctional terminology, physical restriction of a person to a clearly defined area from which he or she is lawfully forbidden to depart and from which departure is usually constrained by architectural barriers and/or guards or other custodians.

confirmation. in drug investigations, the re-analysis of a sample found to be positive in a preliminary test or field test.

confirmation test. a second test by an alternate and more sensitive analytical method to positively identify an unknown substance. A positive result in a preliminary or initial test is called a presumptive positive. A presumptive positive sample that has been tested a second time using the same, similar, or less sensitive analytical method is called a verification. Generally, the term confirmation is reserved for analytical methods that employ definitive technology such as gas chromatography/mass spectrometry (GC/MS).

confiscation. the act of taking private property as a penalty and a forfeit for public use. Also the act of taking contraband.

conflict of interest. a situation where a decision that may be made (or influenced) by an office holder may (or may appear to) be to that office holder's personal benefit.

conformal projection. a mapping method that does not preserve size, distance or area or scale of lengths, but preserves the shapes of the objects depicted.

confrontation. the right of a person to face the witnesses who charge him with a crime. By the first ten amendments to the U.S. Constitution (Bill of Rights), a defendant in any criminal prosecution is entitled to be confronted by the witnesses against him. This means that the defendant shall be given a right and fair opportunity, not necessarily in court, to cross-examine witnesses, either by himself or by counsel.

confusion agent. an individual dispatched by his sponsor to confound the intelligence or counterintelligence apparatus of the opposition, as opposed to the direct task of collecting and transmitting information.

Congressional Assassination Act. a law which makes killing or plotting to kill a member of Congress a federal crime.

conjugal visit. a visit of a spouse with a prisoner in privacy to allow a conjugal (marital) relationship.

connection. a person from whom one can buy or obtain drugs, usually opiate narcotics.

consanguinity. blood relationship; the relationship of persons descended from a common ancestor.

consecutive sentence. a sentence that is one of two or more sentences imposed at the same time, after conviction for more than one offense, and which is served in sequence with the other sentences; a new sentence for a new conviction, imposed upon a person already under sentence for a previous offense, which is added to a previous sentence, thus increasing the maximum time the offender may be confined or under supervision. Also called cumulative sentence or multiple sentence.

consensual crime. a violation of law committed by or between two or more adults with the voluntary consent of each participant, as in the crimes of adultery, sodomy and gambling.

consensual monitoring. the monitoring of conversations between two individuals with the consent and knowledge of one of the individuals.

consent. a concurrence of wills; agreement; voluntarily yielding the will to the proposition of another; a voluntary accord between two people in their contractual relationship.

consent defense. a defense that may be used when consent of the victim is involved. Where consent is offered as a defense, the consent must have been given by a person legally capable of giving it and it must be voluntary.

consent recording. electronic recording of wire or oral communication with the consent of one or more of the participants.

consent to search form. a form used for advising a person of his or her constitutional rights concerning a search, for demonstrating that the rights were understood, and for showing that the rights were waived. The form, which varies from jurisdiction to jurisdiction, contains places for signatures to be affixed by the person granting consent, the search officer, and a witness. A major purpose of this type of form is to demonstrate the voluntariness of a consent search.

consent transmitting. radio transmission of oral communication with the consent of one or more of the participants.

consigliere. a Mafia higherup who serves as a counselor to capi and sottocapi (bosses and underbosses). A consigliere is often retired or partially retired from a successful career in crime as a Mafia leader.

consolidated trial. a trial in which two or more defendants named in separate charging documents are tried together, or where a given defendant is tried on charges contained in two or more charging documents.

conspiracy. a joining together of people to commit an unlawful act; a section of the U.S. Code that makes it a violation of federal law when two or more persons conspire to commit any federal offense, provided that at least one of the conspirators takes some action to effect the object of the conspiracy. The law is found in 18 USC, Section 371.

conspiracy of concealment. efforts to conceal or cover up any evidence of crime or wrongdoing.

constable. In medieval England, the person employed to care for the stables who, when the noble's guards were out of the village, acted as a watchman and caretaker. The constable's duties eventually extended to the pursuit of felons, and later the title applied to an inspector of weapons and equipment. Today, it refers to an elected county official with limited law-enforcement responsibilities. At most, a present-day constable is a parttime peace officer whose compensation is derived from fees he collects. In some jurisdictions, the constable is the acting bailiff of the justice of the peace, serving writs and executive judgments. He is generally without supervision and in most cases a political appointee, with little prestige attached to the office.

constituents of crime. a term relating to a legal concept in which a crime is viewed as having two essential constituents: an external physical action and an internal mental action. The external physical action is the conduct of the offender and its result. The forbidden conduct is set out in the definition for each particular crime. For example, in the crime of murder the conduct is the unlawful killing and the result is the death of the victim. In larceny, it would be the unlawful taking and the permanent loss to the victim of the property taken.

The internal mental action is the intent of the offender to act. Common to all crimes is the requirement that the offender willfully determines to do an act which the law forbids. Although general criminal intent will suffice for many crimes, certain offenses require additional mental intention. For example, the crime of unlawful taking is established when an offender intends to take someone else's property without permission and does so. For the crime to be larceny, a more serious offense, proof must be shown that the offender intended to permanently deprive the owner of the property taken.

In this concept, there can be no crime unless an external act and an internal mental state are present. If a person possesses a criminal intention but does not act on it, he has not committed a crime. If a person commits a forbidden act but does so without intent, there is no crime. A person duped into or insane at the time of performing an unlawful act has not committed a crime. Not only must the external and internal actions be present, they must be united at one and the same time.

constitutional officer. any law enforcement officer specifically and expressly provided for either in the Constitution of the United States or in an individual state's constitution. The offices of sheriff, constable, and coroner are constitutional offices in several states.

Constitutional right. a right guaranteed to the citizens by the Constitution and so guaranteed as to prevent legislative interference therewith.

Constitution of the United States. the basic law of the United States, with which all other federal and state laws must not conflict, lest they be declared null and void on the ground of being unconstitutional.

constriction. a narrowing or compression, especially of eye pupils and blood vessels.

constructively present. a legal term describing the presence at a location other than the crime scene of an aider or abettor. A lookout who functions at a considerable distance from the scene of a burglary may be said to be constructively present.

constructive possession. a condition in which a person, who is not actually in possession of property, is, because of the circumstances of the case, treated as if he or she were in actual possession. For example, illegal drugs found in an automobile are construed to be in the possession of the driver.

constructive sentence. a sentence designed to make the punishment fit the crime.

consumer. a person or agency that uses information or intelligence produced either in-house or obtained from other agencies.

consumer fraud. deception of the public with respect to the cost, quality, purity, safety, durability, performance, effectiveness, dependability, availability and adequacy of choice relating to goods or services offered or furnished, and with respect to credit or other matters relating to terms of sales.

contact gunshot wound. a wound produced when the muzzle is in contact or very close to the victim's body. The edge of the entry hole and the bullet track are burned, and particles of powder and clothing debris can be found inside the wound.

contact high. a phenomenon whereby someone who is not smoking marijuana but is in a confined area where marijuana is being smoked gets or acts high.

contact microphone. a microphone designed to be attached directly to a surface, such as a wall. Also called a spike microphone.

contact wound. a bullet wound made when the muzzle of the gun has been firmly applied to the skin at the instant of firing. When the muzzle is against a bony structure, such as the head, the blast causes a lacerated, charred wound that shows flame burns of the skin and hair from the rapidly expanding explosive gases. Smudges from carbon deposits appear within the subcutaneous tissue, muscle, and bone. A distinct abraded and contused imprint, with the laceration in the shape of a star, will very likely appear on the skin. When the muzzle is in contact with soft flesh, such as the abdomen, the star-shaped laceration and flame burns are not present because the exploding gases of the muzzle blast are dispersed without resistance into the abdominal cavity.

contact writing. impressions or minute tracings of ink from one piece of paper to another that is in contact with it. Pressure marks on paper caused by hand or mechanical writing, along with ink constituents, can be transferred from one document to a contacting document. These marks are often in the form of invisible indentations and chemical traces. By special chemical treatment, contact writing may be developed into legible writing. For example, if an original page is torn or removed from a record book, it may be possible to determine the contents of the missing page by treating the pages above and below the missing page.

containment theory. a theory of criminality, and particularly of juvenile delinquency, which postulates that delinquency and crime occur to the extent that there is a breakdown in "inner" and "outer" containing or restraining forces of society. The inner restraints consist of moral, religious, and superego forces. The outer restraints derive from family, educators, and other potentially disapproving forces.

contaminated print. an impression of a skin surface coated with a foreign substance such as blood or grease. A contaminated print is also known as a patent print.

contamination control station. a place specifically designated for controlling movement of persons and equipment into and from an area contaminated by radiation.

contempt of court. any act which is calculated to embarrass, hinder, obstruct a court, or which is calculated to lessen its authority or dignity. A contempt of court offense is sometimes characterized as "direct contempt" when committed in the immediate presence of the court and "indirect contempt" when committed outside of the court, such as failure or refusal to obey a lawful order, injunction, or decree of the court.

Continental system. the system of criminal prosecution prevailing in most of Europe, Japan and other countries, in contrast to the English and American adversary system. In the Continental system, a judicial officer has the responsibility to investigate and examine, and adjudication is not limited to the facts adduced by the parties. Also called the inquisitorial system.

contingency management. a management style that recognizes that the application of theory to practice must necessarily take into consideration, and be contingent upon, the given situation.

contingency plan. a document that sets forth an organized, planned, and coordinated course of action to be followed in case of an emergency event such as fire, explosion, or release of hazardous waste.

contingency planning. problem solving before the fact; planning to counter emergencies or unexpected occurrences.

contingency procedure. a procedure that is an alternative to a normal procedure when an unusual but anticipated situation occurs. A contingency procedure is usually triggered by an event outside the control of the organization. Contingency procedures would address events such as bomb threat, earthquake, fire, and riot.

continuance. the adjournment or carry-over of a legal proceeding to another scheduled date.

contraband. any article which has been declared illegal to possess. Examples include illegal drugs, stolen property, untaxed whiskey, counterfeit money, and pornographic material.

contra bonos mores. against good morals.

contracting officer. an official with authority to enter into and administer contracts, and make determinations and findings with respect to contracts.

contract parole. a program providing for a form of contract between a prisoner and state prison and parole officials wherein the prisoner undertakes to complete specified self-improvement programs in order to receive a definite parole date, and the agency promises to provide the necessary educational and social services. Also called mutual assistance program.

contra pacem. against the peace.

contributing to the delinquency of a minor. any act or behavior by one or more adults involving a minor, or committed in the presence of a minor, that might reasonably result in delinquent conduct. Examples include encouraging a minor to steal or commit vandalism.

contributory negligence. an act or omission amounting to want of ordinary care on the part of a complaining party, which, concurring with the defendant's negligence, is the proximate cause of injury. Contributory negligence generally applies to a condition of employment, either express or implied, with which an employee agrees that the dangers of injury ordinarily or obviously incident to the discharge of required duties shall be at the employee's own risk.

control group. a group which is not exposed to the independent variable of interest to a researcher, but whose members' background and experience are otherwise like those of the experimental group which is exposed to the independent variable.

controlled burning. the use of fire to destroy marihuana, opium and cocaine yielding crops. Also the destruction by fire of confiscated drugs.

controlled buy. purchase of an illegal drug by a person acting as an agent of the police. Also called a supervised buy.

controlled substances. psychoactive substances covered by laws regulating their sale and possession. The Controlled Substances Act of 1970 defines the term as including all substances subject to the act. The term was developed to replace the previous opiate-depressant-stimulant terminology and is sometimes used to refer only to nonnarcotic drugs such as hallucinogens, amphetamines, and barbiturates, which were first brought under regulatory control with the Drug Abuse Control Amendments of 1965.

Controlled Substances Act of 1970. an act that establishes five schedules or classifications of controlled substances according to their potential for abuse, physical and psychological dependence liability, and currently accepted medical use. Schedule I, the most strictly controlled category, includes heroin, marijuana, and LSD, and other drugs considered to have high abuse potential and not recognized for medical use in the United States; they can be obtained only for limited research purposes under special registration requirements. Schedule II drugs (morphine, methadone, and amphetamines) are primarily different from Schedule I drugs in that they have some currently accepted medical uses. The manufacture and distribution of these drugs are controlled by production quotas, strict security regulations, import and export controls, and nonrefillable prescription requirements. Illicit sale of Schedule I or II narcotic drugs carries a maximum penalty of 15 years imprisonment and a $25,000 fine; for nonnarcotic drugs the penalty is 5 years and a $15,000 fine. Schedule III, IV, and V drugs are considered in descending order to have less abuse potential and dependence liability. There is very little difference in the controls that are imposed on these three schedules, except Schedule V drugs, which are generally sold over the counter and not subject to any refill limitations on prescriptions. Title II of the Drug Abuse Act of 1970 requires registration of all persons involved in the legitimate distribution of controlled drugs and detailed recordkeeping. Illicit sale of Schedule V drugs carries a maximum of 1 year imprisonment and a $5,000 fine. Illicit possession of any of these substances is a misdemeanor on first offense, punishable by 1 year imprisonment and a $5,000 fine.

control material. in crime laboratory testing, a specimen which contains a specifically known ingredient at a precisely known concentration. A laboratory analyst uses the control material to calibrate equipment and ensure that the routine procedures of the laboratory are operating within quality control parameters.

controller. an agent's direct supervisor or case officer; the chief accounting officer of an organization.

control man. in a numbers operation, a person using two or more writers who are submitting their work products to him. A control man usually has an agreement with the backer regarding his personal financial remuneration. He may work on a percentage of play turned in, plus a percentage of the house win.

control question. in polygraphy, a question related to a similar but unconnected issue. It is asked in a general question test in such a manner that the examinee will lie in responding to it. The examiner compares the chart tracings for the control question against tracings related to questions directly relevant to the issue under investigation.

control theory. an explanation of delinquency and crime which postulates that criminal and delinquent acts occur when the bonds that tie people to the law-abiding society are weakened. These bonds include attachment to others, commitment to conventional lines of action, involvement in conventional activity, and belief in the laws governing forbidden behavior.

contusion. a bruise; an injury to any external part of the body by the impact of a fall or the blow of a blunt instrument, without laceration of the flesh and without tearing the skin. A contusion is frequently seen as broken vessels which allow an accumulation of blood in surrounding tissues, producing pain, swelling, tenderness, and often a discoloration as a result of the presence of blood beneath the surface of the skin.

convective column. in firefighting operations, a column of warm air rising above the fire source.

conversion. an ego defense process which converts emotional conflicts into physical illness symptoms.

convict. to find a person guilty of a criminal charge; a prisoner.

conviction. the judgment of a court, based on the verdict of a jury or judicial officer, or on the guilty plea or nolo contendere plea of the defendant, that the defendant is guilty of the offense with which he or she has been charged; the opposite of an acquittal.

conviction rate. the number of convictions, including guilty pleas, as a percentage of the total number of prosecutions in a given area for a given crime.

convict lease system. the practice of selling the labor of prisoners to private employers who pay the state a fee for each of the prisoners, and at the same time assume the responsibility of guarding and feeding them. In exchange, the employer is allowed to retain all or a portion of profits generated by the convicts' labor.

cooker. a small receptacle, such as a spoon or bottle cap, in which heroin is dissolved; any type of container used to hold a drug while it is being heated; the chemist in an illicit drug laboratory.

Cook v. Safeway. a 1973 case in which the Supreme Court of Oregon held that comments made by a Safeway supervisor to three employees to the effect that a former coworker had been discharged for stealing from the company were actionable per se and that a general recovery of damages could be made without proof of harm. Since the comments imputed commission of a crime by the plaintiff and that the plaintiff was unfit to perform the duties of his employment, the plaintiff was entitled to seek redress.

cool blood. the calmness or tranquility of the offender, without the influence of violent passion or frenzy.

Coolidge v. New Hampshire. a case in which the U.S. Supreme Court ruled illegal the search of a person's vehicle parked in his driveway while the person was being arrested inside his home. The Court found that there was no emergency circumstance that prevented the police from obtaining a warrant to search the vehicle. This ruling means that a search of a suspect's vehicle without a warrant is per se unreasonable in the absence of a well-defined exception based on an emergency circumstance.

cooptation. a social process by which people who might otherwise threaten the stability or existence of an organization are brought into the leadership or policy-making structure of that organization.

coordinate method. a method for sketching the scene of a crime through the use of coordinates which determine the position of an object or point by the use of straight lines and angles.

coordination. a formal agreement among government jurisdictions to provide common police services.

copping. the acquisition of heroin or other drugs; a series of events in which goods or money are exchanged for heroin. A "copping area" is a drug distribution site.

coprolalia. the use of obscene language to promote sexual excitement; repetitive use of obscenities in speech, as may occur involuntarily in Gilles de la Tourette syndrome.

coprophilia. sexual excitement derived from defecating; an abnormal interest in feces.

Copyright Act of 1976. an act that became effective on January 1, 1978, replacing an act passed in 1909, which identifies four types of criminal acts: (1) infringement of a copyright willfully and for purposes of commercial advantage or private financial gain, (2) intentional fraudulent use of copyright notice whereby copyright notice is placed on an article when the defendant knows the notice to be false, (3) fraudulent removal of copyright notice, and (4) knowingly making a false representation in copyright application. A significant feature of this law is that computer programs and software are considered copyrightable works.

copyrighted software. any software that is purchased, rented or borrowed and which remains the property of the manufacturer by the terms of agreement. Acquisition of copyrighted software buys the right to use it, not own it.

copyright infringement. a law which makes it a federal crime for anyone who willfully for purposes of commercial advantages and private gain infringes on another's copyright.

coram nobis. a writ issued by a court for the purpose of correcting a judgment entered in the same court, on the ground of error of fact.

COR-ART. the acronym for Central Office for the Repression of Art Thefts, the art theft squad of the French National Police.

cordite. an explosive powder made of nitroglycerin and formed into the shape of string or cord.

core. the approximate center of a fingerprint impression.

core body temperature. the temperature of the internal organs; the predictable rate of loss of body temperature following death.

coroner. an official whose chief duty is to inquire into the cause of the death of persons killed or who die suddenly or unnaturally. A coroner is usually elected, although in some jurisdictions he is appointed for a fixed term. The coroner's examination is made with the aid of a jury, in sight of the body, and at the place where the death occurred. The coroner's responsibilities are often undefined. In cases of crime, he may order autopsies or other scientific procedures to determine the cause of death; subpoena witnesses to appear at an inquest; assume full charge of the body and remove it at his pleasure; and exclude all unauthorized persons from the scene of the crime, even members of the district attorney's office and the police.

corporal punishment. physical punishment as distinguished from pecuniary punishment or a fine; punishment inflicted on the body.

corporate crime. an illegal act or acts committed by a corporate body or by executives or managers acting on behalf of the corporation. Such acts include consumer fraud, price-fixing, and restraint of trade.

corporate fraud. the intentional misstatement of financially material facts for the purpose of deceiving the hearers or readers to their detriment, coupled with or independent of the misapplication of organizational assets by the employees, officers or executives of a publicly held company.

corporation. an artificial legal entity created by government grant and endowed with certain powers; a voluntary organization of persons either actual individuals or legal entities, legally bound to form a business enterprise.

corporation defense. a defense which holds that because a corporation is an artificial creation it is considered incapable of forming the requisite criminal intent. This defense has been largely overcome in recent years. Some crimes, such as rape, bigamy and murder, cannot logically be imputed to a corporation.

corporeal. a term descriptive of things that have an objective, material existence and are therefore perceptible by the senses of sight and touch.

corpus delicti. the body of the crime. The corpus delicti is the actual tangible evidence that proves a crime was committed. The term is often used erroneously to describe the corpse of the victim in a homicide case. Actually, the term relates to the essence of an offense and thus implies that every offense must have a corpus delicti.

In proving an accused's guilt of a specific crime the prosecution establishes three general facts: (1) that an injury or loss particular to the crime involved has taken place, (2) that the injury or loss was brought about by somebody's criminality, meaning that the injury or loss resulted from a criminal act as opposed to an accident or other cause, and (3) that the accused possessing the requisite state of mind (i.e., intent) was the person who caused the injury or loss.

The first two facts constitute the corpus delicti. The third fact simply establishes the identity of the offender. For example, the corpus delicti in a larceny would be (1) the loss of property (2) by an unlawful taking. In an arson offense, it would be (1) a burned house (2) caused by a deliberately set fire.

corpus juris. a body of law.

correctional agency. a federal, state, or local criminal or juvenile justice agency, under a single administrative authority, of which the principal functions are the intake screening, supervision, custody, confinement, treatment, or pre-sentencing or pre-disposition investigation of alleged or adjudicated adult offenders, youthful offenders, delinquents, or status offenders.

correctional day program. a publicly financed and operated nonresidential educational or treatment program for persons required by a judicial officer to participate.

correctional facility. a building or part thereof, set of buildings, or area enclosing a set of buildings or structures, operated by a government agency for the physical custody, or custody and treatment, of sentenced persons or persons subject to criminal proceedings.

correctional officer. a government employee having supervision over alleged or adjudicated offenders in custody. The term is usually not applied to persons supervising juveniles in detention.

correctional reform. a movement to bring about changes in the correctional system, usually involving less punitive and more humane treatment of prisoners, shorter sentences, and the introduction of rehabilitative programs.

corrections. a generic term which includes all government agencies, facilities, programs, procedures, personnel, and techniques concerned with the intake, custody, confinement, supervision, or treatment, or pre-sentencing or pre-disposition investigation of alleged or adjudicated adult offenders, delinquents, or status offenders.

correlation. an observed association between a change in the value of one variable and a change in the value of another variable.

corroborate. to strengthen; to add weight or credibility to a thing by additional and confirming facts or evidence.

corrosive poison. a poison that produces vomiting and severe pain in the gastrointestinal tract. The presence of a corrosive poison is revealed by the strong odor of the victim's breath and any regurgitated material. Corrosive poisons are found in such household items as bleach, solvents, disinfectants, fertilizer and many types of industrial chemicals. Corrosive poisoning can produce shock and coma as well as death.

corruption. the act of an official who unlawfully and wrongfully uses his position to procure some benefit for himself or another person, contrary to duty and the rights of others.

Cosa Nostra. a group of Italian-dominated organized crime leaders and their followers that originated in Sicily.

cost-benefit analysis. any process by which an organization seeks to determine the effectiveness of spending, in relation to costs, in meeting policy objectives.

cotton shot. an injection by a drug addict of water that has been strained through cotton previously used to administer heroin.

Couch v. United States. a 1973 case in which the U.S. Supreme Court ruled that the privilege against self-incrimination does not bar the production of an individual's records entrusted to an accountant for the preparation of tax returns.

counsel. a person trained in the law, admitted to practice before the bar of a given jurisdiction, and authorized to advise, represent, and act for other persons in legal proceedings.

Counselman v. Hitchcock. an 1892 case in which the U.S. Supreme Court ruled that in those instances when an immunity statute merely provides that certain testimony compelled from witnesses will not be used against them in criminal proceedings, such a grant of immunity is not constitutionally adequate to justify the compelling of such testimony. Any use of an immunity statute, therefore, must not only grant immunity as to testimony but also as to evidence which reasonably can be derived therefrom.

count. an allegation in an indictment; a charge; the number of inmates in a particular facility.

counter check. a check used by some banks. It is issued to depositors when they are withdrawing funds from their accounts, and is not good anywhere else. Sometimes a store will have its own counter checks for the convenience of customers. A counter check is not negotiable and is so marked.

counterculture. a specific form of culture whose members reject key norms and values of the larger society.

counterespionage. those aspects of counterintelligence concerned with aggressive operations against another intelligence service to reduce its effectiveness, or to detect and neutralize espionage.

counterfeit. to manufacture or attempt to manufacture a copy or imitation of a negotiable instrument with a value set by law or convention, or to possess such a copy without authorization, with the intent to defraud by claiming the genuineness of the copy. Counterfeit items include bonds, coins, currency, food stamps, postage stamps and similar negotiables. Mere possession without knowledge or criminal intent is not a crime.

counterfeit drug. a substance purported to be a drug but is chemically different from the drug it is purported to be; a drug which, or the container or labeling of which, bears a trademark, trade name, or other identifying mark other than that of the actual manufacturer so as to deceive the buyer.

counterforce car. a heavily-armored, specially equipped, highpower automobile used by persons who have reason to fear capture or assassination.

counterinsurgency. military action planned to oppose guerrilla underground efforts.

counterintelligence. activities conducted to destroy the effectiveness of intelligence operations and to protect information against espionage, subversion and sabotage.

countersniping team. a team specially trained for deployment against a sniper. The team typically consists of an observer and a shooter. The observer, equipped with binoculars and/or special sighting devices, identifies the target, directs the fire, and evaluates the shooter's shots.

court. an agency or unit of the judicial branch of government, authorized or established by statute or constitution, and consisting of one or more judicial officers, which has the authority to decide upon cases, controversies in law, and disputed matters of fact brought before it.

court administrator. the official responsible for supervising and performing administrative tasks for a given court or courts. Duties typically include performing personnel, budget and administrative tasks, compiling and reporting statistical data, and assisting the presiding judge in administrative matters.

court calendar. the court schedule; the list of events comprising the daily or weekly work of a court, including the assignment of the time and place for each hearing or other item of business, or the list of matters which will be taken up in a given court term.

court case. an action brought before a court for adjudication; a set of facts which is the occasion for the exercise of jurisdiction of a court, and which is handled by the court as a procedural unit.

court caseload inventory. an inventory of court cases normally subdivided according to type of case (e.g., civil or criminal), type of filing (e.g., new or re-opened), and manner of disposition (e.g., trial or without trial). For criminal cases, the inventory will usually reflect whether convicted or acquitted.

court clerk. an elected or appointed court officer responsible for maintaining the written records of the court and for supervising or performing the clerical tasks necessary for conducting judicial business; any employee of a court whose principal duties are to perform the clerical tasks necessary for conducting judicial business. Also called clerk of the court.

court decision. any official determination made by a judicial officer; in special judicial usages, any of several specific kinds of determinations made by particular courts. When used in the broadest sense, a court decision may be called a judgment, decree, finding, court order, or opinion.

court disposition. the judicial decision terminating proceedings in a case before judgment is reached, or the judgment itself; the data items for statistical reports representing the outcome of judicial proceedings and the manner in which the outcome was arrived at. In criminal proceedings, the major categories of court dispositions almost always include: jury trial, jury trial with conviction, jury trial with acquittal, nonjury trial, nonjury trial with conviction, nonjury trial with acquittal, dismissal/nolle prosequi, and guilty plea.

courtesy supervision. supervision by the correctional agency of one jurisdiction, of a person placed on probation by a court or on parole by a paroling authority in another jurisdiction, by informal agreement between agencies. Courtesy supervision occurs when a receiving agency agrees to supervise a probationer or parolee through arrangements made without reference to statutory or administratively promulgated rules. The kind of case handled in this fashion is usually one where the offense is not grave, and the practical and rehabilitative needs of the probationer or parolee are best served by residence in a jurisdiction other than the one where adjudication occurred.

court jurisdiction. the legal right or authority of a court to hear a case or controversy.

court-martial. a military court for the trial of members of the armed forces and certain civilians said to be "accompanying the armies in the field."

court of appeals. a court that reviews a trial court's actions, or the decisions of another (but lower-level) appellate court, to determine whether errors have been made and to decide whether to uphold or overturn a verdict.

court of general jurisdiction. a court which has jurisdiction to try all criminal offenses, including all felonies, and which may or may not hear appeals.

court of last resort. an appellate court having final jurisdiction over appeals within a given state; the last court to which a case may be appealed. Although the court of last resort has final jurisdiction over appeals in a given state judicial system, issues of law may exist in some cases that permit subsequent appeal to a federal court. The U.S. Supreme Court is the court of last resort for many kinds of cases.

court of limited jurisdiction. a court of which the trial jurisdiction either includes no felonies or is limited to less than all felonies, and which may or may not hear appeals.

court of record. a court in which a complete and permanent record of all proceedings or specified types of proceedings is kept. For example, a felony trial court is a court of record. Trial proceedings are supposed to be recorded verbatim. The record, usually in the form of a stenotype or short-hand representation of what has been said and done, but sometimes stored on audiotape, is not necessarily transcribed. The court reporter may store such material in the original form and it will not be converted into a typed transcript unless the record pertaining to a case is requested.

court order. a mandate, command or direction issued by a judicial officer in the exercise of his judicial authority. A court order is sometimes referred to as a judgment, but it is more in the nature of the mechanism by which the court, having reached conclusions as to matters of fact and law in a controversy, directs that the actions implementing the judgment occur. Writs and injunctions are court orders.

court ordered release from prison. a provisional exit by judicial authority from a prison facility system of a prisoner who has not served his or her full sentence, whose freedom is conditioned upon an appeal, a special writ, or other special legal proceeding.

court probation. a criminal court requirement that a defendant or offender fulfill specified conditions of behavior in lieu of a sentence to confinement, but without assignment to a probation officer's supervisory caseload. This type of grant of probation is variously called unsupervised probation, summary probation, or informal probation.

court reporter. a person present during judicial proceedings, who records all testimony and other oral statements made during the proceedings. A court reporter is also usually present when proceedings occur outside of the courtroom, e.g., in the judge's chambers. In some jurisdictions, the court reporting function is performed by audio recording and transcription by a typist or typing pool.

cover. a protective guise used by a person, organization, or installation to prevent identification with clandestine activities and to conceal the true affiliation of personnel and the true sponsorship of activities.

covert action. clandestine activity designed to influence the opposition.

covert entry. an entry into or onto premises which if made without a court order allowing such entry would be a violation of a penal code.

covert surveillance. observation by a police officer who is hidden from public view, usually to detect suspicious or illegal activity, and sometimes to aid in traffic enforcement.

crack. a purified form of cocaine that is smoked by inhaling the vapors that are given off as the drug is heated. It is made by boiling cocaine to produce pea-sized crystalline chunks or rocks which are smoked in cigarettes or a special pipe, usually made of glass. The drug gets its name from the sound it makes when heated.

The use of crack is of great concern because it often creates intense dependency and addiction in a relatively short period of use. Prior to the appearance of crack, users who wanted a more potent form of cocaine had to perform the freebasing process themselves.

Crack appears to have spread in popularity among young people partly because it provides the intense high associated with cocaine in an even more intense and rapid manner.

The power and speed of crack are primarily due to purity of the drug and route of administration. Cocaine that is snorted is generally 15 to 25 percent pure, whereas crack will be as much as 90 percent pure. Because crack is inhaled, the vapors go directly to the lungs for immediate absorption into the bloodstream. It is then carried to the brain in a high concentration.

The widely recognized health dangers associated with snorting cocaine (nasal membrane destruction) and injecting heroin (AIDS) may have an effect in leading the hard drug users to crack. Also, the purveyors of crack tout it as the inexpensive, simple, and accessible way to use cocaine.

The effects of crack are produced in 4–6 seconds, are intensely euphoric, and last for 5–7 minutes. When cocaine is snorted, the effects are produced in 1–3 minutes and last 20–30 minutes. Crack's intense, short high is followed by depression which encourages repetitive use. Some users describe these symptoms after effects wear off: (1) a worry about getting the next dose, (2) deep depression, (3) loss of energy and appetite, and (4) self-hate feelings.

The psychological and physiological dangers of crack are similar to those of cocaine. These include the risk of overdose, psychosis, paranoia, sensory hallucinations, heart failure, high blood pressure, weight loss, convulsions, skin problems, and breathing difficulties. Also, the anesthetic qualities of crack tend to mask the body's natural pain signals.

Crack is sold in plastic vials of varying

sizes. It is sold on the street and by invitation at homes, apartments, clubrooms, and storefronts in urban and suburban areas. These locations (called base houses, crack houses, and rock houses) are similar to shooting galleries in that purchasers are invited to use crack on the premises. Pipes are loaned or can be rented.

The primary users of crack appear to be young adults and teenagers. The relatively low cost of crack may account for its attractiveness to young persons. Also called rock, roxanne, base, baseball, and gravel.

crack house. a place where crack is sold or used.

crank. methamphetamine.

crash. to sleep from the use of a drug; to come out from under the influence of a stimulant; a computer system's response to an unstable condition.

crash cushion. a traffic barrier designed to prevent errant vehicles from striking a rigid object located on the roadside, either by smoothly decelerating such vehicles to a stop or by redirecting them away from the rigid object as well as from the opposite flow of traffic. Crash cushions are typically made of plastic or light metal barrels filled with sand or water.

crashing. a period of unpleasantness and depression that follows the sudden sensation (known as a flash or rush) obtained by the administration of a drug, usually intravenously.

crash pad. a term referring to a place (frequently on a college campus) where a drug user undergoing withdrawal, agitation, or a panic reaction can obtain assistance without notice being given to an enforcement agency. Services provided typically consist of emotional support, kindness, understanding, and reassurance.

cravat. the name of a first aid bandage made from a large triangular piece of cloth, usually muslin or cotton.

craving. a term implying both physiological and psychological dependence; the user's desire or need to continue using a drug. This term is often associated with withdrawal and is considered by some to be a main defining characteristic of addiction.

crazed glass. in arson investigations, glass that has been cracked in a particular pattern by fire. The pattern can be interpreted as to the fire's point of origin. Crazed glass also suggests that a fire accelerant was used.

credibility. the believability of a witness at a trial as to his testimony.

credit card fraud. the use of a credit card in order to obtain goods or services with the intent to avoid payment; use with intent to defraud of any credit card, credit plate, charge plate, courtesy card, or other identification card or device issued to the holder which authorizes the holder to obtain credit or to purchase or lease property or services on the credit of the issuer or of the obligor. A credit card is a negotiable instrument through which as many as three different parties (issuer, holder, and seller of goods or services) enter into an agreement.

credit card invoice. a commercial instrument which does or may evidence, create, transfer, terminate, or otherwise affect a legal right, interest, obligation, or status. It is used to show that a sale or service was completed between two parties, the merchant and the cardholder. It represents a promise on the part of the cardholder to repay the merchant or a third party (e.g., a bank that issued the card) according to previously agreed terms.

credit card palming. deliberate retention by an employee of a customer's credit card so that the card can be used for some fraudulent purpose.

credit card swindle. mail-fraud swindle in which the victim is induced to charge an attractive product to a credit card, but the product is not delivered and the charge is billed to the victim's account.

creeper. a pickpocket working in collusion with prostitutes.

crepitus. a noisy discharge of gas; crackling; also a sound or sensation produced by the grating of the ends of a fractured bone.

crib death. a term synonymous with sudden infant death syndrome (SID), a death of an infant while sleeping of an unknown cause.

cricotracheostomy. an incision into the trachea through the cricoid cartilage to obtain an airway in instances of respiratory obstruction.

cricket. marijuana soaked in embalming fluid. Also called clicker.

crime against nature. an unnatural sexual act, such as sodomy or bestiality.

crime analysis. the study of information about criminal incidents to detect patterns or trends of unlawful activity that may be used to predict the need for specific police techniques, such as aggressive patrolling of a given geographic area or placing stakeout teams at likely robbery targets.

crime family. an association of people, related to each other by blood or marriage or having common ties of cultural-ethnic heritage, close bonds, and networks, engaged in ongoing criminal activities.

crime index. an indicator of fluctuations in criminality; a set of numbers indicating the volume and distribution of crimes reported to local law enforcement agencies. In the United States it is based on the number of certain serious crimes known to occur in geographical subdivisions and reported by the FBI in its Uniform Crime Reports. The eight offenses used to construct the crime index are known as the index crimes.

crime in the suites. a play on words to "crime in the streets." It refers to corporate embezzlement, fraud and security thefts by business executives.

crime laboratory. a unit that performs various forensic analyses in support of law enforcement and investigative operations. Every law enforcement agency in the United States is provided crime laboratory services. Smaller agencies obtain forensic examinations from county, state, or federal crime laboratories. Larger agencies, such as major city departments and state bureaus of investigation, operate their own facilities, and all agencies, regardless of size or funding, have access to forensic services provided by the FBI crime laboratory in Washington, D.C.

A crime laboratory typically consists of five sections: (1) biology, (2) criminalistics, (3) documents examination, (4) firearms, and (5) controlled substances.

The biology section performs blood identification by major blood group typing, identification of minor blood groups, isoenzyme identification by electrophoretic methods for the purpose of further analysis of blood types, bloodstain pattern examination to determine origin and direction of blood spatters, spermatazoa identification, differentiation of seminal and vaginal fluids, major grouping of seminal and vaginal fluids, salivary amylase examination for saliva identification, major grouping of body fluids, differentiation of hair species, race identification by hair samples, comparison of evidence hair with known standards, and examination of crime scenes and preservation of evidence.

The criminalistics section identifies and makes flash-point determinations of flammables in arson cases, analyzes urine for drug content, analyzes blood for drug and alcohol content, and examines for the purposes of identification and comparison a wide range of materials including alcoholic beverages, poisons, paints, metals, glass, fibers, and impressions of tires and footwear.

The questioned documents section examines documents to determine age, restore writings on charred or water-damaged papers, identify paper and writing materials, restore erasures, eradications, obliterations and alterations, and determine authorship of writings through comparisons of handwriting and handprinting specimens.

The firearms section is responsible for identifying firearms, identifying unique functional characteristics of particular firearms, linking particular cartridge cases with the firearms that discharged them, linking gunshot residue with particular cartridges or firearms, restoring obliterated serial numbers, comparing toolmark impressions with recovered tools, identifying pick marks on lock cylinders, analyzing shot patterns to determine the distance between firearm and victim at time of discharge, and collecting firearm evidence at a crime scene.

The controlled substances section determines if a specimen contains drugs, determines the quantity of drugs by volume in a specimen, identifies dilutants and impurities in drugs, and matches various drug specimens for the purpose of identifying the common sources of illegal manufacture.

crime of commission. any criminal act involving a specific violation of law, such as burglary or theft.

crime of omission. a failure to fulfill a requirement imposed by law, such as failure to pay a tax.

crime of passion. assault or murder incited by the infidelity of a lover or a mate or a murder committed in the heat of anger or other passionate outburst.

crime of violence. a criminal act involving injury or threat of injury to the victim. Examples include murder, rape, assault and armed robbery.

crime pattern analysis. analysis which seeks to determine what crimes are likely to impact particular targets, the criminals likely to commit the crimes, how the crimes are likely to occur, and when they are likely to occur. The process of analysis typically includes the collection and processing of data related to (1) crime rate by opportunity, (2) the varieties of attack methods, with emphasis on preferred methods, (3) preferred times of attacks by day, week, month and other time variables such as holidays, seasons and special events, (4) characteristics of suspects, (5) general patterns of crimes, and (6) targets preferred by criminals, losses by types, and values of losses.

crime prevention. a general term referring to law enforcement activities that operate under the assumptions that (1) potential crime victims must be helped to take action which reduces their vulnerability to crimes and which reduces the extent of injury or loss should crime impact on them, (2) potential crime victims are limited in the actions they are able to take because of their inability to effectively exercise control over their environments, (3) the environment to be controlled is that of the potential victim, not of the potential criminal, (4) the direct control that a potential victim can exercise over his own environment can reduce criminal motivation, (5) the absence of criminal opportunity means less temptation to commit crime and less chance that a criminal will develop criminal habits, (6) traditional approaches used by the criminal justice system, although response-oriented, do cause criminals to perceive personal risk and thus play an important role in preventing crime, (7) law enforcement agencies have a central but not dominant role in crime prevention, (8) many skill and interest groups in a community must act in concert if crime prevention is to have a comprehensive and lasting effect, (9) crime prevention activities can be both a cause and an effect of efforts to revitalize communities suffering from severe crime problems, (10) crime prevention doctrine is interdisciplinary in nature, is subjected to an ongoing process of discovery and change, and is useful to the extent that it is shared and applied, (11) crime prevention strategies and techniques are not absolutes because what succeeds in one situation may not succeed in other situations.

A goal of a law enforcement crime prevention unit is to reduce crime in a given geographical area. This goal is achieved by planning, implementing and managing a comprehensive program. A program typically involves a wide range of projects and services that operate at three levels: (1) at the client level where the objective is to design crime risk management systems that meet the needs of homes, businesses, institutions and other entities that are owned or managed by individuals or organizations, (2) at the multiple client level where the objective is to design crime risk management projects through which many citizens in neighborhoods, shopping centers, industrial areas and similar localities can collectively work together to improve security, and (3) at the public policy level where the objective is to design crime risk management activities which units of government can carry out to improve security within a large jurisdiction and across jurisdictional lines.

The impact of a crime prevention program is often evaluated and enhanced by (1) measuring the degree of progress made in meeting specific objectives set for the program and progress toward the general goal of crime reduction, (2) identifying weak and strong points of program operations and deriving suggestions for changes, (3) comparing initial program assumptions against assumptions derived from the realities of program operations, (4) suggesting new procedures and approaches, (5) examining depletion of program resources and identifying new resources.

crime prevention activities. activities that are usually community-centered and designed to meet the specific goals of a crime prevention unit. They generally include actions that seek to (1) develop public awareness by informing citizens of crime problems and the services available to them for preventing crime, (2) develop steps to remediate crime problems impacting on specific persons, homes, businesses and organizations, (3) provide teaching and counseling services, with particular attention to key groups that hold leadership positions in the community, (4) develop group projects that harness collective efforts to achieve useful crime prevention activities, (5) interact with builders and code administrators to promote environmental design concepts that encourage active citizen involvement in neighborhoods and which at the same time discourage deviant behavior, and (6) establish Neighborhood Watch programs and similar activities which encourage citizens to watch for crime and report observations to the police.

crime prevention through environmental design. a field of study and experimentation which seeks to develop comprehensive crime risk management systems involving both physical design and social action strategies on a community-wide scale.

crime rate. the number of reported crimes per a specified number (usually 100,000) of inhabitants.

crime rate by opportunity. a comparison of the number of crimes of a particular type with the number of potential targets of that particular crime over a defined period of time.

crime risk management. a concept which holds that all crime risks can be managed to an acceptable level through the application of one or more of five techniques: (1) risk avoidance, (2) risk reduction, (3) risk spreading, (4) risk transfer, and (5) risk acceptance.

Risk avoidance is to avoid the loss of an asset to criminal action by placing it beyond the effective reach of the criminal. A coin collector, for example, applies the technique of risk avoidance when he places all of his coins in a safe deposit box.

Risk reduction is an extension of risk avoidance. Because it is not practical for an owner to place all of his assets under heavy protection, the owner leaves exposed those assets which he has immediate need of and places the remainder in safekeeping.

Risk spreading is the application of physical and procedural safeguards to protect assets from criminal attack.

Risk transfer is the practice of transferring risk to someone else. The purchase of insurance is an example. Another form of risk transfer occurs when a storeowner raises his prices as a consequence of crime losses. In this way the risk is transferred to the customer.

Risk acceptance occurs when the owner of an asset chooses to accept crime losses as a necessary cost of business. All or a portion of the maximum probable loss could be accepted.

crimes against habitations. a general descriptor for referring to offenses affecting homes. Arson and burglary are offenses that fall into this category.

crimes against persons. a general descriptor for referring to offenses that victimize individuals. It is a category of crime in which force or the threat of force is used by the offender. Of the index crimes reported in the Uniform Crime Report, those against persons include murder and non-negligent manslaughter, forcible rape, aggravated assault, and robbery. Arson is classified as a crime against property, although it may result in death or injury to persons.

crimes against property. a category of crime in which force or violence is neither used nor threatened, and where the offender seeks to make unlawful gain from, or do damage to, the property or another. Of the index crimes reported in the Uniform Crime Report, those against property include burglary, larceny-theft, automobile theft, and arson.

crimes and torts. a term that refers to the distinctions made in law between crimes and torts. A crime is a public wrong and a tort is a private wrong. A public wrong is remedied in a criminal proceeding and a private wrong is remedied in a civil proceeding. A single act in some instances will constitute both a crime and a tort. For example, if a person commits an assault and battery upon another, he commits a crime (a public wrong) and a tort (a private wrong). The law will seek to remedy both wrongs, but it will do so in different ways.

The State will move on its own authority to do justice by bringing a criminal action against the offender. The victim is also entitled to bring action against the offender in a civil suit. Tort law gives the victim a cause of action for damages in order that he may obtain sufficient satisfaction. The victim, however, pursues a civil remedy at his own discretion and in his own name. Whether the victim wins his lawsuit or not, the judgment will not prevent prosecution of the offender by the State.

The civil injuries involved in tort cases usually arise from acts of negligence. The fact that the victim by his own negligence contributed to the harm done may afford the offender a defense in a civil action of tort, but it does not constitute a defense to the offender in a criminal prosecution.

The single characteristic that differentiates criminal law from civil law is punishment. Generally, in a civil suit the basic questions are: (1) how much, if at all, has the defendant injured the plaintiff, and (2) what remedies, if any, are appropriate to compensate the plaintiff for his loss. In a criminal case, the questions are: (1) to what extent has the defendant injured society, and (2) what sentence is appropriate to punish the defendant.

crime scene search team. a team of specialists brought together on a formal or an ad hoc basis for the purpose of conducting a comprehensive search of a crime scene, usually a major crime. Team members are typically drawn from the investigations unit, crime lab, and the coroner's office when unnatural death is involved.

The team performs these functions: (1) crime scene and aerial crime scene photography, (2) searching for, photographing, and lifting latent prints, (3) recovering bullets, fragments, and casings, (4) casting footprints, tire marks, and toolmarks, (5) recovering paint scrapings, (6) swabbing for gunpowder residue, (7) testing for and recovering blood evidence, (8) recovering flammables, (9) measuring and sketching the crime scene, (10) marking evidence and transporting it to the crime laboratory, (11) using a metal detector to locate hidden or hard-to-find metallic evidence, (12) collecting trace samples with the use of special vacuum sweeper, (13) gathering hair and fiber samples, and (14) taking fingernail scrapings of suspects and victims.

crimes cleared by arrest. a category in the Uniform Crime Reports that discloses the number and percentage of crimes of a distinct type or in a given area for which an arrest is made and for which the police are satisfied that the crime has been solved.

crime score. a number assigned from an established scale, signifying the seriousness of a given offense with respect to personal injury or damage to property. A prosecuting agency might use a crime score to select cases which need intensive pretrial preparation, and in assuring similar treatment of cases having similar scores.

crimes known to police. all illegal acts that have been observed by or reported to police, or about which the police otherwise become aware.

crimes mala in se. acts immoral or wrong in themselves, such as burglary, larceny, arson, rape, murder; those acts which are wrong by their very nature.

crimes mala prohibita. acts prohibited by statute as infringing on others' rights, though no moral turpitude may attach, and are crimes only because they are so prohibited.

crimes of violence. in Uniform Crime Reports terminology, a subcategory of crime which includes murder, nonnegligent (voluntary) manslaughter, forcible rape, robbery, and aggravated assault.

crime statistics. tabulations of crimes by time period, geography, characteristics of offenders and victims, modus operandi, effectiveness of police response, arrests, convictions, sentences and other data.

crime tax. a phrase referring to the increased price paid by customers of gambling, drug and prostitution operations as a result of higher operating costs caused by vigorous law enforcement efforts.

crime wave. an unusual perceived increase in the total amount of crime committed, or in any single offense or type of crime. It may be caused by increased news media attention, by changes in enforcement or reporting procedures, or by an actual increase in crime.

criminal. one who has committed a crime; one who has been legally convicted of a crime. Also, that which pertains to or is connected with the law of crimes, or the administration of penal justice, or which relates to or has the character of crime.

criminal abortion. illegal termination of pregnancy.

criminal action. the proceedings by which a person charged with a crime is accused and brought to trial and punishment.

criminal anthropology. a school of thought which postulates that criminal types are discernible and identifiable on the basis of human body characteristics.

Criminal Appeals Act. an act which provides that in all criminal cases an appeal by the United States attorney shall lie to a court of appeals from a decision, judgment, or order of a district court dismissing an indictment or information on one or more counts where the defendant has not been put in double jeopardy. In addition, an appeal by the United States Attorney which lies to a court of appeals from a decision or order of a district court suppressing or excluding evidence or requiring the return of seized property in a criminal proceeding, before the verdict or finding on an indictment or information and where the defendant has not been put in double jeopardy, if the United States Attorney certifies to the district court that the appeal is not taken for the purpose of delay and that the evidence is substantial proof of a fact material in the proceeding.

criminal assault. physical attack against another person, typically involving actual or attempted sexual contact. For example, rape is a criminal assault.

criminal biopsychology. a science which investigates the psychosomatic personalities of criminals.

criminal case. a case initiated in a court by the filing of a single charging document containing one or more criminal accusations against one or more identified persons.

criminal commitment. a compulsory treatment program for the detoxification and rehabilitation of addicts who have been arrested and convicted of misdemeanors or felonies. Addicts are confined for a specified period in special treatment facilities, which usually are basically modified prisons.

criminal contempt. any act deemed disrespectful of the authority and dignity of the court.

criminal conversation. an act of adultery; the act of debauching or seducing a wife.

criminal conversion. the conversion or misappropriation for personal gain of another's property or rights.

criminal court. a court having the authority to try persons accused of criminal law violations and to sentence them if they are found guilty.

criminal fence. a receiver of stolen goods or a place where stolen goods are exchanged for money or other considerations.

criminal hacker. a person who seeks to obtain access to a computer system for the purpose of illegal gain.

criminal history information. any information about a person's arrest record, conviction/non-conviction or correctional and release history.

criminal homicide. the causing of the death of another person without justification or excuse; in Uniform Crime Reports terminology, the name of the UCR category which includes and is limited to all offenses of causing the death of another person without justification or excuse. By UCR definition, criminal homicide is subdivided into murder, nonnegligent manslaughter (criminal willful homicide), and manslaughter by negligence (involuntary manslaughter).

criminal informant. an individual who provides information to law enforcement authorities and whose relationships with criminals requires that his or her identity be kept confidential.

criminal information process. a continuous cycle of interrelated activities directed toward converting raw information into material useful for law enforcement purposes. The process has six steps: collection of information, evaluation, analysis, collation, reporting, and dissemination.

Collection involves the identification of the specific information needed and how it can be targeted for acquisition. Priorities are determined and communicated to the collectors (officers, investigators, special agents, et al.) The collectors gather from a variety of open and covert sources.

Evaluation is an examination of the collected information in terms of source reliability. Information is evaluated at the collection level by the collectors who are presumed to be in the best position to judge the reliability of their sources.

Analysis is the interpretation of evaluated information on its own merits and in relation to other information. A central purpose is to answer the question, "What does this mean?" The information can be subjected to various statistical techniques and computer-assisted programs that manipulate the data in a search for trends and patterns.

Collation means to combine many sets of information and develop general hypotheses.

Formatting is to place the processed information into a variety of reports meaningful to the users. Distinctions are made between hard (corroborated) and soft (untested or hypothesized) information.

Dissemination is the function of chanelling reports to users in a controlled fashion, e.g., with restrictions, protections, and on a need-to-know basis.

criminal intelligence. the surreptitious investigation of crime and the gathering of information concerning plans and activities in a criminal subculture or underworld, generally obtained through informants, infiltration, and electronic eavesdropping. The term also applies to crimes committed within a state, or internationally, by organized criminal groups or individuals.

The information used to create criminal intelligence is collected from: (1) undercover investigations, (2) reports submitted by patrol officers and other employees of the department, (3) liaison with other police officials and agencies, (4) modus operandi and criminal personae files, (5) informants, (6) citizens in "listening post" roles, (6) feedback from specific reward offers and "hot line" programs such as Crimestoppers, and (7) liaison with security representatives from business and government organizations.

criminal intent. an intent to do an act which the law denounces, without regard to the motive that prompts the act, and whether or not the offender knows that what he or she is doing is in violation of the law. Criminal intent is the state of mind of the offender, and is generally regarded as falling into two categories: general criminal intent and specific criminal intent. General criminal intent is an essential element in all crimes. It means that when the offender acted, or failed to act, contrary to the law, he did so voluntarily with determination or foresight of the consequences. For example, general criminal intent is shown in the offense of assault and battery when the offender voluntarily applies unlawful force to another with an awareness of its result.

Specific criminal intent requires a particular mental state in addition to that of general criminal intent. The laws relating to certain crimes may describe an additional, specific mental purpose. For example, the crime of murder has a general criminal intent in that the offender voluntarily applies unlawful force with an awareness of its result. In addition, the crime of murder in a particular jurisdiction may require a showing that the offender acted with premeditation to commit murder.

criminalist. a person, such as an evidence technician, who practices criminalistics.

criminalistics. a fact-finding process for detecting crime; police science; scientific detection and investigation of crimes; the use of scientific techniques derived from physics, chemistry, and biology to solve crimes; a field of forensic science that deals with the analysis, identification, individualization, and interpretation of physical evidence by the use of natural sciences. Criminalistics includes ballistics,

blood-stain analyses, and other tests of a scientific nature.

criminalization. the passing of legislation imposing criminal sanctions for commission or omission of an act that had formerly been legal or had been an infraction rather than a crime; a process or influence that affects the development of a criminal.

criminal justice. the entire system of crime prevention and detection, apprehension of suspects, arrest, trial, adjudication of guilt or innocence, and handling of the guilty by correctional agencies, together with the executive, legislative, and judicial rules governing these procedures and processes.

criminal justice agency. any court with criminal jurisdiction and any government agency or identifiable subunit which defends indigents, or which has as its principal duty the performance of criminal justice functions as authorized and required by statute or executive order.

criminal justice process. the series of actions through which a criminal offender may pass in the legal system. A possible sequence is detection, investigation, arrest, booking, indictment, arraignment, trial, conviction, sentencing, incarceration, and eventual release.

criminal law. that branch of public law that is divided into two main parts: substantive and procedural. Substantive law defines what varying types of conduct will constitute crimes, provides for punishments, and lays down rules on such matters as the capacity of persons to commit crimes and the defenses that may be legally employed by charged persons.

Procedural law provides the means and methods by which rights and obligations created by the criminal law are to be vindicated and enforced, that is to say, procedural law defines the manner in which criminal cases are prosecuted. In other words, substantive law tells us what is just, and procedural law tells us how justice is to be carried out.

criminal mischief. intentionally destroying or damaging, or attempting to destroy or damage, the property of another without his consent, usually by means other than burning.

criminal negligence. wanton and willful disregard of the probable harmful consequences of an act.

criminal offense. an act committed or omitted in violation of a law forbidding or commanding it for which the possible penalties for an adult upon conviction include incarceration, for which a corporation can be penalized by fine or forfeit, or for which a juvenile can be adjudicated delinquent or transferred to criminal court for prosecution.

criminal opportunity reduction. the anticipation, recognition, and appraisal of a crime risk and the initiation of some action to remove or reduce it.

criminal possession. having on one's person or under one's effective control objects or substances illegally possessed, such as guns or drugs. Criminal possession applies also to objects legally possessed when there is the intention of using them to commit a crime; for example, a crow bar to be used in a burglary.

criminal proceedings. the regular and orderly steps, as directed or authorized by statute or a court of law, taken to determine whether an adult accused of a crime is guilty or not guilty.

criminal sociopath. a person who has failed to develop a conscience or understand the difference between right and wrong.

criminal syndicalism. advocacy of force, terror and violence to bring about economic or political changes.

criminal target. the place, person or thing that a criminal seeks to take or destroy.

criminal willful homicide. the intentional causing of the death of another person, with or without legal justification. The legal term "willful" embraces murder and voluntary manslaughter, both of which are criminal. Justifiable homicide, which is not criminal, would not be covered under this definition.

criminogenic factor. a factor that is crime-producing. Examples might include the break-up of the family, excessive emphasis on materialism, a lack of ethical standards, lawless abuse of alcohol and other drugs, slum environments, and social disintegration.

criminogenesis. the process by which powerful policymaking groups in a society create the structural conditions that cause other people to commit crimes. Some believe that American social policy toward narcotics is criminogenic to the extent that it stimulates the organization of illegal industry and markets in commodities that had been heretofore lawfully produced and consumed.

criminology. the study of crime causes, prevention, detection and correction; the study of crimes, criminals and victims.

criminosis. psychoneurotic behavior marked by criminal acts or a tendency to engage in criminal activity.

criminotechnol. a descriptor of criminological technology, such as the use of electronic and photographic devices and techniques to apprehend criminals and secure evidence needed for their conviction.

crisis intervention. a formal effort to help an individual experiencing a crisis to re-establish equilibrium; in psychiatry, treatment to help resolve an immediate problem or reduce an emotional trauma, the aim being to restore the person to the precrisis level of functioning.

critical incident review technique. a technique for identifying in a work process any minor tasks which if not performed correctly could have a serious effect on the total process.

critical intelligence. information or intelligence of such urgent importance that it is transmitted at the highest priority before passing through regular evaluative channels.

critical path method. a network-analysis technique for planning and scheduling. The critical path is a sequence of activities that connect the beginning and end of events or program accomplishments.

Crosby v. State. a case in which the Texas Court of Criminal Appeals ruled in 1987 that the police exceeded the authority of an administrative search by conducting the search in a way and at a place unrelated to the purpose of an administrative search. The defendant, a well-known entertainer, was performing at a Dallas nightclub licensed to sell alcoholic beverages. Pursuant to the Alcohol Beverage Code, which permits searches for evidence of liquor violations, the police searched the entertainer's dressing room against his will and found cocaine and a pistol. The Court found that the search was improper because it was not for the purpose of furthering liquor regulations.

cross-dependence. a condition in which one drug can prevent the withdrawal syndrome associated with the use of a different drug.

cross draw holster. a holster worn on the left side of a right-handed person or on the right side of a left-handed person.

cross examination. questions which are asked of a witness by the opposing side in a legal case.

crossover reaction. a hallucinatory experience in which perceptions are scrambled, such as "hearing" colors and "seeing" music.

crosstalk. an undesired signal from a different channel which interferes with the desired signal; the unwanted energy transferred from one circuit, called the disturbing circuit, to another circuit, called the disturbed circuit.

cross-tolerance. a condition in which tolerance to one drug often results in a tolerance to a chemically similar drug; resistance to one or several effects of a compound as a result of tolerance developed to a pharmacologically similar compound. For example, a person who is used to taking large doses of heroin will perceive no effects from small doses of methadone.

crown fire. an intense fire that spreads through the tops of trees.

CRT terminal. a data entry terminal consisting of a keyboard for data entry and a cathode ray tube display screen.

cruel and unusual punishment. punishment which exceeds that normally given for a specific offense; punishment that is inhumane, such as torture or enslavement. It is a phrase used in the Eighth Amendment to the United States Constitution but not defined with specificity by the Supreme Court.

cryptoanalysis. the breaking of codes and ciphers into plaintext without initial knowledge of the key employed in the encryption.

cryptographic algorithm. a set of rules that specify the mathematical steps required to encipher and decipher data.

cryptography. the enciphering of plain text so that it will be unintelligible to an unauthorized recipient; transforming data to conceal its meaning.

crypto key. a code key that encrypts or decrypts data in a cryptographic operation.

cryptology. the science that embraces cryptoanalysis, cryptography, communications intelligence and communications security.

cryptomaterial. the various documents, devices, equipment and apparatus used in the encryption, decryption or authentication of telecommunications.

cryptonym. a name assigned to cover a secret operation or a secret operative; secret name.

cryptosystem. the hardware, firmware, software, documents and/or associated procedures used to effect the encryption and decryption of data.

crystal. a form of heroin so-called because of its resemblance to rock crystal. It is relatively inexpensive, easy to manufacture, and extremely potent. Crystal is a favorite of young persons and those who cannot afford higher-priced drugs.

crystal violet. a tracing powder used to mark objects likely to be touched by a culprit. The powder is converted to a violet colored dye by the skin's natural moisture.

CS agent. the descriptor for orthochlorbenzalmalonitrile, a riot control chemical agent that produces immediate distress on contact with the eyes, the respiratory tract, and the skin. CS agent can be dispensed in grenades, small projectiles, and by pressurized spraying. By comparison with CN agent, CS agent works faster and with stronger effects.

cuff-and-lead chain. a single handcuff attached to a length of chain ending in a ring. It is used for leading prisoners or holding them to some stationary object.

culpability. a state of mind on the part of one who has committed an act which makes him liable to prosecution for that act.

culpable. blamable; censurable; involving the breach of a legal duty or the commission of a fault.

culpable negligence. conscious disregard of the rights of another in the commission of an act.

cultural determinism. the view that the nature of a society is shaped primarily by the ideas and values of the people living in it.

cultural relativism. the view that the customs and ideas of a society must be viewed within the context of that society.

cumulative evidence. additional or corroborative evidence to the same point; that which goes to prove what has already been established by other evidence.

cumulative sentence. a sentence imposed separately and which must be served one after the other.

cunnilingus. a sexual act committed with the mouth and the female sexual organ; oral stimulation of the female sex organ.

Cupp v. Murphy. a 1973 case in which the U.S. Supreme Court ruled that when an emergency search is made it normally cannot be expanded to other areas. Any further search may be unreasonable and any evidence seized could be suppressed.

curfew and loitering laws. in Uniform Crime Reports terminology, the name of the UCR offense category used to record and report arrests made for violations of curfew and loitering laws regulating the behavior of juveniles.

curfew violation. the offense of being found in a public place after a specified hour of the evening, usually established in a local ordinance applying only to persons under a specified age. A curfew violation is usually a status offense.

current intelligence. summaries and analyses of recent events.

current parole eligibility date. that date on which a given offender is currently eligible for parole, which may or may not be the same as the original minimum eligible parole date.

curtilage. the ground adjacent to a dwelling house, and used in connection with it. Usually, curtilage is fenced off, which is necessary and convenient for the use of the occupants of the dwelling house.

custodial interrogation (or interview). questioning initiated by a law enforcement officer of a person who is in custody or whose freedom of movement is restricted in any significant way; incommunicado interrogation in a police-dominated atmosphere; interrogation of a person who is thrust into an unfamiliar atmosphere or environment; interrogation of a person surrounded by antagonistic forces after being taken from familiar surroundings; interrogation of a suspect that is conducted while the suspect is in custody of the police, or is otherwise deprived of his freedom. The term has significance in respect to the rules that issued from the Miranda v. Arizona decision of the U.S. Supreme Court.

custodian. an individual who has possession of or is charged with the responsibility for safeguarding something, such as an evidence custodian.

custody. legal control over a person or property. Custody of a child consists of legal guardianship and the right of physical control of the child's whereabouts. Custody of a juvenile or adult consists of such restraint and/or physical control as is needed to ensure his presence at any legal proceeding, or of responsibility for his detention or imprisonment resulting from a criminal charge or conviction. Custody of property consists of immediate personal care of property not owned by the custodian, who is responsible for guarding and preserving it.

Customs Automatic Data Processing Intelligence Network. a computerized data-bank system concerning known or suspected

Customs Automatic Data Processing Intelligence Network Customs.

Customs waters. a term used in the enforcement of the Customs laws of the United States. It refers to a band of coastal water 12 nautical miles wide from the low-water mark. The U.S. Customs Service and the U.S. Coast Guard share the responsibility for sea enforcement within the Customs waters.

cut card. in a numbers operation, a card that lists the numbers which are currently being accepted by the operation on a cut odds basis. The card will sometimes contain other rules that are laid down by the backer for the information of the writers.

cutis anserina. a goose flesh appearance on the skin of a cadaver.

cut-out. a person who is used to conceal contact between members of a clandestine activity or organization.

cutter. that person in a chopshop/car theft operation who removes the saleable parts of a stolen automobile, usually by cutting, and destroys the remainder.

cut the odds. in a numbers operation, a procedure in which the odds of winning are cut to a lower level in order to protect the backer financially.

cutting. diluting or adulterating a drug. For example, diluting heroin with milk sugar or quinine to make it go further.

cyanosis. a dark bluish or purplish coloration of the skin and mucous membrane resulting from deficient oxygenation of the blood. Cyanosis can be observed in victims at the acute stages of asphyxia (breath stoppage), hypoxia (oxygen deprivation), and hypercapnea (excessive carbon dioxide). A blue or grey color to the tongue, lips, and fingertips is an indication.

cybernetics. the branch of learning that brings together theories and studies on communication and control in living organisms and in machines.

cyclazocine treatment. a program for treating heroin addicts. It involves daily administration of cyclazocine, a long-acting opiate antagonist that blocks the effects of heroin. Cyclazocine is not itself a narcotic. The concept of the program is to lead the addict to a secure and responsible position in society by removing the craving for heroin.

cyclical crime. a crime which occurs with greater or lower frequency at varying times of the year. Robbery, for example, is considered a cyclical crime because it frequently reaches a peak in December and is at its lowest point in May.

CYMBL. an acronym used as a memory jogger when law enforcement officers collect/report information concerning motor vehicles. The letters of the acronym signify color, year, make, body style, and license serial number.

DA. district attorney; an attorney who is the elected or appointed chief of a prosecution agency, and whose official duty is to conduct criminal proceedings on behalf of the people against persons accused of committing criminal offenses. Also called prosecutor, state's attorney, county attorney, and U.S. Attorney.

dactylography. the science of the study of fingerprints as a means of identification.

dactyloscopy. the technique of identifying people by their fingerprints.

daily activity record. a form used to record a police officer's activity during one day's work shift. The officer writes a general account of his official activities so that a later reconstruction can be made of where the officer was and what he was doing at any given time while on duty. This record is also variously called the daily log, daily diary, and field worksheet.

damage. loss, injury, or deterioration, caused by the negligence, design, or accident of one person to another, in respect of the latter's person or property.

damages. money awarded to compensate for financial loss to the injured party in a lawsuit. When one person's tortious act injures another's person or property, the remedy for the injured party is to collect damages. The common law rules of damages for physical harm contain three fundamental ideas: (1) that the plaintiff be restored to his pre-injury condition, so far as it is possible to do so with money and should be reimbursed not only for economic losses, but also for loss of physical and mental well-being, (2) that most economic losses are translatable into dollars, and (3) that when the plaintiff successfully sues for an injury he must recover all of his damages arising from that injury, past and future, in a lump sum and in a single lawsuit.

If the defendant's wrongful conduct is sufficiently serious, the law permits the trier of fact to impose a civil fine as punishment and to deter him and others from similar conduct in the future. Punitive damages (also called exemplary or vindictive damages) are not really damages at all since the plaintiff has been made whole by the compensatory damages awarded in the same action. Punitive damages are justified as: (1) an incentive for bringing the defendant to justice, (2) punishment for offenses which often escape or are beyond the reach of criminal law, (3) compensation for damages not normally compensable, such as hurt feelings, attorneys' fees and expenses of litigation, and (4) the only effective means to force conscienceless defendants to cease practices known to be dangerous and which they would otherwise continue in the absence of an effective deterrent.

dangerous drugs. the old statutory label given to nonnarcotic, controlled drugs such as hallucinogens, amphetamines, and barbiturates, which were brought under regulatory control with the Drug Abuse Control Amendments Act of 1965. The current statutory and preferred term is controlled substances.

dangerous person. a person who, when at large, is believed likely to cause serious harm to himself or to others. The stated grounds for believing that a person is dangerous are usually evidence of past violent behavior and actual infliction of injury.

dangerous weapon. an instrument dangerous to life; an instrument the use of which a fatal wound may probably or possibly be given. Because the manner of use enters into the consideration, the question as to a dangerous weapon is often one of fact for the jury, but not infrequently one of law for the court.

dark figure of crime. a term related to criminal acts that are not observed, reported or recorded in crime statistics, either because they are unknown except to the offenders or because of reluctance by victims or witnesses to make complaints.

data. a representation of facts, concepts, or

instructions in a formalized manner suitable for communication, interpretation, or processing by human or automatic means; representations such as characters or analog quantities to which meaning is, or might be, assigned.

data base management system. a system with management and administrative capabilities for control of record selection, updating and reporting from a data base.

data card. a card sometimes included in close-up pictures of evidence photographed on-scene or in a crime laboratory. The card contains certain identifying data such as case number, date, and name of photographer/investigator. Data cards are also used to record details pertaining to the camera, lens, film, filter, and shutter setting.

data communications. the transmission, reception and validation of data.

data encrypting key. a key used to encipher and decipher data transmitted in a system that uses cryptography.

data leakage. loss of data from a computer system through covert means.

dead bang. a pickpocket's term that refers to being seen or caught in the act of pocket picking.

deadbolt. a type of bolt that is moved in and out of the strike mechanically, as by a thumb latch knob.

dead drop. a hiding place where an agent deposits or collects messages and materials.

dead end. a water main supplied from only one direction, or a fire hydrant served by such a main.

dead lock. a lock equipped with a dead bolt. Also, a key-equipped standard ignition cylinder used by a car thief to replace the original cylinder pulled from its housing by a slapper or slam hammer.

deadly force. a degree of force likely to cause death or serious bodily harm; any force involving a deadly weapon or a physical attack likely to inflict death or grievous bodily harm.

deadly weapon. an instrument designed to inflict serious bodily injury or death, or capable of being used for such a purpose.

A statutory distinction is sometimes made between a deadly weapon, that is, one specifically designed to cause serious injury or death, for example, a gun, and a dangerous weapon, that is, one capable under certain circumstances of causing serious injury or death, for example, a knife. In general usage, the two are often merged. For example, an automobile is not designed to cause injury or death but it may be considered to satisfy the "deadly weapon" criterion for an aggravated assault charge.

dead paper. a term related to the paper used to manufacture U.S. currency, so-called because of its propensity to absorb light. When a genuine U.S. note is placed under an ultraviolet lamp it will not fluoresce.

dead time. time spent in confinement in relation to conviction and sentencing for a given offense, calculated in accord with the rules and conventions specific to a given jurisdiction; total time served under correctional agency jurisdiction. Also called time served.

dead time delay. the interval between a stimulus and a response. For example, the delay experienced between an alarm activation and an alarm response.

dead work. in a numbers operation, slips that are not turned in at the office by an established deadline, or as is the common practice, slips in the possession of trusted pickup men.

deal. to sell drugs.

death. the cessation of life; the ceasing to exist; defined by physicians as a total stoppage of the circulation of the blood, and a cessation of the animal and vital functions consequent thereto, such as respiration and pulsation.

death sentence. a sentence to the custody of a prison facility system while awaiting execution.

death ship. a vessel deliberately destroyed, scuttled or wrecked by its owner in order to collect insurance.

death watch. the period of time, just before execution, that is spent monitoring the activities of a prisoner sentenced to die.

debauchery. excessive indulgence in sensual pleasures; sexual immorality or excesses, or the unlawful indulgence of lust.

debug. a defensive technique designed to detect, prevent or expose the use of electronic audio or visual surveillance devices; to correct the syntax and logic of a computer system.

decelerometer. a brake-testing instrument which measures deceleration. The instrument is essentially a free-moving magnetic pendulum coupled with an armature and designed for attachment to a motor vehicle. When the vehicle is set in motion, the pendulum moves similarly and its angle with the vertical depends upon the speed of the vehicle. When the brakes are applied, the pendulum continues to move forward and its angle of elevation is recorded on dials. There are two separate readings: one is for the braking efficiency of the vehicle and the other for the number of feet before the vehicle comes to a stop after application of the brakes.

deception indicated. a term used by polygraph examiners when giving an opinion that a tested subject was untruthful. Also called DI.

deception response. a deviation from the norm in the chart tracings of a polygraph instrument. It results from emotions produced in the examinee as a consequence of a question.

Deceptograph. the commercial name of a type of polygraph instrument manufactured by the Stoelting Company.

decision table. a presentation in either matrix or tabular form of a set of conditions and their corresponding actions; a table of all contingencies that are to be considered in the description of a problem, together with the actions to be taken for each set of contingencies.

decision tree. a graphic method of presenting various decisional alternatives so that the risks, information needs and courses of action are visually available to the decision-maker. The alternatives are displayed in the form of a tree with nodes and branches. Each branch represents an alternative course of action or decision, leading to a node which represents an event.

Thus, a decision tree shows both the courses of action available as well as their possible outcomes. The steps in constructing a decision tree are: (1) identify the points of decision and alternatives available at each point, (2) identify the points of uncertainty and the type or range of alternative outcomes at each point, (3) estimate the values needed to make the analysis, especially the probabilities of different events or results of action and the costs and gains of various events and actions, and (4) analyze the alternative values to choose a course of action.

deck. a small glassine envelope or folded paper packet containing heroin, morphine or cocaine; a small bindle of drugs.

decoy object. an object marked with a fluorescent substance or dyestuff and placed where it would be touched by a person engaged in a criminal act.

decree. a formal determination of a court, usually made in writing.

decriminalization. the removing of criminal sanctions from formerly criminal behavior; the legal process of revising laws by replacing criminal penalties with civil penalties or reducing the behavior to an infraction or a violation of a local ordinance. Most people believe, for example, that marijuana use should be discouraged, but many also feel that imprisonment for use is too harsh a penalty. Eleven states have changed their drug laws to incorporate civil fines and, sometimes, mandatory drug education programs for offenders. First offenders usually avoid a criminal record under these new laws.

decryption. the process of transforming encrypted data (ciphertext) to intelligible data (plaintext); the process that restores encoded information to its original unencoded form.

dedicated vehicle. a patrol vehicle equipped with two-way radio communication that is used exclusively to provide quick responses to intrusions or alarms.

deductive reasoning. a logical analysis based on facts from which a conclusion may be made; the deriving of a conclusion from reasoning; a process in which a deduction follows from the premises; the reasoning which starts out from an assumption or premise and proceeds by logical steps to deduce a solution to the problem or question.

deep six. to conceal or permanently remove something by dumping it at sea.

de facto. arising out of, or founded upon, fact, although merely apparent or colorable. A de facto officer is one who assumes to be an officer under some color of right, acts as an officer, but in point of law is not a real officer.

defalcation. misappropriation of funds held in a fiduciary capacity.

defamation. a statement made orally or in writing which injures a person's reputation in the community; that which tends to injure the reputation of a living person or the memory of a deceased person and to expose him to public hatred, disgrace, ridicule, or contempt, or to exclude him from society. A statutory distinction is often made between slander, which is defamation by any non-spoken communication, most commonly by some written or printed matter. Defamation is not a criminal offense in all jurisdictions. It can, however, be a cause of action in a civil suit.

default. the failure to appear and defend a lawsuit.

defective delinquent. a juvenile with retarded mental development who commits an act that would constitute juvenile delinquency or criminality if committed by a normal juvenile.

defendant. a person against whom a criminal proceeding is pending. A person becomes a defendant when the formal accusation is entered into the record of the court and remains a defendant until the prosecutor withdraws the prosecution, or the court dismisses the case or otherwise determines that judgment will not be pronounced, or the court pronounces acquittal or conviction.

defendant dispositions. the class of prosecutorial or judicial actions which terminate or provisionally halt proceedings regarding a given defendant in a criminal case after charges have been filed in court. The term is frequently substituted for "court disposition," which has several possible meanings. Use of the word "provisionally" in the definition indicates the contingent nature of a defendant disposition such as probation, which is considered final although further judicial action will be necessary if the conditions of probation are violated.

Defendant Statistical Program File. records maintained by the Drug Enforcement Agency which provide statistical data concerning drug abuse patterns and offender characteristics.

defenestration. suicide by throwing oneself out of a window; tossing a person or a thing out of a window.

defense. the justification interposed by the defendant of a lawsuit which is intended to relieve him of blame and of financial obligation. The law allows many defenses to charges of crime and it is the right of the accused to use any and all of them. The concept of defenses against prosecution may be viewed from two aspects: the basic capacity of the accused to commit the crime charged, and the applicability of certain specifically accepted defenses.

The category of "capacity to commit crime" includes the infancy defense, corporation defense, insanity defense, and intoxication defense.

The infancy defense holds that children are incapable of committing any crime below a certain age; that at a higher age there is a presumption of an incapacity to commit crime; and at an even higher age certain crimes are conclusively presumed to be beyond the capability of a child. For example, it may be presumed that a 13 year old boy is incapable of committing the crime of rape.

The corporation defense holds that because a corporation is an artificial creation it is considered incapable of forming the requisite criminal intent. This defense has been largely overcome in recent years. Some crimes, such as rape, bigamy and murder, cannot logically be imputed to a corporation.

The insanity defense holds that a person cannot be held liable for his criminal act if he was insane at the time of the act. The defense goes to the heart of the fundamental principle of intent, or guilty mind. If the accused did not understand what he was doing or understand that his actions were wrong, he cannot have criminal intent and without intent, there is no crime.

The intoxication defense is similar to that of the insanity defense. It argues that the accused could not have a guilty mind due to intoxication. The fact of voluntary intoxication is generally not accepted as a defense. Involuntary intoxication produced by fraud or coercion of another may be a defense, and insanity produced by intoxicants may be acceptable. Intoxication can also be offered as evidence that an accused was incapable of forming the intent to commit a crime, e.g., the accused was too drunk to entertain the idea of breaking and entering into a house at night for the purpose of committing an offense.

The category of specific defenses includes the alibi defense, the compulsion or necessity defense, self-defense, condonation defense, immunity defense, consent defense, entrapment defense, withdrawal defense, good character defense, ignorance or mistake of fact defense, former jeopardy defense, and statute of limitations defense.

The alibi defense seeks to prove that the accused was elsewhere at the time the offense occurred.

The compulsion or necessity defense argues that a person should not be charged with a crime when the act was committed in response to an imminent, impending and overwhelmingly coercive influence. For example, a person who is ordered to drive a getaway car under the threat of immediate death would not be punishable as a principal to the crime.

The self-defense protection against prosecution relies on the premise that every person has a right to defend himself from harm. The general rule is that a person may use in self-defense that force which, under all the circumstances of the case, reasonably appears necessary to prevent impending injury.

The condonation defense is used in some rare cases where the law allows an accused to be not prosecuted if certain conditions are met. For example, a charge of seduction might be dropped if the parties involved subsequently marry.

The immunity defense grants protection from prosecution in exchange for cooperation by the accused. The required cooperation might be a full disclosure of all facts and testimony at trial.

The consent defense may be used when consent of the victim is involved. Where consent is offered as a defense, the consent must have been given by a person legally capable of giving it and it must be voluntary.

The entrapment defense argues that an accused should not be charged if he was induced to commit a crime for the mere purpose of instituting criminal prosecution against him. Generally, where the criminal intent originates in the mind of the accused and the criminal offense is completed by him, the fact that a law enforcement officer furnished the accused an opportunity for commission does not constitute entrapment. But where the criminal intent originates in the mind of the officer and the accused is lured into the commission, no conviction may be had.

The withdrawal defense may sometimes be used in a prosecution for conspiracy. A conspirator who withdraws from the conspiracy prior to commission of the requisite overt act may attempt a defense based on withdrawal.

The good character defense may seek to offer evidence that the accused is of such good character that it was unlikely he committed the crime charged. This is not a defense as a matter of law, but an attempt to convince a jury it was improbable for the accused to have committed the crime.

The defense of ignorance or mistake of fact argues that the accused had no criminal intent. This defense seeks to excuse the accused because he has misled or was not in possession of all facts at the time of the crime. For example, this defense might be used in a case where a homeowner injured someone who he thought was a burglar in his home but who in fact was the invited guest of another member of the family.

The former jeopardy defense is founded on the principle that a case once terminated upon its merits should not be tried again. Double jeopardy can only be claimed when the second prosecution is brought by the same government as the first. When the act is a violation of the law as to two or more governments, the accused is regarded as having committed separate offenses.

The statute of limitations defense seeks to prevent prosecution on the grounds that the government failed to bring charges within the period of time fixed by a particular enactment. Not all crimes have time limitations for seeking prosecution, and some crimes, such as murder and other major crimes, have no limits whatsoever. As a rule, statutes of limitations are made applicable to misdemeanors and some minor felonies.

defense against sound equipment. electronic and physical means taken to prevent surreptitious monitoring, wiretapping or eavesdropping.

defense attorney. an attorney who represents the defendant in a legal proceeding; a person trained in the law, admitted to practice before the bar or a given jurisdiction, and authorized to advise, represent, and act for other persons in legal proceedings. The defense attorney is the lawyer who advises, represents and acts for the defendant or, in postconviction proceedings, the offender. A defense attorney, depending on how selected and/or compensated, can also be called retained counsel, assigned counsel, or public defender. When a defendant acts as his own defense attorney, he is said to be represented pro se or in propria persona.

Defense Central Index of Investigations. a locator file maintained by the Department of Defense. It identifies the location of files concerning past and present military members, DOD civilian employees, and contractors.

defense of life rule. a general rule derived from English common law which authorizes the use of deadly force in self-defense and in order to apprehend persons committing or fleeing from felonies. In many jurisdictions, the rule has been narrowed by statute so that the use of police firearms is limited only to defense of life situations and to some specific violent felonies, for example, murder, rape, aggravated assault, arson, or burglary.

defense wounds. in homicides and assaults by cutting and stabbing, wounds that are found on the victim's hands and arms. The wounds evidence the manner in which the victim maneuvered to fend off the attacker.

defensible space. a theory which holds that proper physical design of housing encourages residents to extend their social control from their homes and apartments out into the surrounding common areas. In this way, residents change to private territory what had been perceived as semi-public or public territory. Collective care and attention to the common areas results in a form of social control that discourages crime.

deferred sentence. a penalty whose imposition is not disclosed or imposed until a later time. For example, a sentence may be deferred pending preparation of a presentence investigation report.

defibrillation. the arrest of fibrillation (irregular, rapid contractions) of the cardiac muscle with restoration of the normal rhythm.

definite sentence. a sentence to a fixed time of incarceration.

definitive care. a combination of advanced life support techniques usually consisting of electrocardiogram (ECG) monitoring, diagnosis and treatment of cardiac dysrhythmias, defibrillation, and administration of intravenous fluids and drugs.

deflagration. an exothermic (heat, burning) reaction which expands rapidly from burning gases by conduction, convection, and radiation.

defraud. to cheat another person out of what is justly his.

degree. the seriousness of a crime.

degree of care. a duty owed to others which depends on circumstances. For example, persons who invite others on their premises, those who invite children on their premises, and those who sell what might be considered inherently dangerous products are all required to take different degrees of care to prevent harm to others.

de jure. by right of law; rightfully or legally. For example, a corporation de jure is one functioning in law, whereas a corporation de facto is one actually existing, although not necessarily legally.

Delaware v. Prouse. a case in which the U.S. Supreme Court found it unreasonable for the police to stop a car on a highway to check the driver's license and registration absent probable cause or reasonable suspicion that the car was being operated contrary to motor vehicle laws.

The Court held that while the police do have a legal right to stop automobiles, based on reasonable suspicion, the arbitrary stopping of an automobile and detaining the driver in order to check his driver's license and vehicle registration form are unreasonable under the Fourth Amendment. This holding does not preclude the use of spot checks that involve less intrusion or that do not involve the unconstrained exercise of discretion. The use of roadblocks or checkpoints for questioning all oncoming vehicles or every third vehicle are possible alternatives. These options, however, must be uniform, systematic, and applied in a nonarbitrary manner.

delay impact fuse. a bomb fuse designed to function at a predetermined time after impact. The delay allows the explosive ordnance to penetrate the target before detonation. A delay fuse is normally employed when the intended target is constructed of, or protected by, heavy armor plate or reinforced concrete.

delayed dismissal. a dismissal of a criminal charge obtained by the defense but which the prosecution withholds for several weeks or months, as a means of warning the defendant, placating the victim, or allowing public and news media interest to subside.

delegation of authority. the formal assignment of authority to a subordinate to perform specific acts.

delict. a crime, offense, wrong, or injury.

delinquency. in many states, any act that would be a crime if committed by an adult, and therefore a softer synonym for crime; undesirable conduct on the part of a juvenile that is serious enough to come to the attention of the authorities, including truancy, school misconduct, petty offenses, and sometimes serious crimes. Most jurisdictions also include a wide variety of acts which are not illegal if committed by adults. Also, failure, omission, violation of duty; a state or condition of one who fails to perform his duty. Synonymous with misconduct and offense.

delinquent. a juvenile who has been adjudged by a judicial officer of a juvenile court to have committed a delinquent act.

delinquent act. an act committed by a juvenile for which an adult could be prosecuted in a criminal court, but for which a juvenile can be adjudicated in a juvenile court, or prosecuted in a court having criminal jurisdiction if the juvenile court transfers jurisdiction. Also, in some jurisdictions a delinquent act is a felony or misdemeanor level offense.

deliriants. substances capable of producing delirium, often used in reference to the volatile inhalants and the practice called glue sniffing.

delirium. in medical jurisprudence, that state of the mind in which it acts without being directed by the power of volition, which is wholly or partially suspended. A person in delirium is wholly unconscious of surrounding objects, or conceives them to be different from what they really are. In general, a usually brief state of incoherent excitement, confused speech, restlessness, and hallucinations. It may occur in high fever, ingestion of certain toxic substances and drugs, nutritional deficiencies, endocrine imbalance, severe stress, or mental illness.

delirium tremens. a disorder of the nervous system, involving the brain and setting up an attack of temporary delusional insanity, sometimes attended with violent excitement or mania, caused by excessive and long continued indulgence in alcoholic liquors, or by the abrupt cessation of such practice after an intense and protracted episode of use; an acute mental and physical disorder occurring in alcoholics while drinking or as an alcohol-withdrawal syndrome. The onset is marked by tremulousness, nausea, vomiting, weakness, hallucinations, or collapse due to malnutrition from a prolonged diet of liquor.

Delphi technique. a methodology that pieces together various opinions in order to arrive at a consensus on the probability of a future event. The concept involves: (1) asking various informed individuals or groups as to their opinions concerning a possible future event, (2) evaluating the responses by one or more factors (such as the respondents' relative importance or influence on the situation, their expertise or understanding of the situation, and past forecasting accuracy), and (3) calculating from the aggregate of opinions an event probability.

delta. in fingerprint science, that point on a ridge at or in front of and nearest the center of the divergence of the type lines.

delta-9-tetrahydrocannibinol. the full chemical term for tetrahydrocannabinol or THC. It is one 61 chemicals found only in cannabis.

delusion. an erroneous belief or fancy which cannot be corrected by reason; a belief that exists in spite of contrary reason or evidence that would normally be considered sufficient to change it; a firm, fixed idea not amenable to rational explanation.

demand mask. a self-contained breathing apparatus that supplies air to the wearer on a demand basis, i.e., in relation to the wearer's breathing rate.

demand reduction strategy. those federal drug abuse policy goals which are geared toward reducing both the demand and supply of illicit drugs. The demand reduction strategy outlines the federal government's plan for reducing the demand for illicit drugs. The main components of the strategy consist of providing support for treatment and rehabilitation programs, prevention projects, and research and development activities in cooperation with state, local, and private agencies and organizations.

dementia. the loss of rational thought due to functional or organic disorder; mental impairment due to brain damage or degeneration; a progressive state of mental decline, especially of memory function and judgment, often accompanied by disorientation, stupor, and disintegration of the personality. It may be caused by certain metabolic diseases, drug intoxification, or injury, in which cases it is often reversible once the underlying cause is treated. In other cases it is caused by a disease (e.g., Alzheimer's disease), brain injury, or degeneration brought about by aging (senile dementia) that causes irreversible changes.

dementia praecox. a physiologically induced mental disorder that begins at or immediately following puberty. It is characterized by incoherency, lack of judgment, and disassociation with surroundings.

Demerol. the trade name of meperidine (pethidine), a commonly abused synthetic narcotic. It resembles morphine in its analgesic effect, and is probably the most widely prescribed drug for the relief of moderate to severe pain. Tolerance and dependence develop with chronic use, and large doses can result in convulsions or death. Demerol is a Schedule II narcotic.

demography. the scientific study of population size, composition, and distribution, and patterns of change in those features.

demonstrative evidence. an exhibit offered at a trial as a means of explaining or illustrating. Examples are diagrams, maps, plaster casts, models and charts.

demophobia. morbid fear of crowds. Also called ochlophobia.

demurrer. the answer of a defendant to a charge made against him which denies legal responsibility though it may concede the plaintiff's contention; a written objection to being tried on an indictment because of defects in the indictment.

denial of reality. an ego defense process in which an unpleasant reality is avoided through escapist activities such as becoming sick or being preoccupied with other things.

de novo. anew, afresh, as if there had been no earlier decision.

Denver boot. a clamp device which when attached to the wheel of a vehicle will prevent the vehicle from being driven. The device is used to immobilize improperly parked, unattended vehicles and unattended vehicles owned by scofflaw motorists.

dependent and neglected juvenile. a juvenile over whom a juvenile court has assumed jurisdiction and legal control because his or her care by parent, guardian or custodian has not met a legal standard of proper care.

dependent variable. the variable that occurs or changes in a patterned way due to the presence of, or changes in, another variable or variables.

deponent. one who deposes to the truth of certain facts; one who gives under oath testimony which is reduced to writing.

deportation. the act of sending an alien out of the country, and usually banning him from re-entry. Deportation of a criminal alien can take place before a trial, after conviction, or after a sentence has been served.

deposition. the testimony of a witness taken upon oral or written interrogatories, not in open court, after notice to the adverse party for the purpose of enabling him to attend and cross examine the witness. It is reduced to writing and duly authenticated.

depositor's forgery insurance. a type of protection against the forgery or alteration of instruments such as checks, drafts, and promissory notes purported to have been written by the insured.

depreciation. decrease in value of property due to normal wear or the passing of time.

depressant. a drug that acts on the central nervous system producing effects that range from sedation to anesthesia; a drug that acts to depress or decrease respiration, blood pressure and heart rate; any drug that depresses the central nervous system resulting in sedation and a decrease in bodily activity. Not to be confused with the psychological state of depression, these drugs can in fact be mood elevators by lowering inhibitions. Depressants are the largest and most commonly used of all drug types, including the narcotic analgesics, alcohol, barbiturates, proprietary sedative-hypnotics, tranquilizers, and inhalants. All these depressant drugs affect the CNS similarly in a progression depending on dosage from anxiety reduction to sedation, hypnosis (sleep), anesthesia, coma, and even death. Given this similarity in effect, they are classified usually according to the specific purpose for which they are most suitable. Depressants are also additive in their effects. When used together they compound the effects of each and greatly increase the risk of death.

depression. a state of despondency characterized by feelings such as inadequacy, lowered activity, and pessimism about the future. In pathological cases, an extreme state of unresponsiveness to stimuli, together with self-depreciation, delusions of inadequacy, and hopelessness. It frequently consists of chronic sadness over a period of several weeks, plus three or more of the following symptoms: (1) trouble sleeping over a period of several weeks, (2) anorexia leading to weight loss of 8 pounds or more, (3) several weeks of feeling tired for no reason or not able to "get going", (4) thoughts of dying or harming oneself, (5) worry about losing one's mind, and (6) crying spells.

depth of field. in photography, the region in front of and behind the focused distance in which objects still produce an image of acceptable sharpness or resolution. It is the distance between the nearest and farthest objects which gives satisfactory definition in the image plane. The smaller the aperture of a lens, the greater the depth of field. Also, lenses with shorter focal lengths have a greater depth of field than lenses of a longer length when at the same f-stop. Also called depth of focus.

deputy sheriff. a local law enforcement officer employed by a county sheriff's department. Sheriff's department personnel whose permanent duties are primarily custodial or concerned with civil processes are generally excluded from this class.

derivative evidence rule. a rule which bars from trial any evidence obtained during or as a direct result of an unlawful invasion of Fourth Amendment rights. It applies to oral evidence as well as tangible materials. The general application is that not all evidence is excludable simply because it would not have come to light but for the illegal actions of the police. The question is whether, granting the primary illegality, the evidence has been obtained by exploitation of that illegality or, instead, by means sufficiently distinguishable to purge it of the primary taint. Also called the fruit of poisonous tree rule or doctrine.

desecrate. to violate sanctity of, to profane, or put to unworthy use.

desiccation prints. fingerprints obtained from persons with wrinkled and dried skin, as in the case of deceased persons.

designated crimes. those crimes which under federal law can be properly investigated with the aid of electronic surveillance. Federal law allows the states to place into the designated crimes category offenses involving murder, kidnapping, rape, gambling, bribery, narcotics, or other offenses punishable by more than one year in prison.

designer drugs. synthetic drugs, chemically related to legitimate drugs, which are produced inexpensively and sold (sometimes legally) as substitutes for the legitimate products they imitate. The term was originally used to describe drugs designed to meet the tastes of particular clients. A designer drug can be created by adding fluoride or an extra molecule to the chemical structure of a psychoactive drug. The psychoactive effects remain, but because the new variant is no longer exactly the same chemical, it is not subject to the Controlled Substances Act. Fentanyl and its variants are good examples of this process.

destruct line. a line shown in a geographical map to represent the perimeter of destruction caused by an explosive device.

DET. diethyltryptamine, a laboratory-synthesized hallucinogen regulated under the Controlled Substances Act as a Schedule I drug.

detached workers. people assigned to youth gangs in major cities. They seek to transform gang values and organization through individual counseling, influencing interaction within the gang, and developing alternative activities for gang members.

Detacord. a plastic commercial explosive that usually appears in a form similar to a clothesline.

detail sketch. a type of rough sketch prepared at a crime scene or traffic accident scene for the purpose of depicting the exact relative positions of evidential items and other objects of investigative interest.

detainee. a person held in local, very short confinement while awaiting consideration for pretrial release or first appearance for arraignment. The term also refers to persons held in physical custody for lengthy periods while awaiting trial and judgment. Also called detentioner.

detainer. an official notice from a government agency to a correctional agency requesting that an identified person wanted by the first agency, but subject to the correctional agency's jurisdiction, not be released or discharged without notification to the first agency with opportunity to respond.

Detasheet. a plastic commercial explosive that appears as a flat sheet about one-eighth inch thick.

detection powder. any of several powders (or pastes and similar substances) used to mark decoy objects or objects susceptible to theft. The powder, which is usually fluorescent, will transfer to the skin or clothing of persons who handle the marked objects.

detector. any device that detects intrusion, equipment failure, hazards, smoke, fire or other conditions requiring immediate response.

detention. the legally authorized holding in confinement of a person subject to criminal or juvenile court proceedings, until commitment to a correctional facility or release. The reason for custody is sometimes stated as pretrial detention or pre-arraignment lockup. Release from detention can occur prior to trial (pretrial release), or after trial or adjudication as a result of a dismissal of the case, an acquittal, or a sentencing disposition that does not require confinement.

detention center. a government facility that holds a person in confinement pending court disposition.

detention hearing. a proceeding presided over by a judicial officer of a juvenile court to determine whether or not a juvenile is to be detained pending adjudication of his case.

determinate sentence. a prison term for a fixed time, with parole eligibility before the fixed time has expired, and possibly with eligibility for good time.

deterrence theory. the penological theory that the use or threat of legal sanctions or punishment, the knowledge of which is widely disseminated, is the most important method of preventing crime or socially undesirable acts might otherwise be committed. Classical deterrence theory maintains that the likelihood of someone engaging in lawbreaking activity is determined negatively by the certainty, severity, and swiftness of punishment. The more certain, severe, and swift the penalties are, the greater their deterrent effect. This has been called the primary and essential postulate of almost all criminal law systems. Research has also emphasized the role in deterrence of the potential lawbreaker's subjective perceptions regarding the possibility of punishment, whether or not these perceptions are accurate.

detonating cord. a cordlike explosive containing a core of high-explosive material, usually PETN. Also called Primacord and Detacord.

detoxification. supervised withdrawal from drug or alcohol dependence, either with or without medication, usually in a hospital or as an outpatient. Frequently, patients in detoxification programs will live in a highly structured drug or alcohol-free environment. While in itself not considered a very successful treatment method, it is an option that permits the dependent drug user to be seen by some type of center (usually a hospital), to receive medical attention, and to reduce the dependence cycle. Detoxification often leads to other forms of treatment by referral. The most common procedure to relieve the distress caused by heroin withdrawal symptoms during detoxification is that developed at the Public Health Service Hospital at Lexington, Kentucky. Typically, the patient is started on a dose of methadone, consistent with his or her own heroin habit (usually 20mg methadone twice daily or 40mg once a day), and the dose is reduced thereafter by 20 percent per day. Discomfort is thereby held down to roughly that experienced in the course of a mild bout of influenza. Although hospitalization was once considered essential for the treatment of withdrawal symptoms, outpatient detoxification is now used successfully.

developed latent impression. a latent fingerprint impression made visible by powders or chemicals so that it may be preserved and compared. A latent impression is photographed before it is developed.

deviance. conduct, activity, or condition that is disapproved of, stigmatized, and subject to formal and informal punishment.

deviant behavior. generally, behavior that varies markedly from the average or norm, usually pathological in nature, or which elicits condemnation in the social setting in which it takes place. In its widest sense, deviant behavior refers to activities that connote a departure by individuals from accepted standards of conduct or social norms of the dominant group. Deviance is not a quality of an act a person commits, but is defined in terms of a "labeling" phenomenon created by the social group that specifies those infractions constituting deviance. The term antisocial behavior is preferred by some.

Dexedrine. the trade name for dextroamphetamine sulfate which is regulated under the Controlled Substances Act as a Schedule II stimulant. It is considered twice as potent as other amphetamines but with fewer side effects. Dexedrine has been generally replaced as an antidepressant by newer drugs such as amitriptyline hydrochloride (Elavil) and imipramine hydrochloride (Tofranil). It is used as an appetite depressant in dieting, as a mood elevator in minor depression, and for alcoholism and narcolepsy. Dexedrine is also found in Dexamyl. Dexedrine is widely abused, and known on the street as dexies, speed, upper, black beauty, crank, meth, bam, and pink.

dexies. dexedrine capsules or tablets; dextro-amphetamines.

diabetic ketoacidosis. a condition resulting from uncontrolled diabetes, characterized by excessive thirst, hunger, urination, vomiting, and sometimes coma, with the production of ketones in metabolism as well as an excess of organic acids.

diacetylmorphine. heroin; a semisynthetic opiate derivate isolated in 1898 in Germany by the pharmacologist Heinrich Dresser in the search for non-habit-forming analgesics to take the place of morphine. It was named after the German word "heroisch" meaning large, big, powerful. Although heroin was considered nonaddictive when first introduced, by 1924 the U.S. Congress had prohibited its manufacture in the United States. By 1956 all existing stocks on hand were required to be surrendered. Heroin is 2 to 3 times as potent analgesically as morphine, although in equipotent doses the effects are similar. The preference for heroin use over morphine is yet to be thoroughly explained. Whatever physical factors are involved, and the logistics of illicit traffic, heroin is most potent, least bulky and easiest to conceal, and provides greatest profit. Slang names include H, horse, scat, junk, smack, scag, stuff, Harry, and brown sugar.

diagnostic center. a unit within a correctional institution, or a separate facility for persons held in custody, in which an entering convict will be assigned to a specific correctional facility or program; a special place of detention for sex offenders or seriously mentally disturbed convicts.

diagnostic commitment. the action of a court ordering a person subject to criminal or juvenile proceedings to be temporarily placed in a confinement facility, for study and evaluation of personal history and characteristics, usually as a preliminary to a sentencing disposition.

diagonal formation. a riot control formation consisting of police officers moving forward along a diagonal line. Its principal use is to drive rioters in a given direction, such as down a particular street. Also called echelon formation.

dialer. a device that electronically dials one or more prerecorded telephone numbers using digital codes.

diamond formation. a riot control formation used to conduct offensive movements against large groups, for example, to penetrate an unruly crowd for the purpose of taking into custody its leader. Also called triangle formation.

diamond point pencil. a tool used to inscribe identifying marks on metallic evidence items such as firearms and knives.

diaphragm. the musculomembranous partition separating the thoracic and abdominal cavities. When relaxed, it is convex, but flattens on inspiration, thereby enlarging the chest cavity and allowing for expansion of the lungs.

diastole. the dilation of the heart chambers, during which they fill with blood.

dicrotic notch. in polygraphy, a characteristic formation in the descending leg of the cardiosphygmograph tracing. It results from a slight change of blood pressure caused by the closing of the semilunar valves in the left ventricle of the heart.

diethyltryptamine (DET). an hallucinogen classified as a Schedule I controlled substance. It is a synthetic similar chemically and in action to dimethyltryptamine (DMT). DET is frequently used in combination with tobacco, tea, parsley and marihuana.

differential association theory. a major theory in American criminology which postulates that criminal behavior, like normative behavior, is learned, that this learning takes place in association with others already committed to criminality, and that one learns in such association both criminal values and the mechanisms for committing crimes. The fundamental principle holds that criminal behavior is learned and that a person becomes delinquent because of an excess of definitions favorable to law violations. Generally stated, persons who develop criminal behavior differ from those who do not develop criminal behavior in the quantity and quality of their associations with criminal patterns and their relative isolation from anti-criminal patterns. The learning of delinquent role models is due to the availability of delinquent role models in a peer group.

differential police response. a dispatching procedure under which non-emergency calls are classified and assigned for handling and response other than by immediate dispatch of a patrol unit. The procedure is intended to achieve economy in patrol unit deployment without substantial loss of crime control.

differential sentencing. unequal penalties imposed on different persons for the same or similar crimes. The inequalities may reflect such legally irrelevant reasons as race or sex, or different sentencing policies among judges or jurisdictions.

diffused explosion. an explosion characterized by a slow expansion over a relatively wide area into a combustion known as deflagration. Most explosives causing this type of explosion have a pushing rather than a shattering effect, and a twisting and tearing type of deformation results.

digital computer. a computer that operates on discrete data by performing arithmetic and logic processes on these data; a computer that consists of one or more associated processing units and peripheral equipment and that is controlled by internally-stored programs.

digital lock. a type of mechanical lock that is opened by pressing the proper sequence of numbered or lettered push buttons. Also called a cypher lock.

dilation. the process of expanding or enlarging, often associated with the pupils of the eye or blood vessels.

dilatory exception. an exception or motion filed for the purpose of retarding a court case but which does not tend to defeat the charge.

Dilaudid. the trade name for hydromorphone, a semi-synthetic narcotic analgesic. Because it is two to eight times more potent than morphine, it is highly sought by addicts. Dilaudid is a Schedule II substance, and is called K-4 on the street.

dilution. the adulteration of a drug by the addition of an inactive substance; to make less concentrated or to diminish strength. Most dilutants have little or no physiological effect. In drug testing, the addition of a fluid to a urine specimen, rendering it unsuitable for analysis. Such dilution is often the deliberate act of the donor who seeks to mask the presence of a drug or confound the analysis. Dilution of this type is done in two ways: (1) by consuming large volumes of water, tea, vinegar, and other liquids shortly prior to urination, and (2) by directly adding to the specimen a quantity of tap water or other fluid.

dime bag. a quantity of illegal drugs sold for ten dollars.

dimethoxymethamphetamine (DOM). the chemical name for the street drug STP, a synthetic hallucinogen that is chemically related to amphetamine and mescaline and is said to produce an LSD-like experience. Its primary effect is a relentless rush of energy that causes users to tremble. Some hallucinogen users prefer STP because they believe it carries less risk of psychotic reactions than any other hallucinogen. Some users negatively report a long "come down" period of 2 to 3 days on STP, and for that reason prefer to use the shorter-acting LSD.

dimethyltryptamine (DMT). a semisynthetic chemical hallucinogen similar to psilocin. Parsley or some other plant is usually soaked in it, dried, and smoked. Easily synthesized, it is found naturally in a number of plants. Effects are similar to LSD and begin almost immediately but last for under an hour. It is known as the "businessman's trip" or "businessman's lunch hour" because its effect is rapid-acting and of short duration.

DMT is a good example of the correlation between route of administration, intensity of effect, and duration of action. A short-acting drug, introduced directly into the bloodstream by smoking or injection, tends to give a sudden and dramatic change in consciousness (rush). The pursuit of a rush is frequently the basis of addictive use.

Like other psychedelics, DMT loses its effect when taken repetitively over a period of time. The body develops a rapid tolerance that reduces the rush. Many users of DMT save their drugs for special occasions.

diminished capacity. decreased or less-than-normal ability, temporary or permanent, to distinguish right from wrong or to fully appreciate the consequences of one's act. It is a plea used by the defendant for conviction of a lesser degree of a crime, for a lenient sentence, or for mercy or clemency.

dinoly. a type of primary explosive.

dip. a pickpocket.

diphenylaminechloroarsine (DM). a riot control chemical agent that produces severe discomfort and sickness, and for that reason is used only when absolutely necessary. Because it takes several minutes to attain full effect, this agent is usually mixed with chloroacetephenone (CN agent) to produce a more rapid result. Also called and Adamsite.

diphenylamine test. a test that seeks to identify the presence of gunpowder residue on the hands of a person suspected of having recently fired a gun. The suspect's hands are coated with melted paraffin, the paraffin is removed, and diphenylamine is applied to the paraffin that contacted the skin. The examiner evaluates the resulting color reaction. This test is not considered reliable and has almost entirely fallen out of use in modern criminal investigation. Also called the paraffin test.

dipping the till. stealing money from a cash register or cash drawer, usually by an employee.

diprenorphine. a semi-synthetic narcotic made from thebaine, a minor constituent of opium and the principal alkaloid present in another species of poppy called papaver bracteatum. Diprenorphine is regulated under the Controlled Substances Act.

dipsomania. in medical jurisprudence, a mental disease characterized by an uncontrollable desire for intoxicating drinks; an irresistible impulse to indulge in intoxication, either by alcohol or other drugs.

dipsomaniac. a confirmed drunkard; one who has an uncontrollable desire for alcoholic liquors.

direct action. a catch phrase used by protesters. It can mean illegal activity ranging from minor civil disobedience to bombings.

direct approach. an interrogational approach in which the interrogator assumes an air of confidence with regard to the suspect's guilt and stresses the evidence indicative of guilt. The approach is accusatory in nature and seeks to discover why the suspect committed the act, as opposed to learning if the suspect committed the act.

direct drug death. a death that results directly from the taking of a drug at a toxic level.

directed interview. an interview in which the questioner is in full control of the interview content, typically soliciting answers to a variety of specific questions. It is usually employed with a reluctant or uncommunicative witness.

directed patrol. a patrol strategy based on calls for service and on an analysis of the crime workload. This strategy is directed toward specific police problems and goals.

directed verdict. a jury decision rendered by an order of a trial judge. In modern criminal procedure the directed verdict is always to acquit, although it may be limited to specific counts or specific defendants.

direct evidence. that means of proof which tends to show the existence of a fact in question, without the intervention of the proof of any other fact, and is distinguished from circumstantial evidence, which is often called indirect; information which a witness gained through one of the five senses.

direct examination. interrogation of a witness by counsel of the party on whose behalf the witness was called.

directional draw holster. a holster worn on the right side of a right-handed person or on the left side of a left-handed person. When drawn from a directional draw holster, the handgun points at the ground

and then at the target in a natural motion.

directional microphone. a microphone extremely sensitive to audio frequencies arriving from one particular direction, while rejecting those that arrive from other directions.

direct tap. a common form of wiretapping in which a set of wires is attached to a specific phone pair in the phone company's bridge box, usually mounted in the basement or a secluded area of the building where the target telephone is located.

dirty. carrying or using narcotics.

dirty games. insidious work, such as blackmailing a government employee or business executive to force him into espionage.

disaffirm. a legal term meaning to renege or refuse to go through with an agreed transaction.

disaster control. advanced planning and established procedures for handling emergencies. Major considerations include provisions for protecting personnel, evacuating both the injured and uninjured, and care of the incapacitated. Disaster control frequently focuses on threats posed by fire, civil strife, earthquake, explosion, flood, tornado, hurricane, and nuclear accident.

disaster preparedness. any series of actions intended to control and manage major accidents (including nuclear incidents) and bring them to the most satisfactory conclusion possible.

disbar. the act of a court in rescinding an attorney's license to practice at its bar.

discharge gate. a type of valve that controls water flow from a high pressure fire hydrant.

disclosure. the act of making known to the adversary in a criminal case (usually the prosecution) information that might assist in clearing the party making the disclosure (usually the defendant) of alleged guilt.

discovery. a motion, usually made by the defense, calling for disclosure to counsel for the accused all information about a case known to the police and prosecution, or of certain specified information; the disclosure by one party of facts, titles, documents, and other things which are in his knowledge or possession and which are necessary to the party seeking the discovery as a part of a cause of action pending.

discovery sampling. a technique in which a specified level of confidence or precision is stated and one or a few samples are drawn from the population being examined. The objective is to discover a single deviation from the specified level. If a deviation is found, the entire population is examined. This technique is used by auditors looking for fraud.

discretion. the power given to or assumed by officers of the criminal justice system to make decisions, such as whether or not to arrest, negotiate a plea, grant immunity or probation, prosecute, or impose a severe sentence; the freedom of a police officer to decide whether or not to make an arrest, even though a law may have been broken and, implicitly, the assumption of responsibility for the consequences.

discretionary review. an appeal in which the court having appellate jurisdiction may agree or decline to hear, at its own discretion. Procedurally, in these cases, a party wishing to appeal must first make a request to the court for permission to make the appeal, stating the reasons for doing so. The court can grant or deny the request.

discretionary sentencing. the power of the sentencing judge to decide upon the nature and severity of a sentence to be imposed after a plea or a finding of guilt.

discrimination. in equal employment opportunity programs, any active, passive, or neutral employment action which results in a distinction in treatment given an individual or group of individuals because of race, color, religion, sex, handicap, age, national origin, veteran status, or marital status.

disinformation. the spreading of false propaganda and the use of forged documents to create political unrest or scandals.

disinhibition. the temporary absence of inhibition as a result of an outside or irrelevant stimulus. Also, a loss of self-control while under the influence of drugs.

disinterested witness. a qualified witness who is unbiased regarding the case in question.

dismissal. a decision by a judicial officer to terminate a case without a determination of guilt or innocence.

dismissal for want of prosecution. the judicial termination of a case against a defendant, occurring after the filing of a charging document but before the beginning of a trial, on the ground that prosecution has not been continued. A court may dismiss a case for want of prosecution on the motion of the defense or on its own motion. In some jurisdictions, such dismissals are automatic in cases which have not been brought to trial within a specified period of time following the filing of a charging document, unless the defendant has waived the right to have the trial during the specified period.

dismissal in the interest of justice. the judicial termination of a case against a defendant on the ground that the ends of justice would not be served by continuing prosecution.

dismissal without prejudice. the effect of the words "without prejudice" is to prevent the decree of dismissal from operating as a bar to a subsequent suit.

disorderly. contrary to the rules of good order and behavior; violative of the public peace and good order; turbulent, riotous, or indecent.

disorderly conduct. a term of loose and indefinite meaning except as occasionally defined in statutes, but signifying generally any behavior that is contrary to law, and more particularly such as tends to disturb the public peace or decorum, scandalize the community, or shock the public sense of morality. In Uniform Crime Reports terminology, disorderly conduct offenses include affray, unlawful assembly, disturbing the peace, blasphemy, profanity, desecrating the flag, and refusing to assist an officer.

disorderly house. a place where illegal or

immoral activities occur, such as prostitution, gambling or the showing of pornographic materials.

disorientation. a state of mental confusion regarding time, place, or identity.

displacement. a phenomenon in which criminals will move their activities to another location or switch to a different type of crime in response to increased prevention efforts.

displacement reaction. the discharge of pent-up feelings, usually hostile in nature, directed at an object less dangerous than that which initially aroused the emotion.

disposable alcohol screening device. a device used to conduct a one-time qualitative test of blood-alcohol concentration. It typically consists of a small glass tube containing either a column or multiple bands of an alcohol-sensitive reagent and a breath-volume measuring device such as a balloon or plastic bag.

disposition. the final decision of a trial court in the processing of a case, such as a decision to accept a guilty plea, to render a verdict of guilt or innocence, or not to prosecute.

dispositional tolerance. a decrease in the response to a drug dose caused by changes in the physiochemical processes of the body. An increased rate of metabolism will reduce the amount of the drug reaching the receptor cells.

disposition hearing. a hearing in juvenile court, conducted after an adjudicatory hearing and subsequent receipt of the report of any predisposition investigation, to determine the most appropriate form of custody and/or treatment for a juvenile who has been adjudged a delinquent, a status offender, or a dependent.

disprove. to refute; to prove to be false or erroneous, not necessarily by mere denial, but by affirmative evidence to the contrary.

disrepute. loss or want of reputation; ill character; discredit.

dissemination. the distribution of information or intelligence products to legitimate intelligence consumers.

dissenting opinion. an opinion of one or more judges who disagree with the decision of the majority. Also called a minority opinion.

dissociative disorder. a neurosis in which repressed emotional conflict causes a separation in the personality with confusion in identity. Marked by symptoms of amnesia, dream state, or multiple personality, it is treated with psychotherapy, hypnosis, and antianxiety drugs.

dissolute. lacking in restraint; unashamed; lawless; loose in morals and conduct; recklessly abandoned to sensual pleasures; lewd.

distant wound. a wound caused by a bullet that traveled in excess of at least two feet from muzzle to victim. A distant wound is apparent by the absence of flame, smoke, and tattooing marks characteristic of a shot made in contact or in close contact with the victim. When a bullet penetrates the body perpendicular to the skin, it produces a round wound with abraded margins, called a collar abrasion. When a bullet penetrates the skin at an angle, the direction from which it enters the skin is indicated by a triangular abrasion and undermining of the skin. A bullet which grazes but does not penetrate the skin will produce a rectangular abrasion of the skin, called a bullet rub. The shape of an exit wound will vary according to where it exits (whether through a fleshy or bony structure), the shape of the bullet as it exits (whether pristine or flattened), and the motion of the bullet (whether spinning or tumbling). Exit wound shapes include marks that are stellate (star-like), slit-like, everted (inside-out), and irregular.

distinguished visitor. a person who, because of rank or position, may be afforded special protection services to ensure personal safety.

distortion. in polygraphy, a change in chart tracings caused by an unintended outside stimulus; a disturbance of normal polygraph tracings not attributable to a planned stimulus within a test structure. Distortion is usually caused by noises external to the test environment.

district attorney. an attorney who is the elected or appointed chief of a prosecution agency, and whose official duty is to conduct criminal proceedings on behalf of the people against persons accused of committing criminal offenses. Also called a prosecutor, DA, state's attorney, county attorney, and U.S. Attorney.

disturbing the peace. unlawful interruption of the peace, quiet or order of a community, including offenses generally called disorderly conduct, vagrancy, loitering, unlawful assembly and riot.

ditran. a psychedelic hallucinogen, chemically called piperidyl benzilate. Its effects include changes in the user's perception of time, space, hearing, and color, but it does not precipitate any real hallucinations.

divergence. the spreading apart of two lines which have been running parallel or nearly parallel in a fingerprint pattern.

diversion. the official suspension of criminal or juvenile proceedings against an alleged offender at any point after a recorded justice system intake but before the entering of a judgment, and referral of that person to a treatment or care program administered by a non-justice or private agency, or no referral.

Diversion is a criminal justice system reform concept of identifying some criminal defenders in the earliest stages and diverting them into programs that may not involve incarceration. As operationally defined by the American Bar Foundation, it is "the disposition of a complaint without a conviction, the non-criminal disposition being conditioned on either the performance of specified obligations by the defendant, or his participation in counseling or treatment."

As a major nonpunitive alternative to civil commitment, the basis for offender diversion is to remove from the criminal justice system those for whom its processes are thought to be inappropriate or counter-productive. Offenders are generally diverted after arrest but before court disposition. Those who are considered eligible for diversion are offered the opportunity to volunteer. While the offender is in the diversion program, the pending prosecution is suspended or deferred. Upon successful completion of the program, the original charges are generally dismissed.

The term diversion also refers to the redirection of licit, prescription drugs from the normal pharmaceutical marketing system into the illicit street market (especially amphetamine and barbiturate drugs).

diversion investigation. an investigation that seeks to determine how, where, and when legitimate pharmaceutical preparations entered the illegal market. The principal targets of a diversion investigation are members of the health care industry, mainly physicians and pharmacists.

division of labor. the specialization of economic activities, and the tendency for people to become more specialized in what they do; an organization of work in which tasks/functions are grouped or separated so as to achieve efficiency of operation.

divisions of law. a concept which holds that the total body of law consists of systems of rules laid down by the power of government to regulate the conduct of people in society. The law is divided, sometimes arbitrarily, into separate sections. With reference to its subject matter, the law is either private or public.

Private law deals with those relations between individuals with which the government is not directly concerned. It is subdivided for practical purposes into many branches such as property law, domestic relations law, trust law, and tort law.

Public law is that part of the law which deals with the government either by itself or in its relations with individuals. Some of its branches are constitutional law, administrative law, public health law, vehicle and traffic law, and criminal law.

The criminal law is one of the most important branches of public law. It is divided into two main parts: substantive and procedural.

Substantive law defines what varying

types of conduct will constitute crimes, provides for punishments, and lays down rules on such matters as the capacity of persons to commit crimes and the defenses that may be legally employed by charged persons.

Procedural law provides the means and methods by which rights and obligations created by the criminal law are to be vindicated and enforced, i.e., procedural law defines the manner in which criminal cases are prosecuted. Whereas substantive law tells us what is just, procedural law tells us how justice is to be carried out.

DM agent. the descriptor for diphenyl-aminechloroarsine, a riot control chemical agent that produces physiological reactions so severe that it is used with caution and only when absolutely necessary. Also called Adamsite.

DMT. the street name for dimethyltryptamine, a laboratory-synthesized hallucinogen regulated under the Controlled Substances Act as a Schedule I drug.

do a bong. to smoke marihuana or hashish from a modified water pipe called a bong.

docket. a book containing any entry in brief of all the important acts done in court in the conduct of each case, from its inception to conclusion.

documentary evidence. a writing or recording that is significant because of its content. Examples are letters, photographs and tapes.

document examination. a side-by-side comparison of handwriting, typewriting and other written and printed matter for the purpose of determining authorship; a crime laboratory function based on the improbability of any two writings being exactly alike in all characteristics such as style, speed, slant and spacing. Writing involves a mental process, regardless of the skill and habitual performance, as well as muscular coordination.

DOD Weapons Registry. a Department of Defense central registry which lists the serial numbers of small arms in the DOD inventory. It can be used by any police agency seeking information on particular weapons.

dog chain. an iron chain with a ring at one end and a spike at the other end. It is used in firefighting operations to secure a ladder to a window sill.

dog collar. a shoplifting device consisting of a leather strap hung from the neck beneath a loose fitting overcoat. One or two garments on hangers are hooked to the leather strap and concealed under the coat.

Dolophine. the trade name for methadone, a synthetic narcotic used in the treatment of addicts. The effects of Dolophine differ from morphine-based drugs in that its duration will last up to 24 hours, thereby permitting once-a-day administration in detoxification and maintenance programs. Dolophine is a Schedule II narcotic.

DOM. dimethoxyamphetamine, a controlled ingredient that is a chemical variation of amphetamine. When first introduced into the drug culture, it was called STP, after a motor oil additive. DOM, along with DOB, MDA, and MDMA, is one of many chemically-synthesized hallucinogens. These drugs differ from one another in their speed of onset, duration of action, potency, and capacity to modify mood with or without producing hallucinations. They are usually taken orally, sometimes snorted, and rarely taken intravenously. Because they are produced in clandestine laboratories, they are seldom pure, and the dose in a tablet, in a capsule, or on a piece of impregnated paper may be expected to vary considerably.

Donnegan workers. pickpockets and sneak thieves who ply their trade in public restrooms. The typical method of operation is for one of the thieves to distract a victim in a toilet stall while the accomplice steals the victim's billfold, purse, luggage or other valuables.

Doppler Shift. a principle used in alarm operations. In an area to be protected, sound or radio waves are transmitted outward. Upon contact with an intruder, the waves are reflected to the receiver at a different frequency. The frequency differentiation (Doppler Shift) triggers an alarm.

Doriden. the trade name for glutethimide, a depressant regulated under the Controlled Substances Act as a Schedule III drug. Doriden is a barbiturate substitute not having a dependence potential. It is exceptionally difficult to reverse overdoses, which frequently result in death.

dose (or dosage). the amount or quantity of drug administered, usually stated in grams (g), milligrams (mg), or milliliters (ml). The term effective dosage is sometimes used to refer to that dosage which produces a certain effect in 50 percent of the individuals tested, whereas 25 percent felt the same effect at a lesser dosage, and 25 percent required a higher dosage.

dose-effect relationship. a basic principle of pharmacology which holds that the response to a drug differs both in the intensity and the character of the reaction according to the amount of the drug administered. Consideration of the quantity or dose of the drug involved must be taken into account before specific statements about drug effects may be made.

dose-response relationship. a major area of study in behavioral pharmacology in which observations are made over time between the dosage of a drug administered and some measurable behavioral activity of the subject. The observed relations are frequently plotted graphically with the dosage level on one axis and the particular behavior activity level on the other. The line drawn to connect the observations is called the dose-response curve. The inability to fit a curve indicates a poor relationship. The curve may take many shapes. Upward sloping and level curves indicate a direct relationship. Downward sloping curves indicate an indirect relationship. Curves that slope up and then down, or vice versa, are called biphasic dose-response relationships. Alcohol, for example, at low dosage levels may have a disinhibiting, enervating effect, but as the dosage increases these effects may be reversed into an inhibiting, stuporous effect.

dosimetry. the measurement of radiation doses. It applies to the measurement techniques and to the measurement devices (dosimeters).

dossier. a record, case file, or personnel file containing background information as well as materials relating to a crime or a criminal career. The term is applied to espionage and counterespionage.

double. an agent working for two sides at the same time.

double-action. in a numbers operation, a bet on any combination of two of the three digits. Also called a bolita or bleeder.

double bagging. a shoplifting technique in which the thief places one shopping bag inside the other with relatively thin merchandise items concealed between the inner and outer bags.

double banging. a pilferage scheme in which a dishonest retail sales clerk uses a customer's credit card to imprint extra copies of blank sales slips. The sales clerk later fills out the blank sales slips, forges the customer's signature, and removes the equivalent sums in cash from the register.

double-base powder. a rapid burning propellant containing two explosive ingredients, usually nitroglycerine and gunpowder.

double buy. a tactic used in conducting an honesty shopping test. A person posing as a shopper will purchase an item and while receiving change from the cashier will suddenly decide to make an additional purchase. The shopper will place the additional item in the same bag, give the cashier exact payment, and leave before the second sale can be rung up in the presence of the shopper. The shopper later provides to store management the sales slip and other details that will allow the transaction to be examined on the register tape. If the cashier used the opportunity to keep the cash related to the second purchase, it will be apparent by the examination.

double celling. the placement of two inmates in a jail or prison cell originally constructed for the custody of only one.

double female. in firefighting operations,

a hose coupling device having two female swivel couplings that permit hose lines to be attached and laid in opposite or reverse directions.

double indemnity. a separate agreement in an insurance policy which obligates the company to pay twice the face amount of the policy if the insured dies as the result of violent and accidental means.

double-jacketed hose. fire hose having two protective jackets outside the rubber lining or tubing.

double jeopardy. to put a person on trial twice for the same offense. A term relating to the common law principle that a person may not be tried in a court of law more than one time for the same crime by the same sovereign.

double-loaded operation. a criminal activity in which two illegal objectives are accomplished. For example, the combining of organizational and transport capabilities of a narcotics trafficking operation with wide-scale distribution and fencing of stolen goods.

double loop. a fingerprint pattern having two separate loop formations, with two separate and distinct sets of shoulders, and two deltas.

double strip search. a type of search conducted at an outdoor crime scene. The area to be searched is delineated by marking into one or more large rectangles. Two or three searchers proceed at the same pace within fingertip distance along paths parallel to the base of the rectangle. When a piece of evidence is found, all searchers halt until it is processed. The search resumes at a given signal. When the searchers reach the end of the rectangle, they turn and proceed back along adjacent lanes, and continue the process until the entire rectangle has been covered. At this point the searchers repeat the process except that the direction of travel is parallel to the side of the rectangle.

double-throw bolt. a bolt that can be projected beyond its first position, into a second, or fully extended one.

Dover's Powder. a substance containing opium. It is used medically as an analgesic and antidiarrheal. This medication produces high physical and psychological dependence, and has a potential for abuse.

downer. a barbiturate or tranquilizer, often taken to counteract the stimulant effects of amphetamines. Also called a downie.

Doyle v. Ohio. a 1976 case in which the U.S. Supreme Court ruled that silence by a suspect in custodial interrogation cannot later be used to impeach his credibility on the stand at trial. In this case, the defendant testified that he had been framed by a person working with police investigators and that after his arrest he had not informed the investigating officers of this claim. The prosecution argued that Doyle's postarrest silence should be subject to inquiry if the defendant testifies at trial. The Supreme Court disagreed, stating that silence in the wake of Miranda warnings may be nothing more than the arrestee's exercise of these rights and that it would be fundamentally unfair and a deprivation of due process to allow an arrested person's silence to be used to impeach an explanation subsequently offered at trial.

dragon's blood powder. a fingerprint powder made from the resin of the rattan palm. It provides contrast for latent prints found in light, dark, and multi-colored surfaces.

dram shop law. a liquor liability law which provides that a person serving someone who is intoxicated or someone contributing to the intoxication of another may be liable for injury or damage caused by the intoxicated person.

Draper v. United States. a case in which the U.S. Supreme Court held that information obtained from an informant, which is conscientiously corroborated by the police, is sufficient to support an arrest and search incidental to the arrest. In this case, a reliable informant told the police the suspect would arrive on a particular train while carrying a satchel containing narcotics. Other information developed by the police was consistent with the informant's information. The police met the train, identified the suspect on the basis of the informant's description, made an arrest, searched the satchel as part of the arrest, and seized a quantity of narcotics which was introduced as evidence at trial.

dried out. detoxified.

drift. the lateral deviation of the flight of a bullet from its true course; the angular difference between the axis of the bore of a gun from which the bullet is fired and the line of its flight path (drift angle), due for the most part to wind currents.

drilled meter theft of service. a theft of electrical service in which the thief (most usually the subscriber to the service) drills a tiny hole in the glass cover of the electric meter and inserts a wire or nail that acts to slow or stop the meter disk. Electric current will flow through the meter unimpeded but the meter will register only a fraction of total use.

drill job. a general term referring to any safecracking technique that involves the use of a drill. Two types of drills are popular with safecrackers: the high torque drill and the core drill. The high torque drill is typically used to create a pattern of drill holes that permits access to and manipulation of the locking mechanism. The core drill has a hollow cylindrical bit that cuts out a solid core. The diameter of the hole is large enough for the safecracker to reach into the safe and remove the contents by hand.

Driodine. the commercial name of a product used in developing latent prints by iodine dusting. Driodine consists of porous glass saturated with iodine. It is poured onto a surface and where latents are present the characteristic iodine-colored prints will form.

drive off. the act of driving off from a service station without paying.

drive-proof spindle. a cone-shaped or shouldered spindle used on a safe's combination lock. The shape of the spindle prevents it from being driven into the safe by striking blows or a penetrating force.

driving tumbler. the tumbler in a safe or vault lock which is connected to the spindle and actuates the other tumblers by picking them up with pegs, studs or mounted pins.

driving while intoxicated (DWI). the crime of operating a motor vehicle while under the intoxicating influence of alcohol, drugs, or any other substance. Also called driving under the influence (DUI).

drop. a place, where by previous arrangement, messages can be left and picked up in secret.

drop-in mouthpiece. a telephone tap transmitter that has the appearance of a genuine telephone carbon microphone, so-called because it is easily inserted into the mouthpiece of a telephone.

dropping the leather. a scam played on the street by two con artists, A and B. A walks past the victim, V, and appears to accidentally drop a wallet. Before V can react, B comes from behind and grabs the wallet. B offers to split the wallet's contents with V. The wallet contains a few small bills and a counterfeit high-denomination bill. B sells to V his share of the high-denomination bill for change or other valuables in V's possession.

drop the service. an action taken by an electric utility company in response to repeated and flagrant theft of electrical service at a particular subscriber location. The action is to completely remove the entire set of service lines strung between the utility pole and the subscriber's structure.

drug. a substance which alters the structure or functions of a living organism. More commonly, nonfood chemical substances that have mood-altering effects. In general use, there is little consistency in popular conceptions of what constitutes a drug. A multitude of often arbitrary, conflicting definitions of the term has contributed significantly to the controversies and confusions surrounding drug use. Many equate drugs only with those illicit substances used recreationally, viewing them as fundamentally different and more harmful than the licit substances used recreationally, such as tea, alcohol, and tobacco, or the so-called medical drugs, such as tranquilizers, amphetamines, and barbiturates. The confusion is so great, in fact, that some argue that a drug is something that has been arbitrarily defined by certain segments of society. As a result of this confusion, it has become increasingly common to refer to all drugs as psychoactive substances in the hope that use of this new term will help to promote a greater recognition of the similarities among all chemical agents that have mood altering effects and dispel the long-standing misconception that there is something fundamentally different between alcohol, coffee, and tobacco, on the one hand, and "drugs" on the other, or that street drugs act according to entirely different principles from medical drugs.

drug abuse. the use of drugs to one's physical, emotional and/or social detriment without being clinically addicted. This term is unstandardized, value-laden, and used with a great deal of imprecision and confusion, generally implying drug use that is excessive, dangerous, or undesirable to the individual or community and that ought to be modified. Some examples of imprecise definitions are: "The tendency of some people to use some certain drugs in ways which are detrimental to their health, or to the community in which they live, or both" and "Drug use that poses a serious threat to health or to social or psychological functioning." Some believe the use of alcohol and coffee to be abusive. Few agree on what is excessive or dangerous. Generally, the public and the law have defined the recreational use of any illicit psychoactive substance as abuse without any demonstration of individual harm or social consequence necessary.

Most definitions involve some component of nonmedical and/or illicit use, with the clear implication that drug use that is legitimated by the medical or legal authorities is better than that which is

not. For example: "The use, sale, or possession of those substances which are prohibited by the laws of the state; use of a drug in amounts hazardous to individual health or the safety of the community, or when it is illicit, or when taken on one's own initiative rather than on the basis of professional advice; the self-administration of drugs without medical supervision and particularly in large doses that may lead to psychological dependency, tolerance and abnormal behavior; persistent and sporadic excessive drug use inconsistent or unrelated to acceptable medical practice; use outside accepted medical practice; use of a drug beyond medically prescribed necessity; use of a drug for other than therapeutic purposes; and the use, usually by self-administration, of any drug in a manner that deviates from approved medical or social patterns within a culture." The fundamental problem with the term is that "abuse" cannot be precisely defined in reference to an actual phenomenon. What one person or group may deem as harmful or excessive to the individual personally or to society in general may not be perceived as problematic by others or by the drug consumer.

Implicitly, the term abuse has come to be the current equivalent of "badness," or of any use of which one does not approve and this notion has become the most common component of all definitions. As such, the use of this term often depends as much, if not more, on political and moral judgments than on considerations of the actual pharmacological action of a drug on an individual's health and the impact of drug-using actions on social welfare. In fact, some have defined the concept of abuse totally in terms of social disapproval, e.g., "Drug abuse is behavior, as designated by professional and other community representatives, describing the use of particular drugs in particular ways that are contrary to the agreed-upon rituals in a given community at a given point in time" and "The use of chemical agents for purposes considered undesirable by an observer." These definitions do not purport to be a description of an actual drug-using pattern but shift the focus to the response to that pattern, and make it clear that abuse is a relative perception. Indeed, for all of its lack of clarity as a descriptor of an actual phenomenon, because "abuse" has developed such a clear connotation of a personal judgment of bad, deviant or excessive, it remains an apt word to use in reference to an attitudinal response to drug use that incorporates these judgments. Many authorities suggest that the term should be avoided entirely as too polemical and value laden, and too inclusive to be scientifically useful in trying to understand various degrees of drug use. Some emphasize that only the term drug use should be employed, a change which may further draw attention to the need to know more about drug use and how it relates to specific problems of use. Some suggest that the terms nonmedical use (i.e., used for nonmedical purposes) and illicit drug use (i.e., defined as illegal by federal or state laws) would better suggest what is wrong with certain kinds of drug use. Other suggestions include distinguishing between socially acceptable use and unacceptable use or conventional use or unconventional use. As abuse is a term more appropriately applied to people than drugs, the term drug misuse is also often used as a substitute.

Drug Abuse Act of 1970. the Comprehensive Drug Abuse Prevention and Control Act of 1970, the first major federal drug legislation since the Harrison Narcotics Act of 1914. All the regulations advanced since the Harrison Act were repealed and replaced by this new statute. Possession penalties were generally reduced, but the act established strict import and export limitations, extended penalties for trafficking, and imposed new controls on previously unregulated psychoactive drugs. The act was designed to create for the first time a comprehensive framework for the regulation of narcotic and nonnarcotic drugs. Title II of this act is known as the Controlled Substance Act and requires registration of every person in the legitimate chain of drug distribution and detailed recordkeeping.

Drug Abuse Control Amendment of 1965. an amendment to federal food, drug, and cosmetic legislation that classified certain stimulants (amphetamines), depressants (barbiturates), and hallucinogens as dangerous drugs. The amendment shifted the constitutional basis for drug control from taxing power to interstate and commerce powers. Penalties are considerably more lenient than those of the Narcotic Drug Control Act Of 1956. The act is intended to crack down on the trade in amphetamine and barbiturate drugs, and several tranquilizers and nonbarbiturate hypnotics and sedatives. It is also aimed at stopping the underground traffic in hallucinogens, which are mostly manufactured in clandestine laboratories or smuggled in from abroad. Under the act, no person may possess any of the proscribed drugs except for personal or family use or for veterinary purposes. Only authorized manufacturers, suppliers, hospitals, agencies, physicians, or researchers can sell, deliver, or otherwise dispose of the proscribed drugs. Persons who manufacture, process, sell, deliver, or otherwise dispose of these drugs must keep records of all drugs so handled. Prescriptions for these drugs are limited to five refills, and none may be refilled after 6 months. Also called the Harris-Dodd Act.

drug abuse violation. in Uniform Crime Reports terminology, a category used to record and report arrests for offenses relating to growing, manufacturing, making, possessing, using, selling, or distributing narcotic and dangerous nonnarcotic drugs.

Drug Abuse Warning Network (DAWN). a federal program started in 1972 by the Bureau of Narcotics and Dangerous Drugs for the purpose of providing information on medical and psychological problems associated with the effects of drug use. Data are received from facilities in 23 cities that are likely to have contact with drug users with these problems, such as general hospital emergency rooms, medical examiners/coroners, and crisis intervention centers. Whereas CODAP (Client Oriented Data Acquisition Process) describes patients coming into treatment, DAWN describes people experiencing emergencies with drugs, whether or not they are in treatment. The aim of the system is to identify drugs that bring people to the attention of emergency facilities and to identify the patterns with the idea of doing something about it if the problem is severe. Approximately 15,000 new case descriptions are added to the DAWN files each month. Presently funded by DEA and NIDA, reports are issued quarterly.

drug addiction. any habitual use of a substance which leads to psychological and/or physiological dependence. As defined by the World Health Organization, it is "A state of periodic or chronic intoxication produced by the repeated consumption of a drug (natural or synthetic), which produces the following characteristics: (1) an overpowering desire or compulsion to continue taking the drug and to obtain it by any means, (2) a tendency to increase the dosage, showing body tolerance, (3) a psychic and generally a physical dependence on the effects of the drug, and (4) the creation of an individual and social problem."

drug arrest. apprehension for a crime involving either the use, possession, cultivation, transportation, or sale of illicit drugs. Drug arrest data are often used as an indication of the extent of drug use, an assumption questioned by many.

drug automatism. the consumption of drugs without conscious awareness of the amount being consumed. It occurs with heavy users of depressants and is believed accountable for some overdose deaths.

drug controls. any organized effort to influence the ways drugs are consumed, distributed, and generally dealt with in a society. The term refers to those factors which bear on the legal, economic, and physical availability of drugs, whether through punitive, preventative, educational, or therapeutic means.

drug copping. peddling or selling drugs to users, typically at well-known places on the street.

drug dealing. peddling or selling drugs. The seller is called a dealer. Dealing has been defined in some jurisdictions to mean "to sell, exchange, give, or dispose" of drugs to another, or "to offer or agree to do the same."

drug dependence. a state arising from repeated administration of a drug on a periodic or continuous basis. It will vary with the agent involved, and types of dependence are frequently designated; for example, morphine dependence or cannabis dependence. Dependence can be said to exist when an individual must continue to take a drug to avoid withdrawal symptoms and/or to gratify some strong emotional need. The term came into general use in the mid-1960s as a replacement for addiction and habituation to help eliminate the confusions and difficulties inherent in those terms. As defined by the WHO expert committee, "a state of psychic or physical dependence or both, on a drug, arising in a person following administration of that drug on a periodic or continuous basis," with the characteristic of dependence varying with the drug involved (i.e., dependence of the morphine type, barbiturate type, amphetamine type, etc.). In this theoretical scheme psychic or psychological dependence is seen as a feeling of satisfaction and psychic drive that requires periodic or continuous administration of the drug to produce pleasure or avoid discomfort. As such, it was regarded as playing a dominant role in causing people to use drugs compulsively, with physical dependence a powerful reinforcing influence.

drug detection. efforts to determine whether a person has been using a drug. The most frequent method of detection is urinalysis, followed by blood analysis.

drug diversion. the redirection of legally manufactured controlled drugs, substances, and implements (paraphernalia) for the administration of drugs into the illegal market. Drug diversion occurs within the legitimate system for distributing drugs through wholesalers, retailers, hospitals, clinics, research agencies, doctors, and nurses. The principal diverters are unscrupulous doctors and pharmacists.

drug education. any program designed to provide information on the use of drugs conveyed via psychological principles and to change knowledge, attitudes, or behavior in a direction desired by the educator.

drug effects. any physiological or psychological reaction a user experiences after taking a drug. Generally, drugs do not produce the same effect in different individuals, nor do they produce the same effect in the same individual at different times under different circumstances. One of the fundamental problems in assessing an adverse drug reaction is the absence of a clear cause-and-effect relationship between a specific drug and a clinical event. What is loosely referred to as a drug effect is a combination of at least three main factors: (1) the pharmacological properties of the drug, (2) the social setting or environmental context in which the drug is taken, and (3) the personality or character structure, attitudes, and expectations of the user.

drug efficacy. the ability of a drug to safely produce a desired or claimed treatment result.

Drug Enforcement Administration (DEA). the lead agency in narcotic and dangerous drug suppression programs at the national and international levels and in federal drug law enforcement. The DEA was established within the Department of Justice in 1973, replacing the Bureau of Narcotics and Dangerous Drugs. The DEA was created to enforce the controlled substances laws and regulations and to bring to the criminal and civil justice system of the United States or other competent jurisdiction, those organizations and individuals involved in the growing, manufacture, or distribution of controlled substances appearing in or destined for illicit traffic in the United States.

drug experimenter. one who illegally, wrongfully or improperly uses a drug for the purpose of experiencing its effect. The exact number of usages is not necessarily as important in determining the category of user as is the intent of the user, the circumstances of use, and the psychological makeup of the user.

drug free treatment. treatment that calls for complete abstinence from drug use of any kind.

drug law violation. the unlawful sale, purchase, distribution, manufacture, cultivation, transport, possession, or use of a controlled or prohibited drug, or attempt to commit these acts.

drug rehabilitation. the technique of helping drug users give up the use of the drugs to which they are habituated or upon which they are dependent, and making them feel that they can be useful and respected among their families, friends, and communities.

drug-related death. a death that results either directly or indirectly from drug use. Broadly, it refers to anything from an overdose suicide to the presence of some unspecified drug in a person killed in an accident. In direct deaths, the drug is a sufficient and necessary condition or cause of death. In indirect deaths, the drug alone is not a sufficient cause of death, but is a necessary contributor to the death in conjunction with some other drug, condition, or agent. In the Drug Abuse Warning Network (DAWN) system, a drug-involved death is (1) any death involving a drug overdose in which a toxic level is found or suspected; and/or (2) any death in which drug usage is a contributory factor although not necessarily the sole cause (e.g., accidents, diseased state, withdrawal symptoms).

drug-related risk. any risk related to drug taking. Such risks are affected by a wide variety of pharmacological, psychological, and sociocultural variables. Within the concept of drug-related risk are two basic types: (1) risk to health; and (2) risk of drug-induced behavior. Implicit in these risk types are risk to the individual health, welfare, and safety, and risk to society in terms of the public health, wealth, and safety. Risk to the individual and public health is posed by such drug-taking consequences as acute reactions in the form of overdose and psychological trauma, or from diseases that may be directly or indirectly related to drug use and physical or psychological problems of short or long duration. Public safety risks of drug use arise primarily from the behavior induced by the drug experience, such as crime or alterations of perception, judgment, or other mental functions, which may result in disordered or hazardous behavior such as loss of impulse control, which may lead to assaultive, aggressive, or violent acts, or impaired, psychomotor function, which may result in hazardous activities such as inadequate operation of a motor vehicle.

drug resistance. the natural ability of an individual to ward off the effect of a drug.

drug subculture. a subculture of society whose members share norms legitimating the use of drugs that are disapproved by the dominant culture and structured around norms regulating the type of drugs used as well as the frequency and mode of use. Subcultural theorists studying the onset of adolescent drug use stress the importance of interpersonal influences and participation in an adolescent subculture that has a distinctive set of values and conduct norms that are at odds with the more conventional values of the adult or parent culture. Subcultural theorists focus on the shared norms, values, role definitions, and patterns of behavior governing consumption of illicit drugs and thus provide a bridge between sociological and psychological theories. The drug subculture is seen as providing a person with an alternative lifestyle centering around knowledge of how to obtain and use drugs and how to evaluate the experi-

ence. In addition, it provides a set of values and norms and gives respect and admiration to those who adhere to these behavioral prescriptions.

drug survey. a study that selects a sample from some larger population in order to ascertain the prevalence, incidence, and interrelations of selected variables related to drug use. A survey is usually one of three types: descriptive, exploratory, and explanatory.

drug toxicity symptom. a sign indicating a toxic drug reaction, such as depression. Symptoms can be associated with particular drugs.

drug use expectations. the physiological and psychological effects that a drug user expects to experience as the consequence of taking a drug.

drunkenness. the state of being drunk, often also referred to as intoxication, although some consider that drunkenness is a more severe state of inebriation than intoxication. In the United States, drunkenness is covered in state statutes. In Uniform Crime Reports terminology, the name of a category used to record and report arrests made for offenses of public drunkenness or other public intoxication, except for the offense of driving under the influence.

dry-chemical extinguisher. a fire extinguisher containing a chemical agent which extinguishes fire by interrupting the chain reaction wherein the chemicals used prevent the union of free radical particles in the combustion process so that combustion does not continue when the flame front is completely covered with the agent. Three types of base chemical agents are used: sodium bicarbonate, potassium bicarbonate, and ammonium phosphate. These are used primarily on Class B and C fires; however, multipurpose dry chemicals are also effective on Class A fires.

dry firing. a safety-oriented firearms teaching technique in which learners practice the basics of shooting without using live ammunition. The technique helps learners develop psychomotor skills relating to sight alignment, breath control, trigger squeeze, and similar fundamentals before they are permitted to engage in live firing.

drying agent. a material, usually calcium chloride, used to remove moisture from air passing through an iodine fuming gun or tube during the development of latent fingerprints.

dry-powder extinguisher. a fire extinguisher designed for use on combustible metals fires. The principle of extinguishment involves the combination effect of dry-chemical powder.

duces tecum. bring with you. The term is applied to a writ commanding the person to whom it is served to bring certain evidence to court. Thus, we speak of a subpoena duces tecum.

due care. that degree of care or action required to be exercised by a person in relation to a given situation in order to avoid negligence or liability.

due process. the procedures and safeguards which ensure a fair trial or hearing; a Constitutional guarantee that no person shall be deprived of his life, liberty, or property without due process of law.

dummy camera. a genuine-appearing but nonfunctional camera used as a crime deterrent. It is typically mounted out of reach in a conspicuous spot at a premises having a history of employee pilferage, shoplifting, misconduct, robbery, etc. Some models are stationary, some scan, and most are equipped with a red pilot lamp. Also called a simulated camera.

dummy charge. a false or fraudulent claim for payment, typically a bogus or altered invoice.

dummy cylinder. a mock cylinder without an operating mechanism, used for appearance only.

dummy loan. a form of internal bank fraud in which a bank employee, such as a loan officer, will establish a fictitious credit file having the appearance of legitimate transactions. The dishonest employee will steal money loaned to the fictitious borrower, sometimes extending and increasing the loan amount on the renewal date. The crime may go entirely undetected if the dishonest employee can arrange for the unrepaid loan to be written off as a bad debt.

Dunaway v. New York. a case in which the Supreme Court rejected as evidence a voluntary confession from an illegally arrested person. In this case, the defendant was detained by the police upon a reasonable suspicion, was taken into custody, transported to a police station, and then interrogated. The Court ruled this practice unreasonable in the absence of probable cause.

This case makes plain that the detention authority possessed by a police officer is limited to a brief stop at the place of investigation. Further steps, such as transportation of the person or station house interrogation, are tantamount to arrest and therefore require probable cause. Failure to meet this standard may result in exclusion of evidence obtained during custody.

Duquenois analysis. a chemical test for detecting cannabis. A portion of the suspected cannabis is placed in a test tube. The Duquenois reagent, consisting of acetaldehyde, ethyl alcohol, and vanillin, is added along with concentrated hydrochloric acid. If the color in the tube undergoes a series of color changes from pink to violet to deep blue, it is an indication that cannabis is present.

duress. to force a person to do something he doesn't want to do.

duress alarm. a device which enables a person placed under duress to call for help without arousing suspicion.

Durham Rule. a rule enunciated in 1954 by the Federal Court of Appeals for the District of Columbia which holds that an accused is not criminally responsible if his unlawful act was the product of mental disease or mental defect.

duster. a cigarette made of tobacco, mint leaves, marijuana, parsley, and powdered PCP.

dusting. the procedure for developing and preserving latent fingerprints. The usual practice is to dip a camel hair brush into a developing powder and apply it gently across the surface containing the prints. Other dusting techniques employ devices that sift, spray or gently drop small clouds of powder onto the latent prints. Excess powder is variously removed by gentle brushing, blowing light drafts of air across the surface, or by the use of a magnet that picks up metal-based developing powder.

dutchman. a short fold of hose in a fire truck body arranged in such a way to prevent snags when the hose is played out.

dwelling house. any building used as a dwelling, such as an apartment house, tenement house, hotel, boarding room, dormitory, institution, sanitarium, house or structure used or intended for use as a place of habitation by human beings.

dying declaration. a declaration or statement, either in writing or verbal, made to anyone, of the material facts concerning the assault upon him which constituted a homicide. It is made by the declarant under the firm belief that he is about to die without any hope of recovery. This statement, although hearsay, is admissible as an exception to the hearsay rule, on the ground that a person who is about to die is not likely to state a falsehood. Courts have accepted dying declarations as equivalent to a solemn appeal to God upon an oath. However, great caution is exercised before allowing such a statement as evidence. The declaration must not amount to a narration of past events, and it must state facts relating to the circumstances that result in the homicide, and the perpetrator thereof. The requirements for admitting a dying declaration into evidence are: (1) the declarant was in extremis, i.e., dying; (2) the declarant was under a sense of impending death, without any hope of recovery in his mind; (3) the declarant, if living, would have been a competent witness; (4) the declaration must be limited to the circumstances of the death and the perpetrator; and (5) the declarant must die.

dynamite. an explosive compound usually produced in stick form. The explosive charge is surrounded by sawdust entirely wrapped in wax-coated paper. As some dynamite ages it exudes nitroglycerin beads or crystals and in this condition is highly dangerous to handle.

dysfunctional drug use. drug use that results in physical, psychological, economic, legal, and/or social harm to the individual user or to others affected by the drug user's behavior. While not all drug use can be clearly identified as functional or dysfunctional, the effort to link the functionality of drug use to the effects of that use is helpful in that many such effects can be quantified and an estimate of their associated costs generated. It is in relation to such costs that the benefits deriving from effective prevention efforts can be determined.

dyspnea. difficulty or distress in breathing; frequent, rapid, labored breathing. In polygraphy, labored breathing or shortness of breath. It appears on the polygram as suppression or serration of the pneumograph tracing.

early case closure. the suspension of an investigation before its solution.

earth shock. in bomb incident investigations, a detonation wave transmitted through the ground.

easy mark. an unwary or unprotected criminal target.

eavesdropping. an imprecise term that covers two distinct kinds of activity: (1) wiretapping, and (2) mechanical overhearing of a conversation. It is the interception of oral communications in a surreptitious effort to hear what is being said, without knowledge of at least one of the persons speaking. When hidden electronic equipment is used, the process is called bugging, the equipment is a bug, and the premises are said to be bugged.

eccentricity. as used in criminal law and medical jurisprudence, personal or individual peculiarities of mind and disposition which markedly distinguish a person from the ordinary person, but which do not amount to mental unsoundness or insanity.

ecclesiastical law. laws pertaining to the church derived from the canon and civil law; laws that advocate worship in the church and extreme veneration for the authority, forms, and traditions of the church.

echelon formation. a riot control formation consisting of officers moving forward along a diagonal line. Its principal use is to drive an unruly crowd in a given direction, such as down a street. Also called diagonal formation.

echolalia. the constant and senseless repetition of particular words or phrases, recognized as a sign of insanity or of aphasia.

echo suppressor. a line device used to prevent energy from being reflected back to the transmitter.

ecstasy. a derivative of mescaline and amphetamine.

edema. a swelling or accumulation of excessive fluid in cells, tissues, or cavities.

edge marks. marks placed on playing cards between the edge and the design to facilitate cheating.

effective representation. an expansion of the right to counsel requiring that counsel provide a competent defense.

eight-story coat. a coat, similar in design to a bulky hunting jacket, having several tiers of large inner pockets for concealing shoplifted merchandise.

Eilkins v. United States. a 1960 case in which the U.S. Supreme Court ruled that all illegally seized evidence is inadmissible in federal courts. In 1961, the rule was extended to all state and local trials. This case ended the controversial practice by federal police officers of asking state or local officers to seize evidence, frequently illegally, in order to circumvent rules prohibiting the introduction of illegally seized evidence in federal prosecutions.

ejector. the mechanism that throws the cartridge or fired case from a firearm.

ejector marks. the imprints made on a cartridge case by contact with the ejector of a firearm. These imprints help the firearms examiner to match a cartridge case with a particular firearm.

electric dice. dice that can be influenced by an electromagnetic control concealed in a gaming table.

electric Kool-Aid. Kool-Aid or a soft drink laced with LSD.

electric teeth. a name given to police-controlled traffic radar used to detect speeders.

electrocardiogram (ECG or EKG). a graph of the electrical pattern occurring during the contraction and relaxation of the heart muscles.

electrode jelly. in polygraphy, a gelatinous substance used to enhance electrical contact between the galvanic skin response attachments and the examinee's fingers or hands.

electroencephalogram (EEG). a graph of the electrical impulses in the brain.

electron capture detector. a device that captures and analyzes vapors associated with suspected explosives.

electronic countermeasures. defensive techniques designed to detect, prevent or expose the use of electronic audio or visual surveillance devices.

Electronic Funds Transfer Act. an act that defines the rights, liabilities and responsibilities of the various participants in electronic funds transfer systems. The act also provides for penalties for anyone who uses any counterfeit, altered, forged, fictitious, lost, stolen or fraudulently obtained debit instrument.

electronic stethoscope. in electronic surveillance, a contact microphone, such as a spike microphone, or a physician's stethoscope equipped with an electronic amplifier.

electronic surveillance. a generic term that refers to eavesdropping or wiretapping by means of electronic listening and recording devices. Bugging, consent recording, and consent transmitting are activities that fall within the general meaning of electronic surveillance.

electronic theft detection system. any of several types of electronic article surveillance systems used in retail stores, libraries and other places vulnerable to pilferage.

electron microscope. a microscope which uses high-voltage streams of electrons to bring into visibility objects far beyond the range of the most powerful optical microscopes. Magnifications are possible of up to 100,000 times the original size. Its uses in the crime laboratory include: (1) identifying substances, chemically and physically, by particle size, shape, and distribution; (2) determining age of certain substances by noting the structural changes; (3) identifying minute particles of fibers; and (6) comparing different inks, pencil writing, etc.

electrophoresis. a laboratory analysis technique, similar to thin layer chromatography, that is useful in evaluating drugs and blood. The sample to be analyzed is spotted on a plate coated with a thin layer of support material such as silica gel. An electrical charge is passed across the support material. The sample will migrate on the plate and separate into its components. The analyst compares the observed pattern against patterns of known substances. This technique can be used to separate certain proteins or enzymes in blood. For example, it can be used in a crime laboratory to determine whether Sickle cell hemoglobin is present in certain evidence.

elements of the crime. the conduct defined in law to constitute a crime. A single element is often a key element of more than one offense.

eligible for parole. the status of a person committed to the jurisdiction of a federal or state prison system and usually in confinement in an institution, who by a combination of such factors as sentence effective date, statutory credit deductions, and individual sentence, can legally be considered for release from confinement in prison to parole status.

elint. electronic intelligence; the use of electronics technology to intercept messages.

El Paso Intelligence Center (EPIC). a center operated at El Paso, Texas by the Drug Enforcement Administration. The mission of EPIC is to gather intelligence on large-scale drug smuggling activities. Communications with friendly aircraft, ships at sea, and satellites allows EPIC to identify drug staging areas, places of departure used by smugglers, and their routes and destinations. Many of the personnel who work at the center are on loan from other agencies, such as the Customs Service, Coast Guard, Federal Aviation Administration, and Alcohol, Tax and Firearms.

embezzlement. the misappropriation, misapplication or illegal disposal of entrusted property with intent to defraud the owner or beneficiary.

embolus. a plug, composed of a detached clot, air bubble, mass of bacteria, or other foreign body, occluding a blood vessel.

embracery. an attempt to influence a jury corruptly to one side or the other by promises, persuasions, entreaties, entertainments and similar inducements.

embroidery. the pattern of hypodermic-needle abscesses and puncture points commonly found on the arms and legs of drug addicts.

emergency care. the care, packaging, extrication, and transportation of an ill or injured individual by trained personnel until definitive treatment is begun or continued at a medical facility.

emergency descent chair. a conveyance designed to carry a disabled person through a stairwell when elevators are shut down, such as during a fire in a high rise building.

emergency medical technician (EMT). the civilian counterpart of the skilled military paramedic who brings the emergency facility's capabilities closer to the patient. During transport, the EMT manages the life-support systems within a mobile unit and continues treatment and communication with the physician or emergency facility.

emergency response. the response made by firefighters, police, health care personnel and/or other emergency service upon notification of an incident in which human life and/or property may be in jeopardy.

emesis. the act of vomiting expelled stomach contents.

emetic. an agent which will induce vomiting.

eminent domain. the power of the government to acquire land or property of a private individual for a necessary public purpose.

emission. as used in medical jurisprudence, the ejection of any secretion or other matter from the body such as the expulsion of urine, feces or semen.

emission spectrograph. a laboratory instrument that uses optical principles to analyze a wide variety of substances. The sample to be analyzed is burned in an arc between two graphite electrodes. The light emitted in the burning process is passed through a prism or reflected from an optical grating which breaks up the light into its component wave lengths. Since it is known that each element will emit light at wave lengths characteristic of that element and no other, the sample can be precisely identified.

emotion-evoking question. a question that is usually inserted as the last question in a polygraph test. It is designed to elicit a response that will assist the examiner in determining the subject's reaction capacity.

empathetic questioning technique. an interview and interrogation technique in which the questioner empathizes and identifies with the subject's situation. The questioner may (1) describe the crime as being less serious than it is, (2) suggest that many people, the questioner included, have been in a similar situation, (3) suggest that the subject is the victim of circumstances that need to be fully explained in order to be understood, or (4) allow the subject an opportunity to pass moral or ethical (but not legal) blame on the victim or others. For example, in a sexual assault case the questioner might suggest that the decaying moral standards of society inevitably lead to such crimes.

encipher. to scramble data or convert it, prior to transmission, to a secret code that masks the meaning of the data to any unauthorized recipient; to convert plain text into ciphertext.

encryption/decryption process. the process of encoding and decoding information so that its content is not easily obvious to anyone who obtains it. To encrypt is to transform intelligible information, known as plaintext, into a coded and therefore unintelligible form, known as ciphertext. The ciphertext is unintelligible except to those who possess the key to the code and the ability to apply the key in the prescribed manner. The process of applying the key is decryption. It is the reversal of encryption.

In most cryptographic operations, the information that is encrypted is designed to be decrypted. In some cases, however, the extreme sensitivity of information may require that it never be available in plaintext form after its initial generation and distribution. When information of this type has been encrypted, it is not reversible even to authorized persons. This is called a one-way function.

The hardware, firmware, software, documents and associated procedures are called a cryptosystem.

end-of-the-line question. a question asked by an interviewer at the end of a line of questions or at the end of an interview. For instance, "Is that all of what you saw?" or "Is there something you wish to add, change or delete?"

endorsement. writing one's name, either with or without additional words, on a negotiable instrument or on a paper (called an allonge) attached to it. By an endorsement, the endorser becomes liable to all subsequent holders in due course for payment of the instrument if it is not paid by the maker when properly presented and if he is given notice of dishonor.

enforcement index. the ratio of traffic warnings, citations, and arrests to the frequency of traffic accidents, or the ratio of moving traffic violation convictions per traffic accident. Such ratios are useful in evaluating the efficiency of a department in terms of the number of accidents that occur in the community or certain areas of the community. It has been hypothesized that for each moving traffic violation, three warning notices should have been written, and for each injury accident, thirty warning notices or ten such citations. Thus, if 50 accidents occurred in a certain month, the following month should show 1500 warning notices or 500 citations. The rationale for a quota system such as this is based on the fact that moving violations cause accidents, and that steps taken to suppress violations will reduce the number of accidents.

enjoin. require or command, as in the injunction of a court directing a person or person to do or not do certain acts.

Enmund v. Florida. a case in which the U.S. Supreme Court ruled that to impose the death sentence upon an accomplice to capital murder committed in the course of a felony it must be shown at trial that the accomplice killed, attempted to kill, intended that a killing take place, or intended that lethal force be employed.

entrapment. the act of an agent of the government to induce a person to commit a crime which was not contemplated by such person, for the purpose of instituting criminal prosecution. The mere act of furnishing the opportunity to commit a crime where the accused is predisposed to commit the crime is not entrapment.

entrapment defense. a defense against prosecution which argues that an accused should not be charged if he was induced to commit a crime for the mere purpose of instituting criminal prosecution against him. Generally, where the criminal intent originates in the mind of the accused and the criminal offense is completed by him, the fact that a law enforcement officer furnished the accused an opportunity for commission does not constitute entrapment. But where the criminal intent originates in the mind of the officer and the accused is lured into the commission, no conviction may be had.

entry to parole. a release from prison by discretionary action of a paroling authority, conditional upon the parolee's fulfillment of specified conditions of behavior.

enveloping question. in polygraphy, a question inserted at the beginning and end of a probing peak of tension test. An enveloping question is beyond the realm of possibility concerning the issue being evaluated, i.e., it is neutral or irrelevant. Also called a padding question.

EOD incident. the suspected or actual presence of explosive ordinance which constitutes a hazard.

epilepsy. a chronic disorder characterized by sudden attacks of brain dysfunction, usually associated with an alteration of consciousness. The attacks may range from simple impairment of behavior to generalized convulsions.

episodic criminal. a noncriminal person who commits a crime when under extreme emotional stress; a person who breaks down and commits a crime as a single incident during the regular course of natural and normal events. The episodic criminal is seen as being normal in every respect except that under certain stresses he or she cannot adequately cope, and as a result erupts in an explosive manner. For example, a husband who in the heat of jealous passion kills someone he believes to be romantically involved with his wife.

episodic excessive drinker. a classification of alcohol user who becomes intoxicated at a rate of four times per year.

epistaxis. nose bleed; nasal hemorrhage.

equal employment opportunity (EEO). a system of employment practices within an organization under which individuals are not excluded from participation, advancement, or benefit because of race, color, religion, sex, national origin, or other factor which cannot lawfully be the basis for employment actions; an employment system in which neither intentional or unintentional discrimination operates.

Equal Employment Opportunity Commission (EEOC). a federal agency authorized by Congress to enforce federal laws that prohibit discrimination in all aspects of employer and employee relationships on the basis of race, ethnic origin, nationality, language, creed, gender, age, or other specified personal characteristics.

erector-set fraud. a criminal practice in which: (1) an automobile owner arranges for his automobile to be stolen, (2) the owner collects from the insurance company, (3) the automobile is stripped and the skeleton of it is abandoned so it can be found, (4) the automobile owner buys the skeleton from the insurance company for little or nothing, and (5) the owner then rebuilds the automobile with the same parts originally stripped from it.

ergonomics. the study of human characteristics for the appropriate design of the living and work environments. Ergonomics is based on the methodologies of anthropometry, physiology, psychology, engineering and their interrelationships.

ergotin tartrate. an ergot fungus poison used to induce abortion, but which also pro-

duces as side effects diarrhea, convulsions, headache, nausea and vomiting.

error in law. an error by the court in administering the law.

erythroxylon coca. the coca plant which is cultivated in the Andean highlands of South America. Cocaine is derived from the coca plant.

escape. the unlawful departure of a lawfully confined person from official custody.

Escobedo v. Illinois. a case in which the U.S. Supreme Court ruled that a suspect has the right to consult with counsel during interrogation. In this case, the defendant's attorney, who was present at the police station while his client was being interrogated, was not allowed to see or counsel with his client. The Court observed that the police had not warned Escobedo of his right to remain silent which was something that his attorney might well have done had he been present during the interrogation.

Espionage Act. an act that provides criminal penalties for unlawfully accessing and disclosing information.

ethyl bromacetate. a chemical compound that produces severe weeping of the eyes. It is the active ingredient in some types of tear gas grenades.

eupnea. in polygraphy, regular breathing as represented in the inked tracing of the pneumograph component.

euthanasia. mercy killing, such as assisting in or hastening the death of a terminally ill person, with or without the person's consent.

evaluation. the process of determining the value, credibility, reliability, pertinency, accuracy and use of an item of information, an intelligence product, or the performance of an intelligence system.

even money buy. a tactic used in conducting an honesty shopping test. A person posing as a regular shopper will select an item, pay for it with cash in the exact amount, and leave before the sale can be rung up in the shopper's presence. The tactic provides the cashier with an apparently safe opportunity to pocket the cash. Another person also posing as a regular shopper observes the cashier to see if the sale is rung up as would be required by store procedures.

evidence. anything which tends to prove a fact in question in a court of law.

evidence tape. tape specially designed to reveal tampering or breaking. It is used to seal containers in which evidence is placed for safekeeping.

examination before trial. a legal procedure which permits one litigant to make the other answer questions under oath before the actual trial of the case.

exception. a statement made by a counsel in a trial, objecting to a ruling by a judge. The statement is made for the trial record so as to permit appeal on the ground that the ruling was incorrect.

exceptional clearance. an investigative technique in which a criminal's methods of operation are related to other, uncleared crimes.

exception principle. a principle of management in which only exceptional results, good or bad, are brought to the attention of decision-makers.

excessive bail. a sum of money set as bail that is far higher than would be expected under the circumstances of the crime, and in excess of the amount which would reasonably assure the defendant's appearance at subsequent proceedings involving him. Excessive bail is prohibited by the Eighth Amendment to the United States Constitution. Determination of whether bail is excessive is sometimes made by a higher court, which may decrease, confirm, or increase the bail or allow the accused to be released on his own recognizance.

exclusionary rule. a rule which states that any evidence collected during an illegal search will not be accepted in court.

exclusive jurisdiction. a jurisdiction in which the federal government possesses all the authority of the state, and in which the state concerned has not reserved to itself the right to exercise any authority concurrently with the United States, except the right to serve civil or criminal process relating to activities which occurred off the area.

exculpatory clause. a clause in a contract that frees one or more parties from fault or guilt.

excusable homicide. the intentional but justifiable killing of another person or the unintentional killing of another by accident or misadventure, without gross negligence.

ex delicto. arising from a tort.

execute. to put to death by legal means. Also, to carry out or do something, such as to execute a search warrant.

executive. the highest position in a hierarchy; the person who has authority over, and responsibility for, all elements of the organization; in government, the branch that is given the duty of enforcing the laws established by the legislature.

executive action. in espionage, a violent action including assassination or sabotage.

executive action group. a small group or team of government-sponsored experts who specialize in the removal, by assassination or other means, of unfriendly foreign leaders.

executive branch. the segment of government that is responsible for the administration, direction, control, and performance of government. Examples include the President of the United States, state governors, and city mayors. The police and correctional subsystems are under the executive branch.

executive clemency. the sovereign prerogative to extend mercy, exercised in the United States by the President, for federal and military offenses, and within the states by the governor, for violations of the state penal law. Examples of executive clemency include amnesty, commutation of sentence, pardon, and reprieve.

exemplar. a sample the origin of which is known. For example, handwriting samples taken directly from a suspect by an investigator are called handwriting exemplars.

exemplary damages. a sum assessed by the jury in a tort action (over and above the compensatory damages) as punishment in order to make an example of the wrongdoer and to deter like conduct by others. Injuries caused by willful, malicious, wanton, and reckless conduct subject the wrongdoers to exemplary damages. Also called punitive damages.

ex gratia. as a matter of favor.

exhibitionism. sexual gratification obtained through exhibiting the genitals to an involuntary bystander.

exhumation. the digging up of that which has been buried; disinterment of a human body. A body may be removed from its burial place by a court order. The purpose of an exhumation is usually for autopsical purposes, but the chemicals used in embalming are likely to seriously interfere with this process.

exigent circumstances. a situation requiring immediate action which permits certain latitude with regard to arrest, search and seizure.

exit wound. the wound caused by an exiting bullet. The shape of an exit wound will vary according to where it exits (whether through a fleshy or bony structure), the shape of the bullet as it exits (whether pristine or flattened), and the motion of the bullet (whether spinning or tumbling). Exit wound shapes include marks that are stellate (star-like), slit-like, everted (inside-out), and irregular.

ex-offender. an adult who has been convicted of a criminal offense and who is no longer under the jurisdiction of any criminal justice agency.

ex officio. an act done by a person merely by virtue of the office he or she holds.

exonerate. to remove blame from a person.

ex parte. on one side only; by or for one party.

expert testimony. opinion or conclusions given by a witness who has certain unusual qualifications to interpret evidence bearing on a disputed issue. The principal function of an expert witness is to render necessary assistance to the court in the interpretation of evidential facts which have been presented to it. Certain inferences as to material issues may be drawn from those facts, but special training or experience is required to draw the proper inferences. The witness is typically skilled in a particular art, trade or profession or possessed of special knowledge derived from education and/or experience not within the range of common experience, education or knowledge.

expert witness. a person who, on the basis of his training, work or experience as an expert in the field, is qualified to testify on the standard and scientific facts in a particular science, trade or art.

expiration of sentence. the termination of the period of time during which an offender has been required to be under the jurisdiction of a state prison or parole agency as the penalty for an offense.

exploitation. the process of acquiring information from any source and taking full advantage of it.

explosimeter. a device which detects and measures the presence of gas or vapor in an explosive atmosphere.

explosion. a violent bursting or expansion as the result of the release of great pressure. It may be caused by an explosive or by the sudden release of pressure, as in the disruption of a steam boiler. An explosive produces an explosion by virtue of its very rapid self-propagating transformation into more stable substances, accompanied by the liberation of heat and the formation of gas.

explosion-proof device. any device, such as a contact switch, enclosed in an explosion-proof housing to help prevent possible sparking in a potentially volatile environment.

explosive. any chemical compound or chemical mixture that, under the influence of heat pressure, friction or shock, undergoes a sudden chemical change (decomposition) with the liberation of energy in the form of heat and light and accompanied by a large volume of gas.

explosive ordnance. a Department of Defense term meaning munitions containing explosives, nuclear fission, or fusion materials and biological and chemical agents. Included in the term are bombs and warheads, guided and ballistic missiles, artillery, mortars, rocket and small arms ammunition, mines, torpedoes and depth charges, pyrotechnics, cartridges and propellant-actuated devices, electro-explosive devices, clandestine and improvised explosive devices, and all similar or related items or components that are explosive in nature.

explosive ordnance disposal. the detection, identification, field evaluation, rendering safe, recovery, evacuation, and disposal of explosive ordnance which has been fired, dropped, launched, projected, or placed in such a manner as to constitute a hazard to operations, installations, people, or material. It also includes the rendering safe and/or disposal of items which have become hazardous or unserviceable by damage or deterioration when the disposal of such items is beyond the capabilities of technicians normally assigned the responsibility for routine disposition.

explosive range. the percentage of vapor or gas in air by volume which determines the upper and lower limits of explosivity or flammability. For example, the explosive range of propane is 2.2 to 9.5 percent. Any mixture of propane below 2.2 or above 9.5 percent will not ignite. The range below 2.2 is too lean and above 9.5 percent it is too rich.

explosives classifications. classifications established by the U.S. Department of Transportation in which: (1) Class A explosives are materials that possess a detonating hazard (e.g., dynamite, nitroglycerin, picric acid, lead azide, fulminate of mercury, black powder, blasting caps and detonating primers), (2) Class B explosives are materials that possess a flammable hazard (e.g., propellant explosives), and (3) Class C explosives are materials which contain restricted quantities of Class A and/or B explosives.

explosives detector. a device that detects components of explosive devices or explosive compounds by radiographic analysis, by analyzing chemical emissions, or by other methods.

explosive sensitivity. the ease with which an explosive will react to heat, shock or friction.

explosives taggants. small granules added to commercial explosives during manufacture. The taggants are intended to provide investigative leads in criminal bombing cases. A typical taggant is smaller than a grain of sand and will have several layers of different colors. One layer might be sensitive to magnets to aid in retrieval from bomb debris, another layer might be sensitive to ultraviolet light to aid in visual detection at the crime scene, and other layers might contain codes that reveal the manufacturer, lot number and other details useful in identifying the purchaser.

ex post facto. after the fact.

ex post facto law. an unconstitutional law that makes an act a crime when the crime was committed before the law existed.

exposure of person. the intentional exposure in a public place of the naked body or the private parts so performed as to shock the feelings of chastity or to corrupt the morals of the community.

express enactment. a law that affirms, extends, abolishes, or modifies a common law doctrine laid down by the courts. Express enactments of the legislatures are usually called statute law. When conflict exists between common law and statute law, the statute prevails. All of the states have put their common law crimes into some statutory form. Many statutes are simply re-statements of the common law. The criminal statutes are the imperative commands of elected lawmakers.

express questioning. interrogation or its functional equivalent. Express questioning is words or actions on the part of the police that they should know are reasonably likely to elicit an incriminating response from a suspect. The latter part of this definition focuses primarily on the perceptions of the suspect, rather than the intent of the police. The term was used by the U.S. Supreme Court in its discussion of interrogation in the Miranda case.

expulsion grenade. a type of grenade used to deliver a chemical agent to the target.

Upon bursting, the expulsion grenade immediately releases a relatively small but highly concentrated agent cloud. The instantaneous release renders the grenade ineffective if it is thrown back. Also called a bursting grenade.

expunge. the sealing or purging of arrest, criminal or juvenile record information.

exsanguinate. to bleed to death; to hemorrhage so severely that all or most of the blood is expelled from the body.

extenuating circumstances. particular characteristics of an offense or an offender that partially or entirely excuse the offender or serve to reduce the gravity of the crime.

exterior lighting. lighting that is intended to offset the advantages given to the criminal by the cover of darkness. The advantages of darkness to the criminal are: (1) the reduced likelihood that police patrols, residents or passersby will observe criminal activity in progress, (2) the criminal is able to watch a target without being seen and to escape if detected, (3) the natural fear that people have of being out-of-doors at night reduces the opportunity for detection of criminal activity in progress, and (4) the criminal has the element of surprise to gain control over his victims.

external cardiac massage. a rhythmical massage of the heart between the lower sternum in the front and the vertebral column in the back.

external funds. funds available to a police agency from a source other than its parent government.

extort. to gain by wrongful methods; to obtain in an unlawful manner; to compel surrender of money or property by threats of injury to person, property or reputation.

extortion. unlawful demanding or receiving of favors, money or property through the use of fear or force or the authority of office. Blackmail, ransom demands and threats are forms of extortion.

extract. a verbatim portion or combination of portions of an official document.

extractor. the mechanism in a firearm by which a cartridge of a fired case is withdrawn from the chamber.

extractor mark. a mark observable on or near the rim of a fired shell caused by an extractor. An extractor mark is an important identifying characteristic to a firearms examiner.

extradite. to return a fugitive to the place from which he fled.

extradition. the surrender upon request by one jurisdiction to another of an individual accused or convicted of an offense in the requesting jurisdiction; the surrender of a criminal by a foreign state to which he has fled for refuge from prosecution to the demanding state in whose jurisdiction he is charged with having committed a crime.

extrasystole. in polygraphy, a characteristic formation sometimes observed in the cardiographic tracing. It results from a premature contraction of the heart. The cause may be a double heartbeat, as in the case of a cardiac disorder, or a short, emotional surge.

extremis. the state of a person who is near death and beyond hope of recovery.

eyewitness. one who has been present at a crime while it was being committed, or shortly before or after. An eyewitness is usually called to testify as to what he saw or heard.

eyewitness identification. the identification of a defendant in a police lineup or in court. The person making the identification is usually the victim or someone who witnessed the act and the person identified is the person who committed the act.

fabricated evidence. evidence manufactured or arranged so as to intentionally deceive.

fact finder. the individual or group with the obligation and authority to determine the facts in a case. In a jury trial, the jury is the fact finder and is charged with accepting the law as given to it by the judge.

factor analysis. any of several methods of analyzing the intercorrelations among sets of variables.

fail safe. a feature of an alarm system that announces a mechanical breakdown in the system or to any of its component parts.

Fair Credit Reporting Act. an act that provides criminal penalties for unlawfully accessing or disclosing information pertaining to consumers. The act requires that a credit applicant be advised if a consumer report may be requested and be told the scope of the possible inquiry. Should the applicant's request for credit be declined because of information contained in that report, the applicant must be given the name and address of the reporting agency.

fair on its face. a process issued by a court having competent jurisdiction which has the appearance of being legal in every respect. It is not necessary that the process be complete in every detail, only that it contain the substantial parts and is absent anything which might indicate defect or impropriety.

fair preponderance. the measure of evidence required in a civil case for the plaintiff to prevail over the defendant. This is to be distinguished from the requirement in a criminal case that the defendant be found guilty beyond a reasonable doubt.

fallout. the process of precipitation to earth of particulate matter from a nuclear cloud, also applied in a collective sense to the particulate matter itself. Although not necessarily so, such matter is generally radioactive.

false alarm rate. the number of false alarms per installation per month or year. Because false alarms represent a drain on available police resources, many departments have established false alarm reduction programs which include (1) educating subscribers to properly use and care for alarm equipment, (2) educating potential subscribers as to the proper applications of alarms and their limitations, (3) warning potential subscribers concerning poor quality equipment and poor quality installation, (4) enforcing licensing procedures to ensure that alarm dealers and installers meet the established criteria for workmanship, service and quality of equipment, and (5) placing controls on the quality and number of alarms that are in direct connection to the police department.

false alteration. alteration of a written instrument without the authority of anyone entitled to grant it, whether the alteration be in complete or incomplete form, by means of erasure, obliteration, deletion, insertion of new matter, or in any other manner, so that such instrument in the altered form appears or purports to be in all respects an authentic creation of or fully authorized by its apparent maker or drawer.

false arrest. the detention of a person by another who claims to have official authority which is in fact invalid.

false entry. an entry in an official record intentionally made to represent what is not true or does not exist, with intent to deceive or defraud.

false imprisonment. to unlawfully restrain a person's freedom of movement. Also called forcible detainment. When false imprisonment is accompanied by transport of the victim, the offense is sometimes called abduction.

false pretense. a designed misrepresentation of existing fact or condition for the purpose of obtaining another's money or goods.

false representation. a representation which

is untrue, willfully made to deceive another to his injury.

false statement. a statement more than merely untrue or erroneous and made with intention to deceive.

false token. a false document or a sign of the existence of a fact. An example is counterfeit money.

false witness. one who is intentionally rather than merely mistakenly false.

falsify. to counterfeit or forge; to tamper with as in falsifying a record or document.

Fare v. Scott William K. a 1979 case in which the California Supreme Court held that the constitutional provisions of search and seizure extend to minor children. In this case, the Court ruled that neither the parents' authority over minor children nor the parents' consent excused the police from getting a search warrant before opening a locked toolbox in the child's bedroom that he occupied in his parents' home. Police officers arrested the defendant without a warrant at his home on information given to the police by his mother. The arresting officers then obtained consent from the father to search the defendant son's bedroom in the house. The searching officers found nine bags of marihuana in the defendant's locked toolbox. The California Supreme Court held that the defendant, being 17 years old, was able to assert his own rights and that his refusal to allow the police to search his toolbox was effective.

fat doctor. a physician who reaps large profits from prescribing or dispensing excessive quantities of amphetamines, ostensibly for the treatment of weight problems.

feasance. the doing of an act; a performing or performance.

fecal matter identification. a crime laboratory technique for identifying persons through the microscopic examination of fecal matter. Several studies have concluded that a person can be matched to fecal matter; for example, feces found at a crime scene.

Federal Bureau of Investigation (FBI). the general enforcement agency for federal crimes whose enforcement authority is not assigned to another federal agency, such as the Internal Revenue Service. The FBI is also charged with domestic security responsibilities. It compiles and publishes annual statistics on crime.

Federal Bureau of Narcotics (FBN). an agency created in 1930 within the U.S. Treasury Department and made responsible for administering and enforcing those sections of the Internal Revenue Code which placed taxes on narcotics and marihuana. The FBN also enforced the Opium Poppy Control Act of 1942 and the Narcotic Drugs Import and Export Act of 1922. Its goal was to prevent, detect, and investigate violations of laws prohibiting unauthorized possession, sale, or transfer of opium, opium derivatives, synthetic opiates, cocaine, and marihuana. In 1968, the FBN was transferred to the Department of Justice and merged with the Bureau of Drug Abuse Control to create the Bureau of Narcotics and Dangerous Drugs (BNDD).

Federal Communications Act of 1934. an act which in part provides that "no person not being authorized by the sender shall intercept any wire or radio communication and divulge its existence, contents, substance, purport, effect, or meaning," to any person.

Federal Communications Commission (FCC). a board of commissioners appointed by the President under the Federal Communications Act of 1934, having the power to regulate all interstate and foreign electrical telecommunication systems originating in the United States.

Federal Coordinating Officer (FCO). a person appointed by the President of the United States to coordinate the overall federal response to a major nuclear disaster or emergency.

federal crimes. criminal offenses prohibited by acts of the United States Congress. There can be no federal crime unless Congress first makes an act a criminal offense by the passage of a statute, affixes punishment to it, and declares what court will have jurisdiction. This means that all federal crimes are statutory. Although many of the statutes are based on common law, every federal statute is an express enactment of Congress. Nearly all crimes are defined in Title 18 of the United States Code.

Generally speaking, federal crimes fall into three large areas: crimes affecting interstate commerce, crimes committed in places beyond the jurisdiction of any state, and crimes which interfere with the activities of the federal government.

Crimes affecting interstate commerce are described in a variety of acts, e.g., the Mann Act, the Dyer Act, the Lindbergh Act, the Fugitive Felon Act, etc. They cover a wide variety of offenses over which Congress has plenary control.

Crimes committed in places beyond the jurisdiction of any state might include, for example, murder on an American ship on the high seas or on a federal enclave such as a military reservation ceded to the United States by a state. It should be noted that when an offense, not covered by a federal statute, is committed on a federal enclave, the case can be tried in a federal court under the laws of the state where the enclave is located. The offense of murder, for example, is not defined in a federal statute. If murder occurs on a military reservation in Texas, the federal government can prosecute the case using the Texas statute covering murder. This procedure is authorized by the Assimilative Crimes Act.

Crimes which interfere with the activities of the federal government include fraudulent use of the mails, robbery of a federal bank, violation of income tax laws, espionage and many similar offenses. Federal courts have no jurisdiction over crimes against the states, and vice versa. It can happen, however, that an offense will violate both a state law and a federal law, e.g., robbery of a federally insured state bank. In such a case, both the federal and state court will have jurisdiction.

Federal Crime Insurance Program. a federally administered program under which pooling insurance companies write crime insurance for those unable to secure it in the open market.

federal death penalty laws. statutes that have been enacted by the U.S. Congress which if violated can result in the death sentence. These laws include: (1) espionage by a member of the Armed Forces in which information relating to nuclear weaponry, military spacecraft or satellites, early warning systems, war plans, communications intelligence or cryptographic information, or any other major weapons or defense strategy is communicated to a foreign government, (2) death resulting from aircraft hijacking, (3) murder while a member of the Armed Forces, (4) destruction of aircraft, motor vehicles, or related facilities resulting in death, (5) retaliatory murder of a member of the immediate family of a law enforcement official, (6) murder of a member of Congress, an important executive official, or a Supreme Court justice, (7) espionage, (8) destruction of government property resulting in death, (9) first degree murder, (10) mailing of-injurious articles with the intent to kill or resulting in death, (11) assassination or kidnapping resulting in the death of the President or Vice President, (12) willful wrecking of a train resulting in death, (13) murder or kidnapping related to robbery of a bank, and (14) treason.

federal exclusionary rule. a U.S. Supreme Court ruling that any evidence obtained through an unlawful search and seizure by the police is inadmissible in court.

federal judicial circuits. the twelve judicial circuits arranged geographically in the United States, in each of which there is a United States Court of Appeals with appellate jurisdiction over the United States district courts within that circuit.

federal response center. an on-site focal point for coordinating the federal response to a nuclear weapon accident or significant incident.

federal sector. a general term meaning the agencies of federal government.

feedback. in communications, a message or series of messages transmitted in response to a previous message; in computer operations, the return of part of the output of a machine, process, or system to the computer as input for another phase, especially for self-correcting or control purposes.

felonious assault. assault with a deadly weapon.

felony. a criminal offense punishable by death, or by incarceration for a period of which the lower limit is prescribed by statute, typically one year or more.

felony murder. an unlawful killing of a person while committing or attempting to commit another felony, such as robbery. In felony murder, specific intent to kill need not be proved, since it is implied from the intent of the felony associated with the murder.

femoral artery. the main artery supplying the thigh and leg.

fence. a person who receives or buys and then sells stolen goods, usually as a business.

fenethylline. the name of a stimulant drug regulated as a Schedule I controlled substance. Fenethylline is contained in a commercial product called Captagon which is marketed outside of the United States.

fentanyl. an intravenously administered analgesic-anesthetic sold legally as Sublimazer and Innovar. Its effects are similar to morphine but about 100 times as potent. A derivative, sufentanyl, is used for cardiac surgery and is 2000–4000 times as potent as morphine. Carfentanyl, another legally manufactured derivative, has the same general range of potency and is used to immobilize wild animals. Alfentanyl, a less potent variant, is under study for application in minor surgical procedures. Because fentanyl and its analogs have a short duration of action and are difficult to detect in blood and urine specimens, these drugs are favored for doping race horses.

Several illicit variants of fentanyl (sometimes referred to as designer drugs) have been linked to overdose deaths. Alphamethylfentanyl and parafluorofentanyl, first synthesized in the early 1980s, have been brought under the Controlled Substances Act. Other variations of fentanyl continue to be introduced within the illicit trade.

Fentanyl is the active ingredient in such street drugs as China white, Persian white, and Mexican brown. It is usually mixed as one part per 100 parts with lactose and powdered sugar. It is much favored by drug addicts and is the preferred substitute to heroin. Current drug testing techniques cannot always detect fentanyl in urine and blood specimens due to its concentration at the parts-per-billion level. Fentanyl is classified as an opiate and is regulated as a Schedule II controlled substance.

fetal drug toxicity. a condition which occurs when the fetus has an adverse reaction to a drug taken by its mother. The type and severity of adverse effects of a given drug on the fetus depend on a multitude of factors, including the size and frequency of dose, the route of administration, the stage of pregnancy, maternal health and nutritional status, genetic makeup of the mother and fetus, previous obstetrical history, and myriad environmental factors— including concomitant exposure to other drugs, smoking status, and perhaps even environmental pollutants.

feticide. destruction of the fetus; the act by which criminal abortion is produced.

fetishism. the belief in, devotion to, or worship of objects of wearing apparel; pleasure derived from fixing the attention on a part of the body or on a piece of wearing apparel belonging to a person; a form of sexual perversion which gives the fetishist sensual experience and pleasure when in contact with or view of wearing apparel, especially by men of female undergarments.

fetters. shackles for the ankles; handcuffs; chains; irons; manacles. In some jurisdictions, shackles are still used in controlling unruly prisoners.

fiber burning test. a crime laboratory procedure in which a piece of fiber evidence is observed as it is exposed to flame. The smell and whether the fiber burns, melts, forms beads or will not burn are identification indicators.

fictitious informant. a term that refers to a practice of creating a fictitious informant in order to obtain a search warrant. A police officer who does so is open to civil action as well as criminal indictment under the civil rights laws.

fidelity bond. a bond that will reimburse an employer for loss due to the dishonest acts of a covered employee.

field citation. a procedure used in lieu of arrest in which a police officer is empowered to issue summonses for most misdemeanors and some minor felonies. The procedure is intended to unburden overcrowded jails and channel criminal justice resources to more important purposes.

field inquiry. the spontaneous stopping, questioning, or searching of a person on the street by the police, based on a reasonable suspicion that a crime has been committed and that the person under inquiry is involved. This procedure is used by police on patrol to inquire into the activities of a person believed to be involved in a criminal act. The person stopped is asked questions and may be searched if there is reason to believe he is armed. The officer attempts to learn the individual's purpose for being in the area, and files a report. Also called stop and frisk, investigatory stop, field interview, and field interrogation.

field interview report. a report made by a police officer recording an encounter with a citizen who is not known to be connected with a particular crime and including the identity of the citizen and the circumstances related to the encounter.

field notebook. the notebook maintained by a police officer as his or her record of the calls assigned to investigate and the responses made. The notebook is typically small (pocket-size) and is considered in many departments as a standard item of equipment to be carried and used in accordance with established departmental procedures.

field sobriety test. any of several procedures used by police officers to determine whether it is likely that a person suspected of driving while intoxicated is, in fact, intoxicated.

field training. that portion of a training program which takes place outside of an academy or other formal classroom setting and which includes actual experience in police activities by the trainee, usually under the immediate supervision of an experienced officer.

Fifth Amendment. an amendment to the U.S. Constitution that protects individuals from self-incrimination. This amendment guarantees that no person shall be compelled to testify against himself. For this reason, the police are obligated to show that an accused's statements were given voluntarily, without coercion, duress, promise, or inducement.

Figgie Report. a report that examines how crime affects the lifestyles of American citizens.

fighting words. words which tend to incite a breach of the peace.

filing. the initiation of a case in court by formal submission to the court of a document alleging the facts of a matter and requesting relief.

film pirate. a person who sells or uses film produced by another without recording its sale or use so that revenue is unreported or untaxed and royalties unpaid.

final plea. the last plea to a given charge entered in the court record by or for the defendant. By nature of response, a final plea may be not guilty, not guilty by reason of insanity, guilty, and nolo contendere.

find. the discovery of a bug, wire tap or other electronic eavesdropping device.

finding. a conclusion of a court as to an issue of fact, for example, that the defendant is or is not competent to stand trial.

finger lid. the amount of marijuana in a plastic bag represented by the width of one finger.

fingerman. a person who provides information on a truck marked for hijacking by supplying a description of the truck, cargo, plate number, road route, departure time, schedule of stops, arrival time, and similar details of interest to the hijackers; any person who obtains information regarding prospective crime targets and provides it to others who commit the crimes.

fingernail scrapings. residue scraped from under the fingernails of a suspect or deceased victim. The residue may contain traces of skin, hair, fibers, soil and similar materials connected to a crime scene or suspect.

fingerprint identification. the practice of identifying persons by impressions taken of the skin pattern of the inner surface of a finger tip. The practice is extensively used in the identification of unknown persons, such as criminal suspects, and in verifying the identities of parties to commercial transactions. It is the most easily used and positive personal identification of persons known. Fingerprint identification is very reliable because: (1) no two fingerprints are alike, (2) fingerprints are not inherited, (3) they do not change with age, (4) the pattern is not affected by sickness, except by leprosy, and (5) even after obliteration with acid or burns, the pattern will return on new skin.

Fingerprint impressions are usually obtained from living persons by rolling or pressing. A rolled impression is obtained by rolling the fingertip on a glass plate containing a layer of ink and then rolling the fingertip on a sheet of white paper or specially designed card. A pressed or plain impression is obtained in the same manner except that the fingertip is pressed rather than rolled.

fingerprint pattern area. that part of the loop or whorl in which appear the cores, deltas, and ridges used in making a fingerprint classification.

fingerprint reader. a high-security identification device that identifies persons by finger or palmar prints. The system uses a central computer, an optical scanner, and a data base of prints. The unknown prints are placed on a light-sensitive plate.

The prints are read by the optical scanner and compared against file prints.

fingerprint ridge count. the number of ridges intervening between the delta and the core.

fingerprint type lines. the two innermost ridges which start parallel, diverge, and surround or tend to surround the fingerprint pattern area.

finished drawing. a drawing of a crime or accident scene usually prepared for use at trial. It is typically based upon rough sketches, notes, and photographs that were prepared when the scene was initially processed.

fink. a strikebreaker or other person who hires out to help an employer obtain information about unhappy employees; an informant.

firearm frame. that part of a firearm which provides housing for the hammer, bolt or breechblock and firing mechanism, and which is usually threaded at its forward position to receive the barrel. Also called the receiver.

firearms identification. a crime laboratory function which seeks to associate particular bullets, cartridge cases or shotshell casings to a particular weapon to the exclusion of all other weapons.

fire basket. a container, usually of heavy wire, used to carry small pieces of fire fighting equipment. It is sometimes also used as a stretcher.

fire blanket. a fireproof or flameproof heavy cover used to smother fires.

fire bomb. an incendiary device, typically homemade, which when thrown will produce fire upon impact. A fire bomb usually consists of gasoline and a wick in a glass container. The wick is ignited, and the bomb is thrown. When the glass container breaks, a flash explosion occurs. Also called an incendiary bomb or a Molotov cocktail.

fire brigade. an organized group of employees, usually in an industrial setting or a privately owned fire department, who are trained and practiced in basic firefighting operations.

fire cabinet. a cabinet that typically contains a length of fire hose, a nozzle and standpipe connection.

fire cart. a cart for transporting to a fire scene needed equipment such as extinguishers, hoses, ropes, gloves, air packs, and similar items.

fire door. a door tested and rated for resistance to various degrees of fire exposure and utilized to prevent the spread of fire through horizontal and vertical openings. Fire doors remain closed normally or are closed automatically in the presence of fire.

fire extinguisher. a device having characteristics essential for extinguishing flame. Fire extinguishers may contain liquid, dry chemicals or gases. They are tested and rated to indicate their ability to handle specific classes and sizes of fires. The Class A extinguisher is used for ordinary combustibles such as wood, paper and textiles, where a quenching/cooling effect is required. The Class B extinguisher is used for flammable liquids and gases such as oil, gasoline and paint. The Class C extinguisher is used for fires in electrical wiring and equipment. The Class D extinguisher is used for combustible metals.

fireman's key. a key for opening doors or elevators at public premises which is kept in a place known and easily accessible to responding firemen.

fireman's rule. a legal principle which holds that a public servant who is specifically employed for and has accepted the risks of hazardous employment cannot maintain legal actions against another who was negligently responsible for an event which caused the public servant's injuries.

fire point. the lowest temperature at which a flammable liquid, when exposed to a source of heat and in the presence of sufficient air, will give off sufficient vapors and continue to burn. This point is usually a few degrees above the flash point.

fire resistance rating. the time in minutes or hours that a given material or assembly has withstood a fire exposure as established in accordance with specified test procedures.

fire resistant glass. glass plate having an ability to remain intact in its frame during a fire. This characteristic helps reduce the amount of oxygen available to fuel the fire.

fire-resistive. a term applied to properties of materials or designs that are capable of resisting the effects of any fire to which the material or structure may be expected to be subjected.

fire-retardant. a term denoting a substantially lower degree of fire resistance than "fire resistive" and frequently refers to materials or structures which are combustible but which have been subjected to treatments or modifications to prevent or retard ignition or the spread of fire.

fire stair. any enclosed stairway which is part of a fire-resistant exitway.

fire stair door. a door forming part of the fire-resistant fire stair enclosure, and providing access from common corridors to fire stair landings within an exitway.

fire stop. a solid, tight closure of a concealed space which exists to prevent the spread of fire and smoke.

fire wall. a fire-resistant wall designed to prevent the horizontal spread of fire into adjacent areas. It is generally self-supporting and designed to maintain its integrity even if the structure on either side completely collapses.

firing chain. in bomb incident investigations, a chain of four elements necessary to produce an explosion. The four elements are: firing device, primary explosive, booster explosive and main charge. Also called the firing train.

firing device. an item that starts the basic firing chain typical of most explosions. A match, firing pin and safety fuse are types of firing devices.

firing pin. that part of a firearm or a fuse which, on being actuated, strikes the primer or detonator. The firing pin leaves a distinctive mark on the head of a fired shell which can be of help in matching a shell with the weapon that fired it.

firing pin marks. the imprints made on a cartridge case by contact with the firing pin of a firearm. These imprints help the firearms examiner to match a cartridge case with a particular firearm.

first aid. the prompt, efficient care of an individual, whether injured or ill, until medical assistance becomes available.

First Amendment. an amendment to the U.S. Constitution that guarantees rights to free speech. Under the First Amendment, a witness may refuse to answer any questions in a grand jury proceeding if the investigation is searching in nature or is unauthorized either by statute or by special legislation or involves an intrusion into protected First Amendment areas, such as the witness' political or religious beliefs or other constitutionally protected associations.

first degree murder. the most serious and severely punishable crime of killing, usually defined as premeditated, deliberate, and with malice aforethought, or carried out while committing another felony.

first offender. a person who has been convicted for the first time and who therefore might be treated leniently. Although the accused may have committed previous crimes, he is officially categorized as a first offender if he has not been convicted previously.

fiscal year. any consecutive twelve months period selected by an entity as the basis of reporting operating results.

Fisher v. United States. a 1976 case in which the U.S. Supreme Court held that the compulsion by subpoena addressed to an attorney to produce a client's tax returns prepared by an accountant does not constitute a violation of the Fifth Amendment privilege when the subpoena is not addressed to the taxpayer. The Court noted that the tax returns do not represent confidential communication between attorney and client, since they are the work product of a third party, i.e., an accountant.

fishtailing. a sideways slide of a motor vehicle, usually caused by excessive power in relation to road conditions and the ability of the wheels to grip the road surface.

fitting room switch. a shoplifting ploy in which the thief enters a fitting room immediately behind a departing legitimate customer and steals try-on garments left behind.

fix. to inject oneself with narcotics, usually into a vein; an injection or a dose of narcotics; the amount of drug in a bag or packet constituting a single drug dose. Also, to illegally arrange the outcome of a sporting or betting event, or an event which is so arranged.

fixed evidence. items which cannot easily be removed, such as walls of a room, trees and utility poles. Also called immovable evidence.

fixed temperature sensor. a fire detection sensor that works like a thermostat. Typically, a detector sensitive to heat will cause electrical contacts to close when the temperature around it reaches a pre-set, fixed number of degrees. The bi-metallic strip type of detector operates a set of contacts when the sensing element bends due to the different coefficients of expansion of the two metals comprising the strip. A fusible-link type of detector consists of two conductors separated by a material that melts away at a predetermined temperature allowing the conductors to complete a circuit. Bi-metallic strips are restorable after activation, but fusible links require replacement.

flagellation. the act of whipping or being whipped, sometimes to derive sexual pleasure.

flagging. a nervous shoplifter's habit of looking around just prior to the concealment act.

flagrante delicto. in the very act of committing.

flail chest. an injury in which three or more ribs are broken, each in two places. As a result, the segment of chest wall between the breaks collapses with each attempted breath, causing acute respiratory distress.

flame arrester. a device used on vents for flammable liquid or gas tanks, storage containers, cans, gas lines, or flammable liquid pipelines to prevent flashback (movement of flame) through the line or into the container.

flame detector. a sensor that detects the light output from a flame. A photoelectric cell in the sensor responds to light pulses in the 10 Hz region. Flames produce emissions in the 8–12 Hz range.

flame propagation. the spread of flame, independent of the ignition source, throughout a combustible vapor area which may be in a container or across a surface.

flame zone. that area immediately surrounding a bullet wound which has been seared or burned by the muzzle blast of of a firearm discharged in contact with or close to the flesh. A secondary zone of interest is that area on the periphery of the flame zone where tattooing marks have been formed by imbedded powder grains, and are more pronounced with black powder than with smokeless powder. The powder grains, which are hot as they enter the skin, leave tiny burn scars of brownish-red appearance.

flammable liquid burn pattern. in arson investigations, sharp lines of demarcation between areas of burn, usually on floors and walls, which suggest the flowing or splashing of an accelerant.

flaps well down. a term describing an undercover agent who is worried about his future and lying low.

flashback. a spontaneous involuntary recurrence of a hallucinogenic drug experience some time after the drug has worn off. The phenomenon is not fully understood and some argue that flashbacks are a normal neuropsychological event much like the experience of deja vu, which naturally occurs among all people. Flashbacks may occur for weeks or months. Although most involve the visual senses, they may occur in any of the senses, including taste, smell, feel, hearing, time sense, and self-image. Documented cases have indicated that flashbacks may be pleasant, or at the other extreme, they may be terrifying to the point of driving a person to commit suicide. The mechanism responsible for flashbacks is not understood, but there appears to be an inconsistent relationship between the amount and number of times hallucinogens are taken and the occurrence of flashbacks.

flash money. marked money used in undercover operations to bait a criminal into action or to make controlled purchases of illegal drugs or stolen property.

flash paper. a chemically treated paper that self-destructs by rapid burning. It is used in illegal gambling operations.

flashpoint. the lowest temperature of a flammable liquid at which it gives off sufficient vapor to form an ignitable mixture with the air near the surface of the liquid; the minimum temperature at which a liquid fuel will produce enough vapor to burn.

fleeing felon rule. a general rule derived from the English common law which authorizes the use of deadly force in defense of life and in order to apprehend persons committing or fleeing from felonies. In many states, this rule has been further narrowed by statute so that the use of police firearms is limited only to self-defense and to some specific violent felonies, such as murder, rape, aggravated assault, arson, and burglary.

flexcuff. a nylon restraining strap applied to the wrists or ankles of a person in custody. It is removed by cutting and is therefore limited to a single use. Flexcuffs are frequently employed in multiple arrest situations.

floater. a dead body which has been floating in water. A body will rise to the surface in about two weeks, depending on water temperature and depth. Gases formed in the body from the natural processes of putrefaction and decomposition create buoyancy which carries the body to the surface.

floating game. an illegal card or dice game which moves from location to location in order to avoid detection.

Florence reaction test. a preliminary microchemical test which seeks to identify the presence of choline, a constituent of semen. A portion of the stain is dissolved in an iodo-potassium iodide solution and examined under a microscope. The presence of brown rhombic-shaped crystals is an indication of choline, i.e., that semen is present. However, this test is not specific and not conclusive since choline is present in other body fluids and secretions.

flowchart. a pictorial representation of a system or program; a graphical representation of the definition, analysis, or solution of a problem in which symbols are used to represent such things as operations, data, flow, and equipment.

flow control sprinkler. a sprinkler that automatically opens and closes as heat conditions dictate.

flow-through requirements. requirements imposed by a funding agency that are transmitted through intermediary agencies, for example, rules imposed by the federal government upon a state planning agency program which grants federal funds to local police departments for the purchase of equipment.

fluorescein. a tracing powder used to mark objects likely to be touched by a culprit. The powder is invisible in small quantities, but will emit a bright yellow glow when exposed to ultraviolet light.

fluorescence microscope. a microscope that allows an examiner to view with ultraviolet light a sample treated with a fluorescent dye.

fluorescent examination. a crime laboratory technique in which fabrics and other materials are exposed to an ultraviolet or black light so as to make visible stains and other items that cannot be seen in normal light. For example, if the item being examined emits a blue-white glow, the presence of a seminal stain is indicated.

fluorescent powder (or paste). a material used to mark an object in order to transfer a detectable amount to the body or property of a person who handles the object at a later time. An ultraviolet light is used to bring out the fluorescent markings on the skin of the person who handled the object.

fluorocarbons. a large group of chlorinated or fluorinated hydrocarbons now used chiefly as refrigerants. Prior to 1978 they were widely used as aerosol propellants in household products and were subject to abuse because of their intoxicating (anesthetic) effects when inhaled. Fluorocarbons and chlorofluorocarbons were banned from use in household consumer products on March 16, 1978, by the U.S. Environmental Protection Agency under the Toxic Substance Control Act of 1976. The aerosol propellants currently used by industry are pentane, pentene, and other such hydrocarbons. Because of their flammability, they are believed to pose more of a safety than health threat to society.

fluoroscope. a device for observing the shadows of objects shielded from ordinary light, but transparent to X-rays. A fluoroscope consists of a tube or box having at one end a screen coated with a fluorescent substance such as calcium tungstate. When an object is placed between the tube and the screen, the parts which are not transparent to the rays appear as shadows on the screen. When this image is permanently recorded on a photographic emulsion, it is called a radiograph or radiogram.

fob worker. a pickpocket who works from in front of his victim.

focal length. the distance from the optical center of a lens to the focal plane.

focal plane. the area behind a lens where the image is formed.

focal point. the point at which light rays, passing through a lens or reflected from a concave mirror, are concentrated; in fingerprint sciences, the delta or core located within the pattern area of a loop or whorl.

focus. the point at which light rays or an electron beam form a minimum size spot, thus producing the sharpest image.

folk crime. a term sometimes applied to illegal activity that society does not stigmatize; an offense that does not incite a sense of outrage and that is generally thought of as less than criminal; for example, a parking violation.

follow-up investigation. the continuing and

sometimes concluding phase of investigation in which one or more assigned investigators follow-up from basic facts obtained by officers who first arrived at the scene of a reported crime.

footprint. the result of the transference of bodily oils and other substances through the skin on the ridges of a bare foot to an object, thereby leaving an impression. Also, an impression left on a surface by footwear.

foot rail. an inconspicuous hold-up alarm device operated by foot action.

forbearance. giving up the right to enforce what one honestly believes to be a valid claim in return for a promise.

forced choice. a method for evaluating the effectiveness of an employee by forcing an informed person (such as a supervisor) to choose one phrase as more or less descriptive of the employee than another phrase.

forced entry. an unauthorized entry accomplished by the use of force upon the physical components of the premises; breach of an enclosed area usually through a door or window, using tools or muscle power.

force majeure. superior or irresistible force. The term corresponds in a general way to the term "Act of God" such as an earthquake, or the sudden death of a person. If a party to a contract is prevented from executing it by a force majeure, he may not be held liable for damages.

forcible entry and detainer. the use of threat, force, or arms to gain possession of the real property of another and to retain it after surrender has been lawfully demanded. It is a remedy given to a landowner to evict persons unlawfully in possession of his land. A landlord may also use it to evict a tenant in default.

forcible rape. unlawful vaginal penetration of a female of any age, against her will, by force or threat of force, or an attempt at such an act.

Ford v. Wainwright. a case in which the U.S. Supreme Court decided the issue of mental competency of condemned prisoners prior to execution. The case dealt with a prisoner who was mentally competent at the time of the offense, trial, and sentencing but claimed incompetence after he was imprisoned under sentence of death. The state (Florida) law provided for the Governor to appoint three psychiatrists to examine the condemned prisoner. The psychiatrists produced different diagnoses but were unanimous that the prisoner was competent to be executed. The Governor, based on these findings, signed a death warrant without a hearing or further court intervention. The Supreme Court reversed, concluding that a hearing was necessary in order for the defense to challenge the findings of the psychiatrists and to assure that the executive branch (which was responsible for the prosecution) was not also the final determiner of facts as presented by psychiatrists hired by the state.

forecasting. a management tool for long-range planning; an informed estimate about the future based on an analysis of past data and present and future trends.

Foreign Corrupt Practices Act. a law intended to discourage American businessmen from bribing foreign officials in the conduct of their business affairs.

foreign intelligence. in national security terminology, specially caveated information: (1) on the capabilities, intentions, and activities of foreign powers, organizations, or their agents; (2) that concerns activities conducted to protect the United States and its citizens from foreign espionage, sabotage, subversion, assassination, or terrorism; and (3) that concerns methods used to collect foreign human, technical, or other intelligence, and methods and techniques of analysis that are designated by an intelligence community organization of the United States government to require a specific degree of protection against unauthorized disclosure, modification, or destruction for reasons of national security.

foreign national. a person not a citizen of, not a national of, nor an immigrant alien to the United States.

forensic. relating to law, courts, or the judiciary.

forensic anthropology. a branch of anthropology which deals with the examination of skeletal remains, usually for the purpose of identifying dead persons.

forensic auditing. the application of accounting and audit disciplines to matters in litigation or debate.

forensic ballistics. the science of detecting and identifying lethal bullets and the firearms from which they were fired.

forensic chemistry. chemistry applied to questions of law.

forensic medicine. the application of the various branches of medical knowledge to the purposes of the law. Forensic medicine includes anatomy, toxicology, chemistry, botany, and other fields of science that may be used in court to support or dispute a case.

forensic odontology. a branch of dentistry which deals with the analysis of dental evidence, such as teeth, jaw bones, and oral tissues, usually for the purpose of identifying dead persons.

forensic pathology. a specialty in medicine that deals with the determination of the causes of death, especially unnatural deaths. A forensic pathologist is typically a medical examiner or coroner who performs autopsies.

forensic photography. a crime laboratory function which utilizes specialized photographic techniques to make visible latent evidence which is not otherwise visible to the unaided human eye. Forensic photography is typically used to examine alterations and obliterations to documents, laundry marks, and handwriting.

forensic psychiatry. psychiatric knowledge applied to questions of law, as in the determination of insanity. Forensic psychiatry is concerned with psychiatric advice or opinion on a crime, a defendant, or a convicted offender.

forensic science. the application of chemistry, physics and other sciences to the examination of physical evidence within the context of the legal process.

forensic serology. the study and examination of blood and other body fluids in a crime laboratory.

forensic toxicology. the biomedical science that studies the effect of foreign substances introduced into the living body. A forensic toxicologist assists the criminal investigative function by analyzing urine, blood, organs, and tissues for poisons, drugs, alcohol, and other foreign substances.

foreseeability. a legal concept which holds that two key factors determine an organization's liability for a crime committed against invitees on the premises. The factors are: (1) whether the crime was reasonably foreseeable, and if so, (2) whether there was reasonably adequate security in place to prevent the crime.

forfeiture. the loss of goods, property or rights, as punishment for a crime.

forfeiture proceeding. a court action aimed at depriving a defendant of rights or property, such as something taken by the police in a search and seizure.

forged instrument. a written instrument that has been falsely made, completed, or altered. The term includes deeds, wills, contracts, public records, checks, commercial instruments, money, securities, stamps, and prescriptions of a duly licensed physician.

forgery. the act of falsely making or materially altering, with intent to defraud, any writing which, if genuine, might be of legal efficacy or the foundation of a legal liability; a spurious article bearing a false signature, as a painting, sculpture, or book. Forgery includes: (1) false making, counterfeiting, and alteration, erasure, or obliteration of a genuine instrument, in whole or in part, (2) false making or counterfeiting of a signature, as of a party or witness, and (3) placing and connecting together, with intent to defraud, different parts of several genuine instruments. Uttering, which is frequently associated with forgery, is the putting into circulation or disposing of a forged instrument, with intent to defraud, under the pretense that such instrument is genuine, or having in one's possession, with intent to utter, a forged instrument, plate, coin, or other thing.

forgery and counterfeiting. in Uniform Crime Reports terminology, the name of the UCR category used to record and report arrests for offenses of making, manufacturing, altering, possessing, selling, or distributing, or attempting to make, manufacture, alter, sell, distribute, or receive "anything false in the semblance of that which is true."

former jeopardy. a defense plea founded on the common law principle that a man cannot be brought into danger of his life or limb for the same offense more than once. The former jeopardy defense is founded on the principle that a case once terminated upon its merits should not be tried again. Double jeopardy can only be claimed when the second prosecution is brought by the same government as the first. When the act is a violation of the law as to two or more governments, the accused is regarded as having committed separate offenses.

former testimony. testimony given by a witness at a prior legal proceeding which is admissible in a later trial.

Formosa plan. a plan for controlling drug addiction through the issuance of licenses to sell and use drugs in prescribed locations. The plan's name is derived from a system implemented in Formosa to reduce crime by controlling opium smoking. After classifying thousands of crimes committed by Formosans over a period of years, the health commissioner was able to demonstrate that more than 70% of crimes were committed by opium users as compared to about 30% of nonusers.

FORTRAN. an abbreviation of Formula Translation, a programming language primarily used to express computer programs by arithmetic formulas; a programming language primarily designed for applications involving numeric computations.

fortress prison. a maximum-security confinement facility with high walls, guard towers, armed personnel and similar features.

founded offense. a complaint in which the police determine that a criminal offense was committed.

four stages of fire. the natural progression of fire through four distinct stages: (1) the incipient stage in which invisible products of combustion are generated, with no visible evidence of smoke, flame or heat, (2) the smoldering stage in which combustion products are visible as smoke, with no appreciable heat or flame, (3) the flame stage in which flames are visible, with appreciable heat to follow instantaneously, and (4) the heat stage in which intense, uncontrolled heat is accompanied by rapidly expanding air.

Fourth Amendment. an amendment to the U.S. Constitution which states: "The right of the people to be secure in their persons, houses, papers and effects against unreasonable searches and seizures shall not be violated, and no warrant shall issue, but upon probable cause, supported by oath or affirmation, and particularly describing the place to be searched and the persons or things to be seized."

Fourteenth Amendment. a constitutional right of the accused to have the assistance of an attorney at or after the time that judicial proceedings have been initiated, whether by way of formal charge, preliminary hearing, indictment, information, or arraignment.

fracture. a break or rupture in a bone.

fragging. the use of a fragmentation grenade by a subordinate to murder a military superior while in combat or a combat-related situation.

fragile evidence. items that are easily destroyed, contaminated, or will easily deteriorate and therefore require special treatment, handling and protection when gathered.

fragmentation. in bomb investigations, the scattering of the broken, jagged pieces of the bomb case.

franchise fraud. a type of advance fee fraud in which the criminal collects a fee in exchange for the promise of certain services and territorial rights pertaining to the startup of a franchised operation.

frankenpledge. a term describing a system

of self-policing in which participants pledged to be responsible for each other's behavior.

Franks v. Delaware. a case in which the U.S. Supreme Court ruled that a defendant may challenge the truthfulness of factual statements made in an affidavit to a search warrant. If a defendant prevails and shows false or reckless statements in the affidavit, a finding of insufficient probable cause can result and all items seized pursuant to the warrant would be ruled inadmissible as evidence.

fraud. an element of certain offenses, consisting of deceit or intentional misrepresentation with the aim of illegally depriving a person of his property or legal rights; an act which involves bad faith, a breach of honesty, a lack of integrity or moral turpitude. In Uniform Crime Reports terminology, the name of the UCR offense category used to record and report arrests for offenses of conversion or obtaining of money or thing of value by false pretenses, except forgery, counterfeiting and embezzlement.

fraud offenses. a general crime type comprising offenses which share the elements of practice of deceit or intentional misrepresentation of fact, with the intent of unlawfully depriving a person of his property or legal rights.

fraudulent concealment. the hiding or suppression of a material fact or circumstance which a party is legally or morally bound to disclose.

fraudulent conversion. receiving into possession money or property of another and fraudulently withholding, converting or applying the same to or for one's own use and benefit, or the use and benefit of any person other than the one to whom the money or property belongs.

fraudulent conveyance. a conveyance of property by a debtor for the intent and purpose of defrauding his creditors. Such conveyance is of no effect, and such property may be reached by the creditors through appropriate legal proceedings.

fraudulent representation. a false statement as to material fact made with intent that

another rely thereon, which is believed by the other party and on which he relies and by which he is induced to act and does act to his injury.

Frazier v. Cupp. a case in which the U.S. Supreme Court upheld a conviction based in part upon a confession obtained by the police through trickery and deceit. The Court commented that "these cases must be decided by viewing the totality of the circumstances."

freak out. to panic or lose emotional control; an unpleasant reaction to a drug.

freebase. a smokable form of cocaine; to smoke cocaine in the freebase form.

free basing. smoking cocaine after it is converted from its normal form to cocaine base. In its normal form (cocaine hydrochloride), the drug is water soluble to facilitate absorption by the membranes. Cocaine in the hydrochloride form can be converted to cocaine base with a few common chemicals and simple equipment. Because the chemicals are highly flammable, the process is dangerous.

Freedom of Information Act of 1966. an act that provides for making information held by federal agencies available to the public, unless it comes within one of the specific categories of matters exempt from public disclosure. The legislative history of the act (particularly the recent amendments) makes it clear that the primary purpose was to make information maintained by the executive branch of the federal government more available to the public. At the same time, the act recognized that records that cannot be disclosed without impairing rights of privacy or important government operations must be protected from disclosure.

One of the nine specific and narrowly drawn exemptions to the Act relates to law enforcement investigatory files. This exemption excludes investigatory records compiled for law enforcement purposes, but only to the extent that the production of such records would (1) interfere with enforcement proceedings, (2) deprive a person of a right to a fair trial or an impartial adjudication, (3) constitute an unwarranted invasion of personal privacy, (4) disclose the identity of a confidential source and, in the case of a record compiled by a criminal law enforcement authority in the course of a criminal investigation, or by an agency conducting a lawful national security intelligence investigation, confidential information furnished only by the confidential source, (5) disclose investigative techniques and procedures, or (6) endanger the life or physical safety of law enforcement personnel.

free radical assay technique (FRAT). a testing technique that can be used to identify the presence of drugs in urine.

frequency distribution. a term used in the study of statistics. It represents a method of presenting accumulated data by reclassifying the data into subgroups and then presenting again the original facts in terms of these subgroups.

frequency inverter. a voice scrambler that inverts the frequency content of speech. It is usually low cost with good tolerance to poor communication conditions, but is easily broken with an equivalent device and can be defeated by a trained listener.

frequency modulation (FM). a method of converting an analog signal into a tone of varying pitch, which can then be transmitted over radio frequencies.

fresh complaint. a complaint of a victim of a sexual offense made within a short time after the offense was committed. The statements of the victim made during a fresh complaint can be reported in court by witnesses as an exception to the hearsay rule.

freshness rule. a general rule which requires that no more than three weeks may transpire between the date of the last information relating to probable cause in an affidavit and the time the affidavit reaches the person authorized to issue the warrant.

fresh pursuit. immediate, in-sight pursuit of an escaping felon that permits a police officer to depart from his jurisdiction or to intrude on private premises in order to apprehend the felon.

frisk. a brief search of a person by a police officer, usually limited to a "patdown" of the outer clothing, and conducted for the purpose of detecting any weapon that can be used to harm the officer.

frotteur. a person who derives sexual satisfaction from rubbing against the clothing or anatomical parts, usually the buttocks, of a person of the opposite sex. This deviance is practically unknown in females.

fruit of the poisoned tree. a legal concept which holds that evidence may be suppressed at trial if it is tainted by prior illegal conduct on the part of the police. For example, evidence obtained during the search of a defendant at time of arrest may be inadmissible if the arrest was illegally made.

fruits of crime. material objects acquired by means and in consequence of the commission of crime. Swindled money, a stolen watch, and illegally intercepted trade secret information are examples of fruits of crime.

f-stop. the dimensional ratio between a lens aperture and its focal length. For example, a 4-inch lens with an aperture of 0.5 inches equals a ratio of 8 to 1. This corresponds to an f-stop of f-8.

fugitive. a person sought by law enforcement authorities because an arrest warrant has been issued or because he has escaped from custody; a person who is charged with a crime in one jurisdiction and flees to another jurisdiction.

fugitive print. a latent fingerprint that disappears after it has been developed. This occurrence is usually associated with the iodine fuming process of fingerprint development.

fugitive squad. a police unit responsible for the execution of arrest warrants relating to fugitives, violators of probation and parole, misdemeanants, and petty offenders.

full-custody arrest. the taking of a person into physical custody for the purpose of taking him before a judicial officer to answer for a crime, or transporting him to a police facility to answer for a crime, where he will be locked up or will post bond.

full opinion. the official announcement of a

decision of a court, in writing and usually lengthy, presenting in detail the reasons and reasoning leading to the decision.

full pardon. an executive act completely and conditionally absolving a person from all consequences of a crime and conviction. This act is sometimes called an absolute pardon, and can imply that guilt itself is "blotted out." It is an act of forgiveness and is generally accompanied by restoration of civil rights. American law tends to use this executive remedy, instead of judicial proceedings, when serious doubt of guilt or evidence of innocence arises after prosecution.

full-time temporary release. the authorized temporary absence of a prisoner from a confinement facility, for a period of 24 hours or more, for purposes relating to such matters as the prisoner's employment or education, or personal or family welfare.

functional job analysis. a technique of work analysis that measures and describes a position's specific requirements. The technique produces a variety of component descriptions which can be used to accurately illustrate the specific and varied duties actually performed by an incumbent.

functional psychosis. a severe mental disorder in which the afflicted person loses touch with reality as the result of an inability to cope with overwhelming personal problems and conflicts. In this condition, the brain may be organically healthy but functions improperly. Schizophrenia, paranoia, and manic depressive psychosis are forms of functional psychoses.

function key. a key on a keyboard or keypad that has a dedicated function, such as to acknowledge receipt of a signal. Depressing the function key causes the system to respond in some pre-programed manner.

functus officio. an officer who has fulfilled the duties of an office that has expired and who, in consequence, has no further formal authority.

furlough program. a community-based alternative to sentencing of an offender. The aim is to maintain the incarcerated offender's community ties through attendance at work, school and in the home.

Furman v. Georgia. a 1972 case in which the U.S. Supreme Court struck down the death penalty as then applied.

fusible link. a device used in fire detection. When a pre-set temperature is reached, the link will fuse or melt, resulting in an alarm.

fuzee flare. a burning flare placed on or next to the roadway to warn approaching motorists of a hazard, such as a stalled vehicle or traffic accident. The flare has a spike at the bottom end and a cap at the top end.

gage. marijuana.

gag reflex. the elevation of the soft palate and retching elicited by touching the back of the tongue or the wall of the pharynx.

gag rule. formal instructions from a competent authority, usually a judge, to refrain from discussing and/or advocating something.

gait ataxia. lack of coordination in muscle action manifested as unsteady movements and staggering gait. Gait ataxia is one of several manifestations looked for in field sobriety tests as an indicator of impairment by reason of intoxication.

gait pattern identification. an investigative technique in which measurements are made of a series of footprints. Because a person's gait is highly individual, footprint patterns can be useful in connecting a suspect to a crime scene.

galvanic skin response. a change in the electrical resistance of the skin. It is one of three physiological changes measured by the polygraph instrument. Changes of body tissue polarization (neural discharge) and sweat gland activity or circulatory variations which occur as the result of work, emotion, or a combination of either, are recordable by the polygraph instrument. Two metal plates attached to the fingers of the subject pick up the change in electrical resistance. A galvanometer driven by the variations of electrical conductivity is connected to a pen that records the measurements on the polygraph chart.

galvanograph. one of three major components of the polygraph instrument. It records a phenomenon known as the galvanic skin response or electrodermal response.

gambling. staking or wagering of money or other thing of value on a game of chance, or on an uncertain event. In Uniform Crime Reports terminology, the name of the UCR category used to record and report arrests for offenses relating to promoting, permitting, or engaging in gambling. The major forms of gambling offenses are bookmaking (horse and sport book), and numbers and lottery.

ganja. a cannabis preparation, consisting of the resin-rich flowers and top leaves from the female plant. The name is of Indian origin and is the term used in Jamaica for marijuana. Also called ghang.

gaping stab wound. a wound inflicted perpendicular to the direction of tissue fibers. Distortion of skin tension resulting from a separation of the tissue fibers gives the wound a gaping appearance.

garrote. to strangle around the neck with a cord, wire or similar instrument.

Gas Chromatograph Intoximeter. the trade name of a breath testing device used to determine alcohol concentrations in the blood of persons suspected of being under the influence of alcohol.

gas chromatography (GC). a crime laboratory technique for analyzing gas, liquid, and solid samples. The sample is converted to a gaseous state and injected into the gas chromatograph instrument where it passes through a column of absorbent material. The gas is fractionated into compounds according to their chemical and physical properties. The compounds are portrayed as a pattern on a graph which allows comparison with graphs of known samples. Also called gas liquid chromatography (GLC).

gas chromatography/mass spectrometry (GC/MS). a crime laboratory technique which combines the separating power of gas chromatography with the high sensitivity and specificity of spectrometric detection. GC/MS is generally considered to be one of the most conclusive methods for identifying unknown substances.

gas detector. a sensor designed to detect and report the presence of gases or vapors.

gas neutralizer. a product used in riot control operations to neutralize the effect of tear gases. It is usually packaged as an aerosol spray and issued to police personnel.

gate money. money given to a person upon release from prison.

gauge. the size designation of a shot gun. Originally, gauge represented the number of lead balls with the same diameter as the barrel that would make a pound. For example, a 12-gauge shotgun would have a bore diameter of a lead ball $1/642$ of a pound in weight. The only exception is the .410 shotgun, in which bore size is .41 inch.

Gault. a term referring to a decision of the U.S. Supreme Court which afforded to juvenile defendants substantially the same rights given to adults under the rules of due process. These rights are: (1) adequate notice of charges, (2) the right to counsel, (3) right to confrontation and cross-examination, and (4) the privilege against self-incrimination.

gelatin dynamite. a type of commercial dynamite made of nitrocotton (collodion cotton dissolved in nitroglycerin) and nitroglycerin gel. It is usually sticky and rubber-like in appearance.

general appearance file. a police agency file containing photographs and descriptions of criminals known to have engaged in particular types of crimes.

general criminal intent. an intent of the criminal to act contrary to the law with voluntariness and foresight of the consequences.

general intent. the state of mind characterized by recklessness or negligence rather than a specific criminal intent to do what is prohibited.

generalist. an officer who performs all aspects of general police duties or investigations.

generalized anxiety disorder. a personality disorder characterized by diffused and generalized anxiety that is difficult to manage.

general operating procedures. written instructions which concern a department or office as a whole and are applicable to all posts, patrols or jobs therein.

general series test. in polygraphy, a series of questions typically comprised of a combination of relevant, irrelevant and control questions.

general view photograph. a photograph of the general area surrounding a crime or accident scene or of immediately adjacent areas. It shows the scene in relation to its surroundings and is usually taken at eye level in order to give the viewer a perspective similar to that of witnesses to the incident.

generic name. as applied to drugs, the chemical description of the drug class opposed to a commercial brand or trade name for the same compound. The generic name is usually given by the company that first manufactures it and is often a simplified version of the chemical name.

Geneva gauge. an instrument for measuring the curvature of a surface, and is particularly useful to the crime laboratory in identifying the full curvature of an object from only a fragment of the object, for example, in identifying an automobile headlight lens from fragments collected at a hit and run accident scene.

geographic base files. geographically coded calls for service, field-interrogation cards, offense records, citations for moving violations, arrest records, citations for moving violations, arrest records, and so on that are used for computer-assisted dispatch, crime trend analysis, planning, research, and resource allocation.

germ typing. the process of identifying suspects by matching their germs with those found at a crime scene.

ghang. an Indian hemp plant from which hashish is made. Also called ganja.

Gibson v. Florida Legislative Committee. a 1963 case in which the U.S. Supreme Court ruled that under the First Amendment a witness may refuse to answer any questions in a grand jury proceeding if the investigation constitutes a fishing expedition or is unauthorized either by statute or by special legislation or involves an intrusion into protected First Amendment areas, such as the witness' political or religious beliefs or other constitutionally protected associations.

Gideon v. Wainwright. a case in which the U.S. Supreme court ruled in 1963 that the Sixth Amendment's guarantee of counsel requires the states to furnish free lawyers to poor defendants. The Court commented that the assistance of counsel is required in criminal trials since the "noble ideal" in which every defendant stands equal before the law "cannot be realized if the poor man charged with crime has to face his accusers without a lawyer to assist him." In 1964 the Supreme Court returned to this issue by further holding that the right to free counsel would be meaningless if defendants had already confessed to the police before they came to trial. The Court then ruled that a police interrogation of a suspect in custody was a "critical stage" of the case against the suspect, who therefore could not be denied permission to confer with an attorney at that point.

Gilbert v. California. a case in which the U.S. Supreme Court held in 1967 that a suspect may not decline to provide a handwriting sample. The rule enunciated in this case extends to other nontestimonial items such as voice exemplars and blood samples. The prohibition against self-incrimination protects suspects from the compulsion of oral testimony or the production of certain documents.

glazed bricks. in arson investigations, bricks of a burned structure which bear a glossy appearance. Glazed bricks are indicators that the fire was enhanced by an accelerant.

Glickstein v. United States. a 1911 case in which the U.S. Supreme Court ruled that an immunity statute in no way protects from prosecution for offenses not yet committed, including perjury or contempt that may be involved in giving compelled testimony in return for a grant of immunity.

glitch. a problem in a system; a horizontal bar moving vertically on a television monitor; a defect in a tape that causes imperfect playback.

glue sniffing. a major fad that first surfaced in the early 1960s. Glues containing aromatic hydrocarbons, such as toluene, xylene, and the like, were particularly subject to abuse because of their intoxicating properties. While the inhalation of volatile substances continues to be a significant drug-abusing behavior, particularly among youths, the glue sniffing fad has subsided. The practice has diminished for several reasons including the presence and discovery of a cornucopia of household products from nail polish to spray paint that are just as readily available and have the same abuse potential as glues, and the current practice of many glue manufacturers of using harmless additives (e.g., mustard compounds) that have obnoxious scents or the ability to produce nausea, thus discouraging their being sniffed.

glutethimide. a depressant introduced in 1954 as a safe barbiturate substitute, but which has since been found to have no particular advantages and several disadvantages. One disadvantage is that the effects of the drug are of such long duration that it is exceptionally difficult to reverse overdoses, which often result in death. Glutethimide is sold as Doriden and is a Schedule III and IV depressant.

good behavior bond. a promise made to a court by a defendant to maintain good behavior for a specified period of time.

good character defense. a defense against prosecution which seeks to offer evidence that the accused is of such good character that it was unlikely he committed the crime charged. This is not a defense as a matter of law, but an attempt to convince a jury it was improbable for the accused to have committed the crime.

good faith effort. in equal employment opportunity programs, actions taken, being taken, or about to be taken for the purpose of achieving equal employment opportunity within an organization.

good faith exception. an exception to a rule based on the honest belief that the person was acting lawfully and properly. For example, an exception might be granted to allow certain illegally obtained evidence to be introduced at trial if the officer who obtained the evidence had acted in good faith.

Good Head. a drug user.

Good Samaritan. a person other than a police officer who is not directly involved in a crime but who steps in to prevent injury, aid a victim, or apprehend the criminal.

Good Samaritan Act (or law). a statute which provides that a physician or nurse, and sometimes any person, who renders care to accident victims shall be immune from civil damages as a result of ordinary negligence in giving such care.

good time. the amount of time deducted from time to be served in prison on a given sentence contingent upon good behavior or awarded automatically by statute or regulation.

good time law. a law which permits the release of prisoners before the expiration of their sentences because of good behavior while in prison. In New York, as early as 1817, prison boards were authorized to release a first offender sentenced to not more than five years, after serving with good behavior only one-fourth of the sentence. In recent times, prison boards are requiring, in addition to good conduct, a demonstration of reasonable probability that upon release the prisoner will not again violate the law and that the release is compatible with the welfare of society. Also, the release of a prisoner on parole is usually made by the initiative of the prison board and not upon the application of the prisoner.

graft. coerced or voluntary payments made to influence public officials, for example, payments made to the police to overlook illegal gambling.

grain confetti. small paper taggants added to grain in storage for the purpose of identifying stolen grain and discouraging grain theft. Each paper taggant bears a code indicating source and ownership.

grandfather file. a backup record preserved at a location different than the originating location. Grandfather files are almost always used when information is processed by a computer.

grand jury. a body of persons selected and sworn to investigate criminal activity and the conduct of public officials, and to hear evidence against an accused person for the purpose of determining if there is sufficient evidence to bring that person to trial.

grand mal seizure. a generalized motor seizure; a major epileptic seizure attended by loss of consciousness and generalized involuntary body movements.

grant of parole. a release from prison by discretionary action of a paroling authority, conditional upon the parolee's fulfillment of specified conditions of behavior.

grant of probation. a court action requiring that a person fulfill certain conditions of behavior for a specified period of time, often with assignment to a probation agency for supervision, either in lieu of prosecution or judgment, or after conviction, usually in lieu of a sentence to confinement.

Grant v. State. a 1979 case in which the Arkansas Supreme Court held that where a father owned a house and his son resided in the house, paid board, and owned the things in his room, the father had authority to consent to a search of the son's room. The parents' right of access and control over the entire house, including the son's room, gave the father the authority to give a valid consent.

graphic annunciator. a mimic board or CRT display that has special graphics to delineate alarm zones or sensor locations. A graphic annunciator can present an overall picture of a system's status on a map or facility outline and depict the location and current reporting condition of each sensor.

graphologist. a person who analyzes handwriting or handprinting for the purpose of making conclusions concerning the personality or character of the writer.

gratuity. something given freely or without recompense, usually of limited value; something given in expectation of a return favor or consideration.

gravimetric analysis. in chemistry, a form

of quantitative analysis by weighing the substances and precipitates obtained.

grazing. the consumption on store premises of edible or consumable merchandise by customers or employees. Popular grazing items are soft drinks, small food items, aspirins, hairspray and lipstick.

greening. making freshly harvested marihuana ready for smoking by drying it and filtering out debris.

grey propaganda. propaganda which does not specifically identify a source; a mixture of distortions, half-truths and untruths.

grid search. a search of an outdoor crime scene in which the area is divided into grids that are separately and thoroughly examined.

grief work. a normal emotional response to an external loss characterized by stages of resolution, which include denial, anger, bargaining, depression, and acceptance.

Griffin v. Wisconsin. a case in which the U.S. Supreme Court in 1987 ruled reasonable a warrantless search made by the police of a probationer's home pursuant to a regulation that permitted a warrantless search if "reasonable grounds" existed to believe contraband might be found on a probationer's premises. In this case, the police received information that there were or might be guns in the probationer's apartment. A probation officer and other officers searched the apartment and found a gun. The Court Court observed that a probation system presents special needs, and since probation is a form of criminal sanction, probationers do not enjoy the same liberty to which other citizens are entitled. The warrant requirement in this case would be impractical, would unduly interfere with the probation system by inserting a magistrate into the decision-making process, and the delay in obtaining a warrant could be harmful. Also, to require more than "reasonable grounds" (i.e., probable cause) would reduce the deterrent effect of supervision by the probation officer.

grog-shop. a liquor saloon, bar room, or dram shop; a place where intoxicating liquor is sold for consumption on the premises.

grooves. the cavities cut into the barrel of a firearm which impart to the bullet a spiraling motion in flight. By examining the line-like markings (striations) on a bullet, it is possible to match the bullet with the particular firearm that discharged it. It is also possible to identify from striations the make of a firearm by determining the number and width of grooves, and the direction and degree of twist.

gross negligence. the intentional failure to perform a duty in reckless disregard of consequences that may affect the life or property of another; the lack of even slight or ordinary care.

group dynamics. the interactions among members of a group, particularly as they relate to employees and work processes.

group home. a long-term residential facility, usually for juveniles, in which residents are allowed extensive contact with the community, such as attending school or holding a job. Also called a halfway house.

guardian. one who has the control or management of the person, property, or both, of another, who because of infancy, insanity or other reason is incapable of acting in his or her own behalf.

Guaiac analysis. a nonspecific preliminary test for determining the presence of blood on evidence. Guaiac is a greenish-brown resin extracted from a tropical American shrub. The resin is dissolved in ethyl alcohol and the solution is added, with a few drops of hydrogen peroxide, to a saline solution of the suspect blood. A glacial acetic acid is then added. The appearance of a blue color is an indication that the sample is or contains blood.

guardian ad litem. a guardian appointed by the court to either institute or defend a suit in which a minor is involved as a party. In such cases, the guardian is required to give a bond guaranteeing faithful performance.

guidance. the general direction of an intelligence effort, particularly in the area of collection.

guilt complex question. in polygraphy, a question pertaining to a purely hypothetical crime. It is used as a safeguard against misinterpreting the pertinent question responses of an innocent apprehensive person.

guilty plea. a defendant's formal answer in court to the charge contained in a complaint, information, or indictment, admitting that he or she did in fact commit the offense listed.

guilty verdict. the decision by jury or judicial officer on the basis of evidence presented at trial, that the defendant is guilty of the offense for which he or she has been tried. A guilty verdict indicates that it was concluded that the evidence offered of the defendant's guilt was sufficient to prove guilt beyond a reasonable doubt. A guilty plea does not necessarily lead to a judgment of conviction. The judicial officer can enter a judgment of acquittal if the requirements of the law have not been satisfied.

gunshot residue. residues deposited on the thumb, forefinger and web area of the hand when the hand is used to discharge a weapon. Deposits are also made on the face and neck area when a rifle or shotgun is fired. A residue frequently contains antimony and barium which are components of most primer mixtures. Also called primer residue.

gun wallet. a wallet-like device that contains a small handgun, typically a two-shot Derringer. A finger hole cut in the leather around the trigger enables the holder to fire the gun while appearing to be handling a wallet.

Gutzedt analysis. a crime laboratory test that seeks to determine the presence of arsenic in an unknown material. A mixture of zinc, salts of tin and iron, lead acetate, and mercuric chloride are added to the suspect material. The presence of arsenic is indicated if a dark stain appears when examined under ultraviolet rays. The Gutzedt test is regarded as the most delicate of chemical tests for arsenic, and is capable of detection at the range of one part per million.

habeas corpus. an order issued by a judge requiring that a prisoner be released from jail.

habit-forming drug. a drug that may produce either psychological or physical dependence in certain users in certain circumstances. This term is often used by drug manufacturers to mean that prolonged use will result in physical dependence, and specifically that the medicine contains an opiate, opiate derivative, synthetic opiate, or barbiturate. Others use the term to refer to a drug that may be used chronically but does not produce addiction or dependence to the extent of other drugs.

habitual offender. a person sentenced under the provisions of a statute declaring that persons convicted of a given offense, and shown to have previously been convicted of another specified offense, shall receive a more severe penalty than that for the current offense alone.

habituation. a condition resulting from repeated consumption of a drug. It is characterized by a desire to continue taking the drug, little or no tendency to increase the dose, and some degree of psychic dependence. It is an imprecise term generally used to refer to a state of chronic or continuous attachment to drugs, which is less severe or harmful than addiction. It implies a state that is psychological in origin and that is characterized by a desire rather than a compulsion to continue use, with little or no tolerance and no physical dependence. Other definitions include: the physical phenomena of adaptation and mental conditioning to the repetition of an effect; a condition often used as a synonym for psychological dependence in which the habitue desires a drug but suffers no ill effects on its discontinuance; a state of periodic or chronic intoxication produced by the repeated consumption of a drug, the main elements of which are (1) desire, but not a compulsion, to continue taking the drug for the sense of improved well-being it engenders, (2) little or no tendency to increase the dose, (3) some degree of psychic dependence on the effect of the drug, but absence of physical dependence and hence of an abstinence syndrome, and (4) detrimental effects, if any, are primary on the individual as opposed to society; a condition resulting from repeated consumption of a drug, characterized by a desire to continue taking the drug with little or no tendency to increase the dose, and some degree of psychic dependence.

hacker. a person who seeks to gain access to a computer system against the wishes of the owner, sometimes for personal gain. A hacker enthusiast is one who seeks access for the purpose of personal satisfaction as opposed to a criminal motive.

halfway house. a community-located correctional institution in which offenders are supervised under minimum security and which provides therapy, vocational support, and other services. It is used to bridge the gap between prison and unconditional release. Residents live in a group but are permitted to leave the facility during the day and perhaps on weekends. The term was originally given to guidance centers for offenders who are "halfway out" of prison on probation or parole, which sought to assist in the demands of daily participation in community life. Now it applies also to facilities in which a person who recently has been discharged from a mental hospital or drug treatment facility attempts to adjust to living outside the hospital environment. As a basic correctional modality, a halfway house is useful in at least five ways. It serves as: (1) a bridge between a highly structured institutional setting in which a person has little individual initiative and responsibility, (2) a means for providing assistance to the newly released parolee who is precipitously faced with the many and varied problems of being in a community, (3) a place to which inmates who have no satisfactory residence plan may be released, (4) an opportunity for the parole agent to get a better understanding of the parolee by more frequent and intensive observation in the house so that the agent can more effectively provide the needed control, treatment, and assistance, and (5) an alternative to return to a correctional institution (prison) for those parolees who violate the conditions of their release.

hallucination. a perception of sounds, odors, tactile sensations, or visual images that are not caused by external stimuli but arise from within the person; a sensory perception without external stimulation of the relevant sensory organ which has the immediate sense of a true perception.

hallucinogens. a major classification of natural and synthetic drugs whose primary effect is to distort the senses. They can produce hallucinations, i.e., experiences that depart from reality. These drugs may produce profound alterations in sensation, mood, and consciousness at doses that result in comparatively light physiological activity. Although most experiences are visual, they may also involve the sense of hearing, touch, smell, or taste, sometimes simultaneously. They are also variously known as psychedelic drugs, psychotomimetics, illusionogenics, psychotaraxics and psychodysleptics. These terms refer to somewhat overlapping effects alleged to occur with this group of drugs. Included in this group are dimethyltryptamine (DMT), LSD-25, methylenedioxyamphetamine (MDA), mescaline, peyote, phencyclidine (PCP), psilocybin, psilocin, and dimethoxymethamphetamine (STP, DOM). The term has also been applied to the pseudo-hallucinogens such as nutmeg and mace. While other drugs, such as alcohol or cannabis, may produce hallucinations if a very high dose is used, they are not classified as hallucinogens because this is not the usual effect expected or experienced. In low doses, the effects of hallucinogens vary widely depending on variations in drug taken and the unique sensitivity of the user at the time of use. Also, any one of the many varieties of drugs that affect the brain at the cellular level, causing distortions in space, time, color, sound, and feeling, and likely to cause the user to engage in bizarre behavior and lose contact with reality.

hallucinosis. an abnormal mental state characterized by almost continual hallucinations.

halo effect. a bias in ratings arising from the tendency of a rater to be influenced in his or her rating of specific traits by general impressions of the person being rated.

Halon. the trade name of a non-corrosive, chemical agent used for extinguishing fires in areas containing computers and electrical equipment.

hammock carry. a technique for lifting an injured individual onto a stretcher. It is performed by two persons using interlocked arms to support the victim's upper torso and a third person to support the legs. In voice-synchronized movements, the victim is lifted in a manner that minimizes aggravation of the injury.

hand and finger attachment. in polygraphy, a spoon-like metal contact placed on an examinee's hand or finger for the purpose of detecting changes to the skin's resistance to electrical current. This attachment is an element of the galvanograph component of the polygraph instrument.

hand-bagging. a crime scene processing procedure for protecting the hands of a deceased in order to preserve any trace evidence that may be found under the fingernails during the autopsy. A paper bag is preferred over plastic because plastic tends to accelerate putrefaction.

hand down. to announce or file an opinion in a legal cause; to announce a decision by a court upon a case or point reserved for consideration.

handicapped person. in equal employment opportunity programs, a person who has a physical or mental impairment which substantially limits one or more of the person's major life activities (such as self-care or mobility), and has a record of such impairment or is regarded as being so impaired. A handicapped person may be declared capable of performing a particular job with reasonable accommodation to the handicap, and in some organizations involving federal work cannot be discriminated against on the basis of the handicap.

handle. the total amount of money taken in during a specified time by a betting operation.

hand-to-hand. the delivery of an illicit drug at the moment of payment.

handwriting analysis. the evaluation of handwriting and handprinting by a qualified questioned documents examiner. Also, the analysis of handwriting for the purpose of assessing the writer's personality and character. In this latter context, handwriting analysis is synonymous with graphology.

handwriting dynamics. a technique of access control verification which analyzes handwriting velocity, acceleration, and pressure. The technique is also used for accepting or rejecting handwritings for forgery detection and deterrence purposes.

hangfire. the temporary failure of the primer to ignite the powder charge in a cartridge. A hangfire will usually reach ignition within five seconds. Also called misfire.

hanging. an extremely slow response of a computer system. When an active terminal appears to be doing nothing, it is said to be hanging.

hanging jury. a jury selected among persons who have declared their support for the death sentence.

harboring a felon. the crime of hiding or otherwise aiding an escaped or wanted felon for whom the police are searching.

hard copy. the output of a printing device. A computer printout is hard copy.

hard drugs. an ambiguous term generally used to describe drugs legally viewed as narcotics, such as opium and morphine derivatives and their synthetics, and cocaine.

hardware. physical equipment used in data processing, as opposed to programs, procedures, rules, and associated documentation.

hard x-ray examination. a crime laboratory technique in which evidence is examined using x-rays ranging from 25 to 140 kilowatts, which in this range are called hard x-rays. The technique is generally limited to gross metal objects. Soft x-rays, which are in the range of 4 to 25 kilowatts, are generally used to examine paintings, fabrics, papers, inks, gunshot residues, and jewelry.

harmonica bug. an audio amplifier and microphone connected to a telephone line through an audio-tone sensitive relay which is activated by telephoning the bugged premises and sounding the coded tone.

Harris-Dodd Act. an amendment to U.S. food, drug, and cosmetic legislation that classified certain stimulants (amphetamines), depressants (barbiturates), and hallucinogens as dangerous drugs and brought them under federal control, shifting the constitutional basis for drug control from taxing power to interstate and commerce powers.

Harrison Narcotics Act of 1914. the first federal antinarcotics statute and the basis of all subsequent narcotics controls until the passage of the Drug Abuse Act of 1970. Ostensibly, the act was a tax measure designed for the open control and orderly marketing of narcotics, among which were classified the opiates and cocaine. The three central parts of the act stated that (1) anyone engaged in the production or distribution of narcotics had to register with the federal government and keep records of all transactions with these drugs, (2) all parties handling the drugs through either purchase or sales had to pay a nominal tax (1 percent per ounce), and (3) unregistered persons could purchase drugs only on prescriptions from physicians, and such prescriptions had to be for legitimate medical use. The dispensing of narcotics by registered physicians "in the course of their professional practice" was not prohibited. The act's avowed purpose was then primarily to bring the domestic drug traffic into observable channels. However, the possession of untaxed narcotics had become a crime and following the passage of the act, the Treasury Department became responsible for its enforcement and inaugurated a policy of prohibiting the prescribing of narcotics for nonmedical maintenance. In two landmark decisions in 1919 (U.S. v. Doremus and Webb v. U.S.), the U.S. Supreme Court upheld the act's constitutionality and severely restricted the right of doctors to prescribe opiates, asserting that doctors who maintained narcotic users violated the law and that maintenance of a user was illegal unless it was part of an attempt to cure (detoxify) the habit. In Linder v. U.S., the Supreme Court later modified this stand, implying that if done in good faith a physician could prescribe narcotics to a patient. This ruling, however, had little impact. Subsequent legislation that supplemented the Harrison Act were the Narcotic Drugs Import and Export Act of 1922, the Marijuana Tax Act of 1937, the Boggs Amendment of 1951, the Narcotics Drug Control Act of 1956, and the Drug Abuse Control Amendments of 1965. These acts were repealed and replaced by the Drug Abuse Act of 1970.

Harrison process. a technique in which photographic film is pressed against latent fingerprints. When the film is developed, the fingerprint impression is revealed.

Harris v. New York. a case in which the U.S. Supreme Court ruled that although statements taken in violation of the Miranda rule may not be used to prove guilt at trial, they are not barred for all purposes.

In this case, Harris was arrested for selling heroin to an undercover police officer. Immediately following his arrest, he made certain statements to the officers. He had not been advised of his right to appointed counsel. At trial, Harris took the stand in his own defense, and his testimony contrasted sharply with what he told police during his postarrest interrogation. On cross-examination, evidence from the interrogation was admitted to impeach the defendant's credibility. Harris was convicted and he appealed the admission of his prior inconsistent illegally obtained statements for impeachment.

The Supreme Court held that although statements taken in violation of Miranda may not be used to prove guilt, they are not barred for all purposes, and may be admissible to impeach a defendant's credibility where (1) the statements are inconsistent with trial testimony of the accused as they bear directly on the crime charged, and (2) there is no evidence that the statements are otherwise coerced or involuntary.

hash. a slang name for hashish; in communications, an electrical noise.

hashish. the resinous secretions of the cannabis plant, which are collected, dried, and then compressed into a variety of forms, such as balls, cakes, or cookie-like sheets. It contains a higher concentration of THC (up to 14 percent) than marijuana, and has a heavy marijuana odor when burned. It is often smoked in water pipes, which regulate and cool the smoke, or sprinkled on joints or tobacco cigarettes. In India, hashish is known as charas.

hashish oil. a dark viscous liquid yielded through a process of repeated extraction of cannabis plant materials. This highly refined extract contains the highest concentration of THC of all forms of cannabis, up to 40 percent. It is thick and can be dark brown, yellow, reddish-yellow, or clear in color, and is often applied a drop at a time to marijuana tobacco or spread on the paper used to roll joints and cigarettes. It does not have the characteristic smell of marijuana when burned. Crystallized hash oil can have a potency of 60 percent THC. The THC content in hash oil deteriorates rapidly when not properly refrigerated. Hashish oil is a Schedule I substance.

Hass v. Oregon. a 1975 case in which the U.S. Supreme Court ruled that although statements taken in violation of Miranda may not be used to establish the prosecution's case, they are not barred for all purposes, and may be admissible to impeach the defendant's credibility.

In this case, bicycles were stolen from two residences. Hass was identified by an eyewitness in one of the thefts. A police officer arrested Hass and gave him the Miranda warnings. Hass agreed to talk but during questioning requested an attorney. The police officer said to wait until they returned to the office. In the meantime, Hass made some incriminating statements. The trial judge admitted the statements made before Hass asked for an attorney but not those made after it. Hass took the stand in his own defense and his testimony was inconsistent with the statements he made to the officer after he had asked for an attorney. On cross-examination, evidence of those statements was admitted to impeach his credibility. Hass was convicted and he appealed.

The Supreme Court ruled similarly to Harris v. United States by stating "it does not follow from Miranda that evidence inadmissible in the prosecution's case in chief is barred for all purposes provided it is trustworthy and here Hass' statement was not involuntary or coerced."

Hatch Act. a popular name for two federal statutes passed in 1939 and 1940. The 1939 act restricted the political activities of almost all federal employees, whether in the competitive service or not. The 1940 act extended the restrictions to positions in state employment having federal financing.

Hawaiian baby wood rose. a climbing plant of the bindweed family originally grown in Hawaiian and Asian forests. It is now grown and sold in the United States. Hawaiian baby wood rose seeds contain lysergic acid amides and produce hallucinogenic effects when consumed. The fuzz coating on the seeds contains trace amounts of strychnine that can cause nausea and vomiting if not removed before ingestion.

hazardous waste. any materials designated as hazardous by the Environmental Protection Agency.

hazmat. hazardous materials.

header. a verbal statement made at the beginning of a taped recording. The header typically contains details as to time, date, location, offense, and names of persons related to the recording. Such tapes are used to make a record of interviews, interrogations, surveillances, lineups, and the like.

head shop. a store which specializes in selling drug paraphernalia and drug-related materials.

hearing. a proceeding in which arguments, witnesses, or evidence are heard by a judicial officer or administrative body.

hearsay evidence. evidence of a statement which is made other than by a witness. Hearsay cannot be entered into evidence unless the maker of the statement can be cross examined. There are, however, some limited exceptions to the rule against hearsay evidence. A dying declaration is one kind of hearsay that can be accepted in court.

heart of the typewriter. the spacing mechanism of a typewriter which when examined by a questioned documents expert will reveal whether or not certain documents were typed on that particular machine.

heat exhaustion. a disorder caused by overexposure to heat or the sun that results in excessive sweating and loss of large quantities of salt and fluid from the body; prostration caused by excessive loss of water and salt through sweating. It is characterized by cold, clammy skin and a weak, rapid pulse. When salt and body fluid levels fall within the body heat exhaustion can result.

heat of passion. as used in criminal law, a state of violent and uncontrollable rage engendered by provocation. The heat of passion argument is often used to seek a reduction in the charge against a defendant.

heat stroke. a severe life-threatening condition caused by prolonged exposure to heat that results in profound disturbance of the body's heat-regulating mechanism. Persons over 40 and those in poor health are most susceptible to heat stroke. It is characterized by extreme fever, hot and dry skin, bounding pulse, and delirium or coma.

heavy burner. a chronic smoker of marihuana.

hebephrenic reaction. a schizophrenic reaction characterized by shallowness, distortion of fact, and inane behavior.

Heimlich maneuver. a method for dislodging foreign material caught in the throat. In this technique, the rescuer takes a position behind the victim, locks his arms around the victim's upper torso, places one thumb knuckle of clenched hands in the area of the victim's sternum at the upper abdomen, and with the strength of both arms sharply compresses the victim's diaphragm. Air inside the lungs acts as a force for expelling the foreign material.

helping interview. an interview in which the interviewer is an empathic listener rather than an interrogator or recorder of information. The interviewer interjects only as necessary to guide or encourage the flow of information.

hematoma. a localized collection of extravasated blood, usually clotted, in an organ, space, or tissue; a blood clot; the collection of blood in the tissues as the result of injury or a broken blood vessel, usually just below the skin.

hemin crystal test. a laboratory test to determine the presence of blood in a stain or substance of unknown origin. If blood is present, hemin crystals form upon application of a reagent. It is a confirmatory test, i.e., it is used to confirm a test by a different procedure. Also called a Teichmann test.

hemorrhage. bleeding from a ruptured vessel; especially bleeding that is profuse.

hemp. the cannabis plant, particularly the variety cultivated for commercial purposes such as for the making of rope.

Henry system. a fingerprint classification system developed by Sir Edward Richard Henry, former police commissioner of London. The system organizes fingerprints into four main types: arches, loops, whorls, and composites. Arches are divided into plain or tented arches. Loops are called ulnar when the loop opening is toward the ulnar bone or little finger, and radial when the opening is toward the radial bone or thumb. Whorls are classed as inner, meet, and outer. Composites are divided into central pocket loops, twin loops, laterals, and accidentals. Counts are made of friction ridges that intersect an imaginary straight line between the delta and core. A letter-number methodology corresponding to the patterns and ridges allow fingerprints to be classified on a volume basis.

Hering-Breuer reflex. in polygraphy, a reflex characterized by rhythmic control of normal breathing. Quiet, passive expiration is accomplished by relaxation of the external intercostal muscles.

heroin. diacetylmorphine hydrochloride, a semisynthetic opiate derivative isolated in 1898 in Germany by the pharmacologist Heinrich Dreser in the search for non-habit-forming analgesics to take the place of morphine. It was named after the German word "heroisch" meaning large, big, powerful. Although heroin was considered nonaddictive when first introduced, by 1924 the U.S. Congress had prohibited its manufacture in the United States, and by 1956 all existing stocks on hand were required to be surrendered.

Heroin is 2 to 3 times as potent analgesically as morphine, although in equipotent doses the effects are similar. The preference for heroin use over morphine is yet to be thoroughly explained. Pure heroin is a white powder with a bitter taste. It may vary in color from white to dark brown depending on impurities left from the manufacturing process. Pure heroin is almost always diluted, usually with sugars, starch, powdered milk and quinine. Street names include horse, smack and Big H. It appears in the Controlled Substances Act as a Schedule I narcotic. Heroin produces high physical and psychological dependence.

heroin maintenance. the legal prescription of heroin on a regular basis.

hertz. a unit of electrical frequency, mostly used in Europe. One hertz equals one cycle per second.

Herzberg theory. a management theory which holds that employees are motivated by feelings of achievement, the work itself, responsibility, advancement, and personal growth as a contributing member of the organization.

hesitation marks. cutting or stabbing marks on the body of a suicide or attempted suicide victim. The marks indicate the victim's hesitating attempts at self-destruction.

heuristic method. any exploratory method of solving problems in which an evaluation is made of the progress toward an acceptable final result using a series of approximate results.

hidden agenda. unannounced or unconscious goals, personal needs, expectations and strategies that an individual brings with his or her participation in a group.

hidden key. in polygraphy, an item of evidence known only to the victim, perpetrator, investigator, and polygraphist. The polygraphist will use the key in testing suspects. Neutral responses to questions concerning the key are considered indicative of innocence. Deceptive responses suggest knowledge of the key, i.e., guilty knowledge.

hierarchy of needs. a management theory which holds that humans share certain needs, which when satisfied, no longer motivate. From lowest to highest, the needs are: (1) basic physiological survival (food, water, shelter, etc), (2) security against danger, (3) social esteem, (4) independence, and (5) self-actualization.

high. the feeling of euphoria or exhilaration often associated with drug-taking; the continuing state of relaxation and well-being while a drug is in effect, as opposed to the rush, the initial onset of euphoria.

high accident frequency location. a place, intersection or length of roadway where an excessive number of traffic accidents have occurred over a given period of time.

high explosive. an explosive with a rapid burning rate. On detonation, a high explosive will have a shattering effect on objects in the immediate area. TNT, dynamite, and nitroglycerin are types of high explosives.

high-order explosion. an explosion characterized by an extremely rapid combustion, known as detonation reaction, occurring through the action of explosives such as dynamite, TNT, RDX, nitroglycerin, pentaerythritoltetranitrate and various plastic explosives. High-order explosions are those manifesting a velocity of detonation greater than 1000 meters per second.

high-performance liquid chromatography (HPLC). a forensic testing method used to identify the components of a specimen. The technique employs a column through which the sample passes while undergoing equilibration between two liquid phases. The technique measures the time it takes for the specimen to traverse the column at a given solvent flow rate. The speed of movement provides accurate indications as to the drug molecule in the sample. The HPLC technique is often used to identify the presence of drugs in urine and blood.

high pressure fog. a fine mist of water used in fighting fire. It is produced by water being forced by high pressure through a small capacity spray jet.

high port. a position for safely holding or carrying a weapon. At high port, the muzzle of the weapon is pointed in a safe direction, usually upward.

high risk target. a person, object or place which because of actual value, symbolic value, or relative isolation is more likely to be attractive or accessible to criminal action.

hijacking. taking control of a vehicle by the use or threatened use of force or by intimidation; taking a vehicle by stealth, without the use or threatened use of force, in order to steal its cargo.

Himmelsbach test. a test developed and used extensively at the now defunct Addiction Research Center in Lexington, Kentucky, as a means for assessing the severity of a patient's opiate withdrawal syndrome. It consists of assigning points for various symptoms observed over a set time period.

hit. a single drag or inhalation of marijuana smoke; one dose of an illicit drug.

hit and run. unlawful departure by the vehicle operator from the scene of a motor vehicle accident which resulted in injury to a person or damage to the property of another.

hit it. an order given during firefighting operations. It means to attack the source of fire with streams of water or other extinguishing agents.

hit man. a paid assassin; professional killer; hired gun.

hit slip. in a numbers operation, a slip of paper bearing the amount of money bet and the amount of the pay-off.

hit the ceiling. an order in firefighting operations to direct a stream of water so as to strike a ceiling at an angle and thereby deflect and distribute water onto the fire.

hitting up. injecting a drug.

Hobbs Act. federal legislation passed in 1946 that makes it a crime to interfere with interstate commerce by threats or violence. The Hobbs Act has been mainly used to prosecute labor racketeering figures.

hold fast. in firefighting operations, an order to stay in position with a hose line; in military or law enforcement operations, an order to not give ground in the face of attack.

holding. possessing drugs.

hold order. a notation on an inmate's file that another jurisdiction which has charges pending against him or in which he is due to serve time must be informed of his impending release.

hold-over till scheme. a scheme in which a dishonest clerk or cashier retains a portion of money taken in on a shift and when asked to explain the shortage will claim that the money was placed in the till for the next work shift.

hold-up alarm. an audible or silent alarm transmitted from the scene of a hold-up or other emergency for the purpose of summoning assistance.

hold-up switch. a switch used to trigger a hold-up alarm. A hold-up switch is usually located out of sight and capable of being triggered inconspicuously. Panic buttons and foot rails are types of hold-up switches.

hold-up till alarm. an alarm device placed in a till so as to register a silent alarm when money is removed during a robbery. A money clip is a type of hold-up till alarm.

Holger-Neilsen method. a method of artificial respiration used when the victim's air passages may be blocked by a fluid, such as water, blood, or vomit. It has been found effective in drowning and aspiration cases. The rescuer presses downward on the victim's back so that the resulting compression of the lungs creates air to expel fluid from the air passages.

hollow point. a type of bullet designed to expand on impact. In some jurisdictions the use of hollow point bullets is prohibited.

Holmes-Rahe Social Readjustment Scale. a scale used to rate the probability of suicide. The scale rank-orders a series of 43 stressful life events and applies to each event a value. A total of 200 or more points is indicative of a suicide candidate or of suicide in a questionable death case.

holographic document. a writing that is wholly in the handwriting of one person.

homegrown. marijuana grown in or around the home for personal use or sharing with friends, as opposed to growth for commercial purposes. Marijuana is easily cultivated and can be grown undetected in small quantities on balconies, rooftops, gardens, clearings in wooded areas, and even in closets under artificial lights. Under the laws of most states, conviction for growing marijuana is deemed prima facie as "manufacturing with intent to distribute" and carries heavy penalties.

homemade napalm. an improvised incendiary comprised of gasoline in combination with soap, lye, castor oil, blood or salt.

Home Office. a British cabinet office that exercises limited jurisdiction over the police, operates the prison and aftercare systems, and organizes research and statistics on crime.

homicide. a killing of one person by another.

honesty shopping. a general term relating to methods for evaluating the honesty of retail store employees. A common method is to use a specially trained person posing as a shopper who selects an item, pays for it with cash in the exact amount, and leaves before the sale can be rung up. This affords the cashier an opportunity to not ring up the sale and pocket the cash. The transaction is later evaluated by an examination of the cash register tape and information provided by the honesty shopper.

hook. that member of a team of pickpockets who removes items from the mark (victim).

hooked. addicted to drugs; swindled or conned.

hooker. a prostitute.

hook-up. in firefighting operations, a connection between hose lines, pumpers and hydrants.

hophead. a narcotics addict.

hopped up. intoxicated by drugs.

horizontal gaze nystagmus test. a test which measures the ability of the eye to maintain a fixation on objects moving out of the line of vision. The test is based on the principle that the movement of the eyeball as it turns to the side may be aggravated by central nervous system depressants such as barbiturates and alcohol. By observing the onset and quantity of nystagmus (a rapid involuntary oscillation of the eyeball), a trained person may be able to estimate intoxication. The HGN test is used by some police

agencies and employers as an on-scene sobriety test.

horizontal overcharging. the practice of charging an offender with separate offenses for each criminal act in which he or she allegedly participated, thus fragmenting the principal single offense into several component offenses.

horse. heroin.

horse parlor. a place where bets can be made on horse races; a bookie's joint.

horseshoe load. a fire hose wrapped in the form of a horseshoe-shaped loop.

hose jacket. a temporary covering that can be clamped around a burst portion of fire hose to stop a leak.

hose roller. a device that fits over a roof projection, building cornice or window and operates as a pulley for hoisting hose or ladders.

hose strap. a short length of rope with a metal hook at one end. It is used to fasten hose line to banisters, railings and other fixtures so that the line will be stable.

hose tag. a metal plate or disc strapped to a hose line for the purpose of identifying the line as to its source of supply and its use during firefighting operations.

host computer. in a network, a computer that primarily provides services such as computation, data base access, or special programs or programming languages; the primary or controlling computer in a multiple computer installation; a computer used to prepare programs for use on another computer or on another data processing system, for example, a computer used to compile or test programs to be used on another system.

hostile witness. a witness who manifests hostility or prejudice under examination to an extent that the party who has called him to testify will treat him as a witness for the opposite party.

hostility displacement. a displacement of pent-up feelings on objects less dangerous than those which initially aroused the emotions.

hot book. in a numbers operation, a writer who is a particular target of the police.

hot check. a stolen check; fraudulent check; a check knowingly passed without sufficient funds to cover it. Also called a rubber check.

hot check artist. a person who passes worthless checks. Also called a paper hanger.

hot line. a dedicated communication circuit; a telephone line used exclusively for transmitting emergency messages.

hot mike. a microphone in the active mode; a telephone's microphone that has been made active through the use of a third wire or similar surreptitious device even though the hand piece of the telephone is in the "hung up" position.

hot oil. oil produced in violation of state regulations or transported interstate in violation of federal regulations.

hot pursuit law. a law that permits police officers to act under their legal authority outside of their usual jurisdiction if they have directly pursued a suspected criminal who has fled from the original jurisdiction.

hot sheet. the list of stolen vehicles carried by a patrol unit. In some jurisdictions, the hot sheet will include missing or wanted persons, stolen property, and other details relating to recently reported crimes. Also, a list of stolen or fraudulently used credit cards used by cashiers or salespersons when processing sales transactions.

hot spot. an area in a radiation contaminated region in which the level of contamination is considerably greater than in nearby areas within the region.

hot sprinkler. a fire suppression water sprinkler maintained in a charged, or water-filled condition.

hot-stage microscopy. a crime laboratory method for examining the effect of heat on a sample. In fiber examinations, for example, the melting characteristics and relative melting points of various fibers are revealing as to their natural or polymeric properties.

hot surveillance. open tailing or bugging of a target for purposes of harassment or intimidation.

hot wire. a technique for starting a vehicle without the use of a key. Also, an electrical jumper wire used in the technique.

hot wire dispatch. the dispatch of a patrol unit in response to an electric power emergency, such as a fallen power line.

house arrest. restriction of an individual to a specific residence with limitations applied to visitors who may enter. Arrest to quarters is a similar concept that applies to members of the Armed Forces. House arrest is seldom employed in the United States.

housebreaking. a criminal activity in which a house (sometimes merely a structure) is entered by a forcible breaking. Housebreaking in some jurisdictions is synonymous with burglary.

house coach. in traffic enforcement, a vehicle motivated by a power connected therewith or propelled by a power within itself, which is or can be used as the home or living abode or habitation of one or more persons, either temporarily or permanently.

household burglary. the unlawful entry or forcible entry or attempted forcible entry of a residence, usually, but not necessarily, attended by theft.

household larceny. the theft or attempted theft of money or property from a residence or its immediate vicinity.

house of ill fame. a meeting place for performing illegal activity such as gambling, prostitution and drug abuse. Also called house of assignation.

howler. an alarm annunciator which emits a howling sound.

H substance. in crime laboratory examinations, the water soluble substance in body fluids that would be secreted by a person of blood group O. However, it is thought that both A and B substances are made from H substance so that persons of groups A, B, and AB may also secrete some H substance as well.

huckster. a petty criminal; a con artist; a dishonest salesperson; a person who makes false claims for his products or services.

Hudgens v. National Labor Relations Board. a case in which the U.S. Supreme Court held that union pickets have no legal right to enter a privately owned shopping center for the purpose of advertising their strike against one of the retail stores leased from the owner of the center.

hue and cry. a method of policing found in early England. It was a call to action requiring all citizens to participate in the apprehension of an offender.

hung jury. a trial jury so divided in its opinion as to fail to arrive at a verdict; a jury which cannot agree upon any verdict; a dead-locked jury. In such an instance the case may be again tried before another jury.

hush money. money paid to a complainant not to prosecute or report an incident. The term itself is not recognized in law except as bribery or compounding.

hustling. nonviolent means of making money illegally, such as theft, prostitution, pimping, drug selling, and conning.

hybrid computer. a computer that processes both analog and digital data.

hydrant house. a small house containing a hydrant, hose, nozzles, wrenches and other firefighting equipment. It is frequently seen in an industrial setting.

hydrometrograph. an instrument for determining and recording the quantity of water discharged from a pipe in a given time.

hydromorphone hydrochloride. an opioid five times more potent than morphine as an analgesic. Physical dependence develops after prolonged use, and withdrawal symptoms are similar to those of morphine in severity. Two mg provide the analgesia of 10 to 15 mg of morphine. This highly abused semi-synthetic narcotic analgesic is sold in tablet and injectable forms and is a target of theft and acquisition by fraudulent means. Dilaudid is the trade name for hydromorphone which is a Schedule II narcotic.

hydrostatic pressure. the pressure exerted by water or another liquid at rest.

hydrostatic test. the test of a hollow part, such as a hose, for tightness by means of water, oil, or other liquid under pressure; a test made periodically of hose line, fire extinguishers and other equipment susceptible to leakage. The test seeks to insure that such equipment meets certain minimum standards of performance.

hyoid bone. a U-shaped bone at the base of the tongue. A fractured hyoid bone is indicative of manual strangulation.

hypercapnea. a condition in the human body caused when the waste products of respiration are not exhaled. It occurs with the presence of excessive amounts of carbon dioxide in the blood, lungs or vital organs.

hypergolic. self-igniting; a characteristic of certain explosives in which detonation will result from a combining of chemicals contained in a bomb.

hypernea. in polygraphy, rapid or deep breathing as represented in the ink tracings of the pneumograph component.

hypersalivation. drooling; excessive production of saliva, sometimes seen in persons under the influence of PCP.

hypersensitivity. increased or excessive sensitivity to a substance or stimulus.

hypertension. high blood pressure.

hyperventilation. abnormally prolonged and deep breathing, altering the oxygen-carbon dioxide balance in the body. This condition is usually associated with acute anxiety or emotional tension.

hypnotics. a major classification of nonnarcotic depressant drugs with such primary effects as calming, sedation, or induction of sleep (hypnosis). The sedative/hypnotics are usually divided into four categories: (1) barbiturates, (2) alcohol, (3) antianxiety tranquilizers, and (4) nonbarbiturate, proprietary drugs. The antianxiety tranquilizers and the nonbarbiturate sedative/hypnotics are also often called anxiolytic sedatives, or psycholeptics.

hypochondriasis. a neurotic reaction characterized by excessive concern about one's health in the absence of related organic pathology. A person with hypochondriasis has excessive concern about his or her health, and unrealistic interpretations of real or imagined symptoms, often accompanied by anxiety and depression.

hypothetical question. a combination of assumed or proven facts and circumstances, stated in such form as to constitute a coherent and specific situation, upon which the opinion of an expert is asked at trial; a question having the nature of or based on an assumption; a question based on assumed or proved facts and circumstances and stated in such a way that no names or places are specifically mentioned, and upon which an expert witness may answer. In such a case, the expert's answer is based solely on the facts in the question itself and not on any of the evidence that might have been introduced at the trial, though there may be a coincidence with the facts actually proved. Thus, a doctor who has not had any actual knowledge of the defendant's physical ailments, may be asked a hypothetical question based on the facts which allegedly brought about the defendant's illness.

hypothermia. a body temperature significantly below normal. It is either symptomatic of a disease or disorder of the temperature-regulating mechanism of the body, or brought about by exposure to cold environment. Hypothermia is sometimes observed in heavy users of CNS depressants, especially heroin.

hypoxia. a deficiency of oxygen in the tissues of the body. It can occur when other gases replace oxygen in the atmosphere, for example, during a fire.

hysteria. an emotional disturbance characterized by a lack of control over one's emotions; a state of tension or excitement in which there is a temporary loss of control over the emotions. Hysteria is a manifestation of psychoneurosis in which the individual converts anxiety created by emotional conflict into physical symptoms that have no organic basis.

ibogaine. a drug that appears in the Controlled Substances Act as a Schedule I hallucinogen. It is obtained from the root, bark, stems, and leaves of the African shrub, Tabernanthe iboga. Africans are said to use the extract while stalking game to enable them to remain motionless for long periods and still maintain mental alertness. In high doses, it can produce excitement, drunkenness, mental confusion, and hallucinations.

Ibrahim v. The King. a Canadian court case containing a ruling which states: "It has long been established as a positive rule of English criminal law that no statement made by an accused is admissible as evidence against him unless it is shown by the prosecution to have been voluntary in the sense that it has not been obtained from him either by fear or prejudice or hope of advantage exercised or held out by a person in authority."

ICE. an acronym indicating the first aid intervention for strains and sprains. The letters stand for Ice application to site, Compression, and Elevation of the affected part.

ice cream habit. a nonaddictive, irregular drug habit.

identification buy. a tactic used in conducting an honesty shopping test. Two specially trained persons posing as shoppers get in line at a cashier checkpoint. The first shopper makes a purchase, allows it to be bagged, and upon receipt of change suddenly decides to buy an expensive item with exact change. Before the cashier can react, the first shopper leaves the store, thereby providing the cashier with an opportunity to not ring up the sale and keep the cash. The second shopper, who is next in line, takes note of the cashier's actions, makes a normal purchase, obtains a sales slip and leaves. The sales slips of the two shoppers identify on the cash register tape the exact point at which the honesty test occurred and whether or not the cashier responded honestly.

identification reaction. an ego defense mechanism which causes an individual to identify with some other person or institution usually of a successful or illustrative nature.

Identi-Kit. a commercial identification device consisting of a series of photographic transparencies depicting varieties of facial features that can be overlaid to form a human face. An Identi-Kit operator (usually a trained police officer) assembles the transparencies in response to cues received from a witness. The facial likeness produced by the technique is used for suspect identification purposes.

ignition jamming. a car theft technique in which a key blank is inserted in the ignition lock and then forcibly driven into the lock with the use of a hammer. The resulting damage allows access to the ignition wires.

ignition temperature. the lowest temperature of a flammable liquid required to initiate or cause self-sustained combustion in the absence of a spark or flame. This temperature varies considerably, depending upon the nature, size and shape of the ignition, surface, container, and other factors.

ignorance or mistake of fact. a legal defense that seeks to excuse an accused on the grounds that the wrongful act was committed by an honest mistake. For example, the defense might be employed if a homeowner injures a guest in his home who he has mistaken for a burglar.

illegal alien. one who has illegally entered a country of which he is not a citizen, or who, having entered legally, violates the terms of his visa, as by overstaying or by engaging in prohibited activities.

illegal search and seizure. an act in violation of the Fourth Amendment of the U.S. Constitution, which states: "The right of the people to be secure in their persons, houses, papers and effects, against unreasonable searches and seizures, shall not be violated, and no warrants shall issue but upon probable cause, supported by oath or affirmation, and particularly describing the place to be searched and the persons or things to be seized."

illusion. in witness interviewing, a false perception derived from an incorrect interpretation of an observed situation. For example, a witness may experience an illusion by confusing the sound of a car backfire with the sound of a gunshot.

image. a reproduction of an object produced by light rays. An image-forming optical system gathers a beam of light diverging from an object point and transforms it into a beam that converges to another point, thus producing an image.

immaterial. in criminal law, not pertinent or of no significance to an issue.

immaterial question. in polygraphy, a question that is irrelevant or neutral to the issue being evaluated.

immediate precursor. a substance from which another substance can be immediately or directly formed. The term is often used to describe a material, compound, mixture, or preparation containing any substance that can be used to manufacture a controlled substance. Phenylacetone, for example, is an immediate precursor to amphetamine and methamphetamine.

immigrant alien. a person who is lawfully admitted into the U.S. under an immigration visa for permanent residence.

imminent danger. the appearance of threatened and impending injury as would put a reasonable and prudent man to his instant defense. The term is often used as a legal defense to charges of aggravated assault and homicide.

immovable evidence. evidence that cannot easily be collected and transported, such as a blood-spattered wall.

immunity. an exemption from a legal liability. Total or complete immunity means the individual receiving the immunity cannot be held liable for his acts. Qualified immunity refers to a partial grant of immunity to a person by reason of position or a particular activity.

immunity defense. a defense against prosecution which is granted in exchange for cooperation by the accused. The required cooperation might be a full disclosure of all facts and testimony at trial.

immunoassay. an analysis of a body fluid for the purpose of detecting the presence of a drug or drug metabolite. An immunoassay is based on the principle of competition between labeled and unlabeled antigen for binding sites on a specific antibody. An antibody is a protein substance to which a specific drug or drug metabolite will bind. Two types of immunoassays are usually employed: enzyme immunoassay (EIA) and radio-immunoassay (RIA). The EIA utilizes an enzyme as the label, while RIA uses a radioactive label. Because antibodies often cross-react with related drugs, and sometimes with unrelated compounds, confirmation of positive immunoassay results with an independent procedure is imperative for definitive identification.

impact weapon. a nonlethal weapon designed to subdue a subject by delivering to the body a forceful, sometimes painful, impact. The police baton, a defensive tool, is an impact weapon.

impairing the morals of a minor. engaging in sex-related acts (except intercourse) with a minor; for example, taking obscene photographs of the minor or caressing the minor in a lewd manner.

impaled object. an object that has caused a puncture wound and that remains embedded in the wound.

impanel. to select jurors; the act of the clerk of the court in making up a list of jurors who have been selected for the trial of a particular cause.

impeach. to proceed against a public officer for crime or misfeasance, before a proper court, by the presentation of a written accusation called "articles of impeachment." In the law of evidence, to call in question the veracity of a witness, by means of evidence adduced for that purpose.

impending shock. a state of early unconsciousness or depression of the vital processes associated with reduced blood volume and pressure. It is usually caused by severe injuries, burns, or hemorrhage and is reversible if treated promptly. Impending shock is sometimes followed by secondary shock which is profound and frequently fatal. Also called primary shock.

impersonating an officer. pretending to be a police officer, an officer of the armed services, or an official of a federal, state, or local law enforcement agency, usually by wearing a uniform, showing an identification card or badge, and identifying oneself as an officer.

implied answer question. a question phrased so as to imply its answer. In interviewing, it is a type of question to be avoided since it defeats the purpose of determining what the interviewee knows. Also called a leading question.

impound. to take into custody of the law or of a court. A court will sometimes impound a suspected document, when produced at a trial, until a question affecting it is decided.

imputed negligence. negligence that is not directly attributable to the person himself, but which is the negligence of a person who is in privity with him and with whose fault he is chargeable.

inactive supervision. a form of probation in which the probation agency supervises the client on a less than regular basis. Inactive cases are sometimes called banked cases.

inadmissible. that which under the established rules of law cannot be admitted or received into evidence.

in camera. in chambers; in private. A cause is said to be heard in camera when the hearing is had before the judge in his private room or when all spectators are excluded from the courtroom.

incapacitation of criminals. keeping convicted criminals in prison as a means of preventing them from committing further crimes.

incendiarism. an act of malicious fire setting; arson.

incendiary. one guilty of arson; one who maliciously and willfully sets another's property on fire; a device for causing or enhancing a fire.

incest. adultery, fornication, or intermarriage between persons who are within the degrees of consanguinity declared by law to be incestuous and void; sexual intercourse between persons too nearly related for legal marriage. From a very early period incest was banned by the church and in some countries was a capital offense. The degrees within which marriage is permissible so as to be not deemed incestuous are regulated by the statutes of the various states.

inchoate offense. an offense which consists of an action or conduct which is a step to the intended commission of another offense.

incidence of crime. criminality measured in a given population over a defined time span, as during a single day or a single year.

incised wound. a cut or incision on a human body; a wound made by a cutting instrument, such as a razor or knife.

included offense. an offense which is made up of elements which are a subset of the elements of another offense having a greater statutory penalty, and the occurrence of which is established by the same evidence or by some portion of the same evidence which has been offered to establish the occurrence of the greater offense.

incompetency. lack of ability, legal qualification, or fitness to discharge the required duty.

incompetent evidence. evidence which is not admissible under the established rules of evidence.

incompetent to stand trial. the finding by a court that a defendant is mentally incapable of understanding the nature of the charges and proceedings against him or her, of consulting with an attorney, and of aiding in his or her own defense. When a defendant is declared incompetent to stand trial, criminal proceedings are suspended until such time as the defendant may be found competent. Frequently, the court will order periodic examination of the defendant to determine if competency has been regained.

inconclusive. that which may be disproved or rebutted; not shutting out further proof or consideration. Applied to evidence and presumptions.

inconclusive opinion. in polygraphy, a term signifying that the polygraph was unsuccessful in determining if the examinee was truthful or untruthful. The inconclusive opinion usually results from a malfunction of the polygraph instrument, illness of the examinee during the test, or poor test construction due to insufficient information available to the polygraphist.

incontrovertible evidence. evidence which cannot be refuted.

incorrigible. a condition of a juvenile who is habitually delinquent, ungovernable, and unresponsive to rehabilitative efforts.

increased hearing threshold. an increase in hearing perception caused by the use of a drug, such as marihuana.

incriminate. to charge with crime; to expose to an accusation or charge of crime; to involve oneself or another in a criminal prosecution or the danger thereof; as in the rule that a witness is not bound to give testimony which would tend to incriminate him.

incriminating admission. an acknowledgment of facts tending to establish guilt.

incriminating circumstance. a fact or circumstance, collateral to the fact of the commission of a crime, which tends to show either that such a crime has been committed or that some particular person committed it.

incubation period. the period of time in which heat builds up sufficiently to generate a fire. An incubation period precedes a fire caused by a discarded cigarette or spontaneous ignition.

inculpate. to impute blame or guilt; to accuse; to involve in guilt or crime.

indecent assault. sexual assault not amounting to rape, sodomy or carnal abuse; uninvited sex-related touching of another.

indecent exposure. unlawful intentional or reckless exposing to view of the genitals or anus, in a place where another person may be present who is likely to be offended or alarmed by such an act.

indefinite sentence. a prison sentence for a range of time; for example, between one and ten years, or from one year to life.

indemnify. the act of compensating insured individuals for their losses; to restore the victim of a loss to the same position as before the loss occurred.

indented writing. dents or impressions made on the under sheets of writing paper after a writing is made on the top sheet. Thus, where several sheets of paper are stacked one upon another, a writing with pressure on the top sheet will cause a dent or impression on the under sheets. By applying artificial lighting at a sharp angle to the indented impressions, the writing may be read or deciphered by the shadows of the dents caused with the light. Iodine fuming is sometimes used to bring out the impressions by darkening the indentations.

independent variable. the variable whose occurrence or change results in the occurrence or change of another variable; the hypothesized cause of something else.

indeterminate sentence. a type of sentence to imprisonment where the commitment, instead of being for a specified single time quantity, is for a range of time.

index crimes. eight particular crimes whose incidence is reported by the FBI as an index of the extent, nature, and fluctuation of criminality in the United States. The index crimes are murder and non-negligent homicide, forcible rape, robbery, aggravated assault, burglary, larceny-theft, motor vehicle theft, and arson.

indictment. a formal written accusation made by a grand jury and filed in a court alleging that a certain person committed a certain offense.

indirect drug death. a death in which drug use is a contributing factor.

indirect evidence. circumstantial evidence; evidence of a collateral fact, that is, of a fact other than a fact in issue from which, either alone or with other collateral facts, the fact in issue may be inferred. It is a well settled rule in some jurisdictions that where the prosecution relies wholly upon circumstantial evidence to establish the guilt of the accused, the circumstances must be satisfactorily established and must be of such a character as, if true, to exclude to a moral certainty every other hypothesis except that of the accused's guilt.

indirect interrogating approach. a questioning approach that is exploratory in nature, seeking to test the suspect's truthfulness in relation to facts known by the interrogator. This approach is frequently used when interrogating a suspect whose guilt is uncertain or doubtful.

indirect interviewing approach. a method of obtaining information in which the witness or interviewee is asked to "tell the story" and is allowed to speak freely, prompted only as needed and with a minimum of direct questions.

individual characteristics. properties of evidence that can be attributed to a common source with an extremely high degree of certainty. Also, marks made on an object as the result of its use. Such marks, commonly cuts, tears and uneven wearing, can be significant to the analysis of foot and tire prints, tool marks and similar forms of physical evidence.

induction. the process of inducing or bringing in a conclusion or an event by some particular path or course of reasoning; the process of inferring or aiming at the general from observation of the particular; a conclusion reached by inductive reasoning.

induction tap. a wiretap that makes use of a coil placed around or near the telephone instrument or line.

inductive reasoning. a method of reasoning which starts out from specific cases, analyzes them, and reaches conclusions on the basis of the observations; an investigative process in which the investigator develops from observed facts a generalization explaining the relationships between the events under examination.

The process moves by logical steps from the particular to the general.

in evidence. included in the evidence already adduced; facts which have already been proved in the cause.

in extremis. the state of a person who is near death, beyond the hope of recovery.

infamous crime. a crime that is notorious, scandalous, or heinous; a crime for which a punishment may be imposed such as to deprive a person of civil and political rights, or to imprison a person in the state penitentiary or at hard labor. The term infamous crime is generally synonymous with felony crime.

infancy defense. a defense against prosecution which holds that children are incapable of committing any crime below a certain age, and that at a higher age there is a presumption of an incapacity to commit crime. Further, that at an even higher age certain crimes are conclusively presumed to be beyond the capability of a child. For example, it may be presumed that a 2 year old is incapable of stealing and that a 12 year old is incapable of committing the crime of rape.

infanticide. the murder or killing of an infant soon after its birth.

inference. that which is inferred; a deduction or conclusion; implication as a consequence. In law, once a proposition is admitted to be true, any other proposition drawn from it is an inference. For example, it may be inferred that a person fired a gun when it was observed that the person was holding a smoking gun seconds after a gunshot was heard. By contrast, a presumption is a deduction which the law requires to be made from the established facts. For example, flight to escape apprehension is presumptive evidence of guilt.

infiltrate. place an undercover operative within a targeted group or organization.

infinity bug. an audio amplifier and microphone connected to a telephone line through an audio-tone sensitive relay which is activated by telephoning the bugged premises and sounding a coded tone. Also called a harmonica bug.

informal social control. a crime prevention strategy that seeks to develop in a community a network of trust and interdependence built on social relationships of the community's residents. The sense of community cohesiveness exercises informal control of deviant behavior.

This strategy is executed through: (1) intensified use by residents of streets, parks and land around the structures in which they live, (2) increased watchfulness of residents for intruders who manifest unacceptable behavior, (3) an increased tendency of people to look out for the property and well-being of their neighbors and to interact with law enforcement, (4) an enhanced ability to discriminate between outsiders and residents, and an ability to communicate by actions that deviant behavior will not be allowed, and (5) a strong sense of shared interests in improving and maintaining the quality of life in the physical environment and social climate of the area.

informant. a person who wittingly or unwittingly provides information; a person who receives money or other consideration in exchange for information. Informants can be categorized by type, for example: (1) the observer informant is someone whose unique position within or in close proximity to criminal activity is able to report on what he or she sees, but is not necessarily positioned to report reliably on the meaning of the witnessed activity, (2) the eavesdropper informant is someone whose position relative to criminal activity is able to overhear incriminating conversations, or gather hearsay that may be valuable in developing criminal intelligence, and (3) the participating informant is someone actively involved in the criminal activity being reported. Informants are also described according to motive: (1) the out-from-under informant is someone who offers information in exchange for leniency by the criminal justice system, (2) the power informant who is motivated by gratification that stems from a sense of power, (3) the greed or control informant who wants

to use the police to remove business competitors, (4) the jealous informant, (5) the revenge informant, and (6) the paid or professional informant who views cooperation with the police as a strict business arrangement. An informant is also called a source.

informant file. a confidential file that lists information about informants such as personal data, motivations, personality, eccentricities, cases contributed to, successes and failures, areas of operation, reliability, specialties, criminal associates and connections, payments made, and tips on handling. An informant file of this type is usually for exclusive use of the investigator who controls the informants listed in it.

informant master file. a confidential file that identifies and describes all the informants controlled by officers within an investigative unit or department. The master file will contain at least as much information as is reflected in the individual informant files, and in addition will cite informant code names or numbers as they would appear in non-confidential reports. Access to the informant master file is typically restricted to senior members of the unit.

in forma pauperis. a request to waive the payment of legal fees on behalf of an indigent defendant.

information. a formal written accusation made by a prosecutor and filed in a court alleging that a certain person committed a certain offense; in intelligence parlance, raw data obtained from any source which, when processed, produce intelligence.

information overload. a constant flood of details confronting the individual at a rate that exceeds the human ability to process and respond.

information sheet. a file or document containing such data as a subject's arrest record, charges preferred and case dispositions. Also called a rap sheet or criminal history sheet.

informer. a person who intentionally discloses information about persons or activities, not always for financial reward or other considerations. Also called informant or source.

infraction. a violation of a state statute or local ordinance punishable by a fine or other penalty, but not by incarceration, or by a specified, unusually limited term of incarceration.

infrared. light waves that are too low in frequency to be seen by the human eye.

infrared examination. an investigative technique in which objects or events are examined while exposed to infrared radiation. Infrared differs from ultraviolet examination in that there are no fluorescent effects which can be seen by the unaided eye. The appearance of an object or event in the infrared is ordinarily studied through the medium of a photograph. Infrared is useful in examining evidence for tell-tale stains and in nighttime surveillance operations.

infrared fuse. a bomb fuse sensitive to minute increases in heat. The fuse functions when an influence from the target is exerted on a sensitive detecting device within the fuse itself.

infrared viewer. a device that makes infrared light waves visible to the human eye.

inhalants. a major classification of depressant drugs incorporating an aggregate of chemically diverse substances perhaps best described as being volatile (tending to evaporate easily) solvents and gases that are usually inhaled and whose effects are short-lived. Some of these drugs have been called deliriants although delirium is only one of many potential effects and is clearly not restricted to these substances. Many are quite similar in effect to the sedative group, while some have certain psychedelic or hallucinogenic effects. Most of these substances are not used medically, although several have been employed as surgical anesthetics.

inhibition. a mental blockage; a hesitancy to behave, particularly in a somewhat unconventional manner. In neurology, the stopping of an ongoing process or the prevention of a process from starting, as in the inhibition of antagonistic muscles.

initial appearance. the first appearance of an accused person in the first court having jurisdiction over the case.

initial effect. the effect experienced between the time a drug is first administered and the onset of the main or basic effect. It is the first of four stages: initial, main or basic, ending, and withdrawal.

initial plea. the first plea to a given charge entered in the court record by or for the defendant. The acceptance of an initial plea by the court indicates that the arraignment process has been completed.

initiator. that part of an explosive train used to ignite the explosive; the first charge in a firing train.

injection. the process of administering a drug by introducing or forcing it in liquid form into some part of the body usually by means of a syringe or hypodermic needle. Drug injections are classified as intramuscular, intravenous, or subcutaneous.

injunction. an order from a court telling a person or group not to do something; a writ of judicial process issued by a court of equity by which a party is required to do a particular thing or to refrain from doing a particular thing.

in loco parentis. in place of a parent; instead of a parent; charged with a parent's rights, duties, and responsibilities.

inmate code. the code of the inmate subculture; the foundation of prisonization, as in the practice of not informing and not cooperating with correctional authorities.

inmate self-government. the informal self-regulation of an inmate population, usually at the lower levels of decision-making, as in planning and organizing athletic and recreational programs.

inmate subculture. the mores, traditions and customs of an inmate population.

innocent agent. one who performs an act for another without knowledge of the unlawfulness of the act, being merely the instrument of the guilty party in committing the offense. For example, an innocent person may be someone who not knowing the contents of a blackmail letter delivers it to the victim.

innocent passer. a person who passes an

illegal instrument, such as counterfeit money or a bogus check, without guilty knowledge. For example, a store owner who accepts a fraudulent check and passes it along in good faith to a bank would be an innocent passer.

in order of seriousness. a time-honored custom of classifying crimes in order of their seriousness or gravity. In this concept, the common law crimes might be placed into three categories: treasons, felonies, and misdemeanors. Treason is the most serious because it is a crime against one's country. Under early common law it was a breach of faith to the king (high treason) or a killing of a lord by his vassal (petit treason).

Felonies have their roots in the common law crimes of murder, rape, arson, burglary, larceny, robbery and sodomy. In earlier times most felonies were punishable by death. At the present time, whether a crime is classified as a felony or a misdemeanor depends upon the extent of punishment provided by the statute defining the offense.

Misdemeanors were originally known as transgressions and continue today to be regarded as lesser offenses. A misdemeanor is generally defined as an offense not constituting a felony.

inorganic metallic poison. a class of poison which includes arsenic, mercury, lead, and other metals.

inorganic nonmetallic poison. a class of poison which includes cyanide, fluoride, iodine, acids, oxidants, and gases.

in pari delicto. in equal fault.

in personam. a remedy where the proceedings are against the person, as contradistinguished from those against a specific thing; a legal proceeding, the judgment of which binds the defeated party to a personal liability.

inquest. a judicial inquiry to determine the cause and manner of a violent, sudden, mysterious or suspicious death.

inquisitorial system. the system of criminal prosecution prevailing in most of continental Europe, Japan, and other countries, in contrast to the English and American adversary systems. In the inquisitorial system, a judicial officer is assigned to investigate, and adjudication is not limited to the facts adduced by the parties.

in re. a term used in law which means in the matter of, concerning, or in the case of.

In re Gault. a term referring to a landmark decision of the U.S. Supreme Court. The decision held that a juvenile is entitled to substantially the same rights given to an adult under the rules of due process.

in rem. a legal proceeding, the judgment of which binds, affects, or determines the status of property.

insanity. in law, an unsoundness of mental condition sufficient to modify or eliminate legal responsibility or capacity.

insanity defense. a legal defense which rests on the principle that a person who is insane at the time of committing a crime cannot be charged with the crime since an insane person is incapable of forming the requisite intent. This defense goes to the heart of the fundamental principle of intent, or guilty mind. If the accused did not understand what he was doing or understand that his actions were wrong, he cannot have criminal intent and without intent, there is no crime.

inscription. in law of evidence, anything written or engraved upon a metallic or other solid substance intended for great durability such as a tombstone, pillar, tablet, ring or medal.

inside man. the member of a confidence game who is described to the mark (potential victim) as having special knowledge of something that will bring profit. For example, the inside man might play the part of someone who knows that a horse race is fixed or that a major stock market transaction is imminent.

inside worker. a pickpocket who specializes in stealing wallets from inside coat pockets.

INS Master Index. a file maintained in the central offices of the Immigration and Naturalization Service. It contains names and descriptive data of persons admitted to or excluded from the U.S., as well as sponsors of record.

inspection ink. ink that is detectable by ultraviolet light. It is typically used to mark items for control and inspection.

inspector. a police rank, usually superior to that of captain; a functional title in a police agency; a commissioned police officer, usually of superior rank, whose duty is to detect, investigate, and report instances of improper behavior by members of the same organization.

inspector scam. a confidence scheme in which the perpetrator represents himself to a homeowner as an inspector of a local government or utility company. The confidence artist conducts an inspection of some vital service of the house structure, such as electricity, gas or water, and issues a citation or advice that causes the homeowner to believe he is in violation of a law or safety standard. The inspector will recommend a vendor certified to correct the violation. The vendor, who is an accomplice, performs the unnecessary work at a greatly inflated price.

instantaneous crime. a crime consummated by a single act as opposed to one involving a series of acts. Thus, arson is completed at the instant of burning, whereas receiving stolen goods requires the larceny first and then the receipt of the goods with knowledge of the theft.

in statu quo. in the original condition; in the condition in which it was. To place a party in statu quo means to place him in the position he was in before the present situation.

institutional capacity. an officially stated number of inmates which a confinement or residential facility is or was intended to house.

instructions to the jury. verbal and written instructions of a guiding nature given by the judge to the jury. The guidance explains the legal principles that should be applied to the facts of the case when the jury deliberates and reaches a decision.

instrumental analysis examinations. crime laboratory examinations which make use of instrumentation such as infrared spectroscopy, x-ray diffractometry, and emission spectrometry. Paints, plastics, explosives and dyes are typically analyzed by these techniques.

instrument of evidence. any medium, person, or thing through which the evidence of the facts may be conveyed to a jury for deliberation. Thus, a witness is an instrument of evidence as to what he has seen, as a document is an instrument of evidence as to what it purports to be.

insufficient evidence. evidence that is not enough to constitute proof at the level required at a given point in criminal proceedings.

insufflation. the inhaling or snorting of a substance. Psychoactive drugs most commonly insufflated are cocaine, heroin, and the volatile solvents. To be insufflated, the substance must be in either powdered or gaseous form, which is absorbed through the membranes of the nasal and bronchial passages.

insurable interest. any interest a person has in a possible subject of insurance, such as a car or home, or of such a nature that a certain happening might cause him financial loss.

insurgent. one who participates in an insurrection; one who opposes the execution of law by force of arms, or rises in revolt against the constituted authorities.

intaglio process. a printing process in which the design is engraved into the surface of the plate. The ink used in intaglio printing is thicker and coarser than planographic printing ink. Under a stereoscopic microscope, the ink lines of the intaglio process appear to be mounds of ink piled on top of the paper and the grains of the coarse ink can be seen. The intaglio process is used in the printing of U.S. currency and in placing characters on plastic credit cards.

intake. the process by which a juvenile referral is received by personnel of a probation agency, juvenile court or special intake unit, and a decision made to close the case at intake, or refer the juvenile to another agency, or place him or her under some kind of care or supervision, or file a petition in a juvenile court. Intake is the first step in decision-making regarding a juvenile whose behavior is such that a juvenile court could assume jurisdiction. Intake is also the process of admitting a drug abuser into treatment, a routine procedure that usually includes the taking of information on the client's demographics and medical history, a medical examination, an explanation of the program, and in certain cases a detoxification regime.

integrated investigations concept. an organizational concept in which a police agency is structured so that patrol officers and detectives jointly investigate most criminal incidents.

integrated services. police, fire, and related services that are integrated, usually within a single agency called a public safety department. The advantages of integrated services are: (1) more effective use can be made of the resources of the combined groups; (2) overlapping functions can be reduced; (3) salaries, ranks, and benefits can be standardized and inequities removed; and (4) the delivery of services can be better coordinated, especially in major emergencies. The reported disadvantages are: (1) essential specialization may be lost; (2) the integration of services creates problems in supervision and organization; (3) extensive training is required to bring the department into balance among its specialized groups; and (4) friction and competition tend to develop between groups, especially between the superior officers.

intellectualization. an ego defense mechanism by which an individual achieves some measure of isolation from emotional hurt by cutting off or distorting the emotional charge which normally accompanies hurtful situations.

intellectual property. any idea, invention, design, program, work of authorship, and similar information or device generated or collected by or utilized in actual or anticipated business, research or development.

intelligence. the product resulting from the collection, evaluation, analysis, integration and interpretation of information obtained from covert and open sources.

intelligence collection plan. a plan for gathering information from available sources to meet an intelligence requirement.

intelligence cycle. the steps by which information is assembled, converted into intelligence, and made available to consumers. The cycle has four steps: direction, collation, processing, and dissemination.

Direction is the determination of intelligence requirements, preparation of a collection plan, tasking of collection agencies, and a continuous monitoring of collection productivity.

Collation is the exploitation of information sources and the delivery of collected information to the intelligence processing unit for use in producing intelligence.

Processing is the production of intelligence through evaluation, analysis, integration and interpretation of information.

Dissemination is the distribution of information or intelligence products (in oral, written, graphic or other forms) to users.

intelligence data base. all holdings of intelligence data and finished intelligence products at a given department or agency.

intelligence estimate. an appraisal of intelligence elements relating to a specific situation or condition to determine the course of action open to an adversary.

intelligence unit. an element of a police agency whose principal task is to collect and analyze information about criminal behavior, often limited to organized crime.

intensified drug use. long-term, patterned use of drugs at a minimum level of at least once daily, motivated by an individual's perceived need to achieve relief from a persistent problem or stressful situation or by a desire to maintain a certain self-prescribed level of performance. A distinguishing characteristic of this class of behavior is the regular use of one or a combination of drugs, escalating to patterns of consumption that might be defined as drug dependence.

intent. the state of mind or attitude with which an act is carried out; the design, resolve or determination with which a person acts to achieve a certain result.

interactive computer system. a computer system in which the user and the operating system communicate directly by means of a terminal.

interactive display terminal. a CRT display and keyboard that interfaces with a central processing monitor. An operator may enter data and command system functions via the keyboard. Prompting by the computer, with a response from the operator, is called interactive dialogue.

intercept. acquire a communication through the use of an electronic, mechanical, or other device. The term is specially applied to situations in which the acquisition is unlawful or unauthorized and involves the use of surreptitious listening equipment.

intercepted communication. generally, a conversational discussion, whether oral or telephonic, that is intentionally overheard or recorded by instrument, device, or equipment without the consent of any party thereto. This definition, which does not apply in all jurisdictions, would allow consent recordings, such as those made by informants or undercover agents in field assignments.

interface. point of contact; the boundary between organizations, people, jobs and/or systems.

interior common circulation area. an area within a multiple dwelling which is outside the private zones of individual units and is used in common by all residents and the maintenance staff of the building.

interior private area. the interior of a single family house; the interior of an apartment in a multiple dwelling; or the interior of a separate unit within a commercial, public, or institutional building.

interior public area. an interior common-circulation area of common resident-use space within a multiple dwelling to which access is unrestricted.

interior semi-public area. an interior common-circulation area or common resident-use room within a multiple dwelling to which access is possible only with a key or on the approval of a resident via an intercom, buzzer-reply system.

interlocutory appeal. a request, made at some point before judgment in trial court proceedings, that a court having appellate jurisdiction review a pre-judgment decision of the trial court before judgment is reached.

interlocutory decree. an interim decision of a court; a decision issued pending a final decree; a provisional court decision.

intermediate-acting barbiturates. a classification of barbiturates based on the time between administration and the onset of anesthesia. In this classification, barbiturates take effect within 15–40 minutes, with duration up to 6 hours. Pentobarbital (Nembutal), secobarbital (Seconal), amobarbital (Amytal), butabarbital (Butisol), talbutal (Lotusate) and aprobarbital (Alurate) are intermediate-acting barbiturates.

intermittent sentence. a sentence to periods of confinement interrupted by periods of freedom.

International Guide to Missing Treasures (IGMT). a central index used by participating art dealers to record art thefts and disseminate reports and special bulletins to subscribers, legitimate art dealers, key persons in the art community, and law enforcement agencies.

international law. a body of law derived from treaties, decisions of supranational courts (such as the Permanent Court for International Justice), and the charters of the League of Nations and the United Nations; legal precedents and procedures governing multinational corporations, import-export trade, and disputes between nations. In a limited sense, international law governs the conduct of a sovereign nation in matters not entirely internal.

Interpol. a body of police representatives from many countries organized for the purpose of gathering and sharing information about transnational criminal personalities and activities. Interpol also seeks missing persons and identifies unknown dead persons. Its headquarters is in Paris.

interrogating zones. distance zones between interrogator and a respondent which are regarded as being influential in the success or failure of an interrogation. Four zones are hypothesized: (1) The public zone which is an open area, more than 12 feet in any direction, and larger than an average room. This zone is suitable for casual interviewing. (2) The social zone which is roughly equivalent to an average room. It is confining, but not restricting. A social zone is suitable for very mild interrogating. (3) The personal zone which is not larger than an average room. The questioner and respondent are close, but not touching. This zone is appropriate for non-intensive interrogating. (4) The intimate zone which is a more confined space, perhaps half the size of an average room. The questioner is face-to-face with the respondent, well within touching distance. This zone is intended for intensive interrogating.

interrogation. a systematic effort to procure information by direct questioning of a person who is unwilling to provide the information; the extraction of information from a person suspected of having committed a crime or of a person who is reluctant to make a full disclosure. Interrogation involves a process through which the interrogator uses conversation, questioning, and observation as a means of eliciting truth. The process is adversarial in nature and depends upon the application of logic, reasoning, and understanding without violence or coercion.

An interrogation is directed at the achievement of four objectives: (1) obtain valuable facts, (2) eliminate the innocent from consideration as suspects, (3) identify persons who are guilty, and (4) obtain confessions from guilty persons.

As the interrogator moves from the preliminary task of gathering facts to obtaining confessions, there is an increase in the difficulty of acquiring information.

That difficulty, however, is rewarded by an increase in the value of the information.

interrogation distance. the distance between an interrogator and the boundary of the subject's "personal space bubble." At this distance, the interrogator is said to be confrontational and mildly aggressive.

interstate compact. an agreement between two or more states to transfer prisoners, parolees, or probationers from the physical or supervisory custody of one state to the physical or supervisory custody of another, where the correctional agency that first acquired jurisdiction over the person usually retains the legal authority to confine or release the prisoner.

interstitial environment. an urban area isolated by natural or social barriers in which criminal activity flourishes. A ghetto or slum is an interstitial environment.

intervention strategy. any interference that may affect the behavior of others. For example, the intervention strategy to reduce street crime might be the use of frequent and aggressive patrolling in the high crime areas.

interview. in criminal investigation, a structured process of obtaining information when the person being questioned is willing to provide the information. The person being interviewed usually gives in his own manner and words an account of the crime or provides details concerning a suspect or other person connected to the crime. The interviewer seeks to obtain valuable facts, eliminate the innocent from consideration as suspects, and identify persons who are guilty. In intelligence activities, an interview is the gathering of information from a person who knows that he is giving information, although not always with awareness of the true connection or purposes of the interviewer.

interview distance. the distance between the interviewer and the area just outside the interviewee's "personal space bubble." The interviewer who operates from this distance is said to be in a dominating, but not threatening or intimidating position.

intestate. without making a will. A person is said to die intestate when he dies without making a will, or dies without leaving anything to testify what his wishes were with respect to the disposal of his property after his death.

in the order of nature. a term that refers to a traditional custom of classifying crimes according to their nature. Four classes of crime formed by the application of this concept are: (1) Mala in se crimes which are so inherently wrong in their nature that they may be said to be evil in themselves. Crimes like murder, rape, robbery and arson are regarded as mala in se crimes. (2) Mala prohibita crimes which are wrong because statutes declare them to be wrong. Examples would be to violate traffic laws or licensing laws. (3) Infamous crimes which are generally felonies and relate to conduct which call for punishment by loss of civil and political rights, or by imprisonment in a penitentiary or imprisonment at hard labor. (4) Crimes involving moral turpitude which are acts of baseness, vileness, or depravity in the social and private duties a person owes to society in general. The element of moral turpitude may be important in cases involving disbarment of attorneys, revocation of medical licenses, and the deportation of aliens.

intimidation. an offense comparable to extortion, the essential difference being its application to all persons, not just those involved in public official transactions. A person commits intimidation when, with intent to cause another to perform or omit the performance of any act, he communicates to another a threat to inflict physical harm, or to make a criminal accusation, or to expose a person to hatred, contempt, or ridicule, or to bring about or continue a strike or boycott, etc.

intoxication. the offense of being in a public place while intoxicated through consumption of alcohol, or intake of a controlled substance or drug; an abnormal acute or chronic state that in a medical sense is essentially a poisoning; an altered physio-logical state resulting from ingestion of a psychoactive substance in which normal functioning is seriously impeded. Intoxication is most frequently used in reference to drunkenness from the effects of alcohol in the organism, as manifested by such signs as facial flushing, slurred speech, unsteady gait, euphoria, increased activity, emotion, volubility, disorderly conduct, insensibility, or stupefaction. The term does not necessarily imply drunkenness, but rather often refers to a state falling within a continuum between drunkenness and a mild high.

intoxication defense. a defense against prosecution which argues that the accused could not have a guilty mind due to intoxication. The fact of voluntary intoxication is generally not accepted as a defense. Involuntary intoxication produced by fraud or coercion of another may be a defense, and insanity produced by intoxicants may be acceptable. Intoxication can also be offered as evidence that an accused was incapable of forming the intent to commit a crime, e.g., the accused was too drunk to entertain the idea of breaking and entering into a house at night for the purpose of committing an offense.

intradermal injection. a method used by a drug abuser to administer a drug by scratching a hypodermic needle just beneath the skin.

intramuscular (IM). within the muscle of the body.

intramuscular injection. a method used by a drug abuser to administer a drug by inserting a hypodermic needle into the muscle tissue.

intravenous (IV). within a blood vessel.

intravenous injection. hypodermic injection into a vein to instill a fluid or withdraw blood; a method used by a drug abuser to administer a drug by inserting a hypodermic needle into a vein.

introjection. incorporation of external values and standards into the ego structure so that the individual is not at the mercy of external threats.

intrusion. in tort law, interference with the

right to be let alone. Violations can be grouped into four categories: intrusion, appropriation of one's name or likeness, giving unreasonable publicity to private facts, and placing a person in a false light in the public eye. The latter three of these are founded upon improper publicity, usually in the public press or electronic media.

Intrusion is an intentional tort closely related to infliction of emotional distress. Both torts protect a person's interest in his mental tranquility or peace of mind. Privacy is a basic right of a person to choose when and to what extent he will permit others to have knowledge of his personal affairs. Essentially, intrusion is an intentional, improper, unreasonable, and offensive interference with the solitude, seclusion or private life of another. It embraces a broad spectrum of activities, and may consist of an unauthorized entry, an illegal search or seizure, or an unauthorized eavesdropping, with or without electronic aids.

The tort is complete when the intrusion occurs. No publication or publicity of the information obtained is required. It is, of course, essential that the intrusion be into that which is, and is entitled to remain, private. Additionally, the harm must be substantial. The intrusion must be seriously objectionable, not simply bothersome or inconvenient.

intrusion detection system. a system combining mechanical or electric components to perform the functions of sensing, controlling, and announcing unauthorized entry into areas covered by the system. A system of this type has three components: sensor, control, and annunciator.

A sensor detects a condition, but is not able to determine if the condition is in fact an intrusion. Sensors can be grouped according to principles of operation. For example, touch sensors respond to movement, pressure and vibration. Taste/smell sensors detect changes in the chemical makeup of the air or surrounding sub-

stance. Hearing sensors detect changes in airborne sound, and sight sensors detect changes in light patterns.

The control component of an intrusion detection system usually contains power sources to provide operating energy, circuitry to carry the system's signals, and energizing devices to turn the system on and off, program it and test it.

The annunciator component receives signals from the control component and initiates a programmed response. There are four general forms of annunciation: (1) local alarms such as bells, horns, sirens, and flashing lights that activate at the protected area, (2) central station alarm service provided by commercial companies on a subscription basis, (3) direct connection to a response agency such as the police department, fire department, ambulance service, hospital, civil defense, etc., and (4) proprietary station service provided by the owner of the protected area in which the owner or his employees receive the alarms at a central point.

intubation. the act of inserting a tube into the larynx to relieve a respiratory obstruction.

inventory search. a search of a vehicle seized at the time of a legal arrest or impounded for police caretaking. The purpose of the search is to make an inventory of all items found in the vehicle.

inventory shrinkage. a common euphemism for losses due to employee pilfering or shoplifting.

inverted meter theft of service. a theft of electrical service in which the thief, usually the subscriber, removes the electric meter from its socket and then reinserts it upside down. The current flows through the meter but causes the operating dials to operate in reverse.

investigative conference. a conference held periodically, usually daily or weekly, by members of an investigative unit for the purpose of discussing progress made, identifying new leads to be pursued, and exploring opportunities for advancing the investigation. Investigative conferences are more commonly associated with major cases.

investigative consumer report. as used in the Fair Credit Reporting Act, a report pertaining to a consumer's character, general reputation, personal characteristics or mode of living as derived through personal interviews with friends, neighbors or associates.

investigative monitoring. intercepting, listening to, or recording any telephone conversation by use of any electronic, mechanical, or other device without the advance consent of all of the parties to the conversation.

investigative survey. an in-depth probe or test check of a specific operation or activity, usually conducted on a programmed basis, to detect the existence of crime or significant administrative irregularities.

investigatory stop. a procedure used by police on patrol to inquire into the activities of a person believed to be involved in a criminal act. The person stopped is asked questions and may be searched if there is reason to believe he is armed. Also, called stop and frisk or field inquiry.

involuntary manslaughter. causing the death of another person without intent to cause death, with recklessness or gross negligence, including by reckless or grossly negligent operation of a motor vehicle.

iodic acid analysis. a method of testing for the presence of morphine in a substance.

iodine crystals. in fingerprint identification, a product that produces violet fumes when subjected to a small amount of heat. The violet color is absorbed by fatty and oily matter in fingerprint impressions,

thereby making the impressions visible against their background surface.

iodine fuming cabinet. a large glass-walled box used in a crime laboratory to develop latent fingerprint impressions. The item bearing the impressions is placed inside the cabinet, iodine fumes are introduced, the fumes are absorbed by the impressions, and the impressions take on color, making them visible and photographable.

iodoform analysis. a method of testing for the presence of ethyl alcohol in a substance.

ipso facto. by the fact itself.

irrelevant. not relevant; not relating or applicable to the matter in issue; not supporting the issue. Evidence is irrelevant when it has no tendency to prove or disprove the issue involved.

irrelevant question. in polygraphy, a non-threatening question intended to elicit a normal tracing on the test chart. Tracings of irrelevant questions are compared against tracings of relevant questions.

irresistible impulse. a legal defense by which an accused seeks to be fully or partially excused from responsibility on the grounds that although he knew the act was wrong, he was compelled to its execution by an impulse he was powerless to control.

isoquinoline alkaloids. one of two general categories of alkaloids extracted from opium. Alkaloids in this category have no significant influence on the central nervous system and are not regulated under the Controlled Substance Act. The other general category is the phenanthrene alkaloids, represented by morphine and codeine.

Jacob's ladder. a fire rescue device consisting of a lightweight, flexible ladder made of rope, wire or chain.

jail. a short-term confinement facility, usually under the jurisdiction of a county or city government. It is used to house persons awaiting arraignment or trial when no bail has been set or when bail cannot be met. A jail also holds convicted misdemeanants and others sentenced to less than one year confinement, as well as prisoners awaiting transfer and occasionally material witnesses.

jail commitment. a sentence of commitment to the jurisdiction of a confinement facility system for adults which is administered by an agency of local government and of which the custodial authority is usually limited to persons sentenced to a year or less of confinement.

jailhouse lawyer. a prisoner who advises other prisoners on grounds for appeal and on other legal matters, not always with good or correct advice.

jamb peeling. a technique used in forced entry to deform or remove portions of the jamb to disengage the bolt from the strike.

jammer. a frequency generating oscillator that interferes with the operation of electronic audio surveillance.

jamming. the intentional transmission of interfering signals in order to disturb the reception of other signals.

jaw thrust. a maneuver to open the airway of a non-breathing victim by pushing forward on the mandibles.

Jefferson airplane. a crude device for holding a marihuana cigarette butt that is made by splitting a used paper match nearly in half, placing the roach in between, and holding the loose halves together with the fingers.

jeopardy. the danger of conviction and punishment which the defendant in a criminal case incurs when a valid indictment has been found against him and a jury has been impaneled and sworn to try the case and render a verdict; charged with a crime before a properly organized and competent court. If acquitted, the charged person cannot be tried again for the same offense.

jet ax. the commercial name of an explosive device used by firefighters to blow holes in walls. The device has also been used by safecrackers to penetrate safes.

jeweler's mark. a small identifying mark placed at an inconspicuous place on an item of jewelry made or repaired by a jeweler. The mark can be important in an investigation.

jimmy. a pry bar; a burglar's tool.

jimmying. a technique used in forced entry to pry the jamb away from the lock edge of the door a sufficient distance to disengage the bolt from the strike.

jimmy pin. a sturdy projecting screw, which is installed in the hinge edge of a door near a hinge, fits into a hole in the door jamb, and prevents removal of the door if the hinge pins are removed.

jingle key. a key blank milled to fit a particular keyway. Raking and turning the jingle key in the keyway may cause the lock to open. Also called a try key.

job analysis. the systematic study of a job to discover its specifications, frequently for the purposes of determining knowledge, skill and ability requirements, setting wages, and simplifying work procedures.

job hazard analysis. the breaking down into its component parts of any method or procedure to determine the hazards connected therewith and the requirements for performing it safely.

john. a prostitute's customer. Also called a trick.

John Doe. a fictitious name frequently used to indicate a person in legal proceedings until his real name can be ascertained. For example, a John Doe warrant.

joinder. the combining of multiple defendants and/or charges for purposes of any legal step or proceeding; in criminal proceedings, the naming of two or more defendants and/or the listing of two or more charges in a single charging document.

joint. a marihuana cigarette.

Joint Nuclear Accident Coordinating Center (JNACC). a combined Defense Nuclear Agency and Department of Energy center for exchanging information in support of radiological assistance activities during a nuclear accident/incident.

joint tortfeasors. two persons alleged to have committed the same tortious act with a common intent.

joule burn. a burn wound caused by high electrical shock. It is usually brown and has a shape corresponding to the object that made the contact.

joy pop. to take a drug by injection; to inject a drug into a muscle as opposed to a vein.

joyriding. unlawful taking of a motor vehicle with intent to temporarily deprive the owner of possession. This offense is usually codified as unauthorized use of a motor vehicle.

judge advocate. an officer appointed to preside at military court-martials, his duties being to summon witnesses, administer oaths, record minutes of the proceedings, advise the court on points of law, and act as prosecutor. He also has the duty of protecting the accused by preventing him from answering questions which might incriminate him.

judge pro tempore. a judge who sits in lieu of a regularly appointed or elected judge, and who is appointed with full authority to hear all of the cases scheduled for and to exercise all functions of the regular judge. Also called judge pro tem.

Judges Rules of 1912 and 1918. a set of rules followed by Canadian criminal justice authorities in respect to a suspect's confession. The rules require a showing that the confession was voluntary, that the determination of voluntariness was made by the trial judge, and that the trial judge considered all facts and circumstances of the case before determining voluntariness.

judgment. generally, any decision or determination of a court; in specific usage, the statement of the decision of a court that the defendant is acquitted or convicted of the charge.

judicial confession. a confession made during a court proceeding; an admission by a defendant while testifying; a guilty plea entered during a trial.

judicial decision. a decision of the court. Judicial decisions of the courts are frequently referred to as the common law. The law enunciated by the authority of courts is also called case law and unwritten law. The term case law derives from the cases decided by judges, and the term unwritten law derives from the idea that judicial decisions are not written as statutes. In truth, common law is well documented in the reports of decisions handed down since the 13th century. These decisions, and the reasons on which they are based, act as controlling precedents. The actual words of the opinions explaining the principles applied by the courts are not the law itself but an exposition of it.

judicial knowledge. knowledge of that which is so notorious that everybody, including judges, knows it, and hence need not be proved.

judicial notice. the doctrine that a court will, of its own knowledge, assume certain facts to be true without the production of evidence in support of them. A court will usually take judicial notice of facts that are common knowledge.

judicial officer. any person exercising judicial powers in a court of law.

judicial sale. a sale authorized by a court that has jurisdiction to grant such authority. A judicial sale is conducted by an officer of the court.

juggler. a small time numbers game backer who holds all of the small bets, usually up to 25 cents, and lays-off all bets over that amount.

jug mob. a pickpocket team that operates in and around banks.

jugular vein. the main blood vessel collecting the blood from the head and neck.

jumper. any of several types of auto-theft

devices which circumvent the ignition system of a motor vehicle. A jumper may range from a paper clip device to a sophisticated electrical circuit for by-passing the ignition switch. Also, a person who threatens, attempts, or commits suicide by jumping from a high place.

junction. the general area where two or more highways join or cross within which are included the roadway and roadside facilities for traffic movements in the area. A junction may include several intersections of roadways.

junk. heroin; drugs generally.

junkie. a person addicted to heroin; a dope fiend.

jurat. a certificate of an officer or person before whom writing was sworn to; the clause written at the foot of an affidavit, stating when, where, and before whom such affidavit was sworn.

jurisdiction. the authority by which courts take cognizance of and try cases. Also, the territory, subject matter, or person over which authority may be exercised.

jury. a group of citizens impaneled to hear evidence and decide on the facts of a case in a court of law. A petit jury hears criminal cases and decides on the guilt or innocence of the defendant. A grand jury sits in private and decides whether a case should be brought to trial.

jury poll. a poll conducted by a judicial officer or by the clerk of the court after a jury has stated its verdict but before the verdict has been entered in the record of the court, asking each juror individually whether the stated verdict is his own verdict. A jury poll can be initiated by motion of the prosecution or the defense, or the court. If the poll determines that all or the required portion of jurors do not agree on a verdict, then the jury in some jurisdictions may be sent back for further deliberation, or, in others, discharged.

jury sentencing. in criminal proceedings, upon a jury verdict of guilty, the recommendation or determination of a sentence by the jury. Jury sentencing occurs only in those jurisdictions which have

statutes specifically authorizing it, and usually relates only to crimes punishable by death or by life imprisonment.

jury trial. a trial in which a jury is impaneled to determine the issues of fact in a case and to render a verdict of guilty or not guilty. A defendant is guaranteed the right to a jury trial when a serious crime is charged. Practice varies among jurisdictions in cases where a minor offense is charged. The right to a trial jury may be waived by the defense.

jury wheel. a rotary machine or drum in which are placed names of prospective jurors, and from which are drawn, after the drum has been spun, the names of those jurors who are to serve on juries in cases scheduled for hearing in court.

just cause. a good, but not necessarily legal, reason for doing something; in employee relations, a good or fair reason for administering an adverse personnel action such as suspension or termination.

justifiable homicide. the intentional causing of the death of another in the legal performance of an official duty or in circumstances defined by law as constituting legal justification.

juvenile. in the context of the administration of justice, a person subject to juvenile court proceedings because a statutorily defined event or condition caused by or affecting that person was alleged to have occurred while his or her age was below the statutorily specified age limit of original jurisdiction of a juvenile court.

juvenile adjudication. the juvenile court decision terminating an adjudicatory hearing, that the juvenile is a delinquent, status offender, or dependent, or that the allegations are not sustained.

juvenile disposition. the decision of a juvenile court, concluding the disposition hearing, that an adjudicated juvenile be committed to a juvenile correctional facility, or placed in a juvenile residence, shelter, or care or treatment program, or required to meet certain standards of conduct, or released.

juvenile parole. the status or program membership of a juvenile who has been committed to a treatment or confinement facility, conditionally released from the facility, and placed in a supervisory and/or treatment program.

juvenile petition. a document filed in juvenile court, alleging that a juvenile is a delinquent, a status offender, or a dependent, and asking that the court assume jurisdiction, or asking that an alleged delinquent be transferred to a criminal court for prosecution as an adult.

Kansas City study. the name given to a study conducted by the Kansas City, Missouri police department to determine the efficiency of various types of patrol techniques concerning the prevention of crime. A major finding was that no one type of patrol stood out as being more effective than others.

Kastigar v. United States. a 1972 case in which the U.S. Supreme Court ruled that the compelling of testimony by the grant of immunity from prosecution does not violate any Fifth Amendment guarantee provided that the scope of the immunity granted to the witness is coextensive with the scope of the Fifth Amendment privilege against self-incrimination.

Katz v. United States. a 1967 case in which the U.S. Supreme Court ruled that the police may not place listening devices on telephones without first obtaining a search warrant. In this case, the defendant had been making telephone calls from a telephone booth for the purpose of wagering and betting. Federal agents placed an eavesdropping device on the outside of the telephone booth to enable them to overhear the conversations. The Supreme Court found that although the listening device did not penetrate into the telephone booth, there was an intrusion into the privacy that the caller expected in placing a call.

K book. the book used by a numbers writer.

kelly tool. an ax-like tool used by firemen to forcibly enter a structure.

Kentucky Blue. marihuana grown in Kentucky; home grown marihuana; marihuana grown in the U.S.

ketamine. a non-controlled legal drug prescribed for use as an anesthetic. It is chemically similar to phencyclidine (PCP), and like PCP, can produce a dissociative state in which the user's awareness becomes detached from the body and from external reality. Since ketamine is not a controlled substance, it is easily diverted from legal channels into the hands of recreational users, many of whom are medical professionals. Ketamine is manufactured in an injectable form and is usually administered intramuscularly. It produces an altered state of consciousness that begins within a few minutes and lasts about half an hour. The feeling is one of dreamy, floating disconnection from the body. Some enthusiasts like to take it while lying in sensory isolation tanks in attempts to have out-of-body experiences.

ketoacidosis. the condition arising in diabetics whose insulin dose is insufficient to meet their needs, wherein blood sugar reaches high levels, and fat is metabolized to ketones and acids. It is characterized by excessive thirst, urination, nausea, and vomiting, sometimes coma. It may also occur in conditions other than diabetes.

Kevlar. the trade name of a special woven cloth used in bullet-proof vests. It works by stretching upon bullet impact, spreading the bullet's energy, and stopping the bullet before it penetrates.

key event. the first occurrence in a traffic accident that results in appreciable damage or injury; the occurrence determining the time and place of a traffic accident; generally, the first contact in impact concerning a traffic accident.

keyhole effect. the mark made by a bullet on a target when contact is made while the bullet is tumbling or moving sideways in flight. The entry hole is elongated, similar in shape to a keyhole.

keyless system. an entry system that uses a keypad and an electric door strike. Pressing the correct sequential combination of push buttons on the keypad releases the lock to allow entry.

keyway decoder. a tool that when inserted into the keyway of a lock will determine the depth of the cuts on a key to operate the lock. A keyway decoder is a tool of the professional auto thief.

khat. the fresh leaves of the shrubby tree

Catha edulis which are chewed or drunk as tea in Yemen, East Africa, and the Arabian peninsula. It is a stimulant and is often used to produce a feeling of exhilaration. Also called chat, qat, and miraa.

kickback. money or something of value given to an employee by a vendor or contractor in exchange for a consideration. Also, money paid by an employee to a supervisor or third party in exchange for continued employment.

kicked upstairs. removal of a person from a position where his or her performance is not thought satisfactory by promoting the person to a higher position in the organization.

kick-in job. a burglary in which entry is gained by brute physical force, without regard to noise, and a hasty departure from the scene with the stolen goods. So called because the break-in is often achieved by kicking a door loose from the lock or hinges.

kidnapping. unlawful transportation of a person without his consent, or without the consent of his guardian, if a minor.

kidnapping coverage. insurance against the hazard of a person being seized outside the insured premises and forced to return and open the premises or a safe therein, or to give information which will enable the criminal to do so.

kidnap-ransom insurance. insurance written primarily for financial institutions and major corporations confronted with a kidnap-ransom threat. The insurance generally covers named employees for individual or aggregate amounts paid as ransom, with deductibles requiring the insured to participate in a percentage of any loss.

kief. the dried flower pods of the marijuana plant, considered to be somewhat of a delicacy to smoke. In some parts of the Middle East it is used as a general word for marijuana. In Morocco it is the name for a mixture of marijuana and tobacco. It is also spelled kaif, keif, kif, and kiff.

kilo. a kilogram (2.2 pounds). Bulk sales

of marijuana and heroin are often made in kilo lots and the drugs shipped in kilo packages. Also called a lid or a brick.

kindling temperature. the amount of heat required to liberate the flammable gases from a fuel source and cause them to burn.

kinesic interview technique. an interview and interrogational approach in which the subtle unconscious verbal and nonverbal behaviors of the interviewee are diagnosed and exploited.

King's habit. cocaine habit.

kite scheme. a scheme in which a criminal deposits money in a number of banks and then writes checks that exceed the total amount on deposit. The time required to transfer the canceled checks affords the criminal an opportunity to substantially overdraw.

klaxon. an audible signaling device that emits a sound similar to a submarine's signal to dive.

kleptomania. a psychological compulsion to steal; a species of mania consisting of an irresistible propensity to steal.

Knapp Commission. a commission appointed to investigate reports of corruption in the New York City Police Department in the early 1970s.

kneecapping. a form of torture, popular with some terrorist groups, in which the victim is shot in the kneecap or an electric drill is run through the kneecap.

known solution peak of tension test. in polygraphy, a test containing one relevant (hidden key) question pertaining to a known fact about which the examinee has denied knowledge. The relevant question is placed near the center of a group of similar but unrelated, non-relevant questions. The polygraphist compares the examinee's recorded reactions to both the relevant question and the non-relevant questions. The subject's response to the relevant or hidden key question may appear as a peak of tension in the polygrams.

known specimen. an article or material the origin of which is known. It is used as a standard of comparison with a comparable article or material of questionable origin. The character of the known specimen is determined by the circumstances of the investigation. Known specimens might be handwriting samples obtained from a suspected forger or pubic hair samples obtained from a suspected rapist.

known standard. in questioned document examinations, an original sample used to compare against unknown or questioned samples. Known standards include samples of typewriting from various typefaces/machines, watermarked papers, and checkwriter impressions.

kymograph. that component of the polygraph instrument which moves the polygram (chart paper) beneath and in contact with inked pens at a set rate of speed.

LAAM. levo-alpha-acetylmethadol, a synthetic compound closely related chemically to methadone. It is used in the treatment of narcotic addicts, and is regulated under the Controlled Substances Act as a narcotic.

labeling theory. a theory of deviance that focuses on the process by which some people are labeled deviant by others (and thus take on deviant identities), rather than on the nature of the behavior itself.

Labor Management Reporting and Disclosure Act. federal legislation passed in 1959 that provides standards for fair union elections, stipulates reporting and financial disclosure requirements, and provides penalties for fiduciary breaches by union officials and employees. This act provides imprisonment and fines for any person who embezzles, steals, or willfully abstracts any of the monies, funds, securities, or other assets of a labor organization of which he is an officer or employee. A significant section of the law states that any person convicted of certain enumerated offenses is barred from serving in any union capacity for a five year period after conviction or release from imprisonment.

labor racketeer. a broad term that applies to a union leader who uses his or her office as a base for unethical and illegal activities.

labor spy. a union member who spies on union activities on behalf of management.

laceration. a wound made by a tearing or cutting action on the tissues.

La Cosa Nostra. a criminal fraternity whose principal membership is Italian either by birth or national origin. It controls major racket activities in many large cities throughout the U.S., and has international connections as well. La Cosa Nostra operates with great secrecy and adheres to its own body of law and justice. Literally translated, La Cosa Nostra means "our thing." This name has come to be used by its members as a name in lieu of the Mafia.

lacrimator. the ingredient in tear gas that causes watering of the eyes; any chemical compound that produces severe weeping or tearing of the eyes. Ethyl bromacetate and chloroacetephenone are the lacrimators most often used in the construction of tear gas grenades.

La Guardia Report. the short title for a study of marijuana ordered by New York Mayor Fiorello La Guardia in 1938, carried out by the New York Academy of Medicine, with the assistance of the New York Police Department. Headed by George B. Wallace, the committee was composed of 31 eminent physicians, psychiatrists, clinical psychologists, pharmacologists, chemists, and sociologists. The study was in two parts: a clinical study of the effects of marijuana and a sociological study of marijuana users in the city. The report refuted the stepping-stone hypothesis, and generally stressed that the sociological, psychological, and medical ills commonly attributed to marijuana are exaggerated.

laminated padlock. a padlock, the body of which consists of a number of flat plates, all or most of which are of the same contour, superimposed and riveted or brazed together. Holes in the plates provide spaces for the lock mechanism and the ends of the shackle.

laminated safety glass. glass consisting of two layers of plate bonded with a plastic interlayer. When smashed, glass pieces tend to remain connected to the interlayer thereby reducing the hazard of flying glass.

lands. the spaces between the grooves inside the barrel of a firearm. The lands constitute the smooth portion of the barrel after the barrel has been rifled and grooved. The number of lands will vary from four to eight, with the most common types of guns having five or six.

lane line. a line separating two lanes of traffic travelling in the same direction.

189

lapping. an embezzlement technique in which a payment on account is diverted to the embezzler's use. To cover the shortage, a succeeding receipt is credited to the shorted account. For example, an employee who processes incoming cash payments will hold out a $100 payment made at the beginning of the month by Customer A. One week later, Customer B remits $200. The dishonest employee will use $100 to bring Customer A's account into balance and keep the remainder. At this point, the larceny has reached $200 and has not been detected.

larcenous intent. an intent to knowingly take and carry away the goods of another without any claim or pretense of right, with intent wholly to deprive the owner of them or to convert them to personal use.

larceny. unlawful taking of property from the possession of another; the taking and carrying away of the personal property of another with intent to deprive the owner of it permanently.

larceny-theft. in Uniform Crime Reports usage, unlawful taking, carrying, leading, or riding away by stealth of property, other than a motor vehicle, from the possession or constructive possession of another, including attempts.

larynx. the organ of voice production; the upper part of the respiratory tract between the pharynx and the trachea.

laser. a device that generates an intense single-color light beam or frequency.

laser identification. a property identification system in which a laser beam applies to high value items microscopic identification numbers too tiny to be seen by the naked eye. A high value item, such as a diamond, can be marked for ownership purposes without damage to the diamond.

last clear chance. a doctrine on which recovery for injury due to negligence is based. In those states where contributory negligence by the plaintiff defeats his right to recovery, this theory may be used as an exception if the defendant, the person causing the injury, had sufficient notice of the danger to which the plaintiff was exposed and had sufficient opportunity to avoid the accident but did not do so.

last contact. the final touching of objects in a traffic collision before separation; the time and place on a traffic unit or trafficway where final touching occurs. If colliding objects do not separate, there is no last contact.

latent fingerprints. fingerprints which are invisible but detectable; hidden or not visible prints that must be specially developed for them to be seen.

lateral entry. the transfer of a person from one police agency to another at the same or similar rank and position.

lateral pocket loop. a fingerprint pattern of the whorl family in which two or more loops have openings from the same side, usually with two deltas.

Lattes Crust test. a crime laboratory method used to determine what blood group antibody or antibodies of the A, B, O system are present in a dried stain. Also called a blood group agglutinins test.

laudanum. an alcoholic solution containing 10 percent opium; tincture of opium. Laudanum is an early medicinal form of opium which up through the 19th century was sold without prescription and was used widely for a variety of illnesses.

laughing gas. a short-acting gaseous anesthetic sometimes used as an aerosol propellant that is inhaled for its intoxicating effects. It depresses without depressant effects on the spinal cord. When used therapeutically, the effects are those of anesthesia and analgesia. In recreational use, when it is in pure form for less than a minute, its effects are closer to those of the vaporous anesthetics ether and chloroform, making the user giddy or exhilarated for about five minutes. Occasionally hallucinations occur. Excessive doses may cause nausea, vomiting, or unconsciousness, often because of lack of oxygen. Discovered in the 1770s by Joseph Priestly, but not used as an anesthetic until the middle of the 19th century, it was the first really effective modern anesthetic, to be followed by ether and chloroform.

lavage. the therapeutic washing out of an organ; a procedure for washing out the stomach in cases involving the ingestion of poisons.

law enforcement. the generic name for the activities of the agencies responsible for maintaining public order and enforcing the law, particularly prevention, detection and investigation of crime and the apprehension of criminals. The modern preference for "law enforcement" instead of the older term "police" does not represent a difference in meaning. The "police power" is the inherent power of the state to regulate affairs within its jurisdiction in the interests of the safety and welfare of its citizens. A law enforcement agency is the body of professional persons to which a government delegates authority to implement its police power.

Law Enforcement Assistance Administration (LEAA). an agency of the U.S. Department of Justice, established under the Omnibus Safe Streets and Crime Control Act of 1968, among whose responsibilities was the awarding of funds to state criminal justice planning agencies and, in some instances, directly to local police agencies. LEAA was severely reduced in 1979 and effectively abolished thereafter.

law enforcement officer. an employee of a law enforcement agency who is an officer sworn to carry out law enforcement duties; in some jurisdictions, any government employee who is an officer sworn to carry out law enforcement duties, whether or not employed by an agency which primarily performs law enforcement functions. "Sworn personnel" are persons formally authorized to make arrests while acting within the scope of explicit legal authority.

Law Enforcement Teletypewriter Systems (LETS). a noncommercial teletypewriter system which interconnects U.S. law enforcement agencies for the purpose of sending and receiving intrastate and interstate messages of a law enforcement nature. The system uses common carrier land line circuits.

law of crimes. a branch of public law which exists to protect the community as a whole against harms affecting fundamental areas of social life such as public peace, health, safety, welfare, morality, and authority. Law of crimes seeks to protect the individual's person, habitation and property. Also called criminal law.

law of effect. a fundamental concept in learning theory which holds that, all other things being equal, a person will learn those habits leading to satisfaction and will not learn (or learn with greater difficulty) those habits leading to dissatisfaction.

law of the situation. an organizational concept which holds that one person should not give orders to another person, but both should agree to take their action cues (orders) from the situation. To the extent that workers will accept the notion that orders are simply part of the situation, the question of someone giving and someone taking orders does not come up.

law of the road. a general custom or usage which provides that in order to avoid a collision between two vehicles the drivers should attempt to turn their vehicles to the right. Many states have adopted a rule that at an intersection, where there are no signs indicating otherwise, the vehicle proceeding toward the intersection from the right has the right of way.

layer checking. in arson investigations, searching through fire debris by removing one full layer at a time so as to reveal the relative positions of evidentiary items within each single layer.

lay off. the protection a bookie affords himself by placing bets with other bookies in order to reduce the chance of a large loss.

lead azide. a type of primary explosive.

leader line. a fire hose attached to the end of a larger hose; a hose line attached from pump to nozzle as opposed to a line supplying the pump.

leading question. a question so constructed and asked that the listener is led to making a particular response; a question which instructs a witness how to answer or puts into his mouth words to be echoed back. A question is a leading one when it indicates to the witness the real or supposed fact which the examiner expects and desires to have confirmed by the answer. The general rule is, subject to well defined exceptions, that leading questions may not be used in the direct examination of a witness, although they may be used in cross-examination.

lead number. in a numbers operation, the first digit of the three-digit winning number. It is most commonly associated with single-action betting.

lead styphenate. a type of primary explosive.

leap frog surveillance. a vehicle surveillance technique in which surveilling vehicles are stationed at intervals along a particular route expected to be taken by the target vehicle. As the target vehicle goes past the first surveilling station, the surveilling vehicle pulls out, follows, passes and takes up a new position beyond the last surveilling vehicle. The process is repeated all along the route.

leed. the pitch or rate of twist in the rifling of a firearm. The direction of twist moves from the breech to the muzzle, which may be either to the right or to the left. Most pistols with left twist have six lands. The angle of twist is measured from the lands with the angle formed with the longitudinal axis of the flight of the bullet. If that angle is large, the twist is small. The leed is one of the factors taken into consideration when examining a firearm for identification purposes.

legal. an intelligence officer who holds a legitimate embassy post or is attached to another legitimate organization.

legal aid. a system of providing counsel and other legal assistance to indigent defendants through a private or semi-public agency supported by governmental, philanthropic, or other funds.

legal highs. legal herbs, spices, plants, and chemicals with psychoactive properties, or the effects obtained from the use of such substances. There are dozens of substances commonly found in the home, garden and marketplace (e.g., nutmeg, coleus, catnip, hops, broom, hydrangea, and heliotrope) that produce a broad range of pharmacological effects including hallucination, stimulation, and sedation. Each usually requires an extraction process to bring out the active ingredients. Many legal high substances are toxic (even deadly) at high doses or when ingested in an improper form (e.g., broom, nutmeg, parsley) and are often accompanied by unpleasant side effects such as nausea. Most, however, are harmless, milder forms of more potent, illicit psychoactive substances.

legal liability. the responsibility an individual bears for his actions (or inactions), given his obligations to perform a duty or prevent an action or occurrence that is recognized as being a matter that is proper to be heard by and enforced by the courts.

legalization. the rescission of a statute so as to legalize previously illegal or criminal activity. Repeal of Prohibition is an example of legalization.

legend drug. a medicinal product requiring a prescription. Such products bear a legend which says "Caution: federal law prohibits dispensing without prescription."

legging. a shoplifting technique in which merchandise is placed under the dress of the shoplifter and held in place between the upper thighs.

lemonade. poor quality drugs.

lesser included offense. a crime less grave than the one charged but not requiring a separate charge for a guilty verdict, because the less serious offense is automatically implied by the more serious one. For example, a person charged with murder may also be found guilty of inflicting bodily harm.

lethal dose. the amount of a drug that will cause death.

lethargy. a condition of drowsiness resembling profound slumber, from which the person can be aroused, but into which he immediately relapses.

leuco-malachite test. a preliminary, presumptive test for determining the presence of blood in a suspect stain. The reagent consists of leuco-malachite green, glacial acetic acid, and distilled water. A drop of the reagent is placed on the stain. A greenish-blue appearance is indicative of blood.

levels of proof. the degrees of certainty required at different stages in the criminal justice process. For example, to investigate requires a level of "suspicion." To question or superficially search a suspect requires something more than suspicion but less than probable cause. To arrest and prosecute requires "probable cause," and to convict requires a degree of certainty called "proof beyond a reasonable doubt."

lewd and lascivious conduct. a statutory term describing prohibited behavior deemed to be perverse and depraved.

Lexan. the commercial name of a type of bullet-resistant glazing material.

Lexow Committee. a committee appointed by the New York State legislature in 1894 to investigate complaints of corruption in the New York City Police Department. The Committee's findings were an important stimulus to the first major efforts to reform urban police in the United States.

lex talionis. harsh retaliation for a criminal act. Literally translated, the term means "law of the claw."

liability insurance. insurance designed primarily to protect policyholders against financial losses arising out of their legal liability to others as a result of bodily injury, death, or property damage. Generally, such liability can be incurred in two ways: (1) it can be imposed by law as a result of one's own negligent acts, covered under the Law of Torts, and (2) it can be assumed through contractual obligation, which is subject to interpretation under the Law of Contracts.

liaison files. files containing information on various official contacts, to include name, telephone, organization, specific area of value, and remarks on the personal characteristics of the individual.

libel. any statement made in writing which is defamatory and injures the repu-

tation of an individual in the community.

Librium. the trade name for the antianxiety agent chlordiazepoxide. Librium is one of the most widely prescribed and highly abused depressant drugs. Prolonged use of excessive doses may result in physical and psychological dependence. A common mode of abuse is to ingest the drug with alcohol. Librium appears in the Controlled Substances Act as a Schedule IV barbiturate. Street names include barb, downer, blue, yellow jacket, and sleeping pill.

lid. a measure of marihuana.

lie detector. any one of the devices variously called the polygraph, voice stress analyzer, and psychological stress analyzer.

lien. a hold or claim which one person has upon another's property as security for some debt or charge.

life cycle theory. a concept of leadership which holds that the appropriate management style for a particular situation should be primarily dependent upon the maturity level of the employee. Maturity is defined as a function of the employee's general level of education, experience, motivation, desire to work, and willingness to accept responsibility. Leadership is seen as a combination of two types of behavior: directive and supportive.

If an employee is assessed to be immature, the theory suggests that the manager's supervisory style should be high in directive behavior and low in supportive behavior. As the employee matures, the manager's behavior should shift to low direction and high support.

life style inquiry. an investigation to factually determine the sources and amounts of income of a particular person and to compare known income against the person's evident living and spending habits.

lifting box. a box used to shoplift. It has a concealed opening in the bottom which permits it to be placed over the item targeted for theft. When the box is lifted, the item is captured inside the box.

light bulb bomb. an incendiary device made by drilling a small hole in a light bulb and filling it with a highly combustible material. The light bulb is placed in a socket. When the light switch is activated, the electrical arc in the bulb will ignite the combustible.

Likert Scale. a management technique for obtaining useful feedback concerning employee perceptions of the work organization. The Likert Scale (named for Rensis Likert) presents a respondent with a statement calling for a reaction/opinion in one of five or more possible responses. The statement, for example, might be "My supervisor is a good leader." The available responses to choose from might be: (1) strongly agree (2) agree (3) agree somewhat (4) not sure (5) disagree somewhat (6) disagree (7) strongly disagree.

limited-access highway. an expressway or other highway designed for high-speed travel, with access permitted only at designated points and with grade-level intersections eliminated as much as possible.

Linder v. United States. a 1925 Supreme Court case in which the court unanimously vindicated as neither proper nor unwise a physician's prescribing four tablets of morphine and cocaine for relief of a withdrawal condition incident to opiate use. Under this ruling a physician in good faith and according to fair medical standards could give a drug-dependent person moderate amounts of opiates to relieve withdrawal symptoms without violating the Harrison Narcotics Act. At that time, the ruling had no practical effects on law enforcement authorities, who continued to threaten physicians with imprisonment for treating addicts.

line impedance. the impedance of a telecommunication line. It is a function of the resistance, inductance, conductance, and capacitance of the line, and the frequency of the signal. Also called characteristic impedance.

line of demarcation. in arson investigations, the boundary between charred and uncharred material. On floors or rugs, a puddle-shaped line of demarcation indicates a liquid fire accelerant. In the cross section of wood, a sharp, distinct line indicates a rapid, intense fire.

line of sight. in firearms, a straight line from the shooter's eye, through the sighting device of the weapon, to the target.

line smoke detector. a general term describing a type of smoke detector that generates a beam of light transmitted between a sender and a receiver mounted at extreme ends or sides of a protected area. Interruption of the beam by smoke particles causes an alarm.

lineup. a group of people placed together in a line for viewing by a witness or victim for the purpose of identifying the perpetrator of a crime; a line or parade of suspects and criminals in custody for the purpose of allowing law enforcement officers to familiarize themselves with habitual offenders. A lineup is generally used when a suspect is taken into custody and the witness is available to make the identification. There are three predicates for placing a suspect in a lineup: (1) when the suspect consents, (2) when the suspect has been arrested, and (3) when a court orders it.

liquidated damages. an amount the parties to a contract have agreed upon that shall be paid in satisfaction of a loss resulting from a breach of contract. The amount must be in proportion to the actual loss, otherwise the agreement is unenforceable.

liquid debris. debris consisting of liquids from a vehicle or its cargo. In traffic accident investigations, the types of liquid debris include spatter, dribble, puddle, runoff and soak-in. Each may be significant to the investigation.

liquid sulphur. a mixture of melted sulphur and iron filings used as a substitute for plaster of paris when making finely detailed casts of foot and tire prints, tool marks and similar impressions.

liquor laws violation. the name of the Uniform Crime Reports category used to record and report arrests for offenses relating to regulation of the manufacture, sale, distribution, transportation, possession, or use of intoxicating liquor, except public drunkenness and driving under the influence of alcohol.

lis pendens. a notice filed in the office of

the county which advises that a lawsuit is pending against the owner of the designated property and involves that property.

listening post. a location where an eavesdropper monitors receiving equipment during bugging operations.

lividity. an ashy pale coloration of a dead body. Lividity is caused by blood that gravitates downward in a dead body. This draining of the blood to the lower regions leaves an ashy pale appearance in the upper portion. Also, where the body is lying on a flat surface, such as a floor, the weight of the body prevents the gravitational force of blood from reaching that portion which is in contact with the floor. Consequently, this area also will be void of blood and have a pale coloration. In a hanging corpse, the blood drains to the lower region of the body and appears as a bluish red coloration. Generally, lividity will appear in several hours, depending upon whether or not the person was anemic or obese. Also called post mortem lividity or livor mortis.

load up. a fraudulent practice in which a party obtains goods on credit and then declares bankruptcy.

loaf. a kilo (2.2 pounds) of marijuana, so named for its resemblance to a loaf of bread.

loan sharking. criminal usury; the lending of money or property and charging an interest rate substantially in excess of the legal rate. Loan sharking is the illegal business of lending money at exorbitant rates of interest. The lender frequently seeks to perpetuate the interest payments, and uses violence to enforce collection and discourage the borrower from making a report to the police.

local agency check. a Department of Defense review of the criminal, subversive and intelligence files of police departments, county and parish sheriff's offices, and other law enforcement agencies. It may also include other offices such as the Bureau of Vital Statistics, court records, credit agencies and other state or local records repositories.

local files check. a review of records maintained at the Department of Defense installation of assignment (conducted before requesting a personnel security investigation, granting a security clearance or granting information access) to determine the existence or absence of unfavorable information or to verify information provided by an applicant for a security clearance.

lock and load. a command given to shooters immediately prior to aiming and receiving the command to fire.

Lockhart v. McCree. a U.S. Supreme Court decision dealing with the implications for juror selection in capital cases. The defendant, charged with a capital felony murder, objected to juror selection procedures requiring that prospective jurors who stated they could not vote for a death penalty under any circumstances be excluded. The defendant, though convicted and sentenced to life imprisonment, contended that such a jury was more conviction-prone than a jury drawn from a representative cross-section of viewpoints from the community.

The Supreme Court concluded that exclusions based upon shared attitudes toward the death penalty rather than shared characteristics (such as race or ethnicity) were not sufficient to prove that an unbalanced jury had been selected. The Court noted the inherent difficulties that would occur if juries were required to represent a balance of all possible viewpoints. Rather, the Court commented, the "Constitution presupposes that a jury selected from a fair cross-section of the community is impartial, regardless of the mix of individual viewpoints actually represented on the jury, so long as the jurors can conscientiously and properly carry out their sworn duty to apply the law to the facts of the particular case."

lock pick. a tool or instrument, other than the specifically designed key, made for the purpose of manipulating a lock into a locked or unlocked condition.

lock record bar. that part of a polygraph

instrument which prevents the inked pens from moving when the blood pressure cuff is inflated.

lockup. a short-term confinement facility or jail; the holding cells in a police station.

locus criminis. the place or site of the crime; the place where a crime was committed.

locus delicti. the place of the crime or tort.

log in. to enter a computer system. When a user logs in, he or she types an account name and password in response to the appropriate prompts. If the name and password match an account on the system, the user will be permitted access to that account.

logoff. the procedure by which a user ends a terminal session.

logon. the procedure by which a user begins a terminal session.

loiding. a burglary attack method in which a thin, flat, flexible object such as a stiff piece of plastic is inserted between the strike and the latch bolt to depress the latch bolt and release it from the strike. The loiding of windows is accomplished by inserting a thin stiff object between the meeting rails or stiles to move the latch to the open position, or by inserting a thin stiff wire through openings between the stile or rail and the frame to manipulate the sash operator of pivoting windows. The term is derived from the word celluloid. Also called knifing and slip-knifing.

Lombrosian. a term pertaining to the criminological views postulated by Cesare Lombroso (1836–1909) and to adherents of the positivist school of criminology, particularly as they relate to a belief that some people are born criminals and others (called criminaloids) are born with criminal tendencies or predilections.

long-acting barbiturates. a classification of barbiturates based on the time between administration and the onset of anesthesia. In this classification, barbiturates take effect within 1 hour and have a duration time of up to 16 hours. Phenobarbital (Luminal), mephobarbital or methyl-

phenobarbital (Mebaral), and metharbital (Gemonil) are long-acting barbiturates.

long bone measurement. a technique for estimating the height of a deceased person by measuring the length of a skeleton's long bones. These data are correlated to a standard scale and an estimate of height made.

longitudinal study. research involving the collection of data at two or more points in time, usually in relation to the same individuals.

long pause. an interviewing technique in which the interviewer deliberately remains silent for an extended period so that the interviewee will feel compelled to offer further information if only to break the silence.

long-range gunshot wound. a wound caused when the muzzle at time of discharge is more than 24 inches from the victim.

look-alikes. tablets, capsules and powders whose physical appearances mimic prescription drug products and are sold to naive drug buyers. Look-alikes generally contain caffeine, ephedrine, or phenylpropanolamine. They have been linked to deaths from strokes and disturbances of heartbeat. Since caffeine and ephedrine have proven to be relatively safe over an extended period of time, phenylpropanolamine is more likely to account for the bad effects of look-alike stimulants.

look-out message. a radio broadcast which directs patrol officers to look for particularly described persons or objects associated with a recently committed crime.

loop. in fingerprint science, a pattern in which one or more ridges enter on either side of the impression, recurve, touch or pass an imaginary line drawn from the delta to the core, terminate or tend to terminate on or toward the same side of the impression from whence such ridge or ridges entered; one of the three basic groups of fingerprint patterns, the other two being the arch and whorl. The loop pattern has two sub-groups: the radial loop and ulnar loop.

lottery. a game of chance in which money is wagered for a chance to win a set prize.

low belly strippers. playing cards having altered edges so as to facilitate their drawing by a dishonest dealer.

lower flammable explosive limit. the limit at which a low concentration of flammable vapor in a given space is susceptible to explosion.

low-order detonation. an incomplete detonation of an explosive charge.

low-order explosion. an explosion characterized by a slow expansion over a relatively wide area into a combustion known as deflagration. Most explosives of this type have a pushing rather than shattering effect. Damage is characterized by twisting and tearing.

low-order explosive. an explosive with a velocity of detonation less than 1000 meters per second. A low explosive exerts a pushing effect, which propels objects as opposed to shattering them. Black powder and smokeless powder are low-order explosives.

LSD. an abbreviation of the German expression for lysergic acid diethylamide. It is a hallucinogenic drug produced from lysergic acid, a substance derived from the ergot fungus which grows on rye or from lysergic acid amide, a chemical found in morning glory seeds. LSD can cause illusions, poor perception of time and distance, intense psychotomimetic episodes, psychosis, and death. It is orally administered, and known by a wide variety of street names such as acid and microdot. LSD appears in the Controlled Substances Act as a Schedule I drug.

luminol test. a preliminary test used to detect invisible traces of blood by making them glow for a brief period. A common technique is to spray the luminol reagent onto the object or suspect stain under very low light conditions. The appearance of a chemical luminescence (like the flash of a firefly) indicates the presence of blood. The luminescing reaction is sometimes photographed for evidentiary purposes. This test is merely indicative (not conclusive) of blood which may or may not be of human origin.

luminous readers. invisible marks placed on the backs of playing cards by a dishonest gambler. The marks are visible when viewed through special glasses.

lunch hour special. the taking of a short-acting drug, such as DMT, so called because of the popularity of the practice of taking short-acting drugs while on lunch break.

lush worker. an unsophisticated pickpocket who steals from intoxicated or sleeping persons in trains, buses, waiting rooms, and parks.

lycopodium powder. a yellowish fingerprint powder made from spores. It is regarded as being especially effective when mixed with aluminum powder.

lye bomb. a non-exploding, homemade anti-personnel device consisting of a thin-glassed container filled with a liquid lye. It is designed to be thrown and to break upon impact, causing burns to the skin and eyes of the targeted persons.

lysergic acid. a substance derived from the ergot fungus which grows on rye. It can be used to make LSD and is a Schedule III drug.

lysergic acid amide. a chemical found in morning glory seeds which can be used to produce LSD. It is a Schedule III drug.

lysergic acid diethylamide. an hallucinogen classified as a Schedule I controlled substance. It is the technical name of LSD. Also called blotter, purple haze, orange sunshine, acid, microdot, goofies, Snoopy, Mickey Mouse, Donald Duck, window pane, unicorn, and blue star.

3-methylfentanyl. a derivative of fentanyl that is about 2000 times as potent as morphine. It is much sought after by addicts who prefer it to heroin.

Mace. the commercial name of a spray used in riot control operations. It causes dizziness, nausea and tears.

maceration. a softening and separating of skin tissue caused by extended immersion in water. Maceration produces problems when fingerprint and palmar surface impressions are taken from drowning victims.

machinegun. any weapon which shoots, is designed to shoot, or can be readily restored to shoot, automatically more than one shot, without manual reloading, by a single function of the trigger. A machine gun will continue to fire until the magazine is depleted or until the trigger is released. It is generally fired in bursts of three to six shots at a time. Some machine guns are designed to fire either pistol or rifle cartridges. In most states, possession of a machine gun is unlawful.

made. the exposure of a surveillant or undercover operative. Also called blown or burned.

Mafia. a group of Italian-dominated organized crime leaders and their followers that originated in Sicily. The term La Cosa Nostra (our thing) is sometimes used interchangeably with Mafia.

mafioso. a member of the Mafia. In some contexts, mafioso implies a member at the lowest level. The plural is mafiosi.

Maggie's drawers. a red flag displayed at a firing range to signify that the target was not hit.

magic mushroom. a mushroom that contains psilocybin, a natural hallucinogen.

magic paper. a paper favored by bookmakers because it quickly dissolves when immersed in water.

magistrate. a lower-court judge, sometimes called a justice of the peace, municipal judge, or police judge. He is usually assigned to arraignments, preliminary hearings, bail settings, and dispositions of minor offenses.

magnesium ribbon. a product used for developing latent prints. When the ribbon is burned, a white film attaches to an object passed above the burning. When the object is dusted, the powder remains attached to latent prints.

magnetic fuse. a bomb fuse sensitive to minute variations in the earth's magnetic field. The fuse functions when an influence from the target is exerted on a sensitive detecting device within the fuse itself.

magnetic ink character recognition (MICR). a computer technology developed by the American Bankers' Association as a machine language that facilitates the processing of checks, drafts, and similar documents required to be processed through the Federal Reserve System. Special numeric MICR groupings, called "fields," are printed in magnetic ink on the check or other instrument. The numbers identify the Federal Reserve routing code, ABA transit number, account number, and the amount.

magnetic limpet mine. a bomb designed to cling by magnetic energy to the hull of a ship. It is usually of military origin and is a favored tool of terrorists.

mail cover. a practice in which the exterior surfaces of mail moving to and from a subject are examined or copied.

mail fraud. any scheme in which the U.S. Postal System is used to defraud another. Mail fraud is prohibited by 19 USC, Section 1341.

main charge. a quantity of high explosives detonated by a booster explosive. It is the fourth and final element in the basic firing chain of most explosions. The more common materials used as a main charge are TNT, dynamite, and plastic explosives.

main effect. the effect experienced during that period of time when a drug is maximally active in the plasma, causing the typical influence. In the use of a drug, it is the second of four stages: initial, main, ending, and withdrawal. Also called basic effect.

mainframe computer. a large, high-speed computer system consisting of one or more high-speed central processing units, various kinds of memory devices, and devices for the entry and retrieval of information.

mainline. to inject a drug, typically heroin, into a vein.

mainliner. a person who injects illegal drugs into the veins.

maison keying. a specialized keying system, used in apartment houses and other large complexes, that enables all individual unit keys to operate common-use locks such as the main entry and laundry room.

major case prints. recordings of all the friction ridge detail present on the palmar surfaces of the hands and full inner surfaces of the fingers. Major case prints are obtained by inking and then simultaneously pressing the full flat surface of the hand from fingertips to wrist joint. They are used for elimination and identification purposes in major cases.

majority opinion. the opinion of the majority of judges hearing the case. A dissenting or minority opinion is that of one or more judges who disagree with the decision of the majority. A concurring opinion states the reasons and reasoning of one or more judges who agree with the majority decision, but on different grounds.

major tranquilizers. a group of drugs used for treating mental illness and in terminating bad reactions to psychedelic drugs and other states of confusion. In normal circumstances, a small dose of a major tranquilizer will cause drowsiness, lethargy, boredom, and uncomfortable physical effects. This may account for the relative unpopularity of major tranquilizers as recreational drugs.

malachite green. a dye stuff used to mark an object so that a detectable amount will be transferred to the skin or clothing of persons who handled the object.

mala fides. bad faith; the opposite of bona fides.

mala in se. wrongs in themselves; acts morally wrong; offenses against conscience.

mala in se crime. a crime so inherently wrong in nature that it may be said to be bad or evil in itself. Mala in se crimes include murder, rape, robbery, and arson.

mala prohibita. prohibited wrongs or offenses; acts which are made offenses by laws.

mala prohibita crime. a crime that is not necessarily wrong in itself, but is said to be wrong because it is prohibited by statute. Examples would be illegal parking and fishing without a license.

malfeasance. the commission of some act which is unlawful.

malice. a mental state accompanying a criminal act that is performed willfully, intentionally, and without legal justification.

malice aforethought. a knowledge of such circumstances that according to common experience there is a clear and strong likelihood that death will follow a contemplated act. Malice aforethought is usually coupled with an absence of justification for the act.

malicious. done with an evil heart or mind, cruelty or reckless disregard of the consequences.

malicious arrest. an unreasonable arrest done under the color of authority.

malicious mischief. the common law crime of injuring the property of another. If fire or an explosive is used, the offense is arson.

malicious prosecution. the institution of judicial proceedings, civil or criminal, against another, maliciously and without probable cause.

Mallory v. United States. a case in which the U.S. Supreme Court ruled inadmissible a confession obtained from a person who was not promptly arraigned after arrest. Although originally applicable to federal courts, this decision has been applied in state and local jurisdictions.

management by exception. a management control process that requires a subordinate to report to an organizational superior only upon the occurrence of exceptional or unusual events that call for decision-making on the part of the superior.

management by objectives. an approach to managing in which the subordinate and the superior agree on measurable goals to be accomplished by the subordinate (or team) over a set period of time.

management development. any conscious effort on the part of an organization to provide a manager with skills that he might need for future duties, such as rotational assignments or formal educational experiences.

management information system. any formal process in an organization that provides managers with facts they need for decision-making.

management science. an approach to management dating from World War II that seeks to apply scientific methods to managerial problems. Because of its emphasis on mathematical techniques, management science as a term is frequently used interchangeably with operations research.

managerial grid. a graphic gridiron format which has an X axis locating various degrees of orientation toward production and a Y axis locating various degrees of orientation toward people. Individuals scoring themselves on the grid can place themselves at one of 81 available positions that register their relative orientations toward production and people.

managerial psychology. generally, all those concepts of human behavior in organizations that are relevant to managerial problems.

mandamus. a court order that compels the performance of an act.

mandatory prosecution. a system of criminal procedure that denies or limits the prosecutor's discretion not to prosecute. It is used in several European countries.

mandatory sentence. a statutory requirement that a certain penalty shall be set and carried out in all cases upon conviction for a specified offense or series of offenses.

mandatory supervised release. a conditional release from prison required by statute when an inmate has been confined for a time period equal to his full sentence minus statutory good time if any.

manic depressive psychosis. a psychotic reaction characterized by prolonged and alternating periods of euphoria/overactivity and depression/underactivity. In the overactive period, the manic depressive psychotic is likely to be overenthusiastic, self-assertive, boastful, and talkative. The underactive period is marked by melancholia, morbidness, pessimism, and a tendency toward suicide.

manicure. remove stems and undesirable residue from marihuana by filtering or screening.

manslaughter. the unlawful killing of a human being, without malice aforethought.

manual station. a fire alarm initiating device that transmits an alarm signal when manually operated. Sometimes called a pull station.

MAO inhibitors. monoamine oxidase inhibitors. These are antidepressants related chemically to the amphetamines and used as psychic mood elevators, particularly in the treatment of psychotic depression. Potent, unpredictable drugs, they are capable of producing a variety of dangerous side effects.

Mapp v. Ohio. a landmark case in which the U.S. Supreme Court ruled that state police action was subject to the so-called exclusionary rule first enforced in 1914 against the federal police (Weeks v. United States). When first enunciated and made applicable in federal courts, the exclusionary rule prohibited admission at trial of evidence obtained in violation of the Fourth Amendment. The Mapp v. Ohio case applied the rule to the state courts by virtue of the due process clause of the Fourteenth Amendment.

marbling. a preserving treatment applied to the edges of account books. An examination of the marbling pattern may be revealing as to whether pages had been removed or substituted.

marihuana (or marijuana). an ambiguous term related to the varieties of cannabis plants cultivated for their intoxicating properties. Marijuana may refer specifically to the fresh plant or to the dried and shredded preparation made from the flowering tops, stems, and leaves of the female. It is also used to refer generally to all of the various intoxicating cannabis preparations. Also called pot, grass, reefer, herb, weed, Columbian, hemp, joint, Mary Jane, sinsemilla and Acapulco gold.

While marijuana is consumed for its effects, what a user may actually experience is highly variable and uncertain and may range from zero effects to hallucinations and from relaxed euphoria to acute feelings of panic and discomfort. The effect achieved depends upon the environment in which the drug is consumed, user feelings at the time of consumption, and the dose. The dose, in turn, depends upon the route of ingestion —usually smoked or eaten—and THC content (near 0 percent in hemp to 60 percent in crystallized hash oil). It is this broad possible combination of variables that makes the effects of marijuana highly inconsistent between users and for an individual user from one time to the next.

The chemistry of marijuana, a natural, organic substance, is extremely complex. Its chemistry also changes from the fresh plant, to the dried preparation, to the inhaled smoke produced by burning. Dried marijuana contains over 420 chemical compounds, including 61 chemicals (the cannabinoids) that are specific to cannabis. Delta-9-THC is generally cited as the psychoactive ingredient of marijuana, but recent research suggests that other compounds acting independently or interacting with delta-9-THC also contribute to the intoxicating potency of the drug.

Research on the metabolism of marijuana has centered primarily on THC. Like nearly everything else associated with marijuana, the metabolic process is complex and not entirely understood. Because THC is fat soluble, it leaves the bloodstream rapidly changed to 11-

hydroxy-THC, a metabolite that is also psychoactive, and to at least 20 other known metabolic products that are either relatively inactive or have unknown activity. This metabolism mostly occurs in the liver. THC leaves the blood rapidly, not only because it is metabolized but also because of its efficient uptake by tissues. An understanding of the pharmacologic properties of THC is necessarily complex because of its complicated pharmacokinetic behavior, including its formation into metabolites which bind tightly to proteins in the blood and remain for long periods of time in fatty tissues. While stored in body fats, THC and its metabolites are slowly released back into the bloodstream. Thus, 5 days after a single injection of THC, 20 percent of the THC remains stored, while 20 percent of its metabolites remain in the blood. Complete elimination of a single dose can take 30 days. After the passage of about 6 hours, the step that limits the rate of elimination of unchanged THC in the blood is not its metabolism but rather the very slow return to the plasma of THC that has been sequestered in the tissues. Given the slow clearance of cannabinoids, one might predict that repeated administration of marijuana at intervals of less than 8 to 10 days should result in accumulation of THC or its metabolites in the tissues.

The dosage of THC contained in marijuana is extremely variable and, for the ordinary user, unpredictable. The potency of dried leafy marijuana depends upon a number of variables including the genetics of the plant, the soil and climate in which it was grown, when and how it was harvested, its sex, how it was prepared, the parts used, and how it was stored before use. THC content also varies radically across the spectrum of marijuana preparations: hemp and wild U.S. cannabis—less than 0.5 percent; cultivated marijuana—0.5 to 5 percent; hashish—8 to 14 percent; hash oil—15 to 40 percent; hash oil crystals—up to 60 percent. The University of Mississippi School of

Pharmacy, under contract with NIDA, grows, harvests, prepares, and assays an assortment of standardized marijuana strains. The samples are labeled with their exact cannabinoid content and are distributed for use in research projects around the country.

Research on marijuana continues. While few findings on the drug's effects have been definitive, the notion that marijuana is safe is facing a mounting challenge. According to the NIDA, the hesitancy of the scientific community in not drawing unwarranted definitive conclusions from what are preliminary research findings has led many to conclude that marijuana is without serious medical hazard, even for the very young. In reality, the situation is more like that following the popularization of cigarette smoking at the time of World War I. It required 50 years of research for the truly serious implications of cigarette smoking to become apparent. Present evidence clearly indicates that it is not a safe substance. Virtually all clinicians working with children and adolescents agree that regular use of marijuana by youngsters is highly undesirable. There is little serious question that regular use of an intoxicant that blurs reality and encourages a kind of psychological escapism makes growing up more difficult. While there is controversy over the implications of present research concerning adult use, few would argue that every effort should be made to actively discourage use by children and adolescents.

Marihuana Tax Act of 1937. a federal statute which required persons authorized to deal in marihuana to register and pay an occupational tax. The law was designed to locate and control individuals engaged in transactions involving marijuana by requiring all persons who handled the drug to record their transactions. The act provided that (1) all persons using the plant for defined industrial or medical purposes must register and pay a tax of $1.00 per ounce, (2) all those using it for purposes undefined by the act must pay a tax of $100.00 per ounce on unregistered transactions, and (3) all persons failing to comply with the above regulations were subject to penalties of tax evasion (a fine of not more than $2,000 and/or a prison sentence of not more than five years). While theoretically only a means of raising revenue, the act was designed to eliminate recreational use. The law was formulated as a tax measure because many people argued that federal control over drug use and over the prescription practices of the medical profession was unconstitutional.

mark down. a technique in which dishonest employees of a retail operation will mark down price tickets on items purchased by them or their accomplices.

marking for identification. marking evidence at the time of seizure or collection in order to connect the evidence to a particular crime and to demonstrate that fact in court.

mark switch. a switch on a polygraph instrument which when activated instantly places a mark on the galvanic skin response (GSR) tracing. The mark is used to note outside noises or other distractions that occurred during the test. Also called an event marker.

Marme's test. a precipitate test for morphine. When Marme's reagent and hydrochloric acid are added to the alkaloid of morphine, the appearance of a crystalline precipitate under a microscope is indicative of the presence of morphine.

marshal. an appointed law enforcement officer. At one time, a marshal was the principal police officer in outlying jurisdictions, but the term in recent times has been limited to law enforcement agents of the federal court system.

martial law. the exercise of military power to preserve order and insure public safety in domestic territory in times of emergency when a civil government is unable to function or its functioning would itself threaten the public safety.

Mary Ellen worker. a thief who specializes in stealing purses in female rest rooms.

masquerade. to gain unauthorized access

to a computer system by impersonating an authorized user's access identification routine.

Massiah v. United States. a case in which the U.S. Supreme Court ruled that incriminating statements obtained from the defendant after his indictment and in the absence of counsel were not admissible at trial.

In this case, the defendant was arrested and subsequently indicted for federal narcotics violations. He retained a lawyer, pleaded not guilty, and was released on bail. While free on bail and in the absence of counsel, the defendant conversed with a codefendant, unaware that the codefendant was cooperating with federal agents and transmitting his incriminating statements to them. At trial, an agent who overheard the conversation testified as to its contents. The defendant was convicted.

The Supreme Court reversed, holding that incriminating statements deliberately elicited from the defendant after his indictment and in the absence of counsel were not admissible at trial.

mass spectrograph. an apparatus for determining the relative masses of isotopes of an element, and for sorting electrically charged particles in general. A small amount of the substance to be studied is gasified, and the gas is admitted into a vacuum tube where its molecules are ionized by electrons emitted by a thermionic cathode and accelerated. The various types of ions so formed are sent through a combination of electric and magnetic fields which deflects them to different degrees according to their masses, and those of different mass are brought to focus at different places.

master eye. in firearms shooting, that eye of the shooter which dominates and which most strongly influences aiming.

master-servant rule. the rule that employers are obligated to protect the public from the acts of their employees. Courts can hold employers liable for torts committed by employees in the course of their employment.

master station. a station that can select and transmit a message to a slave station.

match bomb. an incendiary device consisting of a lighted cigarette placed between the cover of a pack of safety matches and the matchheads. When the cigarette burns down and reaches the matchheads, a small fire is produced. The match bomb is usually surrounded by highly combustible materials. The match bomb is therefore a delayed action incendiary that allows the arsonist to be well away from the scene when ignition occurs.

matchhead bomb. an explosive device consisting of matchheads packed tightly into a fragmentable container, such as a short length of pipe capped at both ends and drilled to allow insertion of a fuse.

material evidence. any evidence, physical or testimonial, which is relevant to the substantial matters in a dispute, or which has a legitimate and effective influence or bearing on the decision of a case.

material inside information. a term used in federal securities law as relates to the purchase or sale of a company's securities, such as its common stock, by persons possessing information not known to the public. Information may be considered "inside" or "non-public" if it has not been included in the company's Security and Exchange Commission filings, in a press release, or widely reported in the media. Information is considered "material" if it could be expected to affect the investment decision of a reasonable investor or the market price of the company's publicly traded securities.

material question. in polygraphy, a question which when posed to a guilty subject causes a response recordable by the polygraph instrument. Also called a relevant or pertinent question.

matrix organization. any organization using a multiple command system whereby an employee might be accountable to one superior for overall performance as well as to one or more other superiors for specific projects. A contract security guard company can be said to operate on the matrix concept.

maturing out. a term sociologists first applied to adolescent urban gang members who tended to give up their gang association when they entered their twenties. The term was later used in reference to adolescent heroin addicts who were able to give up heroin use after entering adulthood. The hypothesis is that these individuals went through a maturing-out process similar to urban gang members. Research suggests, however, that length of heroin use may be more important than age as a factor in the cessation of heroin use. There is some evidence that extended use may lead, for some persons, to a "burn-out" of heroin use rather than "mature-out" with age.

maximum engagement. in traffic accident investigations, the greatest penetration of one body by another during collision; the instant of greatest force between objects in collision; the position of bodies (such as vehicles) with respect to each other at the instant of collision.

maximum permissible dose. that radiation dose identified as the limiting cumulative dose permitted to be received over a specific period of time by persons exposed to radiation.

maximum security. security measures observed in a custodial institution where utmost efforts are made to prevent escapes. In maximum security institutions, the freedom of inmates and of visitors is restricted more than in other prisons and correctional facilities.

maximum sentence. the maximum penalty provided by law for a given criminal offense, usually stated as a maximum term of imprisonment or a maximum fine.

mayhem. intentional inflicting of injury on another which causes the removal of, or seriously disfigures, or renders useless or seriously impairs the function of, any member or organ of the body.

McAndrew v. Mularchuck. a case in which the New Jersey Supreme Court ruled that a municipality is liable for failing to properly train its police officers in the correct use of firearms.

McCary v. Illinois. a case in which the U.S. Supreme Court held that a police officer who makes an arrest based on information furnished by a reliable informant, and establishes the informant's past reliability or independently corroborates the information need not disclose the informant's identity and the arrest is valid.

This case evolved from the arrest of the defendant for possession of narcotics. Upon testimony by the investigator, it was revealed that an informant had supplied information leading to the arrest. The informant had previously supplied the investigator on fifteen previous occasions. The identity of the informant was requested by the defense counsel, but the trial judge ruled that the sworn officer's testimony would suffice and held that the identity would not be necessary. The trial judge's decision was upheld by the Supreme Court.

McNabb v. United States. a case in which the U.S. Supreme Court ruled that a confession obtained without physical coercion or psychological pressure must be excluded from evidence in a federal court if the suspect confessed prior to being taken before a United States commissioner or a magistrate within a reasonable period of time after arrest. This ruling initially applied only to federal police officers and federal courts, but in recent years has been applied in state courts.

mean time between failures. a statistical figure representing the average time between component or equipment failures.

mean time to failure. a statistical figure representing the average time between initial startup and the first failure of components or pieces of equipment for a given grouping of identical devices.

mean time to repair. a statistical figure representing the average time between component or equipment failure and the completed repair of the unit.

measure of dispersion. any statistical measure showing the extent to which data are concentrated or spread out from a measure of central tendency.

measures of variability. measures that show

the extent to which a distribution of scores is clustered or spread.

mechanic. that member of a pickpocketing team who does the actual taking from the victim. A "stall" distracts the victim as the mechanic lifts and passes the "poke" to a third member of the team.

mechanical fuse. a fuse in which some form of mechanical energy is utilized to cause the fuse to function. In its simplest design, it consists of a striker (firing pin) held away from a detonator by a retaining spring until some external force is applied. When sufficient force is exerted to overcome the retaining spring, the striker is allowed to impinge on the detonator, initiating the firing train.

mechanical imprints. the imprints and markings made on a cartridge case by contact with the firing pin, breechface, extractor and ejector. These imprints assist the firearms examiner to match a cartridge case with a particular firearm.

mechanical initiator. any mechanical device used to initiate a bomb's detonator. A mouse trap and coil spring are common types of mechanical initiators used in homemade bombs.

mechanical stability. the ability of an explosive to withstand mechanical force such as jolting and shaking.

mechanic's lien. a claim created by law for the purpose of securing priority of payment of the price or value of work performed and materials furnished in erecting or repairing a building or structure and as such attaches to the land as well as the building and improvements.

mechanism of injury. the way in which an injury occurred and the forces involved in producing the injury.

mechanistic organization. a form of organizational structure typical to police operations. It is characterized by (1) a high degree of task differentiation and specialization with a precise delineation of rights and responsibilities, (2) a high degree of reliance on the traditional hierarchical structure, (3) a tendency for the top of the hierarchy to control all incoming and outgoing administrative communications, (4) an emphasis on vertical interactions between superiors and subordinates, (5) a demand for loyalty to the organization and to superiors, and (6) a greater importance placed on internal (local) knowledge, experience and skill, as opposed to more general (cosmopolitan) knowledge, experience and skill.

meconic acid test. a test for identifying the presence of opium in a substance. Meconic acid is a natural compound peculiar only to opium, and the presence of it in a substance is the tell-tale mark of opium or its derivative morphine. The test is conducted by placing a particle of the suspected substance in a mixture of nitric acid and ferric chloride. The presence of meconic acid is indicated if a red streak spreads throughout the solution.

Medellin cartel. a drug trafficking network based in Columbia that is believed responsible for the majority of cocaine smuggled into the United States.

median. that portion of a divided highway separating the roadways for traffic in opposite directions.

mediate cause. in traffic accident investigations, a deficiency in the basic attributes of a road, a vehicle, or a person that contributes to an operational factor. An operational factor in the sense used here is a functional failure of a highway transportation system leading to the cause of a traffic accident.

medical fraud. an unlawful practice by medical professionals in which kickbacks are received from laboratories, pharmacies and similar businesses for services or products unnecessarily recommended to patients, or the unlawful practice of billing an insurance carrier for services or products not provided to patients.

medical jurisprudence. medical knowledge applied to legal questions; the application of principles and practices of the different branches of medicine to the elucidation of doubtful questions in a court of justice. Also called forensic medicine.

medium risk commodity. a relatively expensive consumer product with medium resale potential and of interest to thieves and professional fences. Examples are electric typewriters, calculators, musical instruments, power tools, automotive parts and apparel.

medium security. security measures observed in a correctional institution or detention facility where freedom of inmates and visitors is restricted and efforts are made to prevent escapes, but to a lesser extent than in institutions housing more dangerous criminals.

medium view photographs. photographs taken at a crime scene to depict specific objects or locations within the scene, such as point of forcible entry, bloodstains, and signs of struggle. A medium view photograph ideally contains sufficient details to show spatial relationships between the depicted objects or locations within the general crime scene area.

medullary index. the ratio of the diameter of the medulla to the diameter of the whole hair. This index is used in classifying hairs according to thickness. Three general groups are recognized: (1) the narrow medulla, which is characteristic of human hair and the hair of certain monkeys, (2) the medium medulla, which is characteristic of cattle, and (3) the thick medulla, which is characteristic of the hair of all other animals.

memorandum for record. a written record made for the purpose of formalizing the pertinent facts of an event.

memorandum opinion. an opinion of a court, in writing, which briefly states the reasons and reasoning for a decision, without detailed explanation.

Menita. the brand name of a baby laxative used as a cocaine dilutant.

mens rea. a guilty mind; a guilty or wrongful purpose; a criminal intent.

mental retardation. significantly subaverage general intellectual functioning which exists concurrently with deficits in adaptive behavior, and manifested during the developmental period.

menu. a presentation of written or symbolic options from which an individual using a computerized system must select in order to start, continue, or terminate a particular task. A menu is frequently presented on a CRT display.

meperidine hydrochloride. one of the most widely used of the opioids, especially in childbirth and for relief of other severe pains. It is frequently preferred by opiate narcotic abusers in the medical professions. The pharmacological effects are similar to morphine. This drug is manufactured as Demerol.

meprobamate. one of the antianxiety tranquilizers used for muscle relaxation and sedation. Meprobamate is less potent than the minor tranquilizers derived from benzodiazepine such as chlordiazepoxide hydrochloride (Librium) and diazepam (Valium). Meprobamate is manufactured as Miltown and Equanil, and is a Schedule IV controlled substance.

mercury fulminate. a type of primary explosive.

mercury switch bomb. a bomb that will explode when an electrical circuit has been opened or closed by the action of a drop of mercury between contact points. A bomb of this construction is designed to detonate when moved.

merger doctrine. a legal doctrine which holds that when two crimes have been committed by a defendant within the same act, the less serious offense should be merged with the most serious offense charged. For example, the crime of possessing burglar's tools would be merged with the charge of burglary. When a less serious offense is not inherently a part of the larger offense it would be charged separately. This concept also embraces the merging of a murder charge with a felony. In a charge of felony-murder, the doctrine would prevent conviction if the underlying felony is part of the homicide, for example, the prosecution could not rely on aggravated assault as the underlying felony since murder itself is an aggravated assault. When the felony portion of a felony-murder charge is nonassaultive (such as breaking and entering), the merger doctrine would not stand in the way of a conviction.

mescaline. an hallucinogen derived from

the peyote cactus. It is classified as a Schedule I controlled substance. Mescaline is an alkaloid, with hallucinogenic properties, either derived from the heads or "buttons" of the peyote cactus or produced synthetically. It is less potent than LSD, but like LSD it alters perception and can produce hallucinations. Effects appear within 2 to 3 hours and last from 4 to 12 hours or more. Mescaline belongs to the phenylethylalanines and is chemically related to adrenaline.

metabolic disorder theory of action. a drug addiction paradigm that views addiction as a function of the manner in which the drug is metabolized by the body. For example, although initial heroin use may be psychological in origin, it is the variable "imprint" of the drug on the nervous system that causes the protracted addiction syndrome. By treating narcotic addiction as a metabolic disease with the use of a narcotic antagonist such as methadone, the narcotic hunger that results from the physical effects of the opiates is prevented, thus allowing the individual to live a more normal life.

metal detector. a device used to detect the presence of metallic objects. It operates by creating a balanced magnetic field between transmitting and receiving coils. The movement of a sufficient volume of metal through the field causes an imbalance which triggers an alarm. Sensitivity is a function of coil characteristics.

metal foil. a thin strip of metal usually installed on glass. A break in the foil results in an alarm.

metal fracture examination. a crime laboratory examination which seeks to determine if a piece of metal was or was not broken from an object such as a knife or screwdriver.

metallurgical examination. a crime laboratory examination which seeks to determine if two metals or metallic objects came from the same source or from each other. The examination is based on surface and microstructural characteristics, mechanical properties, and composition. For example, a metallurgical examination might seek to match a metal fragment obtained at the scene of a safecracking to safecracking tools found in the possession of a suspect, or the examination might seek to identify from the fragment the type, class, and manufacture of the source object.

metal-mesh grille. a grille of expanded metal or welded metal wires permanently installed across a window or other opening in order to prevent entry through the opening.

meter butcher. a thief who steals electrical or gas service by dismantling, and usually damaging, the meter.

methadone. an opiate classified as a Schedule II controlled substance. It is a synthetic narcotic which prevents withdrawal symptoms and the craving to use other opiates. This opioid is largely used in the maintenance treatment of heroin dependency because (1) it prevents heroin withdrawal symptoms, (2) it fulfills the addict's physical need for the drug, (3) at sufficiently high dosages it blocks the effects of heroin through cross-tolerance, thus canceling the pleasurable effects of street heroin, (4) it is a longer-acting drug than heroin, the average dose lasting 24 hours, thus making it more convenient to administer, (5) it is effective orally, thus breaking the reliance on the ritual of injection, and (6) it can be dispensed at a treatment center.

The ultimate aim is to wean addicts from heroin and the heroin lifestyle and allow them to adjust to a new lifestyle through which they can then withdraw from methadone and live drug free. It is thus often used not only for maintenance but for detoxification from opiate addiction by reducing doses gradually over a short period. Critics argue that because the patient is still dependent on an opiate narcotic, it is doubtful users will ever withdraw from methadone. Data have shown not only that some people can become addicted to methadone in such legal settings, but that some people continue to use heroin and other illicit drugs while taking methadone and that for many methadone has become a drug of preference, thus generating an active illicit market. Some patients complain that methadone and the daily treatment process is just as disruptive as heroin use. A synthetic opiate, LAAM, has been advocated as an alternative to methadone for treatment purposes because daily doses are not needed. Methadone is called dolly on the street and is sold legally as Dolophine.

methadone maintenance. a treatment program for heroin addicts. An addict is administered daily doses of methadone, a synthetic opiate. The methadone blocks the euphoric effects of heroin and does not itself produce distortion in the addict. The concept of this program is to lead the addict to a secure and responsible position in society by removing the craving for heroin. A criticism is that methadone itself is an addictive drug.

methamphetamine. a central nervous system stimulant similar to amphetamine sulfate (benzedrine) but more potent. It is the favored drug among habitual amphetamine users who frequently take it by intravenous injection so as to produce an almost instantaneous onset of the drug's effects, which many users compare to sexual orgasm. Sold as Methedrine and Desoxyn, it is classified as a Schedule III controlled substance. Also called meth, crank, go fast, speed and crystal.

methaqualone. a nonbarbiturate sedative (hypnotic) that produces sleep for about 6 to 8 hours, originally marketed as an alternative to barbiturates. When taken in large doses for purposes other than sleep inducement, it produces muscular relaxation, feelings of contentment, and total passivity, a state somewhat resembling drunkenness. First synthesized in 1951 and introduced in 1965, it was once believed not to have the adverse side effects associated with barbiturates. More recent reports stress that it has no advantages over other sedatives.

Since its introduction, methaqualone has become one of the ten most abused drugs in the United States. Abusers find it more enjoyable and satisfying than barbiturates because it (1) produces rapid, long-lasting effects, (2) reduces inhibitions in social situations, (3) promotes a perpetual state of sedation that eases life's pressures, and (4) is a good substitute for narcotics when they are not available.

Quaalude, the most publicized brand of methaqualone, had become so notorious that many doctors stopped prescribing it and many pharmacies discontinued stocking it. The manufacturer of Quaalude is now marketing a new brand of methaqualone called Mequin which is chemically and therapeutically identical to Quaalude.

The symptoms of methaqualone overdose are: (1) depressed respiratory and cardiovascular activity, (2) increased muscle tone ranging from hypertonia and muscle spasms to convulsions, (3) increased salivation, (4) possible increased pupil reaction to light and rapid changes in pupil size, (5) vomiting, and (6) lack of response to auditory stimulus or pain. High doses of methaqualone can increase a person's pain threshold so that he is unaware of pain, and some users may have a sense of indestructibility.

Trade names include Hymnal, Mandrax, Mequin, Parest, Quaalude, Somnafac, and Sopor. Street names include lude, mandrake, and quad.

methylene blue. a dye stuff used to mark an object so that a detectable amount will be transferred to the body or clothing of a person who handled the object.

methylenedioxyamphetamine (MDA). a synthetic hallucinogen related both to mescaline and the amphetamines, which is usually swallowed. At low dosage, users report a sense of well-being with heightened tactile sensation, intensified feelings, but without hallucinations or distortions. Higher doses produce effects more similar to those of LSD. The effects will last for as long as 10–12 hours. MDA and mescaline belong to the same chemical group (the phenylethylalanines) and are chemically related to adrenaline.

methylenedioxymethylamphetamine (MDM or

MDMA). a synthetic psychedelic chemically related to amphetamine. It is similar to MDA in general effect but lasts 4–6 hours instead of 10–12. A number of similar chemical variations of the amphetamine molecule have been synthesized into drugs with names like MMDA, TMA, and PMA. The names Adam and XTC are sometimes used on the street when referring to MDM.

methylphenidate. a stimulant classified as a Schedule III controlled substance. This drug is a CNS stimulant similar to amphetamine, often prescribed for the treatment of hyperkinesis in children and for weight control in adults, and is manufactured as Ritalin. Adverse effects include loss of appetite, insomnia, nervousness, and allergic reactions.

methyprylon. a depressant classified as a Schedule III controlled substance. This drug is a nonbarbiturate sedative/hypnotic, manufactured as Noludar. Adverse effects include dizziness, gastrointestinal disturbances, headache, paradoxical excitement, and the possibility of dependence.

metro channel. in a law enforcement radio system, a channel or frequency used by all police and public safety agencies within a given jurisdiction so that their separate but complementary activities can be coordinated.

Metropolitan Householders Directory. the trade name for a book that lists within a community all telephone numbers numerically and by street address. Also called Cole's Directory.

Mexican brown. a form of heroin so named for its origin and color. Also, a fentanyl variant mixed with lactose. The fentanyl variant has a brown color that comes from carmelization of the lactose during the heating process used in its manufacture. When uncut, this drug is about 100 times as potent as morphine. Also called Mexican horse.

Mexican reds. barbiturates, usually sodium secobarbital, manufactured in Mexico.

Michigan v. Mosely. a case in which the U.S. Supreme Court addressed in 1975 the issue of what circumstances would allow resumption of police questioning of a suspect after the suspect has exercised the Miranda right to remain silent. In this case, Mosely was arrested in connection with robberies, was advised of rights, and signed a police department form invoking his right to not answer questions. Mosely, however, did not indicate a desire to consult with counsel. The questioning ceased and he was placed in a cell. About two hours later, another detective decided to question Mosely concerning a homicide. Mosely was given a second Miranda advisement, but this time he signed the departmental form indicating his willingness to answer questions. Mosely did not ask for an attorney, and during this second questioning he implicated himself in the homicide. Mosely was convicted of murder, and the Michigan Court of Appeals reversed, holding that the second interview was a violation of the Miranda doctrine.

The U.S. Supreme Court noted that this case did not involve the procedures to be followed if the person in custody asks to consult with a lawyer, as opposed to Mosely's desire only to remain silent and to not have a lawyer. The Court concluded that the main issue was whether or not the police honored Mosely's request in the first interview.

The Court found that Mosely's request to remain silent regarding the robberies was scrupulously honored. The questioning was resumed only after the passage of a significant period of time and the provision of a fresh set of warnings, and restricted the second interrogation to a crime that had not been a subject of the earlier interrogation. The Court concluded that the admission into evidence of Mosely's incriminating statement did not violate the principles of the Miranda decision.

Michigan v. Tyler. a 1978 case in which the U.S. Supreme Court evaluated the constitutionality of a series of searches in an arson case. The initial search began at night while the fire was still being extinguished. The searchers took pictures and removed containers of flammable liquid found in the building. The fire was extinguished at 4:00 AM, and the scene was left unattended until 8:00 AM when the searchers returned. They made a quick examination and decided to make a more thorough search. They left and came back one hour later at which time they found and seized evidence which had not been detectable earlier because of heat, steam, and darkness. Thereafter, on at least three occasions after the day of the fire, further searches and seizures were conducted.

The Supreme Court found that the initial search did not require a search warrant under the emergency circumstances presented by the fire, and that the searches conducted several hours after the fire were also proper because they were a continuation of the original entry and search made under emergency circumstances. The Court held, however, that the searches made several days after the fire had been extinguished were unconstitutional because they were too far separated from the initial emergency.

Mickey Finn. chloral hydrate. When added to an alcoholic drink, this drug will render the imbiber unconscious.

microanalytical examinations. a general name for those crime laboratory examinations which seek to match or determine the origins of unknown objects. Such examinations typically involve fibers, hairs, tool markings, firearms characteristics, and glass.

microcomputer. a small capacity computer with limited memory and functions. It is used for small to mid-sized computerized security systems, and is usually programmed in an upper-level language such as BASIC.

microcrystalline test. a type of test for identifying an unknown substance by an examination of the color and morphology of crystals formed when the substance is mixed with a reagent.

microdot. LSD in a microdot or tiny tablet configuration. Microdot is often manufactured as a tiny speck of LSD on a stamp-size piece of paper that can be placed in the mouth or swallowed. In some cases, the LSD is impregnated in a design on the paper, similar to the tattoo transfers sold in candy stores to children. When placed against the skin, microdots of this type can be absorbed into the bloodstream, and for this reason are dangerous around children and the uninitiated. Microdots are often given other names that correspond to the design on the stamp, e.g., blue star, red pyramid, Superman, and Mickey Mouse.

microgram. one millionth of a gram.

microscope photometry. a crime laboratory technique for comparing samples on the basis of light absorption. By measuring the light absorption of two samples at all wavelengths, an examiner can identify differences which are indistinguishable to the human eye.

microtaggants. tiny magnetized particles mixed with or attached to high-theft items. In addition to being magnetized (to facilitate detection of their presence), microtaggants are coded to provide valuable investigative leads. They are usually added to paints used in marking items, but have also been mixed with animal feed and fertilizers.

Middle East connection. a phrase describing the flow of narcotics from Iran and Turkey through local laboratories via Iranian and Turkish traffickers to distributors in Europe, Canada, the United States, and Mexico.

middle ordinate. in traffic accident investigations, a measurement represented by the perpendicular distance between an arc and its chord at the middle of the chord.

mid-span jump. a theft of electrical service technique in which the thief, after the utility company has discontinued electrical service, will attach a set of automobile booster cables at the point of disconnection so that service will be restored.

military anti-shock trousers (MAST). an inflatable garment applied around the legs and abdomen, used in the treatment of shock.

military jurisdiction. an area within which various individuals, organizations, agencies, or some other instrumentality of the armed forces of the United States exercises the broad police powers of government rather than civilian individuals, organizations, agencies, or other groups normally empowered to do so. The exercise of military jurisdiction is always closely circumscribed and is normally based on either constitutional provisions or international law, including the law of war.

military law. the rules governing military personnel as prescribed by Congress pursuant to its constitutional authority to regulate the armed forces. Offenses against military law are found in the Uniform Code of Military Justice, Title 10 of the United States Code. Violations of rules and regulations which are merely disciplinary in nature, such as absent without leave, are not considered crimes in the usual sense of the word. Military law does, however, cover a wide range of criminal offenses. Breaches of military law are heard and determined by courts-martial. Military persons are bound equally with civilians to strict observance of the criminal laws and are answerable to the ordinary courts for their acts. Military law is different than martial law. Martial law is imposed during extreme emergencies that threaten public order. It is applied equally to civilians and military personnel. Martial law supersedes civil law, and the will of the military commander is supreme.

military offense. an offense applicable within the military environment but which has no parallel offense in the civil environment. Absent without leave, desertion and improper wearing of the uniform are military offenses.

milligram. one thousandth of a gram.

mimetic drug. a drug that imitates the effects of another drug.

Mincey v. Arizona. a case in which the U.S. Supreme Court ruled unconstitutional a warrantless four day search of the defendant's apartment following his arrest after shooting a police officer in the apartment. In the Court's opinion, police officers have a right when they come upon a murder scene to make a prompt warrantless search and to seize any evidence in plain view. A search beyond that, such as a search of desks or drawers, is impermissible if there is time to secure a search warrant.

mineralogy examination. a crime laboratory examination of materials that are mostly inorganic, crystalline or mineral in character. A mineralogy examination is intended to connect a suspect person or objects to a crime scene, prove or disprove an alibi, produce investigative leads or substantiate a theorized claim of events. Materials commonly examined include glass, building materials, soil, debris, industrial dusts, safe insulations, ores, abrasives and gems.

minicomputer. a medium-capacity computer that in scope and function falls between a microcomputer and a mainframe computer.

minimization of interception. a requirement placed on the police to minimize interception of irrelevant conversations when executing an eavesdropping warrant. The general standard is that, as stated in United States v. Tortello, a court should not admit evidence derived from an electronic surveillance order unless, after reviewing the monitoring log and hearing testimony of the monitoring agents, it is left with the conviction that on the whole the agents have shown high regard for the right of privacy and have taken all reasonable steps to avoid unnecessary intrusion.

minimum eligible parole date. the date on which the offender is or was first eligible for parole, as determined at the time of admission to prison or as first set by paroling authority action, depending on the statutes and other rules of the jurisdiction.

minimum-maximum term. a sentence in which the convicted person cannot be released before serving a minimum period, less time off for good behavior, or kept in prison longer than the maximum period, less time off for good behavior. In between the minimum and maximum, the prisoner is eligible for parole.

minimum security. security measures observed in a correctional institution or detention facility where relative freedom is granted to prisoners and visitors, congruent with the concept of involuntary detention, and where lesser emphasis is placed on preventing escapes.

minimum sentence. the minimum penalty provided by law for a given offense, meaning in most contexts, the minimum term of confinement to be served. Like the maximum sentence, the minimum potential term of confinement applicable to a person at time of commitment can be provided by statute, or determined by a court or parole authority within statutory limits. In some jurisdictions there is no officially stated minimum sentence.

Minnesota Multiphasic Personality Inventory. a paper and pencil test that measures degrees of hypochondriasis, depression, hysteria, psychopathic deviation, masculinity-femininity, paranoia, psychasthenia, schizophrenia, hypomania and social introversion.

The MMPI is a personality questionnaire consisting of items answerable by the responses "true," "false," or "cannot say." The responses distinguish certain psychopathological configurations and syndromes as well as normal characteristics. Responses are interpreted using scales each with a different title, alphabetic abbreviation, and numerical code. The MMPI is widely used, often in conjunction with other tests, as a screening tool by schools, employers, and the military. It is also used as a counseling aid, providing a portrait of the respondent's personality characteristics and pathological tendencies.

minority person. a member of an ethnic group that historically has been the victim of discrimination. Under federal law, minority persons are specifically members of the Negro race, persons of Hispanic national origin, persons of Oriental national or ethnic origin, persons of Native American (Indian) and Alaskan native ethnic groups, and certain other specified populations.

Miranda custody. custody in which the detained or arrested person is required to be informed of Miranda rights. Miranda custody exists incident to formal arrest, and absent a formal arrest, courts may make a finding that Miranda rights applied. Miranda is generally not applicable to a temporary investigative detention. One of the more important factors that decide the issue of Miranda custody is the place of interrogation. Miranda has been found to apply in coercive and police-dominated surroundings, and not to apply when the place of questioning is familiar and comfortable to the suspect.

Several standards have been developed to determine if Miranda custody was present in a particular situation. The subjective standard relies on the state of mind of either officer or subject. The probably cause standard uses probable cause. The objective standard grounds its conclusion on a careful appraisal of all pertinent facts surrounding the event in question. The focus standard examines when and if the focus of investigation shifted to the subject.

Miranda rights. the set of rights which a person accused or suspected of having committed a specific offense has during interrogation, and of which he must be informed prior to questioning, as stated by the US Supreme Court in deciding *Miranda v. Arizona* and related cases.

Miranda v. Arizona. a landmark case in which the U.S. Supreme Court ruled that whenever the police are about to interrogate someone who is in their custody or who has "otherwise been deprived by the authorities of his freedom in any significant way" must be given the following warnings: (1) that he has a right to remain silent, and that he need not answer any questions, (2) that if he does answer questions his answers may be used as evidence against him, (3) that he has a right to consult with a lawyer before or during the questioning of him by the police, and (4) that if he cannot afford to hire a lawyer one will be provided for him without costs.

The Miranda decision does not exclude the use of statements "blurted out" by suspects before police have had a reasonable opportunity to advise them of their rights. Neither does it exclude statements made by persons not in custody, or physical or testimonial evidence obtained independent of questioning suspects. For example, if there are witnesses to a crime and police arrest the suspect and seize evidence, and then obtain a confession in violation of Miranda, the only evidence that will be excluded at trial is the confession and any evidence derived from it. A conviction in this example would be attainable based on eyewitness testimony and evidence obtained apart from the confession.

The Miranda decision is therefore an important factor only in cases in which the primary evidence is information obtained from the suspect after being taken into custody.

misapplication. improper, illegal, wrongful or corrupt use or application of funds.

miscarriage of justice. a gross error in the outcome of a criminal case, generally applied to the conviction and punishment of an innocent defendant.

misdemeanor. an offense usually punishable by incarceration for a period of which the upper limit is prescribed by law in a given jurisdiction, typically limited to a year or less.

misfeasance. the improper performance of a lawful act. The law of negligence distinguishes between liability for the consequences of affirmative acts (misfeasance) and liability for merely doing nothing (nonfeasance). Almost any inaction can be characterized as misfeasance if the court is so disposed, and often inaction is substantially the equivalent of active misconduct. For example, the failure to repair defective brakes may be seen as active negligence.

A fundamental question is whether there is a sufficient relationship between the one who failed to act and the one injured as a result. A common example is the absence of a duty to go to the aid of someone needing help (when such help is not required by some pre-existing status or relationship). For example, a person skilled in administering cardiopulmonary resuscitation is not required to aid a victim needing such assistance, unless the person happens to also be a paramedic hired for that purpose.

Duties of affirmative action which would not otherwise exist may be voluntarily assumed. It is commonly held that one who freely undertakes to render aid to another assumes a duty to act with reasonable care, and once the duty is assumed it may not be abandoned. This rule is thought by many to have the negative effect of discouraging rescuers.

misfire. the temporary failure of the primer to ignite the powder charge in a cartridge. A misfire will usually reach ignition within five seconds. Also called hangfire.

misprision. failure in the duty of a citizen to try to prevent a crime, or having knowledge of a crime, fails to reveal it to the proper authorities.

misprision of a felony. receiving or offering to give a monetary or other consideration in return for a promise not to prosecute or aid in the prosecution of a criminal offender. Also known as compounding a crime.

missing person. a person reported missing who is under 18 or who, being 18 or over, is seriously affected mentally or physically, or is absent under circumstances that indicate involuntary disappearance.

mistake of fact defense. a defense against prosecution which seeks to excuse the accused because he was misled or was not in possession of all facts at the time of the crime. For example, this defense might be used in a case where a homeowner injured someone who he thought was a burglar in his home but who in fact was the invited guest of another member of the family.

mistake of law. a defense, rarely allowed, offered by an accused that he did not know his act was criminal or did not comprehend the consequences of his act.

mistrial. a trial terminated or declared void before a verdict is reached, because of some procedural defect, impediment, or error that will prejudice a jury, or because the jury has not been able to agree on a verdict. When there is a mistrial, a new trial can be held without double jeopardy, unless the defendant has objected to the mistrial and an appellate court holds that the mistrial was improperly declared by the trial judge, i.e., that the mistrial was neither necessary or required by the interests of justice.

mitigating circumstances. circumstances that do not constitute a justification or excuse of an offense, but which may be considered as extenuating or reducing the degree of moral culpability. Also called extenuating circumstances.

M'Naghten rule. the rule laid down by the House of Lords after the 1843 verdict of "not guilty by reason of insanity" in the case of Daniel M'Naghten. The rule stated that the perpetrator of the crime is not to be held criminally responsible if, at the time of the act, he suffered from a disease of the mind either making him unable to know the nature of the act he was committing or, if he did know it, making him unable to realize that what he was doing was wrong.

mobile assistance team. a defensive team of U.S. Air Force personnel who perform specialized antiterrorism services in response to a specific need. Team members are typically Air Force Office of Special Investigations (AFOSI) special agents, security policemen, civil engineers, communications specialists and others as the team's mission may dictate.

mobile intensive care unit (MICU). an ambulance staffed and equipped to give advanced life support.

mobile surveillance. the technique of observing from a moving vehicle, such as a patrol car or unmarked vehicle, for the purpose of detecting suspicious or illegal behavior of designated surveillance targets or of the public generally.

Model Arson Law. a statute recommended by the National Fire Protection Association which has been adopted in many states.

Model Penal Code. a statute recommended in 1962 by the American Law Institute which has been adopted in many states.

Model Sentencing Act. a sentencing proposal drawn up in 1963 by the Advisory Council of Judges of the National Council on Crime and Delinquency which has been recommended for adoption by the states.

model statute. a proposed statute, recommended to a legislature for adoption, which can serve several jurisdictions.

modification of probation. a change in the terms and conditions of a probation order, making them more restrictive or less restrictive, as determined by a court.

modified general question technique. in polygraphy, a testing approach consisting of a series of relevant, non-relevant and control questions asked in a planned order.

modifier. in traffic accident investigations, a circumstance that alters an attribute permanently or temporarily. An attribute in this sense is any inherent characteristic of a road, a vehicle, or a person that affects the probability of a traffic accident.

modus operandi. a characteristic pattern of behavior repeated in a series of offenses that coincides with the pattern evidenced by a particular single person, or by a particular group of persons working together.

modus operandi file. a file that records information concerning the distinct techniques applied in crimes of various types and the criminals or groups known to have applied those techniques.

mold. in criminal investigation, a negative impression of an object. Details on the mold will be reversed when the mold and object are viewed together. A mold is used to make a cast, which is a positive representation of the object.

moll buzzer. a pickpocket who specializes in stealing from the purses of lady shoppers in crowded department stores.

molotov cocktail. a bottle or other break-able container containing a flammable liquid into which has been placed a wick or similar igniting device, and which when ignited and thrown will cause a fire or explosion.

momentum. in traffic accident investigations, mass or weight times velocity or speed. Momentum is a vector quantity.

money clip. a hold-up sensor designed to trigger an alarm when paper money is removed from its special clip causing a contact closure. The clip is typically kept in the drawer of a cash register.

monitoring. the act of listening-in or eavesdropping on telephone lines or room conversations.

monitoring by exception. an electronic alerting system which annunciates only when an undesirable act takes place.

monoamine oxidase inhibitor. MAO inhibitor; any of the monoamine oxidase inhibitor group of drugs used to treat depression. Adverse effects include dry mouth, drowsiness, and constipation. The drugs interact with many other drugs and with foods (such as cheeses, red wine, beer, and yogurt) containing tyramine, sometimes causing an acute hypertensive episode with headache and palpitations.

Monroe effect. the concentrating of explosive force through the shape of the charge.

montage synthesizer. a device that creates composite photographs of criminal suspects. It consists of a montage mounting unit, a television camera, and a television monitor. Photographs selected by a witness from a mug shot file are placed on the mounting unit and viewed through the monitor. The camera synthesizes up to four photographs at a time and adjusts for skin tone and texture, allowing any feature mix of gender and racial characteristics. When the victim is satisfied that the composite likeness corresponds to the suspect's likeness, a photograph is taken from the monitor screen.

mood drug. generally, a psychoactive drug; a drug that alters mood, such as a stimulant (cocaine) or a depressant (heroin).

moon walking. walking in a manner similar in appearance to walking in the absence of gravity. It is a manifestation symptomatic of being under the influence, especially of PCP.

moot point. a point or issue not settled by judicial decision. Frequently, a moot point is an abstract question which does not arise upon existing facts or rights in a case.

moral conduct. a form of behavior that involves a consideration of choice of right and wrong, judged in terms of a standard of values or morals, toward which a person recognizes a duty or feels a sense of responsibility. It includes both acceptable and unacceptable or immoral forms of behavior.

moral holidays. occasions when enforcement of the laws is relaxed and the police are indulgent, as during many athletic events, election celebrations, fraternal conventions, the Mardi Gras, and New Year's Eve.

moral offense. a general descriptor for a crime that offends morals or public health. Examples of moral offenses are sodomy, adultery, bigamy, prostitution, desertion, gambling, and drug abuse.

morals squad. a police unit dealing with prostitution, gambling, pornography and other offenses deemed detrimental to the morals of a community. Also called a vice squad.

moral turpitude. a legal term describing a crime found shocking to the sense of decency or to the morals of a community; a showing of conduct contrary to justice, honesty, modesty or good morals.

morbid criminal propensity. a natural inclination or uncontrollable impulse to engage in unlawful behavior.

morning-glory seeds. a source of an hallucinogen used by American Indians and others.

morning report. a report of activities that occurred in the previous 24 hours.

morning shot. an addict's first injection of the day.

morphine. the principal active ingredient in opium. Raw opium is composed of approximately 10 percent morphine by weight. Isolated in 1803 and named after Morpheus, the Greek god of dreams, morphine first received widespread use in the United States during the Civil War. Still one of the most useful of medical drugs, it is considered by some to be superior to all other pain relievers. In addition to pain relief, it reduces drive states and encourages sleep. Since the Harrison Narcotics Act and the spread of heroin use, the recreational use of morphine has declined, although the subjective effects of morphine and heroin in equivalent potencies are almost identical.

Mosaic Code. the law of the Old Testament, particularly as expressed in the Ten Commandments.

motherboard. the primary electronic printed-circuit board in a piece of equipment. It usually interfaces with one or more secondary circuits.

mother ship. a large boat, such as a freighter, used in the smuggling of contraband, mainly drugs. The mother ship typically remains outside territorial waters and offloads its cargo to smaller, high-speed craft which transport the contraband to many different coastal locations.

motile sperm test. a test made of a fluid specimen taken from the posterior vaginal region of a rape victim. The specimen is obtained and visually examined as quickly as possible, frequently at the scene. The examination seeks to identify the presence of motile (moving) sperm.

motion. an oral or written request made by a party to an action, before, during or after a trial, that a court issue a rule or order.

motion for a new trial. a motion by a defendant alleging certain errors committed in the course of his trial. If the trial judge agrees, the conviction is set aside and the defendant may be tried again by a new jury and usually before a different judge. A defendant may also seek a new trial on the grounds of newly discovered evidence favorable to him.

motion-initiated bomb. a bomb engineered to explode when it is moved. It is usually constructed so that movement brings objects or elements into contact, e.g., hypergolic chemicals or contact wires. The motion-initiated bomb is a type of booby trap.

motion to quash an arrest warrant. a motion made before trial by an arrested person alleging that the warrant was defective. If the motion is granted, the arrest is declared illegal and any evidence obtained incident to the arrest cannot be used at trial. However, if the circumstances under which the arrest was made would have justified an arrest without a warrant, the arrest may still be valid and seized evidence admissible.

motion to quash the indictment. a motion by a defendant which questions the legal sufficiency of an indictment. If the court agrees with the motion, the indictment is deemed invalid. The prosecutor can appeal the ruling and/or seek a proper indictment. A subsequent indictment would not violate the constitutional protection against double jeopardy.

motion to suppress evidence. a motion made by the defense attorney, in the absence of the jury, to suppress from introduction into evidence any evidence obtained in violation of the defendant's constitutional rights. Usually such rights are related to the 4th, 5th and 6th Amendments (search and seizure, self-incrimination, right to counsel and right of confrontation with witnesses).

Motivation-Hygiene Theory. a theory developed by Frederick Herzberg which holds that five factors are the chief determinants of job satisfaction: achievement, recognition, the work itself, responsibility, and advancement.

Factors associated with job dissatisfaction were empirically observed by Herzberg to be company policy and administration, supervision, salary, interpersonal relations and working conditions.

The use of the term hygiene in the title of the theory derives from job-content satisfiers such as achievement, advancement, and responsibility. The term hygiene is analogous to the medical use of hygiene to control conditions in the environment.

motive. the reason why something is done. The motive for robbery, for example, would be to get possession of property owned by someone else. Motive and intent are separate concepts in criminal law. Motive is the desire or inducement which tempts or prompts a person to do a criminal act. Intent is a person's resolve or purpose to commit the act. Motive is the reason which leads the mind to desire a certain result. Intent is the determination to achieve the result.

Motive is an important investigative consideration, but is not an essential element of a crime. Intent must be established for a crime to exist. A good motive (as might be represented in a mercy killing) does not keep an act from being a crime, and an evil motive will not necessarily make an act a crime. Furthermore, an accused would not be acquitted simply because a motive could not be discovered. The basic urge that led the offender's mind to want the result of the forbidden act is immaterial as to guilt. Proof of motive, however, may be relevant and admissible on behalf of either side at trial. Motive can be especially pertinent where the evidence in a case is largely circumstantial. In some statutes, proof of motive may be required.

motor vehicle. any vehicle which is self-propelled; any vehicle which is propelled by electric power obtained from overhead trolley wires, but not operated on rails.

motor vehicle accident. an accident involving a motor vehicle in transport, but not involving aircraft or watercraft.

Motor Vehicle Identification Manual. a publication of the National Automobile Theft Bureau which lists state regulations concerning motor vehicle registration, titling, operator licensing, and other details including VIN descriptions.

motor vehicle theft. unlawful taking, or attempted taking, of a self-propelled road vehicle owned by another, with the intent to deprive him of it permanently or temporarily.

motor vehicle traffic accident. any motor vehicle accident that occurs on a trafficway or that occurs after the motor vehicle runs off a roadway but before events are stabilized.

moulage-agar. a colloidal substance of the compound agar used to make finely detailed casts of foot and tire prints, tool marks and parts of the human body.

mounting the gun. bringing a rifle or shotgun to the shoulder preparatory to firing.

mouth habit. an oral drug habit.

mouth-to-mouth resuscitation. a method of artificial respiration in which the rescuer places his mouth over the victim's mouth and/or nose and blows air into the victim's lungs in a timed pattern that simulates natural breathing.

movable evidence. evidence that can be easily collected and transported, such as handguns, knives and documents.

moving coil microphone. a microphone having a movable conductor in the form of a coil. Electric output results from motion of the coil in a magnetic field at an audio frequency rate.

MPTP. the name for 1-methyl-4-phenyl-1,2,3,6-tetrahydropyridine, a highly toxic compound synthesized in clandestine laboratories and sold on the street as a psychoactive drug. MPTP is poisonous to the brain and extremely dangerous.

mugging. a type of strongarm robbery in which the offender approaches the victim from behind, usually suddenly and with stealth.

mug shot. a police-file photograph of a criminal's face, full-view and side-view.

mule. a person who carries or smuggles narcotics, such as cocaine and heroin, on behalf of another; a person who serves as a go between for distributors, dealers, and buyers of drugs.

multiple drug use. the nonmedical use of two or more drugs taken simultaneously or so closely in time that the effects of the first drug have not worn off when the second one or later drugs are taken. The term is not applied to a stepwise progression in the use of different drugs.

multiple flash photography. a crime or accident scene photographic technique in which two or more photoflashes are made in sequence from different positions to increase the illuminated field in low light level situations. The camera lens is covered or the shutter is closed in the intervals between flashes.

multiple personality. a rare dissociative disorder characterized by a division of the personality into two or more complete behavior organizations, each well-defined and highly distinct from the others.

multiple points of origin. in arson investigations, two or more unconnected points where fire started. Since accidental fires have only one point of origin, the existence of multiple starting points is strongly indicative of arson.

multiple reference. the practice of establishing at least two identifiers when determining the identity of an unidentified corpse. Tattoos, scars and dental work are examples of identifiers.

multiple sentence. two or more concurrent or consecutive sentences, or a combination of both. It is possible for a person to be serving one of a set of consecutive sentences while also serving time on a concurrent sentence.

multiplexing. in data transmission, a function that permits two or more data sources to share a common transmission medium such that each data source has its own channel; the division of a transmission facility into two or more channels either by splitting the frequency band transmitted by the channel into narrower bands, each of which is used to constitute a distinct channel (frequency-division multiplexing), or by allotting the common channel to several different information channels, one at a time (time-division multiplexing).

multipurpose dry chemical. a fire extinguishingagent consisting of ammonium phosphate as the base powder plus additives.

multiunit accident. a traffic accident in which more than two traffic units (vehicles, pedacycles, or pedestrians) are involved in collisions, one with another, before there is a stabilized accident situation. A stabilized accident situation is the condition prevailing after motion and other action constituting the events of an accident have ceased.

mummification. a process in which the tissues of the body become dehydrated. The process requires a hot, dry climate, devoid of the moisture required by bacteria. In this process the skin will have a leathery appearance. Infants killed immediately after birth are sterile, limiting bacterial organisms to those that enter from outside the body. Also, the small size of an infant body permits mummification to progress more rapidly than is the case with an adult body.

munchies. a strong desire to eat, often associated with the use of marihuana.

murder. intentionally causing the death of another without reasonable provocation or legal justification, or causing the death of another while committing or attempting to commit another crime.

murder board. a panel of specially selected persons charged to review, evaluate and critique the rehearsal of a briefing, presentation, or public release.

Murphy game. a confidence game wherein money is taken from a customer, often by a pimp, to pay a prostitute who does not show up or slips away before services are rendered.

muscle power attack. the use of brute, physical strength to defeat a physical barrier, usually in connection with a forced entry through a window or door.

muscle relaxant. a drug that reduces the contractility of muscle fibers by blocking the transmission of nerve impulses at neuromuscular junctions, by increasing the time between contractions of fibers, by decreasing the excitability of the motor end plate, by interfering with nerve synapses in the central nervous system, or by interfering with calcium release from muscle or by other actions. These drugs are used to treat muscle spasm and as adjuncts to anesthesia for certain surgical procedures.

Mutt and Jeff technique. an interrogation technique in which a first interrogator presents himself to the subject as being harsh and unsympathetic. A second interrogator takes the side of the subject and seeks to gain his confidence by being kind and sympathetic.

mutual agreement program. a program providing for a form of contract between a prisoner and state prison and parole officials wherein the prisoner undertakes to complete specified self-improvement programs in order to receive a definite parole date, and the agency promises to provide the necessary educational and social services.

muzzle blast. the force produced by the bullet and powder gases exiting a gun barrel when a shot is fired.

muzzle distance. the distance between the muzzle (the front of the barrel) and the object shot. An examination of a gunshot wound may reveal trauma characteristic of muzzle blast, from which an estimate of muzzle distance may be made.

muzzle velocity. the speed of a bullet as it leaves the front of the barrel.

NADDIS. an acronym for Narcotic and Dangerous Drug Intelligence System, a computer-assisted information bank maintained by the Drug Enforcement Administration.

Nalline test. a test based upon the concept that a small dose of nalorphine (Nalline) produces an increase in pupil size in a person actively addicted to narcotics. The subject is placed before a constant lighting source, the pupils are measured, nalorphine is injected subcutaneously, and pupil measurements are taken again at 20, 30, and 40 minutes after the injection. An increase in pupil dilation above 0.5mm is considered a positive test.

nalorphine. a semisynthetic derivative of morphine, manufactured as Nalline. It counters the depression of the central nervous system created by opiate narcotics and is often valuable in the treatment of narcotic overdoses by abolishing respiratory depression. Nalorphine precipitates pupil dilation in the presence of opiates, which is the basis for the Nalline test.

name index file. a file that contains cross-indexing data on subjects, victims, witnesses, organizations, etc. This type of file is usually a locator file that assists in identifying larger records concerning the person or organization under investigation.

Napoleonic Code. the code of laws adopted in France by the regime of Napoleon Bonaparte in 1810 and revised in 1819. The Napoleonic Code became the basis for the criminal code in most continental European and Latin American countries.

Narcan test. a test used to determine opiate dependency, similar to the Nalline test. Both tests rely upon narcotic antagonists to induce visible symptoms when administered to persons with opiates in their systems. These types of tests are frequently used to monitor the use of opiates among inmates in prison. The Narcan test is also known as the naloxone challenge.

narcoanalysis. memory analysis with the assistance of a narcotic such as sodium amytal. The technique usually seeks details concerning a traumatic experience so that associated emotional problems can be treated. It can also be used for criminal investigation purposes when the victim is unable to recall details.

narcolepsy. a condition characterized by fits of sleep or uncontrollable feelings of extreme sleepiness. It may be pathological in nature and may also result as a side effect of certain drugs.

narcoleptic. a substance that produces an uncontrollable desire to sleep; a person with narcolepsy.

narcosis. a reversible state of pathological reduction in responsiveness and a marked slowing down of the physiological system; a state characterized by stupor or insensibility and a feeling of painlessness or well-being.

narcotic. when used in the medical sense, any drug that dulls a person's senses and produces a sense of well-being in small doses, and causes insensibility, stupefaction, and even death in large doses; a drug capable of producing narcosis. The term is sometimes incorrectly used to refer to all CNS depressants, including barbiturates and alcohol, and the belladonna group of hallucinogens. Some insist that only those depressant drugs that both sedate or numb the sensation of pain should be so classified, thus limiting use of the term to opium, the opiates, and the opioids. The term was often used loosely in the 19th century to refer to all nonalcoholic drugs, particularly those that could produce sleep or hallucinations. Beginning in the early 20th century, the term came to be a synonym for disapproved, illicit drugs, or any street drug used recreationally that produced sleep or hallucination and/or appeared addicting or harmful. America's first federal antinarcotics law, the Harrison Narcotics Act of 1914, included cocaine as a narcotic. Marijuana, peyote, and chloral hydrate were soon also legally and popularly classified as narcotics as concerns over their use grew and controls were extended to include them. The term also assumed a social meaning that encompassed debility, addiction, insanity, crime, and death. The United Nations Commission on Narcotic Drugs defines a narcotic as any drug under international control, excluding alcohol and nicotine. Because of the confusion and negative connotations that have developed around the word, most authorities today recommend the term be utilized only to refer to the analgesic depressant opium, the opiates, and the opioids.

Narcotic Addict Rehabilitation Act (NARA). a federal law establishing civil commitment of drug abusers to an in-hospital phase of treatment and an aftercare phase in their home communities. The act also provides for assistance and support to states and municipalities in developing treatment programs and facilities. NARA emphasizes hospitalization plus followup supervision and support to maintain an addict's motivation for rehabilitation upon return to the community. Persons eligible for the program are (1) narcotic addicts charged with certain federal offenses who desire to be committed for treatment in lieu of prosecution, (2) addicts convicted of federal crimes who are committed by the court, and (3) addicts who wish to voluntarily apply for commitment. Both the Department of Justice and the Department of Health and Human Services have recommended repeal of NARA on the grounds that the procedures are cumbersome, certain aspects are infrequently used, it has not proven to be cost beneficial, and in many respects it is incompatible with contemporary treatment approaches.

narcotic analgesic. a drug used clinically to decrease pain. Morphine and other alkaloids of opium are narcotic analgesics.

narcotic antagonist. a drug that blocks or counteracts the effects of opiate narcotics. Many have been derived by chemically altering some aspects of natural or synthetic opiate narcotics. Among the best known antagonists are cyclazocine, naloxone, nalorphine, and naltrexone. In sufficient doses, narcotic antagonists can block the psychological and physiological effects of opiate narcotics, including the development of tolerance and physical dependence, and can reverse or prevent toxic effects. They can also precipitate an intense acute withdrawal syndrome in opiate-narcotic-dependent individuals who have not been detoxified, and this property is sometimes employed for identifying physically dependent persons for medical and legal purposes. Narcotic antagonists may be pure or mixed. The pure narcotic antagonists (e.g., naltrexone and naloxone) in reasonable doses will produce little effect on an opiate-detoxified or non-opiate-dependent person. The mixed, or partial, narcotic antagonists (e.g., cyclazocine, nalorphine, and pentazocine) have slight narcotic agonist properties and their cessation will induce withdrawal symptoms in a user who has developed a physical dependence to opiates.

Narcotic Drug Control Act of 1956. a federal law that specifically outlawed heroin and increased already existing penalties for the transportation, sale, and smuggling of heroin and marijuana into the United States. Restrictions were lessened on tapping phone lines, reading telegrams of known traffickers in drugs, and issuing search warrants in narcotics cases. Agents of the Federal Bureau of Customs were empowered to make arrests without warrants from a court for any narcotics violation committed in their presence. A control record system was established within the Bureau of Narcotics to retain information on all narcotic addicts and violators that was to be made available to federal, state, and local law enforcement officials. Most of the provisions of this act were repealed and replaced by the Drug Abuse Act of 1970.

narcotic farms. a reference to two federal treatment facilities originally established in Lexington, Kentucky, in 1935, and in Fort Worth, Texas, in 1938, which for a quarter of a century carried the major responsibility for the treatment of opiate addiction in the United States. Operated in a manner similar to minimum security penal institutions, the hospital gave priority to the admission of federal prisoners and probationers who were addicts sent for withdrawal and detoxification. Voluntary patients were admitted when and if space was available. In 1945, the hospitals also began providing vocational, counseling, and psychiatric services. Withdrawal treatment was based on the extent of addiction and, at first, routinely consisted of subcutaneous injections of decreasing amounts of morphine over a period of 4 to 10 days. Subsequently, methadone was substituted for morphine, first through subcutaneous and later through oral administration. The hospitals were also authorized to investigate the cause, treatment, and prevention of drug addiction. Until the late 1960s, individuals desiring medical detoxification and withdrawal who could not afford private sanitariums had only these hospitals to which to turn. Soon after the hospitals opened, voluntary patients accounted for 75 percent of admissions, and a total of over 100,000 admissions were made to the hospitals during their years of operation. Although the programs have been criticized for their limited success and their prisonlike conditions, these hospitals did serve the goal of introducing the concept of treatment as a general goal and even as an officially stated government responsibility and provided an atmosphere in which the addict was considered a patient rather than a lawbreaker at a time when addiction was heavily stigmatized.

Narcotic Drug Import and Export Act of 1922. a federal law authorizing the Federal Narcotics Control Board to set import quotas on the amounts of opium, cocaine, and their derivatives needed to fulfill medical needs. In addition, possession without a prescription was made presumptive evidence of concealment of drugs illegally imported in violation of this act, thus making possession for nonmedical use a federal crime. This act was repealed and replaced by the Drug Abuse Act of 1970.

Narcotics Anonymous (NA). a worldwide self-help fellowship for recovered drug abusers who give each other support to remain free of drugs. NA was formed in 1953 and has affiliated chapters throughout the United States. As its name suggests, NA has adopted the Alcoholics Anonymous (AA) model.

narcotism. an obsolete term for narcosis or addiction to narcotics.

National Agency Check and Inquiry (NACI). a Department of Defense personnel security investigation conducted by the Office of Personnel Management, combining a national agency check (NAC) and written inquiries to law enforcement agencies, former employers and supervisors, references and schools.

National Automobile Altered Numbers File. a collection of specimens of altered vehicle identification numbers found on stolen cars, trucks and heavy equipment. The file is maintained by the FBI Laboratory so that comparisons can be made to identify recovered stolen vehicles, and possibly link them with known commercial theft rings.

National Commission on Marihuana and Drug Abuse. a presidential commission that during 1971–1973 studied marihuana and drug abuse affecting the nation. The commission issued two reports that defined the issues, provided data, assessed social impact, and formulated a number of recommendations, including the decriminalization of marihuana.

National Crime Information Center (NCIC). an agency of the federal government, administered by the U.S. Department of Justice, whose responsibility is to collect, index, store, and under prescribed conditions disseminate information about criminals and criminal incidents.

National Crime Survey Program. a statistical program administered by the Bureau of Justice Statistics (formerly the National Criminal Justice Information and Statistics Service of the Law Enforcement Assistance Administration) with data collected by the Bureau of the Census. It provides information on the extent to which persons 12 years of age and older and households have been victimized by selected crimes. Data are collected on the incidence of crimes, and circumstances under which the events occurred, the effects on the victim, and whether or not incidents were reported to the police.

National Defense Area. an area established on non-federal lands located within the United States, its possessions or territories, for the purpose of safeguarding classified defense information, or protecting Department of Defense equipment and/or material. Establishment of a National Defense Area temporarily places such non-federal lands under the effective control of the Department of Defense and results only from an emergency event. The senior Department of Defense representative at the scene defines the boundary, marks it with a physical barrier, and posts warning signs. The land owner's consent and cooperation is obtained whenever possible; however, military necessity dictates the final decision regarding location, shape and size of the area.

National Fraudulent Check File. a collection of checks, writings and other documentary materials maintained by the FBI Laboratory for use in identifying individuals involved in fraudulent check schemes and in determining if questioned documents originated from the same source.

National Institute on Drug Abuse (NIDA). a federal agency created by Congress under the Drug Abuse Office and Treatment Act of 1972. It began operating in 1974 to provide a meaningful response to the growing enigma of illicit drug use. Prior to NIDA, the federal drug effort was scattered across many agencies, and financial support for grassroots treatment programs and drug-related research was plagued with uncertainty. With NIDA's inception the various federal drug programs were in large measure consolidated into a single agency.

NIDA is organizationally a part of the U.S. Department of Health and Human Services. It is associated with counterpart agencies in the areas of alcohol abuse and mental health under the Alcohol, Drug Abuse, and Mental Health Administration (ADAMHA), within the Public Health Service. The vast majority of NIDA's funds are funneled to state and community-based programs in the form of grants and contracts.

National Law Enforcement Telecommunications System (NLETS). a communications system, relying principally on a teletype network, organized and administered by the U.S. Department of Justice, for the communication of information concerning criminal incidents and other law-enforcement matters among federal, state, and local police agencies.

National Organization for the Reform of Marijuana Laws (NORML). a group which actively lobbies for the decriminalization of marijuana, the destruction of criminal records for marijuana law offenders, recognition of the medical uses of marijuana, and research on the effects of marijuana on women of childbearing age. NORML policies, however, are against the abusive use of all drugs, the use of marijuana by children, and driving while under the intoxicating effects of marijuana or any other drug.

National Prisoner Statistics. a national data program which publishes statistical information on federal and state prisons and prisoners. The program was established in 1926, and is currently sponsored by the Bureau of Justice Statistics. The data are collected by the Bureau of Census.

National Security Area. an area established on non-federal lands located within the United States, its possessions, or territories, for the purpose of safeguarding classified and/or restricted data information, or protecting Department of Energy equipment and/or material. Establishment of a NSA temporarily places such non-federal lands under the effective control of the DOE and results only from an emergency event. The senior DOE representative having custody of the material at the scene defines the boundary, marks it with a physical barrier, and posts warning signs. The landowner's consent and cooperation is obtained whenever possible; however, operational necessity dictates the final decision regarding location, shape, and size.

National Stolen Property Act. a federal law which makes it a felony to transport across state lines stolen property valued at $5000 or more, knowing such property to be stolen, or knowingly to receive or conceal property valued at $5000 or more which was stolen from interstate or foreign commerce, or knowingly to pledge or accept such property as security.

National Survey on Drug Abuse. a survey which provides a broad picture of drug abuse in the American population. It is based on information obtained from persons randomly chosen to be representative of those living in U.S. households. It provides a useful indication of the general dimensions of the drug problem in the United States and especially of trends in drug abuse.

National Vehicle Identification Number Standard File. a collection of VIN plates from each factory of the major manufacturers of U.S.-made automobiles. The file is maintained by the FBI Laboratory for the purpose of comparing suspected counterfeit VIN plates against the standards on file.

Native American Church. a religion existing among Native Americans that combines elements of Christianity, native religious rites, and the ritual use of peyote. Peyote use first became apparent among the tribes of the United States in the latter part of the 19th century, when it was used in religious rites and to heal the sick. Gradually a religion developed around the use of the cactus that com-

bined elements of Christianity with the vision-quest ritual typical of the Plains Indians. The religion teaches brotherly love, high moral principles, abstention from alcohol consumption, and considers peyote a sacrament through which God is manifested. Those who practice it have faith in the efficacy of peyote as a cure-all and a true belief in the sacred character of the altered states of consciousness, especially visions, induced by the drug. Although the U.S. Government at first tried to discourage this church, it gradually became recognized that peyotism as practiced by the Indians was a sincere religion, and the courts have upheld it as such under the Bill of Rights. Peyotism does not interest all Native Americans. Many prefer either traditional Christianity or a revival of their own native religions.

natural opiates. a general term referring to opium and its two alkaloids codeine and morphine.

NCIC Agency Identifier. a nine-character code identifying specific law enforcement and criminal justice agencies in the United States and Canada. Assigned by NCIC, these identifiers designate originators of NCIC records and other law enforcement or criminal justice agency transactions.

near contact gunshot wound. a wound caused when the muzzle at time of discharge is approximately two inches or less from the victim but not in contact with the skin. The wound is rounded with inverted abraded edges, surrounded by a zone of scorching, soot deposits, and compact tattooing from powder grains embedded in the skin.

necessity defense. the defense of justification of an otherwise criminal act on the ground that the perpetrator was compelled to commit it because a greater evil would have ensued had he failed to do so. Thus, one could plead necessity if he committed arson to destroy official documents that would otherwise have fallen into the hands of a wartime enemy.

necrophilia. sexual intercourse with a dead

body; literally, love of the dead; morbid perversion which seeks sexual gratification from mutilation of the dead; an erotic attraction to dead bodies.

necropsy. examination of a dead body; an autopsy.

needle habit. the habit of taking drugs by injection. The habit usually follows a progression: intradermal injection (scratchings just under the skin); subcutaneous injection (skin popping); intramuscular injection (piercing into the muscles); and intravenous injection (piercing into the vein).

Needs Hierarchy. a concept of human needs developed by Abraham Maslow which asserts that humans have five sets of goals or needs arranged in a hierarchy of prepotency: (1) physiological needs, (2) safety needs, (3) love or affiliation needs, (4) esteem needs, and (5) the need for self-actualization. Once lower needs are satisfied they cease to be motivators of behavior. Conversely, higher needs cannot motivate until lower needs are satisfied.

negative impression tool mark. a mark made when a tool is pressed against or into a receiving surface.

negative pressure phase. the second phase of a blast wave in which air pressure rapidly decreases to a point less than normal creating a suction effect.

negative proof of arson. a method of proving in court the incendiary origin of a fire by eliminating every potential accidental or natural cause for the fire.

negligence. the doing of that thing which a reasonably prudent person would not have done, or the failure to do that thing which a reasonably prudent person would have done in like or similar circumstances. It is the failure to exercise that degree of care and prudence that reasonably prudent persons would have exercised in similar circumstances. Negligence cases are usually filed under state tort laws.

Tort law has attempted to refine the concept of negligence by subdividing it into narrower categories. Degrees of care and degrees of negligence are closely-related but separate approaches in refining negligence. Degrees of care is the amount of care which is reasonable for a given situation. It depends on various factors, including the relationship between the parties and the nature and extent of the risk inherent in that situation. For example, transporting school children requires a higher degree of care than hauling watermelons.

Degrees of negligence embraces the idea that negligence may be classified as slight or gross. This has been a persistent theme in tort law and criminal law. There are statutes in which the term negligence is preceded by some adjective, such as "slight" or "gross." In most cases, the statute applies only to a particular situation or activity.

Slight negligence is the failure to exercise great care. It is not a slight departure from ordinary care. Technically, it is the failure to exercise greater care than the circumstances would ordinarily require. On the other hand, gross negligence is something more than ordinary negligence but only in degree. It is less than recklessness, which is a different kind of conduct showing a conscious disregard for the safety of others. The distinction is important since contributory negligence is not a defense to wanton misconduct but is to gross negligence. A finding of reckless misconduct will usually support an award of punitive damages whereas gross negligence will not.

negligent conduct. that form of conduct which is an element of various tort causes of action. The components of the cause of action for negligence are: (1) a duty owed by the defendant to the plaintiff, (2) a violation of that duty by defendant's failure to conform to the required standard of conduct, (3) sufficient causal connection between the negligent conduct and the resulting harm, and (4) actual loss or damage. The plaintiff's contributory negligence, if any, will reduce or defeat a claim. In many jurisdictions, contributory negligence is a defense to be pleaded and proved by the defendant, but in some jurisdictions the plaintiff must allege and prove his freedom from contributory negligence as a part of his case.

negligent hiring. a legal concept which holds an employer directly liable for employee conduct on grounds that the employer failed to exercise reasonable care in hiring and retaining an employee who proves to be a danger to others. Although similar to respondeat superior, this concept can extend to situations that occur outside of the workplace. For example, assume that during working hours a police officer makes a date with a female employee. During the date (off the employer's premises and during non-working hours) the officer rapes the other employee. She learns that the employer was aware that this same officer had assaulted other women whom he had met at work, but had hired him anyway without warning her or other female employees. The employer can be charged with failure to exercise reasonable care in the hiring and retention of a dangerous employee.

negligent manslaughter. death resulting from failure to use ordinary care, or from being culpably careless and imprudent.

neighborhood crime prevention. a general term referring to programs that seek to reduce crime within a neighborhood through the coordinated efforts of residents and the police. Such a program might have these objectives: (1) make open areas more easily observable and increase human activity in them, (2) establish workable relationships between residents, businesses and police for the common purpose of eradicating crime, (3) promote a neighborhood identity, develop social cohesion and attract new financial investments to the community, (4) conduct no-cost security surveys to residents and businesses, and provide guidance for implementing survey recommendations, (5) hold public meetings, create special interest groups concerned with reducing particular crimes, and set

up community-manned response units such as a crisis hot line, rape crisis center, rumor control, rap line, and child abuse center, (6) improve the quality of police patrol operations by creating a dialogue between the police and community leaders, and (7) encourage residents to report crimes and criminals.

Action to achieve the neighborhood's crime prevention objectives might include the following described ten-step approach.

Obtain and analyze data relating to the neighborhood. Types of data worthy of analysis include crime and loss patterns, police patrol deployments, census tracts, terrain and topography descriptions, socio-economic and demographic patterns, and political infrastructures. The purpose of the analysis is to identify major crime locations, trends, sources of crime, cultural strengths and weaknesses of residents vis-a-vis the presence of crime, police effectiveness and efficiency, perceptions by the police and of the police, identify leaders and leadership groups in the community, identify resources that exist and that need to be acquired, and assess the divisiveness and/or cohesiveness of the neighborhood.

Identify a comparable neighborhood not planned to be covered under the crime prevention program. Use the comparable neighborhood as a control area against which the success or failure of the program can be measured.

Establish criteria for participation in the program. For example, what percentage of the neighborhood's population should be involved? What residents should be invited to perform organizing roles? What should those roles be? What kinds of projects are appropriate and likely to succeed, especially as first ventures? What kind of resistance can be expected? How do you neutralize it and turn it to your advantage? These are samples of issues to be addressed at this stage in the development of the program.

Approach neighborhood leaders. Those who have been identified as having significant influence should be approached first. The local leaders should be invited to participate in the development of strategy and to act as a sounding board for program effectiveness. The program must be perceived as a neighborhood effort, with neighborhood involvement and direction.

Educate residents through a wide variety of programs. Work through the neighborhood leaders and the groups they lead. Generate interest, support and an awareness of the program. The basic goal is to build a foundation for citizens and police to work together. This implies that police officials, from top on down, also need to be educated concerning program objectives.

Provide feedback to residents and police. The residents need to know how the program is working (e.g., arrests made, convictions obtained, property recovered, victims assisted) and the police need to know how the residents regard the work they are performing (e.g., timeliness of responses, courtesy and visibility).

Formulate crime specific tactics based on accumulating experiences. Ongoing analyses of crime data in the neighborhood will reveal times, places and methods of criminal attack. Preventive and response tactics can be inferred from the analyses.

Implement crime specific tactics as they are developed. Existing tactics will call for modification, new tactics will emerge and combinations of tactics can be attempted. Whatever tactics are selected, they should be applied comprehensively so that criminals will simply not move to another location.

Assess performance of the program's organizers, the residents, and the police. The purpose is not to pass final judgment but to determine what modifications are necessary to improve the program.

Evaluate the impact of the program on crime in the covered neighborhood. The neighborhood selected for comparison serves as a baseline for measurement.

neoclassicism. a trend in the history of criminal justice and criminology that flourished in the early 19th century in Europe. It modified the views of the classical school of criminology by introducing the concepts of diminished criminal responsibility and less severe punishment because of the age or mental condition of the perpetrator.

nervous system. that system of the human body composed of the brain, spinal cord, and nerves. Structurally, the nervous system is divided into the central nervous system (CNS), consisting of the brain and spinal cord, and the peripheral nervous system, consisting of the nerve fibers and cells that connect the brain and spinal cord to the rest of the body. Functionally, the nervous system is divided into the somatic nervous system and the autonomic nervous system. The somatic nervous system deals with functions of the senses and the voluntary muscles. The autonomic nervous system handles involuntary bodily functions such as heartbeat, digestion, and preparation for stress, fight, or flight. The autonomic nervous system is composed of two countervailing parts: the sympathetic and parasympathetic systems. The sympathetic energizes the body for action by processes such as releasing sugars stored in the liver, slowing the digestive process, and increasing heart and breathing rate. The parasympathetic system maintains the normal involuntary muscle, organ, and gland functions within the body such as salivation, pupil dilation and constriction, digestion and elimination, and heartbeat.

neurasthenia. weakness, chronic fatigue, lack of enthusiasm, numerous bodily complaints; a condition of weakness or exhaustion of the general nervous system, giving rise to various forms of mental or bodily inefficiency; nervous prostration.

neurolepsis. an altered state of consciousness marked by indifference to the surroundings; quiescence.

neuroleptic. an antipsychotic tranquilizer or major tranquilizer; any drug that produces neurolepsis. Over 80 neuroleptic substances have been identified. They all have certain common biochemical characteristics in their molecular structure and the pharmacological property of being an antagonist to the brain chemical dopamine. Neuroleptics allow patients to bring their psychoses under control, thus enabling deinstitutionalization under maintenance therapy.

neuroleptic syndrome. a human condition characterized by the reduction of psychotic symptoms such as hallucinations, mental confusion, and delusions; reduction of psychomotor agitation, such as aggressive, assaultive, combative, or destructive behavior; inhibition of panic, fear, and hostility, e.g., relief from emotional tension and excitement; reduction of initiative and increased indifference toward surroundings; and reduction of spontaneous movements, purposeful actions, and normal spinal reflexes.

neurosis. any condition in which a person develops some maladaptive behavior as a protection against unconscious anxiety; an emotional disorder characterized by anxiety, depression, or phobia.

neurotic depressive reaction. a psychoneurotic reaction characterized by persistent dejection and discouragement.

neutral density card. a photographer's tool for checking the density of colors in photographs. A crime scene technician may use it to verify that colors of objects photographed at a crime scene have been faithfully recorded.

neutral density filter. a glass or plastic material tinted grey for the purpose of reducing the amount of light entering a lens. An ND25 filter reduces the overall amount of light transmitted by 25 percent, and an ND50 by 50 percent. A neutral density filter does not affect the color tone of the light. It can be mounted on the front or rear of a lens, and is used where a camera is subject to bright light or high reflectivity.

neutral question. in polygraphy, a question that is not pertinent to the issue for which a subject is tested. It is used to identify the "normal" pattern of reaction to non-threatening issues. Neutral questions are also called non-crucial, immaterial, non-pertinent and irrelevant questions.

neutron activation analysis. an analysis to determine chemical elements in a material by bombarding it with neutrons to produce radioactive atoms whose radiations are characteristic of the elements present. The technique has many forensic applications; for example, to determine the presence of lead, antimony, and barium in residue taken from the skin of a person believed to have fired a gun. Also called activation analysis.

new court commitment. the entry into prison of a person who is being admitted on one or more new sentences to confinement and is not being readmitted on any previous sentence still in effect.

newly discovered evidence. evidence of a new and material fact, or new evidence in relation to a fact in issue, discovered by a party to a cause after the rendition of a verdict or judgment therein; any new evidence, whether the facts existed at the time of the trial or not.

new trial. any trial in which issues of fact and law are examined that have already been the subject of an earlier trial.

New York v. Burger. a 1987 case in which the U.S. Supreme Court held that a warrantless inspection of a closely regulated business is not violative of the Fourth Amendment. In this case, police officers acting pursuant to a statute that permits warrantless inspection of records and premises of automobile salvage dealers entered the establishment of the defendant and requested certain records and documents. When the defendant was unable to produce the requested records, the officers conducted an inspection of the premises and found stolen vehicles and parts. At trial, the defendant moved to suppress the search findings on the ground that the statute was unconstitutional.

The Supreme Court observed that while the Fourth Amendment is applicable to commercial premises as well as private homes, the expectation of privacy at premises of a "closely regulated" business is not as great as in other contexts.

next best evidence. evidence used when the best or better evidence is lost or inaccessible. For example, next best evidence would be oral testimony and/or a copy of an original document that cannot be found.

NHSB National Register Service. a computerized record maintained by the National Highway Safety Bureau which identifies persons whose licenses to drive have been denied, terminated or temporarily withdrawn.

night vision device. any type of viewing device that employs infrared or low-light technology to produce discernible images of objects that are in near total darkness. Light levels as that provided on a dark night by a single star are sufficient for some night vision devices to produce images.

night walker. a person who prowls the streets at night seeking opportunity to commit crime; a prostitute.

nihilist. a person devoted to the destruction of the present political, religious, or social institutions.

nine-eleven (911) system. a telephone system in which the directory number 9-1-1 is reserved for emergency calls, such as calls for police service, fire service, or emergency medical service. This system is usually based at a single location (frequently called The 911 Center) at which all such calls are received and routed to the appropriate response agency.

ninhydrin. a solution used to develop latent fingerprint impressions, usually on paper materials. A color reaction is produced when ninhydrin contacts with amino acids in the perspiration content of fingerprints. Paper containing latent impressions is sprayed with a solution of ninhydrin in acetone and baked in an oven.

nitric acid lift technique. a technique for collecting gunpowder residue from the skin of a suspect. Swabs moistened with a solution of nitric acid are used as the collecting agent. The swabs are later analyzed in the crime laboratory.

nitrocotton. collodion cotton dissolved in nitroglycerin.

nitroglycerin. a highly explosive substance that usually appears as an odorless, oily and milky liquid. It is commonly combined with infusorial earth to form dynamite. Nitroglycerin, or glyceryl trinitrate, is 13 times as powerful as gun powder and will explode when violently struck. Aging destabilizes nitroglycerin, causing it to turn yellow and eventually take on a greenish tint. In a destabilized form it is extremely hazardous. Also called nitro.

nitroglycerin/ammonium nitrate. a type of commercial dynamite made from a combination of nitroglycerin and ammonium sulfate. It is a gelatinous substance that may be sticky and rubber-like in appearance.

nitrous acid test. a nonspecific, preliminary test for identifying morphine or distinguishing morphine from heroin and codeine. The suspected morphine is placed in a tube containing hydrochloric acid, to which sodium nitrite is added. If the solution turns yellow-green, sodium hydroxide is added. A red color reaction indicates morphine.

nitrous oxide. a short-acting gaseous anesthetic sometimes used as an aerosol propellant that is inhaled for its intoxicating effects. When used therapeutically, the effects are those of anesthesia and analgesia. In recreational use, when it is in pure form for less than a minute, its effects are closer to those of the vaporous anesthetics ether and chloroform than other depressants, making the user giddy or exhilarated for about 5 minutes. Occasionally hallucinations occur. Excessive doses may cause nausea, vomiting, or unconsciousness, often because of lack of oxygen. Discovered in the 1770s by Joseph Priestley, but not used as an anesthetic until the middle of the 19th century, it was the first really effective modern anesthetic, to be followed by ether and chloroform. Also called laughing gas or nitrogen monoxide.

no bill. a determination by a grand jury that not enough evidence was found to warrant charging the defendant with a crime. Similar terms include "not found" and "not a true bill."

nodding. the semistuporous state characterized by head bobbing, bowed head, and drooping eyelids experienced by heroin and highdose methadone users after the euphoric effects accompanying ingestions have subsided.

no deception indicated. an opinion reached by a polygraphist based on an interpretation of polygrams. Also called NDI.

noise generator. a device used to cover up voices in a room for the purpose of defeating electronic surveillance. The noise produced is generated randomly and from several alternating frequencies so as to defeat a filter applied to clean up a recording of conversations.

no knock law. a law that empowers the police to enter a place without knocking or announcing identity. The practice usually requires a court order, and is permitted when an announced entry would allow destruction of evidence or when the safety of the police would be imperiled.

nolle prosequi. a formal entry upon the record by the prosecuting officer in a criminal case, by which he declares that he "will not further prosecute" the case, either as to some of the counts, or some of the defendants, or altogether.

nolo contendere. a plea that means "I will not contest it." It has the same legal effect as a plea of guilty, so far as regards all proceedings on the indictment, and on which the defendant may be sentenced. A nolo contendere plea does not debar a defendant from denying the truth of the charges in any other action.

nomograph. generally, a graph on which three or more scales are arranged so that a straight line drawn through values on any two will cross the third at a corresponding value. In law enforcement, a nomograph is used for calculating the speed of a motor vehicle when distance and time are known. Also called a graphic calculator.

no name warrant. a warrant for arrest that does not identify a person by name. It is sometimes called a "John Doe" warrant.

nonappearance. the failure of a defendant to appear in court in answer to a summons or complaint; failure of a defendant to appear on the due date.

non compos mentis. not of sound mind; insane. A general term that embraces all varieties of mental derangement.

nondelay impact fuse. a bomb fuse designed to function upon impact with a hard surface, prior to its complete penetration or ricochet.

nondirective interviewing. an interview in which the interviewer does not guide the discussion, but says only enough to encourage the interviewee to express himself freely.

nonemotional offender. a person who commits crimes without regard to the nature of the crime or the effect of it on the victim. A person who kills for financial gain is considered a non-emotional offender.

nonfeasance. nonperformance of some act which ought to be performed; omission to perform a required duty; neglect of duty.

Nonimmigrant Index. a file maintained by the Immigration and Naturalization Service which contains names and descriptive data of persons admitted to the US for temporary periods of time, and who must eventually depart.

nonjoinder. an omission to join a person as a party to a legal action. It is spoken of as a nonjoinder of parties, meaning that certain persons who should have been joined in action have not done so.

nonlethal weapon. any device intended to exert physical force on a person, such as a belligerent arrestee, without causing serious injury or death.

non-negligent manslaughter. the intentional killing of another in the heat of passion or as a result of provoked anger.

nonprofessional thief. a person who steals to satisfy a personal need or desire. It is estimated that nonprofessional thieves account for a high percentage of shoplifting losses.

nonreactive pupil. a pupil of the eye that does not react in a normal manner to stimuli, such as light, darkness or touching. This condition is indicative of impairment by reason of drug use.

nonrun time. time that does not count as prison time served towards a required term in confinement, or as time served on parole towards total time under correctional jurisdiction. Time elapsed after escape and before apprehension is non-run time. In some jurisdictions, time spent out of confinement pending an appeal decision is non-run time. Also called dead time.

nonsecretor. a person whose blood may be grouped but whose body fluids may not be grouped due to low concentrations of group specific substances.

nonsimultaneous transmission. half duplex, or one-way transmission at a time over a pair. Also referred to as duplex.

no opinion. a conclusion rendered by a polygraphist when an examination cannot be completed and when the polygraphist believes that future testing will be unproductive or unwarranted. A no opinion conclusion can result from uncooperative behavior by the examinee, a lack of emotional response, or the presence of extreme, erratic responses.

no passing line. a line which, when placed parallel to a center or lane line, indicates that all traffic must not cross the line for purposes of overtaking and passing; a double line consisting of two normal solid yellow lines delineating the separation between travel paths in opposite directions where overtaking and passing is prohibited in both directions. Crossing a no passing line is permitted only as a left turn maneuver and only when executed with care. The line is frequently used as a channelizing line in advance of an obstruction which must be passed on the right to form a channelizing island separating traffic in both directions.

normal distribution. a bell-shaped, symmetrical distribution in which mean, median, and mode are the same.

North Carolina v. Butler. a 1979 case in which the U.S. Supreme Court addressed whether, absent an express waiver, a valid waiver of Miranda rights could be inferred from the actions and words of the person interrogated. In this case, the defendant and another shot and paralyzed a gas station attendant while committing a robbery in North Carolina. The defendant was arrested in New York on a fugitive warrant. While in the custody of the FBI, the defendant was read his rights, acknowledged understanding of them, and agreed to talk but would not sign an advice of rights form. The defendant made incriminating statements, he was convicted, and the issue on appeal was whether a specific oral waiver was required or a waiver could be inferred.

The Supreme Court said that an express statement can constitute a waiver and that silence alone after such warnings cannot do so. But such an express statement is not indispensable to a finding of waiver. The Court did find a waiver in this case when it observed: "As was unequivocally said in Miranda, mere silence is not enough. That does not mean that the defendant's silence, coupled with an understanding of his rights and a course of conduct indicating waiver, may never support a conclusion that a defendant has waived his rights. The courts must presume that a defendant did not waive his rights; the prosecution's burden is great; but in at least some cases waiver can be inferred from the actions and words of the person interrogated."

The guidance is that an express waiver, either written or oral, is preferable, but an explicit statement of waiver is not always necessary to support a finding that the right to counsel was waived. In at least some cases, a waiver can be inferred from the actions and words of the person interrogated.

nose candy. cocaine.

no significant reaction. in polygraphy, the absence of a strong deceptive pattern in the polygrams of a tested person.

notary public. a public officer authorized to attest and certify, by his hand and official seal, certain classes of documents, to administer oaths and do other official acts.

notched bullet. a lead bullet which has a portion removed by cutting or filing and which will flatten out upon contact.

not guilty by reason of insanity. the plea of a defendant or the verdict of a jury or judge in a criminal proceeding that the defendant is not guilty of the offense charged because at the time the crime was committed the defendant did not have the mental capacity to be held criminally responsible for his or her actions. A plea or verdict of "not guilty by reason of insanity" differs from other not guilty pleas and verdicts in that the claim or finding is not based on what the defendant is alleged or determined to have done, but rather on the issue of whether he or she possessed the mental capacity to be held responsible for a criminal act. A verdict of "not guilty by reason of insanity" differs from a court finding that a defendant is incompetent to stand trial which concerns only the defendant's mental fitness at the time of trial, and is not related to the question of guilt.

not guilty plea. a defendant's formal answer in court to the charge or charges contained in a complaint, information, or indictment, claiming that he or she did not commit the offense or offenses listed.

not guilty verdict. in criminal proceedings, the decision by a jury or judicial officer on the basis of evidence presented at trial, that the defendant is not guilty of the offense or offenses for which he or she has been tried. A not guilty verdict indicates that the evidence left at least a reasonable doubt as to the defendant's guilt. A not guilty verdict must lead to a judgment of acquittal. The court cannot enter a judgment of conviction unless the defendant has been found guilty or has plead guilty.

notice. a formal communication, as to the defendant in a lawsuit, advising him of what further action is intended.

notice of alibi. information that the defense is required to give to the prosecution before a trial if a defense of alibi will be made, that is, if the defense will contend that the accused was elsewhere at the time of the crime. Such a notice is necessary so that the prosecution may investigate before the trial and be prepared for cross-examination and rebuttal.

no true bill. the decision by a grand jury that it will not return an indictment against the person accused of a crime on the basis of the allegations and evidence presented by the prosecutor. A grand jury finding of no true bill after a complaint has been filed in lower court may be a defendant disposition, terminating criminal justice jurisdiction over the defendant in those jurisdictions where the felony trial phase is initiated by the filing of a grand jury indictment. A grand jury, after its consideration of a case, can decide: to issue an indictment; not to issue an indictment; or to ignore felony charges, but refer the case back to the prosecutor for further prosecution on misdemeanor charges.

Nuclear Emergency Search Team. a Department of Energy team trained in the use of specialized equipment for conducting radiation survey and detection, field communications, explosive ordnance damage support, bomb/weapon diagnostics, hazard prediction, damage mitigation, and decontamination.

nuclear incident. any occurrence within the United States causing bodily injury, sickness, disease, or death, or loss of or damage to property, or for loss of use of property, arising out of or resulting from the radioactive, toxic, explosive, or other hazardous properties of source, special nuclear, or byproduct material.

nuclear radiation. particulate and electromagnetic radiation emitted from atomic nuclei in various nuclear processes. The important nuclear radiations, from the weapons standpoint, are alpha and beta particles, gamma rays, and neutrons. All nuclear radiations are ionizing radiations, but the reverse is not true.

nuclear round. a nuclear weapon (warhead section) and the associated missile and/or propellant required to deliver the weapon on a target.

nuclear safing. the prevention of a nuclear yield in the event of accidental detonation of the high explosive assembly weapon or ignition of the propellant of a gun assembly weapon.

nuclear weapon. a general name given to any weapon in which the explosion results from the energy released by reactions involving atomic nuclei, either fission or fusion, or both.

nuclear weapon preinitiation. the initiation of the fission or fusion chain reaction in the active material of a nuclear weapon at any time earlier than that at which the designed compression or degree of assembly is attained.

nuclear weapon significant incident. an unexpected event involving nuclear weapons or radiological nuclear weapon components which does not fall in the nuclear weapon accident category but results in evident damage to a nuclear weapon or radiological nuclear weapon component to the extent that major rework, complete replacement, or examination or recertification by the Department of Energy is required, immediate action is required in the interest of safety or nuclear weapons security, adverse public reaction (national or international) or premature release of classified information may result, and that the incident could lead to a nuclear weapon accident.

nuclear yield. the energy released in the detonation of a nuclear weapon, measured in terms of the kilotons or megatons of trinitrotoluene (TNT) required to produce an equivalent energy release.

nuisance alarm. a false alarm; an alarm caused by equipment failure or a fault not related to an actual criminal event.

numbers game. an unlawful game of chance in which money is wagered on the occurrence of a chosen number and in which a winner is usually paid at odds. In a numbers game, a person usually bets however much money he chooses on a single number. Any number of people can bet on the same number. The amount to be won is variable, depending on factors such as the amount of the person's bet, the total amount of all bets on the winning number, etc. The winning number is not randomly selected from the numbers bet on, but consists of a set of digits taken from an external source, such as the last three digits of the day's parimutuel gross receipts. Also called the numbers pool.

numerical evaluation. in polygraphy, any of several valid systems which apply numbers or number values to physiological responses graphically represented on polygrams.

nunc pro tunc. now for then. This term is applied to legal acts allowed to be done after the time for the doing of such acts has elapsed. For example, a court may allow the filing of a certain petition even though the time limit for such filing has passed. Such an order would be called a nunc pro tunc order.

nystagmus. involuntary rapid oscillation of the eyeballs, a common symptom of toxic reaction resulting from alcohol consumption or drug use. Nystagmus is looked for in pupillary reaction tests conducted by the police of motorists suspected of driving while intoxicated.

oath. a solemn affirmation, declaration or other promise made under a sense of responsibility to God for the truth of what is stated.

obiter dictum. an observation, casual opinion, comment or remark not pertinent to a question or case at hand made by the presiding judge.

objection. an attempt to exclude evidence or testimony because it is improper. One lawyer might object to another lawyer's question to a witness, or to the answer given by a witness.

object test. in polygraphy, a preliminary test intended to evaluate an examinee's reactions to a known lie. The examinee is asked to take and conceal on his or her person one object from a group of objects. The examinee is told to deny having taken the object when the question is asked during the object test. The deception pattern of the examinee is used by the polygraphist as a base of comparison with relevant questions in a subsequent test.

oblique lighting. a technique of projecting light across a surface at an angle for the purpose of observing and photographing hard-to-see evidence traces such as fingerprints and toolmarks.

obloquy. the state of one who is in disgrace or is spoken ill of; vilification; defamation. To expose one to obloquy is to hold him up to shame and ridicule. The term is often associated with blackmail, extortion, slander, and libel.

obscene matter. materials that appeal to prurient interest of the average person, applying contemporary standards of the community; materials that depict or describe sexual conduct in a patently offensive way; materials that lack serious literary, artistic, political or scientific value.

obsessive compulsive reaction. a psychoneurotic reaction characterized by persistent irrational thoughts and repetitive compulsions.

obstructing a peace officer. willfully standing in the way of the execution of lawful duties by a law enforcement officer. This is usually a misdemeanor, and includes attempts and threats.

obstruction of justice. impeding or retarding the progress of those who seek justice; a deliberate impediment to the administration of justice; interference by act or omission with the proper performance of a judicial act. Examples include destroying records and giving false information. Also called perversion of justice.

occlusion. stoppage of a blood vessel due to a clot or embolus.

oddity file. a file that contains records of physical peculiarities bearing on the identification of suspects and wanted persons. Scars, tattoos, deformities and the like which are attributed to an unknown suspect can be matched against persons identified in the oddity file.

odontology. a branch of dentistry concerned with the examination of dental evidence. The forensic odontologist specializes in comparing dental records against the dental features of unknown dead persons so that positive identifications can be made. The odontologist can also be helpful in a rape or homicide case in which the victim has been bitten by the assailant. Bite mark identification can also extend to cases in which the criminal has bitten into food materials at the crime scene.

Offender-Based State Corrections Information System (OBSCIS). a multi-state program for the development of prisoner information systems for state correctional agencies.

offender-based transaction statistics (OBTS). a centralized system of compiling criminal justice statistics that uses the individual as its unit of measure and tracks the person throughout the criminal justice system. These statistics are derived from information recorded in law enforcement, court and corrections proceedings and are processed in such a way that the identity of the person subject to the proceedings is preserved throughout data collection and analysis. The use of the individual offender as the basic tracking unit provides a mechanism for linking events in the different parts of the criminal justice system.

offenses against public authority. a general descriptor for crimes affecting public authority and government. Examples include escape, perjury, resisting arrest, obstructing justice, misconduct in office, and criminal contempt.

offenses against the family and children. a Uniform Crime Report category used to record and report arrests for offenses relating to desertion, abandonment, nonsupport, neglect or abuse of spouse or child, nonpayment of alimony, and similar acts.

offenses against the public peace. a general descriptor for crimes affecting social order. Examples include breach of peace, unlawful assembly, public nuisance, riot, affray, disorderly conduct, vagrancy, and drunkenness.

offenses known to police. in Uniform Crime Reports terminology, reported occurrences or offenses, which have been verified at the police level.

official records and business entries. a term relating to the admissibility of certain documents as an exception to the hearsay rule. Such a document is an official statement in writing made as a record of fact or event by an individual acting in the performance of an official duty, imposed upon him by law, regulation, or custom, to know or ascertain through appropriate and trustworthy channels of information the truth of the matter and to record it. The document may be admissible to prove the truth of such a matter.

Office of Juvenile Justice and Delinquency Prevention (OJJDP). an office within the U.S. Department of Justice that was created by Congress in 1974 to address the problems of juvenile delinquency. Several of OJJDP's programs emphasize preventing and controlling juvenile drug abuse, and improving the juvenile correctional system.

ogive. the downward slope of the nose of a bullet.

oiled block. a wooden or metal block coated with a thin film of oil. It is applied by a forger to paper to imitate a watermark.

omission. a failure to act that constitutes a crime when it involves nonperformance of an action the person is under a duty to perform as required by the law.

omnibus hearing. a meeting of the opposing parties in a case with the judicial officer prior to trial, for the purposes of stipulating those things which are agreed upon and thus narrowing the trial to things that are in dispute, disclosing the required information about witnesses and evidence, making motions, and generally organizing the presentation of motions, witnesses and evidence. In criminal proceedings, this type of pretrial activity occurs after an arraignment in which the defendant has plead not guilty. It may include consideration of reduction of the charges. Also called a pretrial conference.

onset. in drug research, a term meaning the first time a person uses a particular drug. Age of onset is a major variable often studied by epidemiologists alone and in relation to other variables. Some research suggests an association between the age of onset of heroin use and variables such as the likelihood of continued use, ability to hold a job, criminality, successful rehabilitation, and successful social functioning in general. Onset is also used to refer to the point at which a drug takes effect or begins to wear off (i.e., initiation of the withdrawal syndrome).

on the nod. the feeling experienced by a drug user going back and forth from alertness to drowsiness.

on view arrest. an arrest made without a warrant when the arresting officer has reasonable ground to believe a crime is being committed or has been committed. An on view arrest is based on the direct observations of the officer or when reliable information is presented as to a situation or condition nearby the officer's location.

open bomb. a bomb in which all of the component parts are visible to the naked eye. Also called a straight bomb.

open court. the time period during which a court is in session hearing cases.

open-end questioning. an interviewing technique in which the respondent is asked to tell what he knows in his own words and with minimum interruptions. Questions are constructed and asked so as to encourage a free, uninhibited response. The initial, prompting question is general as opposed to a question that can be answered with a yes or no response. Examples of open-end questions are: "Tell me what you saw," and "What happened then?"

open facility. a correctional facility for juveniles in which access to the community is relatively frequent, in-house restrictions and physical security features are minimal, and entrances and exits are relatively uncontrolled.

open fracture. a break in a bone in which the bone is severed and at least one end protrudes through the skin. Also called a compound fracture.

opening statements. statements made by the prosecuting and defense attorneys in which each outlines what he intends to prove during the trial. The purpose is to acquaint jurors with both sides of a case so it will be easier for them to follow the evidence as it is presented.

open system. any organism or organization that interacts with its environment.

open till pilferage. a technique used by a dishonest employee to steal from a cash register. The employee keeps the cash register drawer open, accepts payments for sales without ringing up the transactions, and steals the cash in excess of the registered ringups.

open to the jury. a part of the procedure of a civil or criminal trial in which each side has an opportunity to present his position to the jury and outline what he intends to prove.

operational factor. in traffic accident investigations, a functional failure of the highway transportation system that contributes to the cause of a traffic accident.

operational intelligence. intelligence required for planning and executing law enforcement and security operations.

operational reports. a general class of police reports which originate at the operational level and relate to routine matters such as incidents, arrests, and complaints. The operational report communicates information laterally among shifts, units or divisions for coordinative and tactical purposes, and vertically to management for control and administrative purposes.

Operation Identification. a crime-deterrent program in which homeowners mark their valuable items so that if stolen they may more readily be recovered by the police.

operative. a person who assumes a false identity for the purpose of obtaining information, usually concerning a criminal activity that cannot be discovered through conventional law enforcement methods.

opiate narcotics. a major subclass of drugs that relieve pain by depressing the central nervous system. Sometimes called simply narcotics or opiates, the term opiate narcotics is generally preferred as it avoids confusion over what constitutes a narcotic and the semantic problem inherent in the terms opium, opiates, and opioids. The nonnarcotic pain relievers such as aspirin differ from the opiate narcotics in having far less CNS depressant effects.

opiates. a group of drugs, sometimes referred to as narcotics, used medically to relieve pain but which also have a high potential for abuse. Opiates derived from the Asian poppy include opium, morphine, heroin and codeine. Synthesized or manufactured opiates include meperidine and pethidine which are sold as Demerol and Mepergan.

opiate withdrawal. a body condition that usually begins within 4–6 hours after the last dose. Symptoms include uneasiness, diarrhea, abdominal cramps, chills, sweating, nausea, and runny eyes and nose. The intensity of symptoms depends on how much of the opiate substance was taken, how often, and for how long. Symptoms are generally strongest 24–72 hours after they begin and subside within 7–10 days.

opinion evidence. evidence of what the witness believes or infers in regard to facts in dispute, as distinguished from personal knowledge of facts. An expert witness might give opinion evidence. As a general rule, a witness can only testify to facts and not opinions or conclusions drawn from facts.

opinion of the court. a statement by which the court sets forth the factual and legal reasons for its decision.

opinion testimony. an exception to the general rule of evidence that prohibits a witness from testifying to anything other than facts of which he has direct knowledge. An opinion is a conclusion drawn by the witness and is admissible when no other description could be more accurate. As an example, witnesses are permitted to testify on such matters as distance, time, speed, size, weight, direction, form, identity, drunkenness, and similar matters, all of which require the witness to state his opinion. It is not essential for the witness to be an expert when he is giving testimony as to evidential.

opioid. a substance that combines the actions of an analgesic, a hypnotic and a euphoriant. An opioid is a synthetic drug manufactured to resemble an opium alkaloid (morphine and codeine and their derivatives) in action and effect. The principal synthetics are meperidine hydrochloride (Demerol) and its related drugs, levorphanol tartrate (Levo-Dromoran), methadone hydrochloride (Dolophine), pentazocine (Talwin), and propoxyphene hydrochloride (Darvon). Although semantically incorrect, opioid is sometimes used as a general term that includes all of the opium and opiumlike derivatives, natural and synthetic.

opium. the narcotic from which all the opiates are derived. It is obtained from drying the milky discharge of the cut, unripe seedpod (capsule) of the opium poppy (papaver somniferum), which appears soon after the petals begin to fall. The major natural alkaloids obtained from opium are morphine (10 percent by weight) and codeine. Opium has been used for centuries as a medicinal and recreational drug. Medically, it was formerly used to treat over 50 different diseases. In 17th-century England it was praised as God's greatest gift to humanity for the relief of suffering, and until the 20th century it was primarily smoked or ingested orally. The development of more effective opiates, opioids, and non-narcotic analgesics has now virtually eliminated its use medically, and recreational users have turned to the intravenous injection of more powerful opiates such as heroin. Opium appears as dark brown chunks or as a powder and is usually smoked or eaten. It is found in Dover's Powder, Parapectolin and paregoric for its analgesic and antidiarrheal effects. Opium produces high physical and psychological dependence, and has a strong potential for abuse.

opportunity reduction. a concept which holds that three ingredients must be present for a crime to be committed: (1) there must be a desire or motivation on the part of the criminal to commit the crime, (2) the criminal must possess the skills, knowledge and tools needed to commit the crime, and (3) there must be an opportunity for the criminal to act. The first two ingredients are difficult to affect in any meaningful preventive way. The third ingredient, however, can be impacted through a variety of preventive actions.

opposite-direction collision. a collision between two traffic units moving in opposite directions on the same roadway. Sometimes called a head-on collision.

oppression. a wrongful act committed upon a person by a public officer under color of office; an act of cruelty, severity or unlawful exaction.

optical character recognition. the scanning of input data with an optical device that translates visual information into electronic impulses.

oral plea. a plea made by word of mouth in a court proceeding. Many jurisdictions require defendants to make oral pleas.

ordinace. a law passed by the law-making body of a city or town.

ordinary care. that care that a prudent man would take under the circumstances of the particular case.

organic brain syndrome. any mental abnormality resulting from transient or permanent disturbance of the structure or function of the brain. It may result from the effects of drugs or other conditions.

organic drug. a plant used as a drug that remains in natural plant form without being subject to extractions or synthetic processing. Organic drugs include peyote, marijuana, psilocybin, and crude opium.

organic nonvolatile poison. a class of poison which includes alkaloids (such as heroin and cocaine), barbiturates, glycosides, synthetic drugs, botulinus toxin and snake venom.

organic organization. a form of organizational structure suitable for operating under unstable, changing conditions. It is characterized by (1) constant reassessment of tasks, assignments and the use of organizational expertise, (2) authority, control and communications are frequently exercised on an ad hoc basis depending upon specific commitments and tasks, (3) communications and interactions between members are both very open and extensive, (4) leadership that stresses consultation and group decisional processes, and (5) greater commitment to the organization's tasks and goals than to traditional hierarchical loyalty.

organic psychosis. a severe mental disorder in which the afflicted person loses touch with reality as a consequence of physiological damage to the brain. The damage may result from infection, drug or alcohol abuse, blood vessel deterioration, physical trauma, and similar organic causes.

organic volatile poison. a class of poison which includes ethyl alcohol, aniline, phenol, gasoline, benzene and chloral hydrate.

organization man. a person within an organization who accepts the values of the organization and finds harmony in conforming to its policies.

organized crime. the criminal activity of persons who engage in crime as a primary source of income and who cooperate and coordinate illegal activity with one another. Organized crime often involves the production, distribution, delivery, and sale of illegal goods and services, such as drugs, prostitution and gambling. It is a complex pattern of activity that also includes offenses of the fraud, theft and extortion groups, and which is uniquely characterized by the planned use of both legitimate and criminal professional expertise. Organized crime frequently has the features of legitimate business, including availability of large capital resources, disciplined management, division of labor, and a focus upon maximum profit.

Organized Crime Intelligence System File. a computerized file and card index maintained by the Department of Justice. It includes financial information, participation in illegal organizations, business connections, associations, habits and other data pertaining to persons believed to be involved in organized crime activities.

original jurisdiction. the lawful authority of a court or an administrative agency to hear or act upon a case from its beginning and to pass judgment on it.

Orozco v. Texas. a case in which the U.S. Supreme Court extended the Miranda rule beyond station house interrogation to situations in which suspects under formal arrest are questioned in their own homes. The decision underscores the concept that it is the custodial nature of the interrogation and not its location that determines the necessity for Miranda warnings. Although in his home, Orozco was sufficiently deprived of his freedom to bring him within the scope of the Miranda rule.

In this case, four police officers went to Orozco's boardinghouse at 4:00 AM, where they were admitted, and began questioning him concerning a murder that occurred earlier in the evening. His responses led to a discovery of the murder weapon. The Miranda warning had not been given, and one officer testified that Orozco was "under arrest" at the time he was questioned. The Court concluded that under the circumstances Orozco had been sufficiently deprived of his freedom to necessitate Miranda warnings.

o-r release. own-recognizance release, a legal device for freeing responsible citizens from going to jail or posting bail bond pending a court hearing.

orthochlorbenzalmalononitrile. a chemical agent used to effect the capture of criminals and break up riots. It is a white powder that can be dispersed in grenades and projectiles or by pressurized cannisters. This agent produces immediate discomfort on contact with the respiratory tract, eyes and skin. Also called CS agent.

ortho-tolidin test. a nonspecific, preliminary laboratory test that seeks to identify the presence of blood in or on an item. A saline solution of the suspected material is added to a mixture of ortho-tolidin, acetic acid, and hydrogen peroxide. If a blue color appears, the presence of blood is indicated.

osmic acid fuming. a technique which uses osmic acid fumes to develop latent fingerprints left on porous surfaces such as unfinished wood and paper.

OTC downer. any of a variety of nonprescription products which promote sleep (Nytol, Sominex) or reduce anxiety (Compoz). OTC downers contain antihistamines, usually pyrilamine or doxylamine, which tend to affect mental function in unpleasant ways. They can produce depression and can be habit-forming.

OTC drugs. over-the-counter drugs; nonprescription drugs.

OTC upper. any of a variety of nonprescription products which purport to provide the stimulating effects of amphetamines. Many contain nothing more than strong doses of caffeine, and one (Caffedrine) is packaged to resemble the more expensive and potent prescription amphetamine called Dexamyl. Examples of OTC uppers are Vivarin and No-Doz whose stimulating effects are within the range of coffee and tea.

output. in communications, the signal level at the output of an amplifier or other device.

outside issue. in polygraphy, a circumstance unrelated to the primary issue being tested which poses a greater threat to the immediate well-being of the examinee than does the primary issue.

outside super-dampening concept. a concept in polygraphy which holds that an examinee may be so concerned over a matter not related to the polygraph examination that he is unable to form a psychological set on either the relevant or the control questions.

overamp. to take too much amphetamine, usually by injection.

over and short record. a log or other written record of overages or shortages pertaining to a particular cashier. The record is used to track individual performance by persons who regularly handle cash.

over-and-under gun. a double-barrelled gun whose barrels are stacked one above the other. Some over-and-under shotgun models offer barrels having different chokes. One choke, for example, might limit the spread of the shot while the other would deliver the shot in a sprayed pattern. Some over-and-under guns combine rifle and shotgun barrels.

overcharging. a police and prosecutor practice of charging or citing an offender with a more serious crime than actually committed or to charge a separate offense for every violation connected with the main offense. An objective of the practice is to strengthen the prosecutor's position in plea bargaining.

overcriminalization. enactment of legislation making marginal acts criminal and creating more criminal laws than can be enforced or are necessary.

overdeflected. a condition of a tire in which the pressure on the road is greater at the edges of the tread than at the middle; an overloaded or underinflated tire condition.

overdose. the administration of a quantity of drug larger than that normally or safely taken at one time, or to which the system has acquired tolerance. The term usually implies some adverse or toxic reaction, whether fatal or not, and is most frequently applied to excessive consumption of opiate or hypnotic-sedative drugs that act to depress the central nervous system causing coma and often death from respiratory depression or complications such as pneumonia or heart failure. Frequent symptoms of nonfatal drug overdose are stupor and agitation. Accidental overdose often occurs through drug automatism or the use of a sedative drug with alcohol, which potentiates its effects. Opiate overdosage can be arrested by the use of a narcotic antagonist such as nalorphine (Nalline). A variety of home remedies may be employed to keep the patient awake and reverse respiratory depression. The widespread use of the word overdose on death certificates has been criticized because there appear to be no consistent toxicologic standards for evaluation of what constitutes a lethal dosage. In practice, police and/or coroners often classify a death as due to overdose if any evidence of heroin use is found.

overindictment. the inclusion in an indictment of charges that are more serious or more numerous than are warranted by the crime. This procedure is sometimes used as a negotiating tactic in plea bargaining.

overlook. in a numbers operation, a winning bet that was misplaced or overlooked in the daily tally.

overreaction. a driver's excessive reaction to a hazardous situation that produces another or an additional hazard. Overreaction is usually a matter of too much steering at a high speed.

overrecommend. to recommend a more severe sentence than would normally be imposed for a given offense so as to gain an advantage during any subsequent plea bargaining.

oversteering. a characteristic of a motor vehicle that results in a tendency to swerve toward the inside of a curve, especially at high speed. A motor vehicle with more weight on the rear wheels than on the front and with too little pressure in the rear tires is likely to oversteer.

overstepping. a condition associated with drug use (especially marihuana and alcohol) in which the loss of depth perception causes the user to overstep when negotiating curbstones, stairs and similar raised platforms.

overt act. an open act which shows the intention of a person to commit a crime; an outward or manifest act from which criminality may be inferred; an act done to carry out a criminal intention, such as would naturally effect that result. It is an essential element of the crime of conspiracy.

over-the-counter drugs. drugs that may be purchased without prescription. There are an estimated 350,000 OTC products. They are subject to abuse, particularly certain cough remedies that contain potent analgesic/euphoric or hallucinogenic substances.

overt intelligence. information collected openly from public or open sources.

overt surveillance. the observation in plain sight of the public or of a specific surveillance target by the police. This tactic is usually applied in high crime areas as a means for discouraging criminal behavior.

pacing. driving at the rear of a moving vehicle for the purpose of determining its speed.

packy. a sneak thief who specializes in interrupting the flow of merchandise being unloaded from a truck and stealing some part of the cargo.

padded book. a numbers book padded with many numbers placed after post time with the connivance of persons inside the numbers operation.

padding question. in polygraphy, a question inserted at the beginning and end of a probing peak of tension test. The padding questions are not relevant to the issue being evaluated. Also called an enveloping question.

palmar print. an impression made by the under surface of the hand. The impression results from the transfer to a surface of bodily oils through the skin on the ridges of the palm.

palming. in shoplifting, the practice of holding in the palm of the hand a small item just prior to concealment. A shoplifter with a palmed item will frequently hold coupons or money in the same hand, reach into a purse or pocket and drop the palmed item inside.

palpation. in emergency care, the act of discerning normality or abnormality by feeling with the fingers.

pamphlet bomb. an explosive device designed to scatter leaflets or pamphlets over crowds of people.

Panama red. marihuana, so called because of its origin and reddish tint.

panderer. a person who procures a female for employment in a house of prostitution.

panel of judges. a group of three or more judicial officers of a court, who jointly hear and decide a case.

panic alarm. a sensor or other device which reports a panic or emergency situation. In commercial applications, a panic alarm is usually called a hold-up alarm.

panic hardware. an exterior door-locking mechanism which is operable from inside the building by pressure on a crash bar or lever.

panic reaction. the most common of the adverse psychological reactions to drug use. Characterized by overwhelming fear, intense anxiety, and possibly immobilization, this reaction accounts for many of the cases that come to the attention of psychiatric personnel. It may be triggered by any drug or may occur seemingly spontaneously at a later time without drug use.

Papaver bracteatum. a species of poppy from which an alkaloid called thebaine is derived. Thebaine is the source of many medically important compounds.

papaverine. a naturally occurring alkaloid of opium that acts to depress the heart and smooth muscles. Unlike morphine and codeine it has no analgesic, euphoric, or other central nervous system effects.

Papaver somniferum. the poppy plant from which opium is produced.

paper acid. LSD impregnated on absorbent paper.

paperhanging. forging checks; passing bad checks.

papillary lines. the lines comprising a fingerprint.

parabolic microphone. a microphone with a large disk-like attachment used for listening to audio from great distances.

paraffin test. a test that identifies the presence of gunpowder residue on the hands of a person suspected of having fired a gun. The suspect's hands are coated with melted paraffin that is allowed to cool and set. The paraffin is removed and diphenylamine is applied to that portion of the paraffin that was in contact with the skin. An examiner evaluates the resulting color reaction. This test is not considered reliable. Also called the diphenylamine test.

para-fluoro fentanyl. a fentanyl derivative that produces effects similar to morphine but is about 100 times as potent. Because it has no approved medical use and carries a high potential for addiction it is classified as a Schedule II controlled substance.

parajudge. a person who performs limited and basic functions of the judicial process such as setting bail and hearing certain kinds of cases. A parajudge might specialize in a particular type of proceeding such as probate, juvenile matters, traffic or domestic relations. In some jurisdictions, certain parole board officials and probation officers are called parajudges.

parallel tap. a wiretap in which a miniature transmitter and a microphone are wired into and draw power from the telephone line.

paramedic. an emergency medical technician trained and authorized to provide advanced life support.

paranoia. a condition characterized by ideas of reference, suspicious thinking, and high levels of anger. In the most extreme forms, paranoia appears as delusions of persecution and/or grandeur. A paranoid personality is characterized by unreasonably lofty ambitions, extreme suspicion of others, and a fixed and inflexible conceit. In severe instances it may be considered a sign of psychosis.

paranoid schizophrenia. a mental disorder characterized by delusions and hallucinations in which the sufferer believes he is the victim of persecution and plotting by imagined enemies.

paraphernalia. the assorted equipment and materials used to store or administer illicit drugs, or to make the drug high more intense. Drug paraphernalia comes in all sizes, shapes, colors, and materials. Some of the more widely used items include cigarette paper, plastic bags, cigarette rolling machines, pipes, strainers, bongs, water pipes or hookahs, and stash boxes for smoking; glassine envelopes, needles, syringes, modified eye droppers, tourniquets (belts, rubber hose, string), spoons, and cotton wads for injecting; plastic bags and vials, razor blades and mirrors or flat hard-surfaced items, straws, dollar bills rolled into cylinder shapes, spoons, and snuff boxes for snorting; and glue, nail polish, gasoline, paint thinner, aerosol products, anesthetics, volatile solvents, paper bags, plastic bags, rags, and balloons for sniffing.

paraprofessional forger. a check forger who possesses a working knowledge of the systems used by banks in processing checks and who uses planning, guile and advance preparation to carry out the crime. A paraprofessional forger typically manufactures his or her own checks, establishes a cover business, and is able to present apparently credible identification.

paraquat. a herbicide. In 1976 paraquat was sprayed over illicit marijuana fields in Mexico by the Mexican Government at the urging of the United States. In 1977 the U.S. Congress prohibited the use of foreign aid for the purchase of paraquat, but Mexico has since continued this form of marijuana eradication on its own. With initiation of the Mexican spraying program, there were fears that anyone smoking marijuana laced with paraquat would be exposed to a serious health threat. Studies sponsored by the Center for Disease Control, however, indicate that the original widespread fear of the health consequences of paraquat spraying was an overreaction.

paraquat poisoning. a toxic condition resulting from the ingestion of the pesticide paraquat characterized by progressive damage to the esophagus, kidneys, and liver, often leading to death.

parasite tap. any type of wiretap device that draws its power from the telephone line.

parasympathetic nervous system. the division of the autonomic nervous system that dominates in relaxed situations. It performs routine "housekeeping" functions, such as digestion and maintenance of body temperature. The parasympathetic nervous system is significant in respect to the theory of polygraphy.

parasympathetic. a substance that produces action similar to the stimulation of the parasympathetic nervous system; having an effect (as from a drug) similar to that caused by stimulation of the parasympathetic nervous system (e.g., slowing heart rate). Also called cholinomimetic.

Parcode. the name of a coding system developed by Parke, Davis and Company to identify Parke-Davis pharmaceuticals. It is available to law enforcement agencies.

pardon. a form of executive clemency in which the punishment of a person is stopped. A full or absolute pardon completely and unconditionally absolves a person from all consequences of a crime and conviction. American law tends to use a full pardon, instead of judicial proceedings, when serious doubt of guilt or evidence of innocence arises after conviction. A conditional pardon releases a person from punishment, contingent upon his or her performance or non-performance of specified acts.

paregoric. a generic medicine containing opium that is used medically as an analgesic and antidiarrheal. Paregoric produces high physical and psychological dependence, and has a potential for abuse.

parens patriae. a duty assumed by the government to care for children who are neglected, delinquent, or without competent parents. In the United States, this duty is carried out at the state level of government.

Parest. a trade name for the controlled ingredient methaqualone, a synthetic sedative. It is regulated under the Controlled Substances Act as a Schedule I depressant.

pari delicto. the fault or blame is shared equally.

Parkinson's Law. a concept which holds that work expands to fill the available time.

parlay. in a numbers operation, a bet on any combination of two of the three digits. Also called a bolita, bleeder, or double action.

parole. a release on certain conditions of a prisoner serving a sentence prior to the expiration of the sentence.

parole revocation. the administrative action of a paroling authority removing a person from parole status in response to a violation of lawfully required conditions of parole including the prohibition against commission of a new offense, and usually resulting in a return to prison.

parol supervision. guidance, treatment or regulation of the behavior of a convicted adult who is obliged to fulfill conditions of parole or other conditional release, authorized and required by statute, performed by a parole agency, and occurring after a period of prison confinement.

parole suspended. the withdrawal by a paroling authority or parole agent of a person's effective parole status, usually accompanied by a return to confinement, pending a determination of whether parole should be revoked, or pending resolution of some problem that may require a temporary return to confinement.

parol evidence rule. a rule which states that a written instrument or contract cannot be modified by an oral agreement. The rule is based on the concept that written contracts should contain all of the facts and agreements between parties and, therefore, should not be allowed to be altered orally at some future date.

parricide. the killing of one's mother, father, or other close relative.

partial impact. in traffic accident investigations, an impact in which motion is continuous between the parts of colliding objects which are in contact with each other; a sideswipe; an impact less than a full impact.

particulars. the details of a claim or the separate items of an account. When stated in a proper form for the information of a defendant, such details are called a bill of particulars.

parties to crimes. all persons culpably concerned in the commission of a crime, whether they directly commit the act constituting the offense, or facilitate, solicit, encourage, aid or attempt to aid, or abet its commission. In some jurisdictions, the concept is extended to include persons who assist one who has committed a crime to avoid arrest, trial, conviction or punishment.

The parties to a felony crime fall into

four categories: (1) principals in the first degree, (2) principals in the second degree, (3) accessories before the fact, and (4) accessories after the fact.

Generally, a principal in the first degree is the actual offender who commits the act. If the offender uses an agent to commit the act for him, he is still a principal in the first degree. There may be more than one principal in the first degree for the same offense.

A principal in the second degree is one who, with knowledge of what is afoot, aids and abets the principal in the first degree at the very time the felony is being committed by rendering aid, assistance or encouragement. A principal in the second degree is typically at the crime scene, nearby or situated in such a way as to render assistance. Under the concept of "constructive presence," a principal in the second degree could be a considerable distance removed from the crime while it is being committed. An example might be a lookout who monitors police radio communications at a remote location and calls his burglar accomplices at the crime scene to alert them of police patrol movements.

An accessory before the fact is a person who, before the time a crime is committed, knows of the particular offense contemplated, assents to or approves of it, and expresses his view of it in a form which operates to encourage the principal to perform the deed. There is a close resemblance between an accessory before the fact and a principal in the second degree. The difference relates to where the accessory was and the nature of the assistance rendered at the time the crime was committed. If a person advises, encourages and gives aid prior to the act but is not present at the act and not giving aid at the time of the act, he would be regarded as an accessory before the fact.

An accessory after the fact is a person who, knowing that a person has committed a felony, subsequently aids the felon to escape in any way or prevents his arrest and prosecution. He may help the felon elude justice by concealing, sheltering or comforting the felon while he is a fugitive, or by supplying him with the means of escape or by destroying evidence. An accessory after the fact must have an intention to assist the felon and must actually do so. Mere knowledge of the felon's offense and a failure to report it does not make a person an accessory after the fact.

Part I offenses. in Uniform Crime Reports, the group of offenses called "major offenses" consisting of criminal homicide, forcible rape, robbery, aggravated assault, burglary, larceny-theft, motor vehicle theft and arson.

Part II offenses. in Uniform Crime Reports, a set of offense categories concerning arrests for less than "major offenses" such as simple assault, drug abuse, and gambling.

part-time temporary release. the authorized temporary regular absence of a prisoner from a confinement facility, for periods of less than 24 hours, for purposes relating to such matters as education or employment.

party-dominated process. an aspect of the adversary system that gives to the judge the passive role of umpire and allows the prosecution and defense to be the major forces in a trial.

passing off. selling an imitation article by claiming it to be genuine.

passive acoustic monitoring. the use of microphones and ancillary equipment to provide surveillance by monitoring sounds.

passive fence. a receiver of stolen goods who customarily accepts everything that is offered and who does not specify to the sellers any preference for particular goods.

passive partner. the person who receives the physical attention during sexual activity. In homosexuality, the person whose genitals are being stimulated by the active partner.

password. a unique word, usually up to eight characters in length, assigned to an authorized computer system user and typically linked to a user ID. Frequently, display of the password is suppressed when it is keyed in during the log on routine.

password protected document. a document in computer memory which cannot be edited, printed, filed or retrieved without the correct password.

pasted counterfeit. a small denomination bill that has been raised to a higher denomination bill by first thinning the original corners on one side and then pasting on new corners of a higher denomination. The new corners have usually been torn, one or two at a time, from other bills that are redeemed at full value.

past posting. in a numbers operation, betting after post time when the winning number is known. The use of a padded book is usually involved.

patch panel. a panel that joins or terminates many different circuits. It features jacks, plug-ins, or simple terminal blocks.

patent ambiguity. an uncertainty in a written instrument that is obvious upon reading.

pathological liar. a person whose lying is compulsive; one who lies for no profit or gain.

pathology. the science or doctrine of diseases; that part of medicine which explains the nature, causes and symptoms of diseases. Forensic pathology is a specialty concerned with the examination of unnatural deaths. The forensic pathologist is frequently a coroner or medical examiner who performs autopsies and works in close conjunction with other forensic specialists and investigators.

patricide. the killing of one's father.

patrol-oriented investigative unit. a unit in a police agency in which nearly all criminal investigations are carried out by patrol officers, with detectives serving primarily as technical advisors. In this organizational concept, the patrol unit dispatched to an incident conducts all or nearly all response and investigative activities required to bring the incident to its appropriate conclusion.

patterned gunshot bruise. a bruise around an entrance wound caused by contact between muzzle and skin. The pattern can sometimes be associated with the weapon used.

pattern of drug use. a sequence of drug-using behavior by an individual or a group; the kind and amount of drug taken as well as the set and setting of drug-taking behavior over a certain period of time. Experts have identified five general patterns differentiated by degree: experimental use, social-recreational use, circumstantial-situational use, intensified use, and compulsive use.

pattern offender. a criminal who commits the same type of crime repeatedly and in a particular pattern. The pattern may be discernible in terms of (1) unique acts committed or unique demands placed on the victim, (2) time, (3) place, (4) approach or departure methods and routes, (5) activities committed before or after the crime, (6) weapons or tools used, and (7) the victims or assets targeted. Patterns are frequently present in sex offenses due to compulsions the offender is unable to resist and unable to not repeat.

Paul v. Davis. a case decision made by the U.S. Supreme Court which addressed the retail security practice of publishing and distributing names and photographs of known shoplifters, passers of bad checks, users of fraudulent credit cards, etc. In this case, a person whose name and photograph appeared in a list of known shoplifters claimed deprivation of the right to due process under the Fourteenth Amendment. The Supreme Court held that the person's due process right does not include protection of one's reputation alone.

pavement. that part of a roadway having a constructed surface for the facilitation of vehicular traffic.

pavement princess. a prostitute, especially one who plies her trade at truckstops.

pawn shop detail. a team of law enforcement officers assigned to periodically visit pawn shops in search of reported stolen property.

pay and switch. a theft by deception technique in which the thief purchases an item, switches the tag with a tag from a similar but more expensive item, and returns the item to the store to exchange it for the higher priced item of a different size or color.

Payton v. United States. a case in which the U.S. Supreme Court in 1980 declared unconstitutional the New York State statutory provisions authorizing police officers to enter a private residence without a warrant and, with force if necessary, to make a felony arrest after probable cause has been established. The Supreme Court emphasized that physical entry into the home is the chief evil against which the Fourth Amendment is directed. This decision established the rule that searches and seizures inside a home, without a warrant, whether for arrest or for search, are presumptively unreasonable.

PCP. the most commonly used street name for phencyclidine, a hallucinogen that can produce in the user a sense of detachment, distance, and estrangement from surroundings. Numbness, slurred or blocked speech, and a loss of coordination may be accompanied by a sense of strength and invulnerability. PCP is unique among popular drugs of abuse in its power to produce psychoses indistinguishable from schizophrenia. It is frequently added to leafy material and smoked. PCP is sold on the street in a variety of pill forms, capsules, dust (usually white), amorphous clumps, and occasionally as a liquid. PCP is known by a variety of names which include angel dust, dust, crystal, crystal joints, hog, CJ, KJ, peace, peaceweed, supergrass, superweed, rocket fuel, elephant tranquilizer, tranks, sheets, surfer, snorts, snuffles, cadillac, cyclosen, soma, mist, goon, TIC, TAC, T, killerweed, embalming fluid, and rocket fuel. The Controlled Substances Act lists it as a Schedule II drug.

peak. to be at the highest point of the effects caused by a drug, usually a stimulant.

peak of tension test. in polygraphy, a test designed to elicit in a guilty subject an emotional response to one specific question related to the crime. All other questions in the test are irrelevant or neutral. The tension in a guilty subject will build as the irrelevant questions are asked, and then peak on the relevant question.

pecking order. a term that describes the comparative ranks that humans hold in their business and social organizations.

peculation. embezzlement, or any wrongful act or illegal appropriation of money or property assigned to one's care.

pecuniary offense. a minor infraction of the law, such as a parking ticket.

pedalcycle. a vehicle operated solely by pedals, and propelled by human power.

pederasty. the unnatural carnal copulation of male with male, particularly of a man with a boy.

pedestrian. any person afoot; any person not in or upon a motor vehicle or other road vehicle.

pedophile. a person who obtains sexual gratification from various forms of sexual intimacies and aberrations involving children.

pedophilia. an abnormal sexual attraction to children.

peel job. a method of safecracking in which a hole is drilled in one corner, a crowbar is inserted, and the exterior surface is ripped off or peeled back. Also called a rip job.

peeping tom. a person who trespasses for the purpose of observing persons inside a dwelling.

penal bond. a bond given by an accused, or by another person in his behalf, for the payment of money if the accused fails to appear in court on a certain day.

penal code. the criminal code of a jurisdiction. It defines criminal conduct and defenses thereto, and determines the punishments to be imposed.

penal sanction. the punishment authorized by law for committing a specific crime within a jurisdiction.

pen and ink counterfeit. a small denomination bill that has been raised to a higher denomination bill by removing the original denomination markings, usually with abrasives, and drawing in the design markings of a higher denomination.

pendente lite. during the period while a legal action is pending.

penetrating gunshot wound. a wound caused when the bullet enters the body or an organ and does not exit.

penetration. as used in criminal law with respect to the offense of rape, the insertion of the penis into the parts of the female, no matter how slight.

penitentiary. a prison originally intended to keep the inmates in isolation both from society and one another, so that they could meditate on their evil past and be penitent. In current usage, the term is synonymous with prison.

pennyweighter. a shoplifter who specializes in stealing jewelry.

penology. the scientific study of corrections, including the justifications, rationalizations, theories, and aims of punishments, types of punishments, and their effectiveness.

pen register. a mechanical or electronic device that attaches to a telephone line and is capable of recording outgoing numbers dialed from that line but is not capable of recording the origin of an incoming communication to that line or the content of a communication carried between that line and another line. Also called a touch-tone recorder.

pentazocine. a narcotic agonist-antagonist used as a specific antidote for narcotic poisoning. It is sold under the trade name Talwin, and because of its morphine-like effects it is regulated under the Controlled Substances Act as a Schedule IV drug. On the street, pentazocine is frequently used in combination with tripelennamine. This combination is commonly referred to as "T's and B's" or "T's and Blues" with "T" referring to Talwin and "B" referring to the blue-colored tripelennamine tablet.

pentobarbital. the generic name of a barbiturate sold under the trade name Nembutal. It is regulated under the Controlled Substances Act as a Schedule II depressant.

Pentothal. the trade name of the controlled ingredient thiopental. It is an ultrashort-acting barbiturate which produces anesthesia within one minute after intravenous administration, and is regulated as a Schedule III depressant.

People v. Howard. a case in which the New York State Court of Appeals ruled that an individual who is stopped by the police upon a reasonable suspicion has a constitutional right not to respond and may remain silent or walk away. The police may attempt to continue interrogation but may not pursue the individual without probable cause to believe that the individual has committed, is committing, or is about to commit a crime.

pep pill. amphetamine pills; uppers.

perception delay. in traffic accident investigations, the time from the point of a driver's possible perception to actual perception.

perceptual barrier. a structure or object that discourages criminal attack by giving the appearance that an attack will be unsuccessful.

Percocet. the trade name of a product combining the controlled ingredient oxycodone, a semi-synthetic narcotic, and acetaminophen. It is listed as a Schedule II drug in the Controlled Substances Act.

Percodan. the trade name of a product containing the controlled ingredient oxycodone, a semi-synthetic narcotic. Addicts take Percodan orally or dissolve it in water, filter out the insoluble material, and "mainline" it. It is a commonly abused drug and is regulated under the Controlled Substances Act as a Schedule II narcotic.

per contra. in opposition.

per curiam. by the court. The term is frequently used to distinguish an opinion of the whole court from an opinion written by one judge.

percussion bomb. an exploding device that detonates upon impact or when struck.

peremptory challenge. a challenge to remove a person from consideration as a juror without assigning a reason or cause. In a trial, both sides have an equal number of peremptory challenges.

peremptory day. a day assigned for trial or hearing in court without further opportunity for postponement.

perforating gunshot wound. a wound caused when the bullet passes completely through the body, leaving both entrance and exit perforations.

perforation. a hole or break in the containing walls or membrane of an organ or structure of the body.

performance bond. a bond that guarantees completion of an endeavor in accordance with a contract.

performance criteria. standards for determining effectiveness or efficiency. They frequently describe steps or products in the work process, and are so stated that workers know at any point what they have achieved, what remains to be achieved, and how their performance will be evaluated.

performance test. a test that evaluates a job incumbent or applicant by requiring the performance of actual or simulated work activities. Also, any test that measures performance as opposed to other factors, such as aptitude or knowledge.

periodic imprisonment. a form of incarceration which allows a prisoner freedom except for certain periods, e.g., weekends.

periodic testing. testing of an employee at periodic intervals of employment for the purpose of evaluating such issues as the employee's honesty, use of drugs, and other matters of concern to the employer. Periodic testing is most often done through the use of the polygraph instrument, but other evaluative techniques are used, such as the so-called pen and paper honesty tests and urinalysis for identifying drug use.

peripheral nervous system. that portion of the human body's nervous system lying outside the central nervous system. The physiological reactions recorded by the polygraph instrument originate in the peripheral nervous system.

perjurer. one who knowingly makes, under oath, a false statement about an issue before a court, legislature, grand jury, or an executive branch of government.

perjury. a lie or false statement made intentionally under oath in a trial.

perpetrator. the chief actor in the commission of a crime, that is, the person who directly commits the criminal act.

perphenazine. an antipsychotic tranquilizer, manufactured as Trilafon and Triavil, used to treat some types of depression, anxiety, and agitation. It is also an antiemetic, used to treat nausea and vomiting in adults. Adverse effects include extrapyramidal signs (e.g., ataxia, dyskinesia) blood abnormalities, and hypersensitivity reactions.

Persian white. a fentanyl analog mixed with a pure white dilutant such as lactose or powdered sugar. Fentanyl produces effects similar to morphine but is about 100 times as potent. It is favored over heroin by many addicts.

personal distance. the distance from about one and a half to four feet that is considered appropriate spacing for close friends and for conversations that concern personal matters. It is a principle of importance in conducting interrogations.

personality disorder. a sociopathic or psychopathic disorder characterized by a marked lack of ethical or moral responsibility and an inability to follow socially approved codes of behavior. A person having a personality disorder knows right from wrong and is in touch with reality, but lacks any feelings of shame or remorse regarding his wrongful actions.

personal protective services. measures that increase the personal protection of a dignitary or important person who may be the target of a criminal or terrorist act.

personal recognition. a system of controlling the movement of people through personal recognition of them.

personal recognizance. a legal device which allows a person to be released from jail pending trial without being under bond. It is based on the promise of the individual to appear as demanded.

personal space. the area that humans actively maintain around themselves, into which others cannot intrude without arousing discomfort. The concept has application to interrogations.

person in need of supervision. one who is remanded to a juvenile facility, mental institution, or other custodial care without having been found guilty of a crime, because a court has determined that without such custodial supervision the individual may be a danger to himself and to others. The term refers primarily to youths. Also called child in need of supervision or juvenile in need of supervision.

personnel investigation. an investigation to determine the character, background, and suitability of a person being considered for a position of trust.

perspective drawing. the representation of an object on a plane surface as it appears to the eye. Because of its pictorial effect, a perspective drawing is sometimes used to elucidate at trial the details of the crime scene.

perspective grid photography. a photographic technique for obtaining accurate measurements of a crime scene or traffic accident scene. Exact measurements are made of any rectangular object that will appear in the picture, or a template whose exact dimensions are known is placed in the field of view. Distances between objects that appear in the photograph can be calculated. The technique can also use discs instead of templates, and for small object photography coins can be used to establish scale.

PERT. an acronym for Program Evaluation and Review Technique, a planning and control process that requires identifying the accomplishments of programs and the time and resources needed to go from one accomplishment to the next.

pertinent question. in polygraphy, a question which when posed to a guilty subject will cause a response recordable by the polygraph instrument. Also called a relevant, critical, guilt-laden, or crucial question.

perturbation. in spectroscopy, an irregularity in the spacing of the lines of a spectrum; a deviation of the values of terms in a spectral series. Perturbation is a phenomenon of concern to a crime laboratory specialist.

petechial eye hemorrhages. in homicide investigations, tiny bleeding areas in the eyeball which correlate with traumatic asphyxia or choking.

Peter Principle. a principle which holds that in a hierarchy every employee tends to rise to his level of incompetence. Corollaries of the principle hold that in time every position tends to be occupied by an employee who is incompetent to carry out its duties, and that productive work is accomplished by those employees who have not yet reached their levels of incompetence.

pethidine. a synthetic narcotic chemically dissimilar to morphine but resembling morphine's effects. It is probably the most widely used drug for the relief of moderate to severe pain. Available in pure form as well as in products containing other medicinal ingredients, it is administered either orally or by injection, the latter method being the most widely abused. Tolerance and dependence develop with chronic use, and large doses can result in convulsions or death. It is also known as meperidine and is a Schedule II controlled substance.

petition. a formal request to an executive or judicial officer to perform some act within his power or authority, as to pardon, commute, reprieve, or adjudicate as delinquent.

petit jury. a statutorily defined number of persons selected according to law and sworn to determine, in accordance with the law as instructed by the court, certain matters of fact based on evidence presented in a trial, and to render a verdict.

petit mal seizure. a relatively mild epileptic attack in which the affected person, frequently a child, loses consciousness only momentarily. Often the only outward signs are twitching of the eyes and mouth and a brief lapse of attention.

PETN. a type of booster explosive.

petrographic analysis. the examination of

mineral composition in substances such as soil, safe insulation, plaster, dust, concrete, and the like. For example, a petrographic analysis may consist of comparing dust found in the clothes of a suspect with dust found at the scene of the crime. A petrographic analysis is conducted by a laboratory specialist, often with the use of a polarizing microscope.

pettifogger. an attorney of low character and integrity.

peyote. a small cactus, Lophophora williamsii, with a spineless head or button, native to north Mexico and Texas, which contains the hallucinogen mescaline. Peyote is sometimes loosely used to refer to mescaline. Its hallucinogenic properties were known to the Aztecs, who considered it divine and called it "peyotl." During the 19th century, based on the continuing belief in its divine, supernatural powers, use spread among Native Americans, who used it in their religious rites as an aid to their traditional search for divine visions, and to heal the sick. Eventually this use developed into a religion incorporating elements of Christianity, which is now known as the Native American Church.

peyote button. the fleshy part of the peyote cactus from which mescaline, a hallucinogen, is derived.

phantom signal. an unexplained alarm signal.

pharmacogenic orgasm. a term that refers to the pleasurable sensation often reported to be experienced by heroin users after intravenous injection of the drug. Some experts believe that the whole mental personality of the addict, together with the drug, represents an autoerotic pleasure apparatus. This view holds that the addict's intense depression immediately prior to heroin administration is relieved by a pharmacogenic elation as the drug takes effect. This elation is characterized by two essential points: (1) it is brought about by the ego itself, at will, and thus gives the addict an omnipotent sense of control over mood; and (2) it resembles and is patterned on an orgasm.

pharmacokinetics. the study of the action of drugs in the body, including the method and rate of absorption and excretion, the duration of effect, and other factors.

pharmacology. the study of the preparation, properties, uses, and effects of drugs.

pharmacopoeia. a book containing a list of all drugs used in medicine and including their preparation, formula, doses, and standards of purity.

pharynx. the throat; the upper portion of the respiratory and digestive tracts below the mouth and nasal cavities and above the esophagus.

phase microscope. a laboratory microscope designed for use in identifying biological specimens (such as blood and semen) at power magnifications in the 100 to 1000X range.

phenanthrene alkaloids. one of two general categories of alkaloids extracted from opium. This category is represented by morphine and codeine. The other general category is the isoquinoline alkaloids.

phencyclidine (PCP). a synthetic depressant drug developed as an anesthetic agent in surgical procedures in the late 1950s, but because of its adverse effects it is now used medically only for veterinary purposes. It is sold and used on the street as a hallucinogen, often represented as THC, mescaline, or psilocybin. A white, crystalline, water-soluble powder, it is used orally, injected and sniffed, but most often smoked after being sprinkled on parsley, marijuana, or tobacco. The risk of adverse reactions to PCP is considered to be great enough to outweigh any usefulness in the treatment of humans. Side effects can include agitation, irritability, extreme excitement, visual disturbances, and delirium. Unlike most hallucinogens, it exerts a CNS depressant effect rather than a stimulant effect. In small doses effects can be very unpredictable, but it generally produces a state resembling drunkenness. When used regularly, memory, perception, concentration, and judgment are often disturbed. In large, chronic doses, it can cause anesthesia, sensory disturbance, and permanent damage to the brain and nervous system. Also called angel dust, dust, crystal, superweed, rocket fuel, goon.

phendimetrazine tartrate. a sympathomimetic amine used as an anorectic. Manufactured as Bacarate, Bontril, Melfiat, Plegine, Prelu-2, SPRX-105, Statobex, Trimstat, Trimtabs, and Wehless-35.

phenmetrazine. a controlled ingredient medically used only as an appetite suppressant. It is sold as Preludin and is widely abused. A common practice of addicts is to dissolve the tablets in water and inject the solution. Complications arising from such use are common since the tablets contain insoluble materials which upon injection block small blood vessels and cause serious damage, especially in the lungs and retina of the eye. Phenmetrazine is regulated under the Controlled Substances Act as a Schedule II stimulant.

phenobarbital. a long-acting, slow onset barbiturate that is especially effective as an anticonvulsant for epilepsy and delirium tremens. Phenobarbital has been in medical use since 1912, and is currently manufactured as Luminal, a commonly abused drug. On the street, phenobarbital is called purple heart.

phenolphthalein test. a preliminary test for identifying the presence of blood in a suspect stain. A positive reaction is the formation of a rose pink color when phenolphthalein is applied to the stain. This test is merely indicative (not conclusive) of blood which may or may not be of human origin.

phentermine. an anorectic (appetite-suppressing) drug with effects similar to those of the amphetamines. It is sold as Ionamin, Adipex-P, and by other names. Phentermine appears in the Controlled Substances Act as a Schedule IV stimulant.

phenylpropanolamine. a nonprescription stimulant that appears in many over-the-counter diet pills, such as Dexatrim. It is also added to cold remedies as a nasal decongestant. The risks of this synthetic drug may be underestimated, especially when it is combined in some products with caffeine and ephedrine or when taken in high doses.

phone business. number bets that are taken by telephone from persons who are not serviced by a pickup man.

phone freak. a person who makes long distance calls at someone else's expense.

phonetic alphabet. an alphabet in which words signify letters, for example, Adam for A, Boy for B, and so forth. There are several phonetic alphabets in use. A standard for police radio transmissions is: Adam, Boy, Charles, David, Edward, Frank, George, Henry, Ida, John, King, Lincoln, Mary, Nora, Ocean, Paul, Queen, Robert, Sam, Tom, Union, Victor, William, X-ray, Young, Zebra.

photoelectric fuse. a bomb fuse sensitive to minute variations in light. The fuse functions when an influence from the target is exerted on a sensitive detecting device within the fuse itself.

Photo Electric Intoximeter. a breath testing device used to determine alcohol concentrations in the blood of drivers suspected of being under the influence of alcohol.

photographic lineup. a form of lineup in which an eyewitness is asked to identify a suspect from a group of photographs depicting persons of the same general description. The rules for conducting a photographic lineup are generally the same as for a live lineup, i.e., that the witness is not led by the police in anyway to select the suspect's photograph from among photographs presented for examination. A photographic lineup is not the examination of a mug shot book or similar file containing photographs of all known criminals. The purpose of a photographic lineup is to match a particular suspect with a particular crime by having an eyewitness select the suspect from among a group of persons who meet the same general physical description. All methods of eyewitness identification are open to challenge by the defense. Also called a rogue's gallery.

photogrammetry. the process of determining measurements from photographs. Its application to police work is in recording crime and accident scenes. It requires the use of two cameras to produce photographs from slightly different but known vantage points. Precise measurements can be made from an analysis of the photographs.

physical anthropology. a study of the physical development of man. The techniques of study center around the examination of skeletal remains. The forensic physical anthropologist will apply these techniques to the examination of bones uncovered by the police in the course of investigating unexplained deaths.

physical dependence. a physiological state of adaptation to a drug normally following the development of tolerance, and resulting in a characteristic withdrawal syndrome peculiar to the drug following abstinence. The extent to which physical dependence occurs in the use of certain drugs and its causes are still a matter of considerable controversy. Physical dependence is generally most closely associated with opiate narcotics, which are believed to produce the most pronounced tolerance and physical dependence of all drugs. However, many researchers now emphasize that dependence does occur among users of other drugs (e.g., barbiturates). It does not always occur the same among all opiate users and it is often impossible to differentiate clearly between physical and psychological dependence. Most theorists now emphasize the predominance of psychological factors in development of dependency on any drug. Often used as a synonym for addiction.

Physicians Desk Reference. a book containing pictures and descriptions of commercial drug products. It is helpful to an investigator when making field (i.e., preliminary and tentative) examinations of suspected controlled substances.

physiological dependence. a physical craving of the body for a drug. If the drug is withdrawn, the body will react with predictable symptoms. The nature and sever-

ity of the symptoms depend on the drug and the dosage level attained.

physiological tolerance. a decrease in the response to a drug dose caused by a change in the receptor cells and related cells.

Picard v. Brennan. a 1973 case in which the Supreme Court of Maine considered the issue of slander per se for a statement that an employee was discharged or fired, without a stated reason for the discharge. Despite the fact that the statement was false, the court held that a general statement that a person was discharged or fired is not slanderous per se, but might be considered slanderous in the case of a statement of discharge of an employee for reasons shown to be false.

pick destructive. a term relating to any lockpicking technique which results in damage to the lock.

pick detectable. a term relating to any lockpicking technique which leaves traces of the picking.

pick gun. a tool used by auto thieves to defeat car door and ignition locks. The handle and trigger are similar to those on a caulking gun. The barrel consists of a lock pick that moves up and down upon activation of the trigger.

pickpocketing. stealthily removing something of value from the pocket of another person, with intent to keep it. Pickpocketing usually carries a more severe penalty than ordinary stealing.

pickup man. in a numbers operation, a person who picks up numbers from writers or at drops and delivers them to persons higher up in the operation.

pieced note. a counterfeit bill created by piecing together a different section cut from each of a number of genuine bills of the same type and denomination. The counterfeiter will cut no more than two-fifths from each genuine bill to ensure they meet the requirements of redemption at full value.

pigeon drop. a bunco scheme committed by a team of con artists in which a wallet or purse containing money is placed so as to be found in the presence of the mark (intended victim) and one of the con artists. The mark is induced to **agree** to share the found money but to first place it and a sum of his own money as collateral with a third party (a member of the team) while an effort is made to locate the owner of the found money. The team separates from the mark, depriving him of his money.

piggyback entry. unauthorized interception and alteration of electronic communication between a computer and its user.

pillow. a rough form of measurement consisting of a plastic bag containing a large quantity (25,000 or more) of illicitly manufactured pills, capsules, or tablets. Pillows are frequently used when transporting illicit drugs from a clandestine laboratory to a distributor.

ping ponging. in health care fraud, providing for unnecessary treatments at the same time needed services are performed.

pinhole lens. a special compressed optical lens used for covert observation. It is typically mounted in a wall so that a person on the back side of the wall can conduct a visual surveillance. The pinhole lens can be straight or right-angled. The right-angle model allows "around the corner viewing."

pink. the street name for a barbiturate.

pin test. a field test for identifying a suspected counterfeit note. The red and blue fibers randomly added to genuine U.S. notes can be picked off the surface of the paper with a pin point. A counterfeit will not have the fibers or will use inks to simulate them.

pip switch. a switch on a polygraph instrument that permits calibration of the galvanic skin response component.

pipe bomb. a short length of pipe capped at both ends and drilled at one end to accept a fuse, which is used to detonate an explosive contained inside the pipe.

pipeman. a messenger or a person who receives and passes on messages in support of a criminal activity.

piquer. a person who derives sexual satisfaction from stabbing his or her victims with sharp instruments.

piracy. the forcible seizure of a seagoing vessel in peacetime. In recent years, piracy has also come to describe the seizure of aircraft, as in skyjacking.

pirate factory. a place where counterfeit products, such as unauthorized reproductions of tapes, records and books, are manufactured in violation of owner rights.

Piso's justice. a punishment that is legally and technically correct but not morally justifiable.

placebo effect. the effect of a neutral or irrelevant aspect of an experiment that is intended to produce the same reaction in a participant as an important or relevant aspect. In drug use, a reaction due to a user's set and setting rather than the pharmacological properties of the substance. The effect, usually beneficial, occurs after the placebo is taken and is not the result of any property of that substance but usually reflects the faith or expectations the person has in the substance. Studies have determined that placebos will fairly consistently give significant relief from symptoms such as severe postoperative wound pain, pain of angina pectoris, headache, cough, mood change, seasickness, anxiety, and the common cold.

placenta. the organ of metabolic interchange between fetus and mother; afterbirth. The placenta is the organ by which the unborn child is attached to the inside of the uterus and through which the body needs of the unborn child are supplied. The placenta is expelled at birth.

Placidyl. a trade name for the controlled ingredient ethchlorvynol. It is used clinically as a hypnotic. Placidyl is especially dangerous in overdose because it is fat soluble and resistive to excretion. This depressant is a Schedule IV substance.

plain arch. a fingerprint pattern in which ridges enter on one side of the impression and flow or tend to flow out the other side with a rise or wave in the center.

plain English. readily understandable written or spoken words as opposed to codes or symbols.

plain impressions. inked fingerprint impressions obtained by simultaneously pressing all of the fingers of the hand and then the thumb. Plain impressions are not rolled impressions.

plaintiff. in law, the person suing the defendant.

plain view doctrine. a rule of law that states it is not a search within the meaning of the Fourth Amendment to observe that which is open to view, provided that the viewing officer has a lawful right to be there. No warrant is required to seize items in plain view. Plain view exists when an officer who had justification for intrusion in the course of official duties inadvertently comes into contact with contraband in open view, and prior to the discovery was unaware of the existence of the contraband before coming upon it unexpectedly.

The plain view doctrine relies on the presumption that the officer has a right to be in a place where evidence or contraband is seen in an area open to plain viewing. An example would be an officer who is called to the scene of an assault and observes cocaine on a coffee table. The officer is legally on the premises and can seize the cocaine. However, if the cocaine was viewed by an officer observing through an open window, not in connection with official police business, the plain view doctrine does not apply. In this case, a search warrant would be required to make a search and seizure.

plain whorl. a fingerprint pattern which has two deltas and at least one ridge making a complete circuit. An imaginary line drawn between the two deltas will touch or cross at least one of the recurving ridges. This pattern is slightly different from a central pocket loop.

plain wrapper. an unmarked police car.

plant. a flammable item or substance placed at or near an arsonist's ignition device. The plant is intended to feed the fire in its early stage. Sometimes plants are placed in a series for the purpose of lead-ing the fire in a desired direction. Newspapers, wood shavings, excelsior, rags, clothing, blankets, and cotton waste are some of the materials used in plants. Accelerants, such as alcohol, lighter fluid, paint thinners, and gasoline are frequently added to plants. The accelerants are called boosters, and a plant that contains an accelerant is sometimes called a boosted plant.

plantar print. an impression made by the under surface of the foot.

plant log. a record of the taped incoming and outgoing calls on a telephone line that is being monitored pursuant to an eavesdropping warrant. Log details would include time and date of call, line number, monitoring officer, and tape reel number. The plant log is required to be made by law and must be available to the defense.

plasma life. that period of time during which a drug produces maximal activity or influence in the plasma. Plasma life varies from drug to drug, for example, 4–6 hours for heroin and 3–6 days for marihuana.

plastic explosive. a putty-like explosive substance that can be molded into various shapes to increase the efficiency of charges. Composition C-4, which is approved for military use only, is a type of plastic explosive.

plasticine. a substance used by a forger to remove graphite from writings on paper.

plastic money. credit cards.

plastic paper. counterfeit money.

plastic print. a fingerprint, tire print, foot print or similar outline visible in a soft surface such as dirt, wax, blood, grease and paint.

platter charge. a concave-shaped steel plate attached to an explosive charge, usually employed to penetrate armor plate. The platter is aimed at a target when the charge is detonated, delivering a force up to 18,000 fps.

plea. a defendant's answer in court to the charges brought against him in a complaint, information or indictment.

plea bargaining. a process of negotiation between a prosecutor and a defense attorney in which the accused voluntarily pleads guilty, usually in exchange for lower charges and sentences.

pleasure-pain principle. the utilitarian concept that people endeavor to maximize pleasure (profit) and minimize pain (loss). Making the anticipated penalty greater than the expected gain is believed to deter rational men from committing crimes.

plenary. absolute, full power regarding the authority or jurisdiction of a court.

plenary confession. a complete and comprehensive confession to a crime.

plethysmograph component. a component on some types of polygraph instruments which electronically records changes in blood volume, pulse rate, and blood oxygen content.

plumbing. services performed in support of covert operations, such as conducting surveillances, operating safehouses, and providing unaccountable funds.

pneumograph component. a major component of a polygraph instrument that records the inhalation and exhalation cycles of the examinee's breathing pattern. One or two hollow tubes that encircle the examinee's chest and/or abdomen expand or contract relative to pressure changes caused by breathing. A bellows apparatus in the polygraph instrument converts the changes to inked tracings on the polygram. The tracings are evaluated by the examiner, especially at points in the test when relevant questions were asked.

point. in fingerprint science, a ridge formed by one of the three basic ridge characteristics, i.e., bifurcation, ridge ending or dot.

point control. the management of vehicle and pedestrian traffic flow at a particular point on a roadway with an emphasis on pedestrian safety.

pointing bulb. in arson investigations, a light bulb distended by heat and pointing in the direction of the heat source, often the fire's point of origin.

point man. the officer situated at the leading position in an offensive riot control formation, such as the wedge, triangle (diamond), or echelon (diagonal). Also called the base man.

point of first contact. in traffic accident investigations, the point of initial touching of objects in a collision. Also called point of impact.

point of intersection. the point at which two straight lines, such as the extensions of two roadway edges, cross each other. Also called intercept point.

point of law. that which is a precedent or an issue to be decided.

point of maximum engagement. in traffic accident investigations, the point of greatest penetration of one body, such as a vehicle, as the consequence of a collision.

point of no escape. the point at which an immediately impending traffic accident cannot be prevented by a driver.

point of origin. in arson investigations, the place where a fire is believed to have started.

point of perception. the point at which a driver comprehends a hazard or risk.

point of possible perception. the point at which a traffic hazard can be perceived by a normal person. It precedes actual perception and is the beginning point of perception delay, i.e., the time between possible perception and perception.

point of tangency. in traffic accident investigations, the point on a curved roadway where a tangent touches. The point of tangency, or PT, is usually located at the spot where a curve begins or ends.

point-to-point search. a crime or accident scene search in which the investigator enters the scene at the logical entrance point, visually examines the scene, goes to the first apparent item of evidence, and processes it. He then goes to the next closest item and does the same until all evidence has been methodically discovered and processed.

poke. the item taken by a pickpocket, e.g., a wallet or change purse.

Poland v. Arizona. a case in which the U.S. Supreme Court addressed the issue of double jeopardy with respect to aggravating circumstances. The case involved a robbery-murder of two armored car guards who were drowned by the two defendants. At the initial sentencing hearing the trial judge concluded that the aggravating circumstance of murder for pecuniary gain only applied to contract murders and was not applicable in this case. He then imposed the death penalty based upon another aggravating circumstance, murder in a cruel and heinous fashion. On appeal, the Arizona Supreme Court reversed the trial court's conviction, finding the evidence insufficient to support the cruel and heinous circumstance. The court also indicated that the pecuniary gain circumstance was not limited to contract murder, as had been concluded by the judge.

Upon remand, the defendants were again convicted of the murders. The trial judge found that both pecuniary gain and cruel and heinous murder circumstances were present, and he sentenced the defendants to death. The defendants appealed on the grounds of double jeopardy, contending they had been acquitted of the death penalty because of the earlier finding by the Arizona Supreme Court that there was insufficient evidence to support the cruel and heinous circumstance. The Arizona Supreme Court again concluded that the evidence did not support the cruel and heinous circumstance but did support the finding of murder for pecuniary gain.

The case went to the U.S. Supreme Court which concluded that the death penalty could be reimposed because the trial judge's initial rejection of the pecuniary gain circumstance did not constitute an acquittal of that circumstance for double jeopardy purposes, and the State Court's rejection of the cruel and heinous circumstance at the first review did not constitute an acquittal of the death penalty.

polar coordinates method. a method for mapping an object in a crime scene sketch by giving its distance from some selected point plus the direction angle taken by the distance line from an axis. For example, if a handgun is found some distance from a house, the closest wall of the house can serve as an axis reference. By measuring from a door or window on the wall, the handgun can be fixed by distance with a tape measure and fixed by angle with a compass aligned to the wall.

polarized-light microscope. a microscope which employs the use of polarized light to determine optical properties such as refractive index. A polarized-light (or polarizing) microscope is useful in identifying minerals, hairs, and fibers. It passes polarized light (light in one plane) through the sample being analyzed, thereby revealing its refractive index and other optical properties. Also called a petrographic microscope for its use in examining dirt, dust, plaster, and similar materials.

pole jump. a theft of electrical service made after the utility company has disconnected the power line from the service pole to the structure. The thief, usually a former subscriber whose account was closed for nonpayment or for prior theft, will string his own power line in order to restore service.

pole trailer. a vehicle without motive power designed to be drawn by another vehicle and attached to the towing vehicle by means of a reach or pole, or by being boomed or otherwise secured to the towing vehicle, and ordinarily used for transporting long or irregularly shaped loads such as poles, pipes, or structural members capable, generally, of sustaining themselves as beams between the supporting connections.

police aide. a paid or unpaid volunteer who is not a commissioned police officer but who performs various routine tasks to assist and support the work of a police agency. Such volunteers are also called community service officers and police cadets.

police connect. an alarm reporting system that is directly wired or channeled to a police station.

police discretion. the power or authority

conferred by law to act in certain situations in accordance with an official's or an official agency's own considered judgment and conscience. For example, a police officer is required to make spontaneous and difficult decisions in unforeseeable situations. Police discretion allows the officer certain defined latitudes in such situations.

police intelligence. processed information relating to criminal activities.

police power. the right of the state to enact laws and enforce them for the order, safety, health, morals and general welfare of the public.

police prosecution system. a system common in the United Kingdom and Ireland in which certain crimes are prosecuted by high-ranking police officials rather than by appointed or elected prosecutors.

police station receiver. an alarm receiver in operation at a police station to receive alarm signals from protected premises.

police sweep. a concentrated effort to clean up a crimeprone neighborhood by making mass arrests of criminals and suspects.

police witness. a police officer who is a witness. He may be the arresting officer, an officer who assisted in the arrest, or an investigating officer.

policy. any one of several widely played games in which players bet money on numbers. Policy is similar to a lottery and is sometimes called the numbers game. Policy is based on some method of choosing winning numbers such as the U.S. Treasury daily balance or parimutuel totals from horse races. A straight bet is based on three digit numbers, 000 to 999; parlay bets on two digit numbers, 00 to 99; and single action bets on one digit, 0 to 9.

polling the jury. a part of trial procedure which permits that each juror be asked if the nonunanimous verdict of the jury is his verdict.

polygram. a moving chart of a polygraph instrument upon which the inked pens place tracings. A polygraphist's opinion is based upon an interpretation of tracings on one or more polygrams.

polygraph examination. an examination of a person by a polygraphist using a polygraph instrument. The procedure includes a pre-test interview, a polygraph test, and a post-test interview.

polygraph instrument. an electronic instrument that continuously records on a moving chart physiological changes that occur in an examinee's body as questions are posed to the examinee. The changes recorded relate to blood pressure, pulse, respiration rate and volume, and galvanic skin resistance. Contemporary polygraph instruments have one or two respiration monitors, a skin resistance monitor, and one or two cardiovascular activity monitors which operate synchronously with a chart drive, graph paper and pen registers.

polygraph technique. a lie detection technique based on the assumption that when an individual experiences apprehension, fear or emotional excitement, his or her respiration rate, blood pressure and galvanic skin resistance will sharply increase. A polygraph instrument records these physiological responses as questions are asked by a trained examiner. The examiner interprets the recordings and renders an opinion as to the truthfulness of the person examined.

polygraph theory. a theory which holds that a conscious mental effort to deceive made by a normal, healthy person will cause certain physiological changes which are recordable by the polygraph instrument.

polygraphy. the science of lie detection or truth verification. It is used to screen job applicants and employees, and to identify possible suspects in criminal cases.

polypharmacy. the act of prescribing or administering more than one drug to a patient, sometimes improperly, unnecessarily, and for gain.

Ponzi operation. a confidence scheme in which money is collected from investors and part of it is paid back with high profits to encourage the early investors and others to increase their investments. When the total amount becomes substantial, the swindlers abscond with the investments. This form of fraud is similar to the pyramid sales scheme in which investors purchase distributorships and rights to sell lower-level distributorships. The scheme collapses when there are no more investors willing to buy in.

pop pills. to ingest drugs in pill form.

poppy straw. parts of the opium poppy plant, except seeds, which remain after mowing. Poppy straw is regulated as a Schedule II controlled substance.

population movement. the entries and exits of adjudicated persons into or from correctional facilities or programs.

pornography. art, expression, implication, speech, suggestion or writing which appeals to the base or sensual desires of a person and is contrary to the established moral code of the society.

poroscopy. the examination of the pores on the palms and fingers of the hand as a means of identification in addition to fingerprint identification. Friction ridges are dotted by pores which differ in position, shape and size. It is possible to discern a pore pattern in a small area of the hand and to use the pattern as a basis for identifying a suspect. Pores are permanent and appear in an infinite variety of patterns, thereby giving to poroscopy a theoretical validity similar to that of fingerprint identification.

portrait parle. a system that uses numerous physical characteristics, such as height, weight and hair color, to describe persons. Also called bertillonage.

POSDCORB. an acronym for a classical management theory which holds that managers carry out their responsibilities by performing tasks associated with the functions of planning, organizing, staffing, directing, coordinating, record keeping, and budgeting. The first letters of the functions form the acronym.

Planning is a continuous process that involves gathering information, analyzing the information, and developing a problem statement. Goals are established which address the problem.

Organizing is the process of creating an organizational structure consistent with the achievement of established goals.

Staffing is the function of identifying, selecting and assigning human beings to the positions that make up the organizational structure.

Directing is to apply the organization's resources to the achievement of established goals. The resources are both human and non-human. Directing implies policies, procedures, training, continuous evaluation, and the use of positive and negative incentives to influence the workforce.

Coordinating is the process of insuring that the various groups and subgroups of the organization are working toward the same goals, in harmony, and cost-effectively.

Record keeping is the maintenance of information in useful and meaningful formats. It is not simply the retention of all information, but of information that has a known or potential value. This process also implies that kept data is to be shared with other managed groups.

Budgeting is the preparation of a request for resources to carry out plans, programs and projects already decided upon. A budget covers a specific period, usually one year.

posed photograph. a photograph used in court to clarify or elucidate the testimony of a witness. It may depict actors representing the accused, victim or witness and other aspects of a scene.

positive correlation. a relationship between two variables in which a high rank on one measure is accompanied by a high rank on the other.

positive pressure phase. that phase of a blast wave in which compressed air moves outward and is bounded by an extremely sharp pressure wave front less than 0.0001-inch thick in which the pressure increases abruptly far above normal. The pressure wave front moves outward with an initial velocity greater than the velocity of sound at sea level (1,110 fps). This front applies a sudden and considerable thrust or push against any obstacle in its path. In water or earth, the same effect takes place and is called water or earth shock.

positive reinforcement. the strengthening of a response by the presentation of a stimulus.

positive sanctions. rewards for socially desired behavior.

positive transfer. transfer of learning that is accelerated and strengthened because it is based on prior learning or experience.

Posse Comitatus Act. an act that forbids the use of military personnel to enforce civilian law. Either military or civilian personnel or both may violate the act. The user of any part of the Army or Air Force for the prohibited purpose is the offender.

possession. a condition of fact under which a person can exercise dominion and control over property. Possession may be actual or constructive.

possible maximum loss. the loss that would be sustained if a given criminal target was totally taken or destroyed. For example, the possible maximum loss for a retail store would be the loss of the entire inventory.

post-conviction remedies. proceedings that may be brought after conviction, such as appeal of the conviction or sentence, request for commutation, pardon, reprieve, or stay of execution.

post-dated check. a check delivered prior to its date, generally payable on sight or on presentation on or after its date. It differs from an ordinary check by carrying on its face implied notice that there is no money on deposit to cover the check prior to the date, but with assurance that money will be on deposit on and after the check's date.

post hoc error. the result of a faulty reasoning process that attributes the cause of a given event to another event that occurred earlier.

post mortem. after death; an autopsy or examination of a dead body to determine the cause of death.

post mortem lividity. a characteristic discoloration of the skin of a deceased person that begins within one-half to two hours after death and continues to increase in intensity while the body is cooling and the blood retains some liquidity. A red to purple discoloration will be visible on the dependent portions of the body, that is, the portions of the body into which the blood will drain and settle. The discoloration will be absent at places where the body has been in contact with a rigid surface, such as would be the case with a person who died on the floor or ground. Discoloration would also not be present where constricting items, such as clothing, belt, or rope, prevented the movement of blood. When the blood of the deceased has completely coagulated, lividity then sets in permanently. At this time pressure on the discolored areas will not blanch. The entire process of post mortem lividity is usually completed within 6 to 12 hours.

Post mortem lividity can be helpful in determining the position of the deceased at the time of death, and in determining if the body was moved after death while the process of lividity was still active. For example, an investigator might conclude that the deceased was moved after death if the pattern of discoloration is inconsistent with the position of the body when it was discovered.

post mortem rigidity. the stiffening of the body after death. Chemical changes within muscle tissue cause the muscles to contract. Also called rigor mortis.

post mortem spoon. a device used to roll individual fingerprints from deformed hands or cadavers. The curved surface of the device (similar in appearance to a shoe horn) allows the finger to remain stable as the spoon rolls across the skin surface. A paper card attached to the face of the spoon captures the fingerprint pattern.

post mortem wound. a wound inflicted after death.

post time. in a numbers operation, the deadline for getting numbers into the hands of a trusted employee operating at a level above that of the bookmaker.

Pot Air Line. a nickname for air operations engaged in smuggling marijuana into the United States.

potato hazer. a homemade weapon made from a potato. Razor blades or nail heads protrude from the surface. It is used for throwing at police in riot situations.

potency. a relative term used to compare the strengths of two or more drugs required to produce a given effect. The more potent the drug, the less is required. The same effect can be achieved by more of a less potent substance, or less of the same substance in a more potent form. Occasionally the term is used to refer to the length or duration of effects.

potentiation. the ability of one drug to increase the activity of another drug taken simultaneously; a synergistic effect in which the effect of two drugs given simultaneously is greater than the effect of them given separately.

pothead. a frequent user of hashish or marijuana.

Powell v. Alabama. a case in which the U.S. Supreme Court in 1932 ruled that the Constitution guarantees the right to counsel in a state court trial whenever the defendant's life is at stake.

power elite. a closely connected group of the corporate rich, political leaders, and military commanders who are presumed by some to decide most key social and political issues.

power of attorney. a document authorizing one person to act as attorney for, or in the place of, the person signing the document.

power skid. a skid by a motor vehicle that results from excessive power in relation to road conditions. An excess of power will cause the driving wheels to spin on the road's surface, thus creating a characteristic sideways slide called fishtailing.

prairie fire. a fast burning fire, usually fed by a high wind, which moves quickly through tall, dried vegetation in open expanses.

prazepam. a controlled drug in the benzodiazepine family of depressants. It is sold as Centrax and is in Schedule IV of the Controlled Substances Act.

pre-alarm signal. a feature of an alarm system in which a visual/audible signal reminds the user to disarm his system upon entry to the protected area.

pre-arraignment lockup. a confinement facility for arrested adults awaiting arraignment or consideration for pretrial release, in which the duration of stay is usually limited by statue to two days, or until the next session of the appropriate court.

precedent. an adjudged case or decision of a court which serves as an example or authority for a later identical or similar case.

precipitin reaction test. a serological test employed to distinguish human blood from blood of other species. In the test, a rabbit is injected with human blood which causes precipitins (antibodies) to form in the rabbit's blood. The injections are administered with increasing dosages over a period of several days. This causes the precipitin serum in the rabbit to increase, and when a sufficient quantity is produced the serum is brought into contact with the suspect blood. If the suspect blood is human, a white ring precipitate is formed. This test can be used to differentiate blood among non-human species, for example, to distinguish between blood of cattle or of canines.

preconcentrator. a device used to collect vapors before they are exposed to analysis by a vapor detector. A preconcentrator is a component of so-called bomb sniffing equipment.

precordial thump. a sharp blow to the midportion of the sternum, usually done by the rescuer to a victim whose heart beat has stopped.

predatory crime. illegal activity in which the criminal preys upon, exploits, attacks, or in any violative way takes advantage of the victim, usually a person unable to defend against the activity.

predatory vandalism. vandalism committed for material gain; destructive acts which produce some form of financial reward for the perpetrator. Breaking into a vending machine to steal coins would be an example.

predictive efficiency. a measure of accuracy of a test or other predictive device in terms of the proportion of its predictions that have been shown to be correct.

predisposing factor. a factor which theoretically causes some individuals to be predisposed to drug use. It has been theorized, but never conclusively demonstrated, that certain individuals are inherently predisposed to use, abuse, and/or addiction to psychoactive drugs. The possibility has been raised that individuals may be predisposed to heroin addiction because of an endorphin deficiency syndrome or as the result of innate metabolic conditions. Other theories hold that elements in the cultural and socioeconomic environment may constitute predisposing factors for drug addiction.

precursor. a substance from which another substance is formed. The term is sometimes applied to those substances used in the manufacture of illicit drugs. A law enforcement agency, for example, might report chemicals seized at a clandestine laboratory as precursors.

predisposition. any factor that, although not the direct cause of an event, insures that the event is more likely to occur in its presence than in its absence. There is a wide range of predisposing factors involved in drug use: personality or psychological make-up of the user; close personal relations and environment in family, school, and peer group; social and economic conditions; and the general attitude of the society toward drug use.

predisposition investigation. an investigation undertaken by a probation agency or other designated authority at the request of a juvenile court, into the past behavior, family background and personality of a juvenile who has been adjudicated a delinquent, status offender, or a dependent, in order to assist the court in determining the most appropriate disposition.

pre-employment polygraph test. a test that uses the polygraph technique to determine if an employment candidate meets requirements set by the employer. The questions typically relate to honesty, drug use, reliability, intentions to remain on the job, driving record, and safety record. The test is usually preceded by three activities: (1) the job applicant completes an employment application and/or prior employment survey which asks for much of the same information that will be covered in the test, (2) the polygraph examiner interviews the applicant concerning the provided information, and (3) the questions that will be asked on the test are reviewed with the applicant. After the test has been completed, the polygraph examiner will analyze the polygrams. If the analysis indicates deception, the examiner may choose to conduct a post-test interview for clarification.

pre-hearing investigation. an investigation made by a probation officer before the adjudication of a minor in a juvenile court. Its aim is to inform the judge of the juvenile's background, apparent reasons for the delinquent behavior, and any other information that might be useful in the judicial procedure.

pre-ignition indicators. in arson investigations, the characteristics of smoke and odor that precede visible flame and which may or may not suggest arson.

PRELIMINARY. an acronym used as a guide for officers who are dispatched to a crime scene. It stands for Proceed to the scene quickly and safely, Render assistance to the injured, Effect the arrest of suspects, Locate and identify witnesses, Interview witnesses, Maintain the crime scene and protect evidence, Interrogate the suspects after giving rights warnings, Note crime scene conditions in writing, Arrange for collection of evidence, Report the incident fully in writing, Yield responsibility to the follow-up investigator.

preliminary crime. a crime which is preparatory in nature and part of a larger purpose. There are three crimes which are preparatory in nature and serve as part of a larger purpose. Each of them is a means of reaching a criminal end. These so-called preliminary crimes are solicitation, attempt, and conspiracy.

Solicitation consists of the offender's oral or written efforts to activate another person to commit a criminal offense. The essence of the crime is to incite by counsel, enticement or inducement. The offense of solicitation is complete if the offender merely urges another to violate the law and otherwise does nothing himself.

Attempt has two elements. First, there must be a specific intent to commit a particular offense, and second, there must be a direct ineffectual overt act toward its commission. There must be some act moving directly toward the act. Mere preparation, such as obtaining tools or weapons, may be insufficient to establish the crime, especially when made at a distance in time or place.

Conspiracy is the combination of two or more persons working in some concerted action to accomplish some criminal or unlawful purpose, or to accomplish some purpose in a criminal or unlawful manner. If there is a common understanding among the participants to achieve a certain purpose or to act in a certain way, a conspiracy exists without regard to whether there is any formal or written statement of purpose, or even though there is no actual speaking of words. There may be merely a tacit understanding without any express agreement.

preliminary detention. the holding of an accused in confinement pending arraignment. If the accused has been arraigned, the term refers to holding him in confinement pending trial because bail has been denied or cannot be met.

preliminary hearing. the proceeding before a judicial officer in which three matters must be decided: whether a crime was committed; whether the crime occurred within the territorial jurisdiction of the court; and whether there are reasonable grounds to believe that the defendant committed the crime.

preliminary interview. an interview conducted of a witness, victim, or complainant at the scene of a crime for the purpose of obtaining the basic facts as quickly as possible. A major purpose of the preliminary interview is to determine the nature of the crime and the identity of the criminal so that immediate action can be taken to effect an arrest.

preliminary investigation. the initial investigation of a report or complaint of a crime which is usually made by the first-responding officer. The preliminary investigation is frequently performed by a patrol officer, with further investigation conducted by a detective.

preliminary search. in patrol operations, a search conducted by a patrol unit for the purpose of locating a reported criminal suspect or evidence of a reported crime. For example, a report of prowling might result in a search for the prowler and then for evidence or factual information that can be used in preparing a complaint report and in assuring the complainant that police action has been or will be taken.

Preludin. a trade name for the controlled ingredient phenmetrazine, a stimulant medically used only as an appetite suppressant. Preludin is widely abused and much sought after by addicts. While the use of Preludin involves both oral and intravenous use, most of the abuse involves the injection of tablets dissolved in water. Complications arising from this practice are common since the tablets contain insoluble materials which upon injection block small blood vessels and cause serious damage, especially in the lungs and retina of the eye. On the street, Preludin is called speed, upper, black beauty, crank, meth, bam, and pink.

premeditated design. the mental purpose or formed intent to commit a crime, particularly the crime of murder.

premeditation. in law, planning in advance to commit a crime.

preponderance of evidence. a term relating to the burden imposed upon a plaintiff in a civil case. The plaintiff, to win, must establish a preponderance of evidence in support of the claim. Also, evidence which is more credible and convincing and which, when fairly considered, produces an impression stronger than opposing evidence.

pre-release orientation. the re-entry training or orientation given to an inmate immediately prior to release from prison. Its purpose is to reduce the difficulties of transition.

prescription. a term applied to a practice by the U.S. Supreme Court in which the police are told in very specific terms what they must do if they wish to introduce the results of interrogations in trials. Prior, the Supreme Court's practice was proscriptive in nature in that its decisions reflected what the police cannot do if they wish to introduce defendants' statements and admissions in prosecutions.

presentence report. a statement drawn up by a probation officer that gives the background information on an offender, including prior criminal record, social and personal history, results of interviews, and recommendations to the judge as to the sentence to be imposed.

presentment. written notice of an offense taken by a grand jury from their own knowledge or observation; alleged facts and charges to a court or grand jury by a prosecutor.

pre-set questioning. an interviewing technique in which all questions have been determined prior to the interview and are the only questions asked.

presiding judge. the title of the judicial officer formally designated for some period as the chief judicial officer of a court.

pressure fuse. a bomb fuse sensitive to minute changes in external pressure. The fuse functions when an influence from the target is exerted on a sensitive detecting device within the fuse itself.

pressure release bomb. an explosive device designed to detonate when pressure on the bomb's container or outer structure has been released or relaxed, as in the case of a bomb having a detonator that will activate when subjected to a change in air pressure; a bomb that will detonate when mechanical pressure on a spring-loaded trigger is released. Also called a pressure sensitive bomb.

presumption. an inference or belief as to the truth or falsity of a matter in the absence of any direct evidence to the contrary; a well-known deduction which may be made from certain facts which the law will allow.

presumption from possession. an inference that a person is guilty of theft when found to be in possession of the stolen property shortly after it was stolen.

presumption of fact. a logical inference which the trier of the facts is authorized, but not required, to draw from the evidence in a case.

presumption of innocence. a conclusion drawn by law in favor of a criminal defendant which requires acquittal unless guilt is established by sufficient evidence.

presumption of law. a rule which requires that a particular inference must be drawn from an ascertained state of facts.

presumption of purposefulness. in hit and run traffic investigations, a presumption by the investigator that the perpetrator at the time of the accident was pursuing some purposeful objective, i.e., that he was going from one place to another by what seemed to be the best route. For example, if a hit and run accident occurred during peak commuter hours, the investigator might presume that the perpetrator was traveling between work and home.

presumptive evidence. evidence which must be received and treated as true until rebutted by other evidence. A statute might provide that certain facts are presumptive evidence of guilt.

presumptive positive. a laboratory test finding that has not been confirmed by an alternate and equally sensitive test. In drug testing, for example, a urine specimen that has been screened by an immunoassay test and found to be positive is considered to be presumptively positive until a second test confirms or refutes the initial finding. The second test often employs the gas chromatography/ mass spectrometry (GC/MS) technique, and the finding from this test is called a confirmation or confirmed result. When the second test is a repeat of the first test or uses a less sensitive or essentially similar methodology, the test finding is called a verification or a verified result.

pretrial conference. a meeting of the opposing parties in a case with the judicial officer prior to trial, for the purposes of stipulating those things which are agreed upon and thus narrowing the trial to the things that are in dispute, disclosing the required information about witnesses and evidence, making motions, and generally organizing the presentation of motions, witnesses and evidence.

pretrial detention. detention until trial is over of one who is eligible for bail, or is unable to raise or post bail; a statutory program authorizing detention of an offender prior to trial where specific findings are made at a public hearing regarding the nature of the charged offense and the prior criminal history of the alleged offender.

pretrial discovery. in criminal proceedings, disclosure by the prosecution or the defense prior to trial of evidence or other information which is intended to be used in the trial.

pretrial identification proceeding. any proceeding prior to trial at which witnesses are called to identify the accused. Examples are lineups, confrontations, and photographic displays.

pretrial motion. a request made to the court before trial. It may cover such issues as change of venue, admissibility of a confession into evidence, and privileged communication.

pretrial procedure. a procedure established in many courts to speed up the disposition of cases by encouraging and assisting settlements before trial.

pretrial publicity. information disseminated concerning a crime, a defendant, or a forthcoming trial that is sometimes claimed by the defense to be prejudicial. It is often used by the defense in its request that the place of trial be moved.

pretrial release. the release of an accused person from custody, for all or part of the time before or during prosecution, upon his or her promise to appear in court when required.

prevention model. any model, program, project, campaign or similar organized effort aimed at the prevention of an undesirable activity, for example, crime or drug abuse.

preventive detention. holding of a person in custody without bail before trial on the ground that such custody keeps the offender from committing further crimes while the charges are pending.

preventive maintenance. a system of conducting regular checks and tests of equipment to permit replacement or repair of weakened or faulty parts before equipment failure results.

preventive patrol. a form of patrol that emphasizes deterrence to crime as opposed to reaction.

Primacord. a brand name for detonating cord, a product used in blasting.

prima facie. at first view. This term refers to evidence which is, according to law, sufficient to establish or prove a point, unless successfully rebutted by other evidence. For example, a signature on a check is prima facie evidence that the check was uttered by the signer.

prima facie proof. the proof which the plaintiff must show at trial before the defendant will be required to prove his defense to the action.

primary cause. in traffic accident investigations, a misnomer loosely applied to the most obvious or easily explained factor in the cause of an accident.

primary explosive. a small quantity of explosive material detonated by a firing device and which in turn detonates a booster explosive. The primary explosive is the second element in the basic firing chain typical of most explosions. The common primary explosive materials are mercury fulminate, lead azide, dinoly and lead styphenate.

primary password. in computer usage, the first user password requested from the user. The computer system may optionally require a secondary password.

primary shock. a state of early unconsciousness or depression of the vital processes associated with reduced blood volume and pressure. It is usually caused by severe injuries, burns, or hemorrhage, and is reversible if treated promptly. Primary shock is sometimes followed by secondary shock which is profound and frequently fatal. Also called impending shock.

primer residue. residue deposited on the thumb, forefinger and web area of the hand when the hand is used to discharge a weapon. Residue may also be deposited on the face and neck area when a rifle or shotgun is fired. Primer residue frequently contains antimony and barium which are components of most primer mixtures. Also called gunshot residue.

principal. a person for whom personal protective services are provided; a chief actor in a crime; an aider and abettor who actually or constructively participates in the commission of a crime, as distinguished from an accessory.

principal agent. an agent or spy who controls and pays others engaged in espionage or undercover investigations.

principal in the first degree. the actual offender; the person who committed the criminal act. There may be more than one principal in the first degree for a single crime, and a principal in the first degree does not have to be present at the crime or personally commit the act. For example, a person who pays another to commit murder would be charged as a principal in the first degree.

principal in the second degree. one who with knowledge afoot, aids and abets the principal in the first degree at the very time the crime is being committed. A driver of a getaway car or a lookout would be a principal in the second degree.

principle of application. a principle which holds that the more an idea is applied and put to use, the more it is understood and remembered.

principle of emotional appeal. a principle which holds that appeals to emotion are communicated more readily than appeals to reason.

principle of line loss. a principle which holds that as the number of people involved in passing a message increases, there is an increase in distortion and delay of the message.

prior restraint order. a court or other government order forbidding or censoring printed matter before publication.

Prisoner Rehabilitation Act of 1965. a federal statute that permits selected federal prisoners to work in the community while still in an inmate status.

prisoner's rights. any rights to which convicts are entitled by law, usually as interpreted by the courts, such as freedom from cruel and unusual punishment, the right to receive visitors, or the right to prepare legal briefs.

prisonization. the process of learning about and adhering to the inmate subculture.

Privacy Act of 1974. a federal statute that reasserts the fundamental right to privacy as derived from the Constitution and provides basic safeguards for the individual to prevent the misuse of personal information by the federal government. The act provides for making known to the public the existence and characteristics of all personal information systems kept by every federal agency. It permits an individual to have access to records containing personal information and allows the individual to control the transfer of that information. Virtually all agencies of the federal government have issued regulations implementing the act. Civil remedies are provided when the requirements of the act are contravened.

The Privacy Act does not apply to records held by state and local governments or private organizations. Also, the Act exempts certain records, i.e., (1) records maintained by the Central Intelligence Agency, (2) records maintained by federal criminal law enforcement agencies which contain data relating to arrest, disposition, sentencing, confinement, release, parole, and probation, or information compiled for the purpose of criminal investigation, or reports identifiable to an individual compiled at any stage in the criminal law process from arrest or indictment through release from supervision, (3) classified documents concerning national defense and foreign policy, (4) investigatory material compiled for law enforcement purposes (other than materials described in the second exemption), (5) U.S. Secret Service intelligence files, (6) files used solely for statistical purposes, (7) investigatory materials used in making decisions concerning federal employment, military service, federal contracts, and security clearances, (8) testing or examination material used solely for employment purposes, and (9) evaluation material used in making decisions regarding promotions in the armed services.

private law. that portion of the total body of laws dealing with those relations between individuals with which the government is not directly concerned. Private law can be divided into several branches such as contract law, property law, law of domestic relations, trust law and the law of torts.

private police. a general descriptor for security officers.

private prosecution. a system prevailing in England and some Continental countries that allows the victim of a crime to initiate criminal proceedings. In practice, unsuccessful private prosecution frequently leads to civil action against the complainant.

private rehabilitation agency. a private organization providing care and treatment services, which may include housing, to convicted persons, juvenile offenders, or persons subject to judicial proceedings.

private search concept. a concept which holds that searches undertaken by private persons are not subject to constitutional regulation. The Bill of Rights, including the Fourth Amendment, apply only to actions of the federal government. The unlawfulness of a private search is irrelevant to the issue of a defendant's entitlement to an exclusionary remedy in criminal proceedings. A wrongful search or seizure conducted by a private party does not deprive the government of the right to use evidence it has acquired lawfully.

private sector. a general term meaning the non-government community; individuals and organizations of private industry.

private security agency. an independent or proprietary commercial organization whose activities include employee clearance investigations, maintaining the security of persons or property and/or performing the functions of detection and investigation of crime and criminals, and apprehension of offenders.

privileged communication. a legal principle based on a confidential relationship between two persons which may be invoked to exclude one from testifying against the other. In some relationships the exercise of the privilege is vested in the defendant. In others it is vested in the witness. The following relationships are generally recognized: husband and wife; attorney and client; physician and patient; and law enforcement officer and informant.

privilege from civil arrest. a privilege granted by statute in some jurisdictions to certain specifically identified parties whose special status requires them to be free of civil arrest. Such parties might be witnesses or litigants duly subpoenaed, diplomats and their families and personal staff, legislators in session, members of the armed forces on active duty, policemen on duty, and firemen on duty.

privileges. in computer usage, a means of protecting the use of certain system functions that can affect system resources and/or integrity. System managers grant privileges according to user needs, and deny privileges as a means of controlling access to functions of the system.

probable cause. a combination of facts and circumstances which would warrant a person of reasonable caution and prudence to believe that a crime has been or is being committed and that the person to be arrested is guilty of such crime. In the context of search and seizure, probable cause is a combination of facts and circumstances derived from credible sources which would warrant a person of reasonable caution and prudence to believe that crime-related evidence may be found in the premises to be searched.

probable cause hearing. a proceeding before a judicial officer in which arguments, witnesses or evidence are presented and in which it is determined whether there is sufficient cause to hold the accused for trial or dismiss the case.

probable maximum loss. the amount of loss a target of criminal attack would likely sustain in a single successful attack.

probation. in the criminal justice system, a procedure meant to encourage good behavior in a person convicted of a crime by releasing him or her before confinement on certain conditions, one of which is that for a stated period of time he or she lead an orderly life. In regard to employees, a status in which a person is employed or assigned to a rank or position temporarily, subject to dismissal or reassignment dependent upon performance.

probation revocation. a court order in response to a violation of conditions of probation, taking away a person's probationary status, and usually withdrawing the conditional freedom associated with the status.

probative fact. a fact which tends to substantiate another fact or issue.

problem drinker. an excessive drinker whose drinking causes personal or public harm. The term is often used as a euphemism for the alcoholic, particularly in business and industrial programs.

procedural law. a subdivision of criminal law that provides the means and methods by which the rights and obligations created by the criminal law are to be vindicated and enforced. It defines the rules in which criminal cases are prosecuted. The laws of arrest and of evidence are examples of procedural law. Also called adjective law.

procedural rights. various protections that all citizens have against arbitrary actions by public officials.

PROCHECK. an FBI-maintained file containing information on prolific bad check passers. The file consists of information culled from existing investigative records and is accessible only to FBI personnel.

pro confesso. as confessed.

product. finished intelligence reports disseminated to users.

Professional Class I Burglar. a burglar who is able to successfully attack most alarm systems and pick locks. His targets usually are high risk commodities such as safes and vaults, cash, jewelry, furs, televisions, stereos, and appliances.

Professional Class II Burglar. a burglar who is able to circumvent alarm systems but is not sufficiently skilled to successfully attack them. He will usually go around an alarm, i.e., gain entry through the roof, floor or a wall. His targets usually are high and medium risk commodities.

Professional Class III Burglar. a relatively unskilled burglar who will avoid alarm systems completely. His targets are usually medium risk commodities.

professional criminal. a person who depends upon criminal activities for at least a substantial portion of his or her income, and who has developed special, related skills.

professional reconstruction. in traffic accident investigations, efforts to determine how an accident happened. The process involves studying results of the accident, considering other circumstances, and applying scientific principles to form opinions relative to events of the accident which are otherwise unknown or are a matter of dispute.

proficiency testing specimen. a laboratory specimen having constituents that are precisely known to an outside agency (such as a licensing agency) but unknown to the testing laboratory or analyst. Proficiency testing specimens are used to evaluate technical competency for purposes of quality control, certification, and licensing.

pro forma. as a matter of form.

Program Evaluation and Review Technique (PERT). an approach to planning, organizing, directing, coordinating, and controlling the work efforts required to achieve the goals of a project of finite duration. PERT can help identify and correct problems that arise during a project. The chief value of the technique is the information that it generates concerning a project's current status. The project manager uses the generated information in exercising control of project activities.

The PERT methodology requires an identification of events to be passed through in order to complete the project. The events represent clusters of work tasks to be performed according to established specifications. The tasks are delineated as to sequence, timing, and in some cases, costs. A PERT chart will depict in a graphical format the project's planned chain of events, the work activities, and time/cost of getting from event to event.

progressive surveillance. a technique in which a subject is followed during a particular phase of his/her daily routine or during a specific period of time in one day. The surveillance is resumed on a later occasion at a phase or time when the previous surveillance was broken off. The several phases of surveillance constituting the subject's full routine are examined for the intelligence data they provide within the context of the investigation. This technique reduces the chance that the subject will spot the surveillance.

projection. an ego defense mechanism in which an individual places the blame for personal problems upon others, or attributes to others his or her own unethical desires and impulses.

projection sketch. a drawing of a crime scene in which the walls of a room or building appear folded out.

Project Label. a system operated by the Drug Enforcement Administration which produces a listing of all marketed drug products containing controlled substances.

promotion of prostitution. the soliciting or aiding in any manner of another to engage in prostitution, or the soliciting or aiding of another to secure the services of a prostitute, or knowingly receiving money or anything of value which is the proceeds of prostitution.

prompt. a message or indication that appears on a CRT display or printer which instructs the operator to take action.

proof beyond a reasonable doubt. proof which precludes every reasonable hypothesis except that which tends to support and which is wholly consistent with a defendant's guilt and inconsistent with any other rational conclusion.

property crime. a category of crime which includes such offenses as burglary, larceny-theft, motor vehicle theft, and arson. The term is frequently used in contradistinction to personal crime and violent crime.

Property Insurance Loss Register. a computerized register maintained by the American Insurance Association for the purpose of detecting false and duplicate claims, detecting fraudulent schemes involving fires, and identifying persons involved in arson-for-profit schemes.

property room. a place in a police department where evidence, lost and stolen property, and other accountable items are safeguarded pending use at trial, return to owners, destruction or other method of lawful disposition.

propoxyphene. a synthetic narcotic closely related to methadone. It is a Schedule II drug, and commercial preparations containing it are in Schedule IV. Darvon contains propoxyphene.

proprietaries. ostensibly private commercial entities established and controlled by intelligence services to conceal government affiliation or sponsorship of certain activities.

proprietary information. information owned by a company or entrusted to it which has not been disclosed publicly and has value.

proprietary drugs. drugs that are protected by some means against free competition as to name, product, composition, or process of manufacture.

proprietary interest. an interest applied where the federal government has acquired some right or title to an area in a state, but has not obtained any measure of the state's authority over the area. Where the federal government has no legislative jurisdiction over its land, it holds such land in a proprietary interest and has the same rights in the land as does any other landowner.

proscription. a term applied to a practice by the U.S. Supreme Court in which the police are told what they cannot do if they wish to introduce the results of interrogations in trials. Proscription is regarded as a "hands off" method for guiding law enforcement. In recent years, the practice has given way to a prescriptive approach in which the Supreme Court has passed down decisions that inform the police in very specific terms what they must do in order for defendants' statements and admissions to be used in prosecutions.

pro se. acting as one's own defense attorney in criminal proceedings; representing oneself.

prosecution withheld. an arrestee disposition in which the prosecutor suspends proceedings conditional upon behavior of the arrestee. Typically, a prosecution withheld disposition is associated with referral of the arrestee to probation or other criminal justice agency.

prosecutor. an attorney employed to initiate and maintain criminal proceedings on behalf of the government (people) against persons accused of committing criminal offenses.

prosecutorial screening decision. the decision of a prosecutor to submit a charging document to a court, or to seek a grand jury indictment, or to decline to prosecute. This process begins with a request by a law enforcement agency or other government agency, or a private citizen, that the prosecutor file a complaint or information or seek an indictment. The prosecutor can grant the request for a complaint, grant the request with some modification of the charges listed in the request, or deny the request.

prosocial behavior. activities associated with the dominant values of the society. A major goal of crime prevention, offender rehabilitation, and treatment of drug abusers is the enhancement of prosocial behaviors, such as seeking and holding a job, education and skill upgrading, and developing meaningful personal relationships.

prostitution. offering or agreeing to engage in, or engaging in, a sex act with another in return for a fee.

prostitution and commercialized vice. the name of a Uniform Crime Reports category used to record and report arrests for offenses relating to the promotion or performance of sexual acts for a fee.

protected class. in equal employment opportunity programs, a group of persons that in the eyes of Congress and the courts is entitled to certain employment protections for the purpose of correcting and reversing the effects of past discriminatory employment practices.

protected executive. a management person whose position in an organization exposes him or her to physical risk, such as assassination, kidnap, or extortion. The protection afforded is typically provided by a dedicated protective unit which functions according to procedures enunciated in a crisis management plan that has been approved by a senior decision making body, such as a board of directors.

protected executive data form. a form containing personal information concerning a key executive who is protected by the organization's crisis management plan. The nature of data on the form is such that it would be helpful in situations involving kidnap, extortion and similar acts directed against the executive and/or immediate family. Typically attached to the form are photographs and handprinting/handwriting examples.

protection racket. a form of extortion in which the victim, frequently a merchant, is forced by violence or the threat of violence to pay a fee for protection. The fee does not necessarily guarantee protection from harm by anyone except the extortionist.

protective custody. detention of an individual not amounting to an arrest. This practice is sometimes used to protect persons from reprisal by criminals.

protective services. measures that increase the personal protection of a dignitary or important person who may be the target of a criminal or terrorist act.

protocol. the official recording of an autopsy. The protocol is prepared by the person who conducts the autopsy, usually a medical examiner, and reflects procedures used in the examination, findings, and cause of death.

proton microscope. an optical apparatus capable of magnification in the range of 600,000, and is thus six times as powerful as the strongest electron microscope.

provisional exit. an authorized temporary exit from prison for appearance in court, work furlough, hospital treatment, appeal proceedings, or other purposes that require departure from prison but with expectation of return.

proxemics. the study of the interpersonal distances humans use in structuring transactions. The distances are: intimate, used where a close relationship exists; personal, which is not defensive but also not close; social, used in small groups and social situations; and public, used when interacting with larger groups. Proxemics has relevance to "personal space" in the context of interrogation.

proximate cause. the effective cause of loss or injury; the cause that sets other causes in operation; a responsible cause of an injury; an unbroken chain of cause and effect between the occurrence of an act and the damage it leads to. For example, improper training of a police officer can be the proximate cause of the officer's illegal actions on the job.

proximity fuse. a fuse designed to activate by radio signals; a bomb fuse designed to detonate at a given range from the target without requiring any physical contact with the target to initiate the firing action.

proximity test. a test used in firearms identification to determine the distance between muzzle and point of bullet contact. It is based on the proposition that a particular weapon, using particular ammunition, will disperse gunpowder residue in a particular pattern. The pattern produced in a proximity test can be compared against a pattern observed in a shooting incident under investigation.

pseudoheroinism. a term referring to the phenomenon whereby a heroin user believes himself to be physiologically addicted when such is not the case. It is possible for a person who uses heroin regularly but in small dosages to experience only minor withdrawal symptoms.

pseudoperforating gunshot wound. a wound in which the bullet does not exit the body and an exit wound is created by a bone fragment.

psilocin. an unstable hallucinogenic alkaloid contained in the Psilocybe mexicana mushroom. It is found with psilocybin, but in a smaller quantity.

psilocybin. a hallucinogenic alkaloid in a number of mushrooms of Mexico with the common name of teonanactyl, such as the Psilocybe mexicana. These mushrooms are used in traditional Indian rites and when eaten they affect mood and perception in a manner similar to mescaline and LSD. Another active ingredient of this mushroom is psilocin, and both can be synthesized chemically. They are listed in the Controlled Substances Act as Schedule I hallucinogens. Both are derivatives of tryptamine and chemically related to LSD and DMT, and usually taken orally. Psilocybin is extremely expensive to synthesize or extract, and most of what passes for it on the street is actually either LSD or a mixture of LSD and phencyclidine (PCP).

psychedelia. a collective term for the world of mindaltering drugs and drug takers as well as drug paraphernalia.

psychedelic drugs. consciousness-expanding or mind-manifesting drugs; the hallucinogens. This term has been widely used in the United States to refer to hallucinogenic drugs and is the preferred term of many users themselves. Others prefer the term hallucinogens, arguing that the term psychedelic incorrectly combines two Greek roots, is biologically unsound, and has acquired meanings beyond the drugs or their effects.

psychedelic experiences. heightened and often inappropriate emotional reactions, mood changes of an extreme character, tactile and visual distortions, and vivid hallucinations.

psychoactive substance. the term preferred by many to refer to drugs that affect the central nervous system and alter mood, perception, or consciousness. It is preferred as a substitute for "drug" because of the value-laden connotations and definitional confusions surrounding the latter term.

psychobabble. indiscriminate use of psychological concepts and terms as an affected style of speech.

psychodysleptic. a hallucinogen that is mind-disrupting.

psychogalvanic skin reflex. a not yet completely understood physiological phenomenon that is measurable with the polygraph instrument. By connecting an examinee's hand or fingers to small electrodes charged with a slight electrical current, the circuit is relayed through a galvanometer which balances the examinee's skin resistance against a fixed resistor. Minute changes in skin resistance are recorded and the polygraphist interprets the recording in forming an opinion.

psychograph. a profile of the human abilities required in the performance of a particular job.

psychological autopsy. an investigative technique used in suspected or apparent suicide cases. The technique attempts to determine whether death resulted from suicide, and if so, the motive. Information obtained from friends, relatives, and records is gathered, collated and analyzed. The technique provides a systematic means to examine social, personal, and physical events leading to the act.

psychological dependence. in regard to drugs, an ill-defined, broad term generally referring to a craving for or compulsion to continue the use of a drug that gives satisfaction or a feeling of well-being. Psychological dependence may vary in intensity from a mild preference to a strong craving or strong compulsion to use the drug. In severe cases, unpleasant psychological symptoms may develop if continued administration of the drug is stopped. The World Health Organization defines psychic dependence as "a feeling of satisfaction and a psychic drive that requires periodic or continuous administration of the drug to produce a desired effect or to avoid discomfort." In most instances, psychological factors are considered more important than any physical factors in maintaining chronic drug use. Psychological dependence is also often called behavioral, psychic, or emotional dependence, and is frequently a synonym for habituation.

psychological models. explanatory models derived from general psychological theories. There are many schools of thought pertaining to crime. In regard to heroin addiction, for example, many experts espouse psychological models which generally hold that (1) those who become abusers are psychologically disturbed, (2) drug abusers do further harm to their psychological state, and (3) sufficient psychological and/or psychiatric therapy and support can eventually enable them to abstain from drugs. Although this has been the most generally accepted model, the validity of each of these positions has been strongly criticized. The major criticism stems from research that indicates no common psychiatric diagnosis among drug abusers, among whom are found all kinds of people.

psychological profile. a description of the personality and characteristics of an individual based on an analysis of acts committed by the individual. The description might include age, race, sex, socioeconomic and marital status, educational level, arrest history, location of residence relative to the scene of the act, and certain personality traits. A profile is based on characteristic patterns of uniqueness that distinguish certain individuals from the general population. Regarding criminal acts, patterns are deduced from a thoughtful analysis of wounds, weapon used, cause of death, position of the body, and similar conditions.

psychological stress analyzer. a lie detector that can be used without the subject knowing he/she is being tested. By analyzing the stress in the subject's voice it purports to determine whether or not the truth is being told. Also called a psychological stress evaluator.

psychological set. in polygraphy, a concept which holds that a person's fears, anxieties and apprehensions will be directed toward the situation which presents the greatest immediate threat to self-preservation or well-being, generally to the exclusion of all other less threatening circumstances.

psychological test. a general term for any effort (usually a standardized test) that is designed to measure the abilities or personality traits of individuals or groups.

psychopath. a person suffering from mental aberrations and disorders, especially one who perceives reality clearly except for his or her own social or moral obligations and seeks instant gratification in criminal or otherwise abnormal behavior.

psychopathology. broadly, that content area within behavioral science that specifies, describes, or predicts disordered or deviant behavior and involves an application of the principles of learning, motivation, perception, biology, and genetics insofar as they contribute to behavior in an effort to arrive at general explanatory laws to account for different kinds of behavior. The study of the significant causes and processes in the development of mental disorders as well as the manifestations of mental disorders.

psychopharmacology. the scientific study of the interactive effect of drugs on psychological and behavioral activity. The term was first used in the 1940s and 1950s but it was not until the discovery of LSD in 1943 and the synthesis of chlorpromazine that a systematic, scientific investigation of drugs that affect the mind became well organized. The science of psychopharmacology links the disciplines of psychiatry, psychology, pharmacology, and neurophysiology.

psychosocial models. explanatory models that define an undesirable activity, such as crime, as a problem associated with both psychological and social factors either as antecedents or consequents. Psychosocial models view crime primarily as a social problem with societal, psychological, and group determinants.

psychosomatic. a term referring to processes that are both somatic (bodily) and psychic (mental) in nature or origin. A psychosomatic disorder is one that is of the body but is psychogenic in nature.

psychotaraxic. a hallucinogen that is mind-disrupting.

psychotherapeutic drugs. drugs that (1) are used as medicines to alleviate psychic distress or as adjuncts to treatment of various physical disorders, and (2) are typically acquired through a doctor's prescription or over the counter at a drugstore. An older and less preferred term for such drugs is psychotropics.

psychotherapy. a technique of treating mental disorders by means of insight, persuasion, suggestion, reassurance, and instruction so that the patients may see themselves and their problems more realistically and have the desire to cope with them. Strictly used, the term includes only techniques such as psychoanalysis or psychodrama that are utilized by specialists. More broadly, it is applied to any informal talk aimed at personal adjustment.

psychotic disorder. a disorder characterized by a generalized failure of functioning in all areas of a person's life.

psychotogenic. producing hallucinations and psychotic behavior.

psychotomimetic. a drug that produces a state similar to or symptomatic of psychoses.

psychotropic drugs. a broad term referring

to psychoactive substances or to psychotherapeutic drugs.

public adjuster. an insurance claims adjuster who represents the policyholder by preparing and presenting claims to underwriters, and who is usually licensed for this purpose.

public defender. an attorney employed by a government agency whose official duty is to represent defendants unable to hire private counsel.

public disclosure. the passing of sensitive information or materials to any member of the public.

public distance. the zone from 12 to 25 feet between individuals. Individuals interacting at this range are considered to be not personally involved.

public law. that part of the law which deals with the government either by itself or in its relations with individuals. Some of its branches are constitutional law, administrative law, public health law, vehicle and traffic law, and criminal law.

public officer. a person vested with a governmental power who performs a function for the benefit of the public.

puddle. in traffic accident investigations, a wet area on the road or roadside where liquid debris accumulates after a vehicle has come to rest. A puddle often marks the final position of a vehicle after an accident.

puddling effect. in arson investigations, irregular burn patterns on floors and sub-floor surfaces caused by the natural flow of a liquid accelerant, such as gasoline.

pugilistic attitude. the posture of a person killed by burning. In this condition, the fists and arms are drawn up similar to a boxer's stance. The pugilistic attitude occurs when the large muscles in the legs and arms are subjected to intense heat, causing them to severely contract and pull inward toward the torso.

puller. a device which when inserted into the keyway of a lock or when attached to the spindle of a combination lock will allow the lock to be forcibly withdrawn. Also called a slammer.

pulmonary arrest. the cessation of spontaneous breathing.

pulmonary edema. an accumulation of fluid in the lungs.

pulverizer. a machine that pulverizes documents beyond recognition. It is usually used to destroy heavy, bulky documents such as ledgers and log books.

punch job. a safecracking technique in which the dial is forcibly removed. The exposed combination lock spindle is then punched into the safe's compartment with a heavy mallet.

puncture wound. a wound made by the insertion into the body of a sharply pointed instrument.

punding. a term referring to behavior, usually caused by massive doses of amphetamines, wherein the abuser loses the capacity to perform complex sequential acts in a rational manner. Instead, the abuser persists in repetitive and compulsive, but subjectively rewarding, manipulative tasks for hours or even days.

punishment concept. a concept of offender rehabilitation that is founded on four purposes: reformation, restraint, retribution, and deterrence.

Reformation is regarded by many criminologists as the most worthwhile goal of punishment. The real criticism of reformation, however, is simply that it hasn't worked. This criticism is supported by much evidence. It can be persuasively argued that the very nature of the prison system is contradictory to reformation.

Restraint is not a debatable proposition. It is necessary to protect society from unreformed criminals. One argument suggests that restraint should be either permanent (life imprisonment) or be coupled with meaningful rehabilitation. The force in this argument is that the penal system should attempt to both reform and restrain rather than merely keep criminals in custody.

Retribution is frequently challenged as a proper purpose of punishment. Opponents contend it is barbaric and inappropriate for a civilized society. Proponents contend it is morally correct to hate criminals and to inflict retribution upon them for their misdeeds. Whether retribution is or is not morally justifiable, most citizens demand it in some fashion. Some experts point out that in the absence of institutionalized retribution there is a danger that people will seek private revenge against criminals.

Deterrence aims at precluding further criminal activity by a defendant. The concept holds that positive sanctions imposed upon one convicted criminal will deter others with similar propensities.

punitive damages. damages awarded over and above compensatory damages which serve to make an example of, or punish, the wrongdoer. Also called exemplary damages.

pupillary reaction test. a test for detecting abnormal pupil dilation/constriction, strabismus, and nystagmus. The test is administered by a specially trained police officer to persons suspected of being under the influence. In identifying pupil dilation/constriction, the officer uses a small flashlight and a pupilometer card to measure the diameter of the pupil. The obtained measurement is compared against the standard (normal) measurement of a nonintoxicated person. The standard adult pupil in normal room light will measure between 2.9 and 6.5 millimeters in diameter. A measurement below or above the standard range is indicative of abnormal dilation or constriction. The testing officer also looks for strabismus and nystagmus. The former is the inability of one eye to attain binocular vision with the other due to an imbalance of eyeball muscles. It causes squinting and is an impairment indicator. Nystagmus is an involuntary rapid eyeball movement, a common indicator of recent drug or alcohol use.

pupilometer card. a file-card size device that contains circles of various diameters which approximate normal eye pupil sizes under various lighting conditions. It is placed on the cheekbone just below the eye so that a comparison can be made of the pupil and the circles on the card. A pupil that is larger or smaller than the circle representing the ambient light conditions is considered indicative of intoxication.

puranan test. a preliminary chemical test for identifying semen in a suspect stain. Puranan reacts to choline, a constituent of semen. However, since choline appears in small quantities in other body fluids, the test is not specific and not conclusive.

purge. the removal of arrest, criminal or juvenile record information from a records system.

purse snatching. grabbing a person's purse with intent to steal it or its contents. Because of the personal danger involved, it is usually punishable more severely than simple larceny or theft. Moreover, if the taker encounters physical resistance and forcibly overcomes it, the offense escalates to the more serious one of robbery.

pursuit driving. a police technique of operating a patrol vehicle so as to overtake and arrest a fugitive who is fleeing in another motor vehicle.

pusher. a drug dealer.

push knife. a thin, flexible blade that can be inserted in the space between a door and jamb to release a spring-loaded bolt.

putrefaction. enzymatic decomposition, especially of proteins, with the production of foul-smelling compounds.

pylorospasm. a spasm of the pylorus, a tubular portion of the stomach, which results in a lowering of the voice. Pylorospasms are sometimes seen in persons under the influence of heroin, or other powerful CNS depressants.

Pyramid Project. a prevention resource network developed by the National Institute on Drug Abuse. Pyramid staff and a nationwide network of resource people provide technical assistance, information, and technology transfer of workable models in prevention. Special areas of consultation are drugs and drug abuse, prevention strategies, prevention curriculum, program planning, needs assessment, community support, staff development, management/ organizational development, evaluation, training, funding, research, conference/ workshop planning, model programs, resource identification, special issues, and other technical services.

pyramid sales scheme. a form of investment fraud in which the victim is offered a distributorship or franchise to market a particular product or service. The contract also authorizes the victim to sell additional franchises. The promoter represents that the marketing of the product or service will result in profits, but that the selling of the franchises will result in a larger and quicker return on investment. The victim consequently expends greater energies on selling franchises than on selling the product or service. Finally, a point is reached where the number of investors is exhausted, leading to the collapse of the pyramid.

The principal indicator of a pyramid sales scheme is the emphasis on the money-making potential of selling distributorships rather than on the earnings possible from selling the product or service itself, which is usually overpriced. Other indicators are claims of enormous profits made by earlier investors, and hard-sell techniques to recruit distributors.

pyrolagnia. sexual pleasure derived from setting fires. Some arsonists have been found to be afflicted with pyrolagnia.

pyrolysis. the decomposition of organic matter by heat.

pyromania. a compulsion or mania to set things on fire.

pyrotechnic grenade. a grenade used to deliver a chemical agent to the target. Upon ignition, the grenade releases an opaque cloud of vaporized agent. The release period will last for 4–5 minutes while the grenade is burning. When the grenade is of a type that is thrown (as opposed to being launched) it may be called a pyrotechnic wand.

Quaalude. the trade name of a widely abused synthetic sedative chemically unrelated to the barbiturates. A large dose can cause convulsions and coma, and chronic use can lead to dependence. Quaalude is usually taken orally or injected. On the street it is called lude and 714. Quaalude is no longer legally manufactured, but supplies of this drug continue to reach the illicit market from clandestine laboratories.

qualified endorsement. an endorsement on a financial instrument that qualifies or limits the liability of the endorser. For example, if an endorser endorses an instrument "without recourse," he does not assume liability in the event the maker fails to pay the instrument when due.

qualitative test. a test that identifies the components of a specimen. A qualitative test seeks to identify specific components, while a quantitative test seeks to measure the amounts or proportions of the components in a specimen.

quality assurance. in crime laboratory operations, practices and protocols designed and enforced to assure accurate findings. Quality assurance techniques include the use of blind samples, spiked samples, and proficiency testing specimens.

quantitative test. a test that determines the amounts or proportions of a specimen. In drug testing, for example, a quantitative test will measure the concentration of a drug in a urine sample. A qualitative test, on the other hand, will identify the drugs that are in the urine but not in terms of amount or volume.

quantity/distance. a term relating to safety standards or directives that control the amounts and kinds of explosives that may be stored and the proximity of such storage to buildings, highways, railways and other facilities.

quantum meruit. the amount deserved. It is the relief in money awarded to a plain-tiff in an action based on a contract implied by law.

quarter piece. one-fourth of an ounce of a drug.

quash. to make void and without effect.

quasi-contract. a legal doctrine applied to situations in which there is no specifically drawn contract. It prevents unjust enrichment or injustice by treating the situation as if a contract actually had been in effect.

quasi-crime. an offense not classified as a crime but is in the nature of a wrong against the public, and which is frequently punished by a fine, forfeiture or similar penalty.

query. in computer operations, the process by which a master station asks a slave station to identify itself and to give its status; an operation at a terminal that elicits a response from the system.

questioned document. a document whose genuineness is questioned, normally because of origin, authenticity, age or the circumstances under which the document was written. A crime laboratory will usually include a questioned documents unit to perform examinations of handprinting, handwriting, typing, the instruments used for making documents, inks, alterations, erasures, and burnt or charred writings.

question spacing. in polygraphy, the elapsed time between an answer given by an examinee and the following question asked by the polygraphist during a test. The elapsed time is usually not less than 15 seconds.

queue. a line or list formed by items in a system waiting for service. For example, patrol assignments to be performed or messages to be transmitted.

quick entry. no-knock entry made by law-enforcement officers.

quick match. cord impregnated with

black powder and used as a fast-burning fuse.

quick plant. an audio bugging transmitter that is easily installed or dropped in the target area.

quickpoint. a type of gun sight designed to eliminate the need to sight down the barrel. The shooter's eye is assisted by a painted dot on the gun sight which when centered on the target provides an accurate sight picture.

quid pro quo. something for something.

quiet air. airwaves undisturbed by radio transmissions. Quiet air is the opposite of busy air.

quill. a folded matchbox cover from which a powdered drug is snorted.

quinine. a substance commonly used to dilute or cut heroin but which also has legitimate uses.

quit claim. a full release and acquittance given by one to another in regard to a certain demand, suit, or right of action. For example, a quit claim deed is a release of the maker's interest in land.

quorum. the number of people which must be present at a meeting before the business of the meeting can be properly transacted.

quo warranto. by what right or authority.

rabies. a disease of the central nervous system affecting all warm-blooded animals. It may be transmitted to humans by bite of the affected animal.

race horse charlie. a long-time narcotic addict; a chronic user of opium or its derivatives.

Racketeer Influenced and Corrupt Organizations Act (RICO). federal legislation passed in 1970 that sets strict penalties relative to patterns of racketeering activity. It enumerates offenses which constitute racketeering, e.g., bribery, counterfeiting, interstate theft, extortionate credit transactions, mail and wire fraud, Hobbs Act violations, and security frauds. A pattern of racketeering requires at least two acts, one of which must have occurred after the statute's effective date, and the oldest of which must have occurred within ten years after the commission of a prior act. The law calls for severe penalties and civil redress provisions, including treble damages to any injured party.

racketeering. obtaining money or other valuables by fraud, illegal use of political advantage, or threat of violence. The term is most often associated with activities of organized crime.

rackets squad. an enforcement and investigative unit that gathers intelligence and conducts investigations, frequently in concert with the prosecutor's office, of racketeering activities, often with emphasis upon corrupt labor organizations, loan sharking operations, and commercial fraud operations.

rad. a measure of the dose of any ionizing radiation to body tissues in terms of the energy absorbed per unit mass of the tissue. One rad is the dose corresponding to the absorption of 100 ergs per gram of tissue.

radiac. a term used to designate various types of radiological measuring instruments or equipment. It is derived from the words "radioactivity detection indication and computation," and is normally used as an adjective.

radial. pertaining to the radius (bone of the forearm) or to the artery found on the thumb side in the forearm, wrist, and hand, the one usually used for taking the pulse.

radial cracks. a spider-web pattern of cracks in glass plate from which a determination can be made as to the direction of force and impact point.

radial loop. a fingerprint pattern in which a loop flows in the direction of the radius bone of the forearm.

radiation dose. the quantity of radiation absorbed, per unit of mass, by the body or by any portion of the body.

radiation fuse. a bomb fuse sensitive to minute detection of nuclear radiation. The actual functioning of the fuse is caused by an influence from the target being exerted on a sensitive detecting device within the fuse itself.

radioactive delay. the gradual diminishing of the quantity of a radioactive substance due to the spontaneous disintegration of nuclei by emission.

radioactive emanation. a gaseous product of the spontaneous disintegration of a radioactive substance. The most important radioactive emanations are actinon, radon and thoron.

radioactive isotope. by common usage, any radioactive nuclide produced in a reactor or in a particle accelerator.

radio frequency bandwidth. a portion of the electromagnetic energy spectrum used to transmit intelligible signals; the information-carrying capacity of a given system of radio communications; a particular group of radio channels.

radiograph. a shadow picture produced by passing x-rays or gamma-rays through an object and recording the variations in the intensity of the emergent rays on a photographic or sensitized film.

radioimmunoassay (RIA). a method of determining the concentration of a protein in

a serum by monitoring the reaction produced by the injection of a radioactive-
labeled substance known to react in a
particular way with the protein being
studied.

radio interference. the inhibition or prevention of clear reception of a broadcast signal.

radiological control area. an area encom-
passing all known or suspected radiological contamination at a nuclear weapon
accident site.

radio spectrum. the entire range of frequencies in which useful radio waves can be
produced. It extends from approximately
15 kiloherz to 30,000 megaherz.

radiotelephone. a communications system
in which voice messages and other information are transmitted over radio
frequencies.

rain barrel effect. sound on an overcom-
pensated (equalized) line.

raising. in forgery, altering a check to
increase the amount payable.

rake gun. a tool used by auto thieves to
defeat car and ignition door locks. The
handle and trigger appear similar to that
on a caulking gun. The barrel of the
device is a lockpicker's rake that slides
forward and backward upon activation
of the trigger.

random access. access of computer data in
a random fashion, without having to consider all irrelevant data on the device, or
in file, that precede the needed data.

random number. a number selected from a
known set of numbers in such a way that
the probability of occurrence of each
number in the set is predetermined; a
number obtained by chance; one of a
sequence of numbers considered appropriate for satisfying certain statistical tests;
one of a sequence of numbers believed to
be free from conditions that might bias
the result of a calculation.

random sample. a sample of units drawn
from a larger population in such a way
that every unit has a known and equal
chance of being selected.

range. the set of values that a quantity
or function may take; the difference
between the highest and lowest value

that a quantity or function may assume.

rape. unlawful sexual intercourse, by force
or without legal or factual consent.

rape kit. any of several types of kits, some
of which are available commercially and
others made from commonly available
materials. A kit typically consists of paper
bags to collect the victim's clothing and
bedsheets, sterile envelopes, vials, microscope slides, and swabs for collecting
debris (hairs, fibers, soil, grass, etc.) and
body fluids (blood, seminal fluid, saliva,
fecal matter, etc.), and a sterile comb for
obtaining pubic hair samples.

rape without force or with consent. sexual
intercourse with a female legally of the
age of consent, but who is unconscious,
or whose ability to judge or control her
conduct is inherently impaired by mental defect, or impaired by intoxicating
substances.

rapid eye examination. an examination made
of the eyes for the purpose of identifying
such drug use indicators as strabismus,
nystagmus, pupil dilation, constriction,
nonreaction, red sclera, and red conjunctiva. Such examinations are frequently
conducted by trained persons (who may
or may not be from the medical field)
incident to "for cause" situations such as
suspected impairment while operating a
motor vehicle.

rap sheet. a file or document containing
such data as a subject's arrest record,
charges preferred and case dispositions.
Also called an information sheet or criminal history sheet.

RDX. a type of booster explosive.

reaction distance. the distance a moving
vehicle travels between the time the driver
perceives a hazard and the time the body
initiates a responsive action, such as
applying the brakes or engaging in a
maneuvering action. For example, if a
driver's reaction time is three-fourths of
a second and the vehicle is traveling at
45 miles per hour, the vehicle will travel
49 feet from the time the driver perceives the hazard and brings his foot into
contact with the brake pedal.

reaction formation. an ego defense mechanism which prevents dangerous desires and impulses from being carried out by fostering opposed types of behavior and attitudes.

reaction time. in traffic accident investigations, the time between a driver's perception of a hazard to an action taken in response to it.

read-out. a means for displaying an electronically transmitted message in a form meaningful to human intelligence.

read/write protection. in computer operations, restriction of access to a data set, file, or storage for reading and writing by a user or program not authorized to do so.

real evidence. evidence furnished by the things themselves as distinguished from a description of them; tangible items of evidence such as a gun, or a bullet.

real-time process. in computer usage, a process that responds to events in related or controlled processes as they occur, rather than when the computer is ready to respond to them.

rear end collision. a collision between two vehicles moving in the same direction on the same roadway. Also called a same-direction collision.

reasonable care. the care that prudent persons would exercise under the same circumstances.

reasonable cause. a combination of facts and circumstances which would warrant a person of reasonable intelligence and prudence to believe that an offense has been or is being committed.

reasonable doubt. any uncertainty in the minds of jurors which would cause them to find a defendant not guilty of a crime. In order to convict, the government must prove that the accused is guilty beyond any reasonable doubt.

reasonable force. the least amount of force that will permit an officer to subdue or arrest a subject while still maintaining a level of safety for himself and the public.

reasonable person concept. a legal concept which applies objective standards of reasonableness when judging whether conduct is negligent. The law does not make special allowance for the particular weaknesses of a person acting negligently. Conduct which creates an unreasonable risk of harm is no less dangerous because the actor lacked the capacity to conform to an acceptable level of performance. While it may seem unfair to hold some people to standards they cannot always meet, it would be more unjust to require the innocent victims of substandard conduct to bear the consequences.

The standard is usually stated as "ordinary care" or "due care" or "reasonable care" measured against the hypothetical conduct of a hypothetical person, i.e., the reasonable man of ordinary prudence. Such a person is not the average or typical person, but an idealized image. He is a composite of the community's judgment as to how the typical citizen ought to behave in circumstances where there is a potential or actual risk of harm. The reasonable person is not perfect or infallible. He is allowed mistakes of judgment, of perception, and he may even be momentarily distracted. Above all, he is human and prone to errors, but such errors must have been reasonable or excusable under the circumstances.

reason to suspect. a combination of facts and circumstances not amounting to probable cause.

rebuttable presumption. a presumption that is open to rebuttal by evidence; a presumption which stands until disproved. For example, the presumption that a 13 year old boy cannot be charged with rape by reason of inability to obtain erection and penetration may be rebutted by proof of his ability to actually do so.

rebound dilation. an eye pupil dilation in which the pupil alternately opens and closes without regard to normal stimuli. It is indicative of impairment by reason of drug use.

rebuttal. the proof presented at a trial by the plaintiff intended to overcome the evidence introduced by the defendant.

receipt of stolen property. the crime of receiving, holding, or concealing property. Also, a section of the U.S. Code that prohibits the receipt, concealment, sale or disposal of goods, wares or merchandise of value of $5,000 or more which have moved in interstate or foreign commerce with the knowledge that the goods had been stolen or unlawfully converted.

receive modem. a device for taking data from a telephone line.

recidivism. repetitive criminal behavior; habitual or confirmed criminality.

reciprocal transfer of evidence. the transfer of evidence, usually trace materials such as hairs and fibers, from criminal to victim and vice versa which occurs during crimes involving bodily contact.

reconciliation procedure. a control procedure that identifies and accounts for any difference between the values of a given balance and its associated control total. Reconciliation procedures, for example, might be used to inventory property in police custody or to audit a petty cash fund.

reconnaissance. a mission undertaken to obtain, by observation or other detection methods, information about the activities of persons or groups.

recording pens. the hollow, stainless steel styli seated in individual cradles atop a polygraph instrument. They are counterbalanced by adjustable nuts, and serve the function of marking the polygraph chart.

record prints. inked finger, palm or sole impressions obtained for identification purposes.

recreational drug use. drug use that, like experimental use, occurs in social settings among friends or acquaintances. Unlike experimental use, recreational use tends to be more patterned but considerably more varied in terms of frequency, intensity, and duration. Also called social use or social-recreational use.

rectangular coordinates method. in crime scene sketching, two measurements made at right angles of an evidential item to the nearest two permanent objects, usually walls. The distances measured are recorded in the crime scene sketch as a means of showing the exact location of the item. For example, if the crime scene is a room and the object to be mapped is a gun on the floor, two mutually perpendicular walls can be used as reference points. A measurement is made from the gun to one wall (north or south) and a measurement is made from the gun to another wall (east or west). The gun is then considered to be fixed or located, and can be shown in a sketch as lying in a particular spot.

red conjunctiva. an inflammation of the mucous membrane lining of the eyelids and the front of the eye (especially the latter). It is indicative of marihuana use.

Reddick v. New York. a case decided in 1980 in which the U.S. Supreme Court declared unconstitutional the New York statutory provisions authorizing police officers to enter a private residence without a warrant and, with force if necessary, to make a felony arrest after probable cause has been established.

redirect examination. the examination of a witness, after cross-examination, by the party which made the initial direct examination. After a redirect examination, the opposing party may make a recross-examination.

reduced charge. a new charge entered by prosecutorial action during the course of proceedings which replaces the original greater charge. It is sometimes called an included offense with respect to the original charge, but in fact can be an offense which has one or more elements which are not elements of the original greater charge.

reduced sentence. a sentence to confinement of which the time duration has been shortened by judicial action; also, a reduced fine or other material penalty.

reduced phenolphthalein test. a test to determine the presence of blood in a stain or substance of unknown origin. Like the benzidine test, it is preliminary in nature and not entirely conclusive.

redundant design. a design of machinery or equipment involving two or more components so arranged that failure of one will call one or more of the others into service.

reefer. a marihuana cigarette.

referee. a person to whom a case is sent by order of the court so that an investigation, examination, or report may be made. The referee is usually instructed to take testimony, hear the parties, and report results to the original court.

reference line. in traffic accident investigations, a line from which measurements are made to locate spots or items of investigative interest. The reference line is usually the edge of a roadway.

reference point. a point from which measurements are made to locate spots or items of investigative interest at the scene of a traffic accident. The reference point is sometimes the intercept of two reference lines, e.g., the point at which two roadways cross. A reference point, or RP, is typically described in notes and sketches in relation to permanent landmarks present at the scene.

referral to intake. a written request by a law enforcement agency, parent, or other agency or person, that an intake officer or unit take appropriate action concerning a juvenile alleged to have committed a delinquent act or status offense, or alleged to be dependent.

reflex action. in traffic accident investigations, an instinctive act resulting from perception of an imminently hazardous situation; an involuntary response to a stimulus.

reformatory. a correctional facility that was originally conceived of as a place where offenders would reform or change their criminal behavior, attitudes and values. In modern usage, it is a place where juvenile offenders are kept in custody.

refractive index. the ratio of the velocity of light in a substance to the velocity of light in a vacuum. Since the refractive index is a specific constant of a substance, it is used as a means of identifying and differentiating between substances. The refractive index principle is an important analytical tool in the crime laboratory.

refractometer. a device for measuring the refractive index of a substance.

refresh the memory. the use of notes or memoranda to stimulate or revive a testifying witness' recollection. Such notes or memoranda can be taken as evidence.

refund operator. a thief who specializes in obtaining cash refunds from a retail store for merchandise that was acquired by shoplifting or the use of bad checks or fraudulent credit cards.

regenerative feedback. a squeal caused by the output of an amplifier feeding back to its own input.

Regina v. Steeves. a Canadian court case in which an appeals court ruling drew a distinction between a person who is compellable by law as a witness to answer questions and could be found in contempt for refusing to do so and a person questioned by the police who is not compelled by law to answer their questions. This ruling emphasizes voluntariness as a qualification of a confession.

register. a showing of blood in a syringe at time of injection which indicates that the needle has punctured the vein.

registered informant. an informant of the police who is registered for the purpose of demonstrating at trial the informant's credibility, reliability, and continuity as a source of information useful to law enforcement and investigations. The manner of registration is determined by the police agency controlling the informant and is formalized to the extent that registration can be shown as a process for differentiating between informants who only provide fragmentary and unreliable data and informants who provide significant and reliable data.

regression analysis. a method for describing the nature of the relationship between two variables, so that the value of one can be predicted if the value of the other is known.

Regulation Z. a term describing rules issued by the Board of Governors of the Federal Reserve System as regards implementation of the Truth-in-Lending Act.

regulatory crime. a crime that violates an order of a federal or state regulatory agency. For example, insider trading is a regulatory crime because it violates regulations enforced by the Securities and Exchange Commission.

regurgitate. to flow backward as with the expulsion of stomach contents or the backflow of blood through a defective heart valve.

rehabilitation. the restoration of a person to the best possible level of functioning after suffering a behavioral disorder; the change of an offender's behavior, mental attitude, and values in such a way that he ceases committing criminal acts.

Reinsch test. a chemical test for determining if a death resulted from arsenic poisoning. The test is applied to the liver, gall bladder, kidneys, and other viscera. Because arsenic will seldom remain in the viscera of living persons longer than 15 days, the earlier presence of it in the body of a deceased may be found in an examination of hair, nails and bone, using a different analytical procedure such as neutron activation analysis.

relation character. a character that expresses a relationship between two operands. For example, the character > means greater than, < means less than, and = means equal to.

relative frequency. in frequency distributions, the frequency of a specific class mark divided by the total number of figures in the data.

release. conditional, temporary, or permanent discharge from custody.

release on bail. a pretrial release in which re-appearance is guaranteed by a pledge that money or property will be forfeited upon nonappearance, with or without payment of a bondsman's fee or deposit of some or all of the pledge with the court.

release on own recognizance. a pretrial release in which the defendant signs a promise to appear but does not pledge anything of value to be forfeited upon nonappearance. Also called ROR.

release to parole. a release from prison by discretionary action of a paroling authority, conditional upon the parolee's fulfill-

ment of specified conditions of behavior.

release to third party. a pretrial release without financial guarantee in which a person or organization other than the defendant assumes responsibility for returning the defendant to court when required.

relevant evidence. evidence having a tendency to make the existence of a fact more probable or less probable than it would be without the evidence; evidence which is directly related to the offense and tends to prove or disprove any fact at issue.

relevant question. in polygraphy, a question pertaining directly to the issue being tested. In theory, a relevant question will produce in the guilty subject a response recordable by the polygraph instrument. Also called a crucial, pertinent or material question.

Relman Report. the report of a 1980–81 government-sponsored study of marihuana research findings. The report concluded that "the weight of evidence from human studies indicates that neither marijuana nor THC cause chromosome damage." The Relman Report was accurate in light of what was known at that time.

remand. to recommit, as when a prisoner's habeas corpus application is dismissed and he is remanded to prison.

remedial law. law concerned with the procedure involved in carrying out substantive law, i.e., the laws of arrest, trial, bail, etc.

remote terminal. a device for communicating with a computer system from a location that is apart from the central computer facility.

removable cylinder revolver. a general class of revolver constructed with the barrel firmly fixed to the frame and a revolving cylinder that is removed for loading/unloading by taking out the cylinder pin on which it rotates.

render safe. to employ particular procedures or modes of action to recover, neutralize and finally dispose of explosive ordnance or other hazardous materials; explosive ordnance procedures which provide for the interruption of functions or separation of essential components to prevent a detonation or function.

rendition. the surrender or delivery of a person by the senior executive of the state or area to which the person has fled.

rent-a-cop. a term describing the practice of hiring police officers to perform security officer duties.

reparole. a release to parole occurring after a return to prison from an earlier release to parole, on the same sentence to confinement.

repeating firearm. a gun, rifle, or pistol designed to discharge several shots without reloading.

replevin. a court action to recover possession of property unlawfully taken or detained. Title to the property must be in the person bringing the action. Thus, if title passes to the buyer and the seller refuses to deliver the goods, the buyer may bring an action in replevin to get possession of the goods. Or the seller, under a conditional sale contract by which he retains title to the goods until payment is made, may recover the goods by an action in replevin if the buyer does not make the payments called for by the contract.

reply. the document submitted by the plaintiff to a lawsuit in answering the counterclaims of the defendant.

reprieve. a stay or delay in the execution of a sentence.

request standards (writing). handwriting or handprinting samples obtained at the request and in the presence of an investigator so that such writings can be compared by a questioned documents examiner with other writings pertinent to the case.

request to appeal case. a case filed in an appellate court by submission of a petition asking that the court review a judgment or decision of a trial court, administrative agency, or intermediate appellate court.

res adjudicata. a legal doctrine which holds that a controversy once having been decided or adjudged upon its merits is forever settled so far as the particular parties involved are concerned. Its purpose is to avoid vexatious lawsuits.

res gestae. things done; transactions.

resident. a prisoner or inmate.

residential treatment center. a residence in which offenders are temporarily living, under conditions less confining than in a jail or prison, and where the major emphasis is on therapy.

residual air. in polygraphy, air remaining in the lungs even after the deepest possible expiration.

res ipsa loquitur. a theory of recovery for personal injury which presumes that under certain conditions the injury would not have occurred if the defendant had been careful.

resisting an officer. resisting or obstructing a law enforcement officer in the performance of an official duty.

res judicata. the legal defense that the issue presented has previously been adjudicated between the same parties.

resonance control. a control on a polygraph instrument that permits the polygraphist to narrow an excessively wide cardiographic tracing.

respiratory arrest. the cessation of spontaneous breathing.

respondeat superior. let the master respond; a legal doctrine that holds an employer liable for negligent acts of his employees that occur while the employee is working within the scope of the employer's authority and in his or her interest. The concept is based on the doctrine that the employee is acting on the employer's behalf as the employer's agent. Another term used in this connection is "vicarious liability," so called because the employer assumes liability for acts performed by someone else.

The courts have developed over the years a doctrine of time, place, and purpose. If the employee's harmful conduct occurred during the employee's normal working hours at a place considered appropriate for the job, and if it resulted from an act whose purpose was to serve the employer's interest, then there is a legal basis for holding the employer accountable under respondeat superior. For example, if a police officer working off duty as a security officer uses excessive force to capture an intruder on the employer's premises, the employer could be held liable on the basis of time (normal working hours), place (employer's premises), and purpose (serving the employer's interests).

A related doctrine is ratification. An employee may have injured someone outside the scope of employment, but if the employer knows about it and in some fashion indicates approval, there can be grounds for imposing liability.

respondent. the person who formally answers the allegations stated in a petition which has been filed in a court; in criminal proceedings, the one who contends against an appeal.

response overload. stimuli so excessive or demanding that the system they are acting upon is unable to respond.

response time. the amount of time between the receipt of a request for police service and the time a police officer arrives to provide the requested service.

restitution. the act of giving back money or property that was stolen. This may be done voluntarily, perhaps in hopes of obtaining a more lenient sentence, or it may be ordered by a court as part of a sentence or as a condition of probation. Restitution does not necessarily relieve an accused of the necessity of standing trial and facing criminal sanctions, but it often does so in practice, or it acts to placate a complainant and to reduce the severity of the sentence.

restraint of trade. illegal action taken to prevent the free flow of goods in a market economy. Restraint of trade may take such forms as the holding back of improved products, the monopolistic control of raw materials, or agreement among corporations to fix prices and to not compete against each other.

restrictive endorsement. an endorsement used in negotiating a negotiable instrument to a person for a specific task such as "for collection only."

resuscitation. the act of reviving an unconscious individual by means of artificial ventilation with or without the use of cardiac massage.

retained counsel. a defense attorney selected and compensated by the defendant or offender, or by other private person or persons.

retentionist. one who favors the retention or reinstitution of capital punishment.

retrial. any trial in which issues of fact and law are examined that have already been the subject of an earlier trial. There are two distinct types of retrials: trial de novo and new trial. Trial de novo takes place in a court having incidental appellate jurisdiction, usually a court of general jurisdiction. A new trial is conducted in the same court in which the earlier trial took place, ordered by that same court or by a higher court having appellate jurisdiction.

retribution. the just-deserts theory of punishment which holds that an offender should suffer to the extent deserved by the seriousness of the crime so that justice may be served.

retrograde amnesia. a loss or impairment of memory usually resulting from an injury. In a traffic accident, a person who has been unconscious for a considerable time or whose injury prevents recollection of events immediately preceding the crash.

return. the endorsement made by an officer upon a warrant, stating that he or she has done what was required by the warrant.

revenge. a motive imputed to a defendant; a motive for punishment; retaliation.

revenge fire. arson motivated by revenge, jealousy, disgruntlement, or similar reason.

reversed gas meter theft of service. a theft of gas service in which the gas meter is disconnected from the gas line piping and is remounted in a reverse configuration. The gas flowing backwards through the meter will cause the meter readings to operate in reverse.

reverse tolerance. a condition in which the response to a certain dose of a drug increases with repeated use.

reversible error. an error sufficient to warrant a reversal of judgment by an appellate court; substantial error claimed as prejudicial to the complaining party's case.

revolver. a handgun with a revolving cylinder holding a number of rounds of ammunition that mechanically brings each bullet in line with the breech of the gun barrel before firing each time the trigger or hammer is activated. Usually, a cylinder holds six rounds of ammunition.

revolving door justice. a term critical of the manner in which the criminal justice system repeatedly releases dangerous defendants.

Rh factor. the name used to describe blood when an antigen is present or absent on the red cells. When the Rh factor is present, the blood is said to be Rh-positive, and when absent, the blood is said to be Rh-negative.

rhodamine B. a tracing powder used to mark objects likely to be touched by a culprit. The powder is converted to a cherry-colored dye by the skin's natural moisture.

Rhode Island v. Innis. a case decided in 1980 in which the U.S. Supreme Court addressed the meaning of "interrogation" as pertains to Miranda. In this case, the defendant at time of his arrest without a warrant for murder was advised of his rights. A second police officer who arrived at the arrest scene made a second rights warning. Neither officer obtained a waiver nor was Innis interrogated. Shortly thereafter a third rights warning was given by a police captain. Innis asked for an attorney, at which point the captain arranged to have him transported to police headquarters. Three officers assigned to the transporting vehicle were instructed to not question Innis or coerce him in any way. Enroute to the police station, two officers engaged in a conversation which suggested that the murder weapon, a shotgun, was most likely concealed near a school for handicapped children and needed to be recovered before it caused injury to a child who might find it. Innis, who clearly heard the conversation, asked the officers to return to the scene of the arrest so he could lead them to the shotgun. At no time were direct questions asked of Innis. Upon arrival at the arrest scene, Innis was given another rights warning. He acknowledged that he understood his rights, wanted to lead the police to the murder weapon, and he did so. The weapon was later introduced at trial and Innis was found guilty.

The Rhode Island Supreme Court reversed the conviction, holding that the conversation of the officers in the presence of Innis amounted to "interrogation" in the context of Miranda. The U.S. Supreme Court disagreed. It defined "interrogation" as either express questioning or its functional equivalent. Functional equivalent was explained as words or actions on the part of the police that they should know are reasonably likely to elicit an incriminating response from the suspect. The latter part of this explanation focuses primarily on the perceptions of the suspect, rather than the intent of the police. In applying this reasoning to the Innis case, the Supreme Court concluded that there was no express questioning or its functional equivalent, i.e., that there was no interrogation within the meaning of Miranda.

rice paper edition. rice paper upon which incriminating information has been written so that the paper can be chewed and swallowed if its owner is in imminent danger of being caught, as in a raid on a numbers racket.

ridge characteristics. ridge endings, bifurcations, enclosures, and other ridge details, which must match in two fingerprints in order for their common origin to be established. Also called minutiae.

ridge count. in fingerprint classification, the number of fingerprint ridges between the core and the delta. The count is made by drawing an imaginary line from the core to the delta. The friction ridges that intersect the line are counted.

riding the wave. under the influence of a narcotic.

rifling characteristics. in firearms identification, the number, dimensions and direction of twist in the barrel of a weapon, plus its caliber. These general features help an examiner match a particular firearm with particular bullets.

righteous dope fiend. a drug user to whom status is allocated by peers according to the size of his or her heroin habit and success as a hustler. Righteous dope fiends prefer heroin above all other drugs and consider themselves members of the elite world of opiate users.

rights of defendant. those powers and privileges which are constitutionally guaranteed to every defendant. At the time of arraignment a defendant is typically informed of the right to remain silent; the right to a court-appointed attorney if the defendant does not have the financial means to privately retain an attorney; the right to release on reasonable bail; the right to a speedy public trial before a jury or judge; the right to the process of the court to subpoena and produce witnesses in the defendant's behalf and to see, hear and question the witnesses appearing before the defendant; and the right not to incriminate himself or herself.

right to counsel. a provision of the Sixth Amendment to the U.S. Constitution which requires that in all prosecutions the accused shall enjoy the right to have the assistance of counsel for his defense. The Supreme Court has held that where incarceration may be a consequence of the prosecution, the defendant is entitled to appointed counsel in the event he cannot afford one.

Right to Financial Privacy Act of 1978. an act that limits government access to private records, specifically financial records, and affords the individual the ability and methods to challenge governmental searches for such records.

rigid borescope. an optical instrument consisting of a series of lenses, mirrors, prisms, and an illumination means (usually a bundle of fibers), all assembled into a rigid tube which allows inspection or surveillance of a field of view. Rigid borescopes were originally developed for use by industry in looking into tightly constricted places, such as the inside of an engine block. Borescopes have been introduced into police work as peephole viewing devices.

rigor mortis. a stiffening of the body's muscles after death in a generally predictable pattern and time frame. It first appears in the face and jaws, before proceeding downward through the neck to the arms, chest and abdomen and finally to the legs and the feet. Rigor mortis of the entire body occurs within eight to twelve hours after death, but eighteen more hours may pass before the body is completely enveloped. Rigor mortis is an indicator of time of death.

riot. the coming together of a group of persons who engage in violent and tumultuous conduct, thereby causing or creating a serious, imminent risk of causing injury to persons or property, or public alarm.

rip job. a method of safecracking in which a hole is drilled in one corner, a crowbar is inserted, and the exterior surface is ripped off or peeled back. Also called a peel job.

riser jumper. a section of cable, sometimes consisting of nothing more than automobile booster cable, used in the theft of electric service. The thief, typically a former subscriber whose account was terminated for nonpayment or prior theft of service, will restore electrical power by attaching a riser jumper at the point where the utility wire leading from the service pole is attached to the roof peak or eaves.

risk assessment. an analytical technique for identifying, evaluating, and documenting the risks to which a facility and system are vulnerable, the control measures available to counter the identified risks, and the value attached to the facility or system should a major loss or disruption occur. This technique produces recommendations for correction of noted vulnerabilities, a plan of action for implementing recommendations, and operating procedures designed to prevent or minimize loss and disruption.

Risk assessment is based on certain common and observable risks in the physical environment. The conditions that produce these risks are (1) inadequate lighting, (2) inadequate physical barriers to individual structures, (3) places of concealment from which criminal attacks can be launched and to which criminals can flee and find refuge within, (4) situations (social, political and otherwise) which create access difficulties for law enforcement, and (5) a growing number of community areas which are difficult for the police to patrol, such as construction sites, transportation depots, shopping malls, parking complexes, parks, playgrounds and housing projects.

risk spreading. a concept in which physical, electronic, and procedural measures are applied singly or in combination to directly oppose criminal attack. The objectives of risk spreading are to deter or discourage the criminal from attacking, detect the criminal if an attack is made and initiate a response, delay the criminal so that the response action can be consummated, and deny the criminal access to the protected targets.

Ritalin. the trade name for a commonly abused amphetamine known generically as methylphenidate, a central nervous system stimulant used in the treatment of attention deficit syndrome in children. On the street it is called speed, upper, black beauty, crank, meth, bam, and pink.

rival hypothesis. an explanation that competes with the original hypothesis in a study.

roach. the butt of a marijuana cigarette or the cigarette itself, so called because after it has been smoked and/or shared it resembles a wet cockroach.

roach clip. a device for holding a hashish or marijuana cigarette so it may be smoked to the very end.

road. that part of the trafficway which includes both the roadway, which is the travelled part, and any shoulder alongside the roadway. Where there are unmountable curbs, the road and roadway are the same. If there is a guardrail, the road is considered to extend to the guardrail.

roadside. that part of a highway or street not occupied by a road or sidewalk.

road space. the path in which a vehicle is legally entitled to travel; a trafficway in which a vehicle may maneuver without interfering with other traffic units.

roadway. that portion of a highway improved, designed, or ordinarily used for vehicular travel, exclusive of the berm or shoulder. If there is a curb, the roadway is considered to extend to the curb, hence roadway may include lanes commonly used for parking. If there is a paved shoulder, the roadway may be distinguished from the shoulder mainly by a painted line marking the edge of the roadway.

robbery. the unlawful taking or attempted taking of property that is in the immediate possession of another, by force or threat of force.

robbery prevention. a combination of techniques that seek to convince the potential robber that in the commission of robbery the personal risks will be high and that the possible gain will be low. Such techniques are for the most part designed for execution by retail businesses that are targeted by robbers, and include these actions: (1) keep in the cash drawer the smallest amount of cash needed to operate, and use a drop safe or similar robbery-resistive container to store excess cash, (2) make bank deposits at least daily, vary the time and route, and use two people to make the deposits or use a courier service, (3) not allow unneeded cash to build up, (4) place notices in prominent places on the premises which announce the cash protection procedures, (5) arrange for maximum visibility of the cashier's counter from outside the premises, (6) provide initial and refresher training to store personnel concerning excess cash, post warning signs, maintain cashier visibility, and provide training on what to do when a robbery occurs, (7) maintain liaison with local law enforcement, especially with those officers who patrol in the immediate neighborhood, and (8) commensurate to the perceived crime risk, install alarm equipment and CCTV or a capability to photograph a robbery in progress, post warning signs that such equipment is installed, and mount cameras so they will serve as psychological deterrents.

Robinson v. California. a landmark 1962 Supreme Court decision resolving the constitutionality of a California statute making it a criminal offense to "be addicted to the use of narcotics." The court explicitly recognized that addiction constituted an illness rather than a crime, and that a sentence even as short as 90 days was cruel and thus unconstitutional if it were imposed as punishment for an illness.

rock. a purified form of cocaine that is smoked by inhaling the vapors that are given off as the drug is heated. It is in the form of small rock-like chunks which can be added to a cigarette or in a pipe, usually made of glass. Rock is more often called crack.

rockhouse. a place where crack, a form of cocaine, is sold and/or used. Also called a crackhouse.

roentgen. a unit of exposure of gamma (X-ray) radiation in the field of dosimetry. One roentgen is essentially equal to one rad.

roentgen equivalent man/mammal (REM). one REM is the quantity of ionizing radiation of any type which, when absorbed by man or other mammals, produces a physiological effect equivalent to that produced by the absorption of one roentgen of gamma radiation.

rogue's gallery. a photographic lineup; a structured environment in which a witness views photographs for the purpose of identifying a suspect. In a rogue's gallery, the witness is asked to pick out the suspect's photograph from a group of photographs of persons of the same general description. A variation is a talking rogue's gallery in which each photograph is accompanied by a taped recording of the photographed person's voice. This technique is usually done with the use of a "sound on slide" audiovisual system.

The rules for conducting a rogue's gallery are generally the same as for a live lineup, i.e., that the witness is not led by the police in anyway to select the suspect's photograph from among photographs presented for examination. A photographic lineup is not the examination of a mug shot book or similar file containing photographs of all known criminals, but is instead an attempt to match a particular suspect with a particular crime by having an eyewitness select the suspect from among a group of persons who meet the same general physical description. All methods of eyewitness identification are open to challenge by the defense. Also called a photographic lineup.

role conflict. a situation in which two or more social roles make incompatible demands on a person.

role expectations. commonly shared norms about how a person is supposed to behave in a particular role.

rolled impressions. inked fingerprint impressions obtained by rolling the fingers from one side to the other. This technique captures maximum ridge detail.

Rolleston Committee. the committee appointed in Britain after passage of the Dangerous Drugs Act in 1920 to recommend procedures for the distribution of opiates and the treatment of opiate addiction by the medical profession.

rolling resistance. the horizontal force required to keep a vehicle in motion on a level surface with the engine disconnected from the wheels and with no brake application; the drag factor produced by friction within a vehicle and deformation of its tires and road surface.

rollover. the motion of a vehicle which has

been retarded at the ground level while the remainder of the vehicle continues moving forward without leaving the ground.

rooter. a pickpocket who works alone, not as a member of team. Also called a single gunner or single cannon.

roper. a pimp; a member of a con artist team who spots and brings a victim into contact with other team members.

roping. undercover work in which the investigator assumes a different identity in order to obtain information.

rosette rivet. a type of rivet, so called because of the rose-like appearance of its cap, used by automobile manufacturers to affix VIN plates. The absence or alteration of rosette rivets on a VIN plate is indicative of vehicle theft.

rough sketch. a hand-drawn sketch made at a crime scene for the purpose of showing the exact relative positions of evidence and other objects.

round down fraud. a theft technique in which the criminal, typically a white collar employee, transfers to a dummy account the rounded-down remainders from the computation of interest pertaining to many accounts. The rounded-down remainder of each account may only be a fraction of one cent, but the total amount stolen can be significant when the number of accounts is large. The dummy account is usually set up in a way that will allow the criminal to make withdrawals without drawing suspicion.

rounder. that member of a shoplifting team who distracts the sales clerk by moving the clerk around and away from the merchandise targeted for theft.

route of administration. the method by which a drug is introduced into the body, such as by oral ingestion, intravenous injection, subcutaneous injection, intramuscular injection, insufflation (snorting), inhaling (smoking, sniffing, breathing), or absorption through the surface of the gums, anus, or genitalia.

rubber gas grenade. a tear gas grenade covered with rubber or soft plastic so as to minimize the possibility of injury when the grenade is fired into a rioting mob.

rubber head. a person having a poor memory as the result of drug abuse; a chronic PCP or marihuana user.

rubber lifter. a material used for lifting latent fingerprints. The material comes in sheet form or as a tape. A removable plastic cover protects the adhesive side of the lifter. The adhesive side is applied to a powdered print and peeled back, capturing the print. Rubber lifters work well on curved surfaces.

rub test. a field test for identifying a suspected counterfeit note. When rubbed with a soft cloth, a genuine note will give off a slight residue of ink which matches the ink color on the note. A counterfeit bill will give no residue or a residue of a slightly different shade.

rule of personal liability. a rule of law that states that everyone is responsible for his or her own negligent acts and that a wrongdoer cannot avoid legal liability for wrongdoing even though another is equally liable.

rule of strict construction. the requirement that a statute be interpreted literally in accordance with its terms, rather than its spirit. The rule is often applied to criminal statutes.

run. a period of continuous, heavy use of a drug. The term especially applies to the injection of amphetamine, which may last 3 to 5 days and usually ends when the user sinks into protracted, exhausted sleep.

runaway. a juvenile who has been adjudicated by a judicial officer of a juvenile court, as having committed the status offense of leaving the custody and home of his or her parents, guardians or custodians without permission and failing to return within a reasonable length of time.

runaway grand jury. a grand jury that asserts its independence of the prosecutor and, often assisted by a special prosecutor, presses investigations over and beyond the desires of the regular prosecutor.

rundown burn pattern. in arson investigations, charring seen on floor joists and other under-floor surfaces which suggests that burning liquid on the floor's surface flowed downward.

runner. a person who serves as a go between for dealers and buyers of drugs; an employee of a central station responsible for restoring an alarm at a subscriber's location and assisting the police or fire department who have responded to the alarm; an employee of a numbers or lottery operation who carries messages.

runoff. in traffic accident investigations, rivulets of liquid debris running downhill toward soak-in at the edge of the pavement. Tire prints can sometimes be observed in runoff which is revealing as to vehicle movement after a collision.

run the trapline. in criminal investigations, to check all sources of information for leads in a particular case.

rush. the initial onset of euphoria and physical well-being felt immediately after a drug has been injected. Rush is not the same as being high, which is the continuing state of relaxation and well-being experienced while the drug is effective. Intravenous injection produces the quickest, most intense rush.

Russian time cube. a sophisticated, yet easy to operate, electronic time delay device used in the construction of terrorist bombs.

rut. in traffic accident investigations, a depression in soft or loose material, such as dirt or snow, made by a rolling tire.

sabotage. the willful and malicious disruption of the normal processes and functions of an organization.

safe house. a meeting place known only to those who meet there which is free of detection or surveillance. A safe house is often a rented apartment or house where a detective can meet with his informant.

safety fuse. a cord containing a core of black powder. It is used to carry a flame at a uniform rate to an explosive charge.

salami technique. a white collar fraud scheme in which small amounts of money, frequently less than a dollar in each instance, are diverted from many separate accounts and credited to an account controlled by the perpetrator, usually with the help of a computer. The salami technique is similar to the lapping technique in which small amounts are debited from many accounts and then later credited back to give the appearance of correct balances when in fact the perpetrator is continuously removing funds from the system.

saliva. a clear, odorless, tasteless fluid produced by certain glands in the body to keep the mouth moist. The presence of saliva can be tested for in a crime laboratory. In secretors, saliva contains large amounts of the blood group substances (A, B, or H). Saliva also contains an enzyme called amylase which may be detected separately in persons who are non-secretors.

salvage switch. a fraud scheme for retitling a stolen vehicle. In this scheme, a badly damaged new vehicle is legally purchased as salvage scrap and the VIN plate is removed. A vehicle of the same make and model is then stolen, and its VIN plate is replaced with the plate from the salvage vehicle. A new title is obtained and the stolen vehicle is sold.

same-direction collision. a collision between two traffic units moving in the same direction on the same roadway. A rear end collision is a same-direction collision.

sandwiching. a shoplifter's practice of holding an item to be shoplifted against the outside of a purse or pocket just prior to concealment.

sanitize. the deletion or revision of a report or document so as to prevent identification of the sources and methods that contributed to or are dealt with in the report.

saponification. decomposition of the tissues of a dead body into adipocere (corpse fat). Saponification is usually seen as a soapy, greasy film on the limbs, chest wall, and buttocks, and is accompanied by a strong odor similar to stale cheese.

satch cotton. cotton used to strain a narcotic solution preparatory to injection.

satisfaction of judgment. a document which states that a recorded judgment has been paid and satisfied.

Saturday-night special. an inexpensive handgun, so called because of its use in robberies (on Saturday nights).

saucer pattern. a cone shaped pattern that appears in glass plate fractured by a penetrating force. In a cross sectional view, the tip of the cone is on the entering side of the glass with the large end of the cone on the exiting side.

sawed off shotgun. a shotgun having one or more shortened barrels, usually less than 18 inches in length.

saw job. a safecracking method in which a high-speed power saw with a diamond or carborundum blade is used to saw a hole into the safe.

scam. a crime, particularly a crime involving trickery. Also, an undercover police operation in which criminals are tricked into revealing their involvement in criminal activities. In the latter context, a scam is also called a sting.

scar. in traffic accident investigations, any mark on the road, ground or fixed object such that surface material is removed or displaced.

scatter diagram. a display of the relationship between variables using dots on a graph.

Schedule I Controlled Substance. a substance which has a high potential for abuse, has no currently accepted medical use, and for which there is a lack of accepted safety for use under medical supervision.

Schedule II Controlled Substance. a substance which has a high potential for abuse, has a currently accepted medical use or a currently accepted medical use with severe restrictions, and which may lead an abuser to severe psychological or physical dependence.

Schedule III Controlled Substance. a substance which has a potential for abuse, is less than the substances in Schedules I and II, has a currently accepted medical use, and which may lead to moderate or low physical dependence or high physiological dependence.

Schedule IV Controlled Substance. a substance which has a low potential for abuse relative to the substances in Schedule III, has a currently accepted medical use, and which may lead an abuser to limited physical dependence or psychological dependence relative to the substances in Schedule III.

Schedule V Controlled Substance. a substance which has a low potential for abuse relative to the substances in Schedule IV, has a currently accepted medical use, and which may lead an abuser to limited physical dependence or psychological dependence relative to the substance in Schedule IV.

schizoid personality. a personality characterized by unsociability, seclusiveness, serious mindedness, and eccentric behavior.

schizophrenia. a group of disorders characterized by thought disturbance that may be accompanied by delusions, hallucinations, attention deficits, and bizarre motor activity.

Schmerber v. California. a case in which the U.S. Supreme Court ruled that extraction of blood from a defendant for the purpose of determining intoxication was a search within the meaning of the Fourth Amendment. This decision has been put forth as a defense in many cases where persons were required to provide biologi-cal specimens such as blood, urine, tissue, hair, and saliva.

Schneckloth v. Bustamonte. a case in which the U.S. Supreme Court ruled that a person who consents to a search waives the Fourth Amendment right to be free from search without a warrant. According to this decision, the consenting party need not be advised of the right to refuse consent but is a factor to be considered by the court in determining voluntariness.

score. to purchase illegal drugs.

Scotch verdict. a verdict in which the charges against the defendant are declared not proved, and which permits the defendant to be charged and tried again if new evidence is found. So called because of its use in Scotland.

Scotland Yard. the popular name for the headquarters of the London Metropolitan Police. The office took its name from the original building's back premises, Scotland Yard, through which the public entered.

scrambler. a device that disguises information so as to make it unintelligible to those who should not obtain it.

scrape. in traffic accident investigations, a broad area of a hard surface covered with many scratches or striations made by a sliding metal part without great pressure.

scrap iron. a drink made from alcohol, mothballs, and hypochlorite.

screamer. in electronic countermeasures, an rf field strength and audio amplifier combination that causes feedback when positioned near a concealed transmitter.

scrimmage wound. a stabbing wound that has been enlarged by movement of the weapon or the victim. A notch along the side of the puncture is a characteristic of a scrimmage wound.

script writer. a physician who willingly prescribes drugs that are not medically justified; a forger of prescriptions.

scuffmark. a friction mark on a pavement made by a tire which is both rotating and slipping. Types of scuffmarks include acceleration scuffs, yawmarks and flat-tire marks.

search. the examination or inspection of a

location, vehicle, or person by a law enforcement officer or other person authorized to do so, for the purpose of locating objects relating to or believed to relate to criminal activities, or wanted persons.

search warrant. an order issued by a judicial officer which directs a law enforcement officer to conduct a search for specified property or persons at a specific location, to seize the property or persons, if found, and to account for the results of the search to the issuing judicial officer.

secobarbital. a commonly abused barbiturate, usually taken orally or injected. Also called barb, downer, blue, yellow jacket and sleeping pill.

secondary deviance theory. a theory which holds that societal reactions to deviant behavior encourage the individual to develop a deviant lifestyle or career, and concomitant self-concept. In this theory, a person publicly labeled as a deviant for some initial behavior will begin to adopt other deviant behavior or a role based on it as a means of defense to the problems created by society's reaction.

secondary evidence. evidence inferior to primary evidence. For example, secondary evidence might be oral testimony or a copy of an original document that cannot be found. Also called next best evidence.

secondary missile wound. a wound caused by a flying fragment created when a bullet or other projectile strikes an object in the environment nearby the victim.

secondary muscular flaccidity. a relaxed and flabby condition of the muscles of a dead body which occurs after the disappearance of rigor mortis and immediately prior to the onset of putrefaction. Secondary muscular flaccidity is a factor considered by the medical examiner in time of death determinations.

secondary password. in computer usage, a user password that may be required at log-in time, immediately after the primary password has been correctly submitted. Primary and secondary passwords can be known by separate users, to ensure that more than one user is present at the log-in.

secondary prevention. intervention to ward off drug abuse or addiction directed at those persons experimenting with drugs who are linked with but not yet absorbed into an addict subculture and for whom the risk of addiction is high.

secondary search. a type of search used after police officers have made a preliminary search in responding to a prowler report and have confirmed that a crime is in progress. A secondary search is usually conducted by four or more officers operating from an understood plan of action designed to effect an arrest of the criminals with minimum risk to human life.

secondary shock. a state of deep unconsciousness or profound depression of the vital processes associated with reduced blood volume and pressure. It is usually caused by severe injuries, burns or hemorrhage, and is frequently fatal. Also called irreversible shock.

second degree murder. killing committed during the course of a quarrel and in the heat of passion.

secretor. a person whose body fluids contain a water soluble form of the antigen of the A, B, O blood group found in his or her red blood cells. Approximately 80% of the population are secretors. The other 20% are called nonsecretors. Human saliva and semen are the two body fluids that contain the largest amounts of these substances.

secret writing. writing which is concealed by including it within the text of other writing or by the use of chemicals.

Section 1983 suit. a civil suit brought under Section 1983 of Title 42, USC, called "Civil Action for Deprivation of Civil Rights." Section 1983 states: "Every person who, under color of any statute, ordinance, regulation, custom, or usage, of any state or territory, subjects or causes to be subjected, any citizen of the United States or other person within the jurisdiction thereof to the deprivation of any rights, privileges or immunities secured by the Constitution and laws, shall be liable to the party injured in an action at law, suit in equity, or other proper proceedings for redress."

A Section 1983 suit is the primary vehicle used by litigants who seek damages and/or injunctive relief from the police (and other public officials) when there is an allegation that one's constitutional or federally protected rights have been violated.

According to the law and court decisions, four elements must be present for the suit to succeed: (1) the defendant must be a natural person (not a company or corporation) or a local government, (2) the defendant must be acting under color of law, (3) the violation must be of a constitutional or a federally protected right as opposed to a state protected right, and (4) the violation must reach constitutional level.

sector search. a type of crime or accident scene search in which the area to be searched is divided into sectors, grids, or quadrants. Individual officers are assigned to search one or more specific sectors. This search method is appropriate for a large area such as a length of highway, an office building, or an open field. Also called an area or zone search.

secure telephone system. a telephone system that uses scramblers and/or line supervision circuitry to enhance security of communications.

security and privacy standards. a set of principles and procedures developed to insure the security and confidentiality of criminal or juvenile record information in order to protect the privacy of the persons identified in such records.

Security File. the name of a file maintained by the U.S. Civil Service Commission. It lists persons who might be ineligible for government clearance because of questioned loyalty or subversive activities. The file is developed from published hearings of federal and state legislative committees, public investigative bodies, reports of investigation, publications of subversive organizations, and various newspapers and periodicals. The file is used by investigative and intelligence officials of federal agencies.

Security Investigations Index. a card file maintained by the U.S. Civil Service Commission. It lists persons investigated by the Commission and other agencies since 1939. Information from the index is available to investigators having a bona fide employment or investigative interest in a listed person.

sedative. an agent that decreases activity and excitability, relieves anxiety, and calms the person. Some sedatives have a general effect while others affect the activities of certain organs, such as the intestines or vasomotor system.

sedative/hypnotics. a major classification of nonnarcotic depressant drugs with such primary effects as calming, sedation, or induction of sleep (hypnosis). The sedative/hypnotics are usually divided into four categories: (1) barbiturates, (2) alcohol, (3) antianxiety-tranquilizers, and (4) nonbarbiturate, proprietary drugs. The antianxiety tranquilizers and the nonbarbiturate sedative/hypnotics are often grouped together and are the most widely used drugs in medicine. The sedative/hypnotics are also often called anxiolytic sedatives, depressants, psychosedatives, or psycholeptics.

sedition. an attempt, short of treason, to excite hostility against a sovereign government among its own citizens.

seizable items. items for which a search warrant may be issued. Examples of seizable items are instruments of a crime to include private papers, stolen or embezzled property, a kidnapped person, a human fetus or corpse, contraband, and other tangible evidence of the commission of a crime.

seizure. the taking into custody of law, by a law enforcement officer or other person authorized to do so, of objects relating to or believed to relate to criminal activity.

selective incapacitation. a sentencing strategy in which individual sentences are based on factors that predict future criminality, and which are used to identify and confine, for an extended period, those offenders who represent the most serious risk to the community.

Selective Traffic Enforcement Program (STEP). a federal program sponsored by the National Highway Traffic Safety Administration in which funds are granted to local police departments in the form of grants administered by state planning agencies. The funds support the attainment of certain objectives delineated by the NHTSA.

self-administration experiment. an experimental program in which drugs are made available to volunteers with histories of drug abuse for ingestion under conditions that permit the gathering of empirical information concerning the patterns and effects of drug self-administration. These experiments are usually conducted over the course of several weeks, and the subject is sequentially exposed to different experimental conditions. These experimental procedures were originally developed in studies made of ethanol self-administration, and have subsequently been extended to studies of other drugs of abuse.

self-defense. the protection of oneself or one's property from unlawful injury or the immediate risk of unlawful injury; the justification for an act which would otherwise constitute an offense on the ground that the person who committed it reasonably believed that the act was necessary to protect self or property from immediate danger. The self-defense protection against prosecution relies on the premise that every person has a right to defend himself from harm. The general rule is that a person may use in self-defense that force which, under all the circumstances of the case, reasonably appears necessary to prevent impending injury.

self-destructing seal. a seal which once in place cannot be removed without destroying it. Evidence tape is a type of self-destructing seal.

self-help group. a group formed to deal with one or more problem areas in which behavior control is the primary reward for participation. Perhaps the most well known self-help group is associated with alcoholism (Alcoholics Anonymous), but scores of groups exist across the country to deal with such varied problems as drug abuse, cigarette smoking, weight control, divorce, neurotic personality, compulsive gambling, ex-prisoner society reentry, family crisis, terminal illness, and the like.

self-incrimination. a testimonial or verbal communication from an individual or his performance of some physical act which requires his conscious mental cooperation, which utterance or act implicates him as being a perpetrator of criminal activity. The Fifth Amendment and the statutes of most states provide that no person can be compelled in a criminal action to be a witness against himself. This guarantee is purely personal and can be invoked only to protect the one required to testify. If the testimony merely tends to hold the witness in disgrace, but does not incriminate him, the privilege does not apply.

self-report study. an investigation by means of a questionnaire or similar device in which the respondent is asked to indicate the nature, extent, and frequency of personal illegal and deviant behavior. For example, the self-report approach might be used to gather data from arrestees and incarcerated persons for the purpose of determining the linkages between drug abuse and crime.

semen. the fluid expelled by the male at sexual climax and which may be detected by a crime laboratory. Semen consists of two parts: spermatazoa and seminal fluid.

semen test. a preliminary, nonconclusive test that uses ultraviolet light to determine if a suspect stain contains semen. The article bearing the stain is placed under an ultraviolet lamp. A whitish luminescing appearance is indicative of semen.

seminal fluid. the liquid portion of semen (male ejaculate) which is present even in men with no detectable spermatazoa. It contains chemicals such as acid phosphatase, spermine, and choline, the A,

B, and H blood group substances in secretions, and other proteins and enzymes which may be tested for in a crime laboratory.

semisynthetic drug. any refined drug whose chemical structure has been altered; a natural drug that has been combined with one or more chemical groups, usually to make it stronger. Cocaine hydrochloride (the powder form of cocaine) is a semi-synthetic drug because it is a transformation of free-base cocaine, a drug made from a natural plant. Heroin is also a semi-synthetic in that it is produced by adding two acetic acid groups to morphine, a derivative of the opium plant. LSD also falls into this category because it is a combination of lysergic acid and a natural chemical found in a fungus called ergot.

semisynthetic opiates. opiates derived from the two opium alkaloids (morphine and codeine), such as heroin and hydro-morphone hydrochloride (Dilaudid).

semitrailer. a vehicle with or without motive power, other than a pole trailer, designed for carrying persons or property and for being drawn by a motor vehicle and so constructed that some part of its weight and that of its load rests upon or is carried by another vehicle.

senile psychosis. a mental illness that results from a reduction in the supply of blood and oxygen to the brain. It is usually caused by hardening and thickening of blood vessels in the brain.

sensation seeking. the process in which the individual actively seeks out stimulation from the environment. Researchers have identified five types: general sensation seeking, thrill adventure seeking, experience seeking, disinhibition, and boredom susceptibility. Drug usage is regarded as an aspect of general sensation, although some will argue that drug use is specifically associated with a high optimum level for fantasies and unusual perceptional feelings.

sensitivity. in crime laboratory operations, the limit or level at which something can be detected according to the test employed. Sensitivity is often expressed as the volume or concentration of a component or ingredient in the specimen examined.

sensitization. the reverse effect of drug tolerance. The effect of increased responsiveness to a drug with repeated use. Subjects may under certain conditions experience sensitization to certain actions of cocaine, for example.

sentence. a judgment in a criminal proceeding.

sentence credit time. time already spent in confinement in relation to a given offense, deducted at the point of admission on a sentence to jail or prison from the maximum jail or prison liability of the sentence for the offense.

sentenced to time served. a sentencing disposition consisting of a sentence to prison or jail, which credits the defendant for an amount of time already spent in confinement equal to the amount of the sentence, and results in release from confinement of the defendant.

sentencing council. a group of judges who meet on a more or less regular basis to discuss sentencing decisions in pending cases in order to render non-binding recommendations to the trial judges, who are usually members of the council.

sentencing disparity. an unwarranted, inappropriate, and unjust variation of punishment from one offender to another. A disparity can be identified by comparing the sentencing practices of judges and jurisdictions, and by applying particular statistical analyzing techniques to offender characteristics.

sentencing hearing. in criminal proceedings, a hearing during which the court or jury considers relevant information, such as evidence concerning aggravating or mitigating circumstances, for the purpose of determining a sentencing disposition for a convicted person.

sequential factors. in traffic accident investigations, factors which follow one another to contribute to the cause of an accident. Sometimes called operational factors.

sequester. to keep a jury in custodial supervision during a trial so as to prevent contact with the public or press; to separate prospective witnesses so that they cannot influence one another's testimony.

sergeans. in medieval England, a watchman assigned to guard a town's or castle's gates. This word is the origin of sergeant.

series radio tap. in electronic countermeasures, a radio transmitter which obtains power from the telephone line to which it is attached and is installed in series or in line with one wire.

serious misdemeanor. a class of misdemeanor having more severe penalties than other misdemeanors, or is procedurally distinct; a statutory name for a type of misdemeanor having a maximum penalty much greater than the customary maximum one year incarceration.

serology. the study of antigen-antibody reactions.

serum. the liquid that separates from the blood when a clot is formed.

service of process. delivering a summons, subpoena or citation upon a person in a legal proceeding.

set. the psychological state or underlying personality of an individual that may affect the qualitative response to a mind-altering drug or response to a questionnaire or other stimuli; that which a person expects to happen as a consequence of taking a drug. It is widely believed that a person's expectations, motivations, and attitudes have a strong influence on drug effects.

setting. the environment in which drug use takes place. The term embraces the physical, social, and cultural aspects of the environment. The effect of a drug can be conditioned by the place in which it is consumed, the people with whom it is shared, and cultural beliefs. During the Vietnam conflict, for example, heroin was extensively used by American soldiers, mainly to escape boredom. Many soldiers stopped using heroin when they returned home, most probably because they had left the special setting of army life in Vietnam. From a purely pharmacological and physiological point of view,

these soldiers should have been drawn to a continued use of the drug.

setup fence. a receiver of stolen property who generates thefts by guiding others to steal designated items from particular victims.

severance. the act of separating the trials of two or more defendants or of two or more charges against a single defendant, rather than holding one trial at which the defendants or charges are tried together.

sex offenses. the name of a broad category of varying content, usually consisting of all offenses having a sexual element except forcible rape and commercial sex offenses.

sex psychopath. a catchall name for persons who repeatedly and compulsively violate sex laws. The term is generally regarded as a stigmatizing label with little precise or scientifically reliable and valid predictive implications.

sex pyro. a person who derives sexual pleasure from starting or watching fires.

sexual assault. touching the body of another with a sexual intent and without the consent of the person being touched.

sexual harassment. the use of the power in one's job to gain sexual favors or punish the refusal of such favors.

sexually anatomically correct (SAC) doll. a doll with parts that represent genitalia and/or orifices of the human body that is used as an aid to interviewing children in sex-related crimes. Also called an anatomical doll.

shackles. handcuffs or handirons.

shaped charge. an explosive charge shaped so as to enable the concentration of the explosive action to have a greater effect in penetrating resistant materials such as steel and concrete.

shaped dice. gambling dice having cut or shaped corners that alter the odds.

SHARP. an acronym indicating Swelling, Heat, Ache, Redness, and Pain, the typical signs and symptoms of a wound infection.

sharp. a cheat; swindler; con artist; bunco artist.

shaving. reducing the score in a sporting

event, usually a basketball game, so as to illegally profit from betting.

shell company. a corporation without assets such as those established by white-collar criminals in bond swindles, money-laundering operations, mutual-fund schemes, and internal business fraud. A common practice is for a company employee, such as a purchasing agent, to use letterhead stationery, printed invoices, and similar documentation to create a fictitious vendor. The employee will authorize payments to be remitted to a postal box address under his control.

shell game. a sleight-of-hand swindling game in which the victim bets on the location of a pea covered by one of three nutshells or thimbles.

shell marks. in firearms identification, the marks observed on a fired shell. These marks, which can be made by the weapon's extractor, ejector, firing pin and other parts, are revealing as to the particular weapon that fired the shell.

shelter. a place providing temporary care or custody for juveniles, battered wives, rape victims, and others. Shelters may also be used for persons in need of supervision, persons charged with minor offenses, or persons held pending adjudication of their cases.

sheriff. usually the chief law enforcement officer in a county and generally charged with keeping the peace, making arrests, executing process of the courts, keeping the jail, opening the sessions of the courts, maintaining order in the courts, and performing other duties prescribed by law.

sheriff's deed. a deed executed by a sheriff pursuant to a court order in connection with the sale of property to satisfy a judgment.

sherman. a cigarette laced with PCP.

shield dial. a type of safe dial constructed with a shield designed to prevent finger smudges that can aid a safecracker in composing test combinations.

shill. that member of a confidence game who encourages or builds up the victim; the assistant of a sidewalk peddler or gambler; a confederate who makes a purchase or bet as an inducement to others to follow suit. Also called a booster or ringer.

shim. a thin, flexible piece of metal or plastic (such as a credit card) which when inserted between the bolt and the strike will defeat the spring bolt lock.

shire reeve. in medieval England, the chief official of a town or village, appointed by the local noble to keep the peace, adjudicate local disputes, and administer the noble's laws and regulations. The title sheriff derives from shire reeve.

shiv. a knife, razor or other sharp instrument used as a weapon.

shoot up. to inject a drug.

shooting gallery. a place where drug addicts go to buy and inject themselves with drugs.

shock. a state of profound mental and physical injury or emotional disturbance.

shock front. that phase of a blast wave which occurs immediately after detonation of a bomb. This front travels with a velocity approximately equal to the speed of sound. The leading edge of the front is expressed in terms of pounds per square inch (psi) above atmospheric pressure. It is the magnitude of this peak pressure which largely determines the degree of damage produced by the blast. Following the peak pressure at the shock front, the pressure gradually drops off to atmospheric, then to a pressure below atmospheric, and finally returns to atmospheric pressure. The blast wave travels outward from the detonation point. As it gets further away, the magnitude of the wave decreases, therefore decreasing the destructive effect.

shock probation. a sentence explicitly requiring the convicted person to serve a period of confinement followed by a period of probation.

shoe. a false passport.

shoe fetishist. a man who derives sexual pleasure from the sight, smell, feel and taste of a female's shoes or feet.

shoemaker. a forger of false passports.

shooting gallery. a place where narcotics users congregate to inject drugs.

short-barreled rifle. a rifle having one or more barrels less than 16 inches in length whether made by design or modification.

short con. a confidence game in which the victim is deprived of only that money or property carried on his or her person.

short package. a package of illegal drugs that is less in weight or quantity than agreed upon by seller and buyer.

short ringup. a ring up on a cash register for less than the full amount of a purchase and thereafter pocketing the difference. For example, the cash sale of a $10 shirt is rung up on the cash register as a $1 sale to cover the subsequent theft from the cash drawer of $9.

short weighing. a practice which involves the packaging stages of production. A producer, for example, might fill containers 90% of their capacity and charge retailers for the entire amount.

short worker. a pickpocket who operates in crowded buses and trains.

shotgun. a light, smooth-bore gun, either single or double-barreled, adapted for the discharge of shot. The muzzle end or choke has a smaller diameter than the rear end which has the effect of confining or controlling the shot as it is discharged. The gauge of a shotgun is determined by the number of shots (pellets) per pound of lead. For example, a 12 gauge shotgun is one that has a bore diameter equal to the diameter of any of the 12 pellets that can be obtained from one pound of lead. A 16 gauge shotgun has a smaller bore because a pellet that is one-sixteenth of a pound of lead is smaller than a one-twelfth pellet.

shotgun microphone. a highly directional microphone with a tube-like appearance.

shotgun wound marks. marks on the body of a shotgun wound victim which are potentially classifiable as to the distance separating the victim and the shotgun muzzle at time of discharge. Four classifications are generally recognized: (1) the direct contact wound which shows an imprint of the muzzle on the skin or which indicates contact by massive destruction of bone and tissue, (2) the up-close or loose-contact wound which shows a small diameter entry pattern having abraded edges surrounded by a zone of considerable scorching, soot, and powder residue, (3) the close-range or near-range wound which has a larger diameter entry pattern consistent with a discharge at 4–6 feet and shows abraded, scalloped margins, wad-impact abrasion, and wide dispersal of powder residue, soot, and smoke stains, and (4) the distance wound which has a very large diameter entry pattern consistent with a discharge at greater than 6 feet and shows scattered, small round pellet holes with abraded margins.

shoulder. that portion of the road contiguous with the roadway for accommodation of stopped vehicles, for emergency use, and for lateral support of the roadway structure. The line between the roadway and the shoulder may be a painted edge line, a change in surface color or material, or a curb. On some modern trafficways, there may be a surfaced shoulder on the right side, and frequently a narrower shoulder on the left side of a one-way roadway. In fingerprinting science, the point at which the recurving ridge of a loop pattern turns inward or curves.

showup. an identification technique in which a single suspect is viewed by a witness. This technique is most often used when a suspect is taken into custody immediately after the crime so that an identification may be made while the incident is fresh in the mind of the witness or when the witness is in danger of death or is seriously incapacitated and time does not allow use of the formal lineup procedure. In other cases, the showup is used when an identification lineup is inappropriate due to some unique visible characteristic of the suspect. The showup is the least desirable method of suspect identification because of its inherent suggestiveness.

shrinkage. a decrease in inventory; loss of volume or bulk. Shrinkage is an accounting term usually applied to a decrease in inventory value by reason of employee pilferage, shoplifting, bookkeeping or production errors, waste, and other common occurrences in business which shrink inventories before sale.

shunting. an interviewing technique intended to overcome digression by the interviewee and to return to the original line of questioning. A shunt consists of a short question that appears to arise out of an interest in what the subject is saying, but is designed to bring the conversation back to an issue of interest to the investigator.

shylocking. loan sharking; loaning cash at an extremely high rate of interest.

shyster. one who uses underhanded tricks; an unethical attorney.

siamese connection. a fire hydrant having a double connection from a single water source.

side-by-side. a shotgun with two barrels positioned side-by-side, as contrasted with the over-under shotgun which has the barrels positioned one on top of the other. Both types offer barrels having different chokes, e.g., one barrel might restrict the spread of shot while the other would deliver the shot in a sprayed pattern.

side effects. all actions produced by a drug given at therapeutic dosage with the exception of the specific action for which the drug was administered.

side scuff. in traffic accident investigations, a scuffmark made while a vehicle is yawing (moving sidewise); a mark made on the road by a rotating tire which is slipping in a direction parallel to the axle of the wheel.

side slip. a sidewise movement of a vehicle in turning; movement of a vehicle in a direction other than that in which it is headed; a sidewise motion produced when centrifugal force exceeds traction force. A side slip is often the result of driver overreaction or excessive speed.

sidewalk. that portion of a street between the curb lines, or the lateral lines of a roadway, and the adjacent property lines, intended for use by pedestrians.

sight. a device for assisting the aim of a shooter. A gun sight is a small protuberance on the top of the barrel which is brought in line with a rear sight located near the shooter's eye. A bore sight is a device with parts attached to the muzzle and breech of a gun that aligns the axis of the bore with the axis of the gun sight. A leaf sight is a type of rear sight that is hinged to allow raising or lowering. A peep sight is a type of rear sight that has a small hole in the center for close aiming.

signature security service. a service designed to provide continuous responsibility for the custody of shipments in transit, so named because a signature and tally are required from each person handling the shipment at each stage of its transit from point of origin to destination.

signature verification system. a computer-aided system that digitizes and compares the dynamic characteristics of a handwritten signature against a known signature on file. The technique analyzes shapes and timing sequences intrinsic to formation of letters in the signature.

sign/countersign. code words used in certain operations, tests or emergencies.

significant reaction. a strong deceptive pattern in the chart of a person tested by the polygraph technique.

sign-on. the procedure performed at a computer terminal while it is in initial mode. The procedure can include entering only the sign-on command, or entering the sign-on command with a password or other user-specified code.

signs of death. the detectable signs that indicate cessation of life. These include: (1) cessation of breath, (2) cessation of pulse, (3) absence of eye reflexes, (4) rigor mortis, (5) lividity, and (6) putrefaction.

silencer. a tube-like device attached to the muzzle of a firearm that significantly reduces the sound of discharge. A silencer is generally constructed with a socket that attaches to the gun, a vortex chamber for the containment of gases and suppression of sound, and a passage groove for the bullet.

silence to an accusation. silence by an accused when an accusation has been made, understood, and an opportunity has been given to reply. Silence in such case may be admissible evidence as an admission. The concept is based on the presumption that an innocent person will reply to an untrue accusation. This concept, however, does not apply when an accusation has been made while the accused is in custody or under formal investigation because under such circumstance the accused has the right to remain silent and silence cannot be counted against him.

silent alarm. a noiseless alarm transmitted from the scene of a hold-up, intrusion or other emergency for the purpose of summoning help.

silent treatment. a subtle form of intimidation in which an interviewer, by silence, suggests that the interviewee should make another answer.

silver nitrate. a solution used to develop latent fingerprint impressions, mainly on paper materials. It will react to sodium chloride (salt) which is present in most latent impressions. A paper believed to contain latent fingerprints is immersed in a silver nitrate solution and then hung to dry in a dark room. After drying, the paper is exposed to light. Fingerprint impressions will gradually appear and then disappear as the paper completely darkens. The prints are photographed while they are most visible. Silver nitrate is also used in a powder or paste form to mark decoy objects which when placed into contact with the skin of the touching person will cause a color reaction to the skin.

silver platter doctrine. the name given to the controversial practice of circumventing rules prohibiting the introduction at federal trials of evidence illegally seized by federal officers. In this practice, federal police officers exploited a loophole in the wording of a 1914 U.S. Supreme Court decision (Weeks v. United States) which said "Evidence illegally seized by federal officers is inadmissible . . . " Until curbed by the Eilkins v. United States decision of the Supreme Court in 1960, federal police officers simply requested state or local officers to make seizures on their behalf.

Silvester method. a method of artificial respiration used to aid a person whose air passages are not obstructed, such as a victim of smoke inhalation. In this method, the rescuer presses downward on the victim's chest to expel air from the lungs and then draws air into the lungs by pulling the arms outward and upward.

simple assault. unlawful intentional threatening, attempted inflicting, or inflicting of less than serious bodily injury, in the absence of a deadly weapon.

simple fracture. a fracture in which the skin is not penetrated by fractured bone; a break in a bone in which the injury is entirely internal with no break in the adjacent tissue or skin. Also called a closed fracture.

simple reaction. in traffic accident investigations, a driver's preplanned reaction to an expected hazard.

simulated camera. a genuine-appearing but nonfunctional camera intended as a crime deterrent. It is typically mounted out of reach in a conspicuous position in an area having a history of employee pilferage, shoplifting, misconduct, robbery, etc. Some models are stationary, some scan, and most are equipped with a red pilot lamp. Also called a dummy camera.

simulated deception responses. in polygraph, physical and mental efforts by the examinee to influence recordings of the polygraph instrument during a test. The examinee's purpose is to create false deception responses that cannot be differentiated from genuine deception responses. Examples of efforts include contraction of the anal sphincture muscle, controlled breathing, and mental concentration on issues other than those being tested.

simultaneous impressions. inked fingerprint impressions obtained by simultaneously pressing all of the fingers of the hand and then the thumb. Also called plain impressions.

simultaneous factors. in traffic accident investigations, factors present together at the same time which contribute to the cause of an accident. Also called condition factors.

sine qua non rule. a rule of law which holds that a defendant's conduct is not the cause of an event if the event would have occurred without it. Also called the "but for" rule.

single action. a name applied to a firearm that is discharged by cocking in one action and releasing the hammer in another action. A double-action firearm will discharge by pulling the trigger which cocks and releases the hammer.

single action man. a numbers writer who specializes in taking single-action bets on any one of the three numbers, and usually writes up to post time for each number.

single gunner. a pickpocket who works alone, not as a member of a team. Also called a rooter or a single cannon.

sink test. the name given to the practice of billing a patient for a medical test that was not performed.

sinsemilla. from the Spanish "sin" (without) and "semilla" (seed). Sinsemilla is the potent flowering top (excised of leaves) of the unpollinated and seedless female marijuana plant. Keeping the female plants unpollinated creates increasing quantities of a sticky substance containing a high concentration of THC (the psychoactive ingredient in marijuana). If the female plant becomes fertilized, it devotes a large portion of its chemical energies to making seeds and in the process lowers its THC content. The growth of sinsemilla requires the identification and weeding out of the male plants before they begin pollination and the harvesting of the female plants at the peak of their pollen-luring secretions, both of which are difficult to determine. This process for cultivating marijuana has been used in Asia for centuries and is, for example, used to grow the marijuana contained in Thai sticks. Its use in the west was popularized after the drug experiences of American soldiers in Viet Nam in the 1960s.

THC concentrations in sinsemilla can reach 6 percent or more, while ordinary street marijuana sometimes contain less than 1 percent. To increase the potency, growers use the Cannabis indica species of marijuana, which contains more THC than its botanical sibling Cannabis sativa.

Sir Francis Drake swindle. a type of mail fraud in which the victim is notified by letter that he is a descendant of Sir Francis Drake (or some other notable person) and is entitled to a share in the estate, but that a sum will be required for litigation.

situational drug use. drug use that is task specific and self-limited. Use is motivated by the perceived need or desire to achieve an effect deemed desirable to cope with a particular situation that is personal or vocational in nature. Examples would be athletes who use steroids to improve performance, and students who use amphetamines while preparing for examinations. Also called circumstantial-situational drug use.

situational management. any management style that recognizes that the application of theory to practice must necessarily take into consideration, and be contingent upon, the given situation.

situation hazard. a circumstance that endangers a traffic unit (vehicle, pedalcycle or pedestrian) and which by conscious action of the driver must be avoided in order to prevent an accident.

Sixth Amendment. an amendment to the U.S. Constitution that accords to citizens the right of counsel. The right-to-counsel doctrine under this amendment has been expanded by Supreme Court decisions to include any judicial proceeding, whether by way of formal charge, preliminary hearing, indictment, information, or arraignment. The Sixth Amendment right to counsel applies to custodial interrogation situations as interpreted by the Supreme Court in several major cases, most notably in Miranda.

skidmark. a friction mark on a pavement

made by a tire that is sliding without rotation. Sliding of the wheels in most cases is due to braking or collision damage.

skills inventory program. a program that collects and examines data on the workforce to determine the composition and level of employees' skills, knowledges, and abilities so that they can be more fully utilized and/or developed to fill the staffing needs of the organization. Skills data are arranged in such a manner that the information gathered can be readily accessible for decision-making purposes. Programs of this type are used in law enforcement departments for the purpose of identifying and fully utilizing officers with particular skills in such areas as SWAT operations, hostage negotiations, crime analysis, crime prevention, and public relations.

skin pop. to inject a narcotic subcutaneously. The onset of the drug's effects is not so immediate as it is with mainlining (injecting intravenously). Skin popping is often used by neophyte users before they progress to mainlining. It is also used by older addicts whose veins can no longer tolerate mainlining.

Skipper v. South Carolina. a case in which the U.S. Supreme Court reversed and remanded a case involving the exclusion of defense witnesses who would have offered mitigating evidence during the sentencing phase of the trial. The witnesses, two jail employees and a frequent visitor to the jail, were prepared to testify on the behavior and conduct of the defendant during the time he was held in jail. South Carolina courts concluded that such evidence was irrelevant and therefore inadmissible. The Supreme Court's decision in this case affirmed the right of defendants in capital cases to present any and all relevant mitigating evidence that is available at the time of sentencing.

skip shooting. a shotgun shooting technique in which the shooter aims at the ground in front of the intended target so that the shot charge will skip or ricochet in a manner intended to reduce the infliction of fatal wounds.

skip skid. a braking skidmark interrupted at frequent intervals, for example, marks made by a bouncing wheel on which brakes keep the wheel from turning.

skip trace. a search made for a person, usually a debtor, who has "skipped town," i.e., left with no forwarding address.

skirmish line. a riot control formation used to confront a mob, advance against it, or block off an area. A skirmish line is not used to attack or make contact with the mob, but to make a display of force, to contain the movement of rioters, and establish a base from which offensive maneuvers can be launched if needed.

slam hammer. a tool used by car thieves to physically pull out the cylinders of ignition locks and by burglars to remove lock cylinders or key cores. It is similar in function to a dent puller which is used to pull dents out of an auto and typically consists of a slender rod with a heavy sliding sleeve. One end of the rod has a screw or claw for inserting into or grasping the lock. The other end has a retaining knob. When the sleeve is jerked away from the lock, striking the retaining knob, the lock cylinder or key core is forcibly pulled out. Also called a slapper or slam puller.

slander. false and defamatory statements about a person.

slave flash. a supplementary photoflash placed at a distance from the master flash to increase the illuminated field in a photograph. The slave flash is actuated by a photoelectric device that responds to light from the master flash.

sleeve sneak. a shoplifting technique in which the thief palms a small article and slips it beneath a sleeve. When the hand is placed inside a pocket or purse, the article is allowed to fall out of the sleeve.

sleeving test. in arson investigations, an examination of the insulation surrounding an electrical conductor that has been exposed to fire. If the insulation is melted onto the conductor, the heat was external. If the insulation is loose on the conductor, the heat was internal, i.e., inside the insulation.

slide-rule discipline. an approach to discipline that eliminates supervisory discretion and sets very specific quantitative standards as the consequences of specific violations. For example, an employee who is late for work more than four times in a 30-day period might be automatically suspended for three days.

sling under. a shoplifting technique in which a female thief will place an item under her dress where it is held by the upper thighs. The thief will walk from the store or to a location in the store where the item can be further concealed.

slip-knifing. a burglary attack method in which a thin, flat, flexible object such as a stiff piece of plastic is inserted between the strike and the latch bolt to depress the latch bolt and release it from the strike. The slip-knifing of windows is accomplished by inserting a thin stiff object between the meeting rails or stiles to move the latch to the open position, or by inserting a thin stiff wire through openings between the stile or rail and the frame to manipulate the sash operator of pivoting windows.

slitter. a pickpocket who uses a razor to cut the pockets or purses of victims. Also called a chopper.

slope. in traffic accident investigation, the change in elevation in unit distance in a specified direction along the center line of a roadway or the path of a vehicle. Slope is the difference in level of two points divided by the distance between the points. It is designated in feet per foot (or meters per meter) of rise or fall per foot (or meter) of distance or in rise or fall as a percent of the level distance. Slope is positive if the surface rises in the specified direction and negative if it falls in that direction. Also called grade.

smack. heroin.

smash. a mixture of marihuana, hashish and acetone. Marihuana is cooked with acetone to obtain oil of cannabis. The oil is added to hashish to form a tar-like material which is rolled into small pellets and smoked.

smash and grab. a criminal method for stealing valuables from a glass enclosed display area such as a counter case or window display area. For example, the criminal might smash the glass plate window of a jewelry store, quickly grab up the jewelry on display, and flee before a response can be made.

Smith v. Maryland. a case in which the U.S. Supreme Court ruled that there was no search or invasion of privacy by the use of a pen register on the ground that a pen register records only the telephone number called by the subscriber and not the conversation. This opinion was based on the view that people have no expectation of privacy regarding the numbers they dial, since this information is recorded by the telephone company. The use of a pen register does not therefore require a search warrant and does not violate Fourth Amendment guarantees.

Smith v. Murray. a case in which the U.S. Supreme Court ruled on psychiatric evidence. In this case, information concerning a prior offense obtained during a pretrial psychiatric examination was introduced during the sentencing phase of the trial. The evidence was used as an aggravating factor by the prosecution, and the jury subsequently recommended the death sentence. On direct appeal, the defense counsel failed to raise the question of the Fifth Amendment protection against self-incrimination, having concluded that such a claim would fail in the state (Virginia) court. A subsequent appeal to the federal courts, however, did raise this claim. The U.S. Supreme Court concluded that the defendant had defaulted on his constitutional challenge to the psychiatric testimony by not raising the issue on appeal before the Virginia Supreme Court and that such a failure was not the result of deficient legal defense because it was a deliberate, tactical decision.

smokeless powder—double base. an explosive consisting of a mixture of nitrocellulose and nitroglycerin.

smokeless powder—single-base. an explosive consisting of nitrocellulose.

smuggling. unlawful movement of goods across a national frontier or state boundary, or into or out of a correctional facility.

snatch squad. in riot control operations, a police team used to capture ring leaders.

sneeze machine. a device used in riot control operations to force people to leave an area. It is mounted in the cargo carrying area of a small truck and disperses a light powder that is irritating to nasal membranes but causes no serious injury or incapacitation.

sniffer. an instrument used to measure the concentration of combustible gases in the air; a dog trained to detect odors characteristic of certain substances, such as drugs and explosives; a tuning device used to determine possible sources of ultrasonic frequencies within a protected area that may cause an ultrasonic detector to initiate a false alarm.

sniffing. inhaling drugs usually of the volatile solvent type, e.g., glue sniffing. Also called insufflation.

snorting. the usual means of abusing cocaine. The drug is sniffed into the nose where it is absorbed by the nasal membranes.

snuff spoon. a tobacco snuff spoon, used also as a cocaine snorting spoon. Also called a coke spoon.

soak-in. in traffic accident investigations, an area on the shoulder or roadside saturated with liquid debris either at the end of runoff or as a puddle marking the rest position of a vehicle after collision.

social control. a deterring effect on criminal activity resulting from the presence of people.

social costs of drug use. the costs to society caused by drug use. Various econometric models have been developed that compute costs to society of addiction based on productivity losses in employment, criminal justice system expenditures such as judicial, penal, and law enforcement expenses and salaries, property crimes, drug education, treatment, and rehabilitation.

social distance. the space that extends from four to twelve feet around an individual, in which most social and business contacts take place. The term has significance in respect to the proximity of an interrogator to the person being questioned, i.e., a proximity closer than the social distance can be intimidating.

social-impact theory. a theory which holds that when social forces affect a situation, the pressure on any one member of a group is lessened because the impact of the social forces is spread over the entire group. As the group increases in size, the pressure on separate members decreases.

social observation. the simple presence of people which has a deterring effect on criminal activity. Also called social control.

social policy objectives. objectives set by government which seek through regulation, taxing or spending to attain broad social goals. Examples of social policy objectives are (1) equitable distribution of income, (2) protection of small businesses and family farms, (3) public transportation services in rural areas, (4) rationing or allocation of scarce resources, (5) consumer protection, (6) price stability, and (7) conservation of natural resources.

social-recreational drug use. drug use that occurs in social settings among friends or acquaintances who wish to share a pleasurable experience. Unlike experimental use, social and recreational use tends to be more patterned but considerably more varied in terms of frequency, intensity, and duration. It is a voluntary act and, regardless of the duration of use, tends not to escalate in either frequency or intensity.

social security number index. a list which matches the first three digits of social security numbers with the states that issued them.

sociogenic drug use. drug use that from inception is simultaneous with participation in a specific social group. The term especially applies to marijuana use. Seven criteria are given for determining when a drug is sociogenic: (1) use is typically in a group; (2) use is shared with intimates; (3) use is shared with those of long-term continuing relations; (4) the group shares many of the same values; (5) value convergence occurs as a result of progressive group involvement; (6) drug use reaffirms group solidarity; and (7) users view use as a legitimate basis for identity.

sociogram. a diagram showing the interactions between members of a group.

sociological models. a term referring to explanatory theories that seek to identify those factors within society and social relations that promote crime. Many sociological models rest on the assumption that people are criminals because of their inability to reach societal goals. Moreover, crime is seen as a problem that is socially defined and perceived differently by different societal groups. Many of these models further stress that social problems such as drug use and prostitution meet certain societal needs and will remain in existence as long as those needs remain. These problems will be eliminated only when the basic societal arrangements that perpetuate them are changed. The main criticism of sociological models is their failure to explain why only some people with a given sociological background become criminals and not others.

sociopathic personality. a personality disorder used to describe chronically antisocial persons who seem unable or unwilling to live within established social and moral frameworks and who tend to pursue self-determined goals regardless of the consequences to self or others. This particular label takes into account the fact that sociocultural norms may be flaunted by individuals so labeled. The term has been used interchangeably with psychopathic personality, and both labels have been replaced by anti-social personality in common usage. It has been thought by some researchers that the nature of the psychopathic/sociopathic personality makes the likelihood of significant improvement in therapy or treatment of any kind minimal.

sodomy. unlawful physical contact between the genitals of one person and the mouth or anus of another person, or with the mouth, anus or genitals of an animal.

soft drug. a psychologically but not physically addictive drug such as hashish, marijuana and related hemp plants and products. It is a vague, imprecise term that is sometimes used to refer to all drugs other than the opiate narcotics, which are labeled hard drugs.

software. programs, procedures, rules and any associated documentation pertaining to the operation of a computer system. Software encompasses the various computer languages and the operating programs written in those languages.

soft x-ray examination. a crime laboratory technique in which objects are examined using x-rays ranging from 4 to 25 kilovolts. Radiographs produced with soft x-rays can reveal characteristics not observable through other techniques. Soft x-ray examination is used to evaluate paintings, fabrics, papers, inks, gunshot residues, and jewelry. Hard x-rays (25 to 140 kilovolts) are used to examine gross, metal objects.

soldato. a "soldier" or rank and file member of the Mafia. A soldato is typically an operator of a Mafia enterprise, such as bookmaking, prostitution, and drug trafficking. A soldato will supervise many employees who may or may not be Mafia members.

solicitation. commanding, encouraging or requesting another person to commit a crime.

solvability factor. information about a crime that can provide the basis for identifying the criminal; a lead; a clue. Certain types of information are considered solvability factors, for example: (1) testimony of a witness, (2) description of a suspect, (3) tracing of property through the use of numbers or marks, (4) unique modus operandi, (5) significant physical evidence, and (6) opportunity for but one person to have committed the crime.

solved case (or offense). a founded criminal offense in which the police have identified the perpetrator. A "solved" determination does not necessarily result from a judicial decision.

somatic. pertaining to the body as opposed to mental or psychological origin.

soporific substance. a generic term for all compounds or drugs used for inducing sleep.

sottocapo. an underboss of a Mafia family or core group. The equivalent in a formal organization would be a vice president or deputy director. The sottocapo is the chief assistant to the capo and acts for him in his absence.

sound spectrograph. an instrument that electronically produces pictorial patterns of speech and other sounds. The spectrograms of a known voice can be compared against the spectrograms of an unknown voice for the purpose of identifying or eliminating suspects. A sound spectrograph is not a lie detection instrument.

source. a person, thing or activity which provides information.

source object. in crime laboratory operations, the object from which a fragment or part has been separated and which is identified by an examination of the separated fragment or part. For example, a source object would be a screwdriver the tip of which was broken off and left at the scene of a forced entry. A metallurgical examination of the tip might result in a match with a screwdriver found in the possession of a suspect.

South Dakota v. Opperman. a case in which the U.S. Supreme Court found legal an inventory search of a vehicle impounded for traffic violations when the purpose is to inventory and list all items found in the vehicle for storage and safekeeping, but did not allow such an examination to consist of a "strip search" of the vehicle.

space cadet. a person whose senses have become dulled from excessive drug use, especially of marijuana.

spaced out. especially high, particularly from a hallucinogen.

spalling effect. in bomb incident investigations, the spalling, scabbing or flaking condition on a steel or concrete surface created by an explosive charge striking the reverse side of the surface; in arson investigations, discoloration, cracks and loosened concrete seen on the remaining concrete structure of a burned building which indicate that the fire was enhanced by an accelerant. Brick exposed to high temperatures (1800 degrees Fahrenheit or higher) will turn pink and cement will get whiter.

Spanish prisoner scheme. a type of mail fraud in which the victim receives a letter from someone claiming to be falsely imprisoned and who offers to share concealed money or valuables in exchange for funds sent to secure the prisoner's release.

span of control. a management principle which holds that a supervisor can be effective in handling from 3 to 6 subordinates. Studies support an assertion that as the number of subordinates increases arithmetically, the number of possible interpersonal interactions increases geometrically.

spatter. a collection of marks on the road made by liquid from a vehicle or its cargo squirted from containers on the vehicle by the force of collision. Spatter areas are irregular in shape and often consist of many small spots.

Special Action Office for Drug Abuse Prevention (SAODAP). a former agency in the Executive Office of the President which reviewed and evaluated the functions and policies of government agencies involved in drug abuse prevention. SAODAP established policies and provided direction necessary to properly coordinate federal efforts in drug abuse treatment, rehabilitation, education, training, and research. The basic mission of the agency was twofold: (1) to reduce drug abuse in the shortest possible time; and (2) to develop a comprehensive long-term federal strategy to combat drug abuse.

special activity. an activity, or functions in support of such activity, conducted in support of national foreign policy objectives abroad that is planned and executed so that the role of the U.S. Government is not apparent.

Special Background Investigation. a

Department of Defense personnel security investigation consisting of all of the components of a Background Investigation plus certain additional investigative requirements.

special bet. in a numbers operation, a bet made with an agreement that if the player wins, the payoff will be at odds higher than normal. Such bets are accepted from only the best customers, and are usually restricted to a dollar minimum.

special deterrence concept. a concept which holds that future crimes by a specific offender can be prevented by imposing a penalty so severe it outweighs the pleasure or profit derived from the crime and convinces the offender to not pursue further criminality.

special endorsement. the designation of a certain person to whom an instrument is payable. Thus, if an instrument is endorsed "Pay to the order of John Jones," followed by the endorser's signature, no one but John Jones can receive payment for the instrument or transfer it.

Special Investigative Inquiry. a Department of Defense supplemental personnel security investigation of limited scope conducted to update or assure completeness of a prior investigation or to prove/disprove relevant allegations that have arisen concerning a person about whom a personnel security determination has been previously made and who, at the time of the allegations, holds a security clearance or sensitive position.

specialist fence. a receiver of stolen property who has a preference for particular goods, excluding most other classes of goods. A specialist fence, for example, might deal only in office equipment or home electronic appliances.

special operating procedures. written instructions which pertain to a specific job or functions within a job.

special weapons and tactics (SWAT) team. a special unit on call for use in unusual crisis situations that have a potential for violence. A SWAT team is usually made up of regularly-assigned officers who have received advanced training in the use of unconventional weapons and tactics.

specific characteristics. in observation and description, the detailed characteristics of a person, e.g., color of hair and eyes, shape of head and face, mannerisms, marks and scars.

specific criminal intent. an intent of the criminal to act with voluntariness, foresight of the consequences, and with a further ulterior purpose in mind. A general criminal intent is present when a person takes another's property voluntarily and with foresight. Specific criminal intent is present when the criminal takes further action to permanently deprive the owner of his property.

specificity. in crime laboratory operations, that quality of an analytical technique which tends to exclude all substances other than that being sought. Specificity or selectivity refers to the ability of a test method to identify a single component in an unknown sample. This characteristic is a function of one or all of the processes of isolation, separation, and detection of a particular component in a matrix.

specific polygraph test. a polygraph test that seeks to resolve a specific, well-defined issue. For example, a specific polygraph test might be administered to determine if the tested person has guilty knowledge of a particular crime under investigation, but would not be used in preemployment screening to evaluate a person's general background.

specimen. a small sample of something; a part of a whole intended upon analysis to reveal characteristics of the whole, e.g., a urine specimen used for urinalysis.

spectral response. the variation in sensitivity of a device to light of different wavelengths.

spectroanalysis. a crime laboratory analytical technique based on the principles of reflection and absorption of light waves. Questioned specimens, such as paint chips, glass fragments and traces of suspected drugs, can be identified by their unique spectra. Spectroanalysis can be performed with the use of several instruments such as the spectrograph, spectro-photometer, and electron microscope.

spectrograph. an apparatus for photographing a spectrum or for forming a representation of the spectrum. This equipment allows analysis of minute particles, and to characterize them by means of their impurities. In the spectrographic technique a particle of an unknown substance is burned. A photograph is made of the light waves emitted during the burning process. This photograph of the light spectrum (hence spectrograph) is compared with the spectra of known substances. In this way it is possible to compare known and unknown samples, and to establish the origin of two specimens.

spectrographic analysis. the qualitative and quantitative analysis of a substance, its composition and properties on the basis of its study with the spectrograph.

spectrophotometer. a laboratory instrument which analyzes an unknown substance according to the substance's capacity to absorb ultraviolet or infrared light. Since many substances of interest to an analyst (such as drugs) will absorb light at specific and unique wavelengths, the analyst compares the wavelengths of the unknown substance against those of the known substances. A finding by spectrophotometer analysis is usually cross-checked with a separate and more specific analytical technique.

spectrum analysis. the study and interpretation of spectra and the investigation and qualitative analysis of substances and bodies through their spectra and spectral lines.

spectrum analyzer. an electronics countermeasure device that detects the presence of radio frequency transmissions characteristic of covertly installed transmitters.

speed. an amphetamine, often Methedrine. In traffic enforcement, distance divided by time if speed is constant. Also called velocity.

speedball. heroin and cocaine or heroin and amphetamine injected as a mixture. The cocaine or amphetamine reportedly enhances rush, while the heroin tempers the unpleasant extremes of the exhilaration and perhaps prolongs the effect.

speed freak. a chronic user of methamphetamine.

speed loader. a device which holds rounds in a pattern aligned with the cylinder of a revolver. All rounds (usually 5 or 6) are inserted simultaneously into the cylinder, thereby speeding the loading process. Also called a multi-loader.

speed tolerance. the margin of deviation over the established speed limit. The purpose of the margin is to remove reasonable doubt concerning speeding violations. For example, where the established speed limit is 55 MPH and the speed tolerance is 10 MPH, speeding tickets would be issued only to motorists operating in excess of 65 MPH.

speedy trial. the right of a defendant to have a prompt trial. It is guaranteed by the Sixth Amendment and is intended to protect an accused from long pretrial detention or from an interminable period of living under the shadow of charges not adjudicated.

Speedy Trial Act of 1974. a statutory scheme that provides time periods within which federal trials must begin. Subject to certain narrow exceptions, a federal trial must commence within 60 days of arraignment.

spermatazoa. the male reproductive cell, the presence of which may be tested for in evidence analyzed by a crime laboratory.

spermine. a chemical found in seminal fluid which is tested for by means of a crystal test called the Barberios test.

sphygmomanometer. an instrument used for measuring arterial blood pressure; a blood pressure cuff. This device is a component of the polygraph instrument.

spike. the needle used to inject illegal drugs.

spike microphone. a contact type microphone with a long, needle-like extension used for listening through walls.

Spinelli v. United States. a case in which the U.S. Supreme Court ruled that an informant's information in an affidavit for a search warrant must be established to be from an informant who is credible and whose past information has been reliable. This test requires an examination of the credibility of the informant and of the reliability of the underlying circumstances on which the informant's conclusion was based.

spiral search. a type of search conducted at an outdoor crime scene. The area to be searched is delineated by markers forming one large circle. Two or three searchers proceed at the same pace within fingertip distance along adjacent paths that spiral in toward the center of the circle. When a piece of evidence is found, all searchers halt until it is processed. At a given signal, the search resumes until the center is reached.

split image lens. a special lens that permits the viewing of two different fields. Two scenes can be photographed by a single camera. It is useful for comparing two different fields, or when an insufficiency of space will allow only one camera where two are needed.

split notes. counterfeit bills created by splitting the paper of higher denomination and lower denomination notes. The halves are pasted together so that each note consists of a high denomination on one side and a low denomination on the other side. The counterfeiter passes all the bills at the higher values.

split sentence. a term in jail or prison with weekend furloughs to be spent with family, or weekdays furloughs so that the offender can continue to work at his regular job. The time spent outside of confinement does not count as time served.

spontaneous combustion. a fire caused by a natural heat-producing process in the presence of sufficient air and fuel; ignition of fire in an object by internal development of heat without the action of an external agent.

spontaneous exclamation. an utterance concerning an event made by an individual in a state of surprise and is not the product of deliberation or design. It is an exception to the hearsay rule and is admissible as evidence. Also called spontaneous declaration.

spook. a spy.

spoon. any of the spoon-like devices used to heat and liquefy illegal drugs for injection. A spoon is part of the drug paraphernalia, or works, used by heroin addicts to prepare their drugs for injection. It is usually made from a teaspoon whose handle is bent back and looped so that a finger may be inserted for a steady holding. The spoon and its contents are heated to prepare an injectable liquid from powdered heroin, or other solid psychoactive drug, and water. The term is also used as a crude unit of measure for the number of doses in a quantity of heroin.

spot. in a numbers operation, a store, apartment, hallway or other fixed location where a writer locates himself to accept bets.

spot analysis technique. in polygraphy, a technique of chart interpretation in which recorded responses to relevant questions are closely analyzed. These spots or locations on the charts are considered extremely important to the polygraphist's opinion.

spot monitoring. in the execution of an eavesdropping warrant, the police practice of listening to a conversation for short intervals in order to differentiate between pertinent and nonpertinent conversations. When a conversation is noted to be nonpertinent, the police listener is required to not listen or tape. The general practice is to spot monitor a conversation for a few seconds every 30 to 60 seconds. Also called minimizing.

spot-plate test. a preliminary, nonconclusive test for determining in a substance the presence of a natural opiate such as morphine, codeine or heroin. A particle of the suspected drug is placed on a tile plate and a formaldehyde solution of sulphuric acid is added. A positive indication will be the appearance of a purple-violet color.

spotter. a person, sometimes an employee, who watches for theft opportunities and sells the information to criminals; a lookout; a person hired by a retail store to watch for and report shoplifters; a person employed by a numbers operator to report the presence of strange persons or police officers nearby the number location or a drop; a person who frequents court buildings and areas near police stations to become familiar with police officers, detectives and undercover officers and to spot informants; that member of a car theft ring who looks for and determines the location of automobiles to be stolen; that member of a hijack team who first locates and points out the targeted truck and, following the hijack, trails the truck as a lookout until it arrives at its planned place of concealment.

spread eagle. a standing or prone position assumed by a person being searched for weapons.

spreading. a technique of forced entry through a door by spreading the door frame apart until the bolt disengages from the strike.

spurious alarm. a false alarm caused by an equipment defect.

squadrol. a mobile police unit, especially a unit equipped and designated for transporting arrested persons.

squib load. a cartridge in which a powder charge has not been loaded, usually as the result of a manufacturing defect.

stabilized accident situation. the condition prevailing after motion and other actions constituting an accident have ceased. An accident situation is said to be stabilized when no further harm will ensue unless a new series of events is initiated.

staggered shifts. a scheduling technique in patrol allocation in which the personnel of one regular shift are divided into two or more subshifts to accommodate variations in the service workload during a part of the day.

stakeout bust. an antifencing enforcement method in which a search warrant is obtained to make an on-premises search after surveillance has confirmed the existence of a fencing operation. A variation of the stakeout bust is the buy-bust

method in which a police undercover agent or informant sells to a fence "bait property" which has been represented as stolen. The transaction is often monitored and taped through the use of a body transmitter so that probable cause can be shown for the arrest and/or search that follows.

stall. that member of a pickpocket team who distracts the victim while the pickpocketing act is performed.

stand-alone computer system. a computer system not connected to a data processing facility and designed to be operated by one person at a time. A personal computer is a type of stand-alone computer.

standard ammunition file. a collection of standard ammunition samples used by a firearms examiner to compare against questioned samples.

standard consolidated statistical area. the area formed by two or more standard metropolitan statistical areas that run together.

standard deviation. in the study of variability or dispersion of a set of observations, the measure of the average of the amounts that the individual numbers deviate from the mean of all the observations. A low standard deviation indicates a tendency of values to cluster about the mean. A high standard deviation indicates a wide variation in values.

standard document. in criminal investigations, a document recognized as proven, genuine or acknowledged that has been obtained from a known and reliable source, such as official records, and is known to be the product of a particular person or machine.

standard federal regions. geographic subdivisions of the U.S. established to achieve more uniformity in the location and geographic jurisdiction of federal field offices as a basis for promoting more systematic coordination among agencies and among federal, state and local governments, and for securing management improvements and economies through greater interagency and intergovernmental cooperation.

standard metropolitan statistical area. a

county or group or counties including at least one city with a population of 50,000 or more. In the New England states, SMSAs consist of towns and cities instead of counties.

standards. in criminal investigations, specimens of handwriting produced in the normal course of events, such as letters, records, reports or checks, and writings that are obtained at the request and in the presence of the investigator. The term is also used in crime laboratory operations to describe authentic samples having a known purity or concentration against which unknown samples can be compared.

standards of comparison. known specimens against which questioned evidence is compared. The character of the articles or materials to be collected as known specimens is determined by the circumstances of the investigation. Known specimens might be handwriting samples obtained from a suspected forger or pubic hair samples obtained from a suspected rapist.

standards of conduct. an organization's formal guidelines for ethical behavior.

standards of performance. statements that tell an employee how well he or she must perform a task to be considered a satisfactory employee. Standards can cover how much, how accurately, in what time period, or in what manner, the various job tasks are to be performed.

standing position search. a search of an arrested person (or prisoner) in which the person is ordered to stand with arms extended high overhead, hands apart, legs apart, and toes pointed outward. When a covering officer is available, the searching officer holsters his weapon and leans the person forward and off-balance by holding the person's belt from behind. The standing position search is similar to the wall search except that a wall is not used.

stand mute. refuse to plead to an indictment. In such case, the accused is proceeded against as if he pleaded not guilty.

Star Chamber Proceedings. the name given to the activities of a former English administrative court with criminal jurisdiction. In modern usage, the term describes court proceedings held without access by public or press and without a publicly available transcript or record.

stare decisis. stand by the decision. The term conveys the idea that the law should adhere to decided cases. The doctrine holds that when a court has laid down a principle of law applicable to a certain set of facts, the court will apply the principle in all future cases where the facts are substantially the same.

stash. a hidden cache of illegal drugs and drug-taking equipment; the drug supply itself.

stash bomb. a homemade bomb that has been constructed to resemble a drug stash. It is intended to injure or kill persons searching for illegal drugs. It frequently appears as a foil-wrapped ball as small as a marble or as large as a baseball. The contents are likely to be a volatile chemical mixture that remains stable while immersed in alcohol. After the bomb is placed in an area where a searcher is likely to look for drugs, the alcohol evaporates causing the mixture to destabilize to the point that the slightest movement will cause detonation.

State Department Lookout File. a computerized file maintained by the Passport Office of the U.S. Department of State. It lists defectors, expatriates, repatriates, criminals, wanted persons, subversives, deserters and other persons whose activities or background justify inquiry. The principal use of the file is to identify those passport applications which require other than routine adjudication in determining eligibility.

state's attorney. an attorney who is the elected or appointed chief of a prosecution agency, and whose official duty is to conduct criminal proceedings on behalf of the people against persons accused of committing criminal offenses. Also called prosecutor, district attorney, U.S. attorney, and county attorney.

state's evidence. testimony given by an

accomplice which incriminates other principals, usually given under an actual or implied promise of immunity.

State v. Bryant. a case in which the Minnesota Supreme Court held that a closed door toilet stall in a department store washroom was a privately protected area, so that the police observations and the pictures taken through a ceiling ventilator could not be used as evidence in the prosecution of an offender.

static discharge. the sudden release of accumulated static. Static discharge can cause damage to relatively delicate components such as integrated circuits.

statistical inference. use of information, observed in a sample, to make predictions about a larger population.

statistical significance. a measure of the likelihood that a change observed in an experiment was due to chance and not to some systematic effect or treatment.

status offense. an act declared by statute to be an offense when committed by a juvenile but not when committed by an adult. Examples are truancy, running away from home, curfew violation, and drinking of alcoholic beverages.

statute law. law derived from enactments of legislatures. Statute law is a source of criminal law.

statute of frauds. a statute, enacted with variations in all the States, providing that certain contracts cannot be enforced unless they are in writing signed by the party against whom the contract is sought to be enforced. The writing need not be a formal document signed by both parties. A written note or memorandum of the transaction signed by the party to be bound by the agreement is sufficient.

statute of limitations. a statute that limits the time within legal action may be brought, either upon a contract or tort. State and federal statutes also limit the time within which certain crimes can be prosecuted. The purpose of the time limitation is to make it impossible to bring suit many years after a cause of action originates, during which time witnesses may have died or important evidence may have been lost. The statute of limitations defense seeks to prevent prosecution on the grounds that the government failed to bring charges within the period of time fixed by a particular enactment. Not all crimes have time limitations for seeking prosecution, and some crimes, such as murder and other major crimes, have no limits whatsoever. As a rule, statutes of limitations are made applicable to misdemeanors and some minor felonies.

statutory law. rules formulated into law by legislative action. The Constitution of the United States and the constitutions of the various states are the fundamental written law. All other law must be in harmony with the constitutions, which define and limit the powers of government. State constitutions must be in harmony with the Constitution of the United States. Congress, cities and towns, and other governmental units find in the constitutions their authority, either express or implied, to enact certain laws. These legislative enactments are called statutes and comprise the greater part of the written or statutory law. Statutory law supplements and supersedes common law.

statutory rape. consensual sexual intercourse between a male and a female who is under the age of consent. In some jurisdictions, the term also applies to consensual sexual intercourse between a custodian and a patient or a custodian and an inmate.

stay awakes. amphetamines used to overcome fatigue and the need for sleep. The term is particularly associated with amphetamine abuse by long-haul truck drivers.

stay of execution. an order to delay the execution of a sentence.

steel-jacketed bullet. a lead bullet encased in a steel jacket for the purpose of increasing its penetrating capacity.

stellate gunshot wound. an entrance wound having a star-shaped appearance. It is caused when the muzzle at time of discharge is against a hard bony surface, such as the forehead. The explosive force of gases produced by the discharge create ragged skin tears that radiate from the bullet hole.

stepping stone hypothesis. the theory that the use of one drug increases the likelihood of the use of other more serious drugs. Often used in the past to connect the use of marijuana to later use of heroin. Although there is no definitive evidence that use of marijuana necessarily leads to the use of heroin or any other drugs, there is evidence that an initial interest in drugs may lead to an expansion of the one-time user's drug interests and possibly to a commitment to a way of life that revolves around or is focused on drugs. The term also implies drug use characterized by progressive experimentation that follows a path from less dangerous to more dangerous substances. Some studies indicate that persons who end up with serious drug problems generally begin by using alcohol or nicotine, and then move on to illegal drugs such as marihuana, PCP, and cocaine. Also called the stepping stone syndrome.

stereobinocular microscope. a relatively low-powered microscope used for making crime laboratory examinations.

stereotype. the persistent repetition of senseless acts or words; a pathological condition in which the individual manifests mannerisms, irrational, and delusional forms of thinking. Some degree of stereotype is characteristic of most of the neuroses and psychoses and often of amphetamine abuse.

sterilize. to remove from material to be used in covert operations any marks which can identify it as originating with the sponsoring organization.

sternum. the long, flat bone located in the midline in the anterior part of the thoracic cage.

stick. a marihuana cigarette.

stimulants. a major classification of drugs that stimulate the central nervous system (CNS) and excite functional activity in the body, producing an elevation of mood (euphoria), a state of wakefulness, increased mental activity, energy, alertness and tension, and suppressing appetite. Sympathetic nervous system effects include increased heart and pulse rates and sweating. Stimulants are often divided into two main subcategories: (1) the primary stimulants, which act mainly on the CNS and only secondarily on the sympathetic nervous system, and include the amphetamines, amphetamine relatives, and cocaine; and (2) the secondary stimulants, which also affect the CNS but exert their primary influence on the sympathetic nervous system, and include nicotine, caffeine, and khat.

stimulation test. in polygraphy, a test intended to stimulate interest on the part of the examinee by demonstrating the accuracy of the polygraph instrument. The test might require the examinee to reply "no" to all questions in a short series. All of the questions are truthfully answered with a "no" except for one. The polygraphist identifies the one untruthful answer, thereby demonstrating to the examinee the accuracy of the polygraph instrument. A stimulation test tends to heighten the anxiety of a guilty subject and ease the anxiety of an innocent subject.

sting operation. a covert operation in which members of the police pose as criminals in order to gather information, obtain evidence, and make arrests of persons engaged in criminal activities.

Stockholm syndrome. sympathy or compassion expressed by a hostage victim on behalf of the abductor, so called because of its appearance in hostages who were held inside a bank vault in Stockholm.

stockpiling. a shoplifter's practice of arranging merchandise in a shopping cart so as to make the theft convenient. For example, a female shoplifter might place a high-value concealable item under her purse in the top section of the cart as a preliminary step to slipping the item into the purse when she is least likely to be observed.

stolen property offenses. a crime category which includes unlawful receiving, buying, distributing, selling, transporting, concealing, or possessing of the property of another by a person who knows that the property has been unlawfully obtained from the owner or lawful possessor.

stoned. a state of drug-induced intoxication, elation, or euphoria.

Stone v. California. a case in which the U.S. Supreme Court ruled invalid a search conducted of a hotel room when police officers obtained consent to the search from the hotel owner, but not from the defendant who was renting the room.

stop and frisk. a procedure used by police on patrol to inquire into the activities of a person reasonably believed to be involved in a criminal act. The stop element is the asking of questions, and the frisk element is a pat-down type search made when the person's answers, conduct or appearance lead the officer to think that the person may be armed. Also called a field inquiry, investigatory stop or investigatory detention.

stop bet. in a numbers operation, a bet across the board on a particular number. The player would win if the selected number came out in any one of the three possible positions.

stopping distance. the distance a moving vehicle will travel from the instant the driver perceives a hazard and the instant the vehicle comes to a full stop. The stopping distance is the sum of reaction distance and braking distance. A stopping distance table can be constructed as aid in making speed of travel estimates. For example, given the conditions that a driver can react to a perceived hazard within three-fourths of a second, is driving an automobile with reasonably good brakes and tires on a straight, dry and level road, and travels a distance of 295 feet before coming to a full stop, the speed of the automobile can be estimated at 70 MPH. Under similar conditions, a stopping distance of 40 feet leads to an estimate that the automobile was traveling 20 MPH at the moment the hazard was perceived.

storefront sting. an antitheft enforcement strategy in which police officers pose as employees of a fencing operation in order to gather information concerning organized theft activities. When sufficient information has been developed to assure prosecution, arrests and searches are made by warrants.

stovepipe boosting. a shoplifting technique in which the thief conceals small items inside a tubular container that appears to be a roll of wrapping paper. One end of the tube has been arranged with a cover that allows quick insertion of merchandise.

STP. the street name for dimethoxy-methamphetamine (DOM). The name is taken from the name of a motor oil additive. STP is a synthetic drug closely resembling mescaline in its chemical structure. It produces a 12-hour intoxication with strong stimulation and may be less euphoric than mescaline. It has been linked to an epidemic of overdoses in which black market tablets contained twenty times the usual dosage.

strabismus. the inability of one eye to attain binocular vision with the other due to an imbalance of eyeball muscles. Strabismus causes squinting and is an impairment indicator looked for in pupillary reaction tests made of persons believed to be under the influence.

straight bomb. a bomb in which all of the component parts are visible to the naked eye. Also called an open bomb.

straight line measurements. in crime scene sketching, measurements made along the same axis from two sides of an item to the nearest two permanent objects. For example, a sofa against a wall can be positioned in a sketch by showing the straight line distances from each end of the sofa to the two corners of the wall.

strangulation by ligature. suicidal or homicidal strangulation with the use of cord, nylon hose, necktie, belt or similar item. The ligature may be looped around the neck and knotted, or twisted in a tourniquet fashion. The ligature mark is usually horizontal, characterized by a groove that encircles the neck at the level of the thyroid cartilage, and most distinct when a firm, rough or coarse ligature is used. In some instances, a coarse ligature will leave a distinct imprint of its texture on the skin. The skin is usually abraded and contused, with scattered hemorrhages. Ligature marks are most apparent when the body is cold. The police investigator will typically photograph the ligature in place at the crime scene and allow it to be removed by the medical examiner at the morgue.

strategic intelligence. information concerning the capabilities, intentions and vulnerabilities of criminals and crime groups, especially of targeted criminal enterprises such as the Mafia.

strategy of defensive driving. a combination of actions such as adjusting speed, controlling movements, and giving signals in relation to perceived potential hazards; maneuvers which facilitate evasive tactics or increase the chance of success in avoiding an accident.

street. the entire width between the boundary lines of a publicly maintained trafficway when any part is open to the use of the public for purposes of vehicular traffic.

street addict. a person belonging to a well-developed street subculture who sees himself as an addict and organizes his behavior around that self-image; a particular type of addict frequently seen as lower class, slum-dwelling, usually a member of a minority group, who adheres to a deviant set of values, and whose chief attributes are self-posturing, conning, and antisocial behavior. The phrase "on the street" implies an idle or homeless person in an urban area who might very well be doing something suited to one's own taste. A distinction is often made between the "physical addict" or upper class addict and the street level or "street addict" by asserting that street addicts belong to a subculture that is insulated from the general culture by a set of unique values and the need to support the habit, whereas upper class addicts still belong to the larger culture because they can afford to support

their habits by legal means. Thus, it is common to lump the street or "subcultural addict" and the criminal addict together. Doing so, however, fails to discriminate between different social patterns of drug involvement on the street scene.

street callbox. a direct-line telephone callbox used by police officers on patrol.

street crime. a class of offenses, sometimes defined with some degree of formality as those which occur in public locations, that are visible and assaultive, and thus constitute a group of crimes which are a special risk to the public and a special target of law enforcement preventive efforts and prosecutorial attention.

street dealer. a middleman in the chain of intermediaries between the importers and the pushers of dangerous drugs.

street time. time spent on conditional release from confinement. If conditional release (such as parole) is revoked, and the person reconfined, street time may not count as time served towards the required term in confinement.

stress interview. an interview in which the questioner deliberately creates a stressful situation for the interviewee in order to elicit observable responses. Common tactics include challenging the veracity of the interviewee, frequently interrupting answers, and silence on the part of the questioner for an extended period.

striated toolmarks. parallel scratches cut into the surface of one material by the harder surface or edge of a tool. The scratches are reproductions of the cutting, prying, or striking surface of the tool that made them. Striated toolmarks can be matched against tools obtained from the possession of a suspect.

striations. marks on bullets produced by rifling in a barrel. As an expended bullet passes thru a barrel it is grooved by the barrel's rifling pattern. Striations on a bullet obtained as evidence can be compared against striations on bullets fired from a suspect weapon, thereby making it possible to link a weapon with a crime. In traffic accident investigations, marks made by friction or abrasion on the roadway or on vehicle parts.

strict construction. the requirement that a statute be interpreted literally in accordance with its terms, rather than its spirit. It is frequently applied to criminal statutes.

strict liability statute. a law based on the concept that one can be held responsible for some acts without the necessity of proving mens rea or blame, fault, or negligence. A strict liability statute categorically forbids a certain act or omission without regard to the offender's state of mind (intent). Strict liability statutes are usually found in the regulatory areas of public health, safety, and welfare. The crimes created by such statutes are often called public torts. Examples are speeding and hunting without a license.

In criminal law the general requirement is that a crime must have an external physical act coupled with an internal mental intent. However, there are some statutory offenses where this doctrine is not applied. They are found in the regulatory areas of public health, safety and welfare which categorically forbid certain acts and omissions without regard to the offender's state of mind. These statutes are based on a view that it is in the best interests of the community to place the burden upon individuals to act or not act at their own peril. Even though a person might not intentionally do or fail to do something, there is no-one else in a better position to prevent the violation. Whether a violator acted intentionally or with knowledge of wrongdoing is immaterial to the question of guilt. For example, strict liability could be applied in the prosecution of a corporate executive whose employees carelessly adulterated food products.

Strict liability statutes usually carry relatively light penalties, as offenders are not generally regarded as criminals in the true sense of the word, and mitigating circumstances are frequently taken into account in assessing penalties.

Examples of strict liability offenses are failure to comply with motor vehicle regulations, food handling violations, alcohol dispensing violations, noncompliance with fish and game laws, and licensing violations.

striker pistol. a non-lethal pistol powered by compressed air which fires pellets containing tear gases or indelible dyes. It is used to mark ring leaders in riot situations.

strip method. a method of searching at an outdoor crime scene. The area to be searched is delineated by markers forming one or more large rectangles. Two or three searchers proceed slowly at the same pace within fingertip distance along paths parallel to one side of a rectangle. When a piece of evidence is found, all searchers halt until it is processed. The search resumes at a given signal. When the searchers reach the end of the rectangle, they turn and proceed back along adjacent lanes, and continue the process until the entire rectangle has been covered.

stripping. a form of theft in which a motor vehicle is stripped of its parts and sold piecemeal.

stroke. the sudden reduction or loss of consciousness, sensation, and voluntary motion caused by rupture or obstruction of an artery of the brain. Also called apoplexy.

strongarm robbery. a robbery in which the offender uses physical force or the threat of it. Also, a type of robbery in which the criminal uses stealth, speed and physical violence, as in a mugging.

structured plea negotiation. a procedure in which the victim of a felony participates with the prosecutor in bargaining the plea of the felon.

strung out. high on drugs.

stupor. a state of semiconsciousness in which the individual is unaware of what is going on in his or her surroundings. Stupor appears as partial or near unconsciousness, or a state of lethargy characterized by diminished responsiveness to stimulation. Stupor is one of the major symptoms of a nonfatal drug overdose.

subculture of violence. a way of life attributed

to large sectors of the lower social classes. In it there is much dependence on force or the threat of force to establish identity and gain status. The subculture of violence may lead to criminality as a method of problem-solving.

subcutaneous. just below the skin, as in subcutaneous injection, a method used by a drug abuser to administer a drug by inserting a hypodermic needle beneath the skin surface.

subliminal perception. the registration of sensory information that influences behavior without producing any conscious experience of the stimulus.

subluxation. an incomplete dislocation in which a bone displaces from its normal site of articulation, but returns spontaneously to its normal position.

subordination. the substitution of one person in place of another with reference to a lawful claim, demand or right so that the substitute succeeds to the rights of the other in relation to the debt or claim, its rights, remedies or securities.

subornation of perjury. an offense in which a witness is induced secretly to provide false testimony.

subpoena. a written order issued by a judicial officer requiring a specified person to appear in a designated court at a specified time in order to serve as a witness in a case under the jurisdiction of that court, or to bring material to that court.

subpoena duces tecum. a process issued out of court requiring a witness to attend and to bring with him certain documents or records in his possession.

subrogation. the legal process by which one party endeavors to recover from a third party the amount paid to an insured under an insurance policy when such third party may have been responsible for causing the loss. Subrogation derives from the common law and is intended to allow an insurer who has paid a claim to assert any rights the policyholder may have against someone who was responsible for the loss.

substantive law. that part of the general body of laws which creates, defines and regulates rights. Adjective or remedial law prescribes methods of enforcing rights and obtaining redress for their invasion. It is a subdivision of criminal law which defines the types of conduct constituting crimes. It also provides for punishment of crimes, and lays down rules on such matters as the capacity of persons to commit crimes and the defenses that persons charged with crimes may legally employ.

sucking chest wound. a wound in which the pneumothorax is open.

suction effect. in bomb incident investigations, a wave of pressure toward the point of detonation which occurs after the blast wave. It is a consequence of a vacuum created when air is powerfully and instantaneously pushed outward by the blast.

sudden heat of passion. a rage or anger provoked by the conduct of another; quick-tempered, rash and impetuous disturbance of a person's emotional stability. Sudden heat of passion is an element of consideration in the crime of manslaughter.

sudden infant death syndrome (SIDS). crib death; the death of an infant after the first few weeks of life, the cause of which cannot be established by careful autopsy.

sudden sniffing death (SSD) syndrome. the most prominent threat to health associated with inhalant abuse. It is related to sniffing the fluorocarbons contained in aerosols and results when the fluorocarbons (particularly trichlorofluoromethane) sensitize the heart to the adrenal hormone epinephrine, which is in itself a strong cardiac stimulant. By potentiating the effect of epinephrine on the heart, wildly erratic heartbeat and increased pulse occur. The use of fluorocarbons as propellants in household aerosol products has been banned by the U.S. Environmental Protection Agency since March 16, 1978.

suicidal cuts. in suicide investigations, parallel and overlapping incisions of varying length and depth. They represent a progression from hesitation to final resolve on the part of the victim. Also called hesitation marks.

sui juris. in one's own right; having the legal capacity to act for one's self.

summary arrest. an arrest made of a suspect at or near the scene of the crime; an arrest without court process. For example, a person in violation of vagrancy laws may be summarily arrested without benefit of a warrant.

summons. a written order requiring a person accused of an offense to appear in a designated court at a specified time to answer the charge.

super dampening concept. in polygraph, a concept which holds that a person is likely to respond randomly, weakly or not at all to relevant questions of a polygraph test if he considers an outside, non-relevant issue to be a greater threat to his well-being than the main relevant issue being tested.

superelevation. the degree to which the outside edge of a roadway is higher than the inside edge at a specified point on a curve; the change in elevation per unit distance across the roadway from the inside of a curve to the outside edge. Superelevation is designated in feet (or meters) of rise or fall per foot (or meter) of level distance from the inside to the outside of a curve. It may also be designated by rise as a percent of level distance.

superficial perforating gunshot wound. a wound in which the skin is torn, giving a lacerated appearance. This type of wound can be mistaken for a wound made by a knife.

super high frequency. a band of the radio spectrum operating between 3000–30,000 megaherz.

superquick impact fuse. a bomb fuse designed to function immediately upon impact, before any penetration, thus giving maximum surface effect. It is normally utilized when the target is of light construction such as aircraft.

supervised buy. a purchase of an illegal drug by a person acting as an agent of the police. Also called a controlled buy.

supervised probation. guidance, treatment or regulation by a probation agency of the behavior of a person who is subject to adjudication or who has been convicted of an offense, resulting from a formal court order or probation agency decision.

supervisory custody. custody of a probationer, parolee or other nonincarcerated person who is subject to the jurisdictional control of a probation or parole agency. Supervisory control does not involve physical control.

supine. lying flat on the back with the face up.

supplemental broadcast. a radio call made to correct errors in an earlier call and to provide newly obtained details for responding officers.

supply reduction strategy. a federal drug abuse strategy geared toward reducing both the demand and the supply of illicit drugs. It outlines the government's plan for reducing the production, importation, and flow of illicit drugs in the country. The domestic component of the supply reduction strategy consists of law enforcement involving the investigation, prosecution, and seizure of assets of drug traffickers. International activities include border interdiction efforts and, through diplomacy and cooperation with foreign governments and international organizations, encouragement of crop eradication programs with income substitution and rural development programs, support of law enforcement programs, support of international narcotics control programs by other governments, and support for international prevention, treatment, and rehabilitation programs.

support fence. a receiver of stolen property who provides tipster, transport, or other services in support of the theft.

suppurative. forming or discharging pus.

suppression. in polygraphy, an indicator of deception which appears as an involuntary reduction in the respiratory amplitude of the pneumograph tracing in response to a stressful question. A trend of four respiratory cycles is commonly regarded as suppression.

suppression hearing. a hearing to determine whether or not the court will prohibit specified statements, documents, or objects from being introduced into evidence in a trial.

Supreme Court of the United States. the highest court in the United States. It consists of nine justices appointed for life, and has ultimate jurisdiction for deciding the constitutionality of state and federal laws and for interpreting the Constitution. Also called the court of last resort.

surveillance. secretly observing the behavior of another, visually or electronically.

surveillance receiver. in electronics countermeasures, a radio receiver used to monitor radio transmitter bugs or beacons.

suspect. a person, adult or juvenile, considered by a criminal justice agency to be one who may have committed a specific criminal offense, but who has not been arrested or charged.

suspect document. any writing which may have been altered, fabricated or forged.

suspended sentence. a sentence imposed by a court but not put into execution.

suspense file. a file which calls attention to work actions required to be performed on certain dates.

suspension lift. a technique for placing onto a stretcher an injured individual who is lying face down. It is performed by one person lifting and stabilizing the victim's head while two other persons are simultaneously lifting from each side of the torso. When the victim is lifted about one foot off the ground, a fourth person slides a stretcher underneath.

suspicion. a belief that a person has committed a criminal offense, based on facts and circumstances that are not sufficient to constitute probable cause.

sustained and coercive detention. a term used to differentiate between an investigatory detention (e.g., street stop or field inquiry) and custodial interrogation within the context of Miranda. When an investigatory detention ceases to be brief and casual and becomes sustained or coercive, Miranda rights apply. The courts generally find that a detained person during an investigatory detention is in no sense an accused but merely one

suspected of misconduct. Because custodial interrogation does not exist, no Miranda warnings need be given. But when suspicion focuses sharply enough to provide probable cause for arrest, then the relationship between the police and the person detained becomes that of accuser and accused, and Miranda warnings must be given and a waiver obtained before any additional statements made by the defendant will be admissible in court.

sweatbox. an interrogation room.

sweep. to search for the presence of electronic eavesdropping devices in a given area with the use of special detection equipment.

swindle. intentional false representation to obtain money or any other thing of value, where deception is accomplished through the victim's belief in the validity of some statement or object presented by the offender.

swing. the degree to which the upper and lower edges of the film in a camera deviate from horizontal when a photograph is made. Swing in crime and accident scene photography may cause the photographs to misrepresent grades and elevations.

swing out cylinder revolver. a general class of revolver constructed with the barrel firmly fixed in the frame and a revolving cylinder that swings out for loading and ejecting.

symbolic assembly language. a computer language that directly interacts with the hardware. Also called a low-level language in contrast to higher level languages such as COBOL and FORTRAN.

symbolic interactionism. an interpretive perspective which says that individuals learn meanings through interaction with others and then organize their lives around these socially created meanings.

sympathetic inks. any of several chemical solutions used to make invisible writings. A sympathetic ink is made visible by a reagent or special light.

sympathetic interrogating (interviewing) approach. a method of obtaining information from a suspect or hostile witness in which the interrogator rationalizes the offense, minimizes the moral implications, and generally portrays the suspect in a favorable light. This approach is often used with first offenders. A sympathetic approach is also applied in interviewing of victims and friendly witnesses who may have difficulty in overcoming psychological trauma or fear. The sympathetic interviewing approach is designed to remove emotional barriers that stand in the way of obtaining accurate information.

sympathetic nervous system. that branch of the involuntary nervous system that prepares the body for fight or flight by speeding up heartbeat and breathing, and at the same time shutting down digestive functions. Nerves of this system leave the middle segments of the spinal cord to connect to many organs, blood vessels, and glands.

sympathomimetic. a drug that primarily produces effects similar to (or that mimic) those resulting from stimulation of the sympathetic nervous system. Sympathomimetic drugs that also excite the central nervous system (such as the amphetamines) are often used as recreational drugs. Also called adrenomimetic drugs.

symptomatic question. in polygraphy, a question designed to determine the existence of an outside issue which might interfere with the successful conduct of the test.

Synanon. a private antidrug addiction society founded in 1958. It uses "attack" therapy and group pressure to overcome the addict's compulsion to use drugs. As originally established, the members remained in the Synanon community as long as they liked and were discouraged from leaving until they were judged capable of remaining off drugs. Synanon has developed into a lifestyle movement as an alternative society and social system.

syncope. fainting; a sudden fall in blood pressure or failure of the heart to contract, resulting in diminished blood flow to the brain and loss of consciousness.

syndicate. an ongoing, coordinated conspiracy, characterized by hierarchy and division of labor, and involving a relatively large number of criminals. The syndicate or organized crime is in partial or total control of numerous illegal activities, such as usury, gambling, prostitution, pornography, drug traffic, extortion, and hijacking. It also controls many legal enterprises, such as restaurants and trucking firms, which are frequently used to conceal the sources of illegally obtained money and to accomplish other criminal purposes.

synergism. cooperative action or reaction by two or more substances whose total effect is greater than the sum of their separate effects. For example, a synergistic effect frequently results from the combined ingestion of drugs and alcohol.

synergist. a substance that augments the activity of another substance, agent, or organ, as one drug augmenting the effect of another.

synthetic drug. a chemically developed drug; a drug not made from natural sources. Demerol, Dolophine, methadone, Valium, PCP, and Seconal are examples of synthetic drugs. Many experts regard synthetics as the most dangerous of all drug types.

synthetic opiates. drugs manufactured to resemble the opium alkaloids morphine and codeine and their derivatives in action and effect. The principal synthetics are meperidine hydrochloride (Demerol) and its related drugs, levorphanol tartrate (Dolophine), pentazocine (Talwin), and propoxyphene hydrochloride (Darvon). Also called opioids.

syphilitic psychosis. a mental illness caused by the syphilitic infection of the spinal cord and brain. Also called paresis.

system. an orderly arrangement of interrelated components operating as an integrated whole.

system architecture. a term referring to the scheme by which various types of equipment are interconnected to form a coherent system.

systemic poison. a poison that acts on the nervous system and organs of the body.

The symptoms of systemic poisoning vary widely. The nature of impairment by systemic poison is related to the amount of poison consumed, the manner of consumption, and whether the victim's body has a built-in tolerance of the poison. Common types of systemic poisons are metal salts, organic poisons and most of the poison gases such as phosgene, hydrogen sulphide and carbon monoxide.

systems analysis. the analysis of an activity to determine precisely what must be accomplished and how to accomplish it; a methodologically rigorous collection, manipulation and evaluation of organizational data in order to determine the best way to improve the functioning of the organization (the system) and to aid a decision-maker in selecting a preferred choice among alternatives.

systems approach. a logical method for problem solving in which a comprehensive solution is developed in relation to a problem having several dimensions. A type of systems approach follows three general steps: assessment of vulnerability, implementation of countermeasures, and evaluation of effectiveness.

systems management. the application of systems theory to managing organizational systems or subsystems. It can refer to management of a particular function or to projects or programs within a larger organization.

systole. the contraction of the heart, especially of the ventricles, by which blood is forced into the aorta and pulmonary artery.

tachycardia. abnormally rapid heart rate, usually taken to be over 100 beats per minute.

tactical intelligence. intelligence immediately useful to the enforcement forces of an agency.

tactical unit. an element of a police organization, sometimes formed on a temporary basis, assigned to perform specific enforcement activities, such as stakeouts at high-risk robbery targets.

tagging. a practice used by auditors to trace a transaction as it moves through an accounting system. Typically, a special code is attached at the beginning point of a transaction, and as the transaction is progresses through the system the code allows it to be monitored for improper processing, violations of control standards, or other indications of fraud.

tagging beeper. a miniature radio transmitter that is concealed on a motor vehicle, aircraft or watercraft for the purpose of tracking such conveyance when visual surveillance is not possible. Used chiefly in drug smuggling enforcement operations, the tagging beeper's signals are monitored by electronic receiving equipment such as the U.S. Customs Airborne Direction Finding Receiving System.

tag switch. a shoplifting technique in which the thief substitutes the price tag from a low-priced article for the price tag on a high-priced article.

tail. that member of a pickpocket team who surreptitiously receives the stolen item from the taker immediately after the taking and departs the scene by a route separate from his accomplices.

tailpit worker. a pickpocket who steals from the side of his victim, e.g., from the side pockets of a jacket.

take a trip. use LSD.

Takayama hemochromogen test. a microcrystal test which is specific for blood. When the Takayama chemical solution is added to dried blood, characteristic red crystals are formed which can be seen under the microscope.

take out. in riot control operations, to neutralize ring leaders by capture or the use of weapons.

taking care of business. engaging in those activities and relationships which allow a street addict to supply his or her drug habit. The term refers to behavior that is directed mainly to the pursuit of the means for obtaining drugs. Many times, such activities include larceny, burglary, robbery, prostitution, and drug dealing.

talbutal. the generic name of a depressant legally sold as Lotusate, and regulated under the Controlled Substances Act as a Schedule III drug.

talking down method. a drug treatment method employed when a drug user is undergoing a panic reaction (bad trip). It involves giving verbal reassurance that the distortions and frightening experiences are related only to the drug itself and do not indicate emotional illness. The goal is to convince the individual that the unpleasant experiences are transitory and will end once the drug has run its course.

talesman. one who is summoned to be added to a jury in order to compensate for a deficient number; any member of a panel from which a jury is to be chosen.

Talwin. the trade name of a narcotic known generically as pentazocine. It is a Schedule IV narcotic.

tampered meter theft of service. a theft of electric or gas service in which the thief, usually the subscriber, will remove the glass face plate covering the meter dials. The thief will turn the dials backwards, remove teeth from gears, or tamper with the recording mechanism in such a way that consumption of service appears to be less than actual.

tangential gunshot wound. a wound caused by a bullet which enters the body at an extreme angle, causing an abrasion and leaving a residue track on the skin.

tape dialer. an automatic dialing device that transmits prerecorded messages over telephone lines to predetermined parties.

tare. the weight of a truck, rail car or other conveyance when empty. The tare is deducted from the gross weight of the loaded conveyance when determining freight charges.

target of opportunity. an entity that becomes available by chance to an intelligence agency for the collection of needed information.

Tarmac. the trade name for concrete cemented with a bituminous material such as tar or asphalt.

TASER. a non-lethal rifle used by the police to subdue violent persons. The rifle fires an electrically charged dart that temporarily immobilizes the offender. TASER is an acronym for Thomas A. Swift Electric Rifle.

task analysis. an analysis of a work process for the purpose of revealing specific tasks, task interrelationships, the work environment, work tools and equipment, work criticalities, time requirements, and the skills, knowledges, and abilities required of the workers.

task force. a temporary organizational unit charged with accomplishing a specific mission.

tattooed gunshot wound. a close-range wound characterized by gunpowder tattooing in and around the bullet hole. The tattooing consists of charring at the entry point, and powder grains and combustion products embedded in the skin.

team policing. a method of law enforcement in which a group or team of police officers are assigned responsibility for all police services in a given geographical area.

tear gas. any of the several chemicals used by the police for the purpose of disabling persons in a nonlethal manner. Tear gas is typically in liquid form and released as an aerosol liquid or gas which upon contact with the target persons produces disorientation, nausea, and other disabling effects of temporary duration. The common form of tear gas is a lacrimator that provokes a copious flow of tears and irritation of the eyes. When discharged, the gas has a blue-white smokey appearance and a strong, sweet odor. The effects last from 5 to 30 minutes depending upon concentration and exposure.

technical listening devices. devices and items of equipment primarily used or designed for wiretap, investigative monitoring, or eavesdropping.

technical preparation. the collection and organization of traffic accident data for study and interpretation relative to an accident under investigation. It includes making measurements, photographs, maps, diagrams, and speed estimates in addition to those prepared on the scene immediately following the accident, matching damage areas, and conducting experiments.

technical services. specialized law-enforcement agency functions such as electronic eavesdropping, wiretapping, communications, identification, laboratory activities, record-keeping, and temporary detention.

technical surveillance. in electronic countermeasures, the bugging, wiretapping, televising or radio tracking of another's activities.

Technology Assessment Program (TAP). a program sponsored by the International Association of Chiefs of Police to test various kinds of police equipment in terms of effectiveness, safety, reliability, and other performance related standards.

Teichmann hemin reaction test. a laboratory test to determine the presence of blood in a stain or substance of unknown origin. If blood is present, hemin crystals form upon application of a reagent. It is a confirmatory test, i.e., it is used to confirm a test by a different procedure. Although conclusive, as opposed to indicative, this test does not differentiate between human blood and blood of other species. It is also called a hemin crystal test.

telephone analyzer. a device that detects electronic eavesdropping equipment present in telephone sets and telephone transmission lines.

telephone boiler room. a room equipped with a bank of telephones used by swindlers to sell worthless bonds, real estate, or stock. Also known as a bucket shop.

telephone dialer. a device that dials a central station or up to about four telephone numbers designated by the subscriber. A telephone dialer is used chiefly to send a recorded message that announces an alarm condition at a protected premises, and is most often a component of a larger system that contains intrusion detectors and a control unit.

telephone line lock-in. a telephone company procedures for "locking in" on the line of a nuisance caller so that a trace can be made to the source of the call.

telephone scrambler. a device used at both the transmit and receive ends of a telephone line for the transmission of scrambled voice communications. Multiple codes are switch-selectable. Speech frequency inversion is a common method of scrambling telephone signals.

teletype system. any of several communications systems in which a typewriter-like device is used to generate coded telegraph signals which are transmitted by wire or by radio-frequency broadcast to receiving units that display the messages on a printer or television-like screen.

teletypewriter exchange service (TWX). teletypewriter service in which teletypewriter stations are provided with lines to a central office for access to other stations throughout the U.S. and Canada.

Telex. the trademark for a communications service of the Western Union Corporation that provides two-way transmission of teletype messages between any two points (terminals) in the Western Union Corporation network worldwide.

temazepam. the generic name of a depressant legally sold as Restoril, and regulated under the Controlled Substances Act as a Schedule IV drug.

tempered glass. a type of windowplate approximately six to seven times more resistive to breaking than standard glass. When fractured, tempered glass shatters into small, comparatively harmless pieces.

template. a precise detailed pattern used as a guide in the mortising and drilling of a door or frame to receive hardware; a stencil-type plate having various shapes symbolizing vehicles, pedestrians and other objects that are typically represented in traffic accident diagrams.

temporary insanity. insanity which existed only at the time of the act; a legal defense.

temporary operating procedures. written instructions issued for a short period of time to cover a situation of limited duration.

ten-code. any of several systems of coded signals, usually transmitted by voice, in which each signal starts with the spoken number, ten, followed by a second number that conveys the sense of the message. For example, 10-4 may be the signal for "acknowledged" or "okay."

tension wrench. an instrument used in picking a lock. It is used to apply torsion to the cylinder core.

tented arch. a fingerprint pattern in which most of the ridges enter upon one side of the impression and flow or tend to flow out the other side. The ridges are arranged on both sides of a spine or axis, and have a sharp upward thrust in the shape of a tent.

terminal box. in electronic countermeasures, the point at which telephone lines are spliced or connected to cables.

territoriality. behavior displayed by an individual or group in connection with the ownership of a place or a geographic area.

terrorism. the unlawful use or threatened use of force or violence by a revolutionary organization against individuals or property for the purpose of coercing or intimidating governments or groups, often for political or ideological causes. Terrorism is distinguished from other criminal acts, psychopathic acts, or acts of warring states.

Terry v. Ohio. a case decided in 1968 by the U.S. Supreme Court which validated the police practice of stopping and making reasonable inquiries of persons reasonably suspected of criminal activity. The Court held that: "Where a police officer observes unusual conduct which leads him reasonably to conclude, in light of his experience, that criminal activity may be afoot and that the persons with whom he is dealing may be armed and presently dangerous; where in the course of investigating this behavior he identifies himself as a policeman and makes reasonable inquiries, and where nothing in the initial stages of the encounter serves to dispel his reasonable fear of his own or another's safety, he is entitled, for the protection of himself and others in the area, to conduct a carefully limited search of the outer clothing of such persons in an attempt to discover weapons which might be used to assault him."

This decision made it clear that accosting an individual under circumstances where the individual is not free to walk away constitutes a limited seizure of that person under the Fourth Amendment. Also, the frisk type of search, although not a complete search, is a serious intrusion upon the sanctity of the individual and is considered a search under the Fourth Amendment. The Court recognized, however, that because a stop of this type is more limited in scope than an arrest and the frisk is less intrusive than a full search, these actions do not fall within the warrant requirement of probable cause.

test graph markings. in polygraphy, the signs and symbols placed by the polygraphist on a moving chart while the examination is in progress. Test graph markings assist the polygraphist at a later time when the chart is interpreted.

testimony. the presentation of evidence by a witness under oath.

testing behavior. provocative acts taken by a juvenile against an authority figure as a means to determine the limits of tolerance.

tetrahydrocannabinol (THC). the psychotoxic ingredient of hashish and marijuana as well as all plants of the genus Cannabis. Considered a mild hallucinogen, it causes sensory and perceptual disturbances, euphoria and other mood changes, decreased motor coordination, and various physiological changes including alterations in pulse rate, respiration rate, and pupil size. It is classified as a Schedule I controlled substance. The term is a shortened version of delta-9-tetrahydrocannabinol, one of the 61 unique chemicals found only in Cannabis. Also called THC.

tetryl. a type of booster explosive.

Thai stick. potent, seedless marihuana grown in Southeast Asia (principally Thailand, Vietnam, and Nepal) that is packaged and tied in a bundle resembling a stick; a short section of bamboo containing marihuana buds.

THC. tetrahydrocannabinol (or delta-9-tetrahydrocannabinol), the active ingredient of Cannabis. Cannabis products are frequently rated and priced in terms of THC content. High-grade marihuana will contain 6–7 percent; hashish about 12 percent; and hashish oil as much as 40 percent. Pure THC is difficult and expensive to produce, and when exposed to air loses its potency rapidly. THC sold on the street is many times not THC at all, but PCP or LSD.

theft. larceny, or in some legal classifications, the group of offenses including robbery, burglary, extortion, fraudulent offense, hijacking, and other offenses sharing the element of larceny.

theft from interstate carrier. the name applied to a law that prohibits embezzling and stealing of goods moving as part of interstate or foreign shipments. It is found in 18 USC, Section 659.

theft of service (TOS). the theft of electric or gas service in which the thief, usually the subscriber, will circumvent or retard the recording mechanisms of the metering equipment. The method of stealing often includes the use of jumpers or conductors to divert electric service around the meter, plumbing devices that bypass the gas meter, or direct tampering with the dials and gears of the meter to show a less than actual consumption of service.

theft-to-order fence. a receiver of stolen property who places orders with thieves for specific kinds of goods, usually on the basis of orders received from buyers.

theory of territoriality. a theory which holds that proper physical design of housing encourages residents to extend their social control from their homes and apartments out into the surrounding common areas. In this way, the residents change what previously had been perceived as semi-public or public territory into private territory. Upgrading the common areas results in increased social control which has the effect of reducing crime. Also called defensible space.

Theory X and Theory Y. opposing sets of assumptions which postulate that under the conditions of contemporary industrial life the potentialities of the average employee are only partially utilized. Theory X assumes that the average employee inherently dislikes work, must be coerced to work toward the achievement of organizational objectives, has little ambition, and wants security above all. In Theory Y, the average employee regards work as natural as play or rest, is self-directed, is committed to organizational objectives to the extent they satisfy personal needs, accepts and seeks responsibility, and is imaginative and creative in solving work problems.

thermal lance. a bar packed with aluminum and magnesium wire or rods, and connected through a regulator to an oxygen container. It burns like a high-powered sparkler and is consumed while being used. A thermal lance is capable of defeating most safes currently manufactured. Also called a burning bar.

thermal viewing device. a portable device that uses the infrared spectrum to detect heat emanations. It can be operated in total darkness and is used to detect heat given off by suspects in hiding, concealed equipment in operation, living disaster victims, and in some instances recently buried bodies.

thin air prescription. a prescription forged by a dishonest pharmacist, usually to account for drugs diverted to the illegal market.

thin layer chromatography (TLC). a laboratory technique for identifying drugs. A glass plate is coated with a thin layer of stationary phase such as silica gel. The suspect drug is spotted on the plate where it is exposed to a solvent that migrates or moves on the plate. The analyst interprets the extent of migration. In the analysis of urine for drug presence, the technique is similar. A drop of chemically treated urine is placed on a specially-coated plate. When a dye solution is added, the spot will migrate and undergo color changes which are interpreted by the analyst.

third wire tap. in electronic countermeasures, the activating of a telephone microphone by adding a third wire to the circuit so that the telephone microphone is in the on mode while the hand set is in the "hung up" position.

thoracic. pertaining to the chest or thorax, i.e., the upper part of the trunk between the neck and abdomen. The skeletal wall of the thorax is formed by 12 dorsal vertebrae and 12 pair of ribs.

threat. the declaration by words or action of an unlawful intent to do some injury to another, together with an apparent ability to do so.

Threatcon Red. a terrorist threat condition declared by U.S. military forces in response to an imminent threat of terrorist acts against U.S. military personnel or facilities in a general geographic area. This threat may be based on information that terrorist elements in an area have plans or preparations for attacks against specific persons or facilities.

Threatcon White. a terrorist threat condition declared by U.S. military forces in response to a non-specific threat against U.S. military personnel or facilities in a general geographic area. This threat may be based on information that terrorist elements in an area have general plans concerning military facilities.

Threatcon Yellow. a terrorist threat condition declared by U.S. military forces in response to a specific threat of terrorism against U.S. military personnel or facilities in a particular geographic area. This threat may be based on information that terrorist elements are actively preparing for operations in a particular area.

threshold inquiry. a brief questioning of an individual, short of an arrest, which gives no right to search the person; a questioning situation in which a Miranda rights warning is not required.

thrill seeking. a process in which an individual actively seeks out stimulation from the environment. Some experts believe that thrill seeking and drug use correlate in that both are associated with persons who tend to fantasize and have unusual perceptual feelings.

thrust. the force against a traffic unit (vehicle, pedalcycle or pedestrian) considered to be concentrated at a particular point on that unit at any instant during a collision.

thumb cuff. in polygraphy, a device placed on an examinee's thumb during testing. It consists of an inflatable cylindrical rubber bladder enclosed in a metal housing. The thumb cuff electronically enhances detected changes in the examinee's blood pressure and pulse rate.

thumbcuffs. a device similar to handcuffs that is placed on the thumbs for the purpose of controlling an unruly person in custody.

tidal volume. the amount of air inhaled or exhaled during normal, quiet breathing; the volume of one breath. In polygraphy, the volume of air moved in or out of the lungs with each respiratory cycle. Tidal volume is a factor associated with measurements made by the pneumograph component of the polygraph instrument.

time delay circuit. a circuit that creates a time delay. For example, a home alarm system might include a time delay for the homeowner to set the alarm and exit without triggering an annunciation.

time interval. in polygraphy, the elapsed time between questions asked during a test. The time interval during a specific test ranges between 15–25 seconds. During a pre-employment screening test the interval is somewhat shorter. The time interval allows the polygraph instrument to record the examinee's full physiological response to the preceding question before the next question is asked.

time lapse imaging. an image-recording system that takes periodic sequential samples of a scene. A time lapse video camera, for example, might record a one second segment every three seconds. This technique places a lesser demand on the taping component of the system.

time limit cutout. a feature of a fire alarm system in which the maximum duration of the alarm signal is limited to not less than 3 minutes and not more than 15 minutes.

time management. a term referring to an assumption that productivity can be enhanced by the application of relatively simple rules that cause workers to concentrate on tasks that are essential as opposed to tasks that are not. An example is the so-called 80/20 rule which hypothesizes that workers tend to spend about 80 percent of their time on tasks that produce 20 percent of the results. Although such activities may make the worker feel a sense of accomplishment, they are not significantly productive. Time management is intended to organize work processes so that maximum time is spent on maximum-value activities.

time-mechanical initiator. a timing device used to initiate a bomb's detonator. An alarm clock and pocket watch are common types of time-mechanical initiators.

time of death determination. in criminal investigations, a determination made by a medical examiner as to the approximate time that a person died in a case under investigation. A time of death determination is based on: (1) body heat, (2) rigor mortis, (3) livor mortis or lividity, and (4) an examination of stomach contents.

Body heat is usually determined by at least two rectal temperature readings made two hours apart. The common formula for calculating time of death is: normal temperature (98.6 degrees Fahrenheit) minus rectal temperature divided by 1.5. The formula is based on the observation that from onset of death the body will cool at a rate of about 1.5 degrees Fahrenheit per hour.

Rigor mortis is revealing in that it develops within 8 to 12 hours, is maintained for 12 to 24 hours, and begins to disappear at the 36 to 48 hours range.

Livor mortis begins about 30 minutes after death and is completed within 8 to 12 hours. The intensity of lividity (color ranging from bright to dark red) is the principal indicator.

Because food requires 3 hours for digestion to occur, stomach contents can be helpful in fixing the time of death.

time served. the total period spent in confinement for a given offense or on a given charge, usually computed as time spent before and after sentencing. In some instances, when persons are held without bail pending trial, the sentence is to time already served, thus permitting immediate discharge.

time sharing. the interleaved use of time on a computer system that enables two or more users to execute computer programs concurrently.

tincture. a medicinal preparation consisting of a drug in an alcohol solution, such as laudanum, which is a tincture of opium.

tintometer. a type of colorimeter used by a questioned documents examiner for the comparison of inks.

TIP. a police-sponsored program which encourages citizens to report suspected drug traffickers, i.e., turn in a pusher.

tissue builder. an undertaker's supply item which when injected into the fingertips of a deceased person will round out wrinkled tips so that fingerprint impressions can be obtained.

tithings. in Saxon England, groups of ten families pledged to be responsible for each other's behavior.

titration. a testing technique in which a reagent is added to a substance until a reaction takes place, and then measuring the volume of reagent so added. In pharmacologic treatment, the method of administering a drug dose in very small increments at a time while carefully gauging the effect of each increment.

TL-15/TL-30. terms used by Underwriters' Laboratories to describe combination-locked steel containers offering 15 or 30 minute protection against an expert burglary attack using common hand tools.

toke. an inhalation of marijuana or hashish smoke, especially from a toke pipe, a short-stemmed pipe favored by the smokers of such substances.

tolerance. a bodily condition that requires ever-increasing amounts of a drug in order to achieve the desired effect, or that a diminished effect results from regular use of the same dosage; a decrease in response to a drug dose that occurs with continued use. Tolerance is caused by both physiological and psychological factors. It has been shown to be both relative and highly subjective to change.

toll call restrictor. an electronic device which when attached to a standard telephone instrument will cause the line to disconnect when an outgoing call is dialed that begins with the number zero, one, or other number that prefixes a toll call. The restrictor can be deactivated by dialing a secret code.

toll the statute. suspend a statute of limitations. A statute can be tolled or suspended if the defendant flees from the state when the crime is committed or if the defendant remains in the state under a false or assumed name. The prosecution is deemed to commence when the defendant returns to the state or is found.

toluene. methyl benzene, the main active ingredient in glue and paint thinner. It is commonly abused by glue sniffers.

toolmark. an impression, cut, scratch, gouge, or abrasion made when a tool is brought into contact with an object. A toolmark may be classified as a negative impression, as an abrasion-type mark, or as a combination of the two. A tool, such as a jimmy, crow bar, hammer, screwdriver or drill, will leave characteristic marks or impressions on any material softer than the tool itself. These impressions can be matched with great accuracy against test impressions made by a tool found in the possession of a suspect. Toolmarks found at a crime scene can also be compared against known impressions on file in a crime laboratory for the purpose of identifying the type or general class of tool used by the criminal.

toolmark classes. the three general classes of toolmarks into which such marks can be placed according to mechanical action, i.e., prying (jimmy, crow bar, tire iron, screwdriver), cutting (bolt and wire cutters, scissors), and gripping (channel locks, pliers, wrench).

toolmark examination. a crime laboratory examination which seeks to determine if a given toolmark was produced by a specific tool. In a broader sense, a toolmark examination includes the analysis of objects which forcibly contacted each other, were joined together under pressure for a period of time and then removed from contact, or were originally a single item before being broken or cut apart. A toolmark is generally considered the result of contact between an object (the tool) and a softer material.

top guard. an overhang of barbed wire strands or barbed tape along the top of a fence or other perimeter barrier, usually facing outward and upward at a 45 degree angle.

top loader. a type of semiautomatic pistol which is loaded by first placing shells in a clip, locking the breechblock open, and stripping the shells from the clip into the magazine located at the top of the pistol.

torch. an arsonist; commit arson.

torch job. a safecracking method in which a cutting torch is used to burn a hole into the side of the container. The cutting tool is usually an oxyacetylene torch, a thermal lance or burning bar, or a thermite grenade. Also called a burn job.

tort. a civil wrong committed when a person's private right is interfered with; a wrongful act committed by one person against another person or his property. It is the breach of a legal duty imposed by law other than by contract. The word tort means "twisted" or "wrong."

Tort law has three main purposes: (1) to compensate persons who sustain a loss as a result of another's conduct, (2) to place the cost of that compensation on those responsible for the loss, and (3) to prevent future harms and losses.

Compensation is predicated on the idea that losses, both tangible and intangible, can be measured in money. If a loss-producing event is a matter of pure chance, the fairest way to relieve the victim of the burden is insurance or governmental compensation. But where a particular person can be identified as responsible for the creation of the risk, it becomes more just to impose the loss on the responsible person (tortfeasor) than to allow it to remain on the victim or the community at large. The third major purpose of tort law is to prevent future torts by regulating human behavior. In concept, the tortfeasor held liable for damages will be more careful in the future, and the general threat of tort liability serves as an incentive to all persons to regulate their conduct appropriately. In this way, tort law supplements criminal law.

tortfeasor. one who commits a tort.

TOS crime. a crime involving theft of service, such as electricity or gas.

toucheur. a person who is irresistibly drawn to touch the body of another person. Male toucheurs are common in large crowds that present opportunities for disguised pinching and caressing of females.

touch-off. arson; to deliberately set a fire, usually for the purpose of making a fraudulent insurance claim.

touch-tone decoder. an electronic device capable of simultaneously recording the number dialed from a telephone instrument and the line to which it is attached. Touch-tone decoders, like pen registers, are used for investigative purposes.

toxic. pertaining to a noxious or poisonous substance.

toxic gas alarm. a system for detecting quantities of toxic substances in the surrounding atmosphere before they become threatening to human life. The system usually employs a continuous-action air sampler.

toxicology examination. an examination to determine the cause of death in a suspected poisoning case. The types of poisons typically looked for are volatile poisons (carbon monoxide, alcohols, cyanide, and solvents), heavy metals (arsenic, mercury, lead, and antimony), solvent soluble compounds (aspirin, nicotine, and drugs of abuse) and miscellaneous poisons (pesticides, inorganic compounds, plants, caustics, and insects).

toxicomania. an extremely strong need or desire to consume toxic substances, including drugs and alcohol.

toxic psychosis. chronic or acute psychotic-like behavior or delirium resulting from impairment of brain function by drugs or poison. Characteristic symptoms are an unpleasant and extreme confusion, disorientation, aggressiveness, depression, or hallucinations.

TR-30/TR-60. terms used by Underwriters' Laboratories to describe combination-locked steel containers offering 30 and 60 minute resistance against an expert burglary attempt utilizing a torch.

trace. an amount of a substance too minute to be measured; a negligible concentration.

trace evidence. evidence so minute as to require special equipment and techniques as to its collection and analysis. Hair, fibers, dust, and small amounts of blood are examples.

trace metal detection. an investigative technique in which a chemical solution (8-hydroxyquinoline in ethyl alcohol) is sprayed on the hands of a suspect believed to have recently handled a heavy metal object such as a gun. The hands are then examined under regular light and ultraviolet light. If the skin had been in recent contact with metal, a shaded discoloration will be apparent. It might also be possible to discern on the skin a pattern corresponding to the shape of the metal object.

tracer. an inquiry forwarded from one place to another; a bullet which leaves a visible line of fire in its wake; a chemical incorporated in certain types of ammunition for ranging, signalling, or incendiary purposes.

trace restore switch. a switch on the polygraph instrument that causes the galvanic skin response pen to return to its base line.

trachea. the air passage, extending from the throat and larynx to the main bronchi. Also called the windpipe.

trachea choke hold. a type of choke hold used to subdue violent subjects. Pressure is applied to the windpipe (trachea) to reduce the subject's air intake. Because this hold is lethal, it is banned by police department policy or law in many jurisdictions.

tracheotomy. the creation of an opening into the trachea by surgical incision through the neck to facilitate the passage of air or evacuation of secretions.

track. in traffic accident investigations, the distance on the ground between the center of the tire tread on one side of the vehicle to the center of the tire tread on the opposite side.

track marks. marks made on the skin of a drug addict by repeated injections of drugs. They are usually seen on the arms and legs.

traction force. the adhesive friction of a body, such as a tire, on a surface, such as a roadway, that keeps the body from slipping on the surface. Slipping begins when another force, such as centrifugal force, exceeds traction force.

trade secret. information that derives independent economic value from not being generally known to and not being readily ascertainable by other persons who can obtain economic value from its disclosure or use, and is the subject of efforts that are reasonable under the circumstances to maintain its secrecy. Examples would be formulas, patterns, compilations, programs, devices, methods, techniques, and processes.

traffic. pedestrians, ridden or herded animals, vehicles, street cars, and other conveyances either singly or together while using any highway for purposes of travel.

traffic enforcement index. a number computed by dividing the number of convictions with penalties resulting from citations or arrests for hazardous moving violations during a given period of time by the number of fatal and personal injury accidents occurring in the same period. This index is used as a management tool for assessing a department's traffic enforcement efforts. The index is based on the premise that an inverse relationship exists between convictions and accidents, that is to say, as convictions go up, accidents go down.

traffic engineering. an engineering discipline that deals with the planning and geometric design of streets, highways and abutting lands, and with traffic operations thereon, to achieve the safe, convenient, and economic transportation of persons and goods.

trafficking. the obtaining, transporting, and selling of illicit drugs for commercial purposes. Also called drug dealing.

traffic offenses. a group of offenses usually informally categorized as such, and usually consisting of those infractions and very minor misdemeanors relating to the operation of self-propelled surface motor vehicles.

traffic unit. an element of traffic such as a pedestrian, pedalcycle or vehicle; a person using a trafficway for travel or transportation.

trafficway. the entire width between property lines, or other boundary lines, of every way or place of which any part is open to the public for purposes of vehicular travel as a matter of right or custom. All highways are trafficways, but trafficways include also some areas on private property such as shopping centers.

trailer. a fuse-like arrangement of combustible materials extending from a fire's point of origin, placed by an arsonist for the purpose of spreading the fire or leading it to a location where accelerants have been placed; in traffic enforcement, a vehicle with or without motive power, other than a pole trailer, designed for carrying persons or property and for being drawn by a motor vehicle and so constructed that no part of its weight rests upon the towing vehicle.

training by objectives. a training method judged to be effective to the extent that the trainees achieve well-defined objectives based on job tasks.

trajectory. the path of a bullet or projectile as it moves through space. The smaller the angle of elevation of the gun from the horizontal, the shorter the time of flight of the projectile and the smaller the maximum height reached. Conversely, the larger the angle, the greater the time of the flight and the greater the maximum height attained by the projectile. If a projectile could move unaffected by air resistance, an angle of 45 degrees would yield the maximum horizontal range.

tranquilizers. a general term for a varied and complex group of drugs that depress the central nervous system, relieving anxiety and tension, and sometimes relaxing the skeletal muscles. Tranquilizers were originally developed as a substitute for the barbiturates and other depressants that had undesirable side effects. However, tranquilizers were found to have undesirable side effects as well, and also to be habituating and subject to widespread misuse. Tranquilizers are particularly dangerous in that they potentiate the effects of other depressants such as the opiates, barbiturates, and alcohol. When taken together, even in small doses, they can cause coma and death. Unlike the barbiturates, tranquilizers do not generally cause sleepiness or loss of alertness (although there are exceptions). Tranquilizers are usually classified into two categories: (1) the antianxiety tranquilizers such as diazepam (Valium) and chlordiazepoxide hydrochloride (Librium), and (2) the antipsychotic tranquilizers such as reserpine (Serpasil) and chlorpromazine (Thorazine).

transactional analysis. an approach to psychotherapy in which the basic unit of social intercourse is defined as a transaction. Transactions emanate from three ego states: parent, adult, and child. A transactional stimulus is any action that consciously or unconsciously acknowledges the presence of other individuals. The transactions between individuals can be classified as complementary, crossed, simple or ulterior, based upon the response that an individual receives to a stimulus.

The TA framework can be used to help managers assess the nature and effectiveness of their interpersonal behavior. By concentrating on developing adult-to-adult transactions, a manager may eliminate many of the "games people play" in work situations.

transactional immunity. complete immunity from criminal prosecution on account of any transaction, matter, or thing about which the witness has testified. Transactional immunity is one of two basic constitutional immunities, the other being called "use and derivative use immunity."

transceiver. a transmitter and receiver mounted in a single housing.

transcript. a verbatim record of the proceedings of a trial or ancillary proceedings. It is required for purposes of possible appeal.

transfer hearing. a preadjudicatory hearing in juvenile court for the purpose of determining whether juvenile court jurisdiction should be retained over a juvenile alleged to have committed a delinquent act, or whether it should be waived and the juvenile transferred to criminal court for prosecution as an adult.

transferred intent. intent that is legally transferred from one act to another. For example, if a defendant kills one person while intending to kill another, his intent to kill is transferred to the person killed.

transfer theory. a theory which holds that when two objects come into contact they transfer to each other some indication of the contact. The theory has application to crime and accident scene processing in which the investigator seeks to discover physical evidence of contact, such as a hand on a doorknob (fingerprints), knife on flesh (bloodstains), foot on soil (footprints), crow bar on window jamb (toolmarks), paint on paint (vehicle collision), tires on roadway (skid marks), etc.

transmission. the sending of information from one location to another by radio, microwave, laser, or other nonconnective methods, as well as by cable, wire, or other connective media.

transmitter. a device that produces a radio frequency or other electrical signal for conveyance to a compatible receiver. A transmitter/receiver is a device capable of maintaining two-way communication.

transnational crime. illegal activity involving more than one sovereign nation, or in which national borders are crossed, as in international terrorism, drug smuggling, and arms trafficking.

transparent lifting tape. a material used to lift latent fingerprints. The adhesive side is rolled flat onto the powdered print and peeled back. The tape is mounted on a card having a background color in contrast to the color of the powder.

transponder warrant. a warrant issued by a competent court that authorizes the placement of a transponder or beeper on a named motor vehicle, aircraft, or watercraft. The language of the warrant also usually authorizes repair and maintenance of the installed transponder or beeper if such is necessary. Also called a beeper warrant.

transportation of stolen property. the name given to a federal law that prohibits the transportation in interstate or foreign commerce of any goods, wares or merchandise of a value of $5,000 or more, with the knowledge that such materials were stolen, converted or taken by fraud. The law is found in 18 USC, Section 2314.

transporter. that member of an auto theft

ring who delivers a stolen car to the buyer.

trauma. an injury, physical or emotional.

traumatic psychosis. a mental illness caused by physical damage (lesions) to the brain.

Travel Act. the name given to a federal law that prohibits travel in interstate or foreign commerce or the use of any facility in the interstate or foreign commerce with the intent to promote, carry on, or facilitate any unlawful activity. The law is found in 18 USC, Section 1952.

Treasury Enforcement Communications Systems (TECS). a computerized information and communications system that services the Customs Service, the Bureau of Alcohol, Tobacco and Firearms (ATF), the Internal Revenue Service (IRS), the Department of State, the Drug Enforcement Administration (DEA), and the Washington, D.C. office of Interpol. The data base of TECS contains information on suspect persons, businesses, vehicles, aircraft, and vessels. TECS interfaces with the computerized files of the National Crime Information Center (NCIC) concerning wanted persons, stolen property, and criminal history files, and with the National Law Enforcement Telecommunications System (NLETS) concerning driving licenses and vehicle registrations. The NLETS interface also allows TECS to communicate messages to all state and local law enforcement agencies.

Treatment Alternatives to Street Crime (TASC). a federally funded pilot program which allows a drug-dependent offender to enter treatment as a condition of release. A court may take into account the offender's cooperation and success in the treatment program and may determine that the offender should remain in treatment as an alternative to prosecution or incarceration.

tremor. a trembling or shaking, usually from weakness or disease; a feeling of uncertainty or insecurity.

Trendelenburg position. the position in which a victim is placed on his back with legs raised and head lowered for the purpose of minimizing or treating shock.

trespass. entering upon the property of another without consent after receiving, immediately prior to entry, notice that entry is prohibited, or remaining upon the property after receiving notice to depart.

triage. the sorting out and classification of casualties of a disaster to determine priority need and proper place of treatment.

trial. the examination in a court of the issues of fact and law in a case, for the purpose of reaching a judgment.

trial by ordeal. proceedings held in ancient times at which the guilt or innocence of an accused was determined by his ability to withstand torture without confessing.

trial de novo. a new trial conducted in a court of record as an appeal of the result of a trial in a lower court not of record.

trial jury. a statutorily defined number of persons selected according to law and sworn to determine, in accordance with the law as instructed by the court, certain matters of fact based on evidence presented in a trial, and to render a verdict. Also called a petit jury.

trial on transcript. a nonjury trial in which the judicial officer makes a decision on the basis of the record of pretrial proceedings in a lower court. Also called trial by the record.

triangle formation. a riot control formation used to conduct offensive movements against large groups, for example, to penetrate a rioting crowd for the purpose of taking its leaders into custody. Also called the diamond formation.

triangulation. a system for locating a spot in an area by measurements from two or more reference points, the locations of which are identified. Triangulation is used to show the exact locations of items in a crime or accident scene.

triazolam. the generic name of a suppressant legally sold as Halcion, and regulated under the Controlled Substances Act as a Schedule IV drug.

tribadism. the derivation of sexual satisfaction by a female from rubbing against the body of another female. Tribadism is practiced by some female homosexuals.

tribal law. the rules of law, generally

unwritten, in a tribe or tribe-like subculture of a nation. Tribal law in some nations has been granted official standing to the extent it does not conflict with other laws.

trichloracetaldehyde. chloral hydrate; a nonbarbiturate sedative-hypnotic derived from ethyl alcohol. When combined with alcohol, it produces acute intoxication. Also called knockout drops and Mickey Finn.

trier of fact. the individual or group with the obligation and authority to determine the facts, as distinct from the law, in a case. In a jury trial, the jury is the trier of fact and is charged with accepting the law as given to it by the judge.

trifurcation. in fingerprinting, the point at which a friction ridge divides itself into a three-forked line.

trigger pull. the amount of pressure, usually expressed in pounds, necessary to fire a weapon by pulling the trigger.

trigger transmitter. a device used to turn on a remotely located bug on command through a switch receiver.

trimethoxyamphetamine (TMA). a synthetic hallucinogen with stimulant properties. It is taken orally or injected, and is regarded as more powerful than mescaline but less powerful than LSD.

trinitrotoluene (TNT). a highly explosive compound usually stable in its cast form. In color it is cream or yellow and is commonly produced in half pound and one pound blocks.

trip. an experience with a psychoactive drug, especially a hallucinogen.

triturate tablet. a medicine tablet formed in a triturate mold, giving the shape of a section cut from a cylinder.

troubleshoot. to detect, locate, and eliminate errors in a program or system.

trover. an action at law to recover the value of personal property wrongfully withheld or converted by another to his own use.

TRTL-30/TRTL-60. terms used by Underwriters' Laboratories to describe combination-locked steel containers offering 30 and 60 minute protection against an expert burglary attack utilizing common hand tools and cutting torches.

truant. a juvenile who has been adjudicated by a judicial officer of a juvenile court, as having committed the status offense of violating a compulsory school attendance law.

truck. a motor vehicle designed, used, or maintained primarily for the transportation of property.

truck tractor. a motor vehicle designed and used primarily for drawing other vehicles and not so constructed as to carry a load other than part of the weight of the vehicle and load so drawn.

true bill. an indictment issued by a grand jury.

trunk line. a telecommunication line that links a private telecommunication system to the public switched network.

trusty. an inmate of a jail or prison who has been entrusted with some custodial responsibilities, or who performs other services assisting in the operation of the facility.

Truth in Lending Act. a federal law enacted in 1970 which provided in part that no credit card could be issued to a person except as the result of a written application, that the maximum liability to a cardholder could not exceed $100, and that the credit card company must place onto the card some means by which the cardholder could be identified.

try keys. a set of keys milled to fit a particular keyway. Each key will have a different common bitting and is used one at a time in an attempt to open the lock. Some try keys have no bittings and are manipulated in the keyway with raking and turning movements that may cause the lock to open. Also called jingle keys.

tryptamine. a nonhallucinogenic chemical from which dimethyltryptamine (DMT), LSD and psilocybin are derived.

Ts and Bs. the street name for an injected compound made from pentazocine (Talwin) and tripelennamine (Pysibenzamine). The first is a pain killer and the second is an antihistamine. When ground, mixed, cooked, and injected intravenously, the compound produces a rush described by users as equal to heroin. It has become popular among heroin addicts because it is less costly and overdose risks are lessened because the user can regulate potency in the mixing stage. Major health risks are blood vessel damage, seizures, and convulsions. Also called Tops and Bottoms and Teddies and Betties.

Tuinal. the trade name for amobarbital, a commonly abused Schedule II controlled substance that is usually taken orally or injected. Also called barb, downer, blue, yellow jacket and sleeping pill.

turned on. under the influence.

turned suspect. a participant in a crime who has agreed to cooperate with law enforcement, usually in exchange for a reduced charge, immunity or some other consideration. A turned suspect is often someone who has been identified to be a lesser, but knowledgeable participant in a crime or conspiracy whose cooperation can significantly advance the investigation and prosecution of the main participants.

Turner v. Murray. a case in which the U.S. Supreme Court dealt with the question of potential racial prejudice among jurors in interracial capital crimes. The defendant, a black male, was indicted for the robbery-murder of a white store proprietor in Virginia. During jury selection the defendant's request to question prospective jurors on racial prejudice was denied by the trial judge, and the defendant was subsequently convicted and sentenced to death. The Supreme Court concluded that a defendant accused of an interracial capital crime is entitled to have prospective jurors informed of the victim's race and questioned on the issue of racial bias.

turn-key. a person who has charge of the keys of a jail.

turn-key system. a system that is supplied to the user in a ready-to-run condition. Preparatory procedures such as installation, setup, and testing are usually performed by the supplier.

turnover. movement of individuals into, through, and out of an organization. The turnover rate can be statistically defined as the total number (or percentage) of separations within a given period of time. The turnover rate is an important indicator of the morale and health of an organization.

turn state's evidence. an agreement by a principal to a crime to testify against one or more other principals, usually in exchange for a reduced charge or immunity.

twin loops. in fingerprinting, two distinct loops that start from opposite sides and overlap one another.

twist off screw (or bolt). a screw or bolt designed to be tightened but once in place any attempt to loosen it will cause the head to twist off, leaving only a flat head that cannot be turned.

two-channel switch. an equipment feature that allows an input/output device to be attached to two channels.

two factor theory. a management theory which holds that two sets of factors determine a worker's motivation. The first set involves the worker's perceptions of job achievement, recognition, satisfaction, responsibility, and advancement. The second set concerns factors in the job environment such as policies, competency of supervisors, compensation, personal relationships with supervisors, and working conditions in general.

two-man carry. a technique for carrying an ill or injured individual when a stretcher is unavailable. The victim is carried by two persons who interlock their arms behind the victim's knees and back.

two-man rule. a rule that requires, within a protected or restricted area, the presence of at least two authorized persons, each capable of monitoring the conduct of the other.

two-part explosive. a substance composed of two chemicals each of which is not explosive until joined together. A terrorist bomb, for example, might be constructed with a decomposable material that separates the two chemicals. When the separating material reaches a point of decomposition, which is time-predictable, the two chemicals are joined and an explosion results.

two-party check. a check issued by one person to a second person who endorses it so that it may be cashed by a third person. A two-party check is most susceptible to fraud because the maker can stop payment at the bank.

two-way alternate communication. communication in which information is transferred in both directions, one direction at a time. Also called either-way communication.

two-way simultaneous communication. communication in which information is transferred in both directions at the same time. Also called both-way communication.

TX-60. a term used by Underwriters' Laboratories to describe a combination-locked steel container offering 60 minute protection against an expert burglary attack utilizing cutting torches and high explosives. A more resistant type of container is the TXTL-60 container which offers 60 minute protection against an expert burglary attack utilizing common hand tools, cutting torches, high explosives, and any combinations thereof.

Tylenol With Codeine. the trade name for a product combining Tylenol with codeine, thereby subjecting it to regulation as a Schedule II drug under the Controlled Substances Act.

type lines. in fingerprint classification, the two innermost ridges which start parallel, diverge and tend to surround the entire pattern area.

typographic printing. a type of printing used in the making of paper currency, stock certificates, and similar items that are susceptible to counterfeiting. The typographic process, for example, allows for overprinting the permanent (intaglio) features with changeable characteristics such as serial numbers, seals, and authorizing signatures.

UCC filings. filings of business transactions made in accordance with regulations of the Uniform Commercial Code, a system for unifying and standardizing business operations among the various states. UCC filings can be valuable sources of information for police investigators, particularly in the area of white collar crime.

Uhlan test. a serological test employed to distinguish human blood from blood of other species. In the test, a rabbit is injected with human blood which causes precipitins (antibodies) to form in the rabbit's blood. The injections are administered with increasing dosages over a period of several days. This causes the precipitin serum in the rabbit to increase, and when a sufficient quantity is produced the serum is brought into contact with the suspect blood. If the suspect blood is human, a white ring precipitate is formed. This test can be used to differentiate blood among non-human species, for example, to distinguish between blood of cattle or of canines. Also called the precipitin reaction test.

ulnar loop. a fingerprint pattern having a loop that flows in the direction of the ulnar bone of the forearm.

ultrahigh frequencies. radio frequencies in the approximate range from 300MHz to 3000 MHz. Commonly called UHF.

ultraviolet analysis. a crime laboratory technique in which ultraviolet light is used to examine evidence, especially concealed writings, stains, and check alterations. Because it reacts well to seminal fluid, it is also used in rape investigations as a searching aid for stains on clothing and bedsheets.

ultraviolet light. light waves too high in frequency to be detected by the human eye. Commonly called UV.

unarmed robbery. the unlawful taking of property in the immediate possession of another by use or threatened use of force without a deadly or dangerous weapon.

unconcealed walkout. in shoplifting, the tak-

ing of merchandise from store premises with no attempt at concealment.

unconditional release. the final release of an offender from the jurisdiction of a correctional agency; final release from the jurisdiction of a court.

uncontrolled final position. a final position reached by a traffic unit after an accident without conscious human intervention.

unconventional drug use. drug use seen as outside the accepted social bounds of drug-using patterns. It is preferred by some as a substitute term for drug abuse.

underbody debris. debris loosened by collision from the underside of a vehicle. It may consist of mud, dust, rust, paint, road tar, grease, and snow. The location and nature of underbody debris can be revealing as to the events in a collision.

undercover buy and bust. an antifencing enforcement method in which an undercover operative purchases from a fence property that is known to have been previously stolen and sold to the fence. The property purchased by the undercover operative and any other evidence, such as conversations monitored or recorded through the use of a body transmitter, are used to establish probable cause for arrest and search.

undercover vehicle. an unmarked police vehicle used by an undercover agent, intended to resemble the sort of vehicle ordinarily associated with the kind of person the undercover agent portrays.

underground chemist. a chemist who unlawfully manufactures psychoactive drugs for sale on the illicit market.

underground economy. a term referring to illegal business practices in which commerce and the income derived from it are unreported. The practices are typically associated with bartering and the sale of goods and services for cash. Drug dealing, prostitution, and gambling are major segments of the underground economy.

underground press. clandestine publishing

ventures which are frequently operated in support of minority ethnic and political interests.

underside burn pattern. in arson investigations, charring seen on the underside of a very low object (such as the bottom of a door) which suggests that a burning liquid was on the floor's surface.

understeer. a characteristic of a motor vehicle as loaded that results in a tendency to swerve toward the outside of a curve. A motor vehicle with more weight on front wheels than on rear wheels or with too little pressure in front tires is likely to understeer at high speed.

under the influence of alcohol. sufficient intoxicating liquor in the body system to impair faculties. A blood alcohol concentration of .10 grams of alcohol per 100 milliliters of blood, or per 210 liters of breath, constitutes the legal presumption for drunk driving under the laws of most jurisdictions.

undue influence. any threat or persuasion which overcomes or destroys a person's consent or will to act for himself.

unfounded offense. a criminal complaint in which the police determine that a criminal offense was not committed or did not occur.

unidentified dead. a deceased person whose true identity is unknown and whose relatives or friends cannot be immediately located.

Uniform Alcoholism and Intoxication Treatment Act. a model law developed by the National Conference of Commissioners on Uniform State Laws in which alcoholism is viewed as an illness, not a crime, and is therefore not a proper issue for arrest and punishment. In states where this act has enacted, the police take publicly intoxicated persons into protective custody for release to public health treatment centers.

Uniform Code of Military Justice. the code of law for the Armed Forces of the United States.

Uniform Commercial Code. a set of regulations governing business transactions, designed to unify methods of conducting business between the various states.

Uniform Controlled Substances Act. a model law based on Title II of the Comprehensive Drug Abuse Prevention and Control Act. Many states have adopted the model with only minor revisions, thereby helping to eliminate inconsistencies in drug enforcement in federal and state jurisdictions.

uniform crime index. an index of crime used for national crime reporting and evaluation purposes. The crimes listed in the index include murder, rape, robbery, aggravated assault, burglary, larceny, and auto theft. Except for murder, attempts are included. Attempted murder is listed as aggravated assault.

Uniform Crime Report. an annual report published by the FBI in which statistics are given for eight uniform crime index offenses.

Uniform Crime Reporting System (UCRS). a system for recording, collecting, and analyzing information about criminal activities and other law enforcement matters. The UCRS is administered by the FBI under the supervision of an advisory committee composed of various law enforcement agencies.

uniform offense classifications. classifications used by the FBI's National Crime Information Center to represent offense types in automated individual criminal history record systems.

uniform sentencing. the practice of imposing equal sentences for crimes of equal seriousness in the same relevant circumstances.

Uniform State Narcotic Drug Act. a model act that was adopted by most states between 1933–1937. It sought to eliminate the many conflicts and weaknesses of state narcotic laws and enforcement procedures. In this act, marijuana was classified as an opiate and cocaine as a narcotic drug.

Uniform Vehicle Code. a specimen or model set of motor vehicle laws, designed and advanced as a comprehensive guide or standard for state motor vehicle and traffic laws.

United States Code. the official law books that contain all federal laws.

United States Court of Appeals. an appellate court without power or jurisdiction to retry criminal cases. Its authority is limited to reviewing the trial court record and correcting errors of law that may have been committed. Thus, on an appeal from a judgment of conviction in the district court, the Court of Appeals will not hear cases anew.

United States Court of Claims. a federal court having jurisdiction over claims, except pensions and certain war claims, against the government, founded upon the Constitution or any federal law. This court determines the validity of claims against the United States, but depends upon the Congress to appropriate money for the payment of them. It convenes in Washington, D.C., and consists of a chief justice and four associate justices. Appeals from this court go directly to the U.S. Supreme Court.

United States v. Chadwick. a case in which the U.S. Supreme Court in 1976 reiterated the expectation of privacy doctrine by ruling unreasonable a government search of luggage without a warrant. This decision is the basis of police procedure which requires that a warrant be obtained to search the luggage (e.g., suitcases and briefcases) of arrested persons.

United States v. Gumerlock. a case in which the U.S. Supreme Court in 1979 found that a search of air shipments which are not subject to security screening, and absent proof that airline employees searched the defendant's package pursuant to government-approved security procedures, is private and thus outside the scope of the Fourth Amendment.

United States v. Matlock. a case in which the U.S. Supreme Court in 1974 held valid a consent to search given by one person who shared common premises with others. In this case, the defendant was convicted on the basis of evidence obtained during the search of an apartment shared by the defendant and other persons, one of whom gave permission to the police to search the apartment's common area. The Court stated: " . . . it is reasonable to recognize that any of the coinhabitants has the right to permit the inspection in his own right and that others have assumed the risk that one of their number might permit the common area to be searched."

United States v. McKinney. a case in which the U.S. Supreme Court ruled that police officers may conduct a search without a warrant when the community would be endangered during the time required to obtain a warrant.

United States v. New York Telephone. a case in which the U.S. Supreme Court in 1977 held that Title III of the Omnibus Crime Control Act was not violated by the use of a pen register and that such use was authorized under the Federal Rules of Criminal Procedure. The decision found that the Federal District Court has the power to authorize the installing of a pen register upon a finding of probable cause. In 1979 the Supreme Court held in Smith v. Maryland that the use of a pen register does not constitute a search or invasion of privacy. Thus, a warrant is not now required to install a pen register. However, the practice of obtaining a warrant continues in some jurisdictions.

United States v. Robinson. a case in which the U.S. Supreme Court ruled in 1975 that any person lawfully arrested by the police, regardless of the nature of the offense, may be subjected to a full search (sometimes called a field search), and whatever incriminating evidence is found on his person or in his clothing may be used against him. The Court stated: "A custodial arrest of a suspect based on probable cause is a reasonable intrusion under the Fourth Amendment; that intrusion being held lawful, a search incident to the arrest requires no additional justification . . . and we hold that in the case of lawful custodial arrest a full search of the person is not only an exception to the warrant requirement of the Fourth Amendment, but is also a reasonable search under that Amendment."

United States v. Santana. a case in which the U.S. Supreme Court held in 1976 that the defendant, who was to be arrested outside his house in a public place, could not defeat the arrest by retreating into a private place.

United States v. Watson. a case in which the U.S. Supreme Court in 1976 ruled that while probable cause is required for arrest, a warrant, even where there are no exigent circumstances, is not required in a public place. In this decision, the Court evaluated the warrant requirement based on an individual's expectation of privacy.

unity of command. a concept that each individual in an organization should be accountable to only a single superior.

unity of direction. a concept that there should be only one head and one plan for each organizational segment.

unregistered informant. an informant whose credibility, reliability, and experience in providing information has not been sufficiently established to warrant status as a registered informant. The difference between a registered and unregistered informant relates chiefly to the use of information in support of affidavits and court testimony. Generally, a registered informant provides substantive and corroborated information that will withstand legal challenge, whereas the unregistered informant provides small bits and pieces of information that cannot be independently verified and is therefore vulnerable to challenge.

unsolved case (or offense). a founded criminal offense in which the perpetrator could not be identified or that the available evidence is insufficient to support a charge against a known suspect.

unwitnessed arrest. in emergency care, a situation in which a first aider finds an individual who is unconscious with no pulse and no breathing.

uranyl phosphate. a fluorescent tracing powder used to mark objects likely to be touched by a culprit. The powder fluoresces brilliantly in ultraviolet light.

urticaria. an itchy skin eruption characterized by well-defined, red-margined, pale-centered wheals. It is often seen in users of heroin.

use and derivative use immunity. one of two basic constitutional immunities, the other being transactional immunity, in which testimony compelled from a witness or any evidence reasonably derived therefrom cannot be used against the witness in any criminal case.

user password. in computer usage, a password that must be correctly supplied when an authorized user attempts to log in and be authenticated for access to the system.

U.S. Pharmacopeia (USP). a widely recognized book of standards for drugs. It contains data concerning strength, purity, and formulas for nearly all drugs currently in use.

usury. a rate of interest charged for the loan of money which is in excess of the rate authorized.

utter. to offer or pass as genuine; to declare that a counterfeit document is genuine.

uxoricide. wife-killing.

vacate a judgment. to reverse a verdict or other decision of a court; to render void a prior verdict or decision.

vacate a plea. to withdraw a previously entered guilty plea.

vacated sentence. a sentence which has been nullified by action of a court.

vaginal smear. a smear obtained by a medical person from the vaginal passage of a rape victim. The presence of sperm in the smear corroborates that the victim had very recent sexual intercourse, but not necessarily that she had been raped.

vagrancy. a Uniform Crime Reports category used to record and report arrests made for offenses relating to being a suspicious character or person, including begging and vagabondage. At common law, a vagrant was a person who lived off charity although able to work. Statutory definitions of vagrancy vary and some have been declared unconstitutional because of vagueness.

vagueness doctrine. the principle that a statute written in an imprecise manner and capable of being invoked arbitrarily may violate due process and hence be unconstitutional, since it does not make clear what is and is not permitted.

Valium. the trade name for diazepam, a commonly abused Schedule IV barbiturate, usually taken orally or injected. Also called barb, downer, blue, yellow jacket and sleeping pill.

value analysis. estimation of the present worth of the future benefits to be derived from an action, such as an investment.

value orientation. a person's disposition toward making certain value choices, observing certain norms, and using certain criteria when taking action in given social situations.

vandalism. a Uniform Crime Reports category used to record and report arrests made for offenses of destroying or damaging, or attempting to destroy or damage, the property of another without his consent, or public property, except by burning. Damaging or destroying by burning is counted as arson.

vanishing window. a larceny scheme in which a thief posing as a security guard stands next to a bank's night depository window and informs depositors that the window's mechanism is out of order and that he has been assigned by the bank to collect the night deposits.

vanity fire. a fire started for the purpose of attracting favorable attention, usually to the person who set it. A security officer, for example, who on his employer's premises starts and extinguishes a fire in order to make him appear diligent in his duties is said to have started a vanity fire.

vapor density. the weight of a vapor or gas compared with an equal volume of air. For comparison, air is assigned the numerical weight of one.

vapor detector. a device that detects explosives by analysis of vapors.

variance. a nonstandard condition which essentially meets but technically varies from a requirement.

vault. a windowless closure with walls, floor, roof and one or more doors designed and constructed to delay penetration from forced entry; in traffic accident investigations, an endwise flip of a vehicle.

vault-type room. a room with one or more doors, all capable of being locked, protected by an intrusion detection system which creates an alarm upon the entry of a person anywhere into the room and upon exit from the room or upon movement of an individual within the room.

vehicle. a device in, upon, or by which a person or property is or may be transported or drawn upon a highway, excepting devices moved by human power or used exclusively upon stationary rails or tracks.

vehicle identification number (VIN). a code consisting of a combination of numbers and letters used for the identification of a vehicle. The VIN is assigned by the manufacturer and appears on a plate mounted with special screws in a place visible from outside the vehicle at the driver seat position. Vehicle identification numbers are not registration numbers.

vehicle tracking system. a system of tracking vehicles in transit by using a computer, radio beacons, and predetermined travel routes.

vehicular manslaughter. causing the death of another by grossly negligent operation of a motor vehicle.

velocity of detonation. the speed of the detonation wave in an explosion.

venireman. a juror or prospective juror.

venous thrombosis. a condition characterized by swollen and blocked veins, often seen among long-term heroin addicts, resulting from frequent injections.

venue. the geographical areas from which the jury is drawn and in which trial is held in a criminal action.

verdict. a decision by a jury to convict or acquit a defendant.

vertical overcharging. a practice of some prosecutors in which a defendant's degree of culpability is raised by charging a higher offense. The practice is used to strengthen the prosecutor's negotiating position in plea bargaining.

very high frequency (VHF). a band of the radio spectrum operating in the approximate range from 30 to 300 megaherz.

very low frequency. a band of the radio spectrum operating between 15–30 kiloherz.

vein. a vessel in which blood flows toward the heart; in systemic circulation, a vessel carrying carbon dioxide and waste products.

vet. examine legally or physically; inspect; inquire, as in a personnel security investigation.

vibration fuze. a bomb fuze sensitive to minute movements or vibrations. The actual functioning of the fuze is caused by an influence from the target being exerted on a sensitive detecting device within the fuze itself.

vicarious liability. a legal principle which holds that not only is an employee civilly liable for his wrongful conduct, but his employer is also liable if the wrongfulness occurred while the employee was acting within the scope of his employment.

vice. any of various types of crimes that involve offenses against the community's moral code, but that generally do not involve crimes against persons or property; the commerce in illegal goods and services.

vice squad. a police unit dealing with prostitution, pornography, gambling, and other offenses deemed detrimental to the morals of a community. Also called a morals squad.

victim compensation. money or other assistance provided to the victim of a crime.

victim impact statement. in the administration of victims' rights, a statement included in the presentence report concerning the person who committed the crime. The report is prepared by a local probation department on the basis of views expressed by the victim.

victimization. the harming through criminal action of a single victim or victim class.

victimization theory. a means of measuring the crime rate by interviewing selected samples of people regarding their victimization or that of members of their families, households, or businesses. Such surveys are used to correct errors in statistics on crimes known to the police by estimating from victim reports the frequency of various types of crimes, injuries, and losses, as well as to learn other information about the acts, the offenders, and the victims.

victimless crime. an illegal activity in which the victim consents to be involved; a violation of law committed by or between two or more adults with the voluntary consent of each participant. Examples include prostitution, gambling, and drug use. Because the actors in these crimes are voluntary and often eager participants, few complaints are made to law enforcement. Attempts to prohibit victimless crime are frequently criticized as an impossible goal and one which inevitably leads to corruption of law enforcement officials. Also called consensual crime.

victimology. a subdiscipline of criminology that studies victims and victimization processes and techniques, victim-offender relationships, victim precipitation, victim vulnerability, restitution, compensation, and similar issues.

victim precipitation. the initiation, encouragement, or escalation by the victim of a criminal act.

victim restitution. restoration of loss to the victim by the offender. This may be done voluntarily, perhaps in hopes of obtaining a more lenient sentence, or it may be ordered by a court as part of a sentence or as a condition of probation. Restitution does not necessarily relieve an accused of the necessity of standing trial and facing criminal sanctions, but it often does so in practice, or it acts to placate a victim and to reduce the severity of the sentence.

victim-witness assistance program. a program established in some jurisdictions to provide special services and support for victims, particularly of rape.

view by jury. an on-site visit of a jury at the crime scene or other place having a material bearing on the issue to be decided.

vigilantism. action taken by the community, neighborhood, or other groups, without authorization by law, to frighten, contain, or take revenge on alleged, suspected, or would-be offenders.

vigorish. the portion of a bet withheld by a bookmaker; the periodic, usually weekly, payment made by a borrower to a loan shark which represents interest but not a reduction of the principal. Also called vig.

vindictive vandalism. vandalism committed to express antagonism or hatred; destructive acts arising from animosity directed at a particular person or group. Damage to company property by laborers on strike is an example.

Vin Mariani. a concoction made from coca leaves and wine, widely used and acclaimed in the latter part of the 19th century. It was created by Angelo Mariani.

violation. the performance of an act forbidden by a statute, or the failure to perform an act commanded by a statute; an act contrary to a local government ordinance; an offense punishable by a fine or other penalty but not by incarceration; an act prohibited by the terms and conditions of probation or parole.

violent crime. a general crime category that includes murder and nonnegligent manslaughter, forcible rape, robbery, and aggravated assault. Also called crime of violence.

viscera. the internal organs, especially the lungs, heart, stomach, and intestines.

vision-restricting dial. a type of safe dial constructed so only the person dialing the combination can easily see the numbers.

vis major. an accident for which no one is responsible; an act of God.

visual-display terminal. in electronic data processing, a terminal capable of receiving output data on a cathode ray tube and, with special provisions, of transmitting data through a keyboard.

vital signs. the signs of life, namely pulse, respiration, and temperature.

vitreous fluid. in criminal investigation, a fluid taken from a deceased victim's eye for analysis to determine time of death.

Vocoder. the trade name of a voice scrambling device that converts speech into a sequence of pulses that are then scrambled by a digital data scrambler.

voice actuated switch. a switch that closes when conversation is impressed at its input. It can be used to turn on and off clandestine listening and recording devices.

voice analysis. a technique of personnel identification that operates on the principle of voice-frequency patterns. A user's voice is digitized into a unique pattern and placed into the memory file of the identification system. When identification is required, the user provides a sample of speech. The sample is compared electronically with the known pattern on file.

voice answer-back. the response by a mechanically created voice from a computer upon an inquiry submitted by means of pushing buttons on a touch-tone telephone.

voice-band. the 300 Hz to 3400 Hz band used on telephone equipment for the transmission of voice and data.

voice driver. an integrated circuit that creates a signal simulating a human voice. The voice is used to give instructions, deter an intruder, or alert response persons to an alarm condition.

voiceprint. a spectrographic sound representation of a person's voice; the aural and visual comparison of one or more identified voice patterns with a questioned or unknown voice for purposes of identification. Voiceprints can be used for identification much like fingerprints, palmprints, and footprints.

voice stress analyzer. a lie detecting instrument that is represented by the manufacturer as being accurate in identifying and measuring stress in the voice of a deceptive person. The operator of the instrument obtains certain recorded measurements which he then interprets. A purported advantage of the instrument is that it can be used without the knowledge of the individual being tested.

voice verification recorder. a multichannel recorder that records all radio and telephone communications in a system, such as that used by a law enforcement or high-security agency to maintain a history of work events.

voir dire. preliminary examination which a court may make of one presented as a witness or juror where his competency or interest is objected to.

volatile chemicals. chemicals that are listed as controlled substances due to their abuse as inhalants. Such chemicals are: toluene, hexane, trichloroethylene, acetone, ethyl acetate, methyl ethyl ketone, tricholorethane, carbon tetrachloride, methanol, methyl isobutyl ketone, methyl cellosolve ketone, cyclohexanone, amyl nitrite, butyl nitrite, chloroform, diethyl ether, petroleum distillate, aliphatic hydrocarbons, ketone solvent, glycol ether solvent, glycol ether intersolvent, xylol, and xylene.

volatile inhalants. a major classification of depressants incorporating an aggregate of chemically diverse substances perhaps best described as being volatile, i.e., tending to evaporate easily. These are typically solvents and gases that are usually inhaled and whose effects are shortlived. Some have been called deliriants although delirium is only one of many potential effects and is clearly not restricted to these substances. Many volatile inhalants are quite similar in effect to the sedative group, and some have certain psychedelic or hallucinogenic effects. Most are not used medically, although several have been used as surgical anesthetics.

voluntary commitment. admission to a correctional, residential, or medical facility or program for care or treatment without a court commitment and by personal choice.

voluntary manslaughter. intentionally causing the death of another with reasonable provocation.

vomitus. matter which is expelled from the body during the process of vomiting.

voyeur. a person who derives sexual pleasure from viewing the genitalia or naked body of another.

V pattern. in arson investigations, V-shaped burn marks on a vertical surface caused by the natural upward movement of fire. The base or point of the V pattern may point to the place where the fire began.

vulnerability assessment. any of several methodological approaches for assessing an organization's vulnerability to loss or disruption by examining the separate criticalities of the organization's components. An approach might feature these steps: (1) identify the components that are minimally essential in order for the organization to operate, (2) determine the reliability of each component to function up to full capacity, (3) identify alternates or substitutions to components that would permit continued operation in the event of component breakdown or loss, (4) identify those key elements of a component (e.g., equipment, materials or persons) that are critical to the functioning of the component or entire organization, (5) identify the extent of exposure (risk) to damage or loss of critical elements, and (6) identify the extent of interdependence among components and how interdependence might be reduced or made resistant to negative influences.

Wagner's test. a preliminary test for identifying morphine. The material suspected to be morphine is dissolved in hydrochloric acid. A drop of Wagner's reagent (potassium iodide in water and iodine) is added. The appearance of a crystalline precipitate is a positive indication.

waive. in law, to give up. For example, an arrested person might voluntarily give up his right to a preliminary hearing. Some rights may not be waived, such as the right not to suffer cruel and unusual punishment.

walkaway. a confined person who fails to return to his or her place of confinement from an authorized temporary absence. Also called a walk-off.

walk-in. a criminal who surrenders to law enforcement authorities and who usually cooperates by providing information or evidence.

walk-in complaint. a complaint made by a victim or complainant at a police location.

wanted person. a person sought by law enforcement authorities because an arrest warrant has been issued or because he has escaped from custody.

war crime. an action ordered or authorized by leaders of a country engaged in a war, or carried out by its military personnel with or without such orders, that violates internationally accepted rules governing the conduct of war. War crimes include wanton killing of civilians, harsh treatment of prisoners, and use of chemical and biological weapons banned by treaties and agreements.

ward boss. an official of a political party whose duty is to promote the party's interests in a ward.

Warden v. Hayden. a case in which the U.S. Supreme Court held in 1967 that police officers do not need a warrant to enter a premises which the suspect they are in "hot pursuit" of has entered to hide. Reasonable belief that weapons may be available to a suspect who is being chased will allow an officer to make a warrantless entry and search of the premises. This decision recognizes the exigent circumstances of a "hot pursuit" which rule out the option to obtain a warrant.

warrant. a process of criminal court which commands search or seizure of persons or property.

wash-up card. a card given to a person exposed to a chemical agent, such as CN. The card gives guidance on how to remove the agent from the body and clothing.

watch list. a list of words, names, phrases, addresses, numbers and similar items which can be screened from a mass of data by a computer or human intelligence.

water cannon. a high-pressure hose device used in riot control operations to split up and disperse large groups of rioters.

watered stock. corporate stock issued by a corporation for property at an overvaluation, or stock issued for which the corporation receives nothing in payment therefor.

water-soluble paper. paper that will rapidly disintegrate when immersed in water. Because it can be quickly destroyed, water-soluble paper is used in illegal gambling operations.

WATS. the acronym for Wide Area Telephone Service, a service that provides a special line on which the subscriber may make unlimited calls to certain zones on a direct-distance-dialing basis for a flat monthly fee.

wax load. a bullet made of wax or plastic. Wax loads are used as an economy measure in close-distance firearms practice. The cartridge cases are primed but have no powder charge. The primer is sufficient to propel a wax load fairly accurately over a short distance.

weapons offense. an offense that relates to the unlawful sale, distribution, manufacture, alteration, transportation, possession, or use of a deadly or dangerous weapon or accessory.

weapons system. a general term that describes a weapon or a combination of weapons and those components required for operation. The components required for operation typically include the weapon itself, the controlling system, and the carrier.

wedge formation. a riot control formation used in clearing rioters from streets and in splitting up large groups and mobs. The wedge is formed by two diagonal lines joined at a point. When a base line is added, the formation is called a triangle or diamond.

weekend sentence. a sentence to a period of confinement interrupted by periods of freedom on weekends. Also called intermittent sentence.

Weeks v. United States. a case in which the U.S. Supreme Court ruled in 1914 that evidence illegally seized by federal law enforcement officers is to be excluded from federal prosecutions. Shortly after this decision, federal officers began introducing into criminal trials evidence illegally seized by state and local officers at the encouragement of federal officers. This practice was called the Silver Platter Doctrine. In 1960, in Eilkins v. United States, the Supreme Court ended this practice when it held that all illegally seized evidence is inadmissible in federal courts.

weight of evidence. the inclination afforded by credible evidence offered in a trial that supports one side of an issue. Weight is not a matter of mathematics but of inducing a belief.

wheel base. the distance from the center of the front wheels to the center of the rear wheels or, if there is a tandem axle, the distance to the midpoint between the two tandem axles.

wheel search. a type of search made of an outdoor crime scene. The area to be searched is delineated by markers so as to form a large wheel with spokes radiating from the hub. The searchers begin at the hub and move outward within the lanes formed by the spokes. A disadvantage of this method is that the lanes become significantly wider as the searchers move away from the hub.

whistle blower. an individual who believes the public interest overrides the interests of the organization and publicly reveals the organization's illegal, fraudulent or harmful activity.

white collar crime. nonviolent crime for financial gain committed by means of deception by persons whose occupational status is entrepreneurial, professional or semi-professional and utilizing their special occupational skills and opportunities; nonviolent crime for financial gain utilizing deception and committed by anyone having special technical and professional knowledge of business and government, irrespective of the person's occupation.

white intelligence. overt information such as that available in books, official reports and periodical literature available to any reader.

white slavery. abduction and enforced prostitution of girls and women and, rarely, of young boys.

whorl pattern. one of the three basic groups of fingerprint patterns, the other two being the arch and loop. The whorl group has sub-groups called the plain or simple whorl, central pocket loop, double or twin loop, lateral pocket loop, and accidental whorl.

willful homicide. the intentional causing of death of another person, with or without legal justification.

willful misconduct. deliberate or intentional failure to comply with rules or regulations.

windchill factor. the effect on the body of low temperatures compounded with high winds, which results in loss of body heat.

windowpane. LSD in the form of a thin square of gelatin.

wind resistance. the force of the atmosphere against a moving vehicle; a combination of forces produced by motion of a vehicle through air and motion of the air itself. Under certain circumstances, wind may assist rather than resist the motion of a vehicle. Also called atmospheric drag factor.

wire communication. a communication transmitted through the aid of wire, cable, or other like connection furnished by a common carrier.

wire fraud. a law that prohibits the devising of a scheme to defraud another or to obtain property by false pretenses when interstate communication facilities are used. The law is found in 18 USC, Section 1343.

wire jumper. an auto theft tool consisting of a short piece of electrical wire with an alligator clamp at each end. One end is attached to a car's battery and the other to the coil. This allows the ignition system to be bypassed. The wire jumper is now somewhat obsolete in that other devices and techniques permit the ignition system to be circumvented from the driver's seat.

wire plant. a clandestine listening/recording device placed on or close to a telephone.

wiretap. a clandestine interception of communications transmitted over wire from a telephone.

withdrawal defense. a defense sometimes used to defend against prosecution for conspiracy. A conspirator who withdraws from the conspiracy prior to commission of the requisite overt act may attempt a defense based on withdrawal.

withdrawal syndrome. the group of physical symptoms experienced by an addict when the addictive drug is withdrawn. The syndrome varies according to the drug abused. In narcotics abuse, the symptoms include watery eyes, runny nose, yawning, and perspiration from 8 to 12 hours after the previous dose. This is followed by restlessness, irritability, loss of appetite, insomnia, goose flesh, tremors, and finally yawning and severe sneezing. These symptoms peak at 48 to 72 hours, and are followed by nausea, vomiting, weakness, stomach cramps, and possibly diarrhea. Heart rate and blood pressure are elevated. Chills alternating with flushing and excessive sweating are characteristic. Pains in the bones and muscles of the back and extremities occur as do muscle spasms and kicking movements. Suicide is a possibility, and without treatment the symptoms may continue for 7 to 10 days. Also called the abstinence syndrome.

Witherspoon v. Illinois. a 1968 case in which the U.S. Supreme Court ruled that juror selection procedures could require exclusion of prospective jurors who stated they could not under any circumstances vote for a death penalty.

witness. a person who directly perceives an event or thing, or who has expert knowledge relevant to a case.

witnessed arrest. in emergency care, a situation in which a first aider is present with a victim at the moment the victim goes into respiratory and circulatory arrest.

witness interview form. a form containing a brief summary of information provided by a witness concerning a crime under investigation, and identification data useful in locating the witness at a later time.

witness relocation program. a program administered by the Department of Justice in which witnesses who have testified against an organized-crime figure are given a change of name, identity, and place of residence. Also called the witness protection program.

wobble area. in firearms shooting, the area over which the shooter's hand, arm or body moves without possibility of control. Also called the area of aim.

Wolf v. Colorado. a case in which the U.S. Supreme Court refused in 1949 to impose the exclusionary rule as a mandatory method of enforcement to deter violations of the Fourth Amendment and left the states free to adopt or not adopt the exclusionary rule. This case was prior to the landmark case of Mapp v. Ohio in which the Supreme Court applied the exclusionary rule to the states by virtue of the due process clause of the Fourteenth Amendment.

Wong Sun v. United States. a case in which the U.S. Supreme Court in 1963 ruled inadmissible a confession from a suspect obtained immediately following an illegal arrest. The Court stated that the confession was "the fruit of the poisonous tree." In the same case, another defendant had also been arrested illegally and then released. He later returned voluntarily to the police station where he made a statement that was used against him at trial. The Court held that the connection between the illegal arrest and the statement had become so attenuated as to to dissipate the taint. This decision means that evidence obtained following an illegal arrest could be used if it was obtained independently of or far removed from the arrest.

work. in a numbers operation, the bet slips that are processed in a single day.

workhouse. a house of detention or correctional facility for short-term confinement of minor offenders.

work measurement. any method used to establish an equitable relationship between the volume of work performed and the human resources devoted to its accomplishment.

work release program. a rehabilitation program in which prisoners are allowed to work and be gainfully employed outside of prison during the latter part of their sentences.

works. a set of drug use paraphernalia for intravenous injection of opiates or other illicit substances. The term usually includes a syringe, a candle and a spoon for cooking the solution, and a string, belt or heavy rubber band for use as a tourniquet.

wound. a bodily injury caused by physical means, with disruption of the normal continuity of structures.

wounded bird ploy. a diversionary tactic used by an interviewee to lead the interviewer away from a subject that the interviewee does not want to discuss.

wrap around. a shoplifting technique in which the thief wraps clothing items around the torso under a loose fitting dress or coat.

wrinkle wound. a cutting or stabbing wound that shows multiple cuts or punctures along the line of the blade, with interspersed areas of uninvolved skin. Wrinkle wounds are usually associated with obese or elderly victims.

writ. a paper issued by a judge which requires or forbids a specified act.

write protection. in computer operations, restriction of writing into a data set, file, or storage area by a user or program not authorized to do so.

writ of error. a document by which appellate review is requested on the ground that a lower court decision was based on one or more errors.

writ of habeas corpus. a document which directs the person detaining a prisoner to bring him or her before a judicial officer to determine the lawfulness of the imprisonment.

writ of mandamus. a document which orders a public official to perform an act that the law requires as his duty, such as to issue a license.

written instrument. any instrument or article containing written or printed matter or its equivalent, used for the purpose of conveying or recording information, or constituting a symbol or evidence of value, right, privilege, or identification which is capable of being used to the advantage or disadvantage of some person. The term includes wills, deeds, credit invoices, driving licenses, checks, currency, securities, public records, and prescriptions. A complete written instrument is one which purports to be genuine and fully drawn with respect to every essential feature. An incomplete written instrument is one which contains some matter by way of content or authentication but which requires additional matter in order to render it a complete written instrument.

wrongful death action. a civil court suit brought by survivors against someone believed responsible, by negligence or intention, for another's death.

x-band. a radio frequency communications band in the 5200 to 11,000 MHz range.

xiphoid process. the pointed process of cartilage that is supported by a core of bone and connected with the lower end of the body of the sternum.

x-ray bomb. a bomb engineered to detonate if an x-ray machine is used to examine it.

x-ray diffraction unit. a laboratory instrument for identifying the molecules and the crystal structures that constitute an element. The unit transmits a beam of x-rays through the unknown specimen, and crystals in the specimen diffract the beam according to the elements it contains. Since the diffraction characteristics of the various elements are known, the analyst has a base for comparison. This technique is considered as specific for a substance as a fingerprint is for an individual.

x-ray radiography examination. a crime laboratory examination that uses x-ray radiography to reveal the interior construction of an object (such as a suspected bomb) and the presence or absence of defects, foreign matter and cavities.

x-ray spectrometer. an instrument for producing an x-ray spectrum and measuring the wavelengths of its components; a type of spectrometer used to measure the angles of diffraction of x-rays produced by reflection from the surface of a crystal.

XYY syndrome. a syndrome in men characterized by unusual aggression, caused by a genetic disorder in which the sufferer has an extra Y chromosome.

yaw. a sidewise movement of a vehicle in turning; movement of a vehicle in a direction other than that in which it is headed; a sidewise motion produced when centrifugal force exceeds traction force. It is often the result of driver overreaction or excessive speed.

yawmark. a scuffmark made on a road surface while a vehicle is yawing; the mark made by a rotating tire which is slipping in a direction parallel to the axle of the wheel.

yellow-dog contract. any agreement between an employer and an employee that calls for the employee to resign from, or refrain from joining, a union.

yellow jacket. the street name for a commonly abused barbiturate, usually a Nembutal capsule. Nembutal is the trade name for pentobarbital which is regulated as a Schedule II controlled substance.

yenhok. a needle-like device used to shape opium gum into pills.

yenshee. the opium residue which collects in the bottom of an opium pipe and which is frequently re-cycled by blending it with fresh opium gum.

yoking. a mugging technique in which the victim is grabbed from behind and held in a stranglehold while one or more accomplices remove the victim's valuables.

youthful offender. a person for whom special correctional commitments and special record sealing procedures are made available by statute.

zebra line. a line, usually drawn on a floor, that demarcates an area that can only be entered after particular requirements have been met. Zebra lines are used to isolate restricted areas in prisons, bioclean areas such as a hospital's operating room, or hazardous areas such as a nuclear radiation laboratory.

zip gun. a homemade gun, usually a pistol constructed of a short length of pipe attached to a handle or the frame of a toy gun. The firing mechanism is made of a nail head and elastic bands.

zone of acceptance. a management concept which holds that authority in an organization stems from the bottom up and is based on a willingness of subordinates to hold in abeyance their own critical faculties and accept the directives of superiors. The zone of acceptance is a theoretical range of tolerance within which organizational members will accept orders without question.

zone of comparison test. in polygraphy, a testing technique in which each relevant question is preceded and followed by at least one non-relevant question. For example, a 10 question test might follow this sequence: (1) neutral question, (2) sacrifice relevant question, (3) symptomatic question, (4) control question, (5) primary relevant question, (6) control question, (7) primary relevant question, (8) symptomatic question, (9) control question or guilt complex question, and (10) secondary relevant question. The polygraphist evaluates the resulting chart by comparing measurements in zones that correspond to the relevant/non-relevant questioning sequence. A zone of comparison test is helpful in disclosing any outside issues, detecting guilt concerning a separate crime, and reducing the subject's concern that surprise questions will be asked during the test.

zone search. a type of search conducted at an outdoor crime scene. The area to be searched is delineated by markers into quadrants. If the area is large, each quadrant may be further sectioned. One searcher is assigned to a quadrant or a subsection. Also called a grid search.

zoning. the process by which a protected structure is divided into zones or areas for alarm reporting purposes. An alarm initiating device installed in a given zone provides a means of identifying the location of the alarm condition.

zoom lens. a single lens with a variable focal range. A zoom lens can be manufactured to extend from wide-angle to telephoto viewing. Zoom lenses are usual components of CCTV systems.

APPENDICES

FELONY DEFINITIONS BY STATE

Alabama. an offense for which a sentence to a term of imprisonment in excess of one year is authorized.

Alaska. not specifically defined.

Arizona. not specifically defined.

Arkansas. not specifically defined.

California. a crime which is punishable by death or by imprisonment in the state prison.

Colorado. any criminal offense punishable by death or imprisonment in the penitentiary, and none other.

Connecticut. an offense for which a person may be sentenced to a term of imprisonment in excess of one year.

Delaware. not specifically defined.

District of Columbia. not specifically defined.

Florida. any criminal offense that is punishable under laws of the State of Florida, or that would be punishable if committed in the State of Florida, by death or imprisonment in a state penitentiary.

Georgia. a crime punishable by death, by imprisonment for life, or by imprisonment for more than 12 months.

Hawaii. any crime so designated as a felony, or a crime if persons convicted thereof may be sentenced to imprisonment for a term in excess of one year.

Idaho. a crime which is punishable with death or by imprisonment in the state prison.

Illinois. an offense for which a sentence to death or a term of imprisonment in a penitentiary for one year or more is provided.

Indiana. a conviction, in any jurisdiction at any time, with respect to which the convicted person might have been imprisoned for more than one year, but not including a conviction with respect to which the person has been pardoned, or a conviction of a Class A misdemeanor.

Iowa. a public offense that has been defined by statute to be a felony.

Kansas. a crime punishable by death or by imprisonment in any state penal institution.

Kentucky. an offense punishable by death or confinement in the penitentiary, whether or not a fine or other penalty may also be assessed.

Louisiana. any crime for which an offender may be sentenced to death or imprisonment at hard labor.

Maine. not specifically defined.

Maryland. not specifically defined.

Massachusetts. a crime punishable by death or imprisonment in the state prison.

Michigan. an offense for which the offender, on conviction may be punished by death, or by imprisonment in the state prison.

Minnesota. a crime for which a sentence of imprisonment for more than one year may be imposed.

Mississippi. any violation of law punished with death or confinement in the penitentiary.

Missouri. a crime which if convicted of may result in a sentence to death or imprisonment for a term in excess of one year.

Montana. an offense in which the sentence imposed upon conviction is death or imprisonment in the state prison for any term exceeding one year.

Nebraska. not specifically defined.

Nevada. every crime which may be punished by death or by imprisonment in the state prison.

New Hampshire. a murder or crime so designated by statute within or outside of the Code or a crime defined by statute outside of the Code where the maximum penalty provided is imprisonment in excess of one year; provided, however, that a crime defined by statute outside of the Code is a felony when committed by a corporation or an unincorporated association if the maximum fine therein is more than $200.

New Jersey. not specifically defined.

New Mexico. a crime if it is so designated by law or if upon conviction thereof a sentence of death or of imprisonment for a term of one year may be imposed.

New York. an offense for which a sentence to a term of imprisonment in excess of one year may be imposed.

North Carolina. a crime which was a felony at common law; is or may be punishable by death; is or may be punishable by imprisonment in the state's prison; or is denominated as a felony by statute.

North Dakota. not specifically defined.

Ohio. regardless of the penalty which may be imposed, any offense specifically classified as a felony is a felony, and any offense specifically classified as a misdemeanor is a misdemeanor. Any offense not specifically classified is a felony if imprisonment for more than one year may be imposed as a penalty.

Oklahoma. a crime which is, or may be, punishable with death, or by imprisonment in the state penitentiary.

Oregon. except as specifically provided, a crime is a felony if it is so designated by state statute or if a person convicted under a state statute may be sentenced to a maximum term of imprisonment of more than one year.

Pennsylvania. not specifically defined.

Rhode Island. unless otherwise provided, any criminal offense which at any given time may be punished by imprisonment for a term of more than one year, or by a fine of more than $1000.

South Carolina. any crime specifically defined by statute as a felony and all other criminal offenses punishable under laws of the state which were felonies under the common law.

South Dakota. a crime which is or may be punishable by death or confinement in a penitentiary.

Tennessee. all violations of law punished by imprisonment in the penitentiary or by the infliction of the death penalty.

Texas. an offense so designated by law or punishable by death or confinement in a penitentiary.

Utah. not specifically defined.

Vermont. any other provision of law notwithstanding, any offense whose maximum term of imprisonment is more than two years, for life, or which may be punished by death.

Virginia. such offenses as are punishable with death of confinement in the penitentiary.

Washington. not specifically defined.

West Virginia. such offenses as are punishable by confinement in the penitentiary.

Wisconsin. a crime punishable by imprisonment in the state prisons.

Wyoming. crimes which may be punished by death or by imprisonment for more than one year.

MINIMUM AND MAXIMUM FELONY SENTENCES BY STATE

State	Minimum	Maximum
Alabama	Greater than 1 year	Death
Alaska	Greater than 1 year	99 years
Arizona	Minimum of 18 months	Death
Arkansas	No minimum exists	Death
California	Greater than 1 year	Death
Colorado	Minimum of 1 year	Death
Connecticut	Minimum of 1 year	Death
Delaware	No minimum exists	Death
Dist. of Columbia	Greater than 1 year	Life
Florida	Greater than 1 year	Death
Georgia	Greater than 1 year	Death
Hawaii	Greater than 1 year	Life
Idaho	No minimum exists	Death
Illinois	Minimum of 1 year	Death
Indiana	Minimum of 1 year	Death
Iowa	Greater than 1 year	Life
Kansas	Minimum of 1 year	Life
Kentucky	Minimum of 1 year	Death
Louisiana	Minimum of 1 year, hard labor	Death
Maine	No minimum exists	Life
Maryland	Minimum of 1 year	Death
Massachusetts	Greater than 30 months	Life
Michigan	Greater than 1 year	Life
Minnesota	Greater than 1 year	Life
Mississippi	Minimum of 1 year	Death
Missouri	Greater than 1 year	Death
Montana	Greater than 1 year	Death
Nebraska	No minimum exists	Death
Nevada	Minimum of 1 year	Death
New Hampshire	Greater than 1 year	Death
New Jersey	Minimum of 3 years	Death
New Mexico	Minimum of 1 year	Death
New York	Minimum of 1 year	Life
North Carolina	Minimum of 1 year	Death
North Dakota	Greater than 1 year	Life
Ohio	Minimum of 6 months	Death
Oklahoma	Minimum of 1 year	Death
Oregon	Greater than 1 year	Death
Pennsylvania	Minimum of 42 months	Death
Rhode Island	Minimum of 1 year	Life
South Carolina	Minimum of 3 months	Death

South Dakota	No minimum exists	Death
Tennessee	Minimum of 1 year	Death
Texas	Minimum of 2 years	Death
Utah	Greater than 1 year	Death
Vermont	No minimum exists	Death
Virginia	Minimum of 1 year	Death
Washington	No minimum exists	Death
West Virginia	Minimum of 1 year	Life
Wisconsin	Minimum of 1 year	Life
Wyoming	Greater than 1 year	Death

CAPITAL OFFENSES BY STATE

As of 1986

Alabama. Murder during kidnapping, robbery, rape, sodomy, burglary, sexual assault, or arson; murder of a peace officer, correctional officer, or public official; murder while under a life sentence; murder for pecuniary gain or contract murder; multiple murders; aircraft piracy; murder by a defendant with a previous murder conviction; murder of a witness to a crime.

Arizona. First-degree murder.

Arkansas. Capital murder as defined by state statute.

California. Treason; aggravated assault by a prisoner serving a life sentence; first degree murder with special circumstances; train wrecking.

Colorado. First-degree murder; first-degree kidnapping.

Connecticut. Murder of a public safety or correctional officer; murder for pecuniary gain; murder in the course of a felony; murder by a defendant with a previous conviction for intentional murder; murder while under a life sentence; murder during a kidnapping; illegal sale of cocaine, methadone, or heroin to a person who dies from using these drugs; murder during first-degree sexual assault; multiple murders.

Delaware. First-degree murder with aggravating circumstances.

Florida. First-degree murder.

Georgia. Murder; kidnapping with bodily injury when the victim dies; aircraft hijacking; treason.

Idaho. First-degree murder; aggravated kidnapping.

Illinois. Murder.

Indiana. Murder.

Kentucky. Aggravated murder; kidnapping when the victim is killed.

Louisiana. First-degree murder.

Maryland. First-degree murder, either premeditated or during the commission of a felony.

Mississippi. Murder of a peace officer or correctional officer; murder while under a life sentence; murder by bomb or explosive; contract murder; murder committed during rape, burglary, kidnaping, arson, robbery, sexual battery, unnatural intercourse with a child, or nonconsensual unnatural intercourse; murder of an elected official; and forcible rape of a child under 14 years by a person 18 years or older.

Missouri. First-degree murder.

Montana. Deliberate homicide; aggravated kidnapping when victim dies; attempted deliberate homicide, aggravated assault, or aggravated kidnapping by a state prison inmate with a prior conviction for deliberate homicide or who has been previously declared a persistent felony offender.

Nebraska. First-degree murder.

Nevada. First-degree murder.

New Hampshire. Contract murder; murder of a law enforcement officer; murder of a kidnap victim.

New Jersey. Purposeful or knowing murder; contract murder; murder during a kidnapping.

New Mexico. First-degree murder.

North Carolina. First-degree murder.

Ohio. Assassination; contract murder; murder during escape; murder while in a correctional facility; murder after conviction of a prior purposeful killing or prior attempted murder; murder of a peace officer; murder arising from rape, kidnapping, arson, robbery, or burglary; murder of a witness to prevent testimony in a criminal proceeding.

Oklahoma. Murder with malice aforethought; murder arising from forcible rape, robbery with a dangerous weapon, kidnapping, escape from lawful custody, first-degree burglary, or arson; murder when the victim is a child.

Oregon. Aggravated murder.

Pennsylvania. First-degree murder.

South Carolina. Murder with statutory aggravating circumstances.

South Dakota. First-degree murder; kidnapping with gross permanent physical injury inflicted on the victim.

Tennessee. First-degree murder.

Texas. Murder of a public safety officer, fireman, or correctional employee; murder during the commission of kidnapping, burglary, robbery, aggravated rape, or arson; murder for remuneration; and multiple murders.

Utah. First-degree murder.

Vermont. Murder of a police officer or correctional officer; kidnapping for ransom.

Virginia. Murder during the commission of abduction, armed robbery, or rape; contract murder; murder by a prisoner while in custody; murder of a law enforcement officer; multiple murders; murder of a child under 12 years old during an abduction.

Washington. First-degree premeditated murder.

Wyoming. First-degree murder including felony murder.

METHOD OF EXECUTION BY STATE

As of 1986

Alabama	Electrocution
Arizona	Lethal gas
Arkansas	Lethal injection; electrocution
California	Lethal gas
Colorado	Lethal gas
Connecticut	Electrocution
Delaware	Lethal injection; hanging
Florida	Electrocution
Georgia	Electrocution
Idaho	Lethal injection; firing squad
Illinois	Lethal injection
Indiana	Electrocution
Kentucky	Electrocution
Louisiana	Electrocution
Maryland	Lethal gas
Mississippi	Lethal gas; lethal injection
Missouri	Lethal gas
Montana	Lethal injection; hanging
Nebraska	Electrocution
Nevada	Lethal injection
New Hampshire	Hanging
New Jersey	Lethal injection
New Mexico	Lethal injection
North Carolina	Lethal injection; lethal gas
Ohio	Electrocution
Oklahoma	Lethal injection
Oregon	Lethal injection
Pennsylvania	Electrocution
South Carolina	Electrocution
South Dakota	Lethal injection
Tennessee	Electrocution
Texas	Lethal injection
Utah	Lethal injection; firing squad
Vermont	Electrocution
Virginia	Electrocution
Washington	Lethal injection; hanging
Wyoming	Lethal injection; lethal gas

SOCIAL SECURITY NUMBER INDEX

The initial numbers (first three digits) in a social security number will identify the state where the number was issued.

Initial Numbers	Issuing State	Initial Numbers	Issuing State
001–003	NH	429–432	AR
004–007	ME	433–439	LA
008–009	VT	440–448	OK
010–034	MA	449–467	TX
035–039	RI	468–477	MN
040–049	CT	478–485	IA
050–134	NY	486–500	MO
135–138	NJ	501–502	ND
159–211	PA	503–504	SD
212–220	MD	505–508	NE
221–222	DE	509–515	KS
223–231	VA	516–517	MT
232–236	WV	518–519	ID
237–246	NC	520	WY
247–251	SC	521–524	CO
252–260	GA	525	NM
261–267	FL	526–527	AZ
268–302	OH	528–529	UT
303–317	IN	530	NV
318–361	IL	531–539	WA
362–386	MI	540–544	OR
387–399	WI	545–573	CA
400–407	KY	574	AK
408–415	TN	575–576	HA
416–424	AL	577–579	DC
425–428	MS		

Air Force Regulation 125-22, Department of the Air Force, Washington, DC, 1976.

Air Force Regulation 205-1, Department of the Air Force, Washington, DC, 1982.

Air Force Regulation 205-16, Department of the Air Force, Washington, DC, 1984.

Air Force Regulation 205-32, Department of the Air Force, Washington, DC, 1982.

Air Force Regulation 208-1, Department of the Air force, Washington, DC, 1982.

Alcohol Abuse in the Hard-to-Reach Work Force, National Institute on Alcohol Abuse and Alcoholism, Rockville, MD, 1982.

Allen, Brandt, "Embezzler's Guide to the Computer," *Harvard Business Review,* July-August, 1975.

Army Regulation 190-5, Department of the Army, Washington, DC, 1973.

Army Regulation 190-16, Department of the Army, Washington, DC, 1984.

Baker, J. Stannard, *Traffic Accident Investigation Manual,* The Traffic Institute of Northwestern University, Chicago, IL, 1975.

Barnard, Robert L., *Intrusion Detection Systems,* Butterworth, Stoneham, MA, 1981.

Bennett-Sandler, G., et al, *Law Enforcement and Criminal Justice,* Houghton Mifflin, Boston, MA, 1979.

Bequai, August, *Computers + Business = Liabilities: A Preventive Guide for Management,* Washington Legal Foundation, Washington, DC, 1984.

Bologna, Jack, *A Guideline for Fraud Auditing,* Odiorne, Plymouth, MI, 1984.

Bomb Incident Management, International Association of Chiefs of Police, Gaithersburg, MD, 1973.

Bombs and Explosives, Federal Law Enforcement Training Center, Department of the Treasury, Brunswick, GA, 1973.

Bomb Threats and Bomb Search Techniques, Federal Law Enforcement Training Center, Department of the Treasury, Brunswick, GA, 1971.

Brockett, W. Don, *New Directions in Corporate Security,* SRI International, Menlo Park, CA, 1984.

Broder, James F., *Risk Analysis and the Security Survey,* Butterworth, Stoneham, MA, 1984.

Brodie, Thomas G., *Bombs and Bombings,* Charles C Thomas, Springfield, IL, 1972.

Buckwalter, Art, *Interviews and Interrogations,* Butterworth, Stoneham, MA, 1983.

Burke, John J., "Searches by Private Persons," *FBI Law Enforcement Bulletin,* October, 1972.

Carroll, John M., *Computer Security,* Butterworth, Stoneham, MA, 1977.

Carroll, John M., *Confidential Information Sources: Public and Private,* Butterworth, Stoneham, MA, 1975.

Chaplin, James P., *Dictionary of Psychology,* Dell, New York, NY, 1975.

Chapman, Charles F., *Medical Dictionary for the Non-Professional,* Barron's Educational Series, New York, NY, 1984.

Clark, John P. and Hollinger, Richard C., *Theft by Employees in Work Organizations,* National Institute of Justice, Washington, D.C., 1983.

Conklin, John E., *Illegal But Not Criminal,* Prentice-Hall, Englewood Cliffs, NJ, 1977.

Corporate Aviation Security, National Business Aircraft Association, Inc., Washington, DC, 1984.

Criminal Law Reference Handbook, Massachusetts Criminal Justice Training Council, Boston, MA, 1980.

Cull, J. G. and Hardy, R. E., *Types of Drug Abusers and Their Abuse,* Charles C Thomas, Springfield, IL, 1974.

Cunningham, William C. and Taylor, Todd H., *Private Security and Police in America,* Chancellor, Portland, OR, 1985.

Daskam, Samuel W., *Eavesdropping Attacks and Countermeasures,* International Security Associates, Stamford, CT.

Dean, William and Evans, David S., *Terms of the Trade,* Random Lengths Publications, Eugene, OR, 1980.

DeSola, Ralph, *Crime Dictionary, Facts on File,* San Diego, CA, 1982.

Department of Defense Industrial Security Program Manual, Defense Investigative Service, Washington, DC, 1984.

Dienstein, William, *Technics for the Crime Investigator,* Charles C Thomas, Springfield, IL, 1970.

Dogoloff, Lee I. and Angarola, Robert R., *Urine Testing in the Workplace,* The American Council for Drug Education, New York, NY, 1985.

Donelan, Charles A., *Principles of Criminal Law for Law Enforcement Officers,* Federal Bureau of Investigation, Washington, DC.

Drug Abuse: Clinical Recognition and Treatment, U.S. Department of the Army, Washington, DC, 1973.

Drug Atlas, Midwest Research Institute, Kansas City, MO, 1971.

Drug Use in Industry, U.S. Department of Health and Human Services, Washington, DC, 1979.

Encyclopedia of Sociology, Dushkin Publishing Group, Guilford, CT, 1981.

Employee Drug Screening: Detection of Drug Use by Urinalysis, U.S. Department of Health and Human Services, Washington, DC, 1986.

Employer's Guide to the Employment of Former Drug and Alcohol Abusers, U.S. Department of Health and Human Services, Washington, D.C., 1983.

Fairchild, H. P., *Dictionary of Sociology and Related Sciences,* Philosophical Library, Totowa, NJ, 1976.

Fay, John, *Approaches to Criminal Justice Training,* University of Georgia Press, Athens, GA, 1979.

Fay, John, *Butterworths Security Dictionary,* Butterworth, Stoneham, MA, 1987.

Fay, John, *Managing Drug Abuse in the Workplace,* Forward Edge, Houston, TX, 1987.

Fay, John, *The Police Instructor's Guide,* The Georgia Peace Officer Standards and Training Council, Atlanta, GA, 1978.

Fay, John, *The Supervisor's Guide for Controlling Workplace Drug and Alcohol Abuse,* Forward Edge, Houston, TX 1987.

Federal Rules: Criminal Procedure, *Evidence and Appellate Procedure,* West, Saint Paul, MN, 1982.

Fennelly Lawrence J., *Handbook of Loss Prevention and Crime Prevention,* Buterworth, Stoneham, MA, 1982.

Fisher, R. B. and Christie, G. A., *A Dictionary of Drugs: The Medicines You Use,* Schocken, New York, NY, 1976.

Fisher Royal P., *Information Systems Security*, Prentice-Hall, Englewood Cliffs, NJ, 1984.

Fitzgerald, Jerry, *Designing Controls into Computerized Systems*, Jerry Fitzgerald and Associates, Redwood City, CA, 1981.

French, William B., et al, *Guide to Real Estate Licensing Examinations*, Warren, Gorham and Lamont, Boston, MA, 1978.

Fuqua, Paul and Wilson, Jerry V., *Terrorism: The Executive's Guide to Survival*, Gulf, Houston, TX, 1978.

Gallati, Robert R. J., *Introduction to Private Security*, Prentice-Hall, Englewood Cliffs, NJ, 1983.

Gaynor, Frank, *Concise Dictionary of Science*, Philosophical Library, New York, NY, 1959.

Gigliotti, Richard and Jason, Ronald, *Security Design for Maximum Protection*, Butterworth, Stoneham, MA, 1984.

Glossaries of Argot Used by Addicts, U.S. Department of Justice, Washington, DC, 1970.

Glossary of Terms in the Drug Culture, Bureau of Narcotics and Dangerous Drugs, Washington, DC, 1970.

Grau, Joseph J., *Criminal and Civil Investigation Handbook*, McGraw-Hill, New York, NY, 1981.

Green, Gion, *Introduction to Security*, Butterworth, Stoneham, MA, 1987.

Green, Thomas, et al, *Glossary of Insurance Terms*, The Merritt Company, Santa Monica, CA, 1980.

A Guide to Security Investigations, American Society for Industrial Security, Arlington, VA, 1975.

Handbook of Forensic Science, Federal Bureau of Investigation, Washington, DC, 1979.

Hardy, R. E. and Cull, J. G., *Drug Language and Lore*, Charles C Thomas, Springfield, IL, 1975.

Haynes, Richard A., "Drugs in the Workplace," *Security Management*, December, 1983.

Hemphill, Charles F., *Security for Business and Industry*, Dow Jones-Irwin, Homewood, IL, 1971.

Hernon, Frederick E., *The White Collar Ripoff*, Management, Akron, OH, 1975.

Hofmeister, Richard A. and Prince, David J., *Security Dictionary*, Howard W. Sams, Indianapolis, IN, 1985.

Inbau, Fred, et al, *Protective Security Law*, Butterworth, Stoneham, MA, 1983.

Jeffrey, C. Ray, *Crime Prevention Through Environmental Design*, Sage, Beverly Hills, CA, 1977.

Kadish, Sanford H., *Encyclopedia of Crime and Justice*, Free Press, New York, NY, 1983.

Kelley, Woody Anderson, *Kelley's Security Thesaussory*, Concept VIII, Gurley, AL, 1977.

Kingsbury, Arthur A., *Introduction to Security and Crime Prevention Surveys*, Charles C Thomas, Springfield, IL, 1973.

Kionka, Edward J., Torts: *Injuries to Persons and Property*, West, Saint Paul, MN, 1983.

Kline, N. S., et al, *Psychotropic Drugs: A Manual for Emergency Management of Overdose*, Medical Economics, Oradell, NJ, 1974.

Kolodny, Leonard, *Outwitting Bad Check Passers*, Small Business Administration, Washington, DC, 1976.

Law Enforcement and Private Security Sources and Areas of Conflict, Department of Justice, Washington, DC, 1976.

Law Enforcement Investigations, FM 19–20, Department of the Army, Washington, DC, 1977.

Lesko, Matthew, *Information USA*, Viking Press, New York, NY, 1983.

"Life Safety Glossary," *Security Systems Administration*, July, 1985.

Lingeman, R., *Drugs From A to Z: A Dictionary*, McGraw-Hill, New York, NY, 1969.

List of Controlled Substances and Drug Code Numbers, Drug Enforcement Administration, Washington, DC, 1987.

Littlejohn, Robert F., *Crisis Management: A Team Approach*, American Management Association, New York, NY, 1983.

Loewy, Arnold H., *Criminal Law*, West, Saint Paul, MN, 1984.

Long Range Planning for Service Organizations, American Management Association Extension Institute, New York, NY, 1982.

Martin, Julian A., *Law Enforcement Vocabulary*, Charles C Thomas, Springfield, IL, 1973.

Maurer, D. W. and Vogel, V. H., *Narcotics and Narcotic Addiction*, Charles C Thomas, Springfield, IL, 1973.

McGowan, Kevin J., "Computer Power Protection," *Data Processing and Communications Security*, May–June, 1985.

Middaugh, J. Kendall, *Transmission Security Threats and Countermeasures*, Georgia State University, Atlanta, GA, 1984.

Montana, Patrick J. and Roukis, George S., *Managing Terrorism*, Quorum, Westport, CN, 1983.

Narcotics and Drug Abuse: A to Z, Social Service Publications, Queen's Village, NY, 1971.

National Criminal Justice Thesaurus, National Institute of Justice, Washington, DC, 1984.

National Strategy for Prevention of Drug Abuse and Drug Trafficking, The White House, Washington, DC, 1984.

Novitt, Mitchell S., *Employer Liability for Employee Misconduct*, Amacom, New York, NY, 1982.

O'Hara, Charles E., *Fundamentals of Criminal Investigation*, Charles C Thomas, Springfield, IL, 1980.

"The Olympics: Terrorism and Disruption Potentials," *Information Digest*, June, 1984.

Opiates, Alcohol, Drug Abuse and Mental Health Administration, Washington, DC, 1983.

Parker, Donn B., *Fighting Computer Crime*, Author's Copy Book Company, Los Altos, CA, 1981.

Part 179 of 27 CFR, Federal Laws and Regulations, Firearms, Department of the Treasury, Washington, DC, 1983.

Patin, Harold C. and Egan, Raymond R., *Industrial Drug Abuse*, Drug Education Associates, Metairie, LA, 1981.

Patterns of Global Terrorism, Department of State, Washington, DC, 1984.

Peanuts and Tea: A Selected Glossary of Terms Used by Drug Addicts, National Institute of Mental Health, Washington, D.C., 1972.

Pendleton, Charles S., *The Employee Handbook on Drug and Alcohol Awareness,* Texas Safety Association, Austin, TX, 1984.

Physical Security, FM 19–30, Department of the Army, Washington, DC, 1979.

Physical Security of Window Assemblies, National Institute of Law Enforcement and Criminal Justice, Washington, DC, 1976.

Physicians' Desk Reference, Medical Economics Company, Oradell, NJ, 1986.

The Police Reference Notebook, International Association of Chiefs of Police, Gaithersburg, MD, 1970.

Pollock, A. J., *The Underworld Speaks: An Insight to Vice, Crime, and Corruption,* Prevent Crime Bureau, San Francisco, CA, 1935.

Pradhan, S. N. and Dutta, S. N., *Drug Abuse: Clinical and Basic Aspects,* Mosby, St. Louis, MO, 1977.

Preventing Drug Abuse in the Workplace, U.S. Department of Health and Human Services, Washington, DC, 1982.

Professional Guide to Drugs, Intermed Communications, Springhouse, PA, 1982.

Purpura, Philip P., *Security and Loss Prevention,* Butterworth Publishers, Stoneham, MA, 1984.

Recognizing Bombs and Explosives, Federal Law Enforcement and Training Center, Department of the Treasury, Brunswick, GA, 1974.

Reference Aid: Glossary of Narcotics Terms, U.S. Department of Commerce, Washington, DC, 1973.

Regulation of Private Security Services, Department of Justice, Washington, DC, 1976.

"Report 695," Business Intelligence Program, *SRI, International,* Menlo Park, CA, 1984.

Report of a Panel Discussion on Drugs in Industry, Burns Security Institute, Briarcliff Manor, NY, 1975.

Research Issue 26, Guide to Drug Abuse Research Terminology, U.S. Department of Health and Human Services, Washington, DC, 1982.

Research Issue 73, Urine Testing for Drugs of Abuse, U.S. Department of Health and Human Services, Washington, DC, 1986.

Ricks, Truett A., et al, *Principles of Security,* Anderson, Cincinnati, OH, 1981.

Reber, Jan and Shaw, Paul, *Executive Protection Manual,* MTI Teleprograms, Schiller Park, IL, 1980.

Romig, Clarence H. A., *The Physical Evidence Technician,* Police Training Institute, Champaign, IL, 1975.

Rothstein, Paul F., *Evidence: State and Federal Rules,* West, Saint Paul, MN, 1983.

Safeguarding Your Business Against Theft and Vandalism, Research Institute of America, New York, NY, 1983.

Saferstein, Richard, *Criminalistics: An Introduction to Forensic Science,* Prentice-Hall, Englewood Cliffs, NJ, 1981.

Salottolo, A. Lawrence, *Modern Police Service Encyclopedia,* ARCO, New York, NY, 1970.

Sanger, John, *The Alarm Dealer's Guide,* Butterworth, Stoneham, MA, 1985.

Schabeck, Tim A., *Emergency Planning Guide for Data Processing Centers*, Assets Protection, Madison, WI, 1979.

Schmidt, J. E., *Narcotics: Lingo and Lore*, Charles C Thomas, Springfield, IL, 1959.

Schools Without Drugs, U.S. Department of Education, Washington, DC, 1986.

Schultz, Donald O., *Principles of Physical Security*, Gulf, Houston, TX, 1978.

The Science of Fingerprints, Federal Bureau of Investigation, Washington, DC.

Scope of Legal Authority of Private Security Personnel, Department of Justice, Washington, DC, 1976.

Sennewald, Charles A., *Effective Security Management*, Butterworth, Stoneham, MA, 1986.

Stone, Alfred R. and DeLuca, Stuart M., *Police Administration*, Wiley, New York, NY, 1985.

Swint, J. Michael and Lairson, David R., "Employee Assistance Programs," *Alcohol Health and Research World*, Winter, 1983/84.

Terrorist Attacks Against US Business, Department of State, Washington, DC, 1982.

Terrorist Bombings, Department of State, Washington, DC, 1983.

Terrorist Incidents Involving Diplomats, Department of State, Washington, DC, 1983.

Texas Drug Laws, Texas Department of Public Safety, Austin, TX, 1985.

Topical Bibliography: Security Officer/Investigator Training and Management, National Institute of Justice, Washington, DC, 1985.

Understanding Crime Prevention, National Crime Prevention Institute, Butterworth Publishers, Stoneham, MA, 1986.

Van Meter, C. H., *Principles of Police Interrogation*, Charles C Thomas, Springfield, IL, 1973.

Vandiver, James V., *Criminal Investigation: A Guide to Techniques and Solutions*, Scarecrow, Metuchen, NJ, 1983.

Vocabulary for Data Processing, Telecommunications, and Office Systems, IBM Corporation, Poughkeepsie, NY, 1981.

Walsh, Dermot and Poole, Adrian, *A Dictionary of Criminology*, Routledge and Kegan Paul, London, England, 1983.

Walsh, Timothy J. and Healy, Richard J., *The Protection of Assets Manual*, Merritt, Santa Monica, CA, 1983.

Weber, Thad L., *Alarms Systems and Theft Prevention*, Butterworth, Stoneham, MA, 1986.

Webster's Ninth New Collegiate Dictionary, Merriam-Webster, Springfield, MA, 1984.

Weil, Andrew, and Rosen, Winifred, *Chocolate to Morphine*, Houghton-Mifflin, Boston, MA, 1983.

White Collar Crime, Chamber of Commerce of the United States, Washington, DC, 1974.

Woodman, Duane J., *Shoplifting: An Illustrated Study*, Security Data Services, Redlands, CA.

Zadrozny, J., *Dictionary of Social Science*, Public Affairs Press, Washington, DC, 1959.